# The Institutional Foundations of
# Ukrainian Democracy

# The Institutional Foundations of Ukrainian Democracy

*Power Sharing, Regionalism, and Authoritarianism*

NATALIYA KIBITA

# OXFORD
## UNIVERSITY PRESS

Great Clarendon Street, Oxford, OX2 6DP,
United Kingdom

Oxford University Press is a department of the University of Oxford.
It furthers the University's objective of excellence in research, scholarship,
and education by publishing worldwide. Oxford is a registered trade mark of
Oxford University Press in the UK and in certain other countries

Published in the United States of America by Oxford University Press
198 Madison Avenue, New York, NY 10016, United States of America

British Library Cataloguing in Publication Data
Data available

Library of Congress Control Number: 2024936499

ISBN 9780192898814

DOI: 10.1093/9780191925351.001.0001

Printed and bound by
CPI Group (UK) Ltd, Croydon, CR0 4YY

*For Adam and Aglaya*

# Preface

This book originated at the end of 2013 and beginning of 2014 when Ukraine revolted against the corrupt Ukrainian state that stubbornly insisted on suppressing pluralism in Ukrainian politics and imposing authoritarianism on Ukrainians. Mass protests went down in history as the Euromaidan, or the Revolution of Dignity. The Revolution of Dignity was Ukraine's third mass protest since it had become an independent state. The first was in 1999, the second one in 2004. By 2014, Russia was under the authoritarian rule of Vladimir Putin. So the question I asked myself in the winter of 2013–2014 was 'What makes Ukraine so different from Russia?', and more specifically, 'Why does Ukraine reject Russia-style authoritarianism?'

By 2013, I had already finished my first monograph on Khrushchev's economic decentralization, the so-called Sovnarkhoz reform, in Ukraine. What I learned from the Khrushchev period was that already in the 1950s and 1960s, behind the façade of officialdom, the Ukrainian party and state apparatus had its own specific political dynamic in the relationship between the Ukrainian central leadership in Kyiv and the regions. This dynamic was driven by Moscow's failure to devise an effective way to delegate powers to the republics, which, in its turn, generated an imbalance between the rights, responsibilities, and powers at the regional and republican levels in Ukraine. The studies on independent Ukraine showed that this imbalance and the general culture of irresponsibility seemed to have successfully survived the disintegration of the system that reared it. In time, this Soviet legacy famously manifested in bourgeoning corruption and the consolidation of the oligarchic system.

As I sought a methodological approach to connect my findings on the Khrushchev era in Ukraine and Ukraine's post-Soviet development, my husband, who is an economist, suggested that I read *Why Nations Fail: The Origins of Power, Prosperity and Poverty* by Daron Acemoglu and James A. Robinson. I cannot thank him enough. Not only was the reading a pleasure, but also I had my broad framework. More reading on the theory of institutions and historical institutionalism followed. Examining the interconnection between economic and political institutions in Soviet Ukraine and the evolution of the Ukrainian institutional system through time seemed to me the way to proceed in order to explain the very mechanisms that not only bred the culture of irresponsibility in Ukraine but also defined the particularities of the Ukrainian state as opposed to Russia.

This is a historical study. However, it was written in the hope that it will also be of interest to policymakers. Today Ukraine has reached one of those rare historic junctures when the circumstances allow for a fundamental change, when Ukraine can break with the negative legacy of the Soviet period. When designing new 'good' policies, one might find it helpful to take a fresh look at the origins of the Ukrainian institutional system.

# Acknowledgements

The work on this book lasted, with varying intensity, for almost nine years and it could not have been written without the support and encouragement of my family, colleagues, friends, and other individuals who inspired me in various, sometimes unusual, ways. My deepest gratitude goes to my husband Adam and my thirteen-year-old daughter Aglaya. To Adam, for being devoted to my work, for being the harshest critic of my arguments and writing, and for giving simply extraordinary care and affection that inspired and motivated me through the years of this solitary exercise. An intellectual of high integrity, he braved the role of a 'single father' for four months to enable me to carry out a fellowship at Harvard to advance my research. This fellowship was crucial to the project. I am grateful to Aglaya for her adult patience and understanding that research takes time, as well as for her curiosity in what I do. Her straightforward 'whys?' and 'hows?' were often more helpful than she or I expected. My thanks also go to my parents, Andrii and Albina Kibita, for helping me to take care of my daughter when she was little and my brother Pavlo who helped me with the online research of Ukrainian- and Russian-language sources.

I was truly blessed with the support of my colleagues. I am heartfully grateful to Geoffrey Swain, who back in early 2014 encouraged me to pursue my research and supported this project from the very early days until the end by generously sharing his time and expertise on Soviet history. He made valuable and insightful comments and suggestions for all chapters, for which I cannot thank him enough. I am grateful to Serhii Plokhy who during my research fellowship at the Harvard Ukrainian Research Institute (HURI) showed great interest in my work, spent many hours discussing my research, generously shared his unique knowledge of Ukrainian history, but also encouraged me to speed up the writing (which proved harder than I thought). After the fellowship in 2019, Serhii continued to provide valuable support.

During a teaching fellowship at the London School of Economics (LSE), I was lucky to receive advice from Janet Hartley and Vladislav Zubok. In the early stages of the research, I considered examining the Ukrainian institutional system since 1861. Janet strongly suggested that I carefully reconsider 1861 as a starting date. I am grateful to her for challenging me on this. Starting the story in 1917 was one of the most important decisions I made with regard to this project. I am truly grateful to Vladislav for his unwavering support for this work, and for all our discussions of Soviet politics and Gorbachev's leadership.

My special thanks go to my former colleagues from the University of Edinburgh who became my personal friends, David Kaufman, Stephan Malinowski, Julius Ruiz, and Luke March. Discussions on the First World War, Nazi Germany, the Spanish Civil War, and post-Soviet politics in Russia were not only informative, but inspirational. Over the years, they read, discussed, and made insightful comments on my research and chapters, and editorial suggestions. David, Stephan, and Julius also provided me with support as they advocated for my affiliation with the School of History, Classics and Archaeology at the University of Edinburgh. Their support was crucial for me to continue working on this monograph during the Covid pandemic. David Smith from the University of Glasgow sponsored my institutional affiliation at the very final stage of work, for which I am grateful.

I would like also to thank Valerii Vasiliev, Semion Lyandres, Terry Martin, Roman Szporluk, Lubomyr Hajda, Volodymyr Dibrova, Mark Kramer, and Ursula Woolley (Griffiths) for discussions and comments. My special thanks go to Paul D'Anieri and Yoram Gorlizki for their feedback on separate parts of the book at different stages of this project. I am grateful to two anonymous reviewers from Oxford University Press whose comments and suggestions induced me to improve the focus of various parts of the book and emphasize the points I wanted to make.

There are several institutions who supported my research. First and foremost, I must thank the Department of International History at LSE for providing a stimulating intellectual environment. I would like to express my gratitude to HURI for a research fellowship in 2019 and for providing an absolutely fantastic research environment. Staff members Tymish Holowinsky and M. J. Scott made my academic stay go smoothly. Librarian and archivist Olha Aleksic found for me rare publications in Ukrainian and in Russian, for which I cannot thank her enough. I am thankful to Kostyantyn Bondarenko for making the maps. As already mentioned, my stay at HURI was indeed crucial to defining the structure and focus of this book.

Collection of archival material would have been much more difficult without the support of the director of the Central State Archive of Public Organizations of Ukraine, Olha Bazhan, who made my archival research at TsDAHOU as speedy and efficient as possible. I would like to thank Viktor Burenkov for helping me find the documents in the State Archive of Zaporizhzhia oblast and Oksana Klymenko for helping me with archival research in the Central State Archive of Supreme Bodies of Power and Government of Ukraine in Kyiv. Natalia Stratonova, my old friend, was able to help me with the technical side of the research up until the full-scale war started, for which I thank her.

Finally, I would like to express my gratitude to Kristina Conroy from HURI who agreed to edit this manuscript. Her comments and editorial advice allowed me to improve the original text considerably. To my editor from Oxford University

Press, Cathryn Steele, I am grateful for the gift of time, for not rushing me with the manuscript. Covid and then the war interfered with my original plans, and I truly appreciate Cathryn letting me finish this book as I intended.

It goes without saying that I take full responsibility for any mistakes the reader finds.

# Contents

# List of Illustrations, Maps, and Table

## Illustrations

## Maps

## Table

# List of Abbreviations and Glossary

*aktiv*  politically active rank-and-file members of the Communist Party

**apparatus**  party and state bureaucracy

*Borbists*  Russian left-wing Socialist Revolutionaries in Ukraine

*Borotbists*  Ukrainian left-wing Socialist Revolutionaries

*buro*  top decision-making body of an organization

**Central Committee**  Central Committee of the Communist Party of the Soviet Union; the bureaucracy of the Communist Party of the Soviet Union

**central Politburo**  supreme decision-making body within the Central Committee of the CPSU

*Commissar*  head of the People's Commissariat

*Commissariat*  government department, predecessor of ministry

**Council of Ministers**  the name of the Soviet government in 1946–1991 (in 1991, the Council of Ministers of the UkSSR was renamed the Cabinet of Ministers of Ukraine)

**CP(b)U**  Communist Party (Bolshevik) of Ukraine in 1918–1952

**CPSU**  Communist Party of the Soviet Union

**CPU**  Communist Party of Ukraine, 1952–1991

**DALO**  State archive of Lviv oblast

**DARO**  State archive of Rivne oblast

**DAZO**  State Archive of Zaporizhzhia oblast

*diktat*  dictatorial, or command-directive, method of administration

**first secretary**  leading party functionary in a party committee

**GARF**  Russian State Archive of the Russian Federation

*glavk*  chief committee or department within the Supreme Sovnarkhoz, later ministr(y/ies)

*(glav)snabsbyt(y)*  (main) branch administration(s) for supplies and sales

*gorkom*  city/town party committee

*Gosagroprom*  State Agro-Industrial Committee

*Gosplan*  State Planning Commission/Committee

*Gossnab*  State Committee for Material and Equipment Supply

*goszakaz(y)*  state order(s)

*gubernia* (Ukr.: *hubernia*)  territorial administrative region, or province, in 1917–1925

*gubkom*  gubernia party committee

*ispolkom*  executive committee of the local soviet, at the gubernia, oblast, raion, or city
   (Rus.: *gorod*) level: *gubispolkom, oblispolkom, raiispolkom, gorispolkom*

*khoziaistvennik(i)*  production manager(s)

*khozraschet*  cost-effectiveness

*kolkhoz(y)*  collective farm(s)

*kolkhoznik*  member of a collective farm

*Komsomol*  Communist Youth League

*krai*  province

*kraikom*  krai party committee

*mestnichestvo*  localism, the tendency to prioritize local interests over all-union or republican interests

MP  Member of the Verkhovna Rada

*Narkomfin*  People's Commissariat of Finances

*Narkomprod*  People's Commissariat of Food

NEP  New Economic Policy

*nomenklatura* **system**  system of appointment to key party and state positions controlled
   by the party

*obkom*  oblast party committee

*oblast*  territorial administrative unit; until 1929, Bolsheviks used the term to refer to the
   entire Ukraine, but after 1929, it referred to a territorial administrative unit below the
   republican level

OGPU  Unified State Political Administration

*okruha* (Rus.: *okrug*)  territorial administrative unit in Ukraine in 1923–1930, smaller
   than a gubernia

*okruzhkom*  okruha party committee

*Orgburo*  Organizational Bureau of the Central Committee

*otaman* (Rus.: *ataman*)  military commander, or leader

*petliurovshchina*  tendency to support independent Ukraine, named after Symon Petliura *plenum*  meeting of a party committee

*Politburo*  political committee of the Central Committee of the Communist Party, effectively the supreme decision-making body in the Central Committee in the period before 1952 and after 1966; called the Presidium (Central Committee Presidium) in 1952–1966

*Presidium*  the supreme decision-making body in an organization, such as the Council of Ministers, the TsIK, or the Supreme Soviet

*Promburo*  Industrial Bureau

*Rabkrin*  People's Commissariat of Workers' and Peasants' Inspectorate

*raikom*  raion party committee

*raion*  territorial administrative unit smaller than a gubernia or oblast

*revkom*  revolutionary committee

*revvoensovet*  revolutionary military council

**RGAE**  Russian State Archive of the Economy

**RGANI**  Russian State Archive of Contemporary History

**RGASPI**  Russian State Archive of Social and Political History

**RKP(b)**  Russian Communist Party (Bolsheviks)

**RSDRP(b)**  Russian Social Democratic Workers' Party (Bolsheviks)

**RSFSR** Russian Socialist Federative Soviet Republic (1918–1936), Russian Soviet Federative Socialist Republic (1936–1991)

*Rukh*  **(Ukr.)** national-democratic movement *Narodnyĭ Rukh Ukraïny*, or People's Movement of Ukraine

*rusapetstvo*  tendency to view ethnic and national peripheries within the Soviet Federation as one, undivided Russia where the peripheries are subjugated to the unconditional rule of the Russian nation

*samostiĭnist'* **(Ukr.)**  independence

**SDs**  Social Democrats

*seredniak*  middling peasant

*shefstvo*  patronage help

*soviet*  council

*sovkhoz(y)*  state farm(s)

*sovnarkhoz(y)*  council(s) of national economy; with regards to the period 1957–1965, the term refers to 'regional economic council(s)'

*Sovnarkom*  Council of People's Commissars, or government

**SRs**  Socialist Revolutionaries

**STO**  Council of Labour and Defence

*trotskyism*: **tendency to support the ideas of Leon Trotsky**

**TsDAEA**  Central State Archive for Audiovisual and Electronic Materials

**TsDAHOU**  Central State Archive of Public Organizations of Ukraine

**TsDAVOU** Central State Archive of Supreme Bodies of Power and Government of Ukraine

*Tsentral'na Rada* (**Ukr.**)  Ukrainian Central Council (Rada)

*Tsentrosoyuz*  All-Russian Central Union of Consumer Cooperative Societies

**TsIK**  Central Executive Committee of Soviets

**Ukrainization**  the policy of indigenization in Ukraine, which included promotion of the Ukrainian language, culture, and elite

*Ukrsovnarkhoz*  republican sovnarkhoz of Ukraine

**UkSSR** Ukrainian Socialist Soviet Republic (1919–1937), Ukrainian Soviet Socialist Republic (1937–1991)

**UN**  United Nations

**UNR**  Ukrainian National Republic

**UPSR**  Ukrainian Party of Socialist Revolutionaries

**URSR**  Ukrainian Soviet Socialist Republic

**USDRP**  Ukrainian Social Democratic Workers' Party

**USSR**  Union of Soviet Socialist Republics

*Verkhovna Rada* (**Ukr.**)  Supreme Council of Ukraine, the parliament in Ukraine

*Vneshtorg*  People's Commissariat of Foreign Trade

*Vukoopspilka* (**Ukr.**)  Ukrainian Association of Consumer Cooperative Organizations

# Note on Transliteration

Primary sources in both Russian and Ukrainian were used for this book, so transliteration is made from both languages. In the text, the Library of Congress system for transliteration of Ukrainian and Russian names and terms was slightly modified. In the majority of words, the soft signs as well as special characters such as -ï- or -ĭ- have been dropped (oblast instead of oblast', Manuilsky instead of Manuïl's'kyĭ (Ukr.)/Manuil'skiĭ (Rus.), Lebid instead of Lebid' (Ukr.)/Lebed' (Rus.)). Surname endings -yi (Ukrainian) and -ii (Russian) are rendered as -y. The names of the majority of non-Russian figures were transliterated from Ukrainian. Geographic locations in Ukraine are all transliterated from Ukrainian (Lviv, Dnipropetrovsk, Kharkiv, Zaporizhzhia). The terminology relating to the functioning of the Soviet party-state system is generally transliterated from Russian (Sovnarkom instead of Radnarkom, and sovnarkhoz instead of radnarhosp). All translations from Russian and Ukrainian were done by this author.

The change we observe is seldom discontinuous...but instead is incremental, and the nature of the incremental institutional change together with the imperfect way by which the actors interpret their environment and make choices accounts for path dependency and makes history relevant.

—Douglass C. North, *Institutions, Institutional Change and Economic Performance*, 1990

# Maps

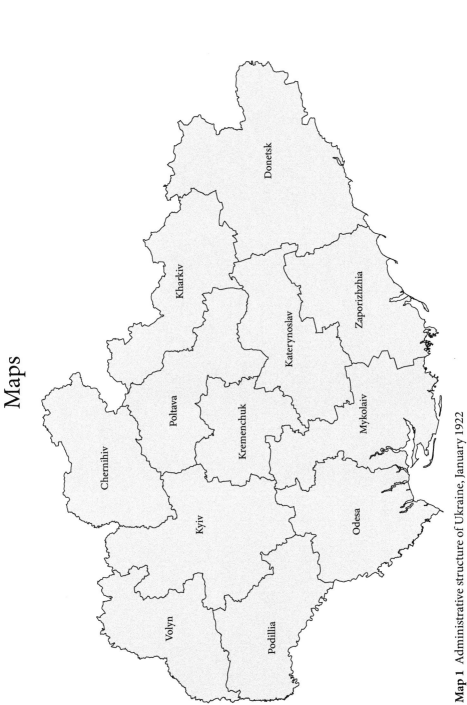

**Map 1** Administrative structure of Ukraine, January 1922

*Source*: Ukrainian Research Institute, Harvard University
© 2023 President and Fellows of Harvard College

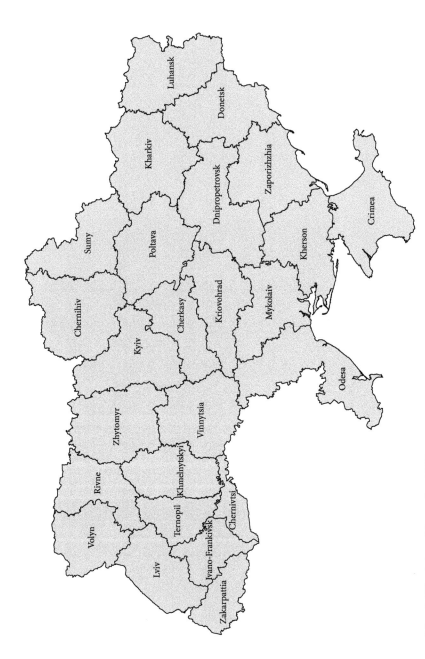

**Map 2** Ukrainian oblasts after 1959

*Source:* Ukrainian Research Institute, Harvard University
© 2023 President and Fellows of Harvard College

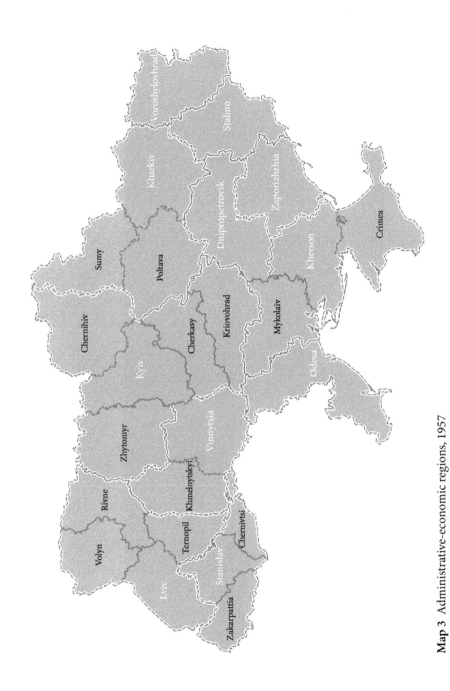

**Map 3** Administrative-economic regions, 1957
*Source:* Ukrainian Research Institute, Harvard University
© 2023 President and Fellows of Harvard College

# Introduction

At the beginning of 2014, the world witnessed an explosion of conflict between two neighbouring countries that were considered by many as culturally, economically, and politically inseparable, Ukraine and Russia. On 24 February 2022, Russia took the conflict to the highest level and launched a full-scale invasion of Ukraine. Apart from security concerns, the Russian military intervention starting in 2014 and the 2022 full-scale war reflected a clash of political cultures between the authoritarian regime of Vladimir Putin and democratic (certainly non-authoritarian) Ukraine. Since the fall of the Soviet Union, Ukraine's democracy has persisted despite several attempts to impose authoritarian rule. By 2014, three out of the four retired presidents of Ukraine, Leonid Kravchuk (1991–1994), Leonid Kuchma (1994–2004) and Viktor Yanukovych (2009–2014), had systematically attempted to bring the Verkhovna Rada under the control of the executive and establish an authoritarian regime. However, they were equally systematically rebuffed, by the population as well as by the political system. Why was this the case?

This monograph takes a new approach to the Soviet legacy. First and foremost, it challenges the concept of 1991 as a break point for Ukraine. Secondly, it expands the analysis of Ukrainian politics beyond the republic level, traditionally analysed through the relationship between Kyiv and Moscow, to include the level of the Ukrainian regions. Bringing a third actor—the Ukrainian regions—into the story of Soviet Ukrainian politics shows that Ukraine had its own specific political dynamic, and that this dynamic influenced the post-Soviet transformation to a far greater extent than the collapse of the unitary party-state system. Examination of this factor makes it clear that treating the fall of the Soviet Union as the starting point for Ukraine's post-Soviet development is a Moscow-centric approach that does not allow for a full understanding of Ukraine's post-Soviet transition.

## Ukraine and Russia during the Post-Soviet Transition

At the moment of the dissolution of the Soviet Union in 1991, the newly independent Ukrainian state appeared similar to its Russian counterpart. Like elsewhere in the post-Soviet space, the Russian and Ukrainian political systems of the early 1990s had weak states, unruly regional authorities, and a powerful parliament, while facing a devastating economic crisis. Like elsewhere in post-Soviet space, politics in both countries were largely based on clans, nepotism, and patronage networks using corrupt practices to sustain governing coalitions.[1] Both Russia and Ukraine were ethnically diverse. Social processes had been unleashed simultaneously in both countries, as manifested in the elites' competition for popular support and the masses' increased political participation.[2] Some analysts saw in these conditions the prospect for institutionalizing democratic processes in Ukraine.[3] However, at the time, the democratic process was not institutionalized in either country. Instead, argued scholars, Russia and Ukraine proceeded with consolidating fundamentally similar authoritarian regimes.[4]

Yet by the end of the 1990s, commentators and scholars could generally agree that in contrast to Russia, the relationship between the executive and legislative branches in Ukraine was driven by consensus-seeking politics, rather than submission to one leader or one party. Ukraine was far from a functional democracy. Ukraine's second president, Leonid Kuchma, built 'competitive', or 'pluralistic', authoritarianism by combining undemocratic practices with competitive elections. But even he failed to turn Ukraine into a fully authoritarian state.[5] By the beginning of the 2000s, commentators were placing Ukraine and Russia in different sub-categories. Russia was viewed as an electoral authoritarian regime, whereas Ukraine was classified as a fairly weak, semi-presidential or semi-authoritarian regime (sometimes referred to as 'hybrid'), where the president was held in the balance between the executive branch, the legislative branch, and the newly formed uncoordinated group of oligarchs.[6] Ukraine enjoyed the most competitive party system within the Commonwealth of Independent States and enjoyed a pluralistic political culture in general. Even disregarding the exact classification of Ukraine, the general consensus was that for most of its existence as an independent state, Ukraine was in a league of its own.[7]

Indeed, the indications that Ukraine was following its own path, different from Russia's, were visible as early as 1989. Already then, in the late perestroika years, Ukrainian politics demonstrated a preference for consensus seeking. Ukraine's independence was the result of an agreement between the national-democratic opposition and the national communists.[8] More significantly, at a very early stage of the transitional period, the presidents of Ukraine and Russia demonstrated a different record of success in asserting presidential power.

In 1993, both Kravchuk and Russian President Boris Yeltsin faced a conflict, in Russia's case a deadlock between the fragmented yet strong parliament and the president. Yeltsin called a referendum, won, ordered the dissolution of the Russian parliament, and called early elections. After overcoming the deadlock with parliament, Yeltsin established a super-presidential constitutional framework, thus laying the foundation for Putin's authoritarianism.[9] Kravchuk's conflict with the Verkhovna Rada over his attempt to install central control over the economy in 1993 did not end in deadlock, nor did it result in him securing domination of the executive over the legislative branch or a new constitutional amendment.[10] Kravchuk resolved the 1993 conflict by skipping the referendum and calling early elections for both the Verkhovna Rada and presidency in 1994, thus setting the stage for a non-violent and democratic transfer of power when Leonid Kuchma won the election. When Kravchuk's successor, Kuchma, tried to handpick his own successor in 2004 as Yeltsin had done with Putin, Kuchma's efforts incited the Orange Revolution and the defeat of his protégé.

The divergence of Yeltsin's and Kravchuk's responses to political crisis appeared to many to be a 'glitch' in the system, rather than a systemic difference between two political environments. It seemed that Kravchuk had the best shot at establishing an authoritarian state but did not push things through. Most often, the 'glitch' was attributed to Kravchuk's personality, his personal choices, and personal mistakes. After all, Kravchuk operated in an environment predisposed to strong presidential power. For more than 300 years, the majority of Ukraine had been fully integrated in the Russian, and then Soviet, state. Ukrainian power elites had been reared in the traditions of the centralized, authoritarian, at times totalitarian, Russian/Soviet state. They were fully integrated with Russian/Soviet politics and enjoyed the same personal privileges as the Russian elites. The majority of Ukraine's early post-Soviet elites were long-time career politicians, coming from what was commonly viewed as one of the most conservative and faithful communist bureaucracies in the Soviet Union and one that was perhaps least likely to pursue democracy.[11] It lagged behind in supporting Mikhail Gorbachev's perestroika, and the upper political echelon remained intact even during the short period between 1989, when Ukraine finally joined the all-union process of political transformation and allowed political opposition to share the political stage and promote the ideas of perestroika, and 1991 when Ukraine proclaimed independence.[12] Although the Ukrainian parliament was elected in 1990, 83 percent was made up by members of the Communist Party of Ukraine (CPU), and it was not dissolved immediately after the August 1991 coup when the CPU was banned, nor after the Ukrainian declaration of independence in December 1991, nor after the formal dissolution of the Soviet Union a few weeks later. The economically and politically conservative majority, which turned out to be pragmatic and driven by self-preservation and the desire to remain in power, formed the so-called 'party of power', a party that, as some scholars concluded, was predisposed to authoritarianism and command-administrative methods.[13] To an equal extent, neither Kravchuk nor the conservative power elites within the executive and legislative branches sought the liberal economic reforms that were necessary for a transition to democracy.[14]

Furthermore, well aware that he was operating in a hospitable political environment, Kravchuk tried to monopolize political control. On 13 December 1991, Kravchuk established the Presidential Administration, the structure of which was similar to the structure of the Central Committee of the Communist Party of Ukraine (hereafter, the 'Ukrainian Central Committee').[15] He tried to imitate

Yeltsin by demanding greater presidential powers from the Verkhovna Rada to manage the economy, by regularly trying to consolidate his power over the legislative branch and the Cabinet of Ministers in 1992–1993, by introducing the institute of presidential representatives as the heads of regional executive power, and by granting significant resources to strategically selected regions. In 1994, Kravchuk attempted to usurp power by cancelling the presidential elections. Some observers considered his chances high. As Lucan Way argued, the interests of the president and the predominantly ex-Soviet political elites whose personal wealth depended on access to state resources were aligned; meanwhile, the economic situation was deteriorating, obstacles from Ukraine's weak civil society were minimal, and the country lacked a democratic history and was relatively isolated internationally.[16] Nonetheless, Kravchuk was effectively rebuffed by the Verkhovna Rada.

When explaining Kravchuk's failure to assert authoritarian control, scholars observed that he was less politically aggressive than Yeltsin.[17] Some argued that Kravchuk inherited a weak state in 1991. The collapse of the Soviet centralized party-state system left Kravchuk 'virtually powerless in all areas except the media'.[18] Kravchuk's inability to establish control over the economy resulted in him lacking the resources to secure the support of the heads of the police and security forces in 1994.[19]

Fragmentation of elites and Kravchuk's failure to unite the elites or to create a personal network are also considered among the factors that determined Kravchuk's short presidency and his failure to leave an authoritarian legacy.[20] Strong regions, or regionalism, to which the fragmentation of the elites is often connected, is a systemic factor that constrained both Yeltsin and Kravchuk.

Regionalism was 'unleashed' during perestroika when the coercive power of the Union centre began to erode. Starting in 1990–1991, the regions in Russia and Ukraine sought to marginalize the role of the central government and maximize their autonomy and economic autarky.[21] Both presidents had problems with the regions, but things worked out very differently in the two countries. After a turbulent relationship with the subjects of federation in the 1990s, Yeltsin, through bargaining, restored centralized control over the regions to a degree sufficient for his successor to proceed with the consolidation of the centralized authoritarian state.[22] Kravchuk, scholars argue, was sensitive to regional diversity. Deprived of a regional base, he tried to rule as a mediator between various ideological and regional groups. However, all *he* could leave to his successor was a 'republic of regions'.[23]

In Ukraine, as the economic crises of the early 1990s and lack of unifying political ideology or instruments of coercion made it difficult for the Ukrainian government to establish its authority and govern, the regions began to 'rediscover, reimagine and formalize their historical pasts'.[24] Regional affinity was reflected in political preferences. The Ukrainian-speaking west of the country for most of the

1990s and 2000s manifested as nationalist and pro-Western; the Russian-speaking east and south as pro-Russian. In between lay the swing centre.[25] Reflecting the regionalizing trends, the majority of the parties formed on a regional basis.[26] Intra-regional ties developed much more strongly than inter-regional ones. No party in the 1990s was able to build an effective organization across the country to win enough votes to avoid making a coalition in the Verkhovna Rada to form a majority. As a result, even though power shifted to the parliament, its composition was fragmented.[27] Regional divisions were widely regarded as a formidable obstacle to the consolidation of the Ukrainian state and political power.[28]

Related to regionalism were regional groups, or regional clans.[29] Unlike political regionalism, the origins of which scholars trace to perestroika and the collapse of the Soviet centralized party-state, regional groups have existed since the beginning of the 1930s.[30] In Ukraine, explains Mikhail Minakov in his influential work, such groups grew strong during the reconstruction period after the Second World War when, in competition for resources from Moscow, the three biggest groups formed around the war-devastated industrial centres of Kharkiv, Stalino/Donetsk, and Dnipropetrovsk: '[a]t the republican level, the regional groups were reaching equilibrium in a balanced hierarchy of First Secretaries and Chairmen of the Council of Ministers'.[31]

During perestroika and Kravchuk's presidency, regional groups allegedly lost their prominence. Political divisions detected by scholars were more pronounced along ideological lines, between national communists and national democrats.[32] The deep economic and political crisis in 1993–1994 caused regional groups, by then referred to as regional clans, to resurface. In Ukraine they proved stronger than elsewhere in the post-Soviet space: '[r]egional clans became a generic form of the emerging new power elites' organization in independent Ukraine'.[33] They grew sufficiently strong to dictate the development of a political system that Minakov dubbed as 'the republic of clans'.

As regional groups re-emerged, regional differences became more pronounced. To win in elections, Kravchuk's contender Leonid Kuchma chose to run on an agenda popular in the east and south of Ukraine, which favoured close ties with Russia, and to obtain the support of the regional elites, thus bringing the regional factor to the fore. It was in the first post-Soviet presidential election of 1994 that the world could first observe a clear and large divide between the pro-Russian east and south and the Ukrainian nationalist west that supported close ties with the West.[34] Due to Ukraine's economic dependence on Russia at the time, some scholars speculated that the east–west divide was a potential source of instability, even a potential reason for Ukraine to break up.[35] The speculations proved incorrect. Firstly, the east–west divide was not neat, and secondly, the majority of the elites still preferred to have a decision- and policymaking centre in Kyiv, rather than in Moscow. Kuchma running and winning in the presidential elections as a representative of the pro-Russian east and south did not change the fact that

Ukraine *was* a republic of regions. Hence, once Kuchma became president, he, too, balanced regional interests and was inclined to compromise rather than attempt to impose the dominance of one regional group over the entirety of Ukraine.[36]

## General Observations

A number of observations can be made on previous studies of the post-Soviet transition in Ukraine that are relevant to this book. First of all, regardless of whether scholars address the question of why Ukraine failed to fully democratize throughout the 1990s, or why it failed to become fully authoritarian and ended up with what some view as a 'hybrid system', for lack of a better term, the scholarly consensus is that the transformation of Ukraine from a Soviet republic into an independent state began during late perestroika and state building began in 1991–1992. Secondly, academic studies explain that Ukraine had a similar start in state building to other post-Soviet states. Like other post-Soviet states, except the Baltics, Ukraine began its transition with old elites and old state structures. Thirdly, scholars tend to assume that Ukraine was predisposed to authoritarianism, but for a variety of reasons—in particular, the character and personal mistakes of President Kravchuk and the rise of regionalism—Ukraine did not follow Russia's path towards authoritarianism. Fourth, scholars seek explanations of Ukraine's political distinctiveness in factors that defined political change, such as liberalization of the economy, the institution of the presidency, the resurrected parliament that, thanks to Gorbachev's perestroika, transformed from a docile decorative Soviet institution into an active policymaking institution,[37] free democratic elections that did not exist in the Soviet Union, the role of elites and political parties in the transformation of Ukraine, as well as the democratization of society, Western and new Russian influences, and the role and the place of oligarchs in Ukrainian politics, a factor more relevant to the Kuchma period than to Kravchuk's. Finally, studies acknowledge the importance of the Soviet legacy in Ukraine's post-Soviet transition, but do not explain how or why the same Soviet legacy or corruption or networks generated different political outcomes in the various post-Soviet states. The scholarly approach to the post-Soviet transition of Ukraine was based on the existing historiographic view of the Soviet Ukraine as one large periphery region of the Soviet Union where the Ukrainian republican leadership had centralized control over the entirety of Ukraine. When considering 'centre–periphery' relations with regard to Ukraine, scholars referred to the relations between the central leadership in Moscow and the Ukrainian republican leadership in Kyiv.[38]

The observations made above leave a student of Ukrainian post-Soviet transition with a few reflections. For example, personalized politics looms large as a crucial factor at the heart of the liberalized political environment or deregulated state. But why was Kravchuk in a weaker position than his counterparts in other republics if they all came from the same system? And why was the Soviet experience of personalized politics instrumental to the restoration of regional groups, but not to the restoration of centralized power in Ukraine? More importantly, if the ex-communist majority in the Verkhovna Rada that formed the so-called party of power was predisposed to authoritarianism, why did it support someone so 'unfit' to install authoritarian control over the state? After all, Kravchuk's personal qualities as a leader were not a secret; he was an 'old cadre' and had a long career at the republican level. He joined the Ukrainian Central Committee in 1970. By October 1988, he was appointed the head of the Ukrainian Central Committee's ideology department. In June 1990, he became a full member of the Ukrainian Politburo, the highest political organ in Soviet Ukraine; in July, he was elected a member of the Central Committee of the Communist Party of the Soviet Union (hereafter, the 'Central Committee'). On 23 July 1990, he became the chairman of the Verkhovna Rada.[39]

When discussing Kravchuk's rise to the presidency, studies have pointed to a major factor that has not yet been mentioned: Ukrainian nationalism. The national-democratic movement *Rukh* that rose in 1989 had quickly grown into a potent force that had prospects of becoming the driving force behind reforms and political and economic liberalization.[40] Such prospects would not materialize, but no one knew that for sure in 1990–1991. Reluctant to remove themselves from power, the old political elites were certain that without a nationwide consensus they would not be able to stand up to Yeltsin's Russia, which became necessary in the summer of 1991, and urgent after Yeltsin's spectacular rise in popularity after the August 1991 coup in Moscow. As the chairman of the Verkhovna Rada, Kravchuk demonstrated an ability to cooperate with the national-democratic movement and orchestrate the gradual rapprochement of the old political elites with the new, anti-communist elites.[41] Viewed from this perspective, favouring Kravchuk for the office of the president was not a mistake, but a rational choice by the old guard. Kravchuk might have lacked the personal qualities to assert authoritarian power, but he was an experienced republic-level leader and was able to forge a national unity behind the idea of consolidating Ukrainian sovereignty within the reformed Soviet Union and, when the context changed, behind Ukraine's separation from Russia. In other words, the choice of Kravchuk for presidency was dictated by the particular historical context that allowed for a tide of nationalism that forced the communist majority to adjust to it.[42]

A tide of nationalism might explain Kravchuk's rise to the presidency. Nationalism and splits in national identity might also help to explain why Kravchuk lost in 1994. But it cannot explain his failure to install an authoritarian regime while in office. The ex-communist majority was predisposed to authoritarianism. Rukh backed Kravchuk's efforts to centralize power, too. It believed that firm control was necessary to protect Ukrainian statehood.[43] In early 1992, Kravchuk secured additional constitutional rights on political reforms and economic policymaking, which showed that regardless of whether he had or did not have the character to be an authoritarian leader, he was certainly prepared to rule with 'a firm hand'. Despite this, according to some scholars, he soon proved reluctant to use these powers, or, according to others, was unable to use them, or bit of both.[44] Splits in national identity played no role in him wanting, trying, and failing to concentrate political control over the state and economy in 1992–1993.

The literature depicts a confusing picture of Ukraine starting state building in the same condition as other post-Soviet states, only weaker, with a new leader ambitious enough to stand up to Gorbachev and Yeltsin, but not ambitious or sufficiently able to use the new powers to assert his own power over the elites, the majority of whom longed for a leader with 'a firm hand'. The regions and political elites were stronger than the state and the president because Kravchuk and the government were too weak.

The understanding of the distinctiveness of the Ukrainian political system is even less clear if we 'zoom out' and look at Ukraine's centuries-long history. Scholars make a convincing case that Ukrainian Cossacks and the Habsburgs left a legacy of liberalism and democracy to the Ukrainian nation. Over centuries, Ukraine developed a tradition of pluralism and political accommodation.[45] Ukraine's resistance to authoritarianism after 1991 came to be viewed as Ukraine's return to its historic traditions of liberalism and democracy. But at least two questions arise. Firstly, how did the democratic tradition survive in the Russian autocratic state and particularly in the Soviet Union—that is, outside the small group of progressive, knowledgeable, and educated intellectuals in the nineteenth century or the group of Ukrainian dissidents in the twentieth? The second question is, if Ukraine has 'democratic DNA', why did it get stuck between dysfunctional democracy and authoritarianism after 1991? Why has the rule of law, the necessary prerequisite of a functional democracy, not prevailed in Ukraine after thirty years of independence and is still to be installed?

One might find it easy to agree with Henry Hale's observation that the existing literature of post-Soviet politics does not give us a good sense of the distinct political system that functions in post-Soviet states, nor of the logic that makes this system a system.[46] And it is when seeking an answer to Hale's observation that we find the absence of an explanation for why the Soviet legacy manifested differently in post-Soviet states. Studies acknowledge the decisive role of the communist legacy. Scholars detect, and many take into account what Synder called the 'institutional wreckage' when examining patterns of exercising power in Ukraine, or the effect of nationalism, cultural diversity, or regional diversity on Ukrainian politics.[47] The Soviet legacy looms particularly large in studies of corruption and network politics.[48] However, in Stephen Kotkin's and Mark Beissinger's words, 'legacy arguments have often been made at a high level of generality, sometimes assume that correlation or similarity is sufficient evidence of a legacy, and frequently fail to trace the actual mechanisms connecting past and present that are implied within them'.[49] Indeed, why did corruption or regional networks—the signature elements of the Russian/Soviet authoritarian system—survive in post-Soviet Ukraine, but Ukraine still did not become authoritarian?

This monograph addresses the observations made by Hale, Kotkin, and Beissinger. It aims to offer a sense of a distinct political system in Ukraine and a sense of the logic that drove politics in post-Soviet Ukraine in the 1990s. Its secondary aim is to provide the missing information on the Soviet period to future researchers who might undertake research on Ukraine's path dependence.[50]

To accomplish these aims, the book takes a new approach to the Soviet legacy. It traces the actual mechanisms that connected the Soviet past with the post-Soviet present and explains how these mechanisms made that connection. To trace these mechanisms, this monograph offers new empirical material and takes a new approach to the interpretation of the empirical archival material.

## Methodological Approach

If at the foundation of the Soviet system lay the party-state configuration, at the foundation of the Ukrainian Soviet and post-Soviet political system lay the centre–periphery configuration between Kyiv and the Ukrainian regions.[51] This monograph makes a historical investigation into regionalism and the institute of leadership in Ukraine. Regionalism is interpreted as the tendency of regional elites to formulate, defend, and prioritize specific local interests over all-union or all-republican interests by available administrative (political after 1991) and economic means and through available institutions.[52] ('Regional elite', also referred to in the text as party–industry alliance, included the first secretary of the territorial party organization (called obkom in an oblast and raikom in a raion), the chairman/chairmen of the territorial executive committee(s) (oblispolkom and/or raiispolkom), and directors of the main industrial enterprises, kolkhozy and sovkhozy. Regional elites also included the heads of security services. However, they are irrelevant to this study.[53])

This book deviates from two existing approaches to the interpretation of the Soviet system and the post-Soviet transition in a Soviet republic. One views the disintegration of the Soviet centralized party-state system as a starting point for the post-Soviet transformation. The second treats 'centre–periphery' relations between the Soviet leadership and Soviet Ukraine as the relationship between Moscow and Kyiv, where Ukraine is one large periphery region with the Ukrainian leadership speaking for it.

Broadly speaking, this monograph is part of the recent innovative reassessment of the Soviet past and post-Soviet developments in the region.[54] Contrary to the existing literature that seeks explanations of the post-Soviet transformation in post-1989 or post-1991 political, social, cultural, or economic developments, this book seeks explanations in the institutional legacy that Ukraine obtained from the preceding Soviet times. At the same time, in analysing the Soviet institutional system in Ukraine, this monograph expands the existing prism of centre–periphery relations, where Moscow is the centre and Kyiv is the periphery, to include a third actor: Ukrainian regions as an uncoordinated group. Arguably for the first time in academic scholarship, this monograph shows that a Soviet republic had its own distinct institutional dynamic and examines the extent of pressure that the regions exerted on the leadership of that republic. By focusing on the pressure from below, the monograph combines and, to a degree, reconciles the view of the Soviet Union as a federation, where subjects of the federation represented 'separate rooms' in a 'communal apartment', with the view of the Soviet Union as a de facto unitary state where political and economic power was centralized.[55]

To examine and offer an explanation of the distinctiveness of the Ukrainian Soviet and post-Soviet political system, the book takes the approach of historical institutionalism. 'At its broadest, historical institutionalism represents an attempt to illuminate how political struggles "are mediated by the institutional setting in which [they] take place".'[56] This book studies the causal impact of the Soviet institutional legacy on the post-Soviet transition in Ukraine.[57] In line with historical institutionalists who seek to explain specific political outcomes using the historical legacy of institutional structures, this book seeks a historical explanation of the efforts and achievements of the Ukrainian leaders during perestroika and after the collapse of the Soviet Union in 1991.

The monograph deviates from narrative political history in that its approach to the analysis of the Ukrainian institutional set-up is guided by the political realities in independent Ukraine, and particularly by Ukraine's simultaneous resistance to authoritarianism and to becoming a fully functional democracy.[58] Thus, the main guiding question of the book is: why did the configuration of 'weak centre, strong regions', to which scholars attribute both Ukraine's failure to fully democratize and its success in not becoming authoritarian, survive the chaos of the 1990s in Ukraine? It is with an eye on this keystone configuration of the relationship between the Ukrainian centre and the Ukrainian regions, which structured Ukrainian politics after the fall of the Soviet Union in 1991, that the analysis is structured and the political and economic developments are contextualized.

Hence, at the centre of this monograph are not political or economic actors, nor political developments as such. (The reader will notice that the monograph pays very little attention to such watershed policies in Soviet history as industrialization, collectivization, the Holodomor, deportations, and de-Stalinization, or to such a crucial phenomenon as Ukrainian nationalism.) At the centre of this monograph are institutions, succinctly defined by Douglass North as 'any form of constraint that human beings devise to shape human interaction', such forms including formal organizations, formal and informal rules and procedures, policies, conventions, and codes of behaviour created or evolved over time.[59] This book is solely concerned with events and developments that are relevant to understanding the origins, changes, and legacies of the political and economic institutions that defined this configuration. In other words, it uses history to explain when and how the configuration 'weak centre, strong regions' was formed and institutionalized, how this configuration survived the dissolution of the Soviet Union and its centralized party-state, and how this configuration affected Kravchuk's choices as president and the behaviour of Ukrainian politicians in the 1990s more broadly.

Based on new empirical archival material and guided by the theory of institutions, this monograph examines how the institutional framework of interlinked political and economic incentives and constraints determined the opportunities and institutional interests of the Ukrainian Soviet and post-Soviet leadership and the leadership of the regions, and how it affected the dynamic of the relationship between these actors. It studies the balance of power between the Ukrainian centre and the Ukrainian regions as an uncoordinated group during the Soviet period and analyses political struggles between the executive branch and the regions in Ukraine during the early post-Soviet transition.[60] Echoing Yoram Gorlizki and Oleg Khlevniuk, the monograph explores how rule following and interest maximizing affected institutional change in the Soviet context. It also explores institutional stability, or path dependency, in the early post-Soviet context.[61]

## Central Argument: Institutional Change versus Institutional Continuity

This monograph argues that the Ukrainian institutional setting evolved throughout the entire Soviet period. The foundations of the system that created the configuration 'weak centre, strong regions' were laid during the period between 1917 and the first half of the 1920s. During Khrushchev's decentralization reforms of the 1950s and early 1960s, and during the first seven years of Brezhnev's rule (1965–1972), the institutional system went through some changes, but not fundamental changes. The fall of the Soviet Union and the disintegration of the centralized party system had an insignificant effect on the existing configuration of 'weak centre, strong uncoordinated group of regions', and the regions maintained low dependence on the Ukrainian leadership in the early post-Soviet period. The old configuration of the relations between Kyiv and the regions continued to structure political outcomes.

## The Soviet Legacy of Weak Presidency

This book scrutinizes the role and place of the Ukrainian leader (first secretary) and the Ukrainian leadership, or the Soviet dual executive, which comprised the Ukrainian Central Committee and the Council of Ministers (the Ukrainian government), in the Soviet administrative structure, and the margins of their power. It challenges the view that Ukrainian republican leaders exercised dictatorial powers over Ukrainian regional leaders.[62] It argues that, in spite of having had such charismatic personalities heading the republic as Nikita (Mykyta) Khrushchev (1938–March 1947; December 1947–1949), Petro Shelest (1963–1972), and Volodymyr Shcherbytsky (1972–1989), the institution of the first secretary was weak.[63] The political weakness of Ukrainian first secretaries was detected as early as 1977 when, based on the patron–client network criteria, Grey Hodnett observed that 'neither Shelest nor Shcherbytsky have come close to being the centre of an all-dominating patron-client network at the top leadership level in the Ukraine'.[64] However, at the heart of the political weakness of Ukrainian Soviet leaders was the institutional weakness of the Ukrainian first secretary, which in its turn was determined by the inconsistency between the responsibilities of the first secretary to fulfil central orders and plan targets by the republic, on the one hand, and his formal (and, by implication, informal) powers, on the other. Due to this inconsistency, the CPU first secretary, regardless of his convictions or personality, relied on the regions for the fulfilment of his direct functions as defined by the Central Committee in Moscow that appointed him.

When political transformation in the Soviet Union forced Ukrainian political elites to create the presidency, they designed the institution of the presidency based on that of the republican first secretary. In contrast to the first secretary, however, the president was a democratically elected official. The president also performed new functions, such as representing Ukraine in the international arena. However, crucially, the first secretary and the president shared a fundamental basic weakness: neither had their functions aligned with their powers. Both were dependent on support of the regions for the fulfilment of their functions. The inconsistency between power and responsibility motivated Kravchuk in January 1992 to seek an expansion of his authority beyond the framework that the Verkhovna Rada had established in the summer of 1991, ironically under his chairmanship.

This monograph agrees with the existing argument that the dual executive, or semi-presidentialism, was not a new form of governance for Ukraine.[65] It argues that the Soviet dual executive was similar to its post-Soviet successor in its lack of access to resources, which determined the margins of authority over the regions for both executive institutions.

## The Soviet Legacy of Regionalism

The book traces the roots of regionalism in Ukraine to the fragmented CPU. Indeed, the CPU was fully integrated into the ideologically monolithic Communist Party of the Soviet Union (CPSU), which was also a special sort of mechanism, 'a system of organs and institutions linked by hierarchical subordination and carrying out activities constituting a state monopoly'.[66] Nonetheless, considered as a regional division of the CPSU, the CPU itself was fragmented. The argument that the CPU was fragmented is not new. Taras Kuzio speculated that the CPU 'was always a factionalised body, with arguably no true existence as a systemic whole'.[67] This monograph substantiates Kuzio's claim and explains why the CPU did not form a systemic whole and how fragmentation of the CPU translated into post-Soviet regionalism.

The CPU's fragmentation was determined by several factors. Firstly, it lacked a unifying Ukrainian party centre. Despite appearances, the Ukrainian Central Committee was not the sole formal or informal authority for the Ukrainian obkoms. The relationship between the Central Committee in Moscow, the Ukrainian Central Committee, and the Ukrainian obkoms as a group was not pyramidal, but triangular, whereby the obkoms had as much access to the Central Committee in Moscow as the Ukrainian Central Committee did, while depending more on the former than the latter.

The second factor was the raison d'être of the obkoms. It had been established that the Soviet prefects, as Jerry Hough famously dubbed the obkom first secretaries, performed the function of economic administrators in their oblasts.[68] Under pressure to fulfil the socio-economic agenda and to ensure their oblasts fulfilled plans, they cooperated with local managers, thus forming party–industry alliances.[69] As the literature on regional networks shows, local party–industry alliances were not specific to Ukraine.[70] What was specific to Ukraine was the existence of an institutionally weak Ukrainian leadership that, due to a lack of resources at its disposal, was unable systematically to assist the regions with the fulfilment of their responsibilities. On an ad hoc basis, Ukrainian leaders, powerful at an all-union level, could satisfy random requests from the obkom first secretaries. However, since the administration of industry was centralized, Ukrainian obkom secretaries systemically depended on the ministries in Moscow for the fulfilment of their main function.

The third factor that contributed to the fragmentation of the CPU was the uneven distribution of heavy industry, which was the priority of the Soviet leadership. Due to the concentration of heavy industry in the eastern and southern oblasts, the obkoms from this region were in a more favourable position to develop their local economies as compared to their counterparts from the agricultural northern, central, and western regions. Some obkoms, like Donetsk,

Dnipropetrovsk, Kharkiv, and Lviv (which Stalin hoped would become the beacon of sovietization in Western Ukraine), had tight connections with Moscow; others, like Sumy, Chernihiv, Volyn, Rivne, and Ternopil, did not. Considering that each obkom was focused on the fulfilment of plans and the socio-economic agenda and had to rely primarily on the producers (and the ministries to which they were subordinated to) for the fulfilment of their principal objectives, the Ukrainian Central Committee was in no position to forge a united CPU.

The institutional fragmentation of the CPU remained concealed until 1989–1990 when the weakening of the CPSU and the decay of centralized economic administration gradually revealed it to the wider public and, most importantly, to the party itself. Perestroika and glasnost put the obkoms on the verge of political extinction. The revitalization of the soviets (councils) initiated by Gorbachev allowed the communist nomenklatura in the periphery to migrate safely into the new centres of authority in the periphery and thus remain in power. However, having transferred power from the obkoms to the soviets, the Soviet leadership did not relieve local soviets of their main responsibilities. The incentives behind alliances between the soviets and managers did not change. The fulfilment of plans no longer dominated the agenda of the soviets (although it remained a decreasing concern for the obkoms), but the pressure from democratization and the new factor of elections forced them to respond to the socio-economic needs of the population in their territories. Under pressure from a declining economy, rapidly decaying centralized administration of the economy, and growing democratization, the obkoms and communists in the soviets urged the Ukrainian leadership to demand the decentralization of control over the economy from Moscow to Kyiv and priority of the interests of the regions over the interests of the all-union centre. The Ukrainian leadership, and First Secretary Shcherbytsky personally, yielded to pressure 'from below' and demanded the decentralization of economic administration—but in vain. Control over the economy remained with the central ministries until the fall of the Soviet Union. In the turbulent years of 1990–1991, support from Kyiv to the regions did not increase, and the regions were left to themselves to fulfil their own agenda. The declaration of independence generated hope among the regions that they would finally have a centre close to them capable of concentrating on their agenda. However, in newly independent Ukraine, their hopes did not materialize.

## The Centre–Region Configuration in Ukraine

The monograph argues that at the foundation of the triangular relationship between Moscow, Kyiv, and the regions in 1917–1991 and the direct relationship between Kyiv and the regions in independent Ukraine was the Bolshevik paradigm that de facto power lay with those who controlled resources, who had 'effective decision-making about the use of resources (i.e., de facto ownership)'.[71] The balance of power between Kyiv and the regions was determined by the correlation between the responsibilities and capabilities of each side. The inability of the Ukrainian leadership to control the distribution of resources determined its institutional weakness and its relationship with the Ukrainian regions. Throughout the entire period under discussion, the Ukrainian leadership was more dependent on the regions for the fulfilment of its responsibilities than the regions were dependent on Kyiv.

The Soviet institutional system, its organizational structure, and the set of incentives and constraints were designed to prevent the Ukrainian leadership from obtaining control over resources or independently accumulating reserves. The main holders of resources were the regions and Moscow. With no resources to manipulate, Kyiv was unable to affect its relationship with the regions. In the realities of 1989–1994, characterized by the dominance of a barter economy, Ukraine's dependence on the Russian rouble, and a deregulated economy, the significance of the Bolshevik paradigm reached new heights. Even more than before, de facto power lay with those who controlled material resources.

Since 1917, the Ukrainian Soviet leadership had envisioned, hoped, and, depending on the general political context, unsuccessfully tried to become the sole intermediary between the Ukrainian regions and the central party-state leadership in Moscow. At the end of perestroika, the Ukrainian leadership finally got its chance to correct the Kyiv–regions balance of power in its favour. Starting in 1989, the regions objectively needed a strong centre and were prepared to support the consolidation of the Ukrainian centre. Kyiv, however, took what this author considers the wrong approach to the consolidation of the Ukrainian centre.

Being institutionally weaker than the regions, to accumulate resources under its control in 1990–1994 Kyiv needed cooperation from the regions. To forge cooperation, it needed to reconfigure the incentive structure that regulated regional control over resources. However, instead of reconfiguring the system of constraints and incentives, the Ukrainian leadership chose to use Moscow's old administrative methods and impose the Soviet top-down model of administration, or *diktat*, over them. The regions, most of which were under the control of the ex-communist nomenklatura, resented *diktat*, not because they resented authoritarian methods per se (on the contrary, they longed for a 'firm hand'), but because unlike Moscow's *diktat* before 1989, Kyiv's did not provide them with political and economic security. Kyiv demanded their submission to its authority while being unable to defend their interests or to punish them. They relied on local businesses to defend their interests. The anger of the population was feared as much as, if not more than, the reprimands of the president. From the perspective of the regions, which as an uncoordinated group controlled material resources, Kyiv's *diktat* was incompatible with the institutional system that existed in Ukraine. Only through cooperation with the regions and the alignment of their interests with central policies could Kyiv consolidate the state and its own power. Hence, throughout 1992–1994, the regions rebuffed *diktat* and concentrated on orchestrating their own survival independently from Kyiv. For the president's representatives, envisaged as his personal network, the incentives to defend regional interests were stronger than their loyalty to the president. The regionalism that had been characteristic of Soviet Ukraine since the 1920s became visible to outside observers.

This book shows that regionalism as a tendency towards autonomy was a reaction not to the dissolution of the centralized party-state, but to the failure of the newly formed executive branch to account for the incentives and constraints to which the regions were subjected in 1992–1994 and its conscious decision to exclude the regions from policymaking. It was in reaction to Kyiv's resentment towards the inclusion of the regions in policymaking that the 1994 parliamentary elections established 'the priority of an active and balanced regional policy in the minds of members of parliament and the electorate. Most members of parliament won their seats based on this issue.'[72]

This monograph further argues that, contrary to the accepted view that all post-Soviet states were at the same starting point after the disintegration of the centralized party-state Soviet system, Ukraine was not. Kravchuk may or may not have inherited a state comparatively weak relative to other non-Russian republics[73] (this remains to be researched), but he certainly inherited a much weaker state than Yeltsin. 'The lack of separation of political and economic power in the Soviet system contributed to a particular intermingling of political and economic power in the new order which has proved a potent mix,'[74] Claire Gordon argued. However, Moscow had full control over political and economic power during the Soviet era, so the task for Yeltsin was to take control over this 'mix'. Soviet Kyiv never had economic power and had only very limited political power. The interlinked political and economic power in Soviet Ukraine lay with the regions, not Kyiv. In the new post-Soviet order, while the Russian state lost control of policies and decisions to the subjects of the federation,[75] the Ukrainian leadership had little control to lose in the first place. The task for Kravchuk and the Ukrainian government was not to restore but to establish political and economic control.

The organizational structure of the post-Soviet Ukrainian state was modified, yet the balance of power between Kyiv and the regions did not change. It remained relatively stable through the entire period between 1917 and 1994. The disintegration of the Soviet system in 1991 did not introduce a fundamental change in the configuration of the relationship between the central leadership in Kyiv, which was institutionally weak, and the regions, which were an uncoordinated group but institutionally stronger. Political change in 1990–1991 was not strong enough to affect the stability of this configuration, nor did the political shock of the disintegration of the Soviet system disrupt 'the development of institution-specific assets such as skills, privileges, knowledge of procedures, and networks with other actors'.[76] For Ukraine, the shock of the fall of the Soviet Union and the centralized party-state, economy, and communist ideology turned out to be more exogenous than endogenous. The events of the Soviet Union's final years had more effect on the ideological setting than on the institutional set-up.

To sum up, this book argues that the keystone configuration of 'weak centre, strong regions' has been at the foundation of Ukrainian politics since 1917 and continued to mediate Ukrainian political actors across space and time.[77] After thirty years of post-Soviet development, the structure has somewhat shifted, bringing more power to the centre. But in the early 1990s, President Kravchuk and his three prime ministers, Vitold Fokin (23 October 1990–1 October 1992), Leonid Kuchma (13 October 1992–21 September 1993), and Yukhym Zviahilsky (22 September 1993–4 June 1994), still operated in an environment of strong institutional inertia. They failed to consolidate control over the state not because they failed to control the factors that determined *change*, but because they refused to tackle the factors that determined *continuity*. The structure of politics that they inherited dictated their actions to a far greater degree than they dictated changes to the political structure.

## Sources

This monograph is primarily based on unpublished primary sources from the Ukrainian central archives, the Central State Archive of Public Organizations of Ukraine (TsDAHOU) and the Central State Archive of Supreme Bodies of Power and Government of Ukraine (TsDAVOU), and regional archives, the state archives of Zaporizhzhia oblast (DAZO), of Rivne oblast (DARO), and Lviv oblast (DALO). The monograph uses documents generated by the central Soviet leadership, including those related to conferences and congresses of the Russian Communist Party (Bolsheviks) (RKP(b)) and the CPSU from the Russian State Archive of Social and Political History (RGASPI), documents related to the Central Committee plenums from the Russian State Archive of Contemporary History (RGANI), and documents generated by the central economic agencies from the Russian State Archive of the Economy (RGAE). For the post-Soviet period, the monograph uses shorthand record reports of the meetings of the Ukrainian parliament, Verkhovna Rada, and other documents available through online databases of Verkhovna Rada, accessed at https://www.rada.gov.ua/meeting/stenogr/ and https://zakon.rada.gov.ua/laws/main.

This monograph embraces several bodies of scholarship. The first is scholarship on Soviet and Ukrainian political and economic history. The monograph makes ample use of the empirical research done by Ukrainian scholars, such as Valerii Vasil'ev [Vasiliev], Mykola Frolov, Hennadii Yefimenko [Efimenko], and

Stanislav Kulchytsky, on Ukrainian political history. The second strand of scholarship used in the monograph is social science works that analysed the Soviet
party-state system of administration. The seminal work of Jerry Hough on the
role of the periphery party organs in economic management, written more than
half a century ago, and John Armstrong's study on the Ukrainian apparatus from
1959 remain relevant.[78] The third strand of scholarship includes works on
Ukrainian early post-Soviet political and economic transformation. Roman
Solchanyk, Taras Kuzio, Paul D'Anieri, Robert S. Kravchuk, Andrew Wilson,
Sarah Whitmore, Kataryna Wolczuk, Gwendolyn Sasse, Oleh Havrylyshyn,
Anders Åslund, and Hans van Zon were among those scholars who laid the
groundwork for understanding the Ukrainian post-Soviet transition and whose
prolific works are amply used in the last chapter. The monograph also uses schol-
arship on Russia's early post-Soviet years. Particularly relevant for this study was
research done by Yoshiko Herrera on Russian regionalism and especially by
David Woodruff on the barter economy.[79]

Finally, the fourth body of studies used for this monograph is the previously
mentioned scholarship on institutionalism. This monograph was conceived as
and remains a historical study, but theoretical work on institutionalism was used
to conceptualize historical findings.

## Overview of the Chapters

The chapters are divided chronologically, according to the 'change–inertia' principle.
Chapters 1, 2, 4, 5, and 7 discuss *change*. Chapters 3, 6, and 8 discuss systemic
*inertia*. All chapters, except Chapter 1, discuss both the central leadership of
Ukraine and the leadership of the regions.

Chapter 1 covers the period that established the institution of centralized
administration in Ukraine in 1917–1920. It de-emphasizes the ideological convictions of the Bolsheviks and focuses on their power ambitions.

Chapter 2 examines formation of the institutional system of Ukraine in
1921–1925. It discusses the efforts of the Ukrainian Soviet leadership to secure and
formalize tangible political and economic powers and thus establish itself as the
only link between the Ukrainian regions and the central leadership in Moscow, as
well as the causes of its failure. The chapter introduces a new actor, 'the regions',
and discusses factors that allowed for the institutionalization of the fragmentation of the Communist Party (Bolshevik) of Ukraine (CP(b)U).

Chapter 3 argues that the institutional framework that regulated the relationship between the all-union centre, the Ukrainian centre, and the regions was
formed by 1925 and did not change until 1954. The policies and events that transformed Soviet state and society had no effect on the division of power between
the all-union centre, the republican centre, and the regions; hence, it had no

effect on the power of the Ukrainian leadership over the Ukrainian regions. At the same time, the priority of heavy industry that was institutionalized from the end of the 1920s and the prioritization of industry branch development over regional development consolidated the institutional weakness of the Ukrainian leadership and the fragmentation of the CPU (formerly the CP(b)U).

Chapter 4 covers the period between 1954 and 1965 and scrutinizes institutional change that was caused by Khrushchev's decentralization reforms. The first part of the chapter assesses how the Sovnarkhoz reform changed the role and involvement of the Ukrainian leadership in economic administration, affecting its authority and its relationship with the regions. The second part discusses how Khrushchev's reforms empowered regional party-industry coalitions and assesses the institutional distinctiveness of Western Ukraine.

Chapter 5 discusses the period between 1965 and 1972. It observes the unequal effect that the restoration of centralized control over the economy had on Ukrainian leadership and the regions.

Chapter 6 describes the period of institutional stability between 1972 and 1989. It discusses the inconsistency between the strong image of the first secretary of Ukraine, Volodymyr Shcherbytsky, and the powers of the institute of the first secretary, the tenacity of fragmentation within the CPU, and continuous marginalization of Western Ukraine. The chapter assesses the effect of perestroika on the triangular relationship between the all-union centre, the Ukrainian leadership, and the regions.

Chapter 7 examines how, in Jack Snyder's words, in the wake of collapse, Ukrainian republican and regional elites sought to adapt 'the institutional wreckage of empire to survive the challenges of social transformation', as they faced the triple challenge of 'the scramble for security in anarchy', 'the widening of political participation', and the challenge posed by economic reform.[80] It argues that the Ukrainian leadership refused to accept Ukraine's institutional realities and thus failed to reconfigure the relationship between Kyiv and the regions in the final years of the Soviet Union, 1990–1991.

Chapter 8 assesses the extent of institutional inertia after Ukraine became independent. It shows that the new Ukrainian executive also refused to reconfigure centre–periphery relations in a way that would reflect the de facto configuration between the weak centre and strong regions and induce cooperation between Kyiv and the regions. Instead, Kyiv chose to use Moscow's administrative method of *diktat* to assert its own power. The chapter looks at why *diktat* did not work in Ukraine in 1992–1994.

The book ends with a general conclusion.

*The Institutional Foundations of Ukrainian Democracy: Power Sharing, Regionalism, and Authoritarianism*. Nataliya Kibita,
Oxford University Press. © Nataliya Kibita 2024. DOI: 10.1093/9780191925351.003.0001

# 1

# Centralized Administration in Ukraine for Ukraine

## Introduction: The Central Rada

For several centuries, Ukrainian gubernias, or provinces, had no Ukrainian territorial administrative centre. Each gubernia was administered by a governor appointed by the Russian Imperial government and the prospects for these gubernias to unite in one polity were dim, until the 1917 February Revolution.[1] Only then, after the abdication of Nicholas II on 2 (15) March 1917, could a group of Kyiv-based Ukrainian intellectuals and socialists create the first all-Ukrainian centre, an organization called the Ukrainian Central Rada (hereafter, the 'Central Rada'). Under the leadership of Professor Mykhailo Hrushevsky, the Central Rada rapidly showed a tendency towards autonomy. On 9 March, it called on Ukrainians to calmly but decisively demand 'the introduction of native language in all schools, from lower to upper, in courts and all governmental institutions', and 'unite in political societies, cultural and economic unions'. On 25 March, the newspaper *Nova Rada* announced that an All-Ukrainian Congress would be held on 6–8 April to discuss 'wide national-territorial autonomy' for Ukraine.[2]

To an outside observer, the Central Rada seemed to appear out of thin air. However, there was nothing sudden or unexpected in either its appearance or its autonomist agenda. As a Hetmanate under the rule of Cossack hetmans, Ukrainian lands enjoyed autonomy until Catherine II imposed centralized imperial control in the early 1780s. After the Napoleonic Wars, the idea emerged to restore Ukraine's autonomy. In 1845, Ukrainian scientist Mykola Hulak, historian and writer Mykola Kostomarov, and journalist Vasyl Bilozersky established the Brotherhood of Saints Cyril and Methodius. A short-lived political organization with a small membership, it aspired to abolish serfdom and advocated for transforming the empire into a federal union of Slavic autonomous peoples, one of which would be Ukrainians, in which each Slavic people would be independent and have people's governance, and each citizen would be equal under the law.[3] After Russia lost the Crimean War to Britain, France, Ottoman Turkey, and Sardinia-Piedmont, Emperor Alexander II initiated the so-called Great Reforms. With the societal changes ushered in by these reforms, the Ukrainian national movement became less focused on political change. Ukrainian nationalist-minded intellectuals focused instead on educating Ukrainian peasants and popularizing Ukrainian language, history, and culture. The Russian imperial government, however, viewed the development of Ukrainian culture and language as no less dangerous for the unity of the empire than the intellectuals' aspirations for Ukraine's autonomy. In 1863, Minister of Internal Affairs Pyotr Valuev issued a directive that prohibited virtually all Ukrainian-language publications, except works of fiction. 'At first considered a temporary measure, the prohibition became permanent in May 1876', when Alexander II issued the Ems Ukase prohibiting all publications in Ukrainian, any importation of Ukrainian-language books from abroad, Ukrainian-language theatre productions, and public performances of Ukrainian songs.[4]

While Alexander II focused on the struggle against Ukrainian language and culture—official restrictions on Ukrainian publications were dropped only in October 1905—the Great Reforms and industrialization that accelerated at the end of the 1880s transformed the political landscape of Ukraine. A plurality of views unknown before the reforms spread beyond groups of the privileged few and transcended romantic thinking about democracy and autonomy. The 1890s witnessed the formation of political parties in Ukraine. At the same time, the reforms induced closer interaction between Russian and Ukrainian revolutionaries and intellectuals. In the minds of Ukrainian nationalist-minded activists, autonomy could not be achieved without transforming Russia, and to transform Russia they needed to act in tandem with Russian progressive groups. This dual transformation of the Ukrainian political landscape gave rise to a new leader of the Ukrainian movement: Mykhailo Hrushevsky.

After the 1905 Russian Revolution, in the First and Second Duma, Ukrainian nationalist-minded intellectuals from St Petersburg and Ukrainian Duma deputies from various political parties promoted political autonomy for Ukraine; the creation of a territorial-legislative branch, Sejm, that would address the land problem in Ukraine; and the introduction of the Ukrainian language in schools, courts, and various administrations. They formed the Ukrainian Duma Society, also known as the Ukrainian parliamentary club.[5] The Ukrainian Duma Society could not fulfil its agenda in the First or Second Duma. After the dispersion of the Second Duma and the introduction of new electoral regulations, a Ukrainian faction could not be formed in the Third Duma. The autonomist agenda could not be brought to the discussion in the Fourth Duma, either. During the First World War, the tsarist authorities suppressed any polemics on the Ukrainian national question, Ukrainian national aspirations, or Ukrainian autonomy, interpreting these topics as separatist.

Once the news of the February Revolution reached Kyiv, there were no second thoughts as to whether to create an all-Ukrainian organization in Ukraine.

At the time of its founding in March 1917, there was no institution in Ukraine that could compete for popularity with the Central Rada. Its popularity and administrative importance were also not challenged by the Provisional Government.

At the beginning of April, the Provisional Government recognized the influence of the Central Rada when Minister of Finance Mikhail Tereshchenko addressed a telegram to the All-Ukrainian National Congress asking for assistance in distributing the 'freedom loan'.[6] At the end of April, the Provisional Government agreed, although reluctantly, to appoint a well-known Ukrainian nationalist, member of the Society of Ukrainian Progressives, and one of the founding members of the Central Rada, Dmytro Doroshenko, to the post of Commissar of Galicia and Bukovina, and to appoint other Ukrainians suggested by the Central Rada to the posts of gubernia and *povit*, or district, commissars. Hrushevsky interpreted the assignment of Doroshenko as 'the dearest gift of the Russian revolution for the restoration of Great Ukraine'.[7] So high were expectations of productive relations between the Central Rada and the Provisional Government that the Provisional Government and Petrograd Soviet's refusal in May 1917 to grant legitimacy to the Central Rada as the Ukrainian territorial administration and recognize Ukraine's autonomist aspirations came as an unexpected surprise.[8]

On 10 June, prompted by popular support from Ukrainian congresses of peasants and soldiers that were held in Kyiv at the end of spring/beginning of summer, the Central Rada issued its First Manifesto. The First Manifesto did not declare autonomy for Ukraine, but it declared centralized administration in Kyiv for Ukraine that would prepare Ukraine for eventual autonomy. On 15 June, the Central Rada formed the first Ukrainian government, the General Secretariat. In July, the Provisional Government recognized the General Secretariat as its territorial representative for five Ukrainian gubernias, instead of nine as the Central Rada expected.[9] The institution of centralized administration in Ukraine for Ukraine was established and formalized. Non-Ukrainian socialist political parties, which until recently had rejected the idea of Ukrainian autonomy, suddenly forgot their antagonism towards the Ukrainian national movement and channelled their efforts into securing as many seats in the Central Rada as possible.[10] On 11 July, Ukrainians and non-Ukrainians held their first joint meeting. Aside from Bolsheviks, all revolutionary-democratic organizations representing Poles, Jews, and Russians sent delegates. They recognized that with Petrograd far away and focused on the war effort, a new administrative centre in autonomous Ukraine was opening new political opportunities.

Similar to non-Ukrainian parties, Ukraine's Bolsheviks at first rejected the Central Rada and its autonomist agenda,[11] partly because they believed that the national agenda distracted workers from the class struggle, but also because in spring 1917 the Bolsheviks did not view Ukraine as a separate administrative unit that needed a territorial administration. However, also similar to non-Ukrainian parties, as the Ukrainian revolution progressed, Ukraine's Bolsheviks, particularly those from Kyiv, realized that a new territorial administration in Kyiv opened new political opportunities for them as well, not so much in Ukraine where they remained in the minority, but within the Russian Social Democratic Workers'

**Illustration 1**  Reading of the First Manifesto of the Ukrainian Central Rada after a prayer at Sofia square in Kyiv, 12 June 1917/© TsDAVOU

After the Russian Revolution of February 1917, a group of prominent Kyiv-based Ukrainian liberal moderates, joined by students, Ukrainian Social Democrats, and representatives of public and professional organizations, created a new All-Ukrainian state institution called Tsentral'na Rada, or Central Rada. On 10 June 1917, the Ukrainian Central Rada issued its First Manifesto, which declared that Ukraine's aim was autonomy within the Russian state. In the photo, the leader of the Ukrainian Socialist Revolutionaries Mykola Kovalevsky reads the First Manifesto to the crowd at Sofia square on 12 June 1917. To his left, the chairman of the Ukrainian Central Rada, Mykhailo Hrushevsky.

Party (Bolsheviks) (RSDRP(b)). They believed that Bolshevik policies would need to be adjusted to the Ukrainian context by local policymakers. The Bolshevik leadership, however, was reluctant to accept Ukraine as one polity. It would take another three years for it to drop the idea of merging Ukraine with Russia and accept the legacy of the Central Rada.

## Transformation of the Bolshevik View on Centralized Administration in Ukraine

In March 1917, Kyiv Bolsheviks observed the growing Ukrainian national movement and realized that Lenin's rhetoric about national self-determination was detrimental to the Bolshevik struggle for power in Ukraine. The separation of Ukraine, which had a small proletariat base, meant that local Bolsheviks had very little chance of coming to power. Therefore, at the Seventh (April) All-Russian

**Illustration 2**  The General Secretariat of the Ukrainian Central Rada, Kyiv, June 1917/© TsDAVOU

On 15 June 1917, the Ukrainian Central Council formed the first Ukrainian government, the General Secretariat. General secretaries left to right, sitting: Ivan Steshenko (education), Khrystofor Baranovsky (finance), Head of the General Secretariat Volodymyr Vynnychenko, Serhii Yefremov (international affairs), Symon Petliura (military affairs); standing: Pavlo Khrystiuk (general chancellor), Mykola Stasiuk (food supplies), Borys Martos (land affairs).

Conference of the RSDRP(b) (24–29 April 1917), the leader of the Kyiv Bolsheviks, Heorhii (Yurii) Piatakov, insisted that the RSDRP(b) should drop the slogan of national self-determination. He argued that the only solution to the nationality problem was open borders.[12] To Lenin, however, the rhetoric of national self-determination served as propaganda against the Provisional Government, as well as against the Petrograd Soviet, which was dominated by the Socialist Revolutionaries (SRs) and the Mensheviks. Lenin's primary concern was power in Petrograd. He replied to the Polish Bolsheviks who, like Ukraine's Bolsheviks, rejected the slogan of national self-determination:

> Why must we, *velikorossy* [Great Russians], who oppressed a greater number of nations than any other nation, refuse to recognise the right to separate by Poland, Ukraine or Finland? They [the Polish Bolsheviks] want us to become chauvinists because this would facilitate the position of the Social Democrats in Poland.[13]

Piatakov soon discovered that Lenin's views on national self-determination were more nuanced than his rhetoric at the April conference suggested. At the meeting of the Kyiv committee of the RSDRP(b) on 4 June, Piatakov mentioned that Lenin had accepted Ukraine's autonomy only under certain conditions, namely after a referendum and only without a legislative body, or a parliament. This revelation was in stark contrast to Lenin's public unconditional support for Ukraine's aspirations for autonomy and the Central Rada, which was viewed by many as a proto parliament.[14] On 4 June, Kyiv Bolsheviks agreed to support a 'territorial, not national, plebiscite' on Ukraine's so-called 'narrow' autonomy. By 'narrow' autonomy, they meant that all legislative power as well as the regulation of economic relations would remain with the Russian government.[15]

After the Central Rada passed its First Manifesto, which in itself was evidence of the growing national movement, the Kyiv Bolsheviks confirmed their position that autonomy could be proclaimed only after a referendum. However, they now accepted 'wide' autonomy, which allowed a legislative body in Ukraine.[16] After the Third Manifesto of the Central Rada on 7 (20) November, which declared the autonomous Ukrainian National Republic (UNR) as part of the (future democratic) Russian Federation, Kyiv Bolsheviks dropped any talk of a plebiscite, accepted Ukraine's autonomy with its own centralized administration, and started taking more decisive steps to fit into the Ukrainian context.

Encouraged by peripheral Bolshevik organizations, on 8 November, the oblast committee of the RSDRP(b) of the south-western region, which had already been formed under the leadership of Evheniia Bosh in April 1917 to unite the Bolshevik organizations of the south-western region, took the initiative of calling a congress of Bolshevik organizations of Ukraine that would 'seriously consider creation of a separate party for Ukraine'.[17] 'Whereas in Russia, revolutionary social-democracy is the leader of the working class…, in Ukraine it is the so-called Ukrainian Social Democratic Workers' Party [USDRP] that claims to perform the role of the leader of the working masses', the Kyiv Bolsheviks reasoned. The Ukrainian Bolshevik centre would be part of the RSDRP(b), 'one of its divisions'; it would respond to local conditions that were specific to Ukraine and 'lead the decisive struggle against the policy of nationalism and chauvinism'.[18]

On 11 November, Bosh asked the Central Committee of the RSDRP(b) (hereafter, the 'Central Committee') for its 'sanctions and instructions', and instructed Heorhii Piatakov, who was in Moscow at the time to personally inform the Council of People's Commissars (Sovnarkom) about the situation in Ukraine.[19] The second chairman of the All-Russian Central Executive Committee of Soviets (TsIK), Yakov Sverdlov, replied to Bosh on 24 (or 25) November that the Central Committee disapproved of the idea of an autonomous Ukrainian 'division of RSDRP(b)' with its own decision-making centre. But he agreed to a 'province congress or conference, which would be viewed [by the Bolshevik leadership] as a regular regional congress of our party'.[20]

It must have been in reaction to this telegram that the south-western oblast committee of RSDRP(b) sent Serhii Bakinsky to Petrograd where, on 27–29 November, he met twice with Lenin. Lenin listened to his arguments for forming a separate party for Ukraine and suggested that Bakinsky discuss the matter with Stalin and Sverdlov. When the Central Committee discussed the organization of the Ukrainian Bolshevik Party at its meeting on 29 November, it did not come to any decision. The issue was passed to the Central Committee Buro, Lenin, Stalin, Sverdlov, and Leon Trotsky. At the beginning of December 1917, the decision was still pending.[21]

## Lenin's Stance on Centralized Administration in Ukraine

What was described as 'studying the issue, while trying to avoid any hasty, unfounded decisions',[22] was Lenin's way of saying that the Central Committee did not need any national Bolshevik Party in Ukraine. Already 'in October 1917, before taking power, Lenin [had] specified that he would not divide the Russian empire into independent socialist national states'.[23] Now in power, he treated each Ukrainian gubernia as an integral part of Russia that should be run directly by the Russian state.[24] He had no plans to create a Ukrainian Soviet republic, and thus did not need a separate Ukrainian Bolshevik Party to dominate the Ukrainian Soviet government in Ukraine.

While publicly unable to deny the principle of national self-determination to Ukrainians, not least because of its propaganda value,[25] in non-public communications, the Bolshevik leadership took a more nuanced approach to applying the principle in Ukraine.

In his 17 November conversations with Bakinsky and Mykola Porsh, representative of the Central Rada and General Secretary for Labour (USDRP), Stalin repeated the Bolshevik official rhetoric about national self-determination. However, when talking to Porsh, Stalin denied the Central Rada's legitimacy by insisting that only the All-Russian Constituent Assembly could legitimize the autonomy of Ukraine.[26] When talking to Bakinsky, Stalin was more straightforward, yet still careful not to blatantly contradict the Bolshevik 'national self-determination' rhetoric. Bakinsky explained that the Kyiv and Kharkiv Bolsheviks insisted on calling an All-Ukrainian congress of soviets (councils) of workers' and soldiers' deputies 'based on the opinion, that until [there is] a *Ukrainian* Constituent Assembly, power cannot stay with the Ukrainian Central Rada'. 'In the region [i.e., in Ukraine], [power] must pass to the congress of soviets of workers' and soldiers' deputies, and in localities [*na mestakh*] to the soviets of workers and soldiers' deputies.' Stalin replied carefully, agreeing that a congress of soviets was necessary. 'The issues of Soviet power in the centre and in the localities are not for discussion. There is no other way to form territorial power', he said. However, while being crystal clear about Soviet power in the periphery, to indicate that the Soviet 'centre' was Petrograd, not Kyiv, he insisted that the autonomy of Ukraine was a future concern. 'The Congress of Soviets of Ukraine must give, by the way, an *opinion* [italics added] about the methods for conducting straw polls about belonging to this or another oblast.'[27] Contrary to the existing interpretation of this conversation,[28] Stalin did not appear to demand that the Congress of Soviets take power from the Central Rada. In fact, he could not, as such a demand would have implied recognition of Ukraine's autonomy. So, Stalin left unanswered Bakinsky's remark that power in Ukraine should belong to the Congress of Soviets. The purpose of the Congress of Soviets was to ensure that the Soviets took power in the periphery, not to form a Ukrainian Soviet government.

The Sovnarkom was more explicit, although still not openly straightforward in rejecting Ukraine's autonomy, in its ultimatum to the Central Rada on 4 December. While making a demand that the Central Rada stop assisting General Alexei Kaledin, who was preparing to fight Bolsheviks in the Don region, the Sovnarkom 'recognize[d] the People's Ukrainian Republic [*sic*] and its right to secede from Russia altogether'. However, it denied legitimacy to the Central Rada by saying it would declare war on the Central Rada 'even if [the Central Rada] were the formally recognized and indisputable organ of the supreme state power of the independent bourgeois Republic of Ukraine'. In other words, the Sovnarkom claimed to recognize the UNR but refused to accept the Central Rada as its government. Significantly, while expressing dissatisfaction that the Rada did not recognize the soviets and the Soviet regime, the ultimatum made no explicit demand that the Central Rada transfer power to the Congress of Soviets of Ukraine. The General Secretariat understood very well what the Sovnarkom was saying. Not only did it refuse to fulfil the Sovnarkom's demands, it stated that: 'it is impossible to simultaneously recognize the right to self-determination, even secession, and at the same time rudely violate this right by imposing your own forms of political organization on the self-determined state'.[29]

### Agenda of the Kyiv Bolsheviks: A Party and a Soviet Government for Ukraine

With no support for organizing Ukrainian Bolshevik organizations into a territorial 'division of RSDRP(b)' or any instruction on forming a Ukrainian Soviet government, Kyiv Bolsheviks nonetheless proceeded with their agenda as dictated by Ukrainian realities. Ukrainian realities demanded a broad socialist coalition.[30]

In November, it looked like a broad socialist coalition might emerge in Ukraine. At the end of November, dissatisfied with the extremely slow pace of reforms, the Ukrainian Party of Socialist Revolutionaries (UPSR), the biggest party in Ukraine, agreed in principle that power in the periphery should lie with the soviets and not with local executive committees that had been formed by the

Provisional Government and were now under jurisdiction of the General Secretariat.[31] To take the lead in a socialist coalition in Ukraine, Bolsheviks who lacked popular support had to at least appear Ukrainian.[32]

On 30 November, Kyiv Bolsheviks Volodymyr Zatonsky, Ivan Kulyk, and others issued a flysheet in Ukrainian, signed 'Social-Democracy of Bolsheviks of Ukraine'. In the flysheet, they called for an All-Ukrainian Bolshevik organization and emphasized that Bolsheviks of Ukraine were 'not *moskali*' (derogatory for Russians). At the oblast congress of RSDRP(b) of the south-western region on 3 December in Kyiv, dominated by the Kyiv Bolsheviks and attended by delegates from many but not all Ukrainian gubernias, Zatonsky and Kulyk were reprehended for issuing a flysheet on behalf of 'Social-Democracy of Ukraine' without 'a decision of the congress'.[33] The delegates agreed that Ukraine was not an integral part of Russia and that they should build the party accordingly. As Leonid Piatakov, brother of Heorhii, summed up, '[I]t is very difficult to work under the title of Russian Bolsheviks, [as] this repulses the masses away from us. If we keep the name, we will always be Russians'. He suggested 'at least temporarily to call the party "RSDRP of Bolsheviks. Social-Democracy of Ukraine"'. Fourteen Bolsheviks were categorically against renaming their party organization, including Bosh. Still, the proposed name for Bolsheviks of Ukraine was accepted by a majority of twenty-three votes.[34]

While there was no consensus on uniting all Bolshevik organizations in Ukraine into a Ukrainian Bolshevik organization, there was a consensus on Ukraine's autonomy and the need for Ukraine to have a soviet government. Vasyl Shakhrai explained:

> The fate of the Ukrainian people took the shape of a federative republic, and this idea took deep roots with the masses of the population. We should conclude that since the Ukrainian nation self-determined as a federal republic, we should certainly recognise it. We should defend soviet federation and organise a Territorial Soviet Council.

Even Arshak Aleksandrov, an opponent of Ukraine's autonomy, recognized Ukraine's autonomy as dictated by objective factors, as an adjustment of state administration of Ukraine to the All-Russian state administration. Bosh was even more explicit. She argued that the *national* movement in Ukraine had a bourgeois character, and thereby class struggle was continuing in Ukraine. Nonetheless, the *territorial* power, which should ultimately belong to the proletariat, should be independent of Russia: 'One should not forget that federation does not mean subordination'. 'With the *Piter* [i.e., Petrograd] government there can be only a contractual relationship',[35] she argued. All agreed that the autonomy of Soviet Ukraine should not extend beyond political governance. Ukraine's Bolsheviks rejected economic federation.

It was from this perspective that Zatonsky assessed the Sovnarkom's ultimatum to the Central Rada, which, the documents suggest, was already known to the Kyiv Bolsheviks on 3 December, and argued that it was necessary to have a Ukrainian Soviet centre despite the lack of instruction from the Sovnarkom in this regard. Indeed, he explained, Ukrainian nationalists and the Central Rada had turned the masses against Soviet power. However, if the Sovnarkom ordered the Central Rada to support the soviets, 'this is a case of international intervention in the domestic affairs' of Ukraine. At present, explained Zatonsky, there was no split among Ukrainians with regard to supporting the Central Rada, and no such split was anticipated. Hence, by declaring war on the Central Rada, the Sovnarkom was declaring 'a war against the Ukrainian people, whereas Bolsheviks form only a small group'. 'We should explain to the [Sovnarkom] that it should carefully ponder this fact. I consider this ultimatum a result of poor information in *Piter*', argued Zatonsky.[36] The Bolshevik congress had little hope of convincing *Piter* to not launch a war against Ukraine. Instead, it passed a resolution proposed by Aleksandrov, stating that since war between Russia and Ukraine was inevitable, it was 'necessary to create a military centre [in Ukraine], because it would be inconvenient for *Piter* to lead the war'.[37]

The First Congress of Ukrainian Soviets convened on 4 December 1917. At this congress the Kyiv Bolsheviks hoped that the UPSR would withdraw its support for the Central Rada and support Soviet power. However, the 2,440 UPSR deputies, against sixty Bolsheviks, while supporting Soviet power in the periphery, refused to replace the Central Rada with a Soviet government. In protest, the Bolsheviks and their supporters left for Kharkiv.[38]

The choice of Kharkiv, the administrative centre of the Sloboda Ukraine gubernia since 1765, was not accidental. By the beginning of the First World War, due to its geographic location and cultural landscape, and as a result of Russia's industrialization, Kharkiv had become the de facto centre of Donbas, serving as the host-city for the Congress of Mining Industrialists of Southern Russia. Founded in 1878, the Congress of Mining Industrialists had an office in St Petersburg and developed close connections with the Russian government. Over the years, it grew into a complex institution with its own Compensation Fund, Mining and Metallurgy Bank, coal and metal bourse, Statistical Bureau, and other bodies. The administrative influence of the Congress of Mining Industrialists spread beyond Katerynoslav to Kherson and Tavria.[39] From the perspective of the Bolsheviks of Ukraine, this industrial centre was a natural proletariat capital of Ukraine. Kharkiv's military and strategic importance as a transportation route between Russia and Ukraine further increased its value for them as the Ukrainian Bolshevik centre.

On 11–12 December, the Bolshevik-dominated Congress of Soviets (re)convened. The Kyiv Bolsheviks were joined by the Kharkiv Bolsheviks and together they secured a resolution that declared Soviet power supreme in Ukraine. The congress elected forty-one members—Bolsheviks, Left SRs, Ukrainian Social Democrats (SDs), and independents—into a newly formed All-Ukrainian TsIK. On 13 December, the All-Ukrainian TsIK elected a temporary presidium of five members. Shortly after, the All-Ukrainian TsIK formed a Ukrainian Soviet government called the People's Secretariat.[40] In their first telegram to the Sovnarkom sent on 13 December, the new presidium introduced itself and expressed strong hope that there would be no military confrontation between the Russian and Ukrainian democracies following the 4 December ultimatum and the refusal of the Central Rada to fulfil its demands.[41]

The Sovnarkom was left with little choice but to recognize the young Soviet republic and play along. On 16 December, Lenin sent a formal telegram greeting the 'true government' of Ukraine.[42] A new institution was not without its advantages. After all, it enabled Lenin to present the political and emerging military conflicts as an internal class struggle between the Ukrainian soviets and the Central Rada.[43] At this point, the Central Committee allowed Ukrainian Bolsheviks to call themselves the Social-Democratic Workers' Party of Ukraine. But they remained fully integrated with the RSDRP(b).[44]

To prevent the All-Ukrainian TsIK or the People's Secretariat from 'assisting the Sovnarkom' without the latter knowing what to expect, on 19 December (1 January) Lenin appointed Grigorii (Sergo) Ordzhonikidze as 'extraordinary commissar of Ukraine for coordinating actions of soviet organizations in Ukraine'.[45] On 22 December, Lenin appointed Mykola Skrypnyk an official 'agent' of the Central Committee to the All-Ukrainian TsIK, although on 15 December, the All-Ukrainian TsIK had already suggested appointing Skrypnyk the secretary of labour.[46] Bolshevik troops remained under the command of Volodymyr Antonov-Ovseenko, who on 5 December was appointed by Lenin to organize the political and military struggle against the Central Rada, but on 8 December received a new order to prepare to fight Kaledin instead.[47] Authority lay with Ordzhonikidze. Together with Antonov-Ovseenko, he had to organize and secure food and fuel deliveries from Ukraine to Russia. Crucially, Ordzhonikidze was the Commissar of the Bank of Ukraine. He managed the money that the Sovnarkom transferred to Ukraine.[48]

## Ukraine's Bolsheviks Try to Consolidate the Ukrainian Soviet Centre

After the UNR signed the Treaty of Brest-Litovsk on 27 January (9 February) 1918, troops of the Central Powers began their advance on Ukraine. According to the treaty, which Bolshevik Russia had also signed, the Sovnarkom was obligated to recognize independent Ukraine and not to meddle in Ukrainian internal affairs. The All-Ukrainian TsIK decided to try once again to unite Ukrainian socialist parties, this time against the Central Powers and the Central Rada.

The Bolshevik leadership accepted the idea of a coalition of socialist forces in Ukraine. However, Lenin insisted that cooperation between the soviets, which included Left SRs and Ukrainian SDs, did not spread beyond military defence.[49] Kyiv Bolsheviks had a different view. They aimed for a much closer coalition of Ukrainian socialist forces.

But first, Kyiv Bolsheviks had to establish unity within the Bolshevik ranks, which were focused on creating their own more local pockets of autonomy. The Bolsheviks who seized power in Crimea at the beginning of 1918 created the Taurida Socialist Soviet Republic on 21 March. On 18 January, Russian Bolsheviks established a Soviet Republic of Odesa. On 9–12 February 1918, Bolsheviks, SRs, Mensheviks, and non-party deputies of Donbas created the Donetsk-Kryvyi Rih Soviet Republic with its centre in Kharkiv and with the charismatic and ambitious Bolshevik Fedor Sergeev (Artyom) at its head.

On 7 March 1918, Skrypnyk, now the chairman of the People's Secretariat, invited all Soviet republics of the south of Russia (i.e., the Don, Donetsk-Kryvyi Rih, Crimean, and Odesa republics) to create a military-political union that would defend Soviet power in the territory controlled by the Central Rada. The Ukrainian Soviet Republic, explained Skrypnyk, was envisaged as a 'more or less independent entity connected with the All-Russian Workers-Peasants Republic by federative ties'. The specifics of these ties were to be defined at more appropriate times, promised Skrypnyk.[50] In the meantime, he insisted, it was necessary to unite to struggle against the Central Rada and Germans. To discuss organizational matters, Skrypnyk invited them to Katerynoslav on 15 March. Skrypnyk needed Bolshevik unity at the forthcoming Congress of Soviets.

The Second All-Ukrainian Congress of Soviets (17–19 March 1918) in Katerynoslav was highly representative, attended by representatives of the Donetsk-Kryvyi Rih Soviet Republic and Crimea, and delegates representing all factions of Ukrainian SDs and SRs, Bund, anarchists, non-party, and undecided. The resolution of the congress recognized a Ukraine that was in federative relationship with Russia and incorporated the autonomous republics of Donetsk-Kryvyi Rih, Odessa and Crimea—that is, the regions included as part of Ukraine in the Central Rada's Third Manifesto. The newly elected All-Ukrainian TsIK included forty-nine Left SRs, forty-seven Bolsheviks, five Left Ukrainian SDs and one member of the Polish Socialist Party. Along with deciding on the organization of the struggle in Ukraine, the congress instructed the All-Ukrainian TsIK to adjust the Sovnarkom's decree on land to Ukrainian conditions, to draft a decree on the eight-hour working day and workers' control over production and distribution, and to draft a manifest to the Ukrainian people.[51]

On 25 March, the All-Ukrainian TsIK decided to send an official delegation to the Sovnarkom. Russian Bolshevik leadership expressed its 'enthusiastic compassion for the heroic struggle of toiling Ukrainians and unshakeable confidence in their victory, hand in hand with the proletariat and peasantry of Russia'.[52]

However, it indicated that it viewed the All-Ukrainian TsIK as a temporary institution. On 4 April 1918, to Zatonsky's suggestion of creating a single monetary system in the south of Russia, the Commissar for Nationalities Stalin famously replied: 'enough playing government and republic,... it is time to stop the game'.[53] To the Bolsheviks in Ukraine, however, centralized administration in Ukraine was unquestionable, as was Ukraine's autonomy and thus the need to cooperate with the Ukrainian left. They replied to Stalin: 'Declarations similar to Stalin's are directed to undermine Soviet power in Ukraine [read "the All-Ukrainian TsIK"] and are unacceptable from a representative of the Soviet government of the neighbouring Republic'.[54] On 18 April, Piatakov suggested combining the All-Ukrainian TsIK Presidium with the People's Secretariat into a Buro of nine members that would conduct the insurgency work in Ukraine. Significantly, four out of nine seats in the new Buro went to the Left SRs.[55]

At the party conference of Ukraine's Bolsheviks in Taganrog (19–20 April 1918), the majority voted for a 'Communist Party (Bolshevik) of Ukraine' (CP(b)U) with an independent central committee that would be connected with the Russian Communist Party (RKP(b)[56] through the Third International. The newly created Orgburo (Organizational Bureau of the Central Committee) was instructed to begin formal negotiations with the Left Ukrainian SDs about unification. The final resolution, nonetheless, declared that the success of Soviet Ukraine's victory over the Central Rada and Germany was fully dependent on 'preservation and consolidation of Soviet power in the Russian Federation and on further advancement of the world socialist revolution'.[57]

Lenin was not pleased with the initiatives of the Kyiv Bolsheviks. Since April 1917, they had demonstrated too much independent thinking and ambition for policymaking and showed little appreciation that Lenin was leading the revolution all over Russia. For him, Ukraine was only one front in the Russian Civil War and Lenin had to coordinate the struggle in Ukraine with the struggle on the southern, eastern, and western fronts as well.[58] As Stalin pointed out to Skrypnyk at the beginning of March 1918, 'The difference between you and us is that you are building Ukraine based on the geography of [Volodymyr] Vynnychenko [as defined by the Third Manifesto], from Podillia to Don and from Gomel to the sea shores, whereas we are building Great Russia, *Velikorossiia*'.[59] Besides, the Bolshevik leadership now wished to strengthen its relationship with Germany 'by offering to sign a wide-ranging economic treaty'.[60] After the German ambassador Count Wilhelm Mirbach arrived in Moscow on 26 April, any excessive state-building enthusiasm among the Ukrainian Bolsheviks was considered damaging to the relationship between Soviet Russia and Germany.

At the end of April 1918, Lenin met with members of the Ukrainian Orgburo, Andrii Bubnov, Zatonsky, Skrypnyk, and others, in order to convince them not to create a separate party. Had Pavlo Skoropadsky not taken power in Ukraine as Hetman on 29 April (supported by the invading Germans), thus pushing Ukraine further away from Bolshevik Russia, Lenin arguably would have insisted on the abolition of the CP(b)U altogether.

Under these circumstances, on 9 May 1918, the Central Committee officially approved the 'separation of the Ukrainian Communist (Bolshevik) Party from the Russian Communist Party', and unofficially specified that the independent stance of the CP(b)U was for public consumption only.[61] The CP(b)U remained a regional, not a national, organization. Any unauthorized initiative, even to sovietize Ukraine, without Moscow's guidance was not welcome, particularly if that initiative included cooperation with the Ukrainian left. An independent Soviet Ukraine with Bolsheviks in the government would have been even more unacceptable for Lenin than a national bourgeois Ukraine. Merging an independent Soviet Ukraine with Soviet Russia would be complicated. Therefore, Soviet power as well as Bolshevik domination in Ukraine had to come from Moscow. Here, Lenin had the support of the right-wing Ukrainian Bolsheviks from Donbas. They opposed the autonomist tendencies of the Kyiv comrades and resented their ambition to be at the head of the Ukrainian Soviet Republic. This stance was clearly demonstrated in their declaration of the Donetsk-Kryvyi Rih Soviet Republic and insistence in Taganrog that the struggle in Ukraine should be held under the centralized leadership of the Central Committee.[62] Kyiv Bolsheviks had little choice but to yield to Lenin's pressure. Indeed, they were politically and militarily too weak to secure an 'independent CP(b)U', or independently to organize a Soviet centre in Ukraine. Kyiv Bolsheviks lacked support from the Donbas comrades for their cause; Ukrainian soviets were prone to cooperate with the Central Rada, whereas the coalition with the left-wing Ukrainian SDs had still to materialize.

At the First CP(b)U Congress held in Moscow on 5–12 July 1918, Lenin secured the status of oblast, as opposed to republican or state, for the Central Committee of the CP(b)U (hereafter, the 'Ukrainian Central Committee'), and placed the Ukrainian Central Committee in direct subordination to the Central Committee. Piatakov was elected first secretary of the leftist Ukrainian Central Committee. The four regional organizations of Ukraine, the South-Western, Donbas, Southern and Crimean, accepted the formal superiority of the Ukrainian Central Committee, but they remained directly subordinate to the Central Committee. The congress agreed that the union between Russia and Ukraine was the main condition for victory over the counter-revolution and formed a Ukrainian Revolutionary Committee (Revkom), subordinated to the Ukrainian Central Committee, to direct the insurgence work in Ukraine.[63]

By November 1918, with Germany embroiled in its own revolution and signing an armistice to end its participation in the First World War, it looked like the Bolshevik leadership might merge Ukraine with Russia once the Red Army invaded Ukraine. Lenin's view of Ukraine as an integral part of Russia had not changed since 1917. To him, the Central Powers had occupied a part of Russia, not an independent Ukraine.[64] In the summer of 1918, Commissar of Foreign Affairs Georgii Chicherin insisted that 'national masses do not wish and do not recognize separation from Russia'.[65] On 25 October, the Central Committee included Stalin, a staunch believer in authoritarian centralization, in the Ukrainian Central Committee. At the beginning of November, Stalin 'castigated those who saw in national resistance "a struggle for national liberation against the "soulless centralism" of the Soviet government"'.[66] In its resolution on annulling the Treaty of Brest-Litovsk from 13 November 1918, the All-Russian TsIK 'while welcoming the population of all regions [oblasts] that were liberated from the yoke of German imperialism...called [the] toiling masses of these oblasts into fraternal union with workers and peasants of Russia and promised them full support in their struggle for establishing [the] socialist power of workers and peasants on their lands',[67] not for establishing socialist states.

On 11 November, the Sovnarkom created an 'army group of the Kursk direction' for military intervention in Ukraine. On 12 November, Trotsky, following Lenin's orders from 11 November, instructed Antonov-Ovseenko to invade Ukraine within ten days.[68] This order had to be revoked. The Red Army was suffering defeats on the Don and in the Baltic states. On 14 November, Ukrainian socialists formed a new government, the Directory. And on 15 November, the Directory called for an uprising against Skoropadsky, which was enthusiastically supported by Ukrainians.[69] Still, on 17 November (12 November according to Mace), the Bolshevik leadership formed a revolutionary military council (revvoensovet), which included Antonov-Ovseenko, Zatonsky, and Stalin. Lenin was preparing to invade Ukraine.[70]

On 20 November, Piatakov and Zatonsky drew up a list of members of the Ukrainian Soviet Provisional Government with Piatakov as the chairman, and Zatonsky, Vasyl Averin, Kliment Voroshilov, Emmanuil Kviring, Yurii Kotsiubynsky, and Fedor Sergeev (Artyom), the leader of the Donbas Bolsheviks, as its members.[71] However, Lenin did not rush to announce the Ukrainian provisional government, indicating that as far as he was concerned, and as the military preparations indicated, the Ukrainian centre was unnecessary.[72] Ukraine's Bolsheviks, on the other hand, needed it, not exclusively or primarily to proceed with military action,[73] but to make sure that a Ukrainian Soviet government was created. Without a Soviet Ukraine, they would remain provincial party functionaries. Only their 'own' republic could elevate their status in the Central Committee and satisfy their political ambitions, or so they believed. So, in the days that followed, Piatakov and Zatonsky, with the support of Kviring and arguably other members of the Ukrainian Soviet Provisional Government, put pressure on Lenin to make the announcement.

Well aware that the Bolshevik leadership resented their policymaking ambitions, Piatakov and Zatonsky assured Lenin in their letters to him that they would not take any unauthorized initiative and would act strictly along the policies

**Illustration 3**  On 14 December 1918, Hetman of Ukraine Pavlo Skoropadsky renounced power/© TsDAVOU

Pavlo Skoropadsky, a descendant of an old Ukrainian noble family and a lieutenant general in the Russian Imperial Army, became Hetman of Ukraine on 29 April 1918. Skoropadsky's political ascent was supported by Germany, which in accordance with the Treaty of Brest-Litovsk (9 February 1918) occupied Ukraine. The withdrawal of Germany from Ukraine in November 1918 undermined Skoropadsky's power. Faced with a popular revolt in Ukraine and in an effort to save Ukrainian statehood and remain in power, he tried to forge a union with the Whites. However, they rejected the idea of a Russian federative state with Ukraine as an autonomous part. On 14 December 1918, Skoropadsky renounced power.

defined by the Sovnarkom. However, they insisted that the Ukrainian Soviet government should have real power to coordinate and manage Soviet work in Ukraine, still within the confines of the policies defined by the Sovnarkom. The rationale for the Ukrainian Soviet government was the chaos and inefficiency caused by uncoordinated independent actions of myriad authorities sent by Moscow to Ukraine.[74] Ukraine needed 'an organ of Soviet power, which would manage, which would be a real centre of Soviet work in Ukraine, to which all Soviet workers would be subordinated and which, therefore, would concentrate all this extremely important [and] complex work of restoration of Soviet power in localities [*na mestakh*]'. 'An absence of such an organ means that in reality there is not any central organ.'[75] Reflecting their power ambitions, Piatakov and Zatonsky argued that conquering Ukraine should not be reduced to a military campaign. Ukraine was a territory with complex politics and 'the issue [was] not so much about a frontal military offensive, but about military support for a political

**Illustration 4**   The Directory arrives in Kyiv, December 1918/© TsDAVOU

The Directory of the Ukrainian People's Republic was formed on 13–14 November 1918 as a temporary organ to lead an uprising against Hetman Skoropadsky. After its success, the Directory transformed into the Ukrainian government. In its early days, the socialist Directory enjoyed wide popular support. The Directory relied on local otamans to overthrow Hetman Skoropadsky. In return, the Directory empowered them and indulged their power ambitions. Ultimately, the Directory failed to bring all Ukrainian regions under its control. In the photo, leaders of the Directory from the USDRP Volodymyr Vynnychenko (2nd left) and Symon Petliura (3rd left) are greeted by the crowds as they arrive in Kyiv.

offensive'. Furthermore, peasants were unable to understand who was 'truly' fighting the Skoropadsky regime and supported the Directory. A Ukrainian Soviet government should be formed to enlighten the peasants.[76]

It took Zatonsky and Piatakov more than one telegram and more than one telephone call with Stalin to convince Lenin to authorize a Ukrainian Soviet provisional government. In one of the telephone conversations with Stalin, Zatonsky stated that the orders coming from the centre were almost always late and were impossible to implement because by the time they arrived the situation had already changed. Implementing them would either be criminal or lead to 'a bigger chaos'. Stalin, in one of his replies, tried to insinuate that Zatonsky's pleas 'to save them from multiple authorities' and create a single centre in Ukraine was an indication of 'disagreements' among the Bolsheviks of Ukraine. Zatonsky strongly objected to this:

> Forgive me, but this is some kind of mockery [*izdevatel'stvo*]. For the third and last time today, I am saying that there is no internal dissension at all among us here….In the name of the Ukrainian Central Committee I am asking you directly: do you authorise us to act?[77]

Lenin finally authorized them to publicly announce the Ukrainian Soviet Provisional Government. Its first meeting was held on 28 November 1918, attended by both the left and the right, Antonov-Ovseenko, Artyom, Zatonsky, Kviring, and Piatakov.[78]

When authorizing the Ukrainian Soviet Provisional Government, Lenin did not plan to make it a functional decision-making centre, as Zatonsky and Piatakov hoped. In their telegram to Commander in Chief Ioakim Vatsetis on 29 November 1918, Lenin and Stalin explained that Soviet provisional governments in Ukraine and the Baltic states served as a façade for the expansion of the Russian Bolshevik centralized state.[79] Their function was to consolidate soviets in the localities, not to build their own governmental infrastructure.[80] The course towards merger remained. At the All-Russian TsIK meeting in mid-December 1918, Stalin stated that the right to independence had been given so as to permit Soviet provisional governments 'to eventually proclaim the unity of the Soviet republic'.[81] In December, Lenin asked Afanasii Zharko, the Commissar of Ukrainian Railways in the Ukrainian Soviet government, whether 'poor peasants in Ukraine were for merging with Russia or against'. Zharko reassured Lenin that, provided the land and food questions were solved in their favour, they would not be against the merger.[82]

Piatakov was not the person to merge Ukraine with Russia. At no point in 1917–1918 did he indicate that he viewed Soviet Ukraine as independent or cared about protecting the interests of the Ukrainian toiling masses. However, since 1917, he had clearly demonstrated the ambitions of a policymaker and, consequently, insisted on policymaking authority for the Ukrainian Bolshevik centre and policies that would benefit the Ukrainian Bolshevik centre.[83] In 1917, in pursuit of his ambition, he put his anti-Ukrainianism aside and, to fit into the Ukrainian political context, he even collaborated with the Central Rada and Ukrainian socialist parties. In 1918, 'the enemy of nationalism was … transformed into the defender of the independence and the specific nature of Ukraine'.[84] As Kulchytsky observed, at the First CP(b)U Congress in Moscow in July 1918, Piatakov understood that if Ukraine were fully merged with Russia, the survival of the Ukrainian Central Committee and his personal position were uncertain. Therefore, while abolishing the Ukrainian Soviet centre, he had to ensure that the Ukrainian Central Committee survived.[85] Piatakov would demonstrate the same institutional loyalty and the same 'taste and capacity for command', as Andrea Graziosi puts it, in his role as the commissar of the State Bank from 17 December 1917 until March 1918, as the chairman of the First Labor Army in the Urals (February–May 1920), and as the vice-chairman of the Supreme Sovnarkhoz (Council of national economy) in 1923–1926, and he would conduct 'a fierce battle in the [Supreme Sovnarkhoz] to remove resources and powers from the Ukrainian [Sovnarkhoz]'.[86] In seeming contradiction to his defence of decision-making powers for the Ukrainian centre, at the Eighth RKP(b) Congress on 18–23 March 1919, Piatakov went as far as to suggest rejecting the slogan of 'self-determination of the toiling masses', just as the party rejected the slogan of 'self-determination of nations'.[87] However, it is worth noting that while he effectively called for the abolition of the Ukrainian republic, he did not call for the abolition of the CP(b)U. He was no longer the chairman of the Ukrainian Sovnarkom, but he was elected onto the Ukrainian Central Committee.

The merger of Ukraine with Russia had to be prepared and duly formalized, as 'a demand from below', by Bolsheviks less ambitious. The Ukrainian Right Bolsheviks were commonly viewed as pro-Moscow, but they also proved to be poor candidates to lead this merger. On 16 January 1919, the Right Bolsheviks removed Piatakov and elected their leader, Artyom, the new head of the Ukrainian Soviet government. Considering that it was the Central Committee that had appointed Piatakov, his unauthorized removal by the Ukrainian Right Bolsheviks indicated that 'pro-Russian' Kviring and Artyom had power ambitions no smaller than Piatakov's.

On 24 January 1919, the Bolshevik leadership appointed Christian Rakovsky as the head of the Ukrainian Soviet government. Rakovsky took on the new assignment with no apparent intent to turn the Ukrainian government into a decision- or policymaking body. At this point in his career, he believed that the Ukrainian Soviet government had been created to 'unconditionally implement all instructions and orders of the [Central Committee]'.[88] Once in safe hands, on 29 January, the Ukrainian Soviet government obtained permanent status and was now called *Sovet Narodnykh Komissarov* (Ukrainian Sovnarkom). The new Ukrainian Sovnarkom included Artyom and Kviring, and even Piatakov, who was now responsible for propaganda. It also included Bolsheviks who had little to no experience of working in Ukraine, the so-called 'Russian Bolsheviks'. For example, Mykola (Rus.: Nikolai) Podvoisky, who had previously worked in the Russian Soviet Federative Socialist Republic (RSFSR), was appointed people's commissar of military affairs, and Oleksandr (Rus.: Aleksandr) Shlikhter, who had also worked in the RSFSR, was made commissar of food provisions. Volodymyr (Rus.: Vladimir) Meshcheriakov was personally invited by Rakovsky to become commissar of land affairs; he also had experience of working in the RSFSR and was not familiar with the particularities of the land issue in Ukraine.[89] The new 'permanent', 'pro-Russian' Sovnarkom, under the 'almost pathologically ambitious' Rakovsky (as described by Jurij Borys), who was known for his hostility to the Ukrainian national movement, was meant to permanently merge Ukraine with Russia.[90]

## Institutional Interests Clash

It very soon became clear that the new pro-Russian government under national nihilist Rakovsky was as defensive of its institutional interests as Piatakov's. While Moscow proceeded with establishing centralized control over resources in the

Ukrainian territory controlled by the Bolsheviks, the Ukrainian Sovnarkom maintained that it, not Moscow's bureaucracy, had the authority to pump resources out of the republic.[91]

In mid-January, Zharko (who had previously assured Lenin that peasants in Ukraine would not be opposed to merging with Russia) refused to implement an order from RSFSR Commissar of Railways Vladimir Nevsky and, instead, issued a decree on the nationalization of Ukrainian railways. Rakovsky supported Zharko.[92]

At the Third CP(b)U Congress (1–6 March 1919), Moscow's appointee Shlikhter agreed that 'food policy in Ukraine cannot be any different from the one in Russia,'[93] thus adhering to a unified party line. But, Shlikhter insisted, the Ukrainian food commissariat 'should be the sole authority in distributing and managing food, and not only food, but all basic products' in Ukraine.[94] Rakovsky similarly fully supported the Bolshevik food policies while viewing the role of the Ukrainian food commissariat as essential. He even welcomed practical advice from the comrades from the periphery on how 'to pump out bread from the [Ukrainian] village', thus signalling to the periphery apparatus that the Ukrainian food commissariat *was* the authority for the republic.[95]

Sharing Shlikhter's position, on 16 April, the All-Ukrainian TsIK Presidium, by then under Moscow's appointee Hryhorii (Rus.: Grigorii) Petrovsky, officially reprimanded Soviet military commander Voroshilov for burning Ukrainian villages during the suppression of peasant uprisings. In this reprimand, the All-Ukrainian TsIK Presidium was not concerned with the well-being of Ukrainian peasants, nor did it object to the Red Army's practice of expropriating food. Rather, the All-Ukrainian TsIK was concerned that burning Ukrainian villages damaged the Soviet power in Ukraine. Voroshilov's primary interests lay with the Bolshevik leadership in Moscow and with Lenin, whose main aim was to expropriate as much food from Ukrainian peasants as quickly as possible to feed the proletariat and the army.[96] So, Voroshilov did not change his methods and the practice of burning villages continued.[97]

Given such instances of resistance to Moscow authority, it was not without reason that A. Nikitin concluded at the Third CP(b)U Congress that, despite the presence of 'healthy' forces, 'the [CP(b)U] congress [was] held under the influence of the left and separatism'.[98] Nikitin had been appointed by the Supreme Sovnarkhoz on 2 January to supervise the organization of industry in the Bolshevik-controlled Ukrainian territory. The accusations of 'separatism' were exaggerated, but the majority of congress members indeed defended the Ukrainian left Bolsheviks' idea that the Ukrainian Central Committee should be a functional party centre with real, formalized powers that would allow it to adjust the Central Committee policies to the Ukrainian context.[99] In reflection of these views, the congress approved the Constitution of the Ukrainian Socialist Soviet Republic (UkSSR), which was 'in general the Constitution of the RSFSR' but adapted to local conditions and which allowed the Congress of Soviets of Ukraine (6–10 March 1919) to instruct the All-Ukrainian TsIK to formalize the Ukrainian republic's relationship with other Soviet republics.[100] On 7 March 1919, consistent with the congressional decisions, the Ukrainian Sovnarkom agreed to unite the Ukrainian Sovnarkhoz with the Supreme Sovnarkhoz, not to eliminate the former, but rather to position it within the centralized economic administration 'so that the Ukrainian Sovnarkhoz received its directives from Moscow'.[101]

In late winter/early spring, Rakovsky and his government showed little enthusiasm for the merger. At the end of March 1919, Rakovsky started showing signs of independence.[102] The Bolshevik leadership, on the other hand, continued to view Ukraine as a temporary phenomenon.[103] As before, Lenin's public stance, certainly in March, was politically correct: the Ukrainian Soviet Republic was in 'the best' relationship with Soviet Russia, but autonomous.[104] However, immediately after the Third CP(b)U Congress, upon the suggestion of Sverdlov (who attended it), Lenin appointed Petrovsky as the chairman of the All-Ukrainian TsIK to balance the Ukrainian left and support 'the healthy forces'.[105] In April 1919, the Central Committee Politburo (hereafter, the 'central Politburo') passed a secret resolution that instructed party officials to 'carefully prepare plans to fuse Ukraine and Russia'. In case of a military retreat of the Bolshevik troops, and should the Ukrainian commissariats be separated from the All-Russian, the Ukrainian commissars 'were to strictly implement only central orders'.[106]

The merger of Ukraine with Russia was becoming all the more urgent as the optimism that the Bolshevik leadership had in April 1919 about the end of the civil war was rapidly fading in May. The rebellion of the Don Cossacks that started in March linked up with the White Army of General Anton Denikin by mid-May. On 23 May, the Latvian Bolsheviks lost Riga to the 'bourgeois' nationalists. Earlier in May, General Nikolai Yudenich began his advance towards Petrograd. On 7 May, Ukrainian otaman of the 'Green Army' Nykyfor Hryhoriv, the most important ally of Antonov-Ovseenko (Lenin's military leader in Ukraine), started a rebellion in retribution for the Bolshevik policies. Smaller uprisings followed. At the end of May, Hryhoriv's uprising was quelled. However, in mid-May, Denikin was already in Donbas. By the end of June, Denikin would occupy the entire Donbas and Don.[107]

On 18 May, Petrovsky delivered 'the initiative from below'. The All-Ukrainian TsIK passed a resolution about the need to centralize control over military and economic resources of all Soviet republics in Moscow.[108]

On 1 June, the All-Russian TsIK ordered the centralization of military, economic, railway, finance, and labour administration in the Soviet republics of Russia, Ukraine, Latvia, Lithuania, and Belorussia.[109] The central Politburo ordered the abolition of the Ukrainian Soviet military command.[110]

As much as he was disappointed about the abolition of the Ukrainian military centre, Podvoisky, the Ukrainian Commissar of Military Affairs and Lenin's appointee, was equally frustrated with the fact that he was not even consulted on the issue. On 10 June, Podvoisky wrote a lengthy letter to Lenin explaining that the decision to abolish Ukrainian military organizations was wrong. It was based on inaccurate information from 'random' reports, which had been written by people poorly informed about the situation in Ukraine, and was 'monstrously harmful' to the revolution. Podvoisky did not lose the perspective of why he had been sent to Ukraine:

> In principle, there can be no two opinions on the military-political union. As I was departing for Ukraine, I told the Revvoensovet that I was not going to culti-vate Ukrainian *samostiïnist'* (i.e., independence), [and that I would] create an organisation that [would] use Ukrainian resources [to extract] people as well as material resources for the defence of the All-Russian, more accurately, world scale. I also declared that in a few months it would be possible to merge [Ukraine and Russia]. However, the time has not yet come to consider the military organ-isation of Ukraine...sufficiently solid as to [consider its centre] unnecessary.

Podvoisky thought he should have been asked first.

> I thought that my year-and-a-half work for the revolution and the Red Army gives me the right to demand that the decision about not only the abolition of the military-organisational administrative centre of Ukraine, but even about its reorganisation would be decided after my report, not based on random reports or even speculations. If my letter convinced you of anything, call me to Moscow for [further discussions].[111]

It did not.

Similar to Podvoisky, Rakovsky did not take the curtailment of his importance, however small it already was, very well either. At the 2 June meeting, the central Politburo allocated 2 trillion, 7 million roubles to Ukraine, 'half to Kharkiv and half to Kyiv', the capital of Ukraine.[112] Rakovsky immediately protested against finances being sent directly to Kharkiv, bypassing the Ukrainian Sovnarkom. His protest was ignored. On the other hand, in July, upon his request, Lenin informed Rakovsky of the sums of money transferred to the Bolshevik centres in Kharkiv, Katerynoslav and Odesa.[113] The decision by the Central Committee to channel financing for the Ukrainian commissariats along the branch lines, as opposed to through the Ukrainian Sovnarkom, was equally met with objection from Rakovsky.[114] He also objected to the decision that the budget of each Ukrainian commissariat had to be approved by the RSFSR Sovnarkom and insisted that the latter approve the budgets only for the All-Russian commissariats; the budgets for other Ukrainian commissariats should be approved only by the Ukrainian Sovnarkom.[115]

At the same Politburo meeting, Rakovsky was rebuffed for his and Shlikhter's initiative to raise money for Ukrainian sugar plants by selling 24,600 metric tons of sugar above the approved norms to Russian cooperatives, the Tsentrosoyuz (All-Russian Central Union of Consumer Cooperative Societies), and United Workers cooperatives for the northern regions. On 1 June, the RSFSR Commissar of Food, Aleksandr Tsiurupa, replied that only the All-Russian Narkomprod (People's Commissariat of Food) could distribute sugar in the north. Distribution of sugar by cooperatives would be considered illegal. At the meeting on 2 June, the central Politburo supported Tsiurupa, effectively calling Rakovsky's initiative illegal.[116] To protect the Ukrainian Sovnarkom from any illegal actions in future, on 14 June, the Central Committee plenum discussed 'the financial and organizational-political subordination of the Ukr[ainian] Narkomprod to the All-Russian [Narkomprod] without public announcement'. The Central Committee thus expanded the list of five areas that the Central Committee had already centralized by the 1 June All-Russian TsIK decree.[117]

During the summer of 1919, the Ukrainian Central Committee was reduced to a political club. Soviet military defeats in Ukraine in the summer of 1919 were undoubtedly a reason. However, there was open neglect of the very existence of the Ukrainian Central Committee on the part of the Central Committee, as the latter made decisions that concerned Ukrainian administration often without communicating them to the Ukrainian Central Committee.[118] At its plenum on 2 August, the Ukrainian Central Committee insisted 'on turning the Ukrainian Central Committee into a real oblast organ of the Central Committee', and on uniting the party work in Ukraine with the work of the RKP(b).[119] The Ukrainian Central Committee wanted the mandate of a 'strong' central Ukrainian organization that would 'systematically apply the experience of Russia' in Ukraine and would also 'coordinate and unite the underground work in the territory occupied by Denikin'. For the latter task, the Ukrainian Central Committee asked for experienced cadres 'whose faces [were] not known in Ukraine', and for money. For finance, Bolsheviks were highly dependent on local Soviet organs, which in many locations remained under the control of the Ukrainian left socialists, the Borotbists, and the Borbists.[120] However, the Ukrainian Central Committee 'felt uncomfortable taking money for the party work from local resources through Ukrainian organs'. The Ukrainian Central Committee needed about 30–40 million roubles. Referring to the fears harboured in Moscow that the Ukrainian comrades had a tendency towards *samostiĭnist'*, the Ukrainian Central Committee promised that its 'financial dependence [on the Central Committee] [would] considerably consolidate [their] relationship'.[121]

The advancement of Denikin and the retreat of the Soviet troops forced the Ukrainian Soviet leadership to leave the territory of Ukraine. On 13 August, the Central Committee instructed Rakovsky 'to shut down all commissariats, except military, food and railways, and to mobilize the state apparatus for military service'. The Ukrainian Sovnarkom, the Soviet of Defence, the All-Ukrainian TsIK, and the Ukrainian Central Committee were to be merged into one organ.[122] In October 1919, Ukraine was occupied by the Whites. The Ukrainian Central Committee and the Ukrainian Sovnarkom 'self-dissolved'.[123]

## Decision on the Centre in 1919

In November 1919, Lenin had to decide whether to resurrect the Ukrainian centre. On the one hand, the UNR had not yet been fully defeated. On the other, the leader of the UNR, Symon Petliura, had failed to unite Ukraine against either the Bolsheviks or Denikin, and the Ukrainian otamans had selected their allies opportunistically with no demand for unifying Ukrainian lands into one polity. These factors arguably suggested to Lenin that Ukrainian statehood might not have been as important for Ukrainian peasants and workers as the Borotbists or the federalist faction within the Ukrainian Central Committee insisted.[124] At the same time, Lenin could not dismiss the Ukrainian national movement, nor the increasing tendency among the Borotbists to create an independent soviet government and 'declare it somewhere in Poltava or Vinnytsia, among Galician soldiers and Ukrainian *muzhichki* [small men]' or create a Ukrainian Red Army. All guerrillas, from Petliura supporters to communists, were in favour of a Ukrainian Red Army, Zatonsky reported at the end of November. More alarmingly, 'many local communist organizations were under the strong influence of the Borotbists'.[125]

As specified in his late November 1919 'Draft Theses of the CC [Central Committee] RKP(b) Concerning Policy in Ukraine', Lenin's solution was to allow a temporary Ukrainian 'centre', not a government, until the convocation of the Congress of Soviets and 'to launch a propaganda campaign for the complete merger [of Ukraine] with the RSFSR'.[126] The 'Resolution of the CC RKP(b) on Soviet power in Ukraine' presented at the Eighth RKP(b) Conference (2–4 December 1919) phrased the provision about the future merger by diplomatically stating that 'the final form of the union [between the Soviet republics] will be decided definitely by the Ukrainian workers and toiling peasants'.[127]

It is quite remarkable that even while suspecting that a Soviet Ukraine might not survive for long, the Ukrainian Bolshevik leaders, who would soon form a restored Ukrainian Central Committee, sought to maximize the authority of the republican centre. Even more remarkable, to make their claim, they were prepared to publicly oppose a central policy. The policy in question was the Central Committee nationality policy presented at the Eighth RKP(b) Conference and the union with the Borotbists.

The new Central Committee nationality policy in Ukraine envisaged support for the Ukrainian language and culture in order to obtain the support of the Ukrainian toiling masses; a less harsh food policy 'with expropriations only at

strictly limited scale' to obtain the support of the Ukrainian peasantry in particular; and no changes to the 1 June merger of the military, economy, and finances.[128]
Political embrace of the Borotbists was necessary to give a national character to
the new Ukrainian government, to pacify the peasantry, and to put an end to the
idea of an independent Ukrainian Soviet republic that the Borotbists so actively
supported.

From the perspective of the Ukrainian Bolshevik leaders, the new nationality
policy left the Ukrainian centre powerless. It had no control over Ukrainian
industry or, by extension, the Ukrainian proletariat. The Bolshevik alliance with
the Borotbists, who were known for their cultural and language agenda, reduced
the authority of the Ukrainian Bolsheviks with regard to culture, language,
agriculture, and the relationship with the non-proletariat population. In the eyes
of a common Ukrainian, the alliance with the Borotbists reduced the status of
Bolsheviks to that of junior partners. Ukrainian Bolsheviks wanted neither to be
nor to be perceived as dependent on the Borotbists. They were happy to depend
solely on the Central Committee. To a different degree of frankness and directness,
they hinted at these concerns when speaking at the Eighth RKP(b) Conference.

Rakovsky, who was appointed the head of the Provisional Buro of the Ukrainian
Central Committee at the end of November,[129] spoke cautiously. He explained his
unwillingness to cooperate with the Borotbists by invoking the experience of the
military struggle in 1919. Indeed, the Bolsheviks had no other choice but to 'liberate Ukraine with help of guerrilla forces', referring to the otamans, many of whom
were Borotbists. But these otamans were not dependent on the Ukrainian
Revkom. Quite the contrary, the Ukrainian Soviet leaders depended on them, as
the otamans 'organized their own supplies, pillaged [villages] and caused popular
outrage against [the Bolsheviks]'. Therefore, Rakovsky said, 'it is the greatest
happiness of Ukraine that this year it will be liberated not by random guerrilla
detachments led by otamans-adventurists, who switched from us to Petliura, and
from Petliura to us—but by the Red Army'.[130]

Rakovsky did not speak against the limitation of the Ukrainian centre's authority.
He accepted, even insisted on, 'strict revolutionary centralization, united
military command, the unity of all human and material resources'. At the same
time, he tried to consolidate the Ukrainian centre by referring to the same
'national factor'. 'When in our ... newspapers they say: Ukraine is ours, Kyiv is
ours and so on—this, comrades, does not create conditions for the correct
approach in Ukraine. Kyiv is Soviet, yes, but one should avoid anything reminiscent of imperialist inclinations'. Thereby, 'anyone who would raise his hand against
the unity of these countries [i.e., Russia and Ukraine] in military, economic or
railways administration would be a traitor of Ukrainian workers and peasants'.
After all, he explained, Russian and Ukrainian workers and peasants have common interests. Nonetheless, the party should clearly indicate to the Ukrainian
toiling masses, 'This is Ukraine.... Here is your independence.' To make sure that

Група керівничих партробітників на Україні в 1919 р.
Зліва направо: Хмільницький, Рухимович, Грановський, Юдовський, Ворошілов, Мещеряков, Подвойський, Балабанова, Раковський, Скрипник, Затонський [нш]

**Illustration 5**  A group of Bolshevik leaders in Ukraine in 1919/© TsDAVOU

Throughout 1919, Bolsheviks who worked in Ukraine concentrated their efforts on securing Ukraine as one territorial administrative unit and institutionalizing the power of the Ukrainian Bolshevik leadership. Front row, left to right: Oleksandr Khmilnytsky, Moisei Rukhymovych, Moisei Hranovsky, Volodymyr Yudovsky, Kliment Voroshilov, Volodymyr Meshcheriakov, Mykola Podvoisky, Anzhelika Balabanova, Christian Rakovsky, Mykola Skrypnyk, Volodymyr Zatonsky.

the Ukrainian toiling masses believed that they had independence was an 'important practical task'. To perform this task, Rakovsky suggested consolidating the CP(b)U, and, by implication, the Ukrainian Sovnarkom and the Ukrainian Central Committee, with strong, experienced Soviet workers.[131]

Other Ukrainian Bolshevik speakers were less diplomatic. Zatonsky insisted that reducing the nationality policy to cooperation with the Borotbists and making concessions on the language issue was simply wrong. The language issue should not be viewed as a concession at all: 'If you go to France or Poland and speak to the French workers in French and Polish worker in Polish—how is this a concession?' Instead of controlling 'language', he insisted, Ukrainian peasants expected the Soviet power to organize their economic life.[132] Alliance with the Borotbists was unnecessary for this. What was necessary was a strong Soviet centre that would organize the trade between Russia and Ukraine.

Dmytro Manuilsky, a Bolshevik revolutionary who was transferred to Ukraine in June 1919, agreed that to conquer the Ukrainian countryside, Bolsheviks needed manufactured goods, whereas the gains from collaborating with the Borotbists were 'unclear'.[133]

For Lenin, the economic solution to the conflict with rural areas was not only more expensive than 'the language and cultural' solution, it also implied decentralization of economic administration, which was out of the question. So, Lenin could not reverse his decision on the union with the Borotbists. In his reply to Rakovsky, Manuilsky, and others who spoke, he insisted that the Ukrainian Soviet Republic would receive cultural, not administrative, authority, although the food policy would be less harsh than before. Furthermore, echoing the confrontation with Piatakov in April 1917, he once again signalled that he understood perfectly well that power ambitions were behind the Ukrainian Central Committee's underlying resentment towards working with the Borotbists and prioritizing cultural and linguistic concessions.

> All those who spoke on the nationality question…, in their criticism of our *tsekistskoĭ* [i.e., of the Central Committee] resolution [on the nationality question] showed that they manifested the same *samostiĭnist'* for which we reprimanded *Kievlian* [the Kyiv comrades, Piatakov, Zatonsky, and others]. Com[rade] Manuilsky is being extremely misled if he thinks that we reprimanded [the Ukrainian Bolsheviks] for national *samostiĭnist'*, in the sense of an independent Ukraine. We reprimanded [them] for *samostiĭnist'* as unwillingness to consider [read: accept] Moscow views, the views of the [Central Committee] that is in Moscow.[134]

His point was very clear: Borotbists or no Borotbists, the Ukrainian centre was not designed as a decision- or policymaking centre, and yes, the authority of the Ukrainian centre would be reduced to culture, language, and the countryside, the three main components of the 'nationality question' as far as the Bolshevik leadership was concerned.

The fact that the Ukrainian Bolshevik leaders challenged the Central Committee on such a major issue in defence of their interests could not but alarm Lenin that they might not follow central instructions. Soon after the restoration of the Ukrainian Central Committee, he submitted a note to the central Politburo suggesting the immediate establishment of 'a practical, short, but meaningful form of reporting (twice a month) from each party worker from Ukraine'. The punishment for not sending these reports: arrest.[135]

On 10 December, the Central Committee restored the Ukrainian secretariat with Stanislav Kosior as its chairman. The central Politburo specified that Ukraine could not have separate ministries 'because [they] would complicate "the future fusion of the two republics"'.[136] The Ukrainian Buro, consisting of Rakovsky, Zatonsky, Kosior, Petrovsky, and Manuilsky, duly composed a 'Draft on the state administration of Ukraine after its liberation from the Whites' and specified that the UkSSR abided by the 1 June military-economic union. It promised not to restore commissariats for military affairs, railways, post and telegraph, food, finances, labour, foreign trade, foreign affairs, internal affairs, nationalities, and the Supreme Sovnarkhoz.[137] The Ukrainian Central Committee was left with agriculture, culture, and language.

## Ukrainian Central Administration: From Temporary to Permanent

In January 1920, the course towards merger continued. On 17 January 1920, the central Politburo officially approved the Ukrainian Central Committee's draft, known as Rakovsky's Thesis, instructed the Ukrainian Central Committee to relocate from Kyiv to Kharkiv, and appointed Rakovsky the head of the Ukrainian Revkom. The Politburo appointed Kosior to Kyiv to organize the party work there and instructed the Ukrainian Central Committee to organize 'a department for work in the village and to pay particular attention to the work on the Right Bank',[138] the territory that remained under the control of the UNR the longest.

However, the events of 1920 made it impossible for Lenin to succeed in merging Ukraine with Russia. On the one hand, domestic pressure to preserve the Ukrainian Soviet Republic remained high, particularly from the Borotbists and federalists who openly longed for de facto autonomy for Ukraine.[139] On the other hand, and probably more importantly, Lenin faced external pressure from Poland.

Since the end of 1919, the UNR had been advancing its efforts to convince Poland to help it liberate Ukraine from the Bolsheviks. Hostilities between Poland and the Bolsheviks, which had begun back in February 1919, could escalate.[140] Being focused on Denikin in January 1920, the Bolshevik leadership believed it could avoid a widespread military confrontation with the Poles.[141] However, in January 1920, Petliura began re-establishing the Ukrainian army in Poland. On 9 February, Chicherin advised the central Politburo 'to localize the conflict [with Poland] by immediately separating' Soviet Ukraine from Soviet Russia by reinstating 'the independence of the Ukrainian Soviet Republic, postponing federation into the future'.[142]

Consequently, on 27 January, the Ukrainian Revkom, with Rakovsky in charge, was still prepared to implement the central Politburo instruction from 17 January to 'unite the activity of the UkSSR and RSFSR'.[143] On 17 February 1920, the central Politburo approved Rakovsky's request to rename the Ukrainian Revkom as the Sovnarkom of the UkSSR (hereafter, the 'Ukrainian Sovnarkom') and to restore the All-Ukrainian TsIK. The latter was not authorized to have its own apparatus and was to remain a decorative institution for public image.[144] Once again, echoing the situation in December 1917 and November 1918, the existence of the Ukrainian Soviet Republic served the diplomatic interests of the Bolshevik leadership. On 17 February, Chicherin suggested to the central Politburo that Rakovsky should inform 'foreign states that the governmental apparatus of the independent UkSSR was being restored'.[145] On 16 March, Lenin sanctioned a Ukrainian Commissariat of Foreign Affairs, with Rakovsky as the Commissar of Foreign Affairs.[146]

Due to the negotiations between Poland and the UNR, the Ukrainian Central Committee decided at its meeting on 19 February to allow the Borotbists to occupy governmental posts. This was a drastic departure from the 11 February decision to 'begin a campaign against them[,]...give them an ultimatum about the dispersion of the central committee of the Borotbists and, at the same time, expel them from the government and local revkoms'.[147] At the Fourth CP(b)U Conference (17–23 March 1920), the Borotbists formally joined the CP(b)U.

With foreign policy favouring the preservation of the UkSSR, the Ukrainian Bolshevik leadership quickly moved to consolidate its position. Well aware that Moscow would not compromise on economic centralization, it proceeded to consolidate the Ukrainian Central Committee as the supreme authority in the republic. On 19 February 1920, the Ukrainian Central Committee decided that 'all principal issues regarding commissariats of Ukraine should be resolved in the Ukrainian Central Committee before being passed to the [RSFSR] Sovnarkom'. The decisions concerning the All-Russian commissariats should be communicated to the Ukrainian Central Committee before being implemented.[148] On 21 (22) April 1920, Poland signed the Treaty of Warsaw, which recognized an independent UNR. On 24 April, Polish troops advanced to Ukraine. The preservation of the UkSSR was now essential for the Bolshevik leadership to deprive the UNR of any legitimate claims for power. However, by June, the merger of Ukraine with Russia still remained on the agenda.[149]

It took a decisive defeat at the Battle of Warsaw (12–25 August) for the Bolshevik leadership to fully accept the UkSSR. On 17 August 1920, in the middle of negotiations with Poland, the RSFSR asked Poland not to tolerate any government claiming to represent part of Soviet Ukraine and to recognize the delegation of the UkSSR as separate from the RSFSR's delegation.[150] By asking for and receiving this concession, the RSFSR had formally recognized the UkSSR. Even though the legal terms of the relationship between the RSFSR and the UkSSR were not quite established, the Ukrainian republic was officially declared to be 'not part of the Russian republic'. 'When the federative relationship between them is formalized', explained Chicherin to Karl Danishevsky, the chairman of the Russian-Ukrainian delegation in Minsk, 'it will be only a tight union with preservation of independence by both sides'.[151] The announcement was not public, but the context in which this assertion was made could not but reassure the Ukrainian Bolshevik leadership that Ukraine would not be merged with Russia any time soon.

## New Status: Expectation of New Power Dynamic

The Soviet defeat in the Polish–Soviet War illustrated that Lenin had overestimated the likelihood of a socialist revolution in neighbouring Poland and could not but induce concerns that national revolution might reignite in Ukraine. This, along with the certainty that the Ukrainian government would be preserved, fundamentally changed the Ukrainian Bolsheviks' power ambitions.[152] From September 1920, the Ukrainian leadership—the Ukrainian Central Committee and the Ukrainian Sovnarkom—would be more assertive in its attempt to obtain tangible authority from the Central Committee.

Thus, on 30 September 1920, the Ukrainian Politburo decided to ask Moscow to increase the autonomy of the Ukrainian office of the Supreme Sovnarkhoz and the Ukrainian Promburo (Industrial Bureau), and to clarify the relationship between the Ukrainian leadership and the Central Committee. On 15 April 1920, the Supreme Sovnarkhoz allowed the UkSSR to expand the size and authority of the Ukrainian Promburo. The latter could open its periphery offices and even obtained the 'right of direct relationship with the Don oblast and the oblast of the Northern Caucasus to receive supplies for Ukrainian industry and deliver food and products manufactured in Ukraine directly to them'.[153] However, the Ukrainian Promburo remained 'hanging between Moscow and Kharkiv'. The Ukrainian Sovnarkom had no influence on it.[154] Now, the Ukrainian Central Committee believed that the Ukrainian Promburo and the Ukrainian Sovnarkom should have autonomy in using Ukrainian resources, that neither of these organs should ask the various glavks (departments) of the Supreme Sovnarkhoz for permission to use their own funds.[155] On 30 September, the Ukrainian Central Committee instructed Vlas Chubar, the head of the Ukrainian Promburo, to draft a detailed proposal on the Promburo. Interestingly, in spring 1919, Chubar had been a proponent of strict centralization and had criticized the UkSSR leadership for 'overestimating the tendencies to "independence" [in reference to the Ukrainian national movement], obstructing "unification of Ukrainian enterprises and industrial branches with ours [i.e., Russian]", and not leading a campaign against worthless "independence" [*nikchemnoï "samostiĭnosti"*]'.[156] Of course, in 1919, Chubar's interests were aligned with the All-Russian institutions as he was running the machine-construction and metal industries in Moscow. In autumn 1920, Chubar had a different institution to protect.

In November 1920, Rakovsky insisted on formalizing the place of the Ukrainian Sovnarkom within the Soviet vertical administration. He insisted that all instructions from the central commissariats in Moscow to the administrations in the Ukrainian periphery should be submitted only through the Ukrainian republican organs, whether through the plenipotentiaries of the All-Russian commissariats to the Ukrainian Sovnarkom, or through the Ukrainian commissariats.[157] On 25 November 1920, the Ukrainian Sovnarkom decided to submit to the RSFSR Sovnarkom a request to open a factory for printing money in Kharkiv, 'as an auxiliary organ to fulfil Ukrainian needs'.[158] The request was to be submitted by Nikolai Tumanov, the plenipotentiary of the RSFSR Narkomfin (People's Commissariat of Finances) in Ukraine, who assumed his post in mid-March 1920 with the agenda to 'unify the financial policy of both republics'.[159]

By November, the Ukrainian Central Committee was prepared to take a more assertive stance vis-à-vis the Central Committee on party matters as well. Since the First CP(b)U Congress in 1918, the loyalty of the administratively impotent

Ukrainian Central Committee lay with the Central Committee that appointed it. At the Fourth CP(b)U Conference on 17–23 March 1920, the aktiv (rank-and-file party members) called the Ukrainian Central Committee a 'signboard' that had nothing behind it.[160] The 'signboard' designation was an accurate description of the Ukrainian Central Committee, whose function was to rubberstamp Central Committee decisions. Yet, among the CP(b)U aktiv, there was a demand for a strong party centre that would lead them in their struggle against the Ukrainian left and make the necessary decisions. Despite Stalin's presence at the Fourth CP(b)U Conference, some even insisted that the Ukrainian Central Committee should be elected or disbanded only by the CP(b)U and should be accountable to it.[161]

By the time the Fifth CP(b)U Congress convened on 20 November 1920, the Ukrainian Central Committee found itself in a triangle between the Central Committee and the CP(b)U. On the one hand, as they were looking towards the period of restoration, many among the aktiv needed a strong CP(b)U with an equally strong Ukrainian Central Committee, even more than in the spring of 1920.[162] The authority of the Ukrainian Central Committee to amend central policies was viewed as essential. 'We should discuss resolutions before drafting and implementing a policy', suggested Skrypnyk, Commissar of the Workers Peasant Inspection of the UkSSR. 'After wide discussions, we might need to go further than the RKP(b) on certain resolutions and implement harsher decisions, or on the contrary, softer policies.'[163]

On the other hand, a policymaking Ukrainian Central Committee was not part of the Central Committee's plans. As President of the Third International Grigorii Zinov'ev succinctly put it at the Fifth CP(b)U Congress, 'How can one run a country without being able to appoint trusted commissioners [*upolnomochennykh*]?'[164]

The Ukrainian Central Committee was inclined to align with the aktiv. At the beginning of the congress, Kosior, in his report on the organizational work of the Ukrainian Central Committee, had already acknowledged the administrative failures of the Ukrainian Central Committee and the weakness of the CP(b)U as an organization, and had promised that the Ukrainian Central Committee would not only 'create the connection with our gubernia and local party organizations', but also 'make it clear that the Ukrainian Central Committee was the highest authority [in the republic]'.[165] In a rather bold effort to project authority, Kosior implied, if not promised, that the Ukrainian Central Committee would take care of the party finances. 'Until now, we lived on the funds of local...organizations.... [I]t is necessary that the Ukrainian Central Committee take upon itself to provide funds to the [local party] organizations....You may consider this issue completely settled.'[166] Kosior did not elaborate from where exactly the Ukrainian Central Committee would procure funds for local party organizations, but it appears that it did indeed hope to obtain control over resources. Rakovsky, in his turn, informed the audience about the Ukrainian Central Committee's request for autonomy for the Ukrainian Promburo and assured them that 'the Central Committee met our expectations'.[167] Rakovsky came close to the position of national communists on the nationality question. Now he, too, publicly insisted that the nationality question was related to economic relations; 'the language [was] a technical aspect of the nationality question'.[168]

Few appointed by Moscow were willing to promote administrative centralization. They focused, instead, on expanding the margins of their own authority. This could not but frustrate the Bolshevik leadership. There were objective reasons for economic decentralization. Since the mid-1920, the glavk system, which centralized control over resources along branch lines, had come under sharp criticism for inefficiency. However, explains Silvana Malle, the Bolshevik leadership closely connected control over the economy with political power. So, it believed that it had 'to concentrate the tasks of economic reconstruction in the hands of the higher organs of the state'. Reconstruction of the economy would be based on heavy industry and transport, coordinated through a single economic plan that 'was to be carried out by the Council of Labour and Defence'.[169] Centralism prevailed.[170] Lenin might have promised Rakovsky to give autonomy to the Ukrainian Promburo, but there would be no practical implementation of this promise. Nonetheless, appearances could not be neglected. The Polish–Soviet War was still not finished, even though the military campaign was over. Petliura was still viewed as a potential military threat and a present political threat, with Ukrainian nationalism not yet defeated.[171] On 28 December 1920, the RSFSR and UkSSR signed a formal treaty. The Ukrainian Sovnarkom was now formally in a position to demand de facto authority.

## Conclusion

The relationship between the Bolshevik leadership in Moscow and the Bolshevik leaders in Ukraine in the period between 1917 and 1920 revealed that the struggle for a common cause and the same ideas did not always mean the struggle for the interests of the same institutions. While fighting for Soviet power, the Bolshevik leadership prioritized the struggle for the All-Russian centre and fought the civil war on the entire territory of the former Russian Empire. For the Bolshevik leaders in Ukraine, who also fought for Soviet power, the Bolshevik ideals, and the world revolution, it was the struggle for Ukraine that mattered first and foremost—but not for nationalist reasons.

Had the Central Rada not been created, the Bolshevik leadership would not have organized nine Ukrainian gubernias into one entity. Yet, once these gubernias formed one polity, local Bolsheviks recognized the political prospects that this polity opened, not in Ukraine, but within the Bolshevik Party. Local Bolsheviks were indifferent to the ideas or aims of the Ukrainian national movement, and of the Ukrainian people in general. They viewed Ukraine as a polity where they could satisfy their political ambitions as policymakers. The Ukrainian national movement offered them a perfect opportunity to insist on the integrity of this polity with Bolshevik leadership, despite Lenin's consistent efforts to merge that polity with Russia.

Hence, Bolshevik leaders in Ukraine defended the integrity of Ukraine and of their respective organizations. Each time Ukraine was in danger of being merged with Russia, they mounted as much resistance as the circumstances allowed. Indeed, it was always a combination of factors that convinced Lenin to restore Soviet Ukraine, first in 1918 and then in 1919, and the pressure from the Bolsheviks of Ukraine might not even have been a defining factor in Lenin's decision. Important is the very fact that regardless of their views on the Ukrainian national movement, regardless of their ethnicity, Bolshevik leaders who worked in Ukraine did not hesitate to profit from the legacy of that very same Ukrainian national movement that the Bolshevik Party as a whole so vigorously tried to eradicate: a central territorial administrative centre. In that sense, Piatakov, Rakovsky, Manuilsky, Podvoisky, and many others simply demonstrated the same state-building talents as the Bolshevik leadership in Moscow, who, as Graziosi observed, were never afraid to bend ideas when confronted with the practical application of power.[172]

*The Institutional Foundations of Ukrainian Democracy: Power Sharing, Regionalism, and Authoritarianism*. Nataliya Kibita, Oxford University Press. © Nataliya Kibita 2024. DOI: 10.1093/9780191925351.003.0002

# 2

# New System

## Introduction

On 28 December 1920, the Russian Socialist Federative Soviet Republic (RSFSR) formally recognized the Ukrainian Socialist Soviet Republic (UkSSR), with its capital in Kharkiv (1919–1934), and the two republics signed a Friendship Treaty. The treaty secured the very existence of the Ukrainian administrative centre. It did not, however, grant it any authority. Apart from propaganda purposes—to illustrate to the world that the Soviet government respected nations' right to self-determination, and to respond to Ukrainians' national sentiments—the purpose of the Ukrainian administrative centre was by design limited to implementing central policies and representing the All-Russian (called 'All-Union' after the creation of the Soviet Union on 30 December 1922) government in Ukraine. In Moscow's view, it was unnecessary to empower the Ukrainian Council of People's Commissars (Sovnarkom) or the Ukrainian Central Committee (hereafter, the 'Ukrainian leadership') with tangible economic or administrative power over the Ukrainian periphery.[1]

The view from Kharkiv was different. For the Ukrainian leadership, Ukraine formed one territorial administrative unit with specific needs requiring the adjustment of central policies. Hence, the Ukrainian centre's authority over the party and state apparatus in the periphery had to be consolidated. In the period between 1921 and 1925, the Ukrainian leadership tried but failed to position itself as the essential link between the Ukrainian periphery and the All-Russian centre.[2] The highly volatile social and economic situation in the republic, in combination with the absence of a formalized division of powers between the Ukrainian and the All-Russian Soviet administrations, provided a favourable background for the Ukrainian leadership to make its case in Moscow.[3] However, for reasons discussed in this chapter, the Ukrainian leadership failed to consolidate its authority. As a result, the Ukrainian Central Committee remained institutionally weak and the Communist Party (Bolshevik) of Ukraine (CP(b)U) fragmented.

## Part I: 1921

### Asserting Distinctiveness

Back in 1919, Christian Rakovsky might have believed that the Soviet government of Ukraine was a temporary organ of the Central Committee that unquestionably

implemented all its instructions and orders,[4] but by 1921, the Ukrainian government he headed was no longer temporary. The certainty over its institutional
survival changed his perception of the authority it should have.

The Ukrainian leadership was well aware of its own weaknesses. Not only did
it lack financial and material resources to command-administrative and economic authority, it also lacked legitimacy with the party and state apparatus. In
Moscow, as well as in Ukraine, the majority of Bolsheviks simply did not view
Ukrainians as a distinct nation that needed its own administration. For them, it
was the south of Russia and could very well be administered from Moscow. The
Ukrainian leadership started to consolidate its authority by asserting the distinctiveness of the very republic that it was appointed to run.

## Ukrainization

In January 1921, the Ukrainian leadership revived the policy of Ukrainization.[5]
As briefly mentioned in Chapter 1, this policy was elucidated at the Eighth
Conference of the Russian Communist Party (Bolsheviks) (RKP(b)) in
December 1919 in the resolution 'About Soviet power in Ukraine', which itself was
based on Lenin's mid-November instruction 'to observe strictly the equality of
the Ukrainian language and culture', and required that all state officials learn
Ukrainian.[6] Lenin's instruction was ignored. There was little scope for
Ukrainization in 1920. At the beginning of 1921, the Central Committee did not
insist on implementing Ukrainization.

Nonetheless, on 11 January 1921, the Ukrainian Politburo instructed Volodymyr
Zatonsky to design a programme to develop Ukrainian culture. On 14 January, it
ordered that the CP(b)U member party cards be written in Ukrainian, and on
15 January, it gave Zatonsky two weeks to present his thesis on the national
question.[7]

During the Tenth Party Congress (8–16 March 1921), Zatonsky hinted at the
role Ukrainization could play in consolidating the Ukrainian administrative
centre. He said:

> We need to obliterate from the heads of comrades the idea that the Soviet feder-
> ation is essentially a Russian [*rossiiskaia*] federation, because the point is not
> that it is Russian, but that it is Soviet. If, for example, Romania becomes Soviet,
> or if there will be Soviet Germany or a number of other federations [*sic*], will
> they be also called Russian? No. The fact that the federation is 'Russian' intro-
> duces enormous confusion in the minds of the party comrades.

The confusion was about power. 'I personally do not know what kind of relationship we, who live in Ukraine, are in with the RSFSR....What to say about the
general masses! According to the latest treaty we are in a federation, [but] we are
not....It is necessary to fight these *rusapetstvo* tendencies.'[8]

Zatonsky argued that if Romania or Germany joined the Soviet Federation, they would not be called 'Russian' because they were linguistically different from Russia. So, in order for Ukraine not to be called Russia, the republic, including its party and state apparatus, had to speak Ukrainian. The Ukrainian leadership should be treated accordingly, as a leadership of a non-Russian Soviet state. For this to happen, state relations between Russia and Ukraine had to be clearly defined and formalized.

But first, the Ukrainian leadership needed to convince the republican party aktiv to accept the distinctiveness of Ukraine. The task was not easy. At the first All-Ukrainian (hereafter, 'Ukrainian') meeting of the CP(b)U held on 2–4 May 1921, the gubkoms of Odesa, Kharkiv, Mykolaiv, and Kyiv effectively accused Rakovsky of nationalist deviations. Nonetheless, after Dmytro Manuilsky's report on the national question, the meeting issued a resolution to steadily implement the December 1919 resolution of the Central Committee on the national question.[9] On 17 May, the Ukrainian Politburo approved the draft of the resolution on the national question and supplemented it with a paragraph on 'formalization of state relations' between Ukraine and Russia.[10] At the end of May 1921, the Ukrainian Politburo instructed Ukrainian Commissar of Education Hryhorii Hrynko to form a commission to reform the Ukrainian literary language and 'bring it closer to the people's language'.[11]

## Asserting Control over Resources

The main motivation for asserting Ukraine's distinctiveness from Russia was control over the economy. Without control over resources, the Ukrainian leadership had little importance to the central bureaucracy in Moscow, nor to the Ukrainian periphery apparatus.

While Zatonsky explained to the Tenth Party Congress that 'Soviet' did not mean 'Russian', the Ukrainian leadership and the Ukrainian commissariats were already in dispute with the All-Russian agencies over authority in Ukraine.[12]

The congress did not introduce any clarity on the relationship between the All-Russian and Ukrainian agencies, but it did launch the New Economic Policy (NEP). The NEP was primarily designed to repair the relationship between the state and the peasantry, which was morally and economically exhausted by the *prodrazverstka*, or surplus appropriation system, of wartime communism. Since 1918 in Russia and 1920 in Ukraine, peasants had delivered foodstuffs by quota and were deprived of the right to retain any surplus over their own consumption.[13] The NEP allowed peasants to trade their surplus after tax deductions. Large-scale industry, including banking and foreign trade, however, remained fully under the control of the state. On 12 August, the Council of Labour and Defence (STO) reduced the number of the branch glavks from fifty-two to sixteen. The state also retained centralized control over heavy industry, railways, wholesale trade, banking, etc.[14] As Mau explained: 'The new system anticipated a number of independent economic subjects—state as well as private—able to openly follow their own interests.... The consolidation of centralism in planning was to be implemented with the decentralization of administration.'[15] In other words, state agencies and private 'capitalists' would be able to implement the centre's plans as they saw fit.

The Tenth Party Congress outlined only general principles of the new system.[16] The Ukrainian leadership decided to capitalize on the principle of decentralization, which, it believed, legitimized its claims for expansion of Ukraine's economic authority and control over resources.

Immediately after the Tenth Party Congress, the Ukrainian leadership made claims on foreign trade.[17] The Soviet state declared its intention to restore 'normal trading relationships' with other countries.[18] In anticipation of a possible relaxation of Moscow's monopoly in foreign trade, on 22 March 1921, the Ukrainian Politburo issued a resolution 'About the relationship between the Vneshtorg and Narkomfin of the UkSSR and RSFSR', where it instructed the People's Commissariat of Finances (Narkomfin) to compose an import–export plan for goods destined for the Ukrainian countryside jointly with the Ukrainian government.[19]

At the 20–21 July 1921 plenum of the Ukrainian Central Committee, the Ukrainian leadership decided to impose its own financial discipline on the state apparatus and instructed the financial commission of the Ukrainian Sovnarkom 'to present a draft of a balanced revenue-spending budget for Ukraine regardless of decisions on the financial policy that will be adopted in Moscow'.[20] At the same plenum, the Ukrainian leadership took steps to assert its control over cooperatives. It passed a resolution that viewed cooperatives as trading agents for the Narkomprod, echoing the RSFSR Sovnarkom decree from 24 May 1921.[21] However, the Ukrainian leadership also allowed the Vukoopspilka (Ukrainian Association of Consumer Cooperative Organizations) to cancel contracts 'in case [there was] a contradiction between local agreements and the general contract signed between the Narkomprod and [Vukoopspilka]'.[22]

The Ukrainian leadership continued to work towards formalizing the relationship between the Ukrainian and central state apparatus.[23] On 20 August 1921 the Ukrainian Orgburo even instructed the Rabkrin (People's Commissariat of Workers' and Peasants' Inspectorate) of Ukraine to tell the inspectors who arrived from the RSFSR 'to go back to the RSFSR and inform their Rabkrin that all investigations in Ukraine were within the jurisdiction of the Rabkrin of Ukraine'.[24] On 20 September 1921, Chairman of the Ukrainian Sovnarkhoz Vlas Chubar signed an instruction stating:

1. Any relationship between the Main Administration [of the Ukrainian Sovnarkhoz] and the gubernia sovnarkhozy with the RSFSR Sovnarkom must

go exclusively through the Ukrainian Sovnarkhoz Presidium. 2. Gubernia sovnarkhozy should not execute the instructions of the RSFSR commissariats if these instructions were not sanctioned by the Ukrainian Sovnarkhoz Presidium. 3. If [the instructions are sent by the RSFSR commissariats] directly [to the gubernia sovnarkhozy], then they should only be taken into consideration.[25]

On 24 September 1921, the Ukrainian Central Executive Committee of Soviets (TsIK) issued a resolution stating that any resolution of the RSFSR TsIK that also applied to Ukraine must first be approved by the Ukrainian TsIK. On 28 September 1921, the Ukrainian Sovnarkom created the Ukrainian Economic Council and subordinated the Ukrainian Gosplan to it. The agenda of the Ukrainian Economic Council was to unite, coordinate, regulate, and control the work of the Ukrainian commissariats as well as the commissioners of the RSFSR commissariats as they drafted and fulfilled economic plans. The Ukrainian Economic Council was of union-republican jurisdiction, as it would become known. It was subordinated to the Ukrainian leadership, as well as to the RSFSR STO. However, the Ukrainian leadership gave the Ukrainian Economic Council the right to delay implementing instructions and resolutions issued by the All-Russian commissariats.[26]

At the Sixth CP(b)U Conference on 10 December 1921, Rakovsky reported on the Ukrainization of education and 'the elaboration of the constitution of the Federation', both in progress, and mentioned that the outlines of a new, fairer, financial relationship between the republics had been set. He was very optimistic about Ukraine's foreign trade, expecting the All-Russian export fund to put '15 or 20 percent' of its financial assets 'entirely at the disposal of the Ukrainian government'.[27]

## The Relationship with the Periphery

The efforts of the Ukrainian leadership to secure its place within the state administration were matched by its efforts to impose its superiority over the Ukrainian gubkoms, the largest territorial party units in the CP(b)U. It began, however, by forcing the gubkoms to accept the authority of the Ukrainian Central Committee, while ignoring the efforts of the gubkoms to communicate their problems to the Ukrainian leadership.[28] The gubkoms resented such leadership.

At the Ukrainian party meeting on 2–4 May 1921, the gubkoms stated that although the political line of the Ukrainian Central Committee was correct—in itself a rather patronizing assertion given that the Ukrainian Central Committee could not have any political line distinct from the one set by the Central Committee—the organizational work of the Ukrainian Central Committee and its connections with the gubkoms remained weak. (To improve these connections, the Ukrainian leadership decided that members of the Ukrainian Central Committee should visit the periphery in person. This effort, however, fell short.)[29]

At the Sixth CP(b)U Conference, Rakovsky admitted that the connection between the Ukrainian centre and the periphery was very weak. Indeed, the periphery lived its own life. However, he was satisfied with the practice of personal visits, 'as the only way to improve communication with the periphery'.[30] Rakovsky was not particularly preoccupied with the condition of the CP(b)U or keeping the gubkoms happy. For him, the gubkoms were there to implement the instructions sent from above and to focus on party work. Gubkoms were not expected to administer the economy. As he announced to the delegates, in line with Moscow's policy that was yet to be officially announced at the Eleventh Party Congress on 27 March–2 April 1922, the Ukrainian leadership was preparing to clearly divide the functions of the party and state apparatus. The party was expected to return to its 'immediate objective of leading the professional movement'.[31] Up until now, 'the party performed state work, and this was unavoidable', but it would no longer be necessary. The party should just issue policy guidance and not perform state work.[32] On the other hand, the power of the Ukrainian leadership should increase, as well as Rakovsky's powers as the chairman of the Ukrainian government. This was necessary because 'in some localities, to please workers, [local authorities] squandered goods [commodities]',[33] explained Rakovsky. Yet, Rakovsky argued, the proletariat would stay in power only if the state industry developed. Therefore, all available resources should be channelled to state industry. In Ukraine, state industry could develop only under the supervision of the Ukrainian government, insisted Rakovsky.[34]

The majority of gubkom secretaries were indignant at the secondary place that Rakovsky assigned to the gubkoms in state administration. They resented the fact that the Ukrainian Sovnarkom and the Ukrainian Economic Council were preparing to regulate the Ukrainian economy, leaving them limited opportunity to influence the economic development of their regions. After all, the gubkoms had no representation in the Ukrainian Sovnarkom. As the Odesa gubkom secretary Oleksandr Odintsov argued, it was 'abnormal' that the NEP was implemented through the Ukrainian Sovnarkom and the Ukrainian Economic Council, even though 'they were party members as well', while the Ukrainian Central Committee took very little part in the implementation of economic policy.[35] 'The new Ukrainian Central Committee should come to grips with economic issues', he insisted. This included establishing new procedures related to the NEP and giving explicit instructions to the periphery.[36]

In line with their resentment towards the Ukrainian Sovnarkom taking the reins in state administration, the periphery secretaries objected to applying the principle of self-financing to the party and the Ukrainian Sovnarkom's instruction from 21 July 1921 to balance their budgets.[37] To balance their books meant cutting expenses, which meant decreasing the size of their paid staff.

The gubkom secretaries again criticized the Ukrainian Central Committee for the Ukrainian Communist Party's organizational disunity, which, many argued, was due to insufficient directives on central policy implementation and lack of regular communication between Kharkiv and the periphery.[38]

However, by far the most alarming criticism that the Ukrainian leadership heard at the conference was that some, if not all, gubkom secretaries objected to being treated as subordinates of the Ukrainian Central Committee. They believed that when implementing central policies, the Ukrainian leadership should not just issue instructions, it should consult the gubkom secretaries and seek their opinion. 'Only when representatives from the periphery, the gubkom secretaries, participate in the discussion of [these] issues and help outline a policy, will they [better] grasp their work', explained the secretary of the Katerynoslav gubkom, Tymofii Simonov. Simonov categorically objected to the superiority of the Ukrainian Central Committee members who were sent by the Ukrainian leadership to the periphery to oversee the gubkoms. The gubkoms were guided by the same directives of the Tenth Party Congress as the Ukrainian Central Committee.

> The directive of the Ukrainian Central Committee that allowed its members who work in the periphery to halt the decision of the gubkoms…[violates] the principle of democratic centralism. Indeed, it is mentioned [in this directive] that the central committee members who work in the periphery should lead all work. But this does not mean that they can halt the decisions of gubkom.[39]

Odintsov agreed. He insisted that the central committee members in the gubkoms should suspend only those decisions that contradicted the party line.[40]

Yet at the same time, the gubkoms believed that the Ukrainian leadership should be more assertive in adapting central policies to the Ukrainian context. The Ukrainian leadership was particularly criticized for reacting to the famine in Ukraine in 1921 only after the central leadership in Moscow acknowledged it. (Interestingly, Mykola Skrypnyk and Manuilsky accepted the criticism.[41]) 'Our central committee was born in the era of storm and stress.…At the time, our central committee did not have authority in the periphery', summarized one gubkom secretary. Now the CP(b)U needed 'a central committee that would be genuinely authoritative for all organizations in Ukraine'[42]—that is, for all party and state organizations.

In 1921, being 'authoritative' was a challenge for the Ukrainian leadership. As Skrypnyk acknowledged in December 1921, 'in every single case [we] have to bargain with the secretaries of ispolkoms [local soviet executive committees] and gubkoms, as well as with other officials. Such leadership lacks the necessary order, decisiveness and foresight.'[43] The Ukrainian leadership equally lacked mechanisms to enforce its directives. It lacked even information on the actual state of affairs in the periphery. This had a damaging effect on its authority, of which it was painfully aware.[44] According to Manuilsky, who in 1921 was appointed first secretary, and Skrypnyk, the way to consolidate the authority of the republican centre was for it to be less of 'the registrar of the instructions of the Central Committee' and instead to 'show more foresight'.[45]

## Part II: 1922

Whether in 1921 the Ukrainian gubkoms truly yearned for a strong party centre in Kharkiv or not remains to be researched. Still, their view of the Ukrainian leadership as weak and inefficient motivated Rakovsky and Manuilsky to work towards empowering the Ukrainian administrative centre.

Rakovsky, with Manuilsky's support, focused on asserting the authority of the Ukrainian commissariats, thus securing their place in the vertical administration of the Soviet state. Manuilsky, with Rakovsky's support, tried to secure a niche for the Ukrainian Central Committee in the party administration.

### Control over Resources

In 1922 the Ukrainian leadership began with an affirmative message and a strong claim over the Ukrainian economy. An opportunity presented itself during a local conflict in Donbas between Heorhii Piatakov, chairman of the Donbas state agency in charge of coal production, and various local groups. Piatakov, tasked with rebuilding the coal industry and providing the country with coal, was given extraordinary powers by Lenin in 1920–1921. The local groups paused their frequent infighting to unite behind the view that an outsider like Piatakov posed a threat to their power. The conflict reached Moscow and, at the end of 1921, the Central Committee sent a delegation headed by Ordzhonikidze to examine the conflict.[46]

In this conflict, the Ukrainian leadership took the side of the anti-Piatakov majority. The Ukrainian leadership also resented Piatakov's authoritarianism and his disregard for the Ukrainian party and state structure. The Ukrainian leadership also considered that it was necessary to restore the entire economy of Donbas, not just the coal industry, and believed that Donbas, being the main industrial region in Ukraine, should not be administered from Moscow.[47] At the beginning of February, Rakovsky, Chubar, and Mikhail Frunze would defend their position in Moscow and insist that Chubar replace Piatakov.[48]

Consistent with its desire to establish control over Ukrainian industry, the Ukrainian leadership was preparing for a considerable increase in its control over the republic's finances.[49] On 14 January, following plenipotentiary Tumanov's financial report, the Ukrainian Sovnarkom instructed Mykhailo Poloz, Ukraine's representative to the STO, to defend an independent budget for Ukraine for both united and republican commissariats and to insist that Ukraine's share of collected taxes be transferred automatically to the Ukrainian Narkomfin. The Ukrainian government would then distribute the funds to the final addressees. To elicit trust that the funds would reach the addressees, the Ukrainian government promised the central leadership that it would report on the fulfilment of the budget and keep an eye on the Ukrainian commissariats. The Ukrainian commissariats were instructed to report twice a month on the state of their budget.[50]

At the same 14 January meeting, the Ukrainian government instructed the Ukrainian Planning Financial Commission to include in its directives a provision about deducting a share of the revenue collected in the republic and setting it aside for the Ukrainian government to create a special fund for republican needs not covered in the budget. It also decided to suggest that the RSFSR Sovnarkom change how banknotes were distributed. Instead of waiting for instructions from the commissariats, the RSFSR Narkomfin should transfer the entire sum of banknotes intended for Ukraine to the Ukrainian government.[51] By mid-April, the Ukrainian government had succeeded in securing an 'endowment fund' of 407 billion roubles and was in a position to provide some financial support to the gubispolkoms and Ukrainian republican administrations.[52]

On 13 January 1921, in response to criticism about how it had handled the famine, the Ukrainian Politburo decided that the gubernias previously designated to supply only to the RSFSR would be allowed to 'supply seeds to the famished gubernias anywhere', 'and [to] temporarily reduce the supply of bread to RSFSR.'[53] After Manuilsky, Chubar, and Ordzhonikidze inspected Donbas, Manuilsky drafted a report that recorded the difficult food situation in Donbas and the 'catastrophic state of railways'. Based on this information, the Ukrainian Politburo instructed the Ukrainian Economic Council to 'inspect the situation with the workers who arrived from the north [i.e., Russia] and take measures to stop their inflow to Donbas.'[54] On 14 January, the Ukrainian Sovnarkom decided to reduce the food tax in some regions and to either replace the food tax with money tax in other regions or completely exempt them from paying food taxes.[55]

In foreign trade, a meeting in Moscow on 8 January 1922 discussed unifying the economic policy of the Union of Soviet Republics. The Ukrainian government approved of declaring the territory of all Soviet Republics a single customs territory, 'which is based on a single trading policy and single economic plan'. However, the Ukrainian government insisted that the All-Union Vneshtorg (People's Commissariat of Foreign Trade) should negotiate the customs tariff with the governments of the republics. Furthermore, a trading treaty concluded by the RSFSR with any other state should not automatically apply to other union republics, and the governments of the latter should have the right to defend their interests and coordinate the defence of their interests with the All-Union Vneshtorg.[56] On 16 January 1922, the Ukrainian Politburo discussed the 'Thesis on Foreign Trade', which announced that the All-Russian leadership would channel all foreign trade transactions through the Vneshtorg and immediately declared its intention to centralize control over foreign trade at the republican level. It categorically forbade all Ukrainian local and republican authorities to send agents abroad without permission from the Ukrainian Central Committee and the Ukrainian Economic Council. The periphery authorities could establish their own relationship with foreign firms, 'but [they should] be cautious and consult the [Ukrainian Commissariat of Foreign Affairs] on each occasion'. Even the Vukoopspilka had to coordinate its export–import transactions with the Ukrainian representative in the Vneshtorg.[57]

To boost trade inside Ukraine, the Ukrainian leadership relied on cooperatives. On 30 January, the Ukrainian Politburo insisted in Moscow that the Tsentrosoyuz should not be allowed to open an office in Ukraine. Members of the Tsentrosoyuz could come work in Ukraine, but only as members of the Vukoopspilka, and they should be approved by the Ukrainian Central Committee.[58] Expecting Moscow's support for its initiatives, the Ukrainian Politburo took steps to consolidate the state apparatus. In January 1922, it drafted the list of members of the Ukrainian Sovnarkhoz Presidium and instructed the Orgburo to draft collegiums for all Ukrainian commissariats.[59]

After the 6 February 1922 Ukrainian plenum, the Ukrainian leadership continued, if not intensified, its efforts to increase its control over resources. In February–March, the Ukrainian Politburo tried to overcome Moscow's resistance to Ukraine having a republican cooperatives bank. On 12 March, it decided to create an agricultural bank in Ukraine. On 13 February, the Ukrainian leadership agreed that it was essential for Ukraine to participate in the federal economic projects and hold a 25–30 percent share in the federal export–import joint stock company. On 28 and 30 April, in response to the prohibition on establishing local taxes—the resolution of the All-Russian TsIK and Sovnarkom from 27 April—the Ukrainian Politburo decided nonetheless to ask the Central Committee for permission to leave between 15 and 25 percent of taxes to local authorities, 'as motivation' for them to collect taxes. (The request would be repeated on 5 June 1922.) On 30 April, the Ukrainian Politburo issued another objection to a new economic regionalization in Ukraine and the 'untimely' abolition of Ukrainian republican central economic administrations.[60]

## Consolidating the Party

In party matters, the Ukrainian leadership was no less assertive. Thus, on 13 January 1922, the Ukrainian Politburo, under Manuilsky's chairmanship, confirmed its decision from one year before that the CP(b)U party cards should be in Ukrainian.[61] Then, in response to the criticism that sounded at the December 1921 conference regarding the Ukrainian Central Committee imposing its cadres on the gubkoms, the Ukrainian Central Committee adopted a conciliatory tone and instructed the Secretariat to take a more personal approach to the appointments. To address the difficult material situation of all party members, but also of the Soviet apparatus, the Narkomprod and the Council for Supplies were instructed to provide basic food supplies for communists most in need.[62]

More importantly, the Ukrainian Central Committee decided to routinize the top-down communication with the gubkoms and start issuing monthly information letters, 'similar to the letters of the Central Committee', about the economic situation in the republic and about the Red Army. To coordinate the party work and connect the gubkoms to the Ukrainian Central Committee in a more tangible way, the Ukrainian Central Committee drafted agendas for its departments and the respective departments in the gubkoms for February, March, and April. Starting in 1922, the Ukrainian Central Committee expected to coordinate party discussions in the gubkoms. On 10 February, Dmytro Lebid, the secretary of the Ukrainian Central Committee, asked Central Committee Secretary Viacheslav Molotov to send the agenda for the forthcoming Eleventh Party Congress scheduled for 27 March–2 April 1922 in Moscow to be discussed beforehand at their gubernia conferences.[63]

Yet no effort to assert the authority of the Ukrainian Central Committee could succeed if the Central Committee continued to communicate with the gubkoms directly. On 4 February 1922, the Ukrainian Central Committee Secretariat asked Molotov 'once again' to establish the exact procedure for transmitting the Central Committee's directives and resolutions to the twelve Ukrainian gubkoms. 'The most correct way would be if all directives, instructions, letters, reports, etc., were mailed only through the Ukrainian Central Committee' and if the Ukrainian Central Committee had the right to introduce certain corrections to the documents issued by the Central Committee.[64]

At the plenum on 6 February 1922, the Ukrainian leadership explained that the initiatives and instructions it had issued so far were only the beginning of the process of consolidating the Ukrainian republican centre. The Ukrainian socialist statehood could develop only in the closest union with Russia and there should be a single economic policy for all republics. However, the economic recovery of the entire state was simply impossible without 'the widest economic autonomy of the Soviet republics',[65] stated Rakovsky in his thesis on the nationality question. Hence, further consolidation of the Ukrainian republican centre was inevitable.

With some editorial changes, including mandatory knowledge of Ukrainian for the state apparatus, the plenum accepted Rakovsky's thesis, thus effectively supporting his vision of an autonomous Ukraine. In line with this decision, the plenum approved further organizational steps to address the famine and decided to emphasize to the Central Committee

that the subordination of the industrial inspection of Donbas to the RSFSR Commissar of Rabkrin deprive[d] the Ukrainian [party] organisation of the possibility of controlling the industry of Donbas through relevant soviet organs, which contradict[ed] the resolution that placed responsibility for the condition of the Donetsk coal industry on the CP(b)U.

Hence, the Central Committee should 'review the decision about the subordination of the rabkrin of Donbas'[66] and subordinate it directly' to the Ukrainian leadership.

To continue consolidating the CP(b)U, the plenum introduced a practice of calling Ukrainian party conferences back-to-back with the party congresses. The Ukrainian Politburo was instructed to prepare a thesis on the issues that were on the agenda for the Eleventh Party Congress; the gubkoms were instructed to open broad discussions.[67]

To build tighter connections between the Ukrainian Central Committee and the gubkoms, the plenum instructed those central committee members who worked in the periphery to send monthly reports about the local situation. In stark contrast with the previous practice that allowed them to overrule the decisions of the gubkoms (a practice that was criticized at the December 1921 CP(b)U Conference), the new rule instructed the central committee members to limit their involvement in local affairs solely to informing the Ukrainian Central Committee Secretariat on the difficulties that the gubkoms were experiencing when implementing central instructions and resolutions.[68]

## An Attempt to Formalize Relations

The All-Russian commissariats had been ignoring their Ukrainian offices and communicated directly with their addressees in the Ukrainian periphery. On 11 March, the Ukrainian Politburo concluded that the time had come to formalize the relationship between the UkSSR and RSFSR and to specify the rights and responsibilities of the UkSSR.[69]

At the 11 May meeting, the central Politburo discussed Ukrainian affairs in the presence of Frunze and Manuilsky, and decided to form a Federal Russian–Ukrainian commission that would regulate the relationship between the RSFSR and UkSSR.[70] The first meeting of the Frunze Commission, named after its chairman, was held on 12 May and attended by its members, Frunze, Stalin, Lev Kamenev, Manuilsky, and Commissar of Internal Affairs of Ukraine Mykola Skrypnyk, as well as those invited: Aleksei Svidersky (member of the collegium of Rabkrin), Mykhailo Kattel from the Ukrainian Narkomprod, Lev Khinchuk from Tsentrosoyuz, and Zatonsky and Vengrov from Vukoopspilka.[71] The composition of attendees had already indicated that the main issue of disagreement was control over resources: industry (Rabkrin) and food (Narkomprod and cooperatives). The Ukrainian side failed to escalate the resolution of urgent unsolved disagreements, such as between the Ukrainian and All-Russian Narkomprod, or between the Tsentrosoyuz and Vukoopspilka, or about the creation of a Ukrainian cooperative bank. Nonetheless, it was reassured that the Ukrainian leadership's status would be defended. The All-Russian organs were instructed to follow the 11 May resolution 'about the inadmissibility of any actions that would practically lead to the liquidation of the UkSSR and the curtailment of the rights of its Central Committee, Sovnarkom, and its central organs'.[72] This instruction applied to the party apparatus as well. Furthermore, privately, Lenin agreed to make an official statement 'at the closest convenient opportunity in the spirit of the outlined decisions and to erase the atmosphere that was unfavourable for Ukraine'.[73]

On 17 June 1922, Manuilsky joined Rakovsky, Frunze, Skrypnyk, and Poloz in signing a 'Supplementary Agreement about the procedure of the passage of legislation of RSFSR through the legislative bodies of UkSSR'. Paragraph 3 of the agreement stated that all laws and decrees, including those relevant to the All-Russian commissariats, in the territory of Ukraine had to be issued by the relevant legislative organs of Ukraine. Any legislative initiative adopted by the RSFSR Sovnarkom could be changed or supplemented by the Ukrainian organs, which had to inform the all-union organs. 'All organs and agents of Soviet power who act in the territory of the UkSSR, act in the name of the UkSSR', except the Red Army, which had to act in the name of both the RSFSR and the UkSSR.[74]

## Unity of the Ukrainian Leadership Broken

Until August 1922, the unity of the Ukrainian republican organs—the Sovnarkom, the Ukrainian Central Committee, the Ukrainian TsIK, and the Ukrainian Economic Council—in defence of their authority in the republic and Kharkiv's access and control over resources seemed unshakeable. Manuilsky viewed the Ukrainian government's effort to secure de facto autonomy for the republic as the best way to protect the interests of the Ukrainian Central Committee. The Central Committee systematically undermined the authority of the Ukrainian Central Committee and its efforts to establish itself as the superior agency for the Ukrainian gubkoms. In the spring of 1922, despite vehement protests from Manuilsky and the second secretary, Lebid, the Central Committee intensified its efforts to establish direct communication with the Ukrainian gubkoms and impose direct control over them. In June 1922, the Central Committee explicitly denied any republican central committee the right to make decisions, appoint main cadres, or 'respond to local needs' of gubkoms. If a gubkom needed help, it should address the Central Committee directly.[75]

Despite its claims, the Central Committee could not provide regular financing to the gubkoms. Gubkoms received their funds either late, or not for the full amounts. It was not uncommon for the party functionaries to go without a salary for two or three months.[76] The Ukrainian Central Committee tried to leverage this situation to consolidate its position in cooperation with the Ukrainian Sovnarkom. The Ukrainian Central Committee did not have its own funds to help the Ukrainian gubkoms directly, but it was able to support them by allowing them to find additional funds where they could and encouraging them to generate their own income 'from the exploitation of agricultural and industrial enterprises'.[77] The ongoing work of the Frunze Commission promised the Ukrainian Central Committee access to the funds of the Ukrainian Sovnarkom, reduced financial dependence on the Central Committee, and more authority over the Ukrainian gubkoms.

However, on 4 September, in a swift pivot, Manuilsky withdrew his support for Rakovsky and the idea of Ukraine controlling its resources. On that day, while on vacation, Manuilsky wrote a secret letter to Stalin where he denounced what he, as a member of the Ukrainian leadership, had defended until now: the position that the NEP required decentralization, that the Ukrainian leadership had to be involved in the management of local resources and have access to the foreign markets, and that Ukrainization was necessary to appease 'the Ukrainian *muzhik*'. He now believed that 'the existing form of the relationship [between Moscow and the republics] has played out and instead of a unified leadership, we have several "masters", which cannot but have a ruinous effect on the economy'. The ongoing conflict between the central and republican agencies was unsustainable because the 'objective situation' could no longer tolerate that 'the responsible comrades were spending three-fourths of their time settling the conflicts'.[78] Hence, the Ukrainian government should have no authority over the Ukrainian economy.

Manuilsky's change of heart was caused by what Pavlova called 'Stalin's secret party-state reform' and happened at the Twelfth RKP(b) Conference on 4–7 August 1922.[79] Stalin's party-state reform, which intensified in 1922–1923, aimed to subordinate the state apparatus to the party. Until the conference, Manuilsky did not have such an aim for the Ukrainian Central Committee. He showed no interest in prioritizing the Ukrainian Central Committee's vertical relationship with the Central Committee over its horizontal relationship with the Ukrainian Sovnarkom. However, at the conference that formalized the new party statute, the interests of the Ukrainian Central Committee were separated from those of the Ukrainian government.

The Twelfth RKP(b) Conference did not offer financial security to the party through party channels. On the contrary, it worsened their financial situation. The conference banned the gubkoms from having their own enterprises. The conference confirmed the decision made at the Eleventh Party Congress to provide financial help to party workers. However, as Molotov explained, the actual funds would not be provided by Moscow. They had to be generated by the periphery party organizations themselves: from the budget of the party organization, from deductions from the party fees of their members, from special transfers 'that can be made by local organizations', and from deductions from the highest salaries of the party staff.[80]

At the same time, the conference confirmed the policy of placing managers under party control and extended party control over trade unions and cooperative trade. Whether or not Manuilsky genuinely sought to place managers under party control, he argued in favour of separating the party from the state and of the Ukrainian Central Committee distancing itself from the Ukrainian Sovnarkom. As he explained, the increasing unemployment among industrial workers was damaging the reputation of the party in Ukraine, but also was instilling fear among the party cadres that they would be made scapegoats for the job cuts. To avoid future cleansing, they would pre-emptively leave the party. Hence, the party had to separate itself from the managers so that workers would not blame the party cadres for the unpopular decisions made by managers.[81]

At the conference, Manuilsky had to choose. He could continue supporting Rakovsky and his version of Ukrainian autonomy, which would make the Ukrainian Sovnarkom the highest authority in the republic. It was yet to be formalized, but Rakovsky's stance defended autonomy for the Ukrainian government and the Ukrainian commissariats, not autonomy for the Ukrainian Central Committee. Alternatively, Manuilsky could support Stalin, who did not conceal his intention to bring the Ukrainian gubkoms under the direct control of the Central Committee, but whose party-state reform promised that the Ukrainian Central Committee would be the highest authority in Ukraine.[82]

Given what is known today about Stalin's way of doing politics, one might also speculate that Stalin may have helped Manuilsky choose by sharing with him the reports of the Central Committee inspectors Kubiak and Sergushev, who, in April to early June 1922, had inspected the gubernias of Kyiv, Odesa, Volyn, Podillia, Kharkiv, Poltava, and Katerynoslav, as well as the Aleksandrivsk okruha. The report of Sergushev on Katerynoslav might have been particularly consequential, as its conclusion aligned with Stalin's own distaste for decentralization.[83]

> The connection with the Ukrainian centre existed, but the centre is always terribly late with its directives, and, because of this, it does not fully win the localities over[.] [W]hereas there is no open animosity of the localities towards [Kharkiv], had it not been for the political motives [i.e., Ukrainian nationalism], [they] would have spoken for Moscow [*vyskazalis' by za Moskvu*], not Kharkiv.[84]

For Stalin, this single paragraph must have validated his efforts to sideline the Ukrainian Central Committee, which had the status of a regional (oblast) party committee, but still showed much ambition to impose its authority over Ukrainian gubkoms. What authority could the Ukrainian leadership insist on if the industrial regions barely tolerated its very existence?

Manuilsky had to act promptly. The Union negotiations seemed to progress in Rakovsky's favour. On 10 August 1922, the Ukrainian leadership enjoyed a small, albeit insecure, victory when the central Politburo instructed the commissariats to be guided by the agreements approved by the Frunze Commission in their interaction with the Ukrainian agencies. Nonetheless, the Politburo did not legitimize these agreements in the Soviet order.[85] On 29 August, the Ukrainian leadership was finally notified of the Narkomfin's 15 June decision permitting the Ukrainian Sovnarkom to raise local taxes in order to increase its own financial resources, 'while informing the Narkomfin RSFSR' of any changes made.[86]

On 4 September 1922, Manuilsky wrote the secret letter to Stalin. His attack on the Ukrainian Sovnarkom specifically, the subsequent inclusion of his letter in Stalin's correspondence to Lenin on 22 September 1922 on the Union project, Manuilsky's subsequent open opposition to Rakovsky during the discussion of the national question at the Twelfth Party Congress on 17–25 April 1923, and the 'secret' meeting of the Central Committee on 9–12 June 1923 that effectively decided on a unitary state—all events scrupulously examined in the scholarly literature—placed this letter and Manuilsky's defection in the context of the Union negotiations and the defeat of Rakovsky.[87]

However, Manuilsky's withdrawal from Rakovsky's autonomy project also marked a watershed in the development of Ukraine's institutional system. As discussed in the rest of this chapter, Manuilsky's new stance not only allowed Stalin to deprive Rakovsky of the support of the Ukrainian Central Committee and the gubkoms in the Union negotiations, resulting in Ukrainian Sovnarkom losing the fight for control over resources. It also allowed Stalin to lay the administrative foundations for a system where the Ukrainian Central Committee would be institutionally weak and the CP(b)U fragmented. Deprived of any policymaking power or resources, and with limited decision-making power, the Ukrainian Central Committee would be unable to overcome this fragmentation. The fragmented CP(b)U would serve as the foundation for economic regionalism in Soviet and independent Ukraine.

## Recentralization of the RKP(b) Continues

After the Twelfth RKP(b) Conference, Stalin intensified his efforts to bring the Ukrainian gubkoms under Moscow's direct control. By doing so, he effectively broke the informal promise to make the Ukrainian Central Committee 'the highest authority in the oblast [i.e., the republic]' that was given at the conference but never clearly explained. However, he upheld the formal legislation in article 30 of the new party statute which stated that the Ukrainian Central Committee was as fully subordinated to the Central Committee as the gubkoms. As far as Stalin and the Central Committee were concerned, the status of the Ukrainian Central

Committee was no different from that of any gubkom, to the dismay of the Ukrainian Central Committee, now without Manuilsky.[88]

In August–September, the secretaries of the gubkoms of Kharkiv, Katerynoslav, and Odesa were summoned to report to the Central Committee Orgburo. Consistent with the policy of placing cooperatives under party control, as announced at the conference, the Orgburo instructed both the Kharkiv gubkom and the Ukrainian Central Committee to consolidate the party work in agricultural cooperation. However, the Ukrainian Central Committee was not appointed by the Orgburo to supervise the Kharkiv gubkom. Nor was it appointed to assist or supervise Simonov, the secretary of the Katerynoslav gubkom, who was instructed to transfer communists to the village. Simonov had to talk directly to Chairman of the Supreme Sovnarkhoz, Pyotr Bogdanov, about the organization of a united metallurgical trust, 'and, in case of a disagreement, to submit suggestions to the Central Committee Secretariat'.[89]

After the conference in August 1922, the Central Committee issued circular no. 60, which reminded the gubkoms to submit one copy of their reports to the Central Committee and another to their republican central committee. The Ukrainian Central Committee, when forwarding the circular to the gubkoms, attached its own circular no. 356, instructing all gubkoms to send both copies of 'the requested materials to the Ukrainian Central Committee. [One copy would be] forwarded to the Central Committee.'[90] (It must be noted that the 'circular wars' between the Central Committee and the Ukrainian Central Committee had somewhat limited effect on the gubkoms, which continued to defy their duty to report regularly on the local situation and focused instead on solving their immediate problems.[91])

On 16 September, Central Committee secretary Valerian Kuibyshev issued a warning 'to the secretaries of the Kharkiv, Kyiv, Podillia, Chernihiv, Poltava, Kremenchuk, Donetsk, Zaporizhzhia, Katerynoslav, Volyn, Odesa, and Mykolaiv gubkoms of the RKP(b)' that failures to report 'will be considered a violation of party discipline and, at the same time, as evidence of the ineffectiveness of the gubkom apparatus, as well as its leader'. On 25 September, Lebid had to inform the gubkoms that the Ukrainian Central Committee no longer required them to submit both copies of their reports to the Ukrainian Central Committee.[92]

The low authority of the Ukrainian Central Committee, particularly visible in party cadre appointments, did not increase after the conference.[93] Before the conference, the Ukrainian Central Committee could relocate a party worker from region to region only after discussing the relocation with the relevant gubkoms. In the summer of 1922, the gubkoms often replied to the Ukrainian Central Committee's instructions to move party functionaries with a brief refusal. None of the Ukrainian gubkoms submitted their lists of responsible party workers, or *otvetstvennykh rabotnikov*, making it difficult for the Ukrainian Central Committee to reallocate the party cadres.[94] After the conference, the Central

Committee continued to assign functionaries directly to the gubkoms. The Ukrainian Central Committee was informed about the new appointments, but with significant delay. The only thing left for Lebid to do was to ask Stalin personally to 'inform us when you assign [party] workers to the gubkoms so that we can keep a record of the [party] workers of our organizations', which he did on behalf of the Ukrainian Central Committee on 7 October 1922.[95]

On financial matters, on 18 September 1922, Lebid 'insistently asked' the Central Committee to send the funds that were supposed to arrive in return for the reports. However, by October, 'the Central Committee had not given a penny' to the Ukrainian Central Committee. So, the Ukrainian gubkoms continued to take funds from local managers. In October 1922, acting on the resolution of the conference, the Ukrainian Central Committee had to order the gubkoms to halt such entrepreneurial activity.[96]

## The Ukrainian Central Committee Weakened

Most of the time, the conflicts and disagreements between the Ukrainian Central Committee and the gubkoms remained an internal affair of the CP(b)U. However, after the Twelfth RKP(b) Conference and Manuilsky's letter, the gubkoms felt no constraint in complaining about the Ukrainian Central Committee to Moscow, often without informing the Ukrainian Central Committee.

Thus, the secretary of the Kharkiv gubkom, Kuprian Kirkizh, complained about the policy of Ukrainization that was being implemented by the Ukrainian leadership, prompting the Central Committee Orgburo to ask the Ukrainian Central Committee to explain 'which measures it took to liquidate the superfluous imposition of the Ukrainian language in the schools of the Kharkiv gubernia by the [Ukrainian Commissariat of Education]'. Odintsov from the Odesa gubkom blamed the Ukrainian Central Committee for not forwarding directives from the Central Committee, prompting the Orgburo to 'suggest to the [Ukrainian Central Committee] Secretariat to explain the reasons for delays in communicating the directives of the Central Committee to the gubkoms of Ukraine and work out measures to eliminate them'.[97] The secretary of the Podillia gubkom, Lev Denis (Starosvetsky), insisted in his 2 October report to the Central Committee Orgburo that he had 'sent the protocols, information reports, and closed letters to the Ukrainian Central Committee to be forwarded to the Central Committee', but that the Ukrainian Central Committee had failed to forward them to Moscow. Denis also complained that the Ukrainian Central Committee had not allocated the party cadres to the Podillia gubkom from the cohort relocated by the Central Committee from central Russia to Ukraine.[98]

After Lebid received information about Denis's complaints, he immediately wrote a letter to Stalin, copied to Molotov, Kuibyshev, and Lazar Kaganovich.

'Dear comrades', he began, 'considering a number of issues that had been raised in connection to Ukrainian gubkoms, secretaries' reports, I find it necessary to give written explanations...'. What followed was an illustration of the new, reversed dynamic in the relationship between Kharkiv and the gubkoms, whereby the Ukrainian Central Committee did not even project superiority over the gubkoms. 'The information that we do not forward the circulars of the Central Committee is incorrect', insisted Lebid. 'The claim that we did not send cadres to the Podillia gubkom...is incorrect.' 'The claim that the [communist] leadership of agricultural cooperatives is weak is completely unfounded.'[99] On 7 October 1922, Lebid wrote a detailed follow-up letter to Stalin insisting that the claims of the Podillia gubkom that the Ukrainian Central Committee mismanaged the cadres did not reflect reality.[100]

Sufficiently concerned about the power of the gubkoms, the Ukrainian Politburo decided on 12 October 1922 that Lebid had to go to Moscow to personally clarify the claims and complaints of the gubkom secretaries, and insisted, once again, 'that a representative of the Ukrainian Central Committee be present during the Ukrainian gubkom secretaries' in-person reports to the Central Committee'.[101]

While the Ukrainian Central Committee and its de facto first secretary, Lebid, were on the defensive—a position diametrically opposed to the one they were in when Manuilsky and Lebid believed they were just one step away from asserting their status as the republican party centre—the central leadership in Moscow outlined the general principles of the future Union Treaty. The Ukrainian leadership became hopeful that Ukraine might secure a share of control over its resources after all.[102]

In a projection of confidence about a beneficial Union, the 16–17 October 1922 plenum of the Ukrainian Central Committee passed several resolutions. Although the Commissariat of Foreign Trade already had all-union status, the plenum decided to 'preserve the existing situation according to which the [Ukrainian] Vneshtorg, guided by the directives of the Ukrainian government, [was] responsible for the export funds of the Ukrainian republic and managed foreign trade at the republican level'. On education policy, despite the fact that the Central Committee Orgburo openly spoke against what it called 'superfluous' Ukrainization, the plenum underlined that deviating from the existing party line on the issue of developing national-Ukrainian culture was out of the question. Knowledge of the Ukrainian language was confirmed as mandatory for government officials. The plenum also gave a directive to the Ukrainian Politburo to create a specific scheme for the relationship between the RSFSR and UkSSR that would reflect a real defence of the interests of Ukraine in various all-union organs. In a blatant effort to counteract the centralization tendency on the part of the all-union leadership, the Ukrainian leadership decided to show that the regions supported a 'real defence of Ukraine's interests'. So, the plenum instructed the

Ukrainian Politburo and the Military High Command in Ukraine, headed by Frunze, to hold a campaign demonstrating that the initiative for defending Ukraine's autonomy came from the periphery. After all, 'our gubernias are struggling [economically] because the organizational interests [of Ukraine] were not represented in the central organs, such as Narkomfin'.[103]

Optimism about Ukraine's future autonomy must have affected the Ukrainian leadership's thinking about the future of the Ukrainian Central Committee. Following Lebid's enthusiastic report to the plenum about the circulars and the resolutions that the Ukrainian Central Committee had issued since May 1922, the plenum adopted a resolution that defied the centralization tendencies diligently pursued by the Central Committee.

> While recognising the need for a most accurate and strict centralised leadership on the part of the Central Committee among the oblast committees and, at the same time, for the organisational and business-like leadership of the party work in the periphery, [we] speak out for full autonomy for the Ukrainian Central Committee, particularly since the Central Committee does not have any reasons not to trust the Ukrainian organisation and, for political reasons, it is not useful to replace an elected [Ukrainian] central committee with an oblast buro.[104]

Did the fact that the plenum adopted the resolutions proposed by the Ukrainian leadership mean that the gubkom secretaries did indeed share the optimism of the Ukrainian government and decided to support the Ukrainian Central Committee's claim to authority? Or did they vote for these resolutions out of precaution, just in case Rakovsky succeeded in securing autonomy for Ukraine? For the Central Committee, the wording 'highest authority' in Stalin's informal plans for the Ukrainian Central Committee did not mean much and certainly did not amount to the 'autonomy' of the Ukrainian Central Committee.

After the plenum, acting on the instruction of the Ukrainian Politburo, Lebid went to Moscow. The results of this trip, reported to the Ukrainian Politburo on 27 October, were devastating for the Ukrainian Central Committee. Lebid brought back the Central Committee's new circular, no. 96, 'About the procedure on written communication between the Central Committee and the gubkoms and obkoms that were members of the oblast [i.e., republican] organizations'. In this circular, the Central Committee finally included the Ukrainian Central Committee in the Moscow–periphery correspondence. The circular even allowed the Ukrainian Central Committee to issue explanatory or supplementary notes to Moscow's circulars and instructions. Only if the Ukrainian Central Committee wanted to change the essence of the document would it need to obtain authorization from the Central Committee. However, all directives that the Ukrainian Central Committee issued to local organizations had to be copied to the Central Committee.[105] This meant the Ukrainian Central Committee was not the only link between the gubkoms and the Central Committee, as it had hoped in the summer 1922. The Ukrainian Central Committee lost any freedom to issue its own instructions to the Ukrainian gubkoms without informing the Central Committee, a power Lebid had exercised in 1921–1922. Indeed, as Pavlova concluded, 'there was no question as to whether local party organs had any independence in making political decisions,'[106] or any decisions, really.

In his 4 November correspondence to Molotov, Lebid tried to convince the Central Committee to change the wording of the circular in a way that would secure a meaningful role for the Ukrainian Central Committee in the chain of communication between the Ukrainian gubkoms and Moscow. 'In general, there is a common view that the Kharkiv centre can be passed over', explained Lebid. At the October plenum of the Ukrainian Central Committee, some gubkom secretaries had voiced their displeasure that there was no clarity in communication procedures.

> This is why the plenum issued a special resolution [i.e., on the full autonomy of the Ukrainian Central Committee], in order to prevent a decrease in the authority of the Ukrainian Central Committee and clearly outline the communication channels. [Circular no. 96] about the procedure on reporting and so on is taken into consideration, and the issue could be considered settled[.] [H]owever, there is no doubt that some gubkom secretaries will take a wrong, from our point of view, approach and will address the Central Committee on all issues while bypassing the Ukrainian Central Committee.[107]

At the end of his report, Lebid implored Molotov to trust the Ukrainian Central Committee and help it to maintain its authority in party cadre management as well. 'All in all, the psychological mood of the functionaries of the Ukrainian Central Committee was very low', he wrote. 'We have an impression, although it could not be formed based on my visit to the Central Committee, that we are treated as the suppliers of the functionaries for the [All-Russian] commissariats. In almost every [Ukrainian] commissariat, they talk about the forthcoming withdrawal of the functionaries.' 'Our decisions about the movement of the cadres are also being questioned.' Providing the cadres was the sacred duty of the party, which the Ukrainian Central Committee could not even perform. 'If you need to be convinced of our need of functionaries', wrote Lebid, referring to the shortage of cadres that handicapped the CP(b)U, 'and in order for everyone to stop considering us as a supplier [of cadres for Moscow], send once again the central committee instructors in order to inspect the gubernias as well as the centre [i.e., Kharkiv]'. To gain trust, Lebid asked Molotov to inspect the CP(b)U, as the Central Committee did in May–June 1922 when his reports on the shortages of funds were verified and confirmed by the Central Committee inspectors.[108]

The Central Committee had no interest in empowering or trusting the Ukrainian Central Committee, not when the Union negotiations were still in progress.[109] Yet the Ukrainian Central Committee had no interest in giving up its claims for power, either. On 11 November, Lebid had to forward circular no. 96 to the Ukrainian gubkoms. Several days earlier, on 6 November 1922, Molotov and Kaganovich issued circular no. 100, which compelled the Central Committee instructors to ensure that the gubkoms implemented the directives of the Central Committee correctly and promptly. The only task that the Central Committee entrusted to the Ukrainian Central Committee was to collect information and write character summaries of the leading staff of the Ukrainian commissariats. In response, the Ukrainian Central Committee issued its own circular, no. 338, which elevated the status of the Ukrainian Central Committee instructors to that of the Central Committee instructors.[110]

Immediately after the plenum, the Ukrainian Central Committee tried to establish control over party finances. Once again, it forbade the gubkoms 'to tax local managers' and 'taxed' the Ukrainian commissariats 285 billion roubles. The local party organs ignored the restriction. The Ukrainian Politburo softened the Ukrainian Central Committee's demand and instructed its Secretariat to draft a general instruction that would regulate, rather than forbid, the taxation of the local industrial organs. At the same time, it tightened control over the gubkoms by forbidding the periphery industrial offices whose central offices were in Kharkiv to freely use the funds the central offices allocated to them. On 2 November, Lebid asked Stalin to increase the financial resources of the CP(b)U.[111]

Reply from Stalin pending, on 10 November, the Ukrainian Central Committee learnt that it would no longer be able to take finance from the Ukrainian commissariats to supply the funds for material help. The central Politburo passed a new resolution stating that those party functionaries 'who took money from the economic organs or the banks' to provide financial help to the party workers would be brought to the party court.[112] Whether the party organizations could take funds from the managers for their organizations remained unspecified.

In response, on 13 November, Lebid sent Molotov a telegram, warning him that unless the Central Committee provided the finance, taxation of the managers was unavoidable. 'There is absolutely no money. The gubkoms continue sending telegrams about their catastrophic situation. The conditions of work are impossible. Immediately send the money, [and] the principles for composing the budget' so that the CP(b)U could start composing its budget for next year, he implored.[113] In a personal letter to Molotov that followed the telegram, Lebid explained the financial situation in the gubkoms in 1922 and the steps the Ukrainian Central Committee had taken to improve it.

At present, the taxation of the commissariats is suspended, but the problem of liquidation of the debts in the Mykolaiv and Kremenchuk gubernias and the problem of creating a special fund for the party workers in 14 famished districts in the Zaporizhzhia, Mykolaiv, Katerynoslav, and Donetsk gubernias remain unresolved because until now we have not received the funds from the Central Committee.[114]

In the postscript, Lebid assured Molotov that none of the Bolshevik managers were taxed in Ukraine.

With no guarantee of funds arriving from Moscow, Lebid nonetheless had to abide by the new rules. At the end of November, the Ukrainian Central Committee issued to the gubkoms yet another 'categorical directive that banned illegal taxation of the managers and cooperatives for party needs'.[115]

By the end of 1922, the Ukrainian Central Committee had dim prospects for asserting its authority over the gubkoms. In the three main areas of communication, cadres, and finances, the Ukrainian Central Committee was of little importance or help to the gubkoms. Even if the Ukrainian government succeeded in obtaining the financial resources at its disposal, the Ukrainian Central Committee would have to violate the new party rules to use them. At the same time, any extension of the Ukrainian government's authority gave it superiority over the Ukrainian Central Committee. Lebid faced the same dilemma as Manuilsky in August. Consolidating Ukrainian autonomy was no longer a shared goal of the Ukrainian leadership. Lebid was now preoccupied with consolidating the power of the Ukrainian Central Committee.

On 24 November, Lebid spoke in favour of a single and centralized financial and taxation policy.[116] On 22 December 1922, he asked Molotov to appoint a permanent deputy chairman of the Ukrainian Sovnarkom. Rakovsky's frequent absence from Ukraine, Lebid insisted, undermined the work of the Ukrainian apparatus.[117]

Whatever doubts Lebid may have had about supporting Rakovsky in the Union negotiations, they would have been dispelled on 5 February 1923, when the All-Russian TsIK Presidium introduced the practice of regular written reports by the 'TsIKs and Sovnarkoms of the national republics, oblasts, and the gubispolkoms', regular inspections of the gubernias and the commissariats, and regular personal reports of the commissars and the chairmen of the gubispolkoms.[118] The resemblance to the party procedures on information was not accidental. On 27 December 1922, the Tenth All-Russian Congress of Soviets elected Stalin a member of the All-Russian TsIK. The next day, the first session of the All-Russian TsIK elected Stalin to the TsIK Presidium and appointed him Commissar of Nationalities. From that moment, neither the All-Russian TsIK nor the Central Committee depended on the republic-level organs for information from the periphery. The arrangement that provided Stalin with centralized control over the party was already in place, and there was little doubt that he was prepared to finish setting up the framework for centralized control over the state organs.

By the time the Central Committee had weakened the Ukrainian Central Committee and Lebid had convinced himself that the Ukrainian Central Committee would be better off if it parted ways with Rakovsky, Stalin was in the process of attracting the support of the gubkoms. Administratively, direct subordination of the gubkoms to the Central Committee was already in place. Yet the party policy of placing the state under party control certainly appealed to the gubkoms. It promised them more power in their territories than Rakovsky's autonomy. Before the Twelfth Party Congress convened, Stalin gave the gubkoms a few more reasons to back him up. On 16 March, the Central Committee Secretariat introduced a special procedure for bringing party secretaries to justice. Before prosecuting a gubkom or obkom secretary, the gubernia prosecutor was obligated to forward all materials and his conclusion to the prosecutor of the republic, who would seek instruction from the Central Committee on how to proceed.[119] On 24 March 1923, appealing to the power ambitions of the gubkom secretaries, Stalin issued a circular letter that instructed 'all party organizations [to survey] that the resolution of the [December 1922 Central Committee] plenum on the monopoly in foreign trade was [being] firmly and steadily implemented'.[120] Rakovsky's insistence on Ukraine's autonomy in foreign trade was well known.

## Rakovsky's Loss

By the time the Ukrainian party aktiv gathered for the Seventh CP(b)U Conference on 5–7 April 1923—convened less than two weeks before the Twelfth Party Congress (17–25 April 1923)—Lebid no longer supported Rakovsky, and the Ukrainian gubkoms had no incentive to support Rakovsky, either. At the conference, Rakovsky finally admitted what the gubkom secretaries had told him all along: to consolidate its authority, the Ukrainian leadership needed support from the gubkoms. Rakovsky asked them for help.

Rakovsky took the floor several times, trying to convince the gubkom secretaries that a strong Ukrainian government would be well placed to assist the CP(b)U apparatus in its relationship with its power base, the proletariat, a matter of great concern for the gubkoms given the ongoing economic crisis. Keeping in line with Stalin's policy of placing the party above the state, which he knew the gubkoms favoured, he no longer sought to limit their role to agitation, propaganda, and the distribution of leaflets. Nor did he seek to separate them from the soviet apparatus. The party was now everywhere; 'it was taking its exam in state affairs'.[121]

The reason why the gubkoms should support the Ukrainian government, he explained, was that the NEP dictated decentralization. Even without the nationality question, the republican governments should be empowered. The unclear relationship between the Union and the Ukrainian organs that prevailed for most of 1922 prevented the party and the Ukrainian leadership from overcoming the hardships caused by the NEP, such as meagre or delayed salaries for metallurgy workers and coal miners. The Union economic agencies' disregard for Ukrainian organs prevented the Ukrainian leadership from placing the trusts under party control.[122]

Rakovsky did not argue for the Ukrainian government to enjoy full autonomy in industrial management. On the contrary, he believed that industries of significance to the entire Soviet Union, such as metallurgy, coal, or sugar, must be administered by the all-union organs. However, he insisted that Ukrainian heavy industry should be much closer to the Ukrainian organs than it was at present and 'that the decisions of Ukraine's central organs on principal questions that concern this heavy industry were obligatory [for fulfilment]'.[123]

Rakovsky needed information and money to make the Ukrainian government influential and truly responsible for industrial development in Ukraine, as well as to place managers under party control, develop heavy industry, support the proletariat financially, and increase the power base of the party.

Information was supposed to come from Moscow. The managers, claimed Rakovsky, did not oppose Kharkiv's supervision. However, they were constrained by the existing procedures, which left the Ukrainian government in the dark about the state of industry. Rakovsky hoped that the central leadership in Moscow would adopt new procedures that would systematically inform the Ukrainian government about the state of Ukrainian industry.[124]

The funds, on the other hand, Rakovsky hoped to receive, at least in part, from the gubernias. Rakovsky suggested that the gubernia authorities contribute to a local Ukrainian fund that would enable the Ukrainian government to help heavy industry and support the proletariat. The Ukrainian government

> can take responsibility neither for managing nor for financing large industry— this is a Union affair.... But are we not able to create a certain reserve and thus have the opportunity to reward those managers who would respect subordination to the party[?] ... The idea is that we, who are on the ground, can sometimes go an extra mile and accelerate the payment of salaries to the workers, who, like in Donbas, are sometimes not paid for two or three months.... If we, comrades, were able to pay salary advances, give equipment, we would be able to eliminate a number of misunderstandings

—the 'misunderstandings' being the mass strikes in the industrial zones caused by redundancies.

> But we cannot do this without help of the gubernias. Where could the Ukrainian Sovnarkom receive funds[?] I think that it could form a fund partially with funds allocated by local authorities. I say 'partially'. This is why I bring this issue

to you. If you want to develop [heavy] industry [and] develop the power base of the proletariat state, then make the relevant conclusions. Be noble.[125]

In return for the gubernias' financial contributions to the Ukrainian fund, Rakovsky promised them more efficient administration and 'a bit of financial support' in place of 'circulars and instructions, the number of which [was] so grand that it [was] impossible to count them'.[126]

Rakovsky effectively admitted that the Ukrainian leadership was financially more dependent on the gubernias than the latter were on the Ukrainian leadership. To correct this, he was fighting in Moscow for the Ukrainian government to have 'sufficient influence on the distribution of the common benefits of the Union', and for Ukraine to have an adequate budget. Without this concession, he admitted, the Ukrainian government would be a superfluous middleman. And he openly asked the gubernias to support him on 'this issue...[when] the structure of the Union will be discussed [at the Twelfth Party Congress]'.[127]

However, he still insisted on a 'top-down' relationship with the gubernias. While seeking the support of the gubkoms, he did not seek to empower the gubernias financially. On the contrary, he condemned the arbitrary taxation that sometimes reached 40 percent above the state taxes in some gubernias, explaining that excessive financial pressure on workers could have undesirable political consequences for the entire party. He shamed some gubkoms for being selfish, for pursuing *mestnichestvo*, or localism, which placed local interests above the authority of the Ukrainian Central Committee or the Central Committee.[128]

Rakovsky failed to gain the support of the majority of the gubkoms. They listened to his argument, but did not react to his plea to support the Ukrainian centre financially, at least not on the record.[129]

The issue of Ukrainization was where they let their sentiment towards the Ukrainian leadership be known. While accepting the foreign policy benefits promised by Ukrainization, they were concerned about its domestic implication. They viewed Ukrainization as a threat from Ukrainian-speaking Bolsheviks both to the party and, being mostly Russian-speakers, to themselves personally. They also viewed it as simply unnecessary, not to mention that the majority of Russian or Russified party secretaries simply despised the Ukrainian language and Ukrainians, who were mostly peasants and were thus viewed as politically inferior to the proletariat. Besides, Ukrainization allowed for the economic and cultural consolidation of kulaks (rich peasant proprietors) as a class.[130]

The party secretaries preferred not to say so on the record, but the logic of the party-state reform and Rakovsky's views indicated that Ukrainization, in combination with the NEP and Rakovsky's plan for economic decentralization, promised to consolidate the authority of the Ukrainian government and give the soviets and managers superiority over the gubkoms.[131] The party-state reform explicitly promised the opposite. How would the party control the soviets and managers in Ukraine if the Ukrainian government had autonomy in state administration? Consolidating the Ukrainian government was thus simply against the party's interests. Instead of Rakovsky, the party secretaries supported Lebid. However, when Lebid told them that the Ukrainian leadership 'was constrained by the Central Committee' and it could only detail Moscow's policies and not make policies of its own, they rebuffed the very idea that the Ukrainian Central Committee should be dismantled because of its powerlessness. After all, the persisting threat of *petliurovshchina* (support for an independent Ukraine) made it necessary to support the existence of the Ukrainian Central Committee. Some even suggested that the Ukrainian Central Committee should have the ability to act more freely and 'should be made a responsible political organ at the national [i.e., Ukrainian] scale'.[132]

## No Clean Victory for Stalin Just Yet

At the Twelfth Party Congress, Stalin further motivated those who hesitated to choose his vision of the party domination over the state rather than Rakovsky's version of autonomy. The congress resolution reasserted the policy of the party dictatorship and specified that 'the task of the party is not only to correctly place its members in various state administrations, but also to set the main guidelines for their work and check the progress of the [state] work'.[133] The gubkoms would not set any guidelines; the Central Committee would. Still, in their gubernias, the gubkom secretaries were expected to be the highest authority. Stalin reassured them: 'The gubkoms are the main foundation of our party, and without them, without the gubkoms, without their leadership of the soviet, as well as the party work, the party would be left as though without legs'.[134] Indeed, for him, the gubkoms were much more important than the republican central committees. In his thirteen-page report, he scarcely acknowledged their existence. Their role in the party administration remained unclear.[135] The Ukrainian gubkom secretaries, already dissatisfied with the weakness of the Ukrainian Central Committee, could not miss Stalin's point.

With party control over the state now official policy, and the direct subordination of the gubkoms to the Central Committee in place, Stalin could safely agree to the request of the Ukrainian government that Ukraine had budgetary rights wider than those of the Ukrainian gubkoms.[136] Stalin could even insist that 'the organs of the national republics and oblasts should be predominantly staffed with locals, who [knew] the language, life, morals, and customs of the respective peoples', and that it was necessary to use the national languages in order to reach non-Russian peasants.[137] To stop Rakovsky, or the Ukrainian leadership in general, from using his support for Ukrainization to reinforce their own position,

Stalin armed the gubkoms with an instruction 'to increase obstacles against the flow of non-proletarian elements [in the party]'.[138]

Stalin sought to avoid an unpleasant surprise from Ukraine until the Union Treaty was secured. In spring–summer 1923, Stalin, with the assistance of First Secretary Emmanuil Kviring, who was appointed on 10 April 1923, began replacing those periphery party functionaries who either shared Rakovsky's views or showed too much initiative.[139]

Ironically, despite Stalin viewing the gubkoms as the main executioners of central policies and the party's all-but-definite control over the state in the new organizational arrangement, the gubkom secretaries were no longer interested in undermining the Ukrainian Central Committee. Quite the contrary, in their empowered position, they needed the Ukrainian Central Committee as the republican authority. The threat of *petliurovshchina*, as they said at the Seventh CP(b)U Conference, was one factor. The other factor was the functional usefulness of the Ukrainian Central Committee. While each gubkom was free to contact the Central Committee on matters of importance, the Ukrainian Central Committee could still assist them in their démarches in Moscow, not to mention that there were still issues that could be solved locally, without involving Moscow. Indeed, as Graeme Gill observed, 'regional political leaders, caught between the imperatives of maintaining their fiefs and of satisfying demands from above, played politics in terms of how they saw their best interests served'.[140]

The gubkom secretaries demonstrated resistance to Stalin's efforts to fully undermine the republican administrative centre at the 20 June 1923 plenum of the Ukrainian Central Committee. The plenum was called immediately after the so-called secret meeting of the Central Committee (9–12 June) that established the main elements of the Soviet unitary state. The Ukrainian plenum was supposed to echo the decisions of the secret meeting. However, the plenum resolution, and specifically the way the plenum voted for it, clearly indicated that the Ukrainian party aktiv, while dissociating from Rakovsky personally, fully intended to continue Rakovsky's agenda of securing a say in state affairs for the Ukrainian leadership, now led by the Ukrainian Central Committee.

Paragraph 1 of the draft resolution on the nationality/Union policy that the Ukrainian Central Committee commission proposed to the plenum struck a conciliatory tone as it stated that the Ukrainian Central Committee 'categorically dissociate[d] itself from the emerging deviations: the great Russian centralism and confederalism'.[141] However, in paragraph 4, the resolution instructed 'the [Ukrainian] Politburo to be guided by the need to provide the republic with sufficiently broad financial, in particular budgetary, rights that would allow [the republic] to manifest [its] own state, administrative, cultural, and economic initiative in the forthcoming clarification of inter-republican relations'. In paragraph 6, the Ukrainian Central Committee objected to the Central Committee's provision permitting the same person to hold the posts of an all-union commissar and a republican commissar simultaneously, 'because this would inevitably lead to the increased significance of the RSFSR over other members of the Union and would thus violate the equality of republic-members of the Union as established by the Twelfth Congress', as well as the equality between the republics and the central power of the Union. In a similar tone, paragraph 7 'decidedly object[ed] to the resolution of the All-Union TsIK commission on the budget, which effectively granted fewer budgetary rights to the republics than to the gubernias, [contradicting] the resolution of the Twelfth Congress'.[142]

This resolution draft, and the vote on it, would have not been of such great importance to the discussion of the institutional system in Ukraine had the plenum not been attended by Manuilsky. On 23 May, per Stalin's instruction, Manuilsky was reinstated into the Ukrainian Politburo. In his capacity as Stalin's ambassador, he disagreed with the entire resolution. The gubkoms disagreed with Manuilsky.

Why did the plenum fail to follow Manuilsky's lead while knowing perfectly well whom he represented? In part, the gubkom secretaries and Kviring might have truly felt empowered by the 'party-over-state' rhetoric and might have been claiming their authority. More likely, however, they understood perfectly that with Rakovsky out of the way, the issue was no longer about the party over the state, but about the centre over the republic. Faced with a blatant effort on the part of the Central Committee to strip the Ukrainian centre of any meaningful authority in the future Union, they chose to defend what they could. This reasoning is likely to have dictated their choice of amendments to accept or reject. The plenum agreed 'to throw away the entirety of paragraph 4', but voted to keep paragraphs 1, 6, and 7.[143]

Manuilsky's amendments threatened the very institution of the Ukrainian republican centre on several levels. Paragraph 4 would have expanded the mandate of the Ukrainian leadership. As discussed in Chapter 1, the central leadership in Moscow never intended the Ukrainian leadership to develop its own policies. Its mandate was strictly limited to implementing central policies in Ukraine, and adjusting them when necessary for the Ukrainian context. Dropping this paragraph on Manuilsky's suggestion bore no threat to the existing status of the Ukrainian leadership. Dropping paragraphs 1, 6, and 7, on the other hand, would have inflicted damage on the existing status of the Ukrainian centre.

Accepting Manuilsky's suggestion for paragraph 1 not to mention the struggle against great Russian centralism and 'dissociate only from confederalism' (the accusation thrown at Rakovsky) would have deprived the Ukrainian leadership of a formal basis on which to confront abuses of power by the all-union commissariats in Ukraine. The plenum's insistence, in the face of Manuilsky's objection, on adopting paragraph 6, which opposed combining the posts of the all-union and RSFSR commissars, had the same motive: to protect the status quo of the

Ukrainian commissars. Retaining paragraph 7 was a clear protest against reducing the status of the Ukrainian administrative centre below that of the gubkoms.

As a result of Stalin's party-state reform, the Ukrainian Central Committee formally became the highest authority in the republic by June 1923. However, as Stalin soon discovered, neither the party-state reform nor the removal of Rakovsky affected the institutional logic of the Ukrainian leadership. Bolsheviks closely linked control over the economy with political power. Hence, with or without Rakovsky, the Ukrainian leadership needed control over resources in order to have administrative weight with the all-union agencies, as well as with the periphery apparatus.

From 1923 through 1925, the Ukrainian leadership persistently and methodically continued to fight for control over resources and the authority to adjust central policies to the Ukrainian context. The Central Committee equally continued withdrawing resources from Kharkiv's control and further weakening the Ukrainian administrative centre. Moscow would win. After two years of administrative struggle, the Ukrainian Central Committee would be definitively weak and the CP(b)U fragmented.

## Part III: 1923–1925

According to Mykola Frolov, removing Rakovsky from Ukraine considerably reduced the tension between the Ukrainian and central leadership. The *troika* of Zinov'ev, Kamenev, and Stalin put loyal people at the top of the Ukrainian leadership. In 1923–1924 it tried to organize a constructive cooperation with new Chairman of the Ukrainian Sovnarkom, Vlas Chubar, First Secretary Kviring, Chairman of the Ukrainian TsIK, Hryhorii Petrovsky, 'and other leaders of the rebellious republic'. 'In 1924 alone, the [Ukrainian] Sovnarkom, headed by Chubar, submitted 330 relatively critical conclusions on the drafts of the all-union laws'. According to Larysa Nahorna, the Central Committee often considered the opinion of the Ukrainian leadership on laws on the budgetary rights of the Union and the republics, Soviet citizenship, local finances, and so on.[144]

Nonetheless, the Ukrainian leadership was not granted control over resources or the authority to implement central policies as it saw fit—quite the contrary. As Frolov observed, centralization of power, economic or administrative, remained on Stalin's agenda.[145] Indeed, with Rakovsky removed from Ukraine, Stalin had little or no incentive to increase the authority of the Ukrainian Central Committee or its control over Ukrainian resources. Yet, with Rakovsky gone, the new Ukrainian leadership had little incentive to drop its claims for tangible powers, either.

Soon after the June 1923 secret meeting, Kviring and Lebid joined the Ukrainian Sovnarkom in its effort to counteract Moscow's pursuit of recentralization and retain control over resources.

Thus, on 1 July 1923 and again on 27 July, the Ukrainian Politburo objected to the Supreme Sovnarkhoz's decision to directly subordinate the large industrial enterprises of Yugostal' and Yugomashtrest to the all-union commissariats in Moscow.[146] The Central Committee, before which the Ukrainian Politburo appealed the decision, ignored the protest. Going to Moscow for clarification, Chubar learnt that the situation was even worse than the Ukrainian leadership thought. Not only did the central commissariats have the support of the Central Committee in centralizing control over heavy industry, they also sought to establish centralized control over other industries, such as salt, textiles, forestry, and sugar, which were run by Ukrainian trusts. At the end of August, Lebid and Chubar objected to the transfer of several Ukrainian trusts to all-union jurisdiction. To put pressure on the central leadership, the Ukrainian leadership decided to send discussion articles to the Moscow press. To appease the Ukrainian leadership, the central leadership agreed to create a special commission that would resolve all issues about Ukraine's trusts and industrial enterprises that were due to be transferred to the direct control of all-union industrial agencies. The commission, however, was a charade and the Ukrainian leadership would begin gradually to lose control over its trusts.[147]

In September 1923, the Ukrainian leadership protested against the 28 August resolution of the Union of Socialist Soviet Republics' (USSR) Sovnarkom, which allowed Union organs to take control over local finances. Such a provision, they argued, 'violated the sovereign rights of the Union republics', and they insisted on its annulment. The central leadership ignored this protest.[148]

On 6 September 1923, Lebid and Chubar joined efforts to secure a say for Ukraine in drafting the legislative acts that concerned the all-union commissariats—a say, however, that the latter were under no obligation to consider. On the same day, Lebid personally wrote to Narkomfin that 'it was impossible to accept the reduction of the budget for the Ukrainian non-union [i.e., republican] commissariats', and insisted that the Ukrainian republican commissariats be allocated at least 19 percent of the all-union budget. After long negotiations, this request was satisfied. However, the Ukrainian government did not become the final authority on approving Ukraine's budget.[149]

By the beginning of 1925, after numerous futile efforts to bring resources under its control, the Ukrainian leadership was in no position to assist the periphery state and party authorities with the low or delayed workers' salaries in the metallurgical, sugar, and coal industries. This issue was of major concern for the gubkoms as it was at the root of the CP(b)U's unpopularity and workers' strikes.[150] It could not assist the railway sector, either,[151] nor could it assist the local authorities in alleviating social tensions due to the rising price of bread.[152] At the Eighth CP(b)U Conference on 12–16 May 1924, the Ukrainian leadership was criticized for not doing enough to reduce private trade, which comprised 50.3 percent of wholesale–retail trade and 91.8 percent of retail in the cities. For the industrial regions, underdeveloped cooperative and state trade was a particularly sensitive issue. Workers, being unable to procure consumer goods and food products in their cooperatives, had to go to the private market where the prices were much higher. At this conference, the gubkoms rejected the Ukrainian Central Committee's resolution defending the private sector and instead voted for their own version of the resolution. They called for a 'resolute direction towards refusing the private trader any state credit', and accepted small merchants 'only in the regions with an underdeveloped cooperative network and if they agree to sell their goods at [state] prices'.[153] In rural areas, the Ukrainian leadership had no consumer goods to offer cooperatives and state shops. Only 18 percent of consumer goods were supplied to villages through cooperatives. In the villages of Kyiv, Volyn, Podillia, and Chernihiv, private traders would retain 100 percent of the trade throughout 1925. On 14 January 1925, the Ukrainian Politburo would ask the Central Committee for more imported goods and a reduction in import duties paid by Ukraine.[154] On 20 February 1925, the Ukrainian Politburo abolished the so-called mandatory commodity loans, which dictated to cooperatives which products they could acquire from industrial producers for their shops.[155]

## The Ukrainian Leadership Institutionally Weak

At the January 1925 plenum of the Ukrainian Central Committee, Kviring had to explain that the Ukrainian leadership simply did not have money to give to the industrial gubernias to pay workers' salaries and that all the Ukrainian Politburo could do was to 'bother Moscow from time to time'. Someone from the audience shouted: 'Then why do we need Ukraine[?]' Andrii Ivanov, chairman of the Odesa gubispolkom, elaborated on this rhetorical question. Commenting on the policy of fixed grain prices that was first imposed by Moscow and then abolished by Moscow after it worsened the economic situation in the gubernias, he said:

> Unfortunately, when we criticise and comment at the Ukrainian Central Committee plenums, we inevitably face the fact that we cannot do anything here [in Ukraine] and all the issues have to be resolved in Moscow. This is, of course, our misfortune [beda], and therefore we can reproach the [Ukrainian] Politburo for not defending its rights energetically enough.[156]

The message that Andrii Ivanov conveyed was unequivocal. If the Ukrainian leadership wanted to become an authoritative institution, it had to command resources and influence policymaking in Moscow. The prospects for both, however, remained slim.

By the beginning of 1925, the Ukrainian leadership had limited access to funds; nor did it have the right to redistribute budgetary funds that Moscow allocated to the regions and economic sectors. Thus, the agricultural fund remained under the centralized administration of the USSR Sovnarkom. Furthermore, starting in 1925, the agricultural fund allocated goods and assigned suppliers, rather than funds. Originally, the Ukrainian leadership had considered ordering agricultural machinery from a Ukrainian factory, but as of January 1925, this was not an option: Ukraine was allocated tractors and agricultural machinery produced in Russia. The central Politburo agreed to increase the capital of the republican branches of the Agricultural Bank. However, the USSR Narkomfin tended to bypass the republican branches, instead working directly with the gubernia offices of the Agricultural Bank. The Ukrainian Central Committee was not holding its breath for the reversal of this decision.

Housing was an acute problem, particularly for the growing cities of Katerynoslav, Odesa, Kyiv, and Donetsk. In an effort to secure funds for housing, the Ukrainian government included communal housing construction in the budget. The USSR Narkomfin removed 'communal housing' from Ukraine's budget and placed the funds for housing construction under the management of the Central Communal Bank. The Ukrainian leadership objected, but in vain. Hence, 'the comrades who expected to receive budgetary money to restore cities, should drop such hopes. They will have to receive these funds through the bank', explained Chubar at the April 1925 plenum of the Ukrainian Central Committee.[157]

The situation with the subvention fund for Ukraine was only slightly better. For 1925, the Ukrainian Sovnarkom asked for 7 million roubles, and received 5.5 million. The funds for teachers, agronomists, and doctors were also only partially fulfilled. This meant that Ukrainian teachers, agronomists, and doctors received lower salaries than their colleagues elsewhere in the Soviet Union.[158]

Under the Ukrainian Central Committee's persistent pressure, the Narkomfin created a rescue fund for industry and cooperatives. However, this was an all-union fund and allocated financial help based on requests directly from the periphery. In Chubar's estimation, such a system would give preference to those living closer to Moscow. Originally, Kharkiv hoped this fund 'would be used to prevent production failures. But with the approach taken by the centre, it will only pay for welfare, and it is possible that we will not receive the help and support for our cooperatives that we expected', explained Chubar.[159]

The Ukrainian leadership was fortunate to secure Moscow's investment in Ukrainian machine-construction factories that would produce machinery for agriculture. However, the launch of metallurgical mills remained fully at Moscow's discretion; the Central Committee and the Supreme Sovnarkhoz made decisions on the development of this sector.[160] It 'bypassed the Ukrainian Central Committee. [And,] as sad as it was,…this question passed by the Ukrainian soviet organizations as well.' Gubkoms were not consulted on economic planning for their gubernias, either.[161]

The Ukrainian leadership's authority as the Ukrainian republican administration was perhaps most damaged by its failure to secure budget funds to meet the deficit in the Volyn, Podillia, and Chernihiv gubernias, which were predominantly agricultural and economically stagnating.[162] In 1924, 57 percent of peasant economies in the Podillia gubernia lacked a horse or any working cattle. 'Dead' inventory—that is, machines and instruments—did not exist either. There were cases of suicide. Soviet currency was in low circulation in Vinnytsia and virtually non-existent in Proskuriv (Khmelnytskyi after 1954), Kamianets-Podilskyi, and Zhmerynka. 'At the market, it [was] replaced with the tsarist silver rouble.'[163] With scarce funds at the disposal of the Ukrainian leadership, the situation was expected to remain difficult.[164] The only consolation for the local party and state apparatus that had to deal with the right-bank (Volyn and Podillia) peasantry, which 'groaned under taxes' and increasingly turned to kulaks for help, was the coming reduction in agricultural tax rates and, despite Stalin's objection, the easing of consequences for those who failed to pay agricultural taxes.[165]

On Chubar's own admission, the Ukrainian leadership was not in a financial position to provide state-building work evenly across Ukraine.[166] The Ukrainian leadership was unable to perform the very task it believed it was meant to perform: to develop the republic as one territorial administrative unit.

Despite their continued frustration with an administratively and financially impotent central committee, the gubkoms faced local problems for which they were held accountable. They did not have any preference as to whether they received funds from Moscow or Kharkiv, as long as the funds were provided. Therefore, when Chubar asked for their support at the January 1925 plenum of the Ukrainian Central Committee, the gubkoms agreed. They supported the Ukrainian leadership's decision to implore the Central Committee to increase the subvention fund enough for Ukraine to pay its teachers and doctors the same salaries as elsewhere in the Union, to distribute the 'rescue' fund based on the economic value of the organizations it was meant to support, to provide Ukraine's agricultural credit in money rather than goods, and to distribute this credit based on the economic value of the regions, as happened elsewhere in the Union.[167]

On 20 March 1925, arguably under pressure, Kviring submitted his resignation letter to the Ukrainian Politburo. The official reason for his resignation, as was discussed at that meeting and later adopted in historiography, was Kviring's failure to suppress *trotskyism* in Ukraine.[168] *Trotskyism* was certainly a convenient excuse for his removal given the political situation in Moscow, but there was another reason for the Ukrainian leadership, and for Stalin, to wish to replace Kviring.[169]

Under Kviring's leadership, the Ukrainian Central Committee had failed to implement two interconnected policies critical to the NEP in Ukraine and the efforts of the central leadership to boost economic growth.[170]

The first was Ukrainization, which Stalin officially embraced in 1923 as necessary to gain the support of the Ukrainian peasants. Its progress remained minimal. The party masses simply 'did not want to speak Ukrainian, did not like [the language], and there was nothing the Ukrainian Central Committee could do to force them to learn it'.[171] The second was a 1924 policy of temporary economic and political reconciliation with seredniaks (middling peasants) and even kulaks, when necessary, under the banner of 'turning the party face to the countryside', or *litsom k derevne*.[172] As elsewhere in the Soviet Union, the party functionaries who worked in the urban areas of Ukraine resented it for ideological and financial reasons.[173] As a result of this discrimination, the presence of the party or Soviet power in the Ukrainian countryside in 1925 was barely noticeable.[174] More importantly, although the policy had come directly from Moscow, the party masses did not hesitate to reject the resolutions and instructions to tolerate private capital and private trade.[175] At the January 1925 plenum, the Ukrainian leadership succeeded in passing the 'village' resolutions. However, the policy remained unpopular with the periphery party secretaries, and the party masses continued to stall its implementation in the months that followed.[176]

Stalin could not be unaware of the CP(b)U's refusal to 'turn towards the countryside'.[177] If the CP(b)U resisted cooperation with the seredniak, it was highly unlikely that it would embrace another necessary economic measure that was being prepared in Moscow and would be approved at the central Politburo meeting on 16 April 1925: the liberalization of labour relationships in the village. The new temporary rules about conditions of using hired labour in the peasant economies legitimized the hiring of peasants by peasants, effectively permitting the kulaks to hire labour.[178]

For their part, the Ukrainian leadership wished to replace Kviring because he was a weak leader at the top of a weak Ukrainian Central Committee. The Ukrainian Central Committee as the party centre had not increased its authority since 1923. The party-state reform secured the formal status of the Ukrainian Central Committee as a representative of the Central Committee. In March 1924, the Central Committee even allowed the Ukrainian Central Committee to have the same departmental structure as the Central Committee.[179] However, Stalin refused to support the Ukrainian Central Committee. The Central Committee could refuse to send its representative to the Ukrainian plenums, which, as Lebid explained in March 1924, deprived the Ukrainian plenums of 'weight'.[180] Consequently, the Central Committee did not believe the Ukrainian Central Committee needed a large apparatus of inspectors. At the beginning of 1924, the Ukrainian control commission included fifteen inspectors. The Moscow city control commission alone included fifty inspectors. The Ukrainian leadership asked the central leadership to expand its staff, but by May 1924, the staff of the Ukrainian control commission had not increased.[181]

Due to the institutional weakness of the Ukrainian Central Committee, it could not enforce cadre appointments. Those whom the Ukrainian Central Committee managed to force the gubkoms to accept adopted the same condescending attitude towards the Ukrainian Central Committee as their predecessors and counterparts from other gubkoms.[182] At the Ukrainian Central Committee plenum on 5–7 April 1925, one such appointed secretary, Pavlo Postyshev, first accused the Ukrainian Central Committee of not trusting his gubkom and then reassured the Ukrainian Central Committee that the Kyiv gubkom would cope with the cadre appointments on its own and would inform the Ukrainian Central Committee of the outcomes.[183] The gubkoms did not bother informing the Ukrainian Central Committee about their personnel in a systemic and expedient way. Hence, the Ukrainian Central Committee struggled to organize something as straightforward as personnel records or to verify systematically that directives were being implemented. Financial reports of the gubkoms were irregular and 'late, except [from] some gubkoms, such as those of Donetsk, Kharkiv, and Katerynoslav'. Records of the Volyn and Podillia gubkoms, on the other hand, remained 'non-existent, because [they] did not send any [financial] information for March [1924], nor for February, nor for January'.[184]

However, of most grave consequence for the Ukrainian Central Committee was its inability to ensure the policies and resolutions of the Central Committee were implemented.[185] In 1925, there was no threat to the existence of the Ukrainian Central Committee, but it was clear that the Central Committee would not enhance its powers. To enforce the central policies of the party and state apparatus in Ukraine, the Ukrainian leadership needed a strong leader whom the gubkoms would simply dare not oppose. So, at the same meeting that accepted Kviring's resignation, the Ukrainian Politburo asked the Central Committee to 'immediately appoint' Viacheslav Molotov, 'as a comrade sufficiently authoritative in the party mass and capable, with his [experience of] leadership in the complex situation of party life, to unite the entire [Ukrainian] organization'.[186] It was no accident that the Ukrainian leadership asked for Molotov. Molotov not only had authority within the party, he was responsible for running it. He was the person who, despite the Ukrainian government's lack of resources, could impose the Ukrainian Central Committee's authority over the gubkoms.

Unwilling to empower the Ukrainian leadership, Stalin still had to satisfy the Ukrainian leadership's request for a new first secretary. Molotov was needed in Moscow. On 26 March 1925, the Central Committee appointed Lazar Kaganovich.

At the Ukrainian Central Committee's 5–7 April 1925 plenum, the periphery secretaries reminded the Ukrainian leadership that instead of resolutions and circulars, they needed capital for cooperatives, goods in satisfactory quantities and assortments, qualified cadres, and a clear, coherent policy whereby the instructions of the Ukrainian Central Committee would not contradict the instructions of the Central Committee.[187]

In response, the second secretary of the Ukrainian Central Committee, Ivan Klymenko, acknowledged the Ukrainian Central Committee's weakness in party administration, and introduced the new General Secretary of Ukraine, Kaganovich, to the party aktiv. At this plenum, with Kaganovich at its helm, the Ukrainian leadership finally aligned with Moscow and passed a resolution reflecting the idea that accumulation of capital in private hands did not threaten socialist construction.[188]

As discussed in the next chapter, Kaganovich's sojourn in Ukraine would boost the authority of the Ukrainian Central Committee, but only temporarily. Since no systemic changes would be introduced to consolidate the institutional authority of the Ukrainian Central Committee, after his departure from Ukraine in 1929, the Ukrainian Central Committee would return to its condition of administrative irrelevance and powerlessness, until 1938 when another authoritative leader, Nikita Khrushchev, would be needed in Ukraine.

## The CP(b)U Fragmented

As had been argued in the scholarly literature, the entire Communist Party of the Soviet Union was fragmented. As Gill explains, the leading political institutions could not maintain the integrity of their institutions or develop institutional strength. Internal discipline and structure were eclipsed by regional politics and personal preferences.[189]

However, the CP(b)U was uniquely fragmented as a result of three interconnected factors: a weak republican centre, the dependence of local party organs on managers, and the prioritization and centralization of heavy industry administration. These factors were arguably also at play in other republics, but only in Ukraine did their interconnection create a completely unique institutional structure.

The economic and administrative weakness of the Ukrainian Central Committee was the primary foundational factor undermining the unity of the CP(b)U after 1920. Although the periphery party organizations were subordinated to the Ukrainian Central Committee in 1918, it had neither the resources nor the repressive mechanisms to impose its authority upon them. The Ukrainian Central Committee had no particularly important function to perform in the communication between the Ukrainian periphery secretaries and the Central Committee. Nor did it have a political agenda that would create a sense of belonging among Ukrainian gubkoms; the policy of Ukrainization failed among the apparatus. The fact that both the gubkoms and the Ukrainian Central Committee had the same source of power—the Central Committee—also detracted from the Ukrainian Central Committee's position as the superior organization.

The fracture between the Ukrainian Central Committee and the periphery organizations was further exacerbated by the difference in their position towards the state organs. Indeed, becoming 'the only party in the real power structure', as I. Anfert'ev put it, was a task for the entire party organization.[190] However, practical application of this policy was not the same at the republican and the periphery levels.

The Ukrainian Central Committee was not expected to assume control of the Ukrainian government or the Ukrainian people's commissars. The trusts, particularly the offices of the all-union trusts such as Yugostal' or Donugol', were specifically outside the reach of the Ukrainian Central Committee, even if it acted as though it had authority over them. It issued directives and instructions and discussed their work at Ukrainian Politburo meetings, but the central leadership had these trusts under its direct supervision.[191]

Furthermore, the Ukrainian Central Committee and the Ukrainian government had, in theory, different functions, with 'the Ukrainian Central Committee giving instructions and the soviet apparatus implementing them'.[192] However, from Moscow's perspective, both institutions existed de facto to facilitate the implementation of central policies in the republic. Moscow viewed the Ukrainian Central Committee and the Ukrainian Sovnarkom, with all its sub-units such as the Ukrainian Economic Council and the Ukrainian Sovnarkhoz, as dual executive bodies. Collectively, the dual executive of the Ukrainian Central Committee and the Ukrainian Sovnarkom were held responsible for the economic performance of Ukraine and the social and political situation in the republic. Collectively, they discussed and addressed party and state issues in the Ukrainian Politburo. However, in contrast to the central Politburo, the Ukrainian Politburo had no policymaking authority. While the central Politburo could hold the USSR Sovnarkom responsible for fulfilling the party's directives, the Ukrainian Central Committee could not hold the Ukrainian Sovnarkom to the same responsibility. The Ukrainian Sovnarkom was subordinated to the USSR Sovnarkom and the central Politburo.

Held equally responsible for the performance of the republic, the Ukrainian Central Committee and the Ukrainian Sovnarkom had the same power ambitions and shared the same aim of consolidating the republican centre vis-à-vis both the regions and the central leadership in Moscow. Hence, as illustrated earlier, the two cooperated while pursuing their aim.

In contrast to the Ukrainian Central Committee, the gubkoms were expected to impose party control over local managers and the soviets. As far as Moscow was concerned, the gubkoms were supposed to be the main regional authorities—that is, the representatives of the central leadership in their territories. However, as discussed below, they largely failed in this mission. Instead of imposing the party's authority on the managers and the soviets, they found themselves in a system where their interests aligned with those they were meant to control. The gubkoms had little choice but to focus on defending local economic interests.

The gubkoms' defence of local economic interests became the second main factor defining the fragmented character of the CP(b)U. The reasons that the periphery party organizations' interests aligned with those of local managers were twofold. On the one hand, the Central Committee held the gubkoms accountable for the economic, political, and social situation in their territories, as well as for the implementation of central policies.[193] On the other hand, the Central Committee did not provide sufficient financing to the periphery party organizations. The combination of these factors encouraged regional leaders to act independently and develop informal networks. Most importantly, it led to the aggrandizement of the gubkoms in industrial regions; because the centre controlled and supported heavy industry, these gubkoms had tighter connections with the Moscow apparatus compared to gubkoms in agricultural regions.

The fundamental problem with the 'responsibility' factor was that the party organizations were held accountable for things over which they had little control. Local social and political situations depended much more on local managers, who had the power to fire, hire, and pay workers, or on the all-union agencies that ultimately decided which industrial enterprises to launch and which to close. Armed merely with propaganda slogans, party committees had little influence on unemployment or food prices, which were the main causes of workers' strikes.

Moscow, of course, could not hold the gubkoms accountable for the industrial performance of enterprises, especially not of those that were directly subordinated to the trusts, and certainly not during the NEP. However, as indicated by the gubkom secretaries' reports, secret letters to the Ukrainian Central Committee and the Central Committee, and personal visits to the Central Committee, the gubkoms had to report on the general situation in their territories and were required to influence the development of industry.[194] They had to report on and were accountable for the so-called party measures they took to solve conflicts between the workers and management, to reduce unemployment, to eliminate delays with salaries, or to prevent the worker unrest that was expected due to inflation after the 1924 currency reform.

However, the gubkoms often struggled to implement party measures because, as they insisted, the periphery party organizations were underfinanced. The Twelfth RKP(b) Conference in August 1922 banned gubkoms from leading economic activity for profit,[195] while failing to ensure sufficient funding for the party committees. The periphery party organizations soon found themselves broke, with insufficient funds to carry out party work, such as agitation, publication of communist newspapers, party education, and so on. They also lacked enough funds for administrative expenditures or staff salaries. To continue their work, the gubkoms relied on financial support from local managers and local budgets. As a result, they found themselves financially dependent on those they were supposed to control and on whom they depended for the socio-economic situation in their territories.

Financial Dependence

Financial dependence was problematic on several levels for the periphery party organizations. The central leadership in Moscow, fully aware that gubkoms throughout the Soviet Union depended financially on the ispolkoms and the managers, attempted to break this relationship. As mentioned above, in November 1922, the central Politburo threatened 'party justice' to those who took money from managers to provide financial help to the party workers. After 1923, the central leadership in Moscow also forbade managers from transferring their own budget funds to local party organizations. On 3 July 1923, the STO 'categorically forbade' any contributions as patronage help from enterprise and state administration budgetary funds. Later, this ban was partially lifted when the USSR Narkomfin allowed donations for 'useful, from the state's view, purposes'. Still, these donations were allowed 'exclusively as voluntary donations from workers or staff wages[, or] from private individuals who come into contact with these administrations and enterprises'; they could not be made from the enterprise accounts.[196] In the period between 26 July 1923 and 11 June 1924, the Supreme Sovnarkhoz issued at least four confirmations of the same order. Still, the requests to allow direct transfers from enterprises to the party organizations continued. So, on 30 June 1924, Felix Dzerzhinsky, the chairman of the Supreme Sovnarkhoz, issued yet another order confirming that the funds had to come from individuals, not enterprises.[197]

Such dependence often increased tensions between the local party and economic authorities. Many Ukrainian managers supported the idea of keeping party finances separate from theirs and tried their best to implement the above-mentioned instructions. However, as Kabanov explained in May 1924, a refusal to comply with the instruction of the party organs, 'given, obviously, not as [an explicit] order', to allocate funds to support this or other party organization, often led to

> a squabble [skloka] between the...[party] secretaries and the director of the factory. One is demanding money, the other does not have the right to give any, and there is created a situation when the manager is ranked as a third-class party member, so to speak, and sometimes is even outcast.[198]

Nonetheless, the gubkoms insisted that they had little choice but to extract funds from the managers. They simply had no money to hold various state campaigns or to provide patronage to the rural party cells.[199]

When reporting on the situation in his gubernia in Moscow on 4 July 1924, Donetsk gubkom secretary Aleksandr Krinitsky explained that the Donetsk party organization had grown considerably since 1922–1923 when the first budgets were drafted, and even then, neither the gubkom nor the gubernia Komsomol (Communist Youth League) received the full amount of their budgets from the

Central Committee. So, 'if we, while not receiving the budget funds [from the Central Committee], stop taking money from the managerial organs and trade unions, we will put our work in a precarious situation'. As the gubkom's finances stood by the end of June 1924, more than half of its funds came from local administrative organs and trade unions. Complaining did not help. At the end of August 1924, faced with a lack of resources for rural party workers, the Donetsk gubkom created 'a commission to find [financial opportunities to finance rural party workers] from the local budget' because 'without solving the financial problem, all talks about fortifying the village with strong party workers, [industrial] workers, etc.,—<u>would remain just a wish</u> [underlined in the document]'.[200]

On 30 October 1924, the central Politburo issued an instruction to all party organizations clarifying that not only were the managers forbidden to transfer budget allocations to the party, but also the party was forbidden to accept any donations from the managers.[201]

It must be emphasized that Stalin did not seek to separate the finances of the entire RKP(b) from those of the state. On the contrary, in the RKP(b) budget for 1928–1929, almost 78 percent of party expenses were covered from the state budget; in the RKP(b) budget for 1929–1930, this share would be reduced to 74.5 percent.[202] However, local party organizations were not supposed to be dependent on the local state budgets.

However, local party organizations continued to ignore Moscow's calls to keep the party and state finances separate. As the Ukrainian Gosplan discovered at the beginning of 1925, the budget of the Chernihiv gubispolkom included funds for the Chernihiv gubkom. The Central Committee inspector Naetr who visited the Donetsk, Katerynoslav, and Odesa gubkoms and the Artemivsk okruha (administrative unit) in February 1925, reported that

> all gubkoms that [he] visited complained that the Central Committee assigned too few financial funds for party work. At the same time,…the means of local party organisations [were] not limited to those allocated by the Central Committee of the party,…approximately the same amount [was] raised from local budgets, enterprises and administrations.[203]

At the April 1925 plenum of the Ukrainian Central Committee, in the presence of Kaganovich, the periphery party secretaries blatantly rebuffed the calls to separate the party funds from the funds of the managers, unless the Central Committee transferred the funds on time and in full.[204]

The reliance on local industry for financing the party organizations, but also for providing jobs and thus securing economic and political stability in their territories, prevented local party organizations from imposing party control on managers and, instead, motivated them to defend the managers and promote their interests. In the heavily proletariat Donbas where industrial development had political significance, the party organs did not shy away from directly med-dling in economic administration through party channels.²⁰⁵

Thus, on 20 June 1924, the Donetsk gubkom plenum asked the Ukrainian Central Committee and the Central Committee to accelerate the 'concentration of coal mines'. The Donetsk gubkom also insisted on participating in drafting the future plan for metallurgy and asked the Ukrainian Central Committee to form a special commission 'that included local [party] organizations (Donetsk and Katerynoslav), that would determine the fate of the Yugostal"s non-operational enterprises'. The gubkom sent several letters to the Ukrainian Central Committee and the Central Committee explaining that it was necessary to find ways to save the equipment from enterprises that the central leadership planned to liquidate. On 11 August, the Donetsk gubkom plenum discussed the coal industry once again and urged Moscow 'not to weaken its attention to and support of Donbas [underlined in the document]'. The plenum spoke categorically against Moscow's idea of letting the market regulate supply and sales of coal and oil. Donbas coal was more expensive than oil. The Donetsk gubkom insisted that Moscow should consider the significance of Donbas not only today but in future, and protect its industry by regulating prices for coal and oil.²⁰⁶

Its reliance on the regional economy was one of the reasons that the Donetsk gubkom resisted the new regionalization in 1924. Detaching the Shakhty and the Taganrog okruhas from the Donetsk gubernia would reduce the income of the Donetsk ispolkom by 400,000 roubles. The remaining territory was to be divided among several okruhas, including those in Stalino (dominated by metallurgical shops), Bakhmut (salt and chemical industry), and Luhansk (metal-processing industry). In spite of two resolutions of the central Politburo, the Donetsk gub-kom still rejected the new regionalization at the 11 August plenum. The main argument in favour of keeping all okruhas tied to Donetsk was that 'Donbas was a single economic unit, it [was] not yet sufficiently strong, therefore [it needed] a strong gubernia centre, authoritative and mighty, that would raise all its prob-lems in Kharkiv and Moscow'.²⁰⁷

While Stalin wanted the party to control economic development, neither he nor the central economic agencies, such as the Supreme Sovnarkhoz, welcomed the initiatives of the gubkoms on the economic development of their regions. Their task was to make sure that the managers fulfilled the party assignments as defined by the central Politburo and the central economic agencies. It was one matter when a gubkom insisted on the workers' salaries being paid on time. It was a different matter when a gubkom insisted that the state launch an enterprise, a mine, or a metallurgical shop. The gubkoms were not supposed to run or admin-ister industry. The party's participation in economic recovery was not supposed to stretch to lobbying the Supreme Sovnarkhoz to change its economic priorities.

It is not surprising, then, that the Supreme Sovnarkhoz opted to withhold a 10 million rouble subsidy originally allocated to Donugol' for political expenses, since Donugol' had misused the funds as regards the ban on the party taking funds from enterprise budgets. Yet, considering the dependence of the Donetsk gubkom on financial contributions from Donugol', it is equally unsurprising that Krinitsky, the secretary of the Donetsk gubkom, objected to the Supreme Sovnarkhoz's decision and insisted that the Ukrainian Central Committee should not allow Donugol' to be deprived of the 10 million rouble subsidy for political expenses.[208] (In the end, the central Politburo approved Krinitsky's request for additional allocations for 'cultural construction' in Donbas. Nonetheless, instead of the 1,300,000 roubles that he requested, the USSR Sovnarkom was instructed to allocate 300,000 through the budget of the Commissariat of Education.[209])

Neither Dzerzhinsky nor Kuibyshev yielded under pressure from Krinitsky, who went to Moscow in August to insist, in person, on forming a special commission—with the participation of the Donetsk and Katerynoslav gubkoms—to study the situation of the non-operational Yugostal' enterprises. On 2 September 1924, upon his return to Donetsk, Krinitsky would again insist that 'only...such a Commission will allow for a correct, [and] reasonable [underlined in the document] resolution of a number of sensitive issues in southern metallurgy'.[210]

Krinitsky's excessive lobbying for industrial interests did not sit well with the Supreme Sovnarkhoz, and in 1924 he was quietly removed from Donbas and appointed to the little industrialized republic of Belorussia as the responsible secretary of the Belorussian central committee.[211]

Krinitsky's removal, however, did not change the relationship between the managers and the Donetsk gubkom, prompting the STO to issue a resolution on 9 February 1925, 'On ceasing the release of funds by the Donugol' to the Donetsk party organization'. On 20 February 1925, the Ukrainian Politburo approved this resolution and ordered that 'any additional allocations by the managers [to the party organizations] should stop as of April [1925]'.[212]

The position of the Ukrainian leadership regarding the dependence of the local party organizations on local managers was somewhat ambiguous. On the one hand, the Ukrainian Central Committee often aligned with the Ukrainian republican economic agencies and refused to support the pleas of the party secretaries to save their local enterprises, thus undermining the lobbying efforts of local party organizations.[213] On the other hand, the Ukrainian leadership encouraged the periphery party secretaries to collect funds from local managers for the same reasons that drove the gubkoms to extract money from the managers: lack of funds. By the beginning of 1925, the CP(b)U remained underfinanced. The CP(b)U drafted its budget for 6 million roubles; it was allocated 3.5 million roubles. (The Central Committee wanted to give it only 2.5 million roubles, the amount it gave to the Caucasian region.) Hence at the January 1925 plenum, the Ukrainian leadership agreed with the gubkom secretaries that it was impossible to perform the party's work with the funds allocated through the party budget, and, whether the party organizations wanted to or not, they had to take funds from the soviets. Chubar openly acknowledged that the managers paid their party secretaries.

> I saw in Moscow a payroll of an economic administration where it was noted: this much for the secretary of the party committee, that much for...the head of [agitation and propaganda] and so on,...—and this document fell into the hands of a functionary of the [Rabkrin], a non-party specialist who went to a member of the Central Control Commission and said that it would seem that according to our laws, the soviet administrations should not pay the party apparatus....The Central Committee decided that the party budget should have certain limits, and that certain work that can be 'distributed' between the administrations should be given to them, should be held though the administrative apparatus and at its expense. For the gubkoms, it would seem, it would be necessary to allocate special funds in the local budgets. This is the only way.[214]

After the arrival of Kaganovich in Ukraine, Chubar had to align his views on the party budget with those of Moscow. On 14 November 1925, the Ukrainian Politburo approved the Ukrainian state and party budgets and issued yet another circular that instructed a strict separation of state and party funds at the local level.[215]

### Differentiation within the CP(b)U

The reliance of the territorial party organizations on local managers and local budgets for finance, along with the focus of the territorial party organizations on the economic interests of their regions, was not unique to Ukraine. However, within the CP(b)U, the prioritization and centralization of the administration of heavy industry—the third defining factor in the fragmentation of the CP(b)U—had placed the Ukrainian gubkoms in an unequal position.

The gubkoms of the geographically compact industrialized regions of Donetsk, Katerynoslav, and Kharkiv had access to a larger number of state-owned industrial enterprises, and thus had access to more resources than their counterparts in agricultural regions. In 1925–1926, the share of all-union investments in the branches of heavy industry in Ukraine was between 85 and 93 percent.[216] The high concentration of the proletariat in these regions made them politically more important to the Central Committee and better connected to it. In contrast, gubkoms in agricultural regions, particularly right-bank Ukraine, had much more limited access to local managerial funds. Due to the absence of a large proletariat base, they were of little interest to the Central Committee and were poorly connected with it. As a result, these gubkoms had a poor reputation and little authority in their territories. In mid-1924, the Podillia gubkom even lost 'basic respect'. 'This is not a gubkom, this is a pest', as the aktiv characterized it. The directives of the Podillia gubkom were not considered mandatory by the lower organizations, which frequently lobbied and influenced the gubkom. The main authority was the gubispolkom. Rural party cells in Podillia fulfilled the assignments and tasks of various state administrative organs. In 1923–1925 in Poltava, an agricultural region in central Ukraine, the gubkom was 'effectively an agitation department of the Poltava gubispolkom'; the gubkom had no influence on the soviet work.[217]

More importantly, the priority of heavy industry had a direct effect on the intra-regional integration of the gubernia/okruha party organizations, through the nascent practice of 'patronage over the village'. Practised all over the Union, patronage over the village, or *shefstvo nad selom*, was a mechanism designed to put into effect the idea that the proletariat was politically superior to the peasantry. Thus, the proletariat had an obligation to influence the peasantry and bring it to socialism while developing a proletarian consciousness among the peasants. In the 1920s, the Soviet leadership relied on patronage as one of the instruments to promote *smychka*, or connection, between urban party organizations and the countryside. Workers were encouraged to form groups and go to villages to set up libraries, organize reading clubs, and so on. In Ukraine, however, patronage was poorly developed. In 1923, connections between the mentoring town party cells and the *podshefnye*, mentees or village party cells, were established in the Kharkiv, Poltava, and other regions. However, delays in workers' salaries undermined the nascent connections.[218]

The 'face to the countryside' policy during the NEP required an intensification of patronage. What was designed by the central leadership as voluntary assistance based on ideological principles had quickly turned into an institutional link between the gubkoms, the okruzhkoms (okruha party committees, after June 1925), and the rural party organizations—a link founded on the informal financial dependence of the rural party organizations on their city patrons. As Katerynoslav gubkom secretary V. Ivanov explained in 1924:

> The financial situation of the party apparatus in the countryside is difficult. The finances that are allocated to them cover only 60 percent of the apparatus. Hence, in order to provide for the party work in the village, [we] have to find ways to satisfy the needs of party workers there.[219]

Like the Donetsk gubkom discussed above, the Katerynoslav gubkom was better positioned 'to find ways' to help its rural cells than the gubkom of Podillia. In Podillia, even the largest industry in the region, the sugar industry, was not well positioned to assist the Podillia gubkom financially. In March 1924, the administration of the sugar industry was reorganized in such a way that the Podillia branch of the sugar trust administered six factories from the Volyn gubernia and two factories from the Kyiv gubernia. The decision might have been justified economically, but it undermined the connections between the Podillia sugar trust and the Podillia gubkom. Not surprisingly, the Podillia gubernia authorities protested against such reorganization, pointing to the rupture between the territorial administration and the administration of the sugar industry, but in vain.[220]

While *shefstvo* was similar to the informal dependence that existed between the gubkoms and the managers, it differed in one key way. Throughout the 1920s, the gubkoms could at least offer political lobbying to the managers, whereas the rural party cells had little or nothing to offer the gubkoms, and thus had no influence over them. Nonetheless, the link was established. At the beginning of the 1930s, unable to satisfy food demand in the cities, yet still unwilling to invest in rural areas, the central leadership would formalize this link by allowing enterprises to sign formal *shefstvo* agreements with the kolkhozy and sovkhozy. The latter could supply food products to enterprises in return for their help with labour, specialists, and spare parts for agricultural machinery.[221] Such formalization would, however, have little effect on the rural party cells in right-bank Ukraine, which was predominantly agricultural.

## A Timid Attempt to Unite the CP(b)U

The damaging effect that the differentiation between the gubkoms had on the integrity of the CP(b)U as an organization, as well as on the authority of the Ukrainian Central Committee, did not go unnoticed by the Ukrainian leadership. With no prospect of establishing control over resources, in 1924, it started working on a new regionalization whereby the gubernias would be abolished and the Ukrainian leadership would be directly connected with forty-one okruhas plus the Moldavian Autonomous Soviet Socialist Republic (which was part of Ukraine until 2 August 1940). On 5 February 1925, the central Politburo approved the new regionalization of Ukraine.[222] On 3 June 1925, the Ukrainian leadership adopted a three-level structure of administration—centre (Kharkiv), okruha, raion—which would be implemented by the end of the year.

The Ukrainian leadership viewed the abolition of the gubernias as an opportunity to increase its administrative control over the periphery. One of the aims of this restructuring was to eliminate the economic and administrative dominance of the gubernia centres, which were the most industrialized cities in their regions, so that 'a number of okruhas with developed industrial and commercial centres [could] considerably increase their budgets and...develop local cultural and economic construction more quickly'.[223] The downside of the new regionalization for the periphery was that a considerable number of budget-deficit okruhas lost the support they had been receiving from the gubernia budget. This is where the Ukrainian leadership expected to increase its authority by asserting itself as a regulatory administration. It was now the task of the Ukrainian government 'to provide full support to these okruhas so that per capita expenditures for cultural, social, and economic needs did not fall behind that of an average okruha'.[224] At the same time, the Ukrainian leadership became more important for Moscow as a regional administration: the Central Committee Secretariat would have had to expand its staff to process communication with forty-one okruhas and Moldavia.

However, redrawing of the territorial administrative map did not yield the expected result. The Ukrainian leadership certainly became the ultimate administrative authority for the deficit and agricultural areas. However, Moscow was not interested in investing in those areas anyway, and it immediately adjusted to the new regionalization and reasserted its control over the industrial okruhas. On 28 August 1925, the Ukrainian Politburo had to 'recognize the necessity for the Central Committee to have direct communication with the okruhas of Kharkiv, Katerynoslav, Kyiv, Luhansk, Stalino (Donetsk), Artemivsk, and Odesa'.[225]

## Conclusion

Between 1921 and 1925, the Ukrainian leadership made a persistent effort to become an indispensable link between Moscow and the Ukrainian periphery, as well as an authoritative institution that adapted central policies to the political and social context of Ukraine and enforced their implementation on the periphery apparatus. The effort failed.

The cause of this failure was twofold. First of all, the Ukrainian leadership relied on Moscow to consolidate its power. It neglected to build a constructive relationship with the periphery whereby the periphery would be interested in consolidating the Ukrainian centre. The top-down model of administration that the Ukrainian leadership tried to implement in Ukraine was inadequate, and Moscow refused to empower the Ukrainian leadership in any meaningful way. Hence, the Ukrainian periphery apparatus simply could not see how the Ukrainian leadership was the highest authority, since it had little decision-making power and no control over resources. Moscow, on the other hand, had both the legitimacy and the resources needed to be recognized as the highest authority.

Secondly, in the Union negotiations, Christian Rakovsky, the de facto leader of Ukraine in 1920–1923, was outmanoeuvred by Stalin. While Rakovsky, driven by the logic of the NEP, rushed to consolidate the Ukrainian government, Stalin first consolidated the party. In the context of Ukraine, this strategic difference played a vital role in Rakovsky's defeat. At the defining moment in spring 1923, Rakovsky lost the support of the Ukrainian Central Committee and the gubkoms. By then, Rakovsky had finally realized that the gubkoms could help him in the Union negotiations, but it was too late. They had already been empowered by Stalin's 'party over the state' policy and had no interest in fighting for Rakovsky's vision of Ukrainian autonomy.

The removal of Rakovsky weakened the Ukrainian leadership, now led by the Ukrainian Central Committee. However, it did not affect its institutional ambition to assert its authority in the republic, nor did it change the central leadership's unwillingness to empower the Ukrainian Central Committee. By 1925, the Ukrainian leadership had been deprived of any institutional authority or ability to project power over the periphery. It now needed an authoritative leader.

The party and state transformation in 1921–1925 could not but affect the CP(b)U. Despite the Bolshevik victory in Ukraine and the establishment of the permanent republican administrative centre, the CP(b)U remained a fragmented 'regional division of the RKP(b)'. The policy of Ukrainization was resented by the majority of the party aktiv. It never became a 'political glue' that defined the distinctiveness of the CP(b)U. At the same time, tied to the Moscow bureaucracy via local managers, and directly to the Central Committee, the gubkoms and later the okruzhkoms from the industrialized regions had no mechanisms or incentives to develop horizontal connections with their counterparts from the agricultural regions, and particularly right-bank Ukraine. Locked into a struggle to defend local interests, each territorial party committee focused on maximizing its power on its own.

In December 1925, the central leadership would announce a new course towards industrialization which would cement the institutional powerlessness of the Ukrainian republican centre, the fragmentation of the CP(b)U, and regionalism in Ukraine. However, by the end of 1925, the institutionally weak Ukrainian Central Committee was already presiding over a network of periphery party committees with varied access to resources, with different levels of access to the Central Committee, and with different political-administrative value for the central leadership in Moscow, yet with the same focus on local interests. The main institutional setting in which the CP(b)U found itself by 1925 would remain in place until the end of the Soviet Union and would serve as the foundation for the regional clans that would flourish after 1953, as well as for the weak presidency and strong regionalism in Ukraine after 1991.

*The Institutional Foundations of Ukrainian Democracy: Power Sharing, Regionalism, and Authoritarianism.* Nataliya Kibita, Oxford University Press. © Nataliya Kibita 2024. DOI: 10.1093/9780191925351.003.0003

# 3
# Industrialization, Collectivization, Centralization
## No Place for the Ukrainian Government

### Introduction

At the beginning of the 1920s, the Ukrainian leadership's institutional weakness was determined by its limited control over financial and material resources either generated by or allocated to the Ukrainian economy. The Communist Party (Bolshevik) of Ukraine (CP(b)U) was fragmented as a result of the Ukrainian Central Committee's lack of administrative superiority over the Ukrainian territorial party organizations, the direct subordination of the gubkoms to the Central Committee, the responsibility of the periphery party secretaries for the socio-economic situation in their territories, and the resulting focus of the gubkoms on defending local economic interests. The prioritization of heavy industry and its centralized administration had created disparity between territorial party organizations from industrial regions and those from agricultural regions. The former enjoyed close connections to the central leadership in Moscow and direct access to large reserves of material and administrative resources to fulfil their agenda. The latter did not.

The transformation of the Soviet Union that slowly began in 1925 did not change this institutional framework. Industrialization, collectivization, rapid social mobility, and cultural changes tied to the famines, the party purges, the Great Terror, and the Second World War (called the Great Patriotic War in the Soviet Union) transformed the Soviet state and society, ushering in new organizations and organizational arrangements. However, the priority of the economic over the political agenda within the party, which was based on the sacred Bolshevik principle that the one who controls resources controls politics, remained in place. The main principles that guided the Soviet leadership in its policy and decision making did not change either. As a result, the role and place of the Ukrainian leadership within the Soviet system remained the same. Ukraine entered a period of institutional inertia.

## General Principles of Governance

### Aversion to Formal Rules

Just like in the first half of the 1920s (indeed, since the Bolshevik coup and the dissolution of the Constituent Assembly by Lenin on 19 January 1918), the central leadership and Stalin personally continued to display an aversion to formal rules after 1925. By the 1930s, 'the attempts to define constitutionally the respective powers of different institutions became ever more difficult'.[1] The leadership also refused to set formal mechanisms that the party or state apparatus could use to protect itself from being arbitrarily accused of committing crimes by the central leadership or being arrested. Stalin appointed trusted emissaries to supervise the implementation of his directives, while disregarding the official administrative set-up or the official post of his emissary. Thus, the central Politburo member Vyacheslav Molotov would supervise grain collection campaigns in Ukraine in 1927–1928 and then in 1932–1933. In 1938, Stalin called on CP(b)U First Secretary Nikita Khrushchev 'to drop everything and return to Moscow' 'to build up the necessary reserves of vegetables to see Moscow through winter', and 'expose enemies' within the Moscow obkom.[2] Similarly, the central planners did not set formal criteria for investment, leaving flexibility for the whims of the leadership. The system of central production and investment plans that was introduced by the first five-year plan (1928–1932) did not provide managers with final plans, the latter being subject to arbitrary change by any superior.[3]

### Centralized Control

Manifested in reliance on personal networks for accomplishing tasks and goals, aversion to formal rules continued to coexist with the principle of centralized control over the party, state, and society.[4]

Local Bolshevik leaders enjoyed a considerable degree of autonomy in 1917. Starting in early 1918, the Bolshevik leadership began extending centralized control over provincial organizations through the state security police (Cheka), 'the Commissariat of Food Supplies, and the Military Councils, armed with "exceptional powers" and accountable only to their superiors in Moscow'.[5] The nomenklatura system that was established during Stalin's party reform in the early 1920s was improved and expanded in the 1930s. It allowed the Central Committee to maintain centralized control over the party and state apparatus, even though the system was full of loopholes and the party did not always dictate the appointment of cadres in the state apparatus. The Central Committee's monopoly over final approval meant just that: simply approval.[6] In the 1930s, a highly centralized and bureaucratized party-state apparatus asserted the priority of vertical over horizontal relationships.[7] With the help of formal party-state structures and procedures, informal politics, and control and surveillance agencies, such as the Unified State Political Administration, Stalin had transformed his rule into a dictatorship.[8]

The principle of centralized state control over resources was tested during the period of war communism and, after a temporary and partial retreat during the New Economic Policy, restored by the beginning of the 1930s. The agricultural sector was collectivized. Sovkhozy and kolkhozy replaced private wholesale producers.[9] The Supreme Sovnarkhoz, the all-union State Planning Commission (Gosplan), and the all-union industrial, or branch, people's commissariats, renamed 'ministries' in 1946, provided the organizational framework for maintaining centralized administration of the economy, whereby plan targets took precedence over cost-effectiveness, or khozraschet.[10] The decentralization of economic administration, which had been necessary during the Second World War, was promptly reversed at the end of the war, even though the periphery managers retained a degree of autonomy and had Stalin's tacit approval for horizontal dealings.[11] On 15 December 1947, in a move towards centralization, the Soviet leadership formed the State Committee for Material and Equipment Supply (Gossnab) 'to organize the distribution of materials among major wholesale users, such as ministries and territorial organizations.'[12]

Regional development, although considered important by Lenin, was not translated into a clearly defined regional policy either in the early 1920s or any time since. Following the organizational arrangements for central planning and economic administration at the end of the 1920s and beginning of the 1930s, sectoral development administered through branch ministries came to predominate over regional.[13] Despite this prioritization, the economic policy of the Stalin epoque did affect the regions.[14] Nonetheless, tellingly, Stalin's last 'five-year plan was put together by the technical planning agencies, Gosplan, Gossnab, and the Ministry of Finance, with no input from those who had to fulfil the plan; namely, the industrial ministries and regional authorities.'[15]

## Priority of Heavy Industry
Priority of heavy industry over agriculture was imbedded in the very ideology of the Bolshevik Party and reflected the fact that industrial proletariat formed the power base of the party. In November 1922, Lenin declared that 'without saving heavy industry, without its reconstruction, we will not be able to build any industry, and without [industry] we will completely perish as an independent country.'[16] In 1928, a process of industrialization began that would see the accelerated growth of heavy industry. It was viewed 'as part of the strategy of constructing socialism in a single country, which was surrounded by a hostile capitalist world.'[17]

In a noticeable departure from the first half of the 1920s, with the start of collectivization, agriculture became one of the main areas of responsibility for the party and a sector of economy where the party 'served as line administrators'.[18] However, fundamentally, neither the function nor the role of the Soviet prefects, as Hough calls regional party secretaries, had changed.[19]

## Responsibility of the Periphery Party Apparatus

During a brief period between November 1917 and March 1919, the Bolshevik leadership governed the country through the executive committees of soviets, while the role of the local party committees was reduced to propaganda. In the next two years, local party organs gradually assumed control over the administrative functions and remained essentially administrative organs, responding to the formal demands of the higher authorities, as well as to the actual conditions on the ground that affected the implementation of policies and directives.[20]

Indeed, Stalin differentiated between party political work and economic work; he also campaigned for the primacy of party political work at the end of the 1930s and after the war.[21] At the highest level there was a clear distinction between the functions of the Sovnarkom of the Union of Soviet Socialist Republics (USSR) and of the central Politburo, whereby the former was primarily responsible for the management of the economy while the Politburo dealt with other issues.[22] The Politburo made policy decisions, while the Council of Ministers broke them down into more detailed directives. However, the party never gave up on overseeing economic affairs. More importantly, Stalin never relieved regional party leaders of the responsibility for the socio-economic development of their territories.[23] During the Second World War, the party was focused on economic affairs, and after the war, the central leadership continued to rely on the regional party leaders to fulfil the tasks and goals by all means necessary, evaluating their performance based on outcomes. When Stalin appointed him first secretary of the Ukrainian Communist Party in March 1947, Kaganovich 'didn't want to accept a plan that wouldn't be fulfilled; he wanted a plan that aimed lower, so that it could be overfulfilled'.[24]

Regional party secretaries were held accountable for economic tasks, yet, as Peter Kirkow observed, they were 'denied the authority, funding, and even information necessary to mitigate imbalances', and, as Armstrong noted, they were also unable to intervene in the management of these tasks. Therefore, to facilitate administration and make up for the deficiencies of central branch economic planning, the regional party secretaries had little choice but to cooperate with the agencies that were directly responsible for the fulfilment of economic tasks.[25] Thus, to help the kolkhozy and sovkhozy fulfil plans, party secretaries organized patronage, or *shefstvo*, from industrial enterprises that could provide labour, agricultural machinery, and even funds.[26] To help industrial producers, party secretaries lobbied through formal channels for additional inputs and funds from central agencies.[27] Lobbying was also done through informal inter-regional clientele networks, often reaching all-union bureaucrats at the end. Party secretaries helped producers by cutting across departmental lines of command and organizing cooperation between enterprises belonging to different branch ministries. As illustrated in the previous chapter, party secretaries had been lobbying for the interests of local producers even before the central planning system was in place. With the start of industrialization, the growth of economy, and thus growth of imbalances, organizing economic life and lobbying for the interests of producers became their main function.

With the central leadership and Stalin personally continuing to rely on regional party leaders to fulfil the tasks and goals, by all means necessary, in a system averse to formal political or economic rules, the Soviet prefects enjoyed relative autonomy in their efforts to facilitate administration by setting up informal regional horizontal cliques of party and state officials and joining informal 'vertical' networks of officials.[28] Hence, as the Soviet state passed through major watersheds, informal practices such as 'clientelism, clan-based politics, and personalized patrimonial understandings of government' remained in place.[29]

The continuity of the principles that guided political and economic processes and practices throughout the 1930s and 1940s resulted in the continuity of Ukraine's institutional set-up after 1925. As discussed below, after industrialization and collectivization, two devastating famines in 1932–1933 and 1946–1947, the Second World War, and the westward territorial expansion of the Ukrainian Soviet Socialist Republic (UkSSR) in 1939–1940, the regulatory decision-making powers of the Ukrainian leadership did not increase, and the CP(b)U did not become organizationally consolidated. Kaganovich and Khrushchev might have been authoritarian and charismatic leaders of Ukraine, but the institutional power of the Ukrainian Politburo, the highest administrative organ in Soviet Ukraine, during their tenures was no greater than that of their predecessors or successors.

## Institutional Inertia in Ukraine

## No Control over Resources

### 1925–1928: Efforts to Stop the Tide of Centralization

When Kaganovich met with the Ukrainian Central Committee for the first time in his capacity of the First (now called 'General') Secretary of the Ukrainian Communist Party in April 1925, he outlined his agenda in Ukraine: to avoid at all costs a divide along national lines between the Russian-speaking CP(b)U and the Ukrainian-speaking soviets in the rural areas, in order to restore industry and consolidate the leadership of the proletariat.[30] In other words, he came to turn the CP(b)U 'towards the countryside' by enforcing the policy of Ukrainization. Kaganovich had other tasks in Ukraine, as well. He had to ensure that the

Ukrainian party apparatus supported the 'correct' position—that is, Stalin's side in his political struggle against Trotsky—and, as Arfon Rees observed, to block demands for greater Ukrainian autonomy.[31] Kaganovich's task was to increase the authority of the republican leadership over the Ukrainian periphery apparatus without increasing its influence over the republican economy. The Ukrainian leaders who welcomed Kaganovich expected exactly the opposite: a tangible expansion of their powers.

Soon after Kaganovich's arrival, the Ukrainian government made yet another attempt to stop the recentralization of the economy and to change 'the dismissive attitude' that the central bureaucracy had towards the interests of all the Union republics, including Ukraine. Writing directly to Stalin in the summer of 1925, Vlas Chubar, chairman of the Ukrainian government (1923–1934), argued that centralization was reaching an unreasonable scale. The central organs had already claimed authority over Ukrainian trusts managing coal, alcohol, and chemical production, and it looked like they would not stop there. The Ukrainian Sovnarkhoz would soon have no trusts under its management. The all-union People's Commissariat of Domestic Trade (Narkomvnutorg) centralized control over commercial bakeries. Now those who wished to open a commercial bakery, regardless of where they lived, had to go to Moscow for a loan. When Ukraine's meatpacking industry asked Narkomvnutorg for assistance, it replied: 'Come to us, become "our" Union organization, and then we will support you.'[32] Control over phone lines and insurance was withdrawn from the republics as well. More importantly, Chubar added, the People's Commissariat of Finances (Narkomfin) violated regulations 'About the budgetary rights of the Union and the Union republics'; hence, 'the participation of the governments of the Union republics in the elaboration of the Union budget reduced almost to zero.'[33]

Of even bigger concern to Chubar was People's Commissar of Finance Grigorii Sokolnikov's intention to divert the republic's share of the industrial tax to the Union budget. If the Narkomfin succeeded in that plan, Chubar explained to Stalin, then Ukraine's revenues would fall and it would 'be deprived of the possibility to redistribute these funds from more industrialized to less industrialized regions.'[34] Besides, the Narkomfin had already centralized control over loans for housing construction. Any small housing cooperative or ispolkom, whether from Odesa or Vladivostok, had to go to Moscow to receive a 5,000–10,000 rouble credit. 'The republican centres [were] completely barred from [the distribution of loans]', yet the republican centres were best positioned to decide whose financial needs had to be prioritized. 'The existing system will inevitably lead to the growth of slick businessmen [lovkachi del'tsy] who know how to snatch what they need',[35] warned Chubar, whereas those who most needed money would be left out. The Ukrainian government did not participate in the distribution of funds for the unemployed, either, and it looked like it would lose control over the funds for agriculture. Sokolnikov was determined to deprive republican agricultural banks of any autonomous function and to turn them into offices of the All-Union Agricultural Bank.[36]

Chubar protested not only against excessive centralization tendencies and the curtailment of the regulatory rights of the republican governments, but also against all-union agencies neglecting formal procedure. 'One can give hundreds of examples [of when the republican organs were ignored or bypassed]. If such tendencies continue, the construction of the Union of Soviet Socialist Republics may suffer greatly, because the situation might aggravate in the direction of unnecessary frictions and loss of time.'[37]

At a meeting on 28 August 1925, with Kaganovich present, the Ukrainian Politburo lined up in support of Chubar's letter. In defiance of Kaganovich, the Ukrainian Politburo 'categorically objected to the transfer of deductions from the industrial tax to the Union budget' and agreed that the republic could not be barred from drafting a budget and that the existing provisional regulations on local finances should be finalized and formalized.[38] On 12–13 September 1925, the Ukrainian budgetary commission included deductions from taxes paid by the all-union industry in Ukraine's budgetary revenues.[39] (The all-union Narkomfin later overruled this provision.)

While fighting Moscow's increasing tendency to centralize control over the economy, the periphery apparatus continued to criticize the Ukrainian leadership for the policies it did not draft and for administrative weaknesses.

At the 21–23 October 1925 plenum of the Ukrainian Central Committee, the party functionaries from agricultural regions expressed their frustration about the lack of financial resources for housing, as well as the lack of tractors and consumer goods. 'Donbas, for example, received 200–300 tractors'; there were three tractors for the entire Chernihiv okruha, and the Vinnytsia okruha did not receive a single tractor in 1925. Imported consumer goods, destined to boost trade, were almost entirely allocated to the industrial okruhas.[40] Pavlo Postyshev from the Kyiv ispolkom—the same Postyshev whom Stalin appointed as second secretary in 1932 to 'supervise' First Secretary Stanislav Kosior—mentioned the inconsistency between the responsibilities and financial abilities of the local authorities in housing construction. He complained that the Ukrainian leadership kept 'much revenue from direct taxes' for the Ukrainian republican budget, whereas the okruhas had forthcoming 'colossal expenditures' for housing construction, schools, and other projects.[41]

The periphery party leaders from the Donetsk basin and the regions of Katerynoslav and Kharkiv had tractors, but an acute housing crisis existed there as well. There was even a 'beskvartirnaia [homelessness] manifestation' in Donbas. They welcomed industrialization but insisted that it was impossible to increase industrial production without improving the housing situation. The Donbas party leaders also insisted that the Ukrainian leadership participate in drafting lists of construction projects.[42]

Polissia, a region in north-western Ukraine, struggled with expensive agricultural loans. In 1925, the famished areas of Polissia received five wagons of grain instead of fifty. The grain was of the best quality and too expensive for peasants to buy.[43] The periphery party secretaries criticized policies for cooperatives, trade, banking, labour, wages (which workers could not understand), grain procurement, and cadres, as well as the way central authorities handled unemployment. Odesa, for example, accounted for more than 30 percent of unemployment in Ukraine. However, they remained in need of help from 'our central organs'.[44] Indeed, all gubernias needed financial help.

As at the previous party forums, Chubar was left to explain the powerlessness of the Ukrainian leadership. The policies and orders issued by the Council of Labour and Defence (STO) overruled any decision that the Ukrainian leadership made, he said, and the Ukrainian leadership did not have any funds for the periphery. 'All industries require investments, but where to get them[?]' philosophized Chubar. He agreed that the main task was to boost industrial development and inject new capital. However, at present, Ukraine was not expecting any large investments from Moscow, either in local urban infrastructure or in local industry or cooperative trade, nor even in large industrial projects like the Dnipro power dam, Dniprobud. 'You', Chubar told the periphery apparatus, 'should rely on your own ability to raise funds to improve the socio-economic situation in your territories and to invest in local industry.'[45]

The presence of Kaganovich did not shield the Ukrainian leadership from criticism by the periphery apparatus. Contrary to the pre-Kaganovich period, they stopped short of suggesting that the Ukrainian Central Committee was a superfluous agency. Nonetheless, the October 1925 plenum of the Ukrainian Central Committee made it clear that control over resources and decision-making powers remained the main criteria for assessing the power of the republican leadership. The Ukrainian leadership continued to struggle to expand the resources at Kharkiv's disposal and to clarify and formalize its regulatory functions. During the first two years of Kaganovich's tenure alone, Ukraine submitted thirty-three demands to cancel or amend decisions that allowed the all-union organs to infringe the republic's constitutional rights on economic matters.[46]

To give a few examples, in November 1925, the Ukrainian leadership objected to the 11 November resolution of the All-Union Central Executive Committee of Soviets (TsIK). Because the resolution was open to interpretation, all-union commissariats took the liberty of bypassing their republican counterparts in communicating with enterprises subordinated to them. Ukraine's protest was rebuffed. In the winter of 1926, the Ukrainian leadership objected to the USSR Sovnarkom's 5 January 1926 decision forbidding the Union republic governments from charging the grain procurement agents' extra fees. The Ukrainian leaders viewed this decision as a violation of article 3 of the USSR Constitution, which did not give the USSR Sovnarkom the right to directly manage (*rukovodit'*) the sovnarkoms of the republics. On 3 August 1926, the All-Union TsIK rejected Ukraine's protest. Grain procurements would be centralized. In May 1926, the Ukrainian government protested the Soviet government's decision to 'allocate finances for the construction of the Palace of Labour in Katerynoslav'. The USSR Sovnarkom rebuffed this protest as well.[47]

Despite the exceedingly clear tendency towards centralizing budgetary expenditures in 1926, the Ukrainian government still hoped to obtain control over Ukraine's budget and the right to distribute republican revenues. In the 'Regulations on the budgetary rights of the Union and Union republics' that it drafted that year, in addition to cultural and social programmes that the republican budget was covering, the Ukrainian government included expenditures for industry within republican jurisdiction, electricity, cooperatives, and agriculture.[48] The central leadership was, however, unwilling to change the main outline of both the republican and the local budgetary systems, which had already been established by October 1924. The central leadership allowed the republican and local periphery authorities some flexibility in expenditures. However, Moscow determined the total expenditure of each budget.[49] All considerable expenditures of the Ukrainian leadership, or the leadership of any other republic, were scrutinized by the all-union Narkomfin and were subject to its approval.[50]

The appointment of Kaganovich did not reduce the Ukrainian leadership's demands for greater autonomy.[51] Remarkably, at the plenum of the Supreme Sovnarkhoz on 21 February 1927, which discussed reorganizing economic administration under the first five-year plan, Chairman of the Ukrainian Sovnarkhoz, Kiril Sukhomlin, argued that the all-union agencies should retain control only over fuel, electro-technical (*elektrotekhnicheskaia*), and metallurgical industries. 'Other industries should be transferred to the administration of the republics.'[52] His suggestion was probably dismissed as naïve. In addition to supervising the all-union industry along branch lines since 1923, the Supreme Sovnarkhoz supervised and planned for industries under republican jurisdiction. In 1926, eight new glavks were organized within the Supreme Sovnarkhoz to run the all-union industry and control republican and local industry.[53] From 1926–1927, the Supreme Sovnarkhoz approved 'new capital investment projects, regardless of whether they would fall under the Union, republican or local jurisdiction'. By 1927, the Ukrainian Sovnarkhoz had already ceased to participate in the preparation of control figures for the all-union industry on its territory.[54]

Until his removal from Ukraine in 1928, Kaganovich remained a strong supporter of industrializing Ukraine.[55] In early spring 1926, he even famously disagreed with Stalin on the expediency of the Dniprobud project and defended the project that was strongly supported by both the Ukrainian government and the party apparatus of Katerynoslav, Zaporizhzhia, and Poltava, the regions that stood to benefit from it the most.[56] However, for all of Kaganovich's political status and 'authoritarian' posturing, his time in office did not see an increase in the institutional power of the first secretary of the CP(b)U, the Ukrainian Central Committee, or the Ukrainian government. The institutional weakness of the Ukrainian leadership was clearly revealed after it failed to procure enough grain in 1927, and the Soviet leadership felt it necessary to send Molotov to Kharkiv to personally orchestrate and supervise the progress of the grain procurement campaign in Ukraine.[57] From Stalin's perspective, Kaganovich did not possess the necessary power to enforce central instructions among the periphery apparatus.

Indeed, the Ukrainian leadership could not command much authority with the periphery apparatus. It was unable to provide funds that the periphery acutely needed. Across the Union in 1928–1929, only 15 percent of the total budgetary expenditure was financed by the republican budgets.[58] The revenue in the Ukrainian budget was insufficient for financing Ukrainian republican industry, and, even then, the Ukrainian leadership did not have the authority to independently distribute funds among enterprises or regions. Lack of a clear separation of budgetary competence between the all-union and the republican governments, which reflected not only Stalin's, but also the entire central bureaucracy's aversion to formal rules, further undermined the regulatory powers of the Ukrainian leadership.[59]

## 1928–1953: Centralization

Stalin's purges of the party and state apparatus in 1929, 1933, and 1937–1938 (the Great Terror) expelled practically the entire central and regional apparatus of the CP(b)U, the Ukrainian Sovnarkom, the Presidium of the Supreme Soviet of the UkSSR, and all chairmen of Ukrainian oblispolkoms, bringing to power a cohort of Stalin loyalists.[60] Furthermore, the Second World War, while allowing for a degree of decentralization in decision making, led to the ideological consolidation of the party. These and other factors disincentivized the Ukrainian provincial leaders from criticizing central policies or the Ukrainian leadership for its administrative weakness. This did not mean that the Ukrainian leadership became an institutionally strong republican administrative and party centre. The first secretaries of the Ukrainian Central Committee, Nikita Khrushchev and then Leonid Melnikov, may have been viewed as, and indeed been, strong authoritarian leaders.[61] However, the main criteria of the Ukrainian leadership's actual authority, control over resources, became characteristic neither of the Ukrainian leadership in general, nor of the first party secretary more specifically, regardless of who occupied the post.

The centralizing tendencies actively pursued by the central bureaucracy in 1925 when Kaganovich arrived in Ukraine were boosted after he left in 1928. With the introduction of a single financial plan in 1929, the republics lost the right to form their own budgets within 'hard limits' of revenues and could only rely on the share of total all-union revenue allocated to them by the Narkomfin.[62] By the end of the first five-year plan (1928–1932), 'all aspects of Soviet economic life were gradually subordinated to the national [Union] economic plan',[63] which itself was devised largely without regard for the republican governments' views on their economies. Any considerable funds that the republic formally possessed, such as the fund of general state revenue in excess of budget or extra-budgetary allocations that could influence the economic situation in a region or industry, could be spent only with Moscow's permission.[64] At the beginning of 1932, Kosior and Chubar tried to increase the Ukrainian leadership's flexibility in managing extra-budgetary funds. On 8 May 1932, their suggestion of creating a Committee of Funds within the Ukrainian Sovnarkom was rejected.[65] This rejection was consistent with the instruction passed by the central Politburo on 4 May 1932, which allocated 19.5 million roubles to Ukraine and specifically instructed the Ukrainian leadership how to distribute the funds: 5 million roubles for the apparatus in the oblasts and housing construction in Vinnytsia and Dnipropetrovsk, 12.5 million roubles to the Commissariat of Heavy Industry for its two projects in Ukraine, and so on.[66] By the end of 1932, the Ukrainian government supervised, rather than controlled, 'only 37.5 percent of all industries located on its territory',[67] the so-called republican and local industry. On 23 March 1932, the central Politburo decided to organize a central administration for republican and local industry.[68]

**Illustration 6** Ukrainian Soviet leaders at the Ukrainian front during the Second World War, March 1943/© TsDAHOU (f. 240 op. 1 spr. 52 ark. 20)

Left to right: Ukrainian Central Committee secretary Demian Korotchenko, CP(b)U First Secretary Nikita Khrushchev, Deputy Chairman of the Ukrainian Sovnarkom Vasyl Starchenko, Chairman of the Ukrainian Sovnarkom Leonid Korniets.

After the war, the Ukrainian leadership had even less control over Ukraine's economy. In 1945, Ukrainian industry constituted only 26 percent of its pre-war level; in comparison, the industry of the entire Soviet Union was at 92 percent of its pre-war level. In 1946–1950, the Soviet leadership allocated 6.7 billion roubles to invest in the Ukrainian economy, which amounted to 19.2 percent of all investments injected into the Soviet economy.[69] However, a mere 11 percent of this investment was allocated to portions of the economy subordinated directly to the Ukrainian government.[70] Control over financial and material resources was divided between the local managers who 'sat' on the actual resources—that is, had direct physical access to the resources generated in Ukraine—and the all-union ministries that had regulatory control over resources and funding.

Consequently, Ukrainian leaders had to turn to local and central assistance for industrial projects. When faced with the problem of reconstructing housing in Ukraine in 1945, First Secretary Khrushchev could only urge the Ukrainian periphery apparatus to seek local resources and ask Moscow for permission to cut wood. Khrushchev had no cement, wood, or any other material to give.[71] To address an inefficient use of resources within the sugar industry in 1950, Leonid Melnikov (Khrushchev's successor) and Demian Korotchenko (the chairman of the Ukrainian government) had to write to Stalin personally asking for funds, materials, 'and relevant instructions' to the all-union agencies to organize a khozraschet trust. To complete the construction of irrigation systems in the south of Ukraine, Melnikov had to personally ask Stalin to instruct the all-union Gossnab and the all-union Ministry of Agriculture to allocate the materials and equipment that the republic needed.[72] Officially, the Ukrainian leadership was supposed to supervise the construction of the Kakhovka hydroelectric station and the South Ukrainian Canal, which had been approved by the central leadership in September 1950. However, in September 1951, the Ukrainian leadership needed the USSR Gosplan's permission to store local materials in volumes sufficient to continue construction during winter, and it was on the all-union Ministry of Railways that the Ukrainian leadership had to rely to transport these materials.[73]

### Agriculture: Responsibility with No Rights

As elsewhere in the Soviet Union, with the beginning of industrialization and collectivization, it was agriculture, not industry, that became the primary responsibility of the republican leadership.

To emphasize the managerial role of the Ukrainian leadership in agriculture, the central leadership moved the capital of the UkSSR from Kharkiv to Kyiv in 1934. By 1934, the administration in the main industrial regions of Donbas, Kharkiv, and Dnipropetrovsk, as well as Moscow's control over them, was well established. On 20 January 1934, the central Politburo instructed the Ukrainian leadership to move the party and republican soviet apparatus to Kyiv, another large industrialized centre, in order to be closer both 'to the most important agricultural regions, which are the regions located in right-bank Ukraine', and to Ukraine's natural geographic centre.[74] When appointing Khrushchev to lead Ukraine in late 1937, Stalin 'warned him "not to spend all [his] time in the Donbas" at the expense of "[his] agricultural responsibilities"'.[75] During the next twelve years, Khrushchev personally supervised the harvest and procurement of grain.[76]

Although the Ukrainian leadership had to focus on agriculture, it had little control over the financial or material input or the output of this sector of the economy. The very concept of collective farms manifested the tendency towards centralized control, as they 'enabled Moscow to replace local decision making with its own detailed plans, instructions, and formal, but often transient rules'.[77] This, in turn, made it easier to extract agricultural produce from rural areas. As with culture and education, Stalin accepted the national particularities of 'specific customs and land-use patterns that varied by republic'. So, the agricultural com-missariats were republican. However, in 1929, the Ukrainian Commissariat of Agriculture was subordinated to the newly established all-union Commissariat of Agriculture (Narkomzem).[78]

By the end of 1932, observes Vasil'ev, the Ukrainian leadership had lost its relative autonomy in grain procurement, or rather grain collection. Starting on 29 October 1932, when the Central Commission led by Molotov arrived in Kharkiv, the grain procurement campaign in Ukraine came under the direct supervision of the central leadership. On 16 January 1933, the Central Committee created committees to organize sowing campaigns in Ukraine and the north Caucasus.[79] From January 1933, political departments were created in the machine-tractor stations that serviced agricultural machinery for kolkhozy and sovkhozy. Subordinated directly to the political administration within the all-union Narkomzem, which in turn was subordinated directly to the central Politburo,[80] the political departments of machine-tractor stations were outside the jurisdiction of the raion party committees (raikoms) or the Ukrainian Central Committee, although sometimes they formed informal connections with the raikoms.

As with industrial resources, the central leadership did not allow the Ukrainian leadership any control over the distribution of grain or the seed bank that was stored in the territory of Ukraine.[81] (As Khrushchev explained in his memoirs, 'once grain was handed over to the state collection centres, [he] no longer had any authority over it'.[82] He had to ask Stalin for permission to issue ration cards in 1946.[83]) The tragic outcome of Moscow's control over the grain was the Great Famine and an outright genocide of the Ukrainian people in 1932–1933, also known as Holodomor.[84]

The Ukrainian leadership was likewise deprived of any regulatory authority in managing non-grain agricultural produce. The procurements of non-grain agri-cultural produce were to be held strictly in the territories where the procurement agencies were located. The STO committee for procurement of agricultural produce could give only the largest procurement agents permission to procure outside of their territories. The largest agents included unions of consumer cooperatives or industrial enterprises, as well as 'the largest state trade or public catering organizations, primarily those of the industrial centres of Moscow, Leningrad, Donbas, Ural, and Baku'. The procurement organizations in non-industrial regions were allowed to procure agricultural products only from the neighbouring territories. In 1950, the Ukrainian government needed approval from the Soviet government and Stalin personally to 'loan' potatoes from the Ukrainian state supply to the kolkhozy of Donbas or southern oblasts of Ukraine, or to supply potatoes from other Ukrainian oblasts to the Stalino and Voroshylovhrad oblasts.[85]

The Ukrainian leadership was just as constrained in decision making and resource management in its other areas of responsibility: education, ideology, and culture, as well as the sovietization of the annexed areas of Western Ukraine after 1939–1940. In 1934, the central Politburo reprimanded the Ukrainian Politburo for allocating 10,000 places in the agricultural technical schools and institutes to the *kolkhozniks*, reducing this number to 6,000 places. Apparently, the central Politburo reduced the quota because it was 'wrong that the Ukrainian Central Committee issued this resolution without consulting the Central Committee'.[86] Whether it was to expand the print run of the Ukrainian weekly newspaper *Literaturna hazeta*, or to create a Science Secretariat in the Ukrainian Academy of Sciences, Melnikov and Korotchenko needed Moscow's permission. To build a theatre in Zhdanov, Melnikov had to ask the Soviet government for financing and permission for the Azovstal'bud trust of the all-union Ministry of Construction of Enterprises of Heavy Industry to construct the theatre.[87]

Stalin personally supervised the struggle against nationalist resistance in the western oblasts. Khrushchev and the secretaries of the western Ukrainian oblasts reported to Stalin on the progress and measures that had been taken.[88] The funding for sovietizing the newly annexed territories was allocated and regulated by Moscow.[89] On 4 December 1945, the Central Committee instructed the Ukrainian Central Committee to create a department for the western, Izmail, and Zakarpattia oblasts that would assist the local party organs with the party-ideological work and with 'improving control over the fulfilment of the decisions of the party and the government on the further restoration and full development of all economic branches by the commissariats and republican organizations'.[90] The industrialization of Lviv was orchestrated and administered by the central bureaucracy, as well. The Ukrainian leadership supervised Lviv's urban infrastructure, water-pipes, public transport, streetlights, reconstruction of housing, and domestic gas supply. The first secretary reported on the progress of industrialization in Lviv and suggested what was yet to be done. In 1951, the Ukrainian government asked the all-union Gossnab and the USSR Gosplan to allocate financial and material resources to start constructing a car-repairing factory in Lviv.[91]

## Dual Executive

Throughout the Stalinist period, the Ukrainian Central Committee and the Ukrainian Sovnarkom remained the de facto dual executive. The separation of powers that existed between the central Politburo, the Central Committee, and the USSR Sovnarkom was mirrored at the republican level only to the extent that the Ukrainian Central Committee and the Ukrainian Sovnarkom often had different specific tasks.[92] The Ukrainian Central Committee was sometimes treated as superior to the Ukrainian Sovnarkom.[93] The Ukrainian Politburo, on the other hand, did not match the central Politburo in decision- or policymaking, even within the margins of its authority, as the decisions of the Ukrainian Politburo were valid only if the central leadership approved them. First secretaries Kosior, Khrushchev, and Melnikov could propose projects or initiatives, and they could lobby for additional material or financial resources. However, they did not control the resources necessary for their initiatives, nor did they decide whether the project would be implemented at all. Contrary to the arrangement in Moscow, the Ukrainian Politburo did not maintain tight control over the Ukrainian Sovnarkom or appoint or reprimand its chairman.[94]

Instead, the Ukrainian Central Committee and the Ukrainian Sovnarkom continued to be held jointly responsible for the fulfilment of plans and implementation of central policies and instructions, preferably at no extra cost to the state, by mobilizing locally available material and human resources.[95] When the central leadership decided in 1947 to abolish the card system, the Ukrainian Central Committee and the Ukrainian government had to work together to prepare the Ukrainian retail network for free trade in food products.[96] Stalin did not differentiate between Kosior and Chubar when demanding that Ukraine fulfil the grain-procurement targets in 1932–1933.[97] Briefly, between 1944 and 1947, Khrushchev combined the post of the CP(b)U first secretary and the chairman of the Ukrainian government. On 3 March 1947, Stalin returned Kaganovich to Ukraine as first secretary. By September, after a brief period during which Stalin's trust in Khrushchev was allegedly shaken, Stalin demanded that Kaganovich no longer submit memorandums without Khrushchev's signature.[98]

Even then, the Ukrainian leadership rarely had sole responsibility for fulfilling and implementing the centre's demands. To supervise the construction of factories, the Ukrainian leadership was often instructed to cooperate with local territorial authorities and central economic agencies. In 1950, for example, the Ukrainian leadership was instructed to cooperate with the Stalino and Voroshylovhrad obkoms, as well as the all-union Ministry of the Coal Industry, in implementing the Soviet government's instructions to increase labour productivity and consolidate technical guidance in the Donbas mines. The Ukrainian Central Committee and the two obkoms were equally responsible for supervising the implementation of this resolution.[99]

## Fragmentation of the Ukrainian Communist Party

On 27 June 1928, the Ukrainian Central Committee gathered to say goodbye to Kaganovich. At the meeting, Molotov declared that Kaganovich had consolidated the CP(b)U and put an end to the *otamanshchina*, a practice in which, as previously discussed, regional groups consolidated around a regional leader, quasi autonomous in his actions. Not all present at the meeting agreed with Molotov. Some argued that the unity was superficial, that the CP(b)U as an organization was not consolidated, that the CP(b)U would now be even more disunited than before Kaganovich arrived in Ukraine in 1925, and that the fiefdoms of Kyiv, Dnipropetrovsk, Odesa, Kharkiv, and Donbas would be restored.[100]

Pessimism about the CP(b)U's unity was not unfounded. The unity of the CP(b)U that Molotov was talking about was not so much unity as it was absence of open dissent, which itself was a result of the party cleansing that Kaganovich, on Stalin's instruction, began as soon as he took over the post in 1925. The CP(b)U became more obedient, but it did not become organizationally united.[101] Indeed, there were no reasons for the Ukrainian party apparatus to unite. The factors that determined the fragmentation of the CP(b)U in the first half of the 1920s remained and would endure until the fall of the Soviet Union.

### No Strong Centre

The institutional weakness of the Ukrainian leadership remained the main factor determining the fragmentation of the CP(b)U, which oversaw Ukraine's economic affairs as an integrated part of the Communist Party of the Soviet Union. There is little doubt that the Ukrainian Politburo, the Ukrainian Central Committee, and the Ukrainian government had their roles to play in the Soviet administrative system. They coordinated the efforts of various agencies and mobilized the masses and the party for the fulfilment of central policies and instructions. Education, culture, and social policies remained under the purview of the Ukrainian leadership, as well. The Ukrainian leadership continued to be useful for the central leadership's foreign policy agenda. In 1945 Ukraine joined the United Nations as a founding member.

However, the Ukrainian Central Committee did not become the sole party authority in the republic, as the Ukrainian obkoms remained under the double jurisdiction of the Central Committee and the Ukrainian Central Committee and maintained a direct relationship with the former.[102] In 1950, the Central Committee asked the Ukrainian obkoms directly for something as trivial as the lists of revision commission members elected at the latest party conference or congress.[103] Likewise, the Ukrainian Politburo lacked the regulatory powers that would have enabled it to consolidate its own authority over the periphery or the CP(b)U as an organization. As already illustrated at length, neither the

Ukrainian Politburo nor the Ukrainian government controlled resources for industrial branches or for the economic development of the regions.

As a result, the obkom secretaries, focused on their economic agenda, brought their requests for material supplies and financial investments directly to the central party and state apparatus in Moscow. In 1933–1934, the Dnipropetrovsk obkom and oblispolkom negotiated food deliveries from the oblast to the state directly with the central Politburo. In 1935, the oblasts of Kyiv, Kharkiv, and Chernihiv directly approached Chubar, now the deputy chairman of the USSR Sovnarkom, for permission to build factories to manufacture synthetic fibre in their territories. In June 1933, the secretary of the Donetsk obkom, Ivan Akulov, asked the Central Committee's permission to organize aquaculture in Donbas. After Akulov signalled his perfect understanding of the line of command, the Central Committee passed his suggestion to the Ukrainian Central Committee for examination, thus once again emphasizing the executive status of the Ukrainian Central Committee.[104]

Industrialization, collectivization, and economic recovery after the war were administered in Ukraine through direct communication between the central and oblast authorities. The Central Committee's commissioners supervised industrialization in Kharkiv and Donbas; food supplies to the Ukrainian industrial areas were centralized.[105]

## Prioritizing Growth of Heavy Industry

Forcefully supported with investment allocations, the policy of prioritizing heavy industry maintained the gap in industrial development between economic regions in Ukraine. With the economic agenda prioritized over the ideological within the party, this polarization 'spilled' into the CP(b)U. By the time of Stalin's death, the Ukrainian obkoms were de facto divided between the privileged 'industrial' and underprivileged 'agricultural'.

During the early stages of industrialization, the Soviet leadership tried to decrease inter-regional inequality.[106] However, in Ukraine, these efforts were of little consequence. In the period between 1929 and 1935, the already industrialized south-east, also called the Donetsk-Prydniprovsk economic region, which included the oblasts of Dnipropetrovsk, Donetsk and Kharkiv, received between 88.2 and 90.8 percent of all investments allocated to Ukraine. The traditionally agricultural south-western region, which included the oblasts of Kyiv, Vinnytsia, and Chernihiv, received between 5.7 and 8.7 percent of all investments allocated to Ukraine. The share of the southern economic region, which included the Odesa oblast and the Moldavia autonomous republic, constituted between 2.6 and 3.7 percent (corresponding to this region's share of Ukraine's population and economy).[107] By 1939, 'the split between Ukraine's eastern and southern industrial areas and its western and central agricultural regions' had been reinforced.[108]

After eastern Galicia, Volhynia, and Bukovina (and Transcarpathia in 1945) were incorporated into the UkSSR, the Soviet leadership invested in their industrialization. On average, the total gross output of industry in these regions (comprising the oblasts of Lviv, Ivano-Frankivsk, Ternopil, Volyn, Rivne, Chernivtsi, and Zakarpattia) increased by 64 percent in the period between 1940 and 1950, as compared to a 15 percent increase in 'old' Soviet Ukraine. Stalin singled out Lviv as 'the hub and symbol of the Sovietization of Western Ukraine', as Tarik Cyril Amar observes, and personally watched how the city would make a 'leap from backwardness to progress'. In 1945, the share of plants under central control increased from less than 8 percent to 40 percent. By 1950, central planners estimated that total output of enterprises in Lviv would increase by 330–390 percent in republican and local industries, and by more than 3,200 percent in all-union industries.[109]

Lviv industry never achieved the growth that central planners predicted. Nonetheless, with an increase of 192 percent in the period between 1940 and 1950, Lviv saw the highest growth rate of industrial gross output in the newly annexed region. 'Lviv became an important centre of electronic, metal-working, and machine-building industries for the Ukrainian SSR as well as for the USSR.' To compare, the gross industrial output increased by 10 percent in the Ternopil oblast, 32 percent in Volyn, 69 percent in Stanislav (renamed Ivano-Frankivsk in 1962), 66 percent in Rivne, and 77 percent in Chernivtsi. The Zakarpattia oblast's industrial gross output remained at the level of 1940.[110] 'The most isolated of the newly acquired Ukrainian territories', Zakarpattia was the first to complete its collectivization (by spring 1949).[111]

In the period between 1940 and 1955, industrial employment in the south-western economic region (which now incorporated the annexed territories) decreased from 48 to 44 per thousand persons. The downward tendency was characteristic of the entire Ukraine, falling from 79 to 73 per thousand in Ukraine on average. However, in the Donetsk-Prydniprovsk region, it decreased from 173 to 116, and in the southern region, from 88 to 71.[112] Despite the growth of industry, the south-western economic region remained the least industrialized. In mid-1950s, with 46.5 percent of the Ukrainian population, the region accounted for only 27.7 percent of Ukraine's gross industrial output. The respective numbers for the southern region were 12 and 11.6 percent; for the Donetsk-Prydniprovsk they were 41.5 and 60.7 percent.[113]

The level of industrialization of an oblast had several effects on its obkom and the organizational unity of the CP(b)U. As in the 1920s, having heavy industry enterprises in their oblasts helped the obkom secretaries with their agenda. In particular, the obkoms from industrialized oblasts had a larger pool of enterprises to rely on in developing agriculture during collectivization and after the war. The Soviet leadership's 9 March 1946 resolution obligated industrial enterprises to help the machine-tractor stations, kolkhozy, and sovkhozy with agricultural machinery, spare parts, construction, etc.[114]

The obkoms in the industrial regions were better positioned for building housing and urban infrastructure, as well. In the 1930s, as Donald Filtzer explained, the presence of heavy industry enterprises did not always guarantee the city a developed infrastructure,[115] but having heavy industry in the oblast had its benefits. As the chairman of the Chernihiv oblispolkom explained to Chubar in 1935, 'construction of a [synthetic fabric] factory in Chernihiv should at least to some extent elevate [*oblagorodit'*] the oblast centre'. The small amount of funding that the city of Chernihiv was to receive in 1936 for urban infrastructure, which was 1.1 million roubles out of the all-Ukrainian fund of 132 million roubles, would leave Chernihiv 'without the sewerage, without [running] water and if the TPS [i.e., heat and power plant] of the [local] textile factory will be supplied the way it is supplied today, then [the city will be] without electricity as well'.[116] Construction of a factory could bring additional funds to the city budget. After the war, the Soviet leadership channelled the meagre resources it was willing to allocate in housing construction and urban infrastructure to the industrial areas. In the period between 1948 and 1950, 72.8 percent of housing construction was planned for the industrial oblasts of Stalino, Voroshylovhrad, Dnipropetrovsk, Zaporizhzhia, and Kharkiv, including 45 percent of housing planned for Donbas, which accounted for only 15 percent of the Ukrainian population in 1956.[117]

The financial well-being of the obkom and of the obkom secretary also depended on the industrial importance of the oblast. On the one hand, the more the oblast was industrialized, the higher its place in the Central Committee classification of obkoms and the higher its first secretary's salary.[118] The July 1939 classification divided the sixteen Ukrainian obkoms into four groups. The classification was based on the size of the obkom staff, which itself reflected the scale of industrialization in the oblast as well as the size of the proletariat and the party organization. The Kyiv, Stalino, and Kharkiv obkoms, with their oblasts delivering the highest volumes of heavy industry gross output in 1937 and 1940, were placed in the first category; Voroshylovhrad, Dnipropetrovsk, Zaporizhzhia, and Odesa were in the second category; Vinnytsia, Zhytomyr, Kamianets-Podilskyi, Kirovohrad, Mykolaiv, Poltava, Sumy, and Chernihiv were in the third group; the fourth group included only the obkom of Moldavia.[119]

On the other hand, the presence of heavy industry provided more informal finance to the territorial party organizations for their official, but also unofficial, expenses. Throughout the 1930s and the 1940s, 'local party leaders struggled with insufficient funding from the center', established Belova and Lazarev. In 1938, the Soviet Communist Party generated a mere 15 percent of its revenue; 'nearly 85 percent of the revenues came from federal sources'. It was only by the mid-1950s that 'the party moved toward financial self-sufficiency by significantly raising its revenues from membership dues and the party's publishing business'.[120] Therefore, the party's 'taxation' of enterprises, widely practised in the 1920s, continued throughout the entire Stalinist period. In the 1940s, explains Moshe Lewin, industrial ministries also willingly included the highly placed regional party leaders on their renumeration lists, thus, arguably, paying them for their lobbying services.[121] The industrial ministries had little reason to pay the obkom secretary of primarily agricultural oblasts.

Of more importance for this discussion was the political effect of prioritizing the growth of heavy industry. As has been observed in the literature, the more industrialized the oblast was, the higher the status of its obkom first secretary and the more political weight he carried.[122] (And the more political weight a regional party secretary had, the more investments he could secure for the region.) Fully in line with the priority of heavy industry over agriculture, this principle was reflected in the composition of the Ukrainian Politburo, which for all its limited powers was nonetheless the highest administrative organ in the republic. All obkom secretaries were members of the Ukrainian Central Committee. However, only several, sometimes even just one, joined the Ukrainian Politburo. Until 1925, the Ukrainian Politburo generally did not include any periphery party secretaries. With the appointment of Kaganovich in 1925, the periphery secretaries became regularly included in the Ukrainian Politburo. In 1947–1952, the Ukrainian Politburo did not include a single obkom secretary. In September 1952, the Ukrainian Politburo included first secretaries of the Kyiv, Kharkiv, Lviv, and Stalino obkoms.[123] The reasons why the periphery secretaries became regular members or candidate-members of the Ukrainian Politburo specifically in 1925, and why they were excluded from the Ukrainian Politburo in 1947–1952 when Ukraine was entrusted to Stalin's loyalists Kaganovich, Khrushchev, and Melnikov, remain to be researched. For our discussion, it is sufficient to emphasize that, apart from the first secretary of the Vinnytsia obkom, no other secretary from an agricultural oblast was a member or candidate-member of the Ukrainian Politburo in the period between 1925 and 1952.[124] Yet, all obkom first secretaries were appointed by the Central Committee, and agriculture remained one of the main responsibilities of the party apparatus. Out of twenty-three issues discussed at the Ukrainian Central Committee plenums between 1950 and 1953, thirteen were devoted to the development of agriculture.[125]

## Conclusion

The period of transformation of the Soviet Union was a period of institutional inertia in Ukraine. By 1953, the Ukrainian leadership was not administratively or economically any stronger than it was before 1925. Appointed by Stalin, such leaders as Kaganovich and Khrushchev projected charisma and authority. They could undoubtedly get things done. Yet 'the things' were of an ad hoc nature. The policymaking or regulatory powers of the CP(b)U first secretary, or the Ukrainian government, or the Ukrainian Politburo did not expand after 1925. As designed at the beginning of the 1920s, the Ukrainian Central Committee and the Ukrainian government remained two executive branches jointly responsible for the fulfilment of tasks they were assigned. This shared responsibility pushed them to cooperation, or 'collective leadership'.[126]

Despite its persistent efforts since the beginning of the 1920s, the Ukrainian leadership failed to expand the sectors under its purview. By the beginning of the 1950s, the Ukrainian leadership had a certain degree of influence on culture and education. With the start of collectivization, it carried out managerial functions in the agricultural sector. However, access to material and financial resources for industry and agriculture, which was still the main criterion of power and authority, remained out of its reach. Control over resources was divided between the local managers, who had physical control over production, and the central bureaucracy. In other words, although it was responsible for fulfilling economic plans, the Ukrainian leadership had no leverage over the producers upon whom it depended to fulfil the plans. As the next chapter illustrates, during the decentralization reform, the Ukrainian leadership would find itself subordinate to the industrial regions.

The party's focus on the economic agenda made the institutional weakness of the Ukrainian leadership a decisive factor in the fragmentation of the CP(b)U. The policy of prioritizing the growth of heavy industry while also prioritizing branch over regional development divided the obkoms into 'privileged' and 'underprivileged', depending on their oblast's specialization. The privileged, industrial oblasts found themselves closely tied to the central party and state apparatus, with greater access to resources. Reflecting the all-union tendency, the interests of the horizontal regional clientele groups merged with the departmental interests of the branch ministries.[127] To all intents and purposes, and certainly as far as the fulfilment of economic directives was concerned, the industrial oblasts viewed the Ukrainian leadership as a largely superfluous administrative link whose powers were not tangibly greater than theirs.

*The Institutional Foundations of Ukrainian Democracy: Power Sharing, Regionalism, and Authoritarianism.* Nataliya Kibita, Oxford University Press. © Nataliya Kibita 2024. DOI: 10.1093/9780191925351.003.0004

# 4

# Institutional Change

## The Sovnarkhoz Reform

### Introduction

To address the set of problems that the Soviet Union had accumulated by the time of Stalin's death in March 1953, the new Soviet leadership needed to deviate from Stalin's policies. In the spring of 1953, Lavrentii Beria began to abolish the laws and decrees from the 1930s–1950s that violated 'socialist legality', launched a new nationality policy, and even suggested the de-Stalinization of the relationship with the Soviet bloc. At the fifth session of the Supreme Soviet of the USSR in August 1953, the new chairman of the USSR Council of Ministers (hereafter, the 'central government'), Georgii Malenkov, spoke openly in favour of prioritizing light industry.[1]

Yet, it was Nikita Khrushchev who called for institutional change. At first timidly in August 1953, and then increasingly assertively in the following years, Khrushchev (who was appointed First Secretary of the Communist Party of the Soviet Union on 14 September 1953) deviated from the hyper-centralized system of vertical administration characteristic of the Stalinist period and advocated the decentralization of economic administration. The decentralization dynamic reached its peak in 1957 when Khrushchev shocked the central bureaucracy with the Sovnarkhoz reform, which abolished most of the industrial branch ministries, emphasized the territorial principle in economic administration, and allowed for decentralized control over resources.[2]

The Sovnarkhoz reform transferred industrial and construction enterprises to the direct management of regional economic councils within the republics. The new economic councils (*sovety narodnogo khoziaĭstva*, or *sovnarkhozy*) of the 105 newly formed economic regions were placed under the jurisdiction of their respective republican governments. Seventy economic regions were formed in Russia, nine in Kazakhstan, four in Uzbekistan, and eleven in Ukraine. The remaining eleven republics each constituted one economic region.[3]

The administration and control over resources that were previously managed by 141 abolished ministries was divided between the USSR Gosplan and its glavsnabsbyty; the gosplans of the republics, and the sovnarkhozy and oblispolkoms, depending on the importance of the produce and the location of its producer and customer. Republican gosplans expanded their staff to assume responsibility for planning the economies of their republics, managing supplies allocated to their republics, and controlling and regulating the activity of their sovnarkhozy. Similarly to the USSR Gosplan, the republican gosplans organized their work along branch lines.

The reform sought to reduce unnecessary expenditures by improving coopera-tion between industries. The departmentalism within branch ministries had led to closed production cycles, which prevented ministries from cooperating in ways that could have increased efficiency and cost-effectiveness. The reform was also a response to inefficient planning, whereby central planners, detached from the production sites, composed plans that did not reflect factual production capacities and resources available in the periphery. Khrushchev hoped to improve the Soviet economic system and boost economic growth by combining central-ized planning for industrial branches with decentralized territorial management of production. He hoped that the proximity of the sovnarkhozy to the local party and soviet organizations would increase the involvement of the party in eco-nomic administration and that the obkoms would be able to influence managers as well as the plan indices and fulfilment.[4] In Khrushchev's scenario, the obkoms would, of course, defend the all-union interests as defined by the central leader-ship and central planners.

The insertion of a territorial element in branch administration of the economy did not increase the influence of the obkoms on the managers. It did, however, have a profound effect on the regions. The reform provided favourable conditions for party–industry alliances; the obkoms depended on the sovnarkhozy for own agenda and the interests of the obkoms and the managers were tightly connected.[5]

At the same time, the republican leadership took on an unprecedented level of involvement in economic administration as the reforms increased its role dra-matically. For the first time, the republican leadership became an active partici-pant in state administration. Across the Soviet Union, practically all industries, including enterprises working for defence, were placed under the jurisdiction of the republican governments.[6] The republics were now formally responsible for the fulfilment of plans and the general socio-economic development of their republics. 'While republican governments had accounted for only 6 per cent of budgetary expenditure on industry in 1950, their share had increased to 76 per cent by 1958. In agriculture, they provided only 26 per cent of expenditure in 1950, but by 1958 they accounted for 95 per cent.'[7] (This did not mean that the republics were free to use these funds as they pleased. Moscow still supervised the expenditures.) Formal procedures no longer allowed the central apparatus to communicate directly with the sovnarkhozy or enterprises. It was obligated to go through the republican authorities. The central leadership relied on the latter to control the fulfilment of production plans, enforce inter-republican deliveries and deliveries for export by their sovnarkhozy, and use allocated funds as central plans dictated. It relied on them to suppress all manifestations of *mestnichestvo* (localism) and protect all-union interests as defined by the central leadership. As Khrushchev said in May 1957, the reform was about 'transferring the centralism nearer to the localities where the immediate economic process develops, i.e., not less, but more centralization'.[8] In other words, the role of the republican authorities and regional authorities in Russia was to bring centralization closer to the production sites.

During the next two years, the central leadership discovered that the republics were willing to fight localism pursued by their regions' sovnarkhozy and obkoms, but they were just as prone to prioritize their republics' interests over those of other republics. The first revelation came in autumn 1957, when the republics submitted the drafts of their 1958 production plans composed 'from below'. Khrushchev expected that the enterprises, sovnarkhozy, and republican gosplans would include in their production plan targets the material resources and production capacities that existed in their territories. Instead, contrary to the expectations of the central leadership, the republics requested lower-than-expected production targets, higher-than-expected investment targets, and investments in industries not prioritized by the central leadership. Without asking the USSR Gosplan, the Council of Ministers of Ukraine (hereafter, the 'Ukrainian government'), for example, reduced capital investment in the coal industry by 249 million roubles and in ferrous metallurgy by 53 million roubles in 1957, and directed 'these funds for other needs, including communal construction'.[9] Planning 'from above' was swiftly restored. From now on the republics would be required to draft plans for their sovnarkhozy based on the so-called control numbers they were given.

The new administrative set-up failed to prevent producers from ignoring the delivery orders issued by the higher authorities or from siphoning resources in the same way the abolished ministries had. Indeed, the sovnarkhozy tended towards *mestnichestvo* for the same reasons the ministries had become characterized by departmentalism, or *vedomstvennost'*: they were 'looking after their own interests'.[10] Both *mestnichestvo* and *vedomstvennost'* were developed in response to the deficiencies of the planned economy. The difference was that the hoarded resources were now managed by the regions, as opposed to the branch ministries and decentralizing the administration of production looked like a promising way to boost economic growth. In October 1959, the head of the USSR Central Statistical Agency, Vladimir Starovsky, reported that the sovnarkhozy performed better than the ministries based on such criteria as gross output, above-plan production, productivity, reduction in the cost of production, and so on. In the year before the reform, the total gross output of industrial production had increased by 9.6 percent over the previous year. In the first year of the reform, from July 1957 until June 1958, the total gross output in the Soviet Union increased by 10.4 percent, in the second year by 10.7 percent, and in the nine months of 1959 by 11 percent.[11] In Ukraine, the growth rate of value added in industry was 8.3 percent in 1957 compared to 1956, and 14.8 percent in 1958 compared to 1957.[12]

Nonetheless, two years into the reform, the central leadership began a slow process of recentralization. The official explanation for recentralization was that the sovnarkhozy undermined the development of the industrial branches. Less official was the localism and autarkic tendencies that had developed.[13] The effect of localism on industries aside, the central apparatus and the central leadership had yet another reason to curtail the reform. By 1959, the central leadership and apparatus were under growing pressure from the republics to formalize the administrative relationship between the central and republican apparatus and further devolve control over material and financial resources to the republican governments. Indeed, the sovnarkhozy prioritized deliveries to the customers from their own economic regions; they did not rush to reveal hidden production capacities or increase productivity. However, the republics argued they had limited possibilities to tackle localism due to their limited control over material and financial resources and the unclear separation of responsibilities between the central and republican supply agencies.

After the shock of the 1957 reform, which had pushed the devolution of control over production, and the revelations from the exercise in planning 'from below', the central state apparatus had no intention to empower the republican governments further. The republican governments had, at the very early stage of the reform, demonstrated that they prioritized their own republican economies. Therefore, if the centre gave them the necessary power to suppress localism, where was the guarantee that the republican leadership would not impose the territorial principle of administration over the branch principle? How would the central leadership retain control over the economy if the republican governments controlled production? And where, then, would the political relationship between the republics and the centre be?[14]

Whether Khrushchev and Aleksei Kosygin, whom Khrushchev appointed in 1959 as the chairman of the USSR Gosplan, thought along these lines or not, the insistence of the republican governments on broadening the scope of the nationality policy to include economic relations, as Ukraine and Georgia had in 1922–1923, was hard to miss. Like Stalin in 1922–1923, to protect the power of the centre, Khrushchev could not allow the economy to become another component of the nationality policy. The principle that the one who controls resources controls politics was not a subject for de-Stalinization.[15]

At the November 1962 Central Committee plenum, Khrushchev announced that economic administration would be recentralized along branch lines but the sovnarkhoz system would not be abolished. The sovnarkhozy continued to manage production, and republican leadership maintained an important role in economic administration.

Khrushchev's decentralization reforms had a significant effect on Ukraine's institutional system. Firstly, the Ukrainian leadership became the de facto authority in the republic. It did not become the supreme authority in the republic, as Rakovsky and Manuilsky once dreamt. The central leadership maintained a direct relationship with the Ukrainian periphery along state and party lines. There was no change to the double subordination of the obkoms to both the Ukrainian Central Committee and the Central Committee. The formal status of the Ukrainian Central Committee also remained the same, that of an obkom. Policymaking remained firmly with the central leadership. The Ukrainian Central Committee and the Ukrainian government remained 'the dual executive'. However, the first part of this chapter will discuss how, in its role as executive, the Ukrainian leadership had meaningful decision-making powers and meaningful functions to perform in the economic administration. It could now influence policy implementation. For the first time in Soviet history, the Ukrainian leadership was anything but a superfluous link in the administrative system.

Secondly, as discussed in the second part of the chapter, these reforms empowered regional party–industry alliances. The obkoms remained marginal in the struggle against localism and, by the end of the reform, their interests were ever more deeply vested in the economy of their oblasts. At the same time, due to the particularities of the regionalization in Ukraine, whereby heavy and defence industry was concentrated in the south-east of the republic, the reform led to a deepening of the fragmentation of the Communist Party of Ukraine (CPU) and the consolidation of differentiation among the oblasts. Western Ukraine, a region with a distinct cultural and historical heritage, also became an institutionally distinct region.

## Part I: The Rise of the Ukrainian Leadership

### 1953–1956: High Hopes for Decentralization

As soon as the Ukrainian leadership saw an opportunity to ask for an expansion of its powers, it acted on it. The opportunity came soon after Stalin's death on 5 March 1953. On 15 March, the USSR Supreme Soviet passed the law 'On the reorganization of the ministries of the USSR'. The Ukrainian leadership immediately resurrected a constitutional provision that stated that the transformation of the ministerial system in Ukraine was within the competence of the Supreme Soviet of the Ukrainian Soviet Socialist Republic (UkSSR). Hence, argued the Ukrainian leadership, the non-constitutional committees and administrations attached to the Ukrainian government must be abolished or merged by the Ukrainian government.[16]

By the summer of 1953, CPSU First Secretary Nikita Khrushchev, had formulated the idea of devolution of the branch ministries' managerial authority to the lower administrations. On 11 August 1953, at the meeting of a commission formed to expand the rights of republican ministers, Khrushchev explained that decentralization was a longstanding idea, but 'it was impossible to realistically implement' it under Stalin. Now the time had come for regional authorities to be actively involved in the administration of trade, even coal and metallurgy, and 'undoubtedly' construction.[17] Khrushchev did not seek to empower the republican leadership for the benefit of the republics. He sought to optimize the central planning system by separating the 'executive' and 'control', or supervision, functions. Echoing ideas from the first plenum of the Supreme Sovnarkhoz in February 1927 about centralized leadership and control and decentralized operations,[18] he suggested freeing the central bureaucracy from the tasks that he believed the republican agencies could fulfil and allowing the central apparatus to focus on broader economic policies and control. Formal decentralization would increase the responsibility of the republics for the fulfilment of the plans, whereas the central apparatus would be better able to control the fulfilment of the plans.[19] Of course, Khrushchev knew, based on his own experience, that the republics were already held responsible for fulfilling production plans and supplying the population with food and housing. For them, the issue was not responsibility, but formal authority.

After the 11 August 1953 meeting, the state apparatus embarked on a long and tedious process of dividing the rights and responsibilities for the economy between the centre and the republics. For Ukraine, the first piecemeal step was made in the winter of 1954. The central leadership sanctioned two union–republican ministries in Ukraine: the Ministry of Ferrous Metallurgy on 8 February 1954 and the Ministry of Coal Mining on 19 April. Tellingly, the ministries were created not in Kyiv, the capital of the UkSSR, but in Dnipropetrovsk and Donetsk, respectively, which is where these industries were concentrated. The central offices of these two industries delegated a number of managerial functions to their Ukrainian counterparts without releasing centralized control over the industries. The Ukrainian leadership did not gain any authority over them.

Reminiscent of the early 1920s, the Ukrainian leadership took a systematic approach to decentralization and argued that not only should the republic expand its administrative system, but also it should have greater decision-making authority. On 8 May 1954, the Ukrainian leadership submitted extensive proposals on the extension of the rights and responsibilities of the governmental organs that the Ukrainian leadership considered desirable to obtain from the centre. In addition to the ministries for coal and metallurgy, they argued, the republic should create four new union–republican ministries, to administer communication, electric power stations, rural construction and higher education. The Ukrainian government should have access to the raw statistical data that the Central

Statistical Agency collected in Ukraine. The republican supply system should expand and manage chemical production, paper, metal, construction materials, and electricity. Central planners should allocate general funds to the republic and let republican glavsnabsbyty distribute material resources to all enterprises located in Ukraine, regardless of their status as union or republican enterprises. To enable the Ukrainian government to control the fulfilment of production plans by manufacturers, Ukraine should also have its own republican branches of the State Bank, the Industrial Bank, the Agricultural Bank, and the Commerce Bank. Plan targets should be aggregate. The republic would reformulate them for the industrial branches and enterprises. The republic should have the right to reallocate credits for capital investments and should be able to review the republican and local budgets, issue short-terms loans to enterprises, and set certain prices.[20] The reserve fund of the republic should be increased from 0.1 percent of its budget to 3 percent, and the republic should be free to spend it without consulting Moscow.[21]

In other words, Kyiv suggested that Moscow need only tell the republics what to produce, and then let them organize the production. In anticipation of the expansion of its economic rights, on 8 April 1954, CPU First Secretary Oleksii Kyrychenko and the Chairman of the Ukrainian Government Nykyfor Kalchenko asked Malenkov and Khrushchev to allow the Ukrainian government to build a new Permanent Mission of the UkSSR to the Soviet government. The one that had opened in 1923, they argued, was too small to cope with the increasing volume of work.[22]

To say that Ukraine's proposal was radical for the central apparatus would be an understatement. The extent to which Moscow was unprepared for any of the above was reflected in the fact that, in 1954, the central leadership limited the expansion of Ukraine's economic authority to the creation of ministries for communication, rural construction, and higher education, as well as the transfer of more enterprises from all-union to republican jurisdiction. Ukraine could take responsibility for these enterprises, but its economic rights remained the same and the central apparatus in Moscow maintained control over resources.

By the beginning of 1955, the other republics had submitted their proposals. Ukraine resubmitted the provisions that had been rejected in 1954. On 4 May 1955, the central government issued a resolution 'On changes in the procedures for state planning and financing the economies of the Union republics', which was based on a draft composed by an inter-republican commission under the chairmanship of Kosygin that included representatives of Russia, Belorussia, Kazakhstan, Georgia, Uzbekistan, and Ukraine. The resolution expanded the decision-making authority of the republican governments and republican ministries in planning and in distributing material funds between the ministries and administrations. The republics could distribute the entire output of enterprises under their jurisdiction. They could spend the surplus income to finance housing, communal services, and social-cultural events. They could also sell 50 percent of the construction materials produced by enterprises of all-union ministries on their territory, so long as it was sold to the population. The republican governments could order agricultural machinery from the all-union ministries. Ukraine was allowed to open republican offices of the State Bank, Industrial Bank, Agricultural Bank, and Commerce Bank.[23] At the same time, Kosygin still did not approve of Ukrainian supply offices for metal production, construction materials, or electricity. He refused to place the Ukrainian Statistical Agency under the double jurisdiction of the Ukrainian government and the central government, to allow the Ukrainian government to issue loans, even through the State Bank, to reduce prices for goods in low demand, or to allow the kolkhozy to delay payment for machine-tractor station services. The Ukrainian government did not obtain the 3 percent reserve fund either.[24]

All in all, the Kosygin commission approved of the republics channelling surplus materials and finances generated in their republics to meet the needs of the population in housing and consumer goods. But the republics had no power over industrial investments, financial matters, credit, pricing, or supplies for industrial branches.[25] Food distribution also remained under Moscow's control.[26]

In 1955, 53 percent of enterprises in the Soviet Union were under union jurisdiction, down from 67 percent in 1950. However, the transfer of enterprises from union to republican jurisdiction was a ritual exercise with no effect on the centre's control over the republics' financial and material resources. Indeed, instead of expanding the decision-making authority of the republican governments, the central leadership expanded the authority of the all-union ministries.[27]

The Twentieth Party Congress (14–25 February 1956) confirmed the chosen course of decentralizing economic administration and called for further expansion of the republics' economic rights. In an important departure from the past, the Soviet leadership instructed central planners to consider territorial development as well as branch development.

Inspired by the congress, and arguably Khrushchev's 'secret speech' denouncing the crimes of Stalin, the Ukrainian leadership drafted further suggestions on decentralizing administration and formalizing economic relations. Kyiv argued that the republic should also assume responsibility for operational controls, such as monitoring performance and efficiency. It should have full access to the raw statistical data collected in Ukraine. It should develop its own economic research and study Ukraine as a single economic complex. By the beginning of April 1956, the Ukrainian leadership had submitted an extensive proposal to expand republican economic rights in pricing, managing surplus production, issuing loans to industries, distributing credits for technological innovation and retail trade, setting the turnover tax on consumer goods not yet priced by the central government,

**Illustration 7** Members of the Ukrainian Soviet leadership among delegates to the Nineteenth CPU Congress, 17–21 January 1956/© TsDAEA (2-155442)

The Nineteenth CPU Congress was held one month before the Twentieth CPSU Congress. Left to right: first row—Olha Ivashchenko (2nd), Ivan Nazarenko, Chairman of the Ukrainian Government Nykyfor Kalchenko, CPU First Secretary Oleksii Kyrychenko, Demian Korotchenko, Mykola Pidhorny, Ivan Senin, Mykhailo Hrechukha (10th), Vasyl Chuikov (11th); second row—Ivan Kazanets (2nd), Ivan Hrushetsky (7th); third row—Volodymyr Shcherbytsky (11th).

and setting the level of investment in construction. Kyiv asked for a reserve fund of 5 to 7 percent of the Ukrainian republic's budget, an increase from the 3 percent that the republic was refused in 1955. Echoing the call for territory-based planning, the Ukrainian leadership insisted that central planners should treat Ukraine as a single economic complex.[28]

On 22 February 1956, as the Twentieth Party Congress was finishing its work, at a meeting of the Central Committee Presidium (hereafter, 'central Presidium'), CPU First Secretary Kyrychenko infringed on the centre's sacred monopoly on foreign connections by objecting to the central apparatus making all visits to foreign exhibitions and fairs. After the congress, Ukrainian Minister of Commerce Heorhii Sakhnovsky suggested decentralizing 'the procedures for purchasing merchandise abroad'. To obtain better prices, delivery terms, and quality, and even to bypass the embargo that the West imposed on selling strategic products to the countries of Eastern Europe and the Soviet Union, the central leadership should allow 'cooperative unions, cities, industrial trusts, and specialized trade organizations to buy goods abroad'.[29]

After the congress, the Ukrainian leadership returned its attention to formalizing deliveries. On 5 March 1956, Kyrychenko and Kalchenko submitted their suggestions on Moscow's proposal, 'Changes of the procedures for supplying the population with meat products', and insisted on formalizing meat product supply. In the original proposal, they argued, 'there is no objective criteria based on which [the central organs] decide the share and size [of deliveries] supplied by each republic to the all-union fund'. The terms for participation in state deliveries and in the all-union fund should be the same for all republics, and the republic's share in state deliveries should be the same as its share in the all-union reserve fund. Insistence on 'fair share' was Ukraine's diplomatic way of saying that it resented the existing arrangement whereby Georgia and Azerbaijan were exempt from deliveries to the all-union fund whereas their production of meat per capita, including urban population, was the same as the per capita production in the republics that were not exempt from the deliveries.[30] There was also a problem of annual changes to the republican deliveries of meat to the all-union fund, which made it impossible for the republics to improve supplies of food to the local population. A five-year fixed size of deliveries would be preferable, argued Kyiv. It was also desirable for the republics to be free 'to decide for themselves what products to produce with the meat, milk, and eggs that the central planners allocated to them'.[31] The Ukrainian leadership expected transparency, fairness, predictability, and formalized criteria in the republics' delivery of supplies to the all-union meat fund.

The pressure from Kyiv, and arguably from other republics, had little effect on the central leadership. At the end of May 1956, instead of expanding the decision-making powers of the republics, the central leadership further reshuffled the ministerial system, reorganizing thirteen ministries and transferring their enterprises to republican jurisdiction. The main decision-making authority, including for technological policy and control over supplies and investments for enterprises, remained with the Moscow offices of the new union-republican ministries.[32]

Decentralization was pushed further only after the 20–24 December 1956 plenum of the Central Committee and after Khrushchev concluded that the plan for 1957 was wrong and the system needed further adjustment. The plenum launched an attack on the planning organs. Shortcomings in planning slowed down the implementation of economic programmes, insisted Nikolai Bulganin, the new chairman of the central government. Excessive centralization in economic administration continued to stifle the initiative of local managers. Kyrychenko could not agree more. Had central planners considered the plan targets proposed by the republic, the available production capacities would have been reflected in the plan. The discrepancy between the production targets and the financial and material inputs necessary for meeting them would have been eliminated. To improve the plans, central planners simply had to rely on the republics.

After the December 1956 plenum, Ukrainian ministers grew increasingly impatient with the piecemeal transfer of enterprises to their jurisdiction. Ukrainian Minister of Coal Mining Oleksandr Zasiadko went so far as to claim that the existing planning procedure, in which the central planners ignored republics' proposals, was unconstitutional. He insisted that the Ukrainian government should have enough financial resources to be able to provide emergency help to the republican ministries and organizations. Ukrainian Minister of Construction Mykola Horbas insisted on decentralizing control over material resources and suggested organizing a Ukrainian Ministry of Material and Technical Supplies.[33]

By 1956, 78.6 percent of industry located on Ukrainian territory had been subordinated to the Ukrainian government, a remarkable increase from 36 percent in 1953. The economy was rapidly growing. With de-Stalinization in the air, a full-scale decentralization seemed imminent, and indeed it was. However, what followed was not what the Ukrainian leadership or the Ukrainian republican apparatus expected.

## The Ukrainian Leadership during the Sovnarkhoz Reform

As already mentioned, the Sovnarkhoz reform increased the economic power of the republican leaderships. In Ukraine, in reflection of Khrushchev's reliance on the party to move the state forward, the Ukrainian Central Committee became the main administrative centre for organizing the sovnarkhoz system, albeit with approval from the Central Committee, and remained in charge of implementing the reform. The eleven sovnarkhozy in Ukraine were subordinated to the Ukrainian government (see Map 3).

With a staff four times larger than before the reform, the Ukrainian Gosplan now planned 96.2 percent of the republic's gross industrial output, a significant jump from the 10 percent it had planned before 1957. It included thirty-four branch departments and nineteen Ukrainian glavsnabsbyty. The Ukrainian Gosplan drafted plans and distributed funds for all economic actors for all funds allocated by the state. The USSR Gosplan held its Ukrainian counterpart responsible for ensuring that the sovnarkhozy fulfilled their supply obligations for export, to all republics, but also for customers inside Ukraine.[34]

In practice, however, from the outset of the reform, the economic authority of the Ukrainian leadership was more limited than the initial formal set-up suggested.

**Illustration 8**  Khrushchev and the Ukrainian leadership, 1957/© TsDAEA
(2-151329)

In 1957, Khrushchev tested the capacity of the Soviet economic administration to reform and
launched the Sovnarkhoz reform. The reform was welcomed in Ukraine, as in other republics. In the
photo, Khrushchev is in the company of Ukrainian leaders. Left to right: sitting—Olha Ivashchenko,
Demian Korotchenko, CPU First Secretary Oleksii Kyrychenko, Nikita Khrushchev, Mykola
Pidhorny, Nykyfor Kalchenko; standing—Volodymyr Shcherbytsky (6th).

## Limitations from Above

From above, the authority of the Ukrainian leadership was limited by the double
subordination of the Ukrainian Gosplan. In 1957, the Ukrainian Gosplan was formally subordinated to the Ukrainian government, but in spring 1958, it was just
as formally appointed as the sole representative of the USSR Gosplan in Ukraine.
The structure of the Ukrainian Gosplan mimicked the structure of the USSR
Gosplan, which remained organized along branch lines. Supplies continued to be
distributed along branch lines as well. The branch organization of the USSR and
Ukrainian Gosplans was at odds with the territorial administration of production, an inconsistency which the Ukrainian sovnarkhozy did not hesitate to
emphasize, but which the Ukrainian leadership could not address.

The persistent lack of clarity in the functions of the all-union and republican
supply agencies, poor communication between the central and republican planners, and violations of existing formal procedures by the central apparatus would

continue to frustrate Kyiv. From the early days of the reform, central planners aimed to minimize the formalization of the economic relationship. In violation of the existing procedures, they neglected to inform Ukrainian planners about detailed plans for inter-republican deliveries or ad hoc delivery orders. They often communicated changes to the delivery orders directly to the sovnarkhozy, and even to enterprises, much to the chagrin of the Ukrainian planners. Often uninformed of such changes, the Ukrainian Gosplan was in no position to monitor deliveries, or join the sovnarkhozy in protesting against the uncoordinated disruptions to the plan programme.[35]

More importantly, contrary to its pre-reform expectations, the Ukrainian leadership did not become the main holder of financial and material resources allocated to Ukrainian industry, which accounted for almost half of Ukraine's national income: 48.7 percent in 1956 and 49.8 percent in 1963. Nor was it the main repository of information on Ukraine's economy.[36] (Resources for agriculture, as well as the output of the agricultural sector, were not affected by the reform and remained centrally controlled.[37])

The USSR Gosplan retained control over all types of raw materials and equipment, inter-republican deliveries, and the production classified as 'the most important'. For Ukraine, this meant that from the start of the reform, almost 50 percent of its industrial output remained under the management of the USSR Gosplan, despite the formal function of the Ukrainian Gosplan to draft plans and distribute resources for almost all Ukrainian economic actors. Consequently, these producers maintained direct relations with the Moscow apparatus. In 1958, the 'USSR Gosplan expanded the list of centrally distributed nomenclature to include products that were originally on the Ukrainian Gosplan's list. In 1959, when the USSR Gosplan began recentralization, more than 80 percent of domestic production was to some extent dependent on the USSR Gosplan or its glavsnabsbyty.'[38]

### Limitations from Below

At the same time, the authority of the Ukrainian leadership was limited from below by the newly empowered economic regions. Of the 96.2 percent of industrial production that had been placed under republican control in 1957, only 22.9 percent was placed under the direct control of the Ukrainian ministries, whereas 73.3 percent was administered by the sovnarkhozy. The share of industry under the control of the sovnarkhozy would increase every year, reaching 86.6 percent in 1965.[39] Formally, the republican leadership could not communicate directly with enterprises under the jurisdiction of the sovnarkhozy. Branch departments of the Ukrainian Gosplan could only recommend that the sovnarkhozy produce certain goods; they had no mechanisms in place to force the sovnarkhozy to share their resources with other economic regions. The sovnarkhozy had the right to refuse the republican planners' production requests, and they could refuse to share their resources with others. Likewise, the Ukrainian leadership could not control the distribution of supplies to the periphery enterprises. In 1957, the Ukrainian leadership placed the Ukrainian network of supply offices and warehouses under the control of the Ukrainian Gosplan. However, in July 1958, the central leadership transferred to the sovnarkhozy the network of periphery supply offices and warehouses that serviced industries administered by the sovnarkhozy. The Ukrainian Gosplan 'retained control over the supply offices for non-ferrous metallurgy, salvage metal, automobiles and tractors, bearings, wood and paper, oil, equipment, and military production', the latter being tightly supervised by Moscow.[40]

Access to information was another problematic area for the Ukrainian leadership. Only in 1960 did the central leadership place the Ukrainian Statistical Agency under the double jurisdiction of the Central Statistical Agency and the Ukrainian government. At the beginning of the reform, Ukrainian planners had to rely on central planners and the sovnarkhozy to provide the information necessary to compile the plan drafts, and both were often unwilling to share it with Kyiv.[41]

*Mestnichestvo*

By mid-1958, control over production and resources was mainly shared between the central apparatus in Moscow and the sovnarkhozy. At the same time, while the central apparatus controlled 'orders', 'plan targets', and the funds, the sovnarkhozy controlled the actual production. As a result, they acquired a lot of leverage over the all-union and the republican authorities. In summer 1957, the sovnarkhozy and the regional party–industry alliances more broadly found themselves in a favourable position to prioritize their own economic needs over the needs of others as defined by the planners. This dynamic was particularly strong in large and complex economic regions such as Donetsk, Dnipropetrovsk, Kharkiv, Kyiv, and Odesa.

Able to manoeuvre all resources and production capacities that had previously been dispersed between various ministries, the sovnarkhozy could increase local consumption and profits by optimizing production and producing surplus amounts of the necessary inputs, by rechannelling investment funds into industries that the regional authorities sought to boost, and by using the available resources for barter exchange, sometimes semi-formal, with other regions. The sovnarkhozy could build small workshops to provide the necessary inputs or finished products. The loopholes in the pricing system offered further possibilities to hoard the necessary products or obtain above-plan profits. The sovnarkhozy would often satisfy local demand by blatantly ignoring orders to deliver outside of their regions. This practice, by far the most irritating to the higher authorities, was a prime example of localism.[42]

Accumulated funds and resources could be spent on the formal and informal needs of the regions and their authorities.[43] The degree of economic comfort experienced by the industrial regions was well expressed by Nikolai Tikhonov (the chairman of the Dnipropetrovsk sovnarkhoz and former USSR Deputy Minister of Ferrous Metallurgy, 1955–1957) at a Ukrainian Central Committee meeting on 4 July 1958. He said that if the Ukrainian government did not have the funds to finance the water supply in Kryvyi Rih, it could take them from his sovnarkhoz.[44]

Yet, it was the Ukrainian leadership that was responsible for ensuring the sovnarkhozy fulfilled their inter-republican supply obligations and the republic fulfilled its production and investment plans. Consequently, the Ukrainian leadership fought against localism by any means available. In July 1958, based on the results of the May 1958 audits that the centre commissioned of the Dnipropetrovsk, Stalino, Luhansk, and Lviv sovnarkhozy, the Ukrainian Central Committee reprimanded the chairmen of these sovnarkhozy: Nikolai Tikhonov, Ivan Dyadyk, Anton Kuzmich and Ivan Ivonin respectively. The reprimands were issued for the arbitrary reduction of capital investments in ferrous metallurgy, coal, chemical, and other industries, and for channelling almost 118 million roubles into the 'development of secondary branches' and 52 million roubles into 'other branches'. The sovnarkhozy were instructed to return the funds to the branches to which they had been originally allocated, and warned of harsher measures in case of repeated violations.[45]

The sovnarkhozy had no fear of 'harsher' measures. Already in November 1958, Dyadyk, the chairman of the Stalino oblast-sovnarkhoz, violated the delivery orders for supplies outside the Stalino region and even legitimized these violations by issuing a resolution that instructed local producers to prioritize local customers. The scandal reached the office of the chairman of the Ukrainian Gosplan, Petro Rozenko. However, not only had Dyadyk failed to take 'the necessary measures' to correct this violation, but 'on 16 March 1959 [he] issued a similar resolution'. Knowing where Dyadyk's power lay, the Ukrainian Gosplan functionaries asserted that such violations would not have been possible had the supply network remained under the control of the Ukrainian Gosplan, as they had insisted in spring 1958.[46] Ironically, prior to the Sovnarkhoz reform in 1957, Dyadyk occupied the post of the second secretary of the Stalino obkom. In fact, Dyadyk was the only Ukrainian sovnarkhoz chairman appointed from the party apparatus. The other ten chairmen came from the all-union or republican ministerial apparatus.[47]

As the Ukrainian leadership reprimanded the sovnarkhozy for localism, it could not have been unaware that localism reflected their understanding that the reform was designed to improve local economies. The sovnarkhozy indicated this in the 1958 plan drafts that they submitted to the Ukrainian Gosplan in summer 1957. At the time, Ukrainian planners had dismissed the targets proposed by the regions as they did not reflect all-Ukrainian needs. Instead, they drafted the plan for Ukraine without input from the regions, thus causing the first major conflict between Kyiv and the regions, while demonstrating the Ukrainian leadership's tendency to mimic Moscow's *diktat*.[48]

Similarly, Kyiv could not have been unaware that localism was the regions' reaction to the difficulties related to plan fulfilment or to local socio-economic problems. For example, in the case of the above-mentioned diversion of investments to 'secondary branches', Dyadyk withdrew 24.4 million roubles of investments from the coal industry. However, he channelled these funds to build housing, a kindergarten, and other social projects in 1958. The coal industry had a chronic shortage of labour. In April 1955, the Ukrainian Central Committee had to ask the Central Committee for permission to draft 15,000 young people for permanent work in the coal mines of Donbas.[49] In 1958, in light of the regular annual increases of coal production targets and the estimated coal production target for the forthcoming seven-year plan (1959–1965), which was deemed 'above realistic possibilities', the Stalino sovnarkhoz needed 30,000 workers. Without providing housing for the labour force, fulfilling production plans would be 'very difficult', argued Dyadyk. The Lviv sovnarkhoz used 39.6 million roubles of the coal money to provide the industry with construction materials. The sovnarkhozy of Kyiv, Vinnytsia, and Kharkiv diverted a share of investments originally allocated to the food industry into other branches to meet the output targets set for these branches.[50]

The Ukrainian leadership must also have known that random audits and reprimands would not help it gain authority with the regions. As the chairmen of the Ukrainian sovnarkhozy explained at the Ukrainian Central Committee meeting on 4 July 1958, such audits only undermined the relationship between the republican authorities and the sovnarkhozy. The latter needed correlated plans, flexibility in managing funds, and assistance from the Ukrainian Gosplan. Instead, as Tikhonov explained, the Ukrainian Gosplan was assigning plan targets 'that were impossible to fulfil', while it was unable to solve problematic supply issues without involving the USSR Gosplan.[51]

Hence, in 1958–1959, along with tightening control over the sovnarkhozy, the Ukrainian leadership continued to insist in Moscow that its decision-making authority should be expanded and aligned with its responsibilities. It could not fight localism effectively without increased control over material and financial resources, without clearly defined boundaries between the functions of the republican and central apparatus, and without the central apparatus respecting existing formal procedures. Furthermore, it was difficult for the Ukrainian Gosplan to enforce deliveries or report on their fulfilment if Moscow did not communicate the relevant information. 'We do not have a plan for inter-republican deliveries, and we never had it. Yet, the responsibility [for the fulfilment of the plan] lies with the republic',[52] lamented Ukrainian planners at the end of December 1959.

While the Ukrainian leadership argued in favour of further devolution of economic decision-making authority and handing control over resources to the republics, the central leadership had quietly turned towards re-establishing fully centralized control over the economy. In 1959, Khrushchev appointed Kosygin as the chairman of the USSR Gosplan. Kosygin was a true believer in a centralized ministerial system that, he believed, had allowed the Soviet Union to win the war. With the arrival of Kosygin at the USSR Gosplan, the Sovnarkhoz reform began to reverse course.[53] In 1960, the central leadership initiated a new organizational reshuffle and regrouped seventy-eight sovnarkhozy into thirteen large new economic regions. The three largest republics, Russia, Kazakhstan, and Ukraine, were instructed to organize republican sovnarkhozy to coordinate the work of their regional sovnarkhozy.

## Ukraine Delays Recentralization

For all the limitations on its power, in 1960 the Ukrainian leadership was strong enough to successfully delay the implementation of the recentralization in the republic. Until 1963, the Ukrainian Central Committee and the Ukrainian government were at the peak of their executive authority. The republican leadership did not have financial or material resources at its disposal in the same volumes as the central agencies or the regions, so it had limited economic authority. However, it had accumulated sufficient administrative authority, and that was valued by the regions.

Thus, the Ukrainian leadership had a strong hold on the nomenklatura. It could issue reprimands or hold a state or party official personally responsible for any failures. It could also shield any official from responsibility for an economic failure by issuing a vague directive 'to improve measures'.[54]

Although the central leadership abandoned the idea of planning 'from below', the plans were not dictated to the republics, as in the 1940s, either. Ukraine's objections and requests were not always met in Moscow, but its opinion was not completely dismissed.[55] To obtain favourable plans, the regions had to convince the Ukrainian leadership to accept their plan targets or include their project in the republican plan first.

The central government resolution from 29 December 1958 authorized the sovnarkhozy, oblispolkoms, the Ukrainian Gosplan, and any other authority to make changes to the quarterly plans of an enterprise within forty-five days of the end of the quarter.[56] Hence, the Ukrainian Gosplan could increase a production target, but it could also decrease it, thus allowing a sovnarkhoz to sell the surplus production to the state at a higher price and receive bonuses for over-fulfilling the plan.[57] The sovnarkhozy also relied on the Ukrainian Gosplan not to act on procedural violations.[58] Of course, the republican authorities did not always diligently seek to enforce state discipline, particularly when Moscow allowed the republic to keep a share of the surplus production. For example, the combination of the 29 December 1958 and 10 December 1959 resolutions that allowed the UkSSR to use 50 percent of rolled steel produced above plan for the needs of the republic motivated the Ukrainian Gosplan to overlook any procedural violations by sovnarkhozy that produced rolled steel.[59]

The sovnarkhozy, oblispolkoms, and the remaining ministries addressed their requests to the Ukrainian leadership. The Ukrainian leadership decided whether to provide assistance or to refuse.[60] If the Ukrainian leadership considered it necessary to assist but could not, it sent a request to the relevant all-union organs. Chances were high that an issue would be solved in Ukraine's favour. For example, in 1962, the Ukrainian leadership submitted a total of 2,690 letters and reports to the Central Committee, central government, USSR Gosplan, and all-union ministries and administrations: 170 documents co-signed by the CPU first secretary and the chairman of the Ukrainian government, and 2,520 documents signed by vice-chairmen of the Ukrainian government. Of those documents, 954 letters and reports concerned industry and construction and 576 concerned material funds. By 1 January 1963, the central agencies had made decisions on 2,334 documents, of which 90.8 percent, or 2,117 letters and reports were 'resolved positively' and 9.2 percent were either dismissed or 'resolved not positively'.[61] Throughout the period, the central leadership and apparatus were willing to satisfy the requests of the Ukrainian leadership for additional resources on an ad hoc basis, particularly when the requests coincided with Moscow's branch priorities, which motivated the Ukrainian leadership to focus on Moscow's priorities.[62]

Moscow controlled who would produce what and where. Nonetheless, in 1961, the Ukrainian Central Committee was widely viewed as the only administration that 'could solve a problem' in Ukraine.[63] In a system that was averse to formalizing responsibility and in which accountability was heavily reliant on informal relationships, this was arguably the highest praise the Ukrainian leadership could receive from the regions.

The Ukrainian leadership's administrative powers were insufficient to claim authoritarian control over the regions.[64] However, they were sufficiently vast for the Ukrainian leadership to forge a close relationship with the regions and use this relationship to defend its own power and regional interests when Moscow started recentralization.

Thus, in 1960, despite the general trend towards merging economic regions across the Soviet Union, the Ukrainian Central Committee succeeded in convincing Moscow to increase the number of sovnarkhozy to fourteen at the regions' request. In 1963, the Ukrainian leadership had another administrative victory as the centre continued to merge economic regions: Ukraine's regions were reduced only by half (from fourteen to seven), whereas the number of sovnarkhozy in Russia was reduced from seventy to twenty-four and the entire country retained only forty-seven economic regions by 1963.[65]

More illustratively, the Ukrainian leadership successfully prevented the newly created Ukrsovnarkhoz from asserting its power in the Ukrainian administrative system. From the moment Ukrsovnarkhoz was formed in August 1960, the regions and the Ukrainian leadership viewed it as a superfluous agency. The Ukrainian leadership resented another economic administration that was created without its input and tasked by Moscow with taking over the administrative functions of the Ukrainian Gosplan, an organization that had defended Ukraine's interests in Moscow. Sovnarkhozy, too, in their majority resented and ignored the new administration, which imposed its authority but could not bring resources or solve problems. As a result, until 1963, Ukrsovnarkhoz remained marginalized. In 1963, when Kyiv had to mimic Moscow's reorganization and elevate the role of Ukrsovnarkhoz, Ukrainian Gosplan Chairman Petro Rozenko and his staff left Ukrainian Gosplan to work at Ukrsovnarkhoz.[66]

Recentralization

At the 19–23 November 1962 plenum of the Central Committee, Khrushchev insisted the economy's technological advancement should be promoted through centralized branch vertical administration. He thus publicly signalled that he supported recentralizing branch development administration, even if he still adhered to the principle of territorial administration of production and still believed that managerial decision making should be decentralized. At the central Presidium meeting on 12 October 1962, Khrushchev even criticized the USSR Gosplan for inefficient planning and for ignoring the ideas proposed by the republics.[67]

Khrushchev's October–November pronouncements were old news for the central apparatus. Disregarding the tacit recentralization launched with Kosygin's appointment to the USSR Gosplan in 1959, Khrushchev expressed his support for recentralization in July 1962. Then, the central leadership issued a resolution, 'On further improvement of the apparatus for administration and specialization in machine building, construction, and other branches of the economy', which increased centralized control over the named branches. At the central Presidium meeting on 26 July, Khrushchev emphasized that branch development must not be stopped by 'national frontiers'. At the 29 November Presidium meeting after the plenum, he explained that the planners were no longer required to prioritize the complex development of republics or large economic regions. He now expected complex centralized development of industrial branches to counteract the danger that 'every republic would act as it pleases'.[68]

Still, Khrushchev insisted that the recentralization was partial. The operational economic rights of the sovnarkhozy, enterprises, and the republics should even be enhanced. 'Of course, one should consider localism and *rvachestvo* [grabbing/ snatching] by the republics; however, still, comrades, the republics define, direct, and provide [*opredeliaiut, napravliaiut i obespechivaiut*]'. This is why the USSR

Gosplan should include a small apparatus only to combine and correlate the republican plans with 'our needs, our possibilities, and correct distribution [of resources] between the territories'.[69]

The day after the November 1962 plenum, the central leadership created the USSR Sovnarkhoz and put it in charge of current planning. The USSR Gosplan was instructed to focus on perspective planning. The 'very centralized, union-republican' USSR State Construction Committee regained control over construction. State branch committees continued to replace ministries for the most important branches, such as the aircraft industry and radio electronics, reaching thirty in number after the plenum. The state branch committees were tasked with restoring centralized control over research and technological advancement for the branches, enabling some of them to claim control over enterprises.[70]

In Ukraine, in line with Khrushchev's insistence that republican rights be expanded, the recently empowered Ukrsovnarkhoz and its glavsnabsbyty, which together replaced the Ukrainian Gosplan as the main planning agency, increased the portfolio of products they managed. However, the portfolio expanded primarily to include products previously managed directly by the sovnarkhozy, not the USSR Gosplan. Ukrsovnarkhoz took over the management of exports, special deliveries, and material and technical supply for the most important construction sites. The branch departments of the Ukrsovnarkhoz might have been particularly hopeful of expanding their authority because they had already taken on some of the administrative functions previously performed by the all-union supply offices. The Ukrainian main administration for metal supplies and sales, for example, placed production orders for cast iron, ferroalloys, and coke-chemical with the Ukrainian metallurgical mills. But Ukrsovnarkhoz still did not issue delivery orders.[71] In other words, it could issue production instructions but not control how the product would be distributed. Starting on 8 February 1963, the central government allowed republican governments to increase the expenses of the sovnarkhozy, ministries, and administrations for capital renovations of main production funds. The increased expenditure could be paid for with the funds from the depreciation deductions that had been allocated for the full restoration of capital funds.[72]

With all of Khrushchev's efforts to strike a balance between centralized planning and decentralized management of production, the prevailing dynamic was nonetheless recentralized control over resources. In Ukraine, the republican leadership was losing control over resources much faster than the regions. According to the new regulations on the sovnarkhozy, finished by a USSR commission led by Kosygin at the beginning of 1963, the sovnarkhozy were no longer under the sole jurisdiction of the republican governments. In a significant departure from the 1957 system, the sovnarkhozy were placed under the double jurisdiction of the republican governments and the USSR Sovnarkhoz. The sovnarkhozy were now obligated to implement the instructions issued by the

USSR Sovnarkhoz on all aspects of production management. The sovnarkhozy were not, however, obliged to act through their republic-level authorities on issues related to the development of new technology, and they had to communicate directly with the state branch committees. At the same time, the central leadership began transferring local industry that had traditionally been run by local soviets to the sovnarkhozy.

In January 1963, the USSR Sovnarkhoz 'reduced the list of centrally planned products that were negotiated between the centre and the republics and increased the list of products managed by [the all-union supply agencies] and branch committees'. The republics were requested to submit more detailed information on the distribution of resources.[73] In April, the status of Ukrsovnarkhoz, the Ukrainian Gosplan, and several other republican organizations changed from republican to union-republican. They were no longer subordinated solely to the Ukrainian government. They were now subordinated to the Ukrainian government and the respective central agencies in Moscow.[74]

### Kyiv Aligns with the Regions

The new organizational framework provided the central leadership with increased control over resources, but the rearrangement of economic administration did not improve the supply system. The sovnarkhozy continued to break delivery contracts, conceal resources, accumulate above-norm stocks, and commit other violations characterized as localism.[75] To enforce the delivery contracts, the central apparatus had little choice but to rely on the Ukrainian leadership that was still officially in charge of almost the entire Ukrainian economy. However, the economic power of the Ukrainian leadership and thus its influence on the sovnarkhozy remained limited. The central apparatus continued to 'bar republican supply organs from defining production targets, [even though] it was the responsibility of the republics to ensure inter-republican supplies'. Reallocation of investments from one industry to another could be done only with Moscow's permission. In September 1963, the 1961 central resolution that required all-union organs to involve the republican organs while assigning production targets for inter-republican deliveries and manage the targets only for the main types of products remained to be implemented.[76] Formalizing the Ukrainian leadership's functions could increase its standing with the regions. However, the central apparatus preferred the flexibility of managing its relations with the republics without being bound by formal rules.

The Ukrainian leadership's financial possibilities remained modest. It could not invest independently from Moscow even when it managed to accumulate some funds.[77] The Ukrainian leadership had limited possibilities to provide financial assistance to those in need. Finances of the republic and the sovnarkhozy remained strictly centralized throughout the period, with the Ukrainian Ministry of Finance, which took orders from its all-union counterpart, guarding the books.[78] The hopes for a fixed 5–7 percent reserve fund, let alone a 3 percent reserve fund, had completely evaporated. Moreover, the USSR Ministry of Finance refused to set aside a fixed percentage of the budget for the reserve fund, instead confirming it each year at the same time as the republic's budget. In 1958, Ukraine's reserve fund constituted 1.96 percent of its budget.[79] In 1963, it constituted 1.88 percent.[80] In 1962, it constituted 1.87 percent, or 143,057 roubles. To put this number in perspective, the budget of the Kharkiv sovnarkhoz for 1962 was 116,333 roubles, the budget of the Dnipropetrovsk sovnarkhoz was 341,194.5 roubles, and that of the Donetsk sovnarkhoz was 502,774 roubles.[81] Furthermore, contrary to the Ukrainian leadership, the sovnarkhozy could create additional funds to provide financial help to organizations and administrations within their economic regions and bonus funds using 'no more than 0.05 percent of the entire wage fund of the enterprises [under its jurisdiction]'. No such funds existed at the disposal of the Ukrainian government. At the beginning of 1964, Ukrsovnarkhoz asked the central government for permission to create parallel republican funds, echoing Rakovsky's 1923 suggestion to the gubkoms to support the Ukrainian government financially. The republican funds would be filled by taking a percentage of the parallel funds formed by the sovnarkhozy: 25 percent of each sovnarkhoz fund for assisting enterprises would go into the republican fund for the same purpose and 15 percent of each sovnarkhoz bonus fund would go into the republican bonus fund.[82]

With recentralization in progress, the best way for the Ukrainian leadership to retain its authority as an indispensable middle-level administration was to position itself as 'the agent of the regions' and defend the interests of the sovnarkhozy, which, as a group, were institutionally stronger than the Ukrainian leadership (more on this in the second part of this chapter).[83]

In 1960, along with shielding the sovnarkhozy from excessive oversight from Ukrsovnarkhoz, the Ukrainian leadership defended the sovnarkhozy's choice not to deliver products outside the republic or their regions. It argued that classifying all inter-republican deliveries as most important was not always economically justified. Deliveries inside an economic region or the republic could be just as important.[84]

At the end of October 1962, acting on Khrushchev's public support for increasing the economic rights of the sovnarkhozy and enterprises, the Ukrainian leadership drafted a proposal. By now it was no longer asking to enlarge the rights of the sovnarkhozy, but to restore the rights that had been granted to them in September 1957. These rights, such as the right to redistribute funds between industry branches or between construction sites, had been increasingly withheld as the reform progressed.[85]

Due to the prioritization of heavy and defence industry, the Ukrainian leadership focused on the needs of the south-eastern industrialized oblasts. Numerous requests to allocate or ensure the delivery of goods to producers in these oblasts contributed to, but did not fully account for, the fact that from 1959 to 1962 state investments in Ukraine exceeded the control number by 700 million roubles for a total of 12.8 billion roubles. By 1964, 18.6 billion roubles were invested in Ukraine's industry.[86] More than 50 percent of capital investments in Ukrainian industry was allocated to heavy industry 'geographically connected to the Donbas [oblasts of Stalino/Donetsk and Voroshylovhrad/Luhansk] and Prydniprovsk [oblasts of Dnipropetrovsk and Zaporizhzhia], whereas machine-construction, chemical, and light industries developed slowly in Ukraine.'[87]

Tellingly, in June 1963, the Ukrainian government put the responsibility for the Ukrainian sovnarkhozy's non-deliveries (which had been revealed in an audit) on the USSR Sovnarkhoz and the All-Union Administration of Metallurgical Production, deviating from traditional explanations such as its own 'lack of control' or the 'wilful decision of a sovnarkhoz to retain resources in its region'. Specifically, Kyiv explained, the USSR Sovnarkhoz had reduced republican funds rather than making up for a shortage of inputs as the republic had requested. Hence, Ukraine could not fulfil its delivery plan.[88]

Pointing to shortcomings in the work of central planners who systematically failed to correlate production plans with supply plans was not new. Since 1954, the Ukrainian leadership had argued that it was best positioned to determine the needs of Ukrainian producers and manage the funds.

What was new was the Ukrainian leadership's insistence on holding the central apparatus responsible for the malfunctioning of the supply system. Granted, the Ukrainian leadership did not make excuses for the Ukrainian producers, sovnarkhozy, or obkoms when the violations were indeed wilful, and it issued reprimands or stern warnings when necessary.[89] However, if the sovnarkhozy did not deliver because the central planners did not provide the necessary inputs, whether in terms of quantity, quality, or timing, the non-delivery was the responsibility of the central apparatus, not the sovnarkhozy. Similarly, the sovnarkhozy could not always be held accountable for concealing material resources or accumulating production stocks above the plan norms. Often, the sovnarkhozy had to hoard the inputs or the output because the all-union supply agencies failed to issue delivery orders on time or for the total output. The Ukrainian leadership argued that frequent and random changes of production targets after the plan was approved, modifications in construction projects that required cancellation of previous orders, and deliveries ahead of schedule were among the causes of a poorly functioning supply system. Moscow could not hold the sovnarkhozy solely responsible for problems with deliveries. In 1964, the Ukrainian government openly stated that hoarding products was often the fault of the all-union planning organizations, which should be held responsible for forcing the sovnarkhozy to accumulate resources. Output targets and bonuses for exceeding plan targets remained among the traditional reasons for hoarding. On 24 April 1965, Ukrsovnarkhoz requested the Ukrainian government to ask the central government to allow the sovnarkhozy to redistribute funds allocated for capital renovations among enterprises and organizations.[90]

Return to Moscow as a Source of Power

As long as the central leadership adhered to the territorial principle in economic administration, the Ukrainian leadership could reasonably expect that it might still increase its authority by aligning with the regions that controlled production, as well as by defending those regions' interests in Moscow. However, in summer 1965, CPU First Secretary Petro Shelest learned that the General Secretary of the Communist Party Leonid Brezhnev and Kosygin, the chairman of the central government, had decided to fully restore centralized branch administration.[91] Fearful that Kyiv might lose the authority it had accumulated since 1954, the Ukrainian leadership distanced itself from the sovnarkhozy.

Thus, when reporting on measures taken to realize above-norm stock of equipment and materials in September 1965, the Ukrainian leadership repeated its conclusion that the main causes for hoarding resources did not lie with the producers and illustrated how the republican government reduced excess stock. However, this time, the tone of the report was less confrontational.[92] At the 21 September 1965 meeting of the Ukrainian government, when Oleh Soich, the chairman of the Kharkiv sovnarkhoz, insisted that the sovnarkhoz producers lacked inputs to meet production targets, Ivan Kazanets, chairman of the Ukrainian government, instructed him to pay more attention to 'the organizational work'. A similar instruction was given to other chairmen of the sovnarkhozy.[93] Earlier that month, the Ukrainian leadership informed the chairmen of the Donetsk and the Prydniprovsk sovnarkhozy, Mykola Khudosovtsev and Leonid Lukich, respectively, along with the vice-chairman of the Kyiv sovnarkhoz, Vasyl Stepanchenko, that it was holding them personally responsible for fulfilling state orders for agricultural machinery, equipment, and spare parts for agricultural machinery by enterprises of their sovnarkhozy. They would also be held responsible for investigating the reasons behind any failed deliveries.[94]

The change in rhetoric did not mean that the republican leadership gave up on insisting that Moscow expand its economic rights or requesting additional inputs and capital investments. This change only meant that after a brief period of flirting with the idea of building power 'from below' and trying to consolidate its authority by aligning with the regions, the Ukrainian leadership returned to viewing Moscow as the sole source of its power.

## Part II: The Sovnarkhoz Reform and the Regions

Compared to the republican leadership, the effect of the Sovnarkhoz reform on the regions was more profound and longer lasting. Having empowered the regions economically, Khrushchev provided an institutional foundation for regional party–industry alliances. After the abolition of the sovnarkhoz system, these alliances would serve the 'regional and functional cleavages...characteristic of the Soviet political system under Brezhnev'.[95]

The factors behind party–industry alliances were several. On the one hand, the Sovnarkhoz reform did not release local party and soviet authorities from responsibility for plan fulfilment, implementation of central directives and instructions in their territories, or their territory's socio-economic situation—or, as Khrushchev liked to repeat throughout the entire period, for providing 'concrete results'. Moreover, as Andrei Markevich and Ekaterina Zhuravskaia argued, the sovnarkhoz system connected each region's industrial performance to the career advancement of its leaders.[96]

On the other hand, the reform provided for the rise of *khoziaistvenniki*, or managers, in the periphery.[97] The sovnarkhozy now controlled production, resources, and information on industry, but they no longer had to fulfil the plan at all costs. As mentioned earlier, the reform allowed a number of agencies to modify plans, including the sovnarkhozy and republican Gosplans. Fulfilment 'at all costs' was now often replaced by negotiating a new target, as opposed to mobilizing all available labour and material resources.

Whatever expectation Khrushchev might have had for the obkoms controlling or supervising the managers during the Sovnarkhoz reform, the dominance of the economic over the ideological agenda rendered it counter-intuitive for the obkoms to fulfil the 'party duty' and fight against localism. The sovnarkhozy increasingly controlled access to resources. The obkoms continued to struggle with traditional problems plaguing their areas of responsibility, such as chronic scarcity and insecurity of supplies or insufficient funding for urban infrastructure, housing, or agriculture.[98] Compared to the pre-sovnarkhoz period, the obkoms were more incentivized to ensure their oblasts performed well economically, and they had more opportunities to address their formal, informal, and personal agendas.[99] Under these circumstances, alliance and cooperation constituted a more appropriate type of relationship between the obkoms and the sovnarkhozy.[100] The pre-1957 regional alliances between the party apparatus and the enterprise managers grew into regional alliances between the obkoms/gorkoms and the sovnarkhozy. The obkoms cultivated 'a very close "family" relationship with those on whom they [were] to check'.[101]

## No Party Control over Managers

In Ukraine, from the start, the reform precluded party control over managers. Firstly, the new regionalization grouped twenty-six oblasts into eleven economic regions (see Map 3). Not every obkom was in a position to supervise the sovnarkhoz that administered its oblast's industry and construction.[102] There were only five economic regions in Ukraine that comprised a single oblast: Stalino, Dnipropetrovsk, Voroshylovhrad, Zaporizhzhia, and Odesa. The remaining six economic regions—Kharkiv, Kherson, Kyiv, Lviv, Stanislav, and Vinnytsia—included two or more oblasts. For logistical reasons, only the obkoms of the oblasts that physically hosted the sovnarkhozy could supervise them.[103] More importantly, regardless of the geographic proximity of the obkom to its sovnarkhoz, the obkoms had no interest in supervising either the sovnarkhozy or the managers of enterprises on their territories. As elsewhere in the Soviet Union, the obkoms and oblispolkoms relied on industry to assist with housing, urban infrastructure, agricultural equipment, spare parts for agricultural machinery, and generally with the fulfilment of agricultural plans.[104]

When the Ukrainian Central Committee gathered on 20 February 1957 to discuss the new economic regions that would be created during the reform, the obkom secretaries hinted that their main concern would not be controlling and supervising managers. In response to CPU First Secretary Kyrychenko's question 'How will the obkoms influence the sovnarkhozy?' Kazanets, first secretary of the Stalino obkom, reassured him that 'the influence of the party organization would be the same as before'.[105] But 'the same as before' was not good enough. Just two days earlier, on 18 February, Oleksandr Burmistrov, the Ukrainian Central Committee secretary for heavy industry, had reported to Kyrychenko that the obkoms of the Dnipropetrovsk, Stalino, Zaporizhzhia, and Voroshylovhrad oblasts (four out of the five oblasts that would form oblast-sovnarkhozy) concerned themselves very little with ferrous metallurgy and were less demanding of enterprises.[106] The entire purpose of the reform was to ensure that the party finally brought managers under its control, so, Kyrychenko insisted, the obkoms would have to boost supervision of the sovnarkhozy, particularly where one oblast formed one economic region. Furthermore, organizational work did matter, he argued. The coal industry of the Stalino and Voroshylovhrad oblasts had the same production problems, but the Voroshylovhrad obkom worked better and the oblast fulfilled the plan. The Stalino oblast, on the other hand, did not fulfil the coal production plan 'because the buro of the obkom…[did] not visit the mines, [did] not work with people', Kyrychenko concluded. Similarly, the main reason for the 'bad situation with metal' in the oblasts of Zaporizhzhia, Dnipropetrovsk, Donetsk, and Voroshylovhrad was 'poor organization' of the party work at industrial enterprises.[107]

No obkom secretary openly contradicted Kyrychenko regarding the role of the party in economic administration. However, the exchange of remarks between Volodymyr Shcherbytsky, first obkom secretary of the Dnipropetrovsk oblast, and Anton Haiovy, first obkom secretary of the smaller, neighbouring Zaporizhzhia oblast, indicated that the obkoms were primarily concerned with access to resources.

Haiovy was inclined to merge Dnipropetrovsk and Zaporizhzhia into one eco-nomic region, but Shcherbytsky objected. Had the sovnarkhoz been limited in its activity to industry alone, the two obkoms 'would not argue'. The Ukrainian Ministry of Metallurgical Industry, which was based in Dnipropetrovsk, had mainly concentrated on these two metallurgical oblasts. However, merging the oblasts in the context of the Sovnarkhoz reform, explained Shcherbytsky, meant coordinating agricultural activity as well: 'If [we] unite the production of grain in Zaporizhzhia and Dnipropetrovsk, this is 4 million hectares of land. That will be difficult [for one sovnarkhoz to manage].'[108] To Shcherbytsky, as to Haiovy, the obkom and the sovnarkhoz were to jointly run the entire oblast economy, indus-try, social infrastructure, and agriculture, as one complex.

Hence, no meaningful control on the part of the obkoms over the sovnarkhozy followed. Nor, after the reform started, was such control expected by the Ukrainian leadership or the Ukrainian Central Committee secretaries. On 4 July 1958, the Ukrainian Central Committee met with the sovnarkhoz chairmen. When replying to the chairmen's complaints that they had been audited 'too much', Ukrainian Central Committee secretary Leontii Naidek disappointed them by promising 'on the contrary, to increase control by the republican and other organizations'. However, obkoms were not singled out as the main control-lers. The Ukrainian Central Committee intended to control the sovnarkhozy directly from Kyiv, not through the obkoms. As an indication of such intent, the obkom secretaries had not been invited to the 4 July meeting, which had been called on the initiative of the sovnarkhoz chairmen to discuss 'the thorny issues' in economic administration.[109]

At the Twenty-First (Extraordinary) Party Congress (27 January–5 February 1959), Khrushchev, who had also been the chairman of the central government since March 1958, did not insist on party control over industry and downplayed the involvement of territorial party committees in economic administration, although he still did not release them from responsibility for their regions' economic performance.[110] He now aimed to reassert centralized control over the economy directly from Moscow, not through Kyiv. After the November 1962 Central Committee plenum, Khrushchev urged the party apparatus to focus on the political and organizational leadership of the masses, rather than economic administration.[111]

## Obkoms and Sovnarkhozy Working Together

In the meantime, the interests of the obkoms and the sovnarkhozy had aligned. Since 1957, the obkoms and sovnarkhozy had worked separately and together to attract and retain as many resources as possible in their regions. For example, in October 1958, first secretary of the Drohobych obkom, Volodymyr Druzhynin (echoing the gubkom secretaries in the 1920s), suggested that the oblasts first satisfy local demand for their products, and only then supply to customers in other oblasts. He also suggested that the oblasts keep the above-plan production manufactured on their territories. The second secretary of the Chernivtsi obkom, Oleksii Hryhorenko, asked the Ukrainian leadership to enforce the fulfilment of deliveries. Around the same time, to facilitate the management of resources available in their region, the Lviv sovnarkhoz and obkom argued that all financial funds allocated to an economic region for 'social-cultural activities' should be allocated to the sovnarkhoz, 'without separating them between enterprises, organizations, or administrations'.[112]

By the summer of 1964, Ukrainian enterprises were hoarding 31 percent of the total production stock that was officially classified as 'unnecessary'.[113] These resources, accumulated or obtained from the higher authorities, were not always used to fulfil state tasks as defined by planners. Often, this stock was used for barter exchanges that were facilitated, if not organized, by the obkoms.

By 1965, the obkoms and managers had fully coalesced, and the regions grew sufficiently powerful to protect their resources. The integrity of regional alliances was laid bare at the 19 June 1965 plenum of the Ukrainian Central Committee. CPU First Secretary Shelest had just recently learned that the ministerial system would be restored. Worried about the negative effect that returning to branch administration would have on the authority of the Ukrainian leadership, Shelest demonstrated his resolve to impose state discipline on producers. So, he launched an attack on regional party–industry alliances and the obkoms in particular for their lack of control over managers.

'The plan for capital investments in light industry was only 86 percent fulfilled in the first five months of 1965', stated Shelest. Construction of light industry enterprises progressed particularly slowly in the Donetsk economic region, which fulfilled the plan by 42 percent, the Lviv economic region, by 70 percent, and the Podillia economic region, by 76 percent. 'Yet it is necessary to remind [you] that the Donetsk, Luhansk, and Lviv obkoms repeatedly asked, and continue to ask, the Ukrainian leadership to increase investment in light industry in their oblasts.' The Ukrainian leadership found additional funds for development of the light industry in these oblasts and the Ukrainian Gosplan made relevant changes in the plans. 'How should we understand you?' Shelest asked Volodymyr Dehtiariov, Volodymyr Shevchenko, and Vasyl Kutsevol, the secretaries of the Donetsk, Luhansk, and Lviv obkoms, respectively. 'You are asking for additional funds…but you do not demand that the managers who are responsible for construction of light industry facilities fulfil the plan.' When the Novo-Kakhovka factory failed to start producing electric engines for gas drainage machines to be used in coal mines, the Chornomorsky sovnarkhoz showed 'unacceptable indifference' and the Kherson obkom did not intervene either.[114]

The attitude of the regional authorities to the defence industry was no more conscientious, lamented Shelest.

The 25 December 1964 resolution of the Central Committee and the central government stated that fulfilling the production plan for the defence industry was a critically important task for the economic, soviet, and party organs.... However, because of the insufficient attention to this issue on the part of some obkoms and sovnarkhozy, enterprises of Ukraine did not fulfil plans for seventy-two titles of the military equipment in the last five months of this year. The Donetsk sovnarkhoz and the Donetsk obkom unsatisfactorily produce and control production of military equipment.

The two factories that were instructed to speedily produce 'very important components for special equipment not only failed to fulfil this assignment, but did not fulfil the main, planned, deliveries. Instead of holding the directors of these factories accountable, the Donetsk obkom and sovnarkhoz put one of these factories forward for the Red Challenge Banner award of the Council of Ministers of Ukraine.' Defence enterprises were not being constructed according to schedule in other oblasts either. 'After five months, thirty-six out of seventy-two defence enterprises did not fulfil the plan of capital investment', Shelest continued. How could the chairmen of the sovnarkhozy and the obkom secretaries 'explain such an attitude to the defence industry?'[115]

The relationship between the obkoms and sovnarkhozy was just as tight in central and western Ukraine. The decision to organize the production of refrigerators for meat and meat products was prepared and discussed with the sovnarkhozy of Kyiv, Ivano-Frankivsk, and Lviv, and with the obkom secretaries of the oblasts involved. However, the decision was never carried out. According to Shelest, 'the failure to fulfil this decision was due to irresponsibility on the part of the managers and absence of the necessary party control'.[116]

Shelest might have sounded authoritative in his criticism of the regions, but what he conveyed was the vulnerability and dependence of the Ukrainian leadership on the regions for the republic's fulfilment of plans. The criticism itself was an acknowledgment of the lack of mechanisms at the disposal of the Ukrainian leadership to enforce state discipline in economic affairs. All Shelest could realistically do was to insist, even ask, that they fulfil the state assignments for which the Ukrainian leadership was accountable in Moscow. At a certain point, Shelest blatantly admitted that he relied on the goodwill of the regions not to undermine the reputation of the Ukrainian leadership. In his comments on the obkoms' requests to include 'unrealistic' investment allocation targets in the next production plan, Shelest implored his audience 'to have the feeling of reality in these questions'. Acknowledging that the leadership could not satisfy all demands for investment allocation, Shelest noted that the obkoms should not make demands that would create the impression that the Gosplan, Council of Ministers, and Central Committee did not support the toiling masses. 'You cannot do that, comrades.'[117]

In their replies to Shelest, the regional authorities explained that the reason behind party–industry alliances in the periphery was the mutual responsibility for fulfilling plans, that the sovnarkhozy pursued localism for objective reasons, and that, indeed, the Ukrainian leadership had no leverage over them.

Khudosovtsev, the chairman of the Donetsk sovnarkhoz (which included the Donetsk and Luhansk oblasts), explained that the Donetsk sovnarkhoz and Donetsk and Luhansk obkoms fully agreed on all economic issues.[118]

Oleksii Titarenko, first secretary of the Zaporizhzhia obkom, agreed with Shelest in principle that the party should control the managers, but he could not follow it. In response to the criticism about the failure to launch electric furnaces, Titarenko explained: 'We cannot say that comrades from the sovnarkhoz did not work on this problem. They worked a lot.' But in order to launch electric furnaces they first had to receive them. They still had not, so there was nothing for the Zaporizhzhia obkom to control.[119]

Kutsevol, first secretary of the Lviv obkom, had a similar situation at a factory that did not receive engines on time from the Likhachov factory in Moscow. Construction plans could not be fulfilled without a solid construction industry capable of building large enterprises in the region. Therefore, the obkom had little to control in this sector either. In response to the criticism of the Lviv obkom's failure to oversee the technological process at a construction site, Kutsevol admitted that, indeed, the obkom knew that the technological process had not been tested and had failed to insist on testing before implementing it. He further admitted that the obkom had failed to 'inform the Central Committee or the relevant departments of the Gosplan or the government' of this error. But he accepted the consequences. 'We paid for this now', Kutsevol said, referring to the criticism at the plenum, which, it would appear, he viewed as fair punishment for construction based on 'imperfect blueprints'. To the criticism of the region's progress in light industry, Kutsevol philosophically replied: 'I think that we are all probably falling short here; we do not inform the Central Committee in a timely manner, whereas the relevant branch departments in Ukrsovnarkhoz and Gosplan also demonstrate a certain passivity, I would say.'[120] Indeed, there was little Kutsevol could say about the Lviv obkom controlling the Lviv sovnarkhoz. Since 1957, the Lviv sovnarkhoz had run its affairs independently from the obkom.[121] The obkom could only offer its support. In 1965, Kutsevol seems to have been content with the arrangement. Considering that Kutsevol would remain in his chair until 1973, Shelest must have been content with the arrangement as well.

The obkom secretaries and the chairmen of the sovnarkhozy did not offer alternative explanations as to why the obkoms would overlook various violations committed by managers. However, the chairman of the Ukrainian Association for the Administration of Agricultural Machinery (Ukrselkhoztekhnika), Volodymyr Krivosheev, did see some reasons why such violations would be overlooked. He explained that although agricultural machinery was included in production plans, the kolkhozy and sovnarkhozy had to rely on the goodwill of local enterprises for any necessary repairs.

> Today, there are 276 repair shops. Based on the decision of the Central Committee, a considerable number of industrial enterprises, particularly in the sovnarkhozy of Kharkiv, Kyiv, [and] Chornomorsky, conscientiously provide patronage and practical help to [the kolkhozy and sovkhozy] in reconstructing and equipping these repair shops. Unfortunately, the same cannot be said about enterprises in the Prydniprovsk, Donetsk, and Lviv sovnarkhozy. They offer very little help.[122]

During the 1950s, the pressure on enterprises to provide patronage to the kolkhozy and sovkhozy increased. By 1965, patronage had become one of the functions that enterprises and the sovnarkhozy had to systematically provide, and the obkoms and the leadership counted on it. On 5 January 1965, the buro of the Dnipropetrovsk obkom stated that some enterprises did not provide the necessary patronage to the kolkhozy and sovkhozy for 'the labour-intensive processes of repairing agricultural machinery' and instructed the relevant obkom departments 'to maintain the good tradition of manufacturing spare parts and equipment for the kolkhozy and sovkhozy using the internal reserves of enterprises'. At its meeting on 29 January 1965, the buro of the Dnipropetrovsk obkom passed a resolution that tied towns to villages 'to provide patronage help to the kolkhozy

**Illustration 9**   CPSU First Secretary Nikita Khrushchev in Ukraine, end of the 1950s–beginning of the 1960s/© TsDAHOU (f. 240 op. 1 spr. 56 ark. 90)
Khrushchev promotes his corn campaign. To his left: Petro Shelest.

and sovkhozy', and instructed the enterprise directors, kolkhozy, and sovkhozy to schedule the volumes and deadlines for necessary works. In particular, they had to focus on constructing 'the simplest irrigation systems'. On 31 May 1965, the Ukrainian leadership issued a resolution 'obligating Ukrselkhoztekhnika, Ukrsovnarkhoz, and the sovnarkhozy to take measures to fundamentally improve patronage help on the part of industrial enterprises'.[123]

Hence, Khudosovtsev felt obligated to clear the good name of his sovnarkhoz. In response to Krivosheev, he denied that the Donetsk sovnarkhoz had neglected its patronage obligations.

> We coped with all plans and tasks for agriculture, agricultural machinery, spare parts, etc. Moreover, last year our enterprises produced 500 sprinkling machines as patronage help. This year, agricultural workers asked for cultivators, and we manufactured 1,500 cultivators that were not included in the plan[.] Another 1,000 cultivators will be produced this year upon the request of the agricultural workers of the Luhansk oblast[.] [In total,] we will produce 2,500 cultivators that were not anticipated by the plan.[124]

## Economic Differentiation of the Oblasts

Of course, not all oblasts had the same access to resources that were managed by their sovnarkhoz, and not all obkoms developed a close relationship with the sovnarkhozy, influenced the distribution of resources, or relied on patronage from industry to the same extent as the obkoms of Luhansk and Donetsk. The oblasts that hosted the sovnarkhozy and were the most industrialized within their economic regions generally received priority.[125]

Pavlo Kozyr, first secretary of the Vinnytsia obkom, was satisfied with the Podillia sovnarkhoz.[126]

> During the years of the seven-year plan [1959–1965], the volume of the industrial production of [the Vinnytsia] oblast had increased by 70 percent instead of 63 percent as planned. Forty new industrial enterprises had been built during this period...[;] 167 million roubles were spent on the restoration and expansion of the existing production capacity of the sugar, alcohol, machine-construction, chemical, and other industrial branches. This is a considerable amount for us.[127]

In August 1965, the Ukrainian leadership would congratulate the Vinnytsia obkom, oblispolkom, and its *kolkhozniks* on the fulfilment of state grain procurement targets by all raions 'thanks to dedicated creative work of the village toilers [*trudiashchiesia sela*]' and party organizations, and thanks to 'large patronage help provided by industrial enterprises to the kolkhozy and sovkhozy'.[128]

Hryhorii Shevchuk, first secretary of the Ternopil obkom, was less enthusiastic about the economic development of the Ternopil oblast, which never hosted a sovnarkhoz. Although its industrial production in 1965 reached seven times what it had been in 1945, the Ternopil oblast remained the least industrialized in Ukraine. In the seven-year plan (1959–1965) for the Lviv sovnarkhoz, which administered Ternopil's industry in 1957–1963, only 4 percent of capital investments for industrial construction were allocated to the Ternopil oblast. Shevchuk explained:

> When drafting annual plans, the [Lviv] sovnarkhoz systematically reduced the volume of investments [for the Ternopil oblast], delayed the starting dates for construction projects, and even completely excluded a number of important enterprises from the construction plan, namely the factories for manufacturing plastic and synthetic fibre, silicate bricks, synthetic cleansers, and pharmaceuticals. The situation did not improve when the oblast was transferred to the Podillia sovnarkhoz [in 1963], either.[129]

Unsurprisingly, the Ukrainian leadership's August 1965 telegram to the Ternopil obkom regarding the harvest did not include any mention of the patronage from enterprises to the kolkhozy. This was also omitted from the telegrams sent by the Ukrainian Central Committee to the obkoms of Cherkasy, Khmelnytskyi, Zhytomyr, and Rivne. Crimean enterprises, in contrast, received praise from the Ukrainian leadership for providing labour to the local kolkhozy.[130]

Interestingly, data collected by Ukrainian statisticians indicated that the presence of the sovnarkhoz had no considerable effect on the economy of the oblast where it was located. Out of fourteen oblast centres that hosted a sovnarkhoz at some point during the reform, seven of them increased their share of Ukraine's industrial output in the period between 1954 and 1963, five decreased, and two retained the same share (Table 1). However, the changes were not significant and did not affect the balance that existed between the oblasts before the reform. The ten most industrialized oblasts remained Stalino, Dnipropetrovsk, Kharkiv, Voroshylovhrad, Kyiv, Odesa, Zaporizhzhia, Lviv, Crimea, and Poltava.

**Table 1** Share of oblasts in Ukraine's industrial output (%)

| Oblast | 1954 | 1963 | 1990 |
|---|---|---|---|
| Stalino[a] | 20.0 | 15.85 | 13.06 |
| Dnipropetrovsk | 10.8 | 11.26 | 10.72 |
| Kharkiv[b] | 10.2 | 9.72 | 7.56 |
| Voroshylovhrad[c] | 8.0 | 7.88 | 6.96 |

| | | | |
|---|---|---|---|
| Kyiv[d] | 7.9 | 8.69 | 9.88 |
| Odesa | 5.9 | 5.36 | 4.26 |
| Zaporizhzhia | 5.8 | 6.92 | 5.82 |
| Lviv | 3.0 | 4.97 | 5.78 |
| Crimea | 2.6 | 3.34 | 3.31 |
| Poltava | 2.5 | 2.81 | 3.49 |
| Sumy | 2.4 | 2.38 | 2.66 |
| Vinnytsia | 2.4 | 2.31 | 2.54 |
| Mykolaiv | 2.1 | 2.10 | 1.98 |
| Zhytomyr | 1.9 | 1.93 | 2.05 |
| Cherkasy | 1.8 | 1.80 | 2.58 |
| Chernihiv | 1.8 | 1.83 | 2.20 |
| Kirovohrad | 1.5 | 1.70 | 1.63 |
| Khmelnytskyi[e] | 1.4 | 1.38 | 2.09 |
| Kherson | 1.4 | 2.07 | 1.94 |
| Zakarpattia | 1.3 | 1.08 | 1.72 |
| Chernivtsi | 1.3 | 1.18 | 1.35 |
| Stanislav[f] | 1.1 | 1.07 | 2.28 |
| Drohobych[g] | 1.2 | n/a | n/a |
| Rivne | 0.7 | 0.88 | 1.47 |
| Ternopil | 0.5 | 0.72 | 1.53 |
| Volyn | 0.5 | 0.78 | 1.14 |
| Total | 100 | 100 | 100 |

[a] Renamed Donetsk in 1961
[b] Including the city of Kharkiv
[c] Called Luhansk before 1935, in 1958–1970, and after 1990 until present
[d] Including the city of Kyiv
[e] Called Kamianets-Podilskyi oblast in 1937–1954
[f] Renamed Ivano-Frankivsk in 1962
[g] Merged with the Lviv oblast in 1959

*Sources*: TsDAHOU f. 1 op. 31 spr. 859 ark. 7–8; op. 6 spr. 3911 ark. 46, 47; Popovkin et al. (1994: 32).

The three western oblasts of Rivne, Volyn, and Ternopil remained the least industrialized in Ukraine throughout the reform. When these are combined with Chernivtsi, Zakarpattia, and Ivano-Frankivsk, the six western oblasts contributed a mere 5.7 percent of Ukraine's industrial output, slightly more than the Lviv oblast alone. The share of these six oblasts in the total output of Ukraine, agricultural and industrial, was 7.7 percent. To put this number in perspective, in 1964, up to 30–40 percent of the working population of Western Ukraine, including Lviv, was not employed by the state; the majority was occupied in housework and farming household plots.[131] Certainly in these western oblasts, the reform failed to unveil concealed production resources as intended.

The branch investment policy orchestrated in Moscow was of greater significance to the oblasts than the reform. The Kherson oblast, for example, benefited from an increase in the average annual rate of investment in the food, light, and defence industries, for which Kherson produced ships and submarines. The share of the Kherson oblast in Ukraine's textile industry, for example, increased from

3.4 percent in 1955 to 17 percent in 1960.[132] The oblasts of Dnipropetrovsk and Zaporizhzhia increased their share in Ukraine's total industrial output thanks to the growth of average annual capital investment in ferrous metallurgy from 105.3 percent in 1952–1956 to 111.9 percent in 1959–1964. In 1957, these two oblasts produced 92.7 percent of ore in Ukraine. The average growth rate of capital investments in the coal industry decreased from 113.8 percent in 1952–1956 to 97.2 percent in 1959–1964, reducing the coal industry's share in Ukraine's total industry from 7.5 percent in 1958 to 5.54 percent in 1965. This reduction affected the Stalino and Voroshylovhrad oblast-sovnarkhozy, which had accounted for 92.2 percent of Ukraine's coal mining in 1957.[133]

Despite the relatively low impact of hosting a sovnarkhoz, the obkom secretaries preferred to have one in their oblast. In 1960, the first obkom secretary of Cherkasy joined his counterparts from Kirovohrad, Poltava, and Crimea in petitioning Kyiv for separate economic regions for their oblasts. Only Kirovohrad was refused. The new Crimean and Poltava economic regions consisted of one oblast each. The Cherkasy economic region united two oblasts, Kirovohrad and Cherkasy.[134] The number of the sovnarkhozy increased from eleven to fourteen. In October 1962, one month before Khrushchev announced recentralization, the obkoms of the Kyiv, Volyn, Khmelnytskyi, Chernihiv, Sumy, Kirovohrad, Zakarpattia, Chernivtsi, and Rivne suggested that each oblast form a separate economic region and created a sovnarkhoz.[135] At the end of 1962, when the oblasts were regrouped into seven economic regions, half of the oblast-sovnarkhozy lost their privileged access to resources. At the same time, the oblispolkoms lost control over local industry to the newly enlarged sovnarkhozy, as the obkoms insisted that the new sovnarkhozy create separate departments for their oblasts.[136] The Poltava obkom asked the Ukrainian Central Committee to expand the structure of the Kharkiv sovnarkhoz, which now administered the economy of the Poltava oblast, to include departments for Poltava's leading industries of food, meat, milk, and fish. The Zaporizhzhia obkom had a similar request regarding the Prydniprovsk sovnarkhoz: the newly formed administration should 'administer the enterprises that are in their majority located in the Zaporizhzhia oblast'. The Kherson and Mykolaiv obkom secretaries asked the Ukrainian Central Committee to authorize a department for wine production in the new Chornomorsky sovnarkhoz with headquarters in Odesa to take over the wine-producing industry in their oblasts. 'The [wine-branch] department, in addition to administering industry and agriculture, will also maintain a relationship with the [Kherson and Mykolaiv] party organs and implement their resolutions.'[137]

## Divisions in the CPU

During the decentralization reforms, the CPU continued to develop its specific character. The obkoms' continuous focus on the economic agenda after 1953, the reliance of the obkoms on the sovnarkhozy for the fulfilment of their agenda, and the oblasts' unequal access to resources managed by the sovnarkhozy exacerbated the institutional fragmentation of the CPU.

The continuous prioritization and centralized administration of heavy and defence industry continued to elevate the status of the obkom secretaries of large industrialized oblasts from south-eastern Ukraine and, to a lesser extent, Lviv. They maintained a direct relationship with the central party and state apparatus throughout the reform. In 1962, the sovnarkhozy of Donetsk and Dnipropetrovsk were audited directly by the USSR Gosplan.[138] Being at the helm of the oblasts that managed more than 50 percent of investments allocated to Ukraine's industry, the first obkom secretaries of the Donbas and Prydniprovsk oblasts received the highest salaries in the CPU and were regular speakers at the Ukrainian party forums. With the start of the Sovnarkhoz reform, they were elected to the highest Ukrainian party organs. To name a few, in December 1957, the Dnipropetrovsk first obkom secretary Volodymyr Shcherbytsky moved to Kyiv as a secretary of the Ukrainian Central Committee and was elected to be a member of the Ukrainian Presidium. Haiovy from the neighbouring Zaporizhzhia was appointed first obkom secretary of Dnipropetrovsk and also joined the Ukrainian Presidium. Haiovy was the first obkom secretary to join the Ukrainian Presidium. The first obkom secretary of Donetsk, Kazanets, became CPU Second Secretary and a member of the Ukrainian Presidium at the Twenty-First CPU Congress in 1960. In 1963, Kazanets was appointed the chairman of the Ukrainian government.[139]

The influence and political standing of the Donetsk party–industry alliance was anchored in the dominance of the coal industry and had been established as 'a partially distinct unit before 1953'.[140] During the discussion of the plan and budget for 1965 at the fifth session of the USSR Supreme Soviet on 9–11 December 1964, Kazanets, the chairman of the Ukrainian government, and Khudosovtsev, the chairman of the Donetsk sovnarkhoz, were among four speakers who spoke on behalf of Ukraine. Curiously, Kazanets and Khudosovtsev were listed as representing 'Donetskaia oblast' and 'Luganskaia oblast', respectively. The other two speakers, Vasyl Drozdenko, the Kyiv obkom first secretary, and Illia Lomako, the chairman of a kolkhoz from the Donetsk oblast, were listed as representing the 'Ukrainskaia SSR'.[141]

After the return to branch administration, Kazanets became the USSR Minister of Ferrous Metallurgy and retained this post until 1986. Khudosovtsev became the Minister of the Coal Industry of Ukraine in October 1965 and remained in this post until 1974. The prominence of Donetsk would remain high throughout the rest of the Soviet period, although with the ascendance of Brezhnev in 1964 and the replacement of Shelest with Shcherbytsky in 1972, Donetsk would give seniority to Dnipropetrovsk, which saw the standing of its 'regional family' rise rapidly in the 1950s.[142]

On the other end of the scale were the six obkoms of the western Ukrainian oblasts of Ternopil, Stanislav, Volyn, Rivne, Zakarpattia, and Chernivtsi. Despite the growth of industry in Western Ukraine and some progress with sovietization of the region in the 1950s, the economic profile of these oblasts and, consequently, the political profile of the obkoms remained low. The opinion of the first obkom secretaries from these oblasts was not required at the Ukrainian party forums, unless the matter under discussion was ideology or agriculture.[143] Despite the region's ideological and strategic significance, none of these secretaries was invited to join the Ukrainian Presidium. Ivan Hrushetsky, who for a long time worked in Western Ukraine and was the first secretary of Lviv obkom in 1961–1962, was elected candidate member in the Ukrainian Presidium after he left Lviv and became the chairman of the Ukrainian committee of party-state control.[144] The obkoms of the six western oblasts had the smallest staff. In 1962, their staff ranged from fifty-two staff members in Ternopil to forty staff members in Chernivtsi. That same year, the obkoms of the Volyn and Zakarpattia did not have a secretary for industry. Volyn also lacked a secretary for construction.[145] In 1957, of the seven western obkoms (the Drohobych oblast merged with the Lviv oblast in 1959) only the staff of the Drohobych and Zakarpattia obkoms were in the second-highest group by salaries, according to the pay scale of obkom staff across the Soviet Union. The staff of the Volyn, Stanislav, Rivne, Ternopil, and Chernivtsi obkoms formed the third (lowest) group by salaries. No other Ukrainian obkom was in it.[146] In the Ukrainian Central Committee, the six western obkoms were viewed as administratively and politically weak.[147] The low level of complex industrialization deprived these obkom secretaries of strong connections with the Moscow party and state apparatus.[148]

## Conclusion

Years of Stalinist hyper-centralization could not suppress the Ukrainian leadership's desire to become a meaningful power centre. As soon as the opportunity presented itself, it sought to expand the nationality policy to include economic relations.

From 1953 until 1965, the Ukrainian leadership sought to increase its control over resources in Ukraine, to formalize its relationship with Moscow (whereby the republic would have authority over its areas of responsibility and the central agencies would be responsible for decisions they made), and to convince Moscow that Ukraine should be treated as a single economic complex.

Kyiv did not accomplish any of the above. Treating Ukraine as one economic complex was not on Moscow's agenda. For the purpose of spatial planning, Ukraine was divided into three large economic regions, Donetsk-Prydniprovsk, South-Western, and Southern.[149] Branch administration survived the Sovnarkhoz reform and, after 1962, dominated. Throughout the entire period, control over resources was largely shared between the central apparatus in Moscow and the regions. Moscow was willing to satisfy the requests of the Ukrainian leadership for additional resources on an ad hoc basis.[150] However, it refused to systematize any future distribution of resources. The formalization of economic functions and division of responsibilities between the central and republican apparatus did not happen either. From Moscow's perspective, formalization risked increasing the power of the Ukrainian leadership over the economy and, by implication, over the regions. The central leadership was prepared to empower the Ukrainian leadership but only if such empowerment did not interfere with the centre's direct access to the Ukrainian economy and Ukrainian regions.

To assert its authority and align it with its duties, the Ukrainian leadership tried to capitalize on its administrative powers and its position between Moscow and the regions. As long as the principle of territorial administration and the trend towards decentralization prevailed, the Ukrainian leadership imposed its authority over the regions by asserting itself in its traditional role as the direct representative of the central leadership. It was prepared to fight regional localism that undermined all-union interests as defined by Moscow. After the central leadership reversed the course of the reform and the Ukrainian leadership understood that the central leadership would not expand its authority, the Ukrainian leadership aligned its interests with the regions. The concept of localism was re-evaluated. Kyiv began protecting regional economic interests in Moscow, particularly the interests of industrialized regions. When Kyiv learned that the territorial principle would be abandoned altogether, it returned to defending all-union interests.

The extent to which the Ukrainian leadership was empowered during the decentralization reforms was insufficient to forge the CPU into a 'united regional division of the CPSU' (not that the Ukrainian Central Committee ever considered such forging necessary). The transfer of resources to the sovnarkhozy exacerbated the fragmentation of the CPU. The obkoms still relied on local managers to finance the party agenda, such as propaganda, party education, party buildings, and the party apparatus, yet to a lesser extent than in the 1930s.[151] At the same time, with the economic agenda dominating any other and the Ukrainian centre economically weak, the obkoms became ever more dependent on regional economic authorities to ensure their oblasts fulfilled the plans. The obkoms' interests were more aligned with those of the local managers than with the party task to fight localism. At the same time, centralized branch administration combined with the prioritization of heavy industry allowed party–industry alliances from Donetsk and Dnipropetrovsk to rise in prominence. Western Ukraine, except Lviv, on the other hand, remained industrially backward and was yet to be fully sovietized. By 1965 Western Ukraine was on a path to political marginalization.

The Sovnarkhoz reform was a disappointment to all but the regions. The central leadership was disappointed because localism had led to a dispersion of resources among the regions. The economy was growing, but the de-sacralization of the principle of plan fulfilment at all costs affected central control over economic development. For the Ukrainian leadership, the reform was a disappointment because the regions were empowered more than Kyiv. Kyiv did not become the main administrative centre with decision-making powers, as it had hoped. The regions maintained their direct communication with Moscow. Still, Kyiv was no longer an institutionally superfluous link between the regions and Moscow. Despite its limitations, during the years of the Sovnarkhoz reform, the Ukrainian leadership was as economically powerful as it ever was or would be.

Khrushchev's choice to transfer control over production directly to the economic regions instead of the republican centre set Ukraine on a path of institutional development different from other republics. Until the Sovnarkhoz reform, Ukraine's institutional set-up was no different from any other republic, except Russia which did not have its own central committee. The reform changed that. On the one hand, the reform institutionalized regionalism in Ukraine, arguably contrary to all other republics except Russia. On the other, in contrast to Russia, which did not have its own central committee, the Ukrainian Central Committee became a meaningful, albeit weak, republican authority. As discussed in the following chapters, when the reform was reversed, the authority of the Ukrainian leadership shrank. The power of the regions did not. After the sovnarkhoz experiment, Ukraine was firmly on the path of strong regionalism and weak centralized power.

*The Institutional Foundations of Ukrainian Democracy: Power Sharing, Regionalism, and Authoritarianism.* Nataliya Kibita, Oxford University Press. © Nataliya Kibita 2024. DOI: 10.1093/9780191925351.003.0005

# 5

# Economic Recentralization and the Ukrainian Leadership

## Introduction

In 1964, Nikita Khrushchev was full of energy and enthusiasm to further reorganise state institutions. His colleagues in the central Presidium and the entire party and state apparatus were not. At the 13–14 October 1964 plenum of the Central Committee, Khrushchev was criticized for his policies and his leadership style and was removed from all posts. During the discussion, the sovnarkhoz system, although mentioned, was not presented as his largest sin.[1] Nor was the system immediately abolished after his removal. In contrast to Khrushchev's controversial idea to bifurcate the party organs into agricultural and industrial, which irritated the party apparatus, the sovnarkhoz system provided the republican leaderships and large regions with tangible, if limited, economic power.[2] Leonid Brezhnev and Aleksey Kosygin did not want to alienate the republican leaderships or the obkom secretaries before securing Khrushchev's removal. Only one year later, after Brezhnev and Kosygin were firmly installed as first secretary of the CPSU and chairman of the Soviet government, respectively, they demolished the sovnarkhoz system and restored the centralized branch administration of production. The republics lost control over their economies, although not to the degree that existed before 1954.

First Secretary of the CPU Petro Shelest was among Nikita Khrushchev's critics at the October 1964 plenum. He criticized Khrushchev for curtailing republican economic rights. As discussed in the previous chapter, the authority of the republican leadership began to decline from 1960 when the all-union managers began reclaiming control over material resources. Of even greater significance for the Ukrainian leadership was the obkoms' economic dependence on the industrial managers, while the latter became more closely connected to the all-union bureaucracy. Still, as long as the sovnarkhozy were subordinated to the Ukrainian government and the Ukrainian government controlled the distribution of almost 50 percent of Ukraine's output, there could be no threat to the Ukrainian leadership's authority or the first secretary's power over the regional party–industry alliances.

However, by the end of 1965, the sovnarkhozy had been abolished and the Ukrainian leadership had been stripped of any meaningful influence over its economy. The majority of ministries that were created in Ukraine had union-republican status with double subordination to the Ukrainian government and the main Moscow-based offices. Fully returning to the branch principle in economic administration meant that the main offices of these ministries in Moscow not only set the planning targets for their Ukrainian offices but also allocated material supplies and determined investments.[3] The Ukrainian leadership had limited authority over the few Ukrainian industrial ministries of republican status and had no control over resources that would flow along branch channels. To remind Kyiv that heavy industry remained Moscow's priority and indicate that the Ukrainian republican leadership was not an essential link in administering heavy industry, Moscow placed the Ukrainian union-republican ministries for coal and metallurgy in Donetsk and Dnipropetrovsk, respectively; the same cities that hosted them in 1954. All heavy industry—but also light industry, and even food, meat, and milk industries that used primarily local raw resources—was run by union-republican ministries. In sum, as Motyl and Krawchenko observed, 'until 1990, 95 percent of Ukraine's economy [would be] controlled by Moscow'.[4]

As this chapter shows, as soon as the Ukrainian leadership lost control over resources, its position weakened; the position of the regional party–industry alliances did not. They survived the abolition of the sovnarkhoz system, grew stronger, and developed a deeper, direct relationship with the Moscow industrial bureaucracy.

## Part I: Kyiv Resists Recentralization

To Shelest, by 1964 the republics had responsibilities but no rights.[5] Yet, at no point in the period leading up to the 1964 coup did Shelest think that removing Khrushchev would lead to economic recentralization, or even the abolition of the sovnarkhozy, despite economic slowdown. The June 1957 attempted coup against Khrushchev had ended with Khrushchev's victory, not least because Khrushchev presented himself as a proponent of economic decentralization. The fact that the plotters of Khrushchev's removal in 1964 relied on republican party secretaries led Shelest and others to believe that Moscow would not curtail their economic rights. Instead, they figured that the new leadership might even reverse recentralization efforts that Khrushchev had started in 1959–1960. Shelest's certitude that the republican leadership would benefit from Khrushchev's removal was so strong that in the summer of 1964 he gave instructions to create a Chamber of Commerce in Kyiv, in preparation for Ukraine to obtain a degree of autonomy in foreign trade.[6]

Soon after Khrushchev was removed, the central leadership indicated that it was looking into two possible ways to reorganize the economic administration. The first possible approach was to continue running industry through republican governments based on production plans adopted by the central government. The second approach entailed restoring the centralized ministerial system. Neither had room for the sovnarkhozy. The fact that the sovnarkhozy would be abolished did not bother Shelest. As shown in the previous chapter, he was critical of the regional *mestnichestvo* and resented the power of regional party–industry alliances. Abolishing the sovnarkhozy might even result in the Ukrainian government gaining more control over Ukrainian industry. However, this would not be the case if Moscow restored the pre-1954 ministerial system.

At the beginning of November 1964, the republican sovnarkhoz of Ukraine, Ukrsovnarkhoz, submitted a document to the Ukrainian Central Committee that explained the advantages of having the republican governments run the republican industries. Ukrsovnarkhoz rejected outright the idea of creating union-republican ministries. These ministries would restore closed economies by restoring barriers between ministries. The republican government would be unable to regulate territorial inter-branch cooperation, which was viewed as the biggest achievement of the sovnarkhoz system, or create a common supply system within the republic. The influence of the republican governments on the fulfilment of plans would drastically decrease.[7]

The leaderships of other republics must have shared the Ukrainian leadership's unwillingness to cede control over their republics' economies. So, the central Soviet leadership proceeded slowly in the direction of recentralization. On 16 November 1964, the Central Committee plenum voted to abolish the sovnarkhozy, despite the positive evaluation of the sovnarkhozy by the participants.[8] However, the extent to which abolishing the sovnarkhozy would affect the economic rights of the republics remained unclear, which prompted Shelest to continue to insist that the republican governments were better positioned to run the republican economies than the central bureaucracy in Moscow. Thus, writing to the Central Committee on 13 April 1965, Shelest stated that the central planners did not always satisfy the material and spare parts needs of Ukrainian enterprises in the metallurgical, coal, and chemical industries, in construction, and in agricultural machinery manufacturing. Central planners blamed insufficient supplies of necessary materials on a deficit of those materials. However, Ukraine had the capacity to organize the production of material and spare parts in excess of planned quantities. The key to overcoming the deficit, argued Shelest and the Ukrainian Presidium, was to increase the incentives for the republics to produce more. The republican right to use its excess production should be increased.[9] The republics should be allowed to organize the above-plan production of deficit products, and to organize new production of 'raw materials, other materials, machinery, equipment'. The 'new' production should remain at the full disposal of the republic during the first three years, and only in the fourth year be included in the nomenklatura of the all-union resources, if necessary, and only to a point: between 50 and 100 percent of above-plan production should remain at the disposal of the republican governments in the fourth year.[10] The new quotas of production remaining at the disposal of the republican governments would have been a considerable increase on the existing quotas, which generally did not exceed 50 percent of above-plan production.[11]

When the Central Committee announced its plan to recentralize the economy at the September 1965 plenum, Shelest probably thought his April letter was naïve. As progressive as his ideas about stimulating above-plan production might have seemed to Shelest, they could not but frustrate the central planners. After all, not only did he blatantly tell them that they did not have accurate information on the industrial capacity of the state, but also he admitted that without proper stimulus, the republican leadership would not go the extra mile to boost production of deficit goods. At the same time, central planners were probably thankful that Shelest had confirmed their claims that the sovnarkhozy and the republican governments were pursuing localism.

By mid-summer 1965, the Ukrainian leadership was already sceptical about retaining the same level of control over resources. To the regions, Shelest continued to project confidence about the impossibility of returning to centralized economic administration.[12] In private, he harboured no illusions that sooner or later Kosygin, the staunch opponent of territorial administration, would recentralize control over the economy and sideline Kyiv from influencing the republic's economy.[13] If that were to happen, the regions would have even fewer reasons to view the Ukrainian leadership as the de facto authority. After all, the value of the republican leadership in the vertical administration of the republic was determined by its ability to influence both production and distribution of resources. As he would say in 1989, 'it is necessary that the local power, starting at the raion level, has its own money, its own [material] funds. Otherwise, [local power] is nothing but a name.'[14] In July 1965, he tried to convince Moscow not to completely abandon the principle of territorial administration. In its official proposal on future economic administration, the Ukrainian leadership insisted that it was both possible and in the common interest of the state, the republics, and Moscow to correctly correlate branch and territorial development. To achieve the balance between territorial and branch administration, the new system of plan indices for enterprises should be drafted simultaneously with the plans for the republics. 'Material balances composed for republics for group nomenclature, [i.e.,] that include practically all production [manufactured in the republic,] should be used as the basis for the planned volumes of production and capital construction.' The plans should be composed first for the republics, with the participation of the republican governments, and only then for the industrial branches.[15]

Before the new system took shape, Shelest tried to secure the Ukrainian leadership's access to at least some resources. Shelest focused on areas that cut across branch divisions and regional boundaries. These included Ukraine's direct access to foreign markets and the implementation of new technology in production.

Shelest also addressed a problem which, if successfully resolved, would have boosted his political power with the obkoms: unemployment.

## Foreign Trade

By the summer of 1965, Shelest's plans to create a Chamber of Commerce in Kyiv and provide Ukraine with direct access to foreign markets had not materialized. At the beginning of July 1965, Shelest returned to foreign trade, now in the context of the forthcoming so-called Kosygin reform. He suggested implementing Kosygin's new incentive system to increase foreign trade by allowing enterprises to keep a share of the profits from exports and use these profits to buy necessary equipment on the foreign market. The republics, in their turn, could assist the USSR Ministry of Foreign Trade with the increased volumes of trade. They could organize the enterprises' foreign trade relations. For this, they 'should have the right to sign trade deals with socialist countries in agreement with the USSR Ministry of Foreign Trade, and with capitalist countries through the USSR Ministry of Foreign Trade.'[16]

In his follow-up two-page letter on 30 July, Shelest provided more details of the proposal. His initiative, he explained, was not arbitrary or groundless. It originated in the informal conversations that the Ukrainian delegates had had with representatives of a number of developing and capitalist countries at international conferences and sessions of the United Nations (UN).[17] The representatives of capitalist countries had explained that they could not trade directly with the Soviet Union 'because their governments have not settled a number of issues with the government of the USSR'. Therefore, they had to trade with the Soviet Union through neutral countries, which caused significant difficulties. 'Trade through the Ukrainian SSR, which was a UN member, would eliminate these difficulties and have a positive influence on the development of [Soviet] foreign trade', concluded Shelest. Shelest insisted that this idea deserved attention. Lately, he continued, the authority of Soviet Ukraine 'as a sovereign state that is a founding member of the UN and a participant in numerous international organizations' had increased considerably. Besides, Ukraine was one of the largest exporters in the Soviet Union. But the republic's capabilities to develop foreign trade were insufficiently used, while the all-union agencies that managed foreign trade were not coping with the increased volume and the increased demand. They were inefficient in uncovering additional commodities 'which [were] produced in the republics...and which could increase the [foreign] currency reserves of the state if they were used in full and in a timely manner'. 'Thus, it has become necessary to improve the organizational forms of foreign trade...by using all favourable conditions for economically beneficial trade. More active participation of the governments of the Union republics in the organization of foreign trade could help achieve this goal.' Partial decentralization of foreign trade was in the interest of the entire Union, argued Shelest.[18]

De-monopolization of Soviet foreign trade was a long-cherished idea of the Ukrainian leadership. Shelest was at least the fourth Ukrainian leader who argued that Ukraine should become an actor in Soviet foreign trade.[19] The previous attempt was made in 1956 by Ukrainian Minister of Commerce Heorhii Sakhnovsky with the support of CPU First Secretary Oleksii Kyrychenko. Back then, Sakhnovsky suggested allowing 'cooperative unions, cities, industrial trusts, and specialized trade organizations to buy goods abroad.'[20] Ukrainian planners supported him. They also complained that the USSR Ministry of Foreign Trade refused to accept a number of Ukrainian products for export, and they insisted that Ukraine, not the USSR Ministry of Foreign Trade, should decide what Ukraine exported and imported.[21] Such independent discernment was forbidden by Khrushchev.

## New Technology

The June 1965 draft of the Kosygin reform did not prioritize the implementation of new technology in industrial production. The Ukrainian planners considered this a mistake that would have long-term negative consequences for industry.[22] Shelest saw this disagreement as an opportunity to expand the authority of the republican leadership.

On 20 July 1965, the Ukrainian Presidium passed a resolution 'About increasing the efficiency of scientific and research organizations of the Ukrainian SSR', which established Ukraine's control over the implementation of any new technology in industrial production, regardless of which authority funded the research. The resolution aimed to reclaim the republic's control over research and the implementation of science and technology in production that it had enjoyed in the short period between 1957 and 1962.[23] The resolution stated that licensing, evaluation, and implementation of scientific discoveries in Ukraine had to be performed in accordance with Ukrainian regulations. The decision about whether to implement a scientific or technological discovery in Ukrainian industry lay solely with the Ukrainian State Committee for the Coordination of Scientific and Research Work. Any disputes between Ukrainian ministries, administrations, sovnarkhozy, or other agencies with regard to the evaluation or implementation of new discoveries in production had to be resolved by the Ukrainian State Committee. However, if the dispute involved an agency of all-union jurisdiction, the decision of the Ukrainian State Committee had to be approved by the USSR State Committee for the Coordination of Scientific and Research Work.[24]

## Unemployment

Shelest's approach to unemployment is probably the best illustration of his under-standing of how Kyiv's control over resources and its authority with the obkoms were connected. Although well informed about the problem, particularly since taking office on 23 June 1963, Shelest did not take a categorical stance against the central planners or begin to explore other ways to tackle unemployment until late July 1965.

As elsewhere in the Soviet Union, the problem of unemployment was never solved in Ukraine.[25] In 1961, CPU First Secretary Mykola Pidhorny (Rus.: Nikolai Podgorny) indicated that unemployment existed in Ukraine and had to be addressed when he insisted on lower productivity targets and higher labour force targets in industry and construction in the draft of Ukraine's production plan for 1962.[26] At the beginning of 1963, soon after the November 1962 Central Committee plenum that announced the recentralization of industrial administration along branch lines, Pidhorny criticized the Institute of Economics of the Ukrainian Academy of Sciences for not paying enough attention to 'finding ways for the most efficient usage of material and labour resources'. In February 1963, he declared 'studying productive forces' as a factor in the complex development of economic regions to be the priority of economic research in Ukraine.[27]

By the end of 1963, Ukrainian economists had determined that the cause of 'inefficient usage of labour force' was the Soviet investment policy. As they reported to the Ukrainian leadership, by then led by Shelest, 'in the afterwar years, the main investments were channelled to the reconstruction and expansion of the existing enterprises, located mainly in the industrialized oblasts, large cit-ies, and the oblast centres'. For example, 40 percent of all investments allocated to the Kharkiv economic region in 1959–1965 were channelled to develop the indus-try of the city of Kharkiv; about 30 percent of all investments allocated to the Kyiv economic region were used to develop the industry of Kyiv; 75 percent of all allocations to the Odesa and Zaporizhzhia oblasts were used to develop indus-tries of the cities of Odesa and Zaporizhzhia. As a result, these cities faced a shortage of labour, whereas small towns faced the rise of unemployment. 'Every day, more than 140,000 people travelled from the suburbs to Kharkiv for work; about 100,000 people travelled from the suburbs to Kyiv; about 35,000 to Dnipropetrovsk; about 30,000 to Lviv.'[28]

Based on this information, in December 1963, the Ukrainian leadership issued a resolution that restricted investments in large cities and prioritized small and mid-sized cities. The resolution had no effect. 'The investments that were allo-cated to Ukraine by central planners [continued to be] directed primarily to the enlargement and reconstruction of the existing enterprises that were concen-trated in large industrial centres, whereas in many small and mid-sized towns, industry developed poorly.'[29] Indeed, as Malle observed, 'decisions on production capacity are by and large adopted without consideration for the availability of labour and services.'[30]

In his 22 September 1964 comments on the central leadership's draft of 'Main directions in the economic development of the USSR for 1966–1970', Shelest reminded the central leadership of this problem. However, he limited his criticism to the central planners' insufficient consideration of the 'critical' issue of employment, 'particularly in the western oblasts, where up to 30–40 percent of the employable [*trudosposobnogo*] population [was] not occupied in socialist production.'[31]

Immediately after Khrushchev's removal, Shelest focused more closely on the problem of unemployment, although he still did not go beyond surveying it. On 16 December 1964, the Central Statistical Agency of Ukraine submitted to Shelest a detailed report on the economic situation in the republic that included information on unemployment and personal income by oblast. Ten days later, Shelest discovered that Moscow was already well informed of the problem. On 26 December, he received a copy of a seven-page report, 'On the letters of citizens from the Ukrainian SSR about employment', that was originally submitted to Anastas Mikoian, the chairman of the Presidium of the USSR Supreme Soviet. The report contained extracts from letters written by Ukrainians to the Supreme Soviet describing the difficulties of finding jobs in Ukraine. Mikoian concluded that 'the question deserve[d] attention' and forwarded the letter to the Ukrainian Central Committee. On the same day that Shelest received Mikoian's message, he received a follow-up report from Ukrainian statisticians on the growth of employment in Ukraine since 1958 that further detailed the effect of Soviet investment policy and the prioritization of heavy industry on unemployment in Ukraine.[32]

On 23 January 1965, Ukrainian planners reported to Shelest that 19.8 percent of the labour force in Ukraine was not involved in socialist production.[33] The highest percentage of people unemployed in socialist production was in the southwestern region,[34] particularly the western oblasts,[35] with Zakarpattia leading the way with 38.2 percent. Anton Kochubei, the chairman of the Ukrainian Gosplan, confirmed that the reason for the high concentration of unemployment in the western oblasts was the prioritization of heavy industry in the eastern oblasts and insufficient investments in the south-western region. At the same time, Kochubei did not expect any structural changes in the Ukrainian economy in the foreseeable future. Therefore, even though the Ukrainian Gosplan planned, or rather asked Moscow to plan, high growth rates for the south-western region, Kochubei still expected about a million persons to need jobs in 1970, mainly in the southwestern region. Coal and metallurgy would develop at an accelerated pace, stated Kochubei, which 'of course limits the republic's ability to increase industrialization in the south-western region.'[36]

One solution to unemployment, suggested Kochubei, was to let Moscow tackle the problem at the all-union level, through a special union-republican organ that could 'register and regulate the distribution of labour resources between repub-lics, economic regions, oblasts, and industrial branches, based on the agencies of organized recruitment [*orgnabor*] and resettlement'. (As Malle observed, such an organ—the first job placement buro—was indeed formed in 1969.[37]) Additionally, the republic could organize small enterprises in the towns to produce consumer goods with local material resources; the kolkhozy and sovkhozy could organize agricultural produce processing. The republic could also encourage folk craftwork by offering benefits.[38] Still, the republic could not solve the problem alone.

On 4 March 1965, the central government instructed statisticians to collect employment information in towns with under 100,000 inhabitants. Ukrainian statisticians established that 15.5 percent of the labour force was not working or studying in these towns. More than half (50.8 percent) of these 15.5 percent needed employment. In these small towns, women made up 95.6 percent of unemployed and non-studying people. Shelest received this information on 25 July 1965.[39]

In his letter to Moscow on 9 June 1965, Shelest asked central planners to build several heavy and light industry enterprises in the south-western region, explain-ing that with a population of almost 20 million, this remained one of the most backward regions of the Soviet Union in terms of industrial development and employment. If current investments were not increased, he argued, the 'usage of labour' in the western oblasts in particular was expected not only not to improve, but to worsen. 'All the problems set out here had already been presented to the USSR Gosplan during the elaboration of the draft of control numbers for 1966–1970', stated Shelest. 'However, none of them was taken into consideration or resolved positively.'[40]

It was only after Brezhnev and Kosygin announced that the restoration of ministries would accompany the Kosygin reform, which would expand the enter-prises' economic rights, that Shelest shifted from a somewhat passive observer of the unemployment problem to a proactive actor determined to take an active part in the solution of the problem.

On 5 July, a Ukrainian commission led by Oleksandr Liashko, the Ukrainian Central Committee secretary, confirmed Kochubei's January estimate of those not involved in socialist production at the level of 19 percent, or 4.4 million, and stated that almost one third of this number, or 1.5 million people, urgently required jobs.

> The employment situation is particularly difficult in the south-western economic region, where 2.4 million people are not involved in social[ist] production, or 23 percent of the working age population. In the western oblasts of this region, Zakarpattia, Volyn, Ivano-Frankivsk, Rivne, Ternopil, and Chernivtsi, 30–40 percent of the population is unemployed.

In the Ternopil oblast in 1965, 'only 8.2 percent of the total working-age population [was] occupied in industry, which is three times less than on average in Ukraine. Almost 25 percent of the working-age population [was] not occupied in any social[ist] production.'[41]

On 20 July, the Ukrainian Presidium wrote to the Central Committee and not only provided a more detailed description of the situation of labour in Ukraine, but explicitly pointed to the source of the problem.

> [The difficult] situation with employment in western oblasts and generally in the south-western economic region was due to the fact that more than half of investments that are allocated to the republic's industry is invested in the coal, mining, and metallurgical industries, which are located in Donbas and Prydniprovsk, whereas enterprises of light, food, and machine construction, which could solve the problem of unemployment in the south-west, had insufficient growth in the republic.

Yet even the industrialized zones did not have full employment.

> There was a difficult situation with the employment of women in a number of cities and towns of the Donetsk and the Kryvyi Rih basins. This is explained by the fact that at present, female labour is not used in the underground works, whereas food and light industries are poorly developed in this region.

The Ukrainian Presidium reminded the central Presidium in Moscow that Ukraine's negotiations with the USSR Gosplan about additional investments did not bring any results and asked for assistance in convincing the USSR Gosplan to expand industrial construction in Ukraine.[42]

This time, the Ukrainian leadership went beyond pleas with the central leadership. It followed Kochubei's recommendation from seven months before to use locally available resources to increase employment. On 20 July, the Ukrainian Presidium instructed the obkoms and oblispolkoms of Ukraine, in cooperation with the sovnarkhozy,[43] territorial construction administrations, and other economic organizations, to draft specific measures aiming to involve as much of the working-age population in socialist production in 1965–1966 as possible.[44] According to the estimates of Ukrainian planners, the oblasts could provide jobs to more than 350,000 people. New enterprises would increase the income of local budgets. On 17 August 1965, the Ukrainian Presidium gave a boost to its January decision to restore the system of local industry in Ukraine and started the process of organizing the Ukrainian Ministry of Local Industry, which would work closely with the oblispolkoms.[45] Being directly responsible for the socio-economic situation in their oblasts, the obkoms could not but appreciate Shelest's assistance on the matter.

## Moscow's Reply to Shelest's Initiatives and the Kosygin Reform

Moscow first answered Shelest's initiative on foreign trade. It is difficult to say whether it was Shelest calling Ukraine a *derzhava* ('sovereign state'), or the fact that he had the support of all the main Ukrainian administrations to challenge Moscow's monopoly on foreign trade, or his insinuation that the USSR Ministry of Foreign Trade was not aware of which resources were available for export in the republics, but Shelest was categorically rebuffed by the central leadership. '2 September. It was the meeting of the [central] Presidium....As soon as I arrived..., I noticed a certain wariness towards me', Shelest noted in his diary.

> At the end of the meeting, Brezhnev announced that there was one more, unofficial matter to be discussed: the question of com. Shelest's note about foreign policy (about the work of foreign trade)....A lot of 'sharp criticism' sounded in my address: they talked about my gaffe [*neobachnist'*], immaturity, that my note could be used by class enemies. That my note aimed to undermine the monopoly in foreign trade, to undermine the unity of the people.[46]

Secretary of the Ukrainian Central Committee Heorhii Kriuchkov also described this meeting in his memoirs. He specified that Kosygin spoke harshly against Shelest's suggestions. Mikoian emphasized that the question of the state's monopoly in foreign trade was settled more than forty years ago. 'Then', continued Kriuchkov, '[they] reminded N. V. Pidhorny [who was viewed as the protector of Ukraine and Shelest personally] and P. E. Shelest of everything they could [remember]: the high level of meat consumption in Ukraine and the flourishing of [Ukrainian] nationalism.'[47] 'Only when they started mentioning that Ukraine leads a weak struggle against manifestations of bourgeois nationalism, that ideological work is performed poorly, particularly among the youth, that propaganda of the friendship of the peoples and international education are organized poorly, everything became clear', explained Shelest. 'It was all invented, not true, and shameless lies.' 'Some even went as far as declaring the Ukrainian language a spoilt Russian. In all this was manifested the craziest chauvinism, particularly in the speeches of [Aleksandr] Shelepin, [Mikhail] Suslov, [Pyotr] Demichev, Kosygin...' 'In the meantime, the reality showed that Ukraine's interests in foreign policy were ignored. Whereas chambers of commerce were organized in the republics of Uzbekistan, Kazakhstan, Turkmenistan, Tajikistan, Kirghizstan, Georgia, Armenia, and Azerbaijan by 1961, this issue was not resolved for Ukraine.'[48]

This was not the first time 'bourgeois nationalism' had been used in the struggle for power between Moscow and Kyiv. In the autumn of 1919, 'the struggle against Ukrainian bourgeois nationalism' was a factor in Lenin's decision to allow Ukraine to have its Soviet government. In 1922–1923, Rakovsky used 'the struggle against bourgeois nationalism' to try to convince Moscow to grant autonomy to the Ukrainian ministries. According to Kriuchkov, Oleksii Kyrychenko, CPU first secretary in 1953–1957, was removed for introducing the Ukrainian language in the party and state apparatus and for the Ukrainization of schools, which was viewed in Moscow as an attempt to increase his own personal power in the republic.[49] In February 1970, Shelest would argue that Ukraine should have its own delegation at a symposium in Helsinki because 'Ukrainian bourgeois nationalists will undoubtedly try to use the absence of a Ukrainian delegation in their dastardly purposes, since Ukraine was a member of UNESCO [the United Nations Educational, Scientific and Cultural Organization]'.[50] 'Bourgeois nationalism' or 'nationalistic distortions' would sound again in spring 1972, when, following Shelest's assault on the centralized ministerial system, the central leadership would finally remove him from his post.[51]

At the 29 September 1965 Central Committee plenum, as well as through a number of resolutions that followed, Shelest received answers to his other initiatives—namely, control over excess production, the implementation of new technology in production, unemployment, and territorial administration. The responses, in short, were negative.

The September 1965 plenum launched the so-called Kosygin reform. The aim of the reform was to boost economic growth by establishing a set of incentives that would motivate production enterprises to be more efficient and, at the same time, reduce the monitoring cost for the central planners. The number of compulsory plan indicators would be reduced, and enterprises would not make their own decisions on certain investment-related matters. Harrison observed:

> A parallel intention was to update and enlarge the concept of the Soviet 'firm' from a single-plant enterprise to an integrated multi-plant corporation that could internalise the coordination of the stages of production, distribution, research and development (R&D), and innovation, generate its own finance, borrow from state credit institutions on its own responsibility, and become financially self-reliant, halting the drain of subsidies on the state budget.[52]

The new administrative system first and foremost restored the dominance of the branch principle over the territorial by abolishing the sovnarkhozy and drastically reducing the influence of the republican governments on their economies. Control over production was shared between the industrial ministries and production enterprises. The USSR Gosplan regulated capital investments, while the Gossnab controlled material resources.[53] Shelest's request to expand the republics' access to excess production was rejected. At the most, republics would be allowed to distribute 50 percent of a limited nomenklatura of important products.[54] In his speech, Kosygin gave no details on the Union republics' new rights in planning, capital construction, financing, labour, or wages. Kosygin was specific on two issues, though: the development of local industry, 'which [had] great importance for servicing the population', and the cadres. Kosygin relied on the central committees of the republican communist parties to make personnel appointments.[55]

The provision that the gosplans of the Union republics would compose plan-drafts for all industrial enterprises regardless of their jurisdiction, in order to provide correct territorial planning and complex usage of natural, labour, energy, and other resources in economic regions,[56] sounded promising. However, it was up to the USSR Gosplan to combine the branch development with the territorial.[57] Furthermore, the fact that the USSR Gosplan had union-republican status meant that the republican gosplans would be subordinated directly to the USSR Gosplan. The influence of the republican leaderships on their respective gosplans would be limited.[58]

The implementation of new technology in mass production was on Kosygin's agenda. However, it was not viewed as the main driving factor behind economic growth. Rather than technology fuelling economic growth, economic growth had to fuel technological progress. Indeed, socialist and capitalist countries would now compete in the world of scientific-technological revolution, noted Kosygin in his speech. But first, it was necessary to create huge reserves for capital invest-ments and, at the same time, increase the material well-being of the people. To achieve these goals, it was necessary to expand the growth of existing resources. Later in his speech, however, Kosygin appeared to contradict himself by admit-ting that the implementation of new technology and new scientific discoveries in production increasingly determined economic growth. Regardless, Kosygin relied on the industrial ministries, not the republican governments, to fulfil these plans. In response to Shelest and other republican leaders who hoped to have a say in the implementation of scientific research and new technology in produc-tion, Kosygin stated that the USSR State Committee for the Coordination of Scientific Work would be transformed into the All-Union State Committee for Science and Technology. This meant that the committees for the coordination of scientific work in the Union republics would be abolished.[59]

Regarding unemployment, Kosygin stated that 85 percent of the total employ-able population was occupied in either socialist production or education, includ-ing 72 percent of employable women, and acknowledged 'that there [were] possibilities to attract additional labour in social[ist] production and services. Considerable reserves of labour [were] available in small towns, particularly in western regions of Ukraine, Belorussia, a number of regions of Transcaucasia, and some central regions of the country'. Kosygin relied on the USSR Gosplan to address the problem and to 'plan production and capital construction in a way that would provide the fullest possible usage of labour resources'.[60]

Brezhnev, in his speech, was more straightforward about the new role of the republican governments in economic administration: it would be limited. The republican leaderships had no one to blame for the curtailment of republican economic rights but themselves. Under the sovnarkhoz system, the republican party organizations had weakened their attention to the cadres, while it was the cadres in the sovnarkhozy who pursued localism.

> We [often had] a situation where, for example, one republic produced deficit production and when it [came] to distributing it, then the real care [was] shown towards satisfying the needs and requests of its 'own' republican customers.... [W]here the attitude towards supplying other republics [was] allowed to be indifferent, the inter-republican deliveries were often not made.... It happen[ed] sometimes that the leadership of an economic region [was] absolutely determined to organise production of this or that type of equipment, even if it was more profitable to organise this production in a different region.[61]

Putting the blame for localism, slow implementation of technology in production, and slow economic growth on the sovnarkhozy could not conceal Brezhnev's true aim: to curtail the power of the republican leaderships. The sovnarkhozy were subordinated to the republican governments and it was the latter who were responsible for the fulfilment of inter-republican deliveries and who often challenged the authority of the central planners.

Brezhnev agreed with Kosygin that it was up to the newly created industrial ministries to implement technological innovation in industrial production.[62] He saw no room for the republics in managing this or any other aspect of economic development.

All in all, Brezhnev fully supported the restoration of centralized branch administration, and if anyone was considering challenging the central leadership on recentralization, they would have to take it up with Lenin himself (figuratively speaking). 'While preparing its suggestions for this plenum', explained Brezhnev,

> the Presidium of the Central Committee was guided by the ideas of Vladimir Illich Lenin, who viewed our Soviet economy as unified, [who] considered it necessary to provide a tight economic union of the Union republics, and the main [thing] that was required was to strictly follow 'the tendency towards formation of a single economy, based on a common plan and regulated by the proletariat of all nations'.

Brezhnev continued:

> Lenin repeatedly indicated that in organising the economy we do not need democratic centralism in general, but such democratic centralism that requires the construction of industry by branches, that conveys the unity of economy on the scale of the entire country. Vladimir Illich energetically emphasised that the refusal to subordinate all enterprises of each industrial branch to a single centre would mean not communism, but 'regional anarcho-syndicalism'. It is necessary

to remember the importance that Vladimir Illich gave to the <u>unity of the will</u> in economic administration [underlined in the document]. Without it, he emphasised, no large machine industry can exist. As experience showed, these requirements could not be met when industry was administered by the sovnarkhozy.[63]

What was the role of republican party organizations in the new system? They served to appoint qualified cadres, 'raise the enthusiasm of workers', explain the decisions of the plenum to every worker, and ensure that 'the principles of material stimulus and other economic methods were properly implemented'.[64] The last task that Brezhnev assigned to the party would provide Shelest with the perfect excuse to attempt to impose party control over industry in Ukraine.

In his speech to the Central Committee plenum, Shelest could not but support the enlargement of enterprises' economic rights. Nonetheless, he pointed to the positive accomplishments of the sovnarkhoz system and defended Soviet economic achievements by attacking 'the fake bourgeois propaganda about the so-called crisis and technological stagnation that supposedly takes place in our industry'. Unsurprisingly, Shelest defended the role of the republican governments in running their economies.

> The party organisation of Ukraine [led] considerable work for furthering technical perfection of all industrial branches, for implementing the achievements of science and technology in production....In the last few years, thousands of new, more modern machines, equipment, and materials that correspond to the modern technical level had been created and implemented [in Ukraine].

Shelest argued that it was necessary to continue with the territorial administration of the economy and take territorial inter-branch cooperation further. 'This will allow us to avoid long cross transportations, which were characteristic of the former ministries when cooperation developed mainly inside the same branch.'[65] Ivan Spiridonov, former first secretary of the Leningrad obkom and now the chairman of the Soviet of the Union of the USSR Supreme Soviet (*Sovet Soiuza Verkhovnogo Soveta SSSR*), sent a note to the plenum presidium wondering

> whether it would not be useful, at the initial stage [of the reform], to create a special organ (a ministry, or a main administration, etc.) in each republic that would unite and administer enterprises of inter-branch cooperation, about which comrade Shelest was talking in his speech....The need for such organs would become unnecessary when direct relationships between enterprises were consolidated.[66]

In contrast to Kosygin and Brezhnev, who attributed a relatively minor role to the party in the new manifestation of the old system, Shelest was determined to have the CPU lead the implementation of the Kosygin reforms. 'Communists of Ukraine will do everything', promised Shelest, to eliminate the shortcomings that have been uncovered at this plenum and resolutely improve the work of industry, accelerate technological progress, and achieve the increase of labour productivity and culture of production. We will perform this task first of all by improving the work of each enterprise, because, in the end, the success of our industry in general is dependent on the work of each individual enterprise.[67]

Shelest's promises, or hopes, could not change the fact that the new Soviet leadership did not need the republican governments to manage resources and did not rely on the party to increase economic growth. So, the leadership would allow the ministries to 'dominate the republican authorities and impose their own interests'.[68]

Foreign trade was not discussed at the September 1965 plenum, but Shelest already knew by then that there was no prospect for Kyiv to participate in this area. Nonetheless, as if the 2 September meeting had been insufficient, on 21 October 1965, 'at Brezhnev's behest, the CPSU Presidium [now formally] rebuked Shelest for having sent a note to the Presidium in early August 1965 proposing that the Ukrainian government be allowed to establish its own foreign economic ties'.[69]

## Shelest Loses the Struggle for Resources

Of all the areas that interested Shelest in the summer of 1965, unemployment was both the most sensitive and the most promising in terms of securing the republican leadership's influence on resource distribution in Ukraine. The socio-economic situation was the primary responsibility of the party, so Shelest could legitimately insist that the central planners consider the republic's views.[70] Besides, at the Ukrainian Central Committee plenum that gathered on 19–20 October 1965 to discuss the Kosygin reform, some obkom first secretaries emphasized that the problem of labour remained at the centre of their attention. The Vinnytsia, Chernihiv, and Lviv obkom secretaries, for example, stated that they had to solve the problem of unemployment, whereas the secretaries of other oblasts, such as Kherson, were struggling with a shortage of labour.[71] In his closing statement to the plenum, Shelest assured the audience that he shared their concerns but admitted that the possibility of securing additional funds from Moscow was limited. Therefore, the republic should try to rely on internal resources.

'Several comrades raised the question of employment. This is a correct question', Shelest said. It was discussed in the Ukrainian Presidium and, based on information from the oblasts, suggestions were sent to the central Presidium in Moscow. 'But I must say', he continued,

that the way some comrades are demanding [to solve it], this question will not be solved any time soon, neither today, nor tomorrow, nor in a year. We cannot immediately build the [necessary] number of new enterprises that would employ all unemployed persons in this or another oblast....There is no doubt, we will try to construct some enterprises in some oblasts, but we will consider the interests of the republic and the state in general. At the same time, I think that we also need to pay more attention to local industry, so that it develops as it should and thus would be able to use the available local raw materials and employ more people in small enterprises working with local raw materials. We should amply use this opportunity in each oblast.[72]

Shelest did not leave the problem there. On 22 January 1966, he wrote to Moscow that 'the USSR Gosplan should take a substantial labour force and fixed assets in the south-western part of the Soviet Union into account' and consider 'further development of productive forces primarily by reconstructing...the existing production sites as well as by constructing new enterprises of labour-intensive industries'.[73]

By March, Shelest had managed to secure the allocation of some funds from central planners to Western Ukraine. This allowed the Ukrainian party apparatus to focus on unemployment in other parts of Ukraine at the Twenty-Third Ukrainian Party Congress that was held on 15–18 March 1966, shortly before the Twenty-Third Party Congress (29 March–8 April 1966). Unemployment in Western Ukraine was not mentioned at all. Furthermore, neither western oblasts nor their obkom secretaries were mentioned in Shelest's report to the Central Committee about the Twenty-Third Ukrainian Party Congress.[74]

However, after the Twenty-Third Party Congress, the USSR Gosplan and several all-union ministries changed their mind about allocating funds to Western Ukraine. Without explaining their reasons, they ignored Ukraine's requests for labour and 'cancelled the decisions that had previously been made about the location of new enterprises [in Western Ukraine and the Donbas coal basin]'. As Shelest explained in his letter to the Central Committee on 30 July 1966, 'in the south-western region, there were projects to build factories for automobile manufacturing in Uman [Cherkasy oblast], Sambir [Lviv oblast], Uzhhorod [and Mukachevo] [Zakarpattia oblast], Stryi [Lviv oblast], Ivano-Frankivsk, [and] Shepetivka [Khmelnytskyi oblast]'. However,

the Ministry of Automobile Industry and the USSR Gosplan decided to construct these enterprises in other republics. As light industry investments were distributed among the republics, factories in Volodymyr-Volynsk, Khmelnytskyi, Uzhhorod, Komunarsk (today Alchevsk), and Krasnyi Luch in the Luhansk oblast, [as well as] eight flax-processing plants and a number of other factories that had been planned for the south-western region were taken off the list of new construction sites.[75]

As a major rebuff, and very much contrary to the Ukrainian leadership's expectation that the USSR Gosplan would invest in labour-intensive industries, the

Ukrainian leadership had to promise in July 1966 that '70 percent of the production growth would be achieved by increasing productivity'.[76]

In his closing speech at the 15 December 1969 Central Committee plenum, Brezhnev reported that nine out of ten employable persons were either working or studying. Shortage of labour was everywhere in the Soviet Union. By 1969, the average unemployment rate in Ukraine was 12 percent. However, according to Ukrainian statisticians, in Western Ukraine, unemployment remained between 18 and 30 percent, depending on the oblast. Gross output of industrial production in the western oblasts was 1.7 times smaller than in the rest of Ukraine. Monetary income of the population of the western oblasts was 15–20 percent lower than the republic average. Shelest again asked to build labour-intensive industrial enterprises and construction sites in this region.[77]

By the summer of 1966, the Ukrainian leadership had lost its influence on the distribution of material resources, whether they were generated in Ukraine or allocated to it. Of 4,312.7 million roubles that were formally allocated to parts of the Ukrainian economy that fell under the de jure jurisdiction of the Ukrainian government—that is, of union-republican or republican status (including construction)—1,824.5 million, or 42.3 percent, were channelled through the Ukrainian government. The amount seemed considerable. However, it included investments in such areas as agriculture (549.8 million roubles), transport (146.8 million) and housing (501.1 million).[78] The Ukrainian government could allocate only 9.17 percent of the 1,824.5 million roubles to industrial production. (The share of industrial output manufactured by enterprises of republican jurisdiction was 13.6 percent.)[79]

On 14 June 1966, the Ukrainian Politburo[80] instructed the Ministry of Local Industry to prepare a proposal on how to increase local production and, in particular, how to address the problem of unemployment.[81] On 5 August 1966, Ukrainian Minister of Local Industry Anatolii Yeriomenko reported to Shelest that he planned to increase local production by 170 percent from 1965 levels by 1970. He planned to increase production of construction materials from local raw materials and construction lime to 3.8 times the 1965 levels.[82]

(Yeriomenko's readiness to increase production of construction materials was not accidental. As the former chairman of the Lviv sovnarkhoz, he was fully aware of the need for construction materials in Western Ukraine. Besides, at the October 1965 Ukrainian Central Committee plenum, the first secretary of the Lviv obkom, Kutsevol, had insisted that unemployment in his oblast could have been lower had the planners invested in production of local construction materials.[83] As described in the previous chapter, under the sovnarkhoz system, Kutsevol and Yeriomenko formed a regional party–industry alliance. After 1965, they maintained a good relationship.)

To fulfil the five-year plan, continued Yeriomenko in his letter to Shelest, his ministry planned to allocate 215 million roubles to capital construction; he planned to construct 223 new enterprises and reconstruct 323. 'Eighty-seven new industrial combines will be organized in the regions of the republic with available labour, local raw materials, and production wastes',[84] promised Yeriomenko.

Still, the Ministry of Local Industry had very limited ability to reduce unemployment. Its share in the total industrial output of Ukraine in 1966, including production enterprises of the all-union jurisdiction, was a meagre 1.5 percent, a sharp decrease from 12 percent of total industrial output in 1962. In the years to follow, its capabilities would decline further as the union and union-republican ministries would start producing simple goods which had traditionally been produced by the local industry.[85]

For years to come, Shelest continued to insist that the role of the Ukrainian leadership in the administration of the economy should be increased.[86] The central leadership remained reluctant. As a way of preventing the Ukrainian leadership from influencing industry, the central leadership refused to clearly divide rights and responsibilities between the union-republican ministries and the councils of ministers of the republics where the relevant union-republican ministries were formed.[87] In spite of Kyiv's requests, there were no regulations defining the relationship between the all-union ministries and the republican governments, either. In 1968, Shelest asked Moscow to include two paragraphs in the Central Committee resolution 'About finishing the transfer of industry to the new planning system and economic stimulus', which would require all-union economic agencies to set out regulations only after approval by republican governments. The central leadership ignored his pleas.[88] As a result, the Ukrainian leadership was held responsible for decisions upon which it had no influence. With the main flow of resources out of its reach, the only way in which the Ukrainian leadership could still be useful to the industrial managers was to defend their interests in Moscow. During his time in office, Shelest sent numerous letters asking to increase investments in this or that industry. The most common argument that Shelest used in his letters was the impossibility of meeting plan targets without sufficient resources.

A rare exception was Shelest's 1968 request to Moscow when he used the 'socio-economic' factor to argue for funds for Western Ukraine. The argument concerned the production of DT-20 tractors. Central planners had decided to move the manufacturing of this tractor from Kharkiv to a non-Ukrainian factory. In August 1968, and then again on 15 October 1968, Shelest insisted on moving production to the Ternopil machine-construction factory. 'The per capita GDP in the Ternopil oblast is five times less than the average in Ukraine', explained Shelest, 'whereas the number of industrial personnel per 1,000 persons is 2.5 times lower. The percentage of the population that is not occupied in socialist production is increasing every year and will reach 25 percent of total labour resources in 1970.' Besides, argued Shelest, the Ternopil factory had the capacity to organize the production of DT-20 tractors, and the mechanical parts that the

**Illustration 10**  Ukrainian Soviet leaders, 1960s/© TsDAEA (0-243321)
Ukrainian Soviet leaders in one of the pavilions at the Exhibition of Achievements of the National Economy of the Ukrainian SSR. Right to left: Chairman of the Ukrainian Government Volodymyr Shcherbytsky (2nd), CPU First Secretary Petro Shelest, member of the Ukrainian Politburo and future chairman of the Ukrainian government (1972–1987) Oleksandr Liashko.

Ternopil factory did not produce could be supplied from the Rivne factory, which produced spare parts for tractors, and the Lozova forging-mechanical plant (Kharkiv oblast).[89] Central planners rejected Shelest's suggestion. They determined that it would be faster and more cost-effective to transfer the production of DT-20 tractors to the Vladimir factory in Russia.[90]

The continuous priority of heavy industry and the Soviet investment policy that prioritized the existing industrial centres in Ukraine led Shelest to focus on the needs of the industrialized oblasts of eastern Ukraine. Of the areas that Shelest wrote most about to Moscow, ferrous metallurgy was third to agriculture and cadres.[91]

Shelest's attention to the heavy industry branches undoubtedly reflected his aim to ensure that Ukraine fulfilled production plans, for which the Ukrainian leadership remained accountable. It also reflected his effort to remain useful to the eastern Ukrainian obkoms. However, Shelest's efforts did not always bring positive results. In his letter to the Central Committee on 23 March 1972, in what could almost be viewed as despair, Shelest complained that even though Ukraine had harmonized its suggestions on the resolution 'The measures on further development of iron-ore industry and comprehensive improvement of ore production' with the positions of the USSR Gosplan, the USSR Ministry of Ferrous

Metallurgy, and the central government, the updated version of the government's resolution did not include these suggestions.[92]

Certainly by 1970, the obkoms of the industrialized oblasts knew that Shelest's lobbying did not guarantee a positive outcome. So, the obkoms wrote directly to the relevant all-union ministries in Moscow and the Central Committee when seeking to secure resources for the main industries of their oblasts.[93] The Ukrainian Central Committee was only one of the addressees.

## Part II: The CPU

### Asserting Party Control over the Economy: Breaking Regional Party–Industry Alliances

Asserting party control over industry was Shelest's second strategy to impose the power of the republic's centre over the regions. The context for insisting on party control over the economy was seemingly favourable. The unity of party organizations that Khrushchev had bifurcated into industrial and agricultural in 1962 was restored. The Twenty-Third Party Congress emphasized the role of the party in economic supervision.[94]

To restore party control over industry, Shelest first tried to split regional party–industry alliances. As discussed in the previous chapters, the main reason behind regional party–industry alliances was the financial dependence of the obkoms on industrial enterprises for the fulfilment of agricultural plans and social programmes and, at the same time, the accountability of the obkoms for the fulfilment of industrial plans by their oblasts. In 1965, Shelest could not relieve the obkoms of their responsibility, nor could he freely financially assist the obkoms and oblispolkoms. Not only was the republican leadership losing its influence over Ukrainian heavy industry, it had no influence on oblast budgets.[95] So, Shelest relied mainly on rhetoric that called for 'party discipline'.

At the 19 June 1965 Ukrainian Central Committee plenum, Shelest indicated that he did not favour regional party–industry alliances. He insisted that the failures of the sovnarkhozy—which were the official justification for economic recentralization—were due as much to the lack of responsibility among industrial managers as to the lack of industrial oversight on the part of the obkoms.[96] At the Ukrainian Central Committee plenum of 19–20 October 1965, which discussed economic recentralization, Shelest repeated that the obkoms were responsible for industrial failures in their oblasts and insisted that, at the regional level, the interests of the obkoms and those of the managers were very different. The managers were responsible for production. The party's interest was to uncover shortcomings in the work of industrial enterprises, not to cover up for them, and not to ignore any violations. The message that Shelest tried to convey was that the party could and must interfere with industrial management, but not replace it. Echoing Brezhnev's speech at the September 1965 plenum, Shelest explained:

> Under the new conditions, the party organisations must deal more with issues of industrial production [than when the sovnarkhozy were in place]. They must ensure that the principles of material stimulus are implemented correctly, [and they must] struggle for the rational usage of financial, material, and labour resources. It is necessary to increase control…over the economic activity of production enterprises…[97]

Shelest went as far as to instruct the obkoms to make sure that industrial and construction enterprises were properly prepared for winter. 'Particular attention should be paid to stocking the sufficient volume of raw materials, other materials, and fuel.' A similar instruction was given to all party organizations. The role and the responsibility of the grassroots party cells and party organizations in enterprises, construction sites, ministries, and administrations for the fulfilment of the decisions of the September Central Committee plenum had to be considerably increased, as well.[98]

Shelest had good reasons to believe regional party–industry alliances could be broken. Starting in 1965, the new Soviet leadership sought to boost investment in agriculture, an area traditionally under the party purview. At the 24–26 March 1965 Central Committee plenum, Brezhnev announced that the state would invest in agriculture in the 1966–1970 period as much as in the previous nineteen years.[99] The 25–27 May 1966 Central Committee plenum boosted the programme of land melioration that had been launched under Khrushchev. The five-year plan for 1966–1970 allocated 10 billion roubles to the irrigation and drainage of lands in the Soviet Union.[100] Ukraine's share was 5.3 billion roubles, which included funds to procure fertilizers and new agricultural machinery, but also investments in a number of industries, such as heavy, chemical, light, food processing, and machine construction, and a number of construction organizations involved in irrigation and drainage works. According to the 1966–1970 plan, the area of irrigated and drained agricultural lands in Ukraine was to expand by 2.5 times compared to 1961–1965 and investments in irrigated and drained lands were to increase by four times compared to 1961–1965.[101] Increased investment in agriculture suggested that the Ukrainian leadership would be able to assist the obkoms and oblispolkoms with the fulfilment of agricultural and other plans, and thus reduce, if not completely eliminate, the financial dependence of the obkoms on local industrial managers.

However, the increase in agricultural investment did not increase the authority of the Ukrainian leadership vis-à-vis the obkoms and thus did not affect regional party–industry alliances. Firstly, the Ukrainian republican leadership had limited say in the distribution of the funds allocated to the production of agricultural output. Secondly, the Ukrainian government could not freely distribute the funds that had been allocated to Ukraine for land melioration works. In theory, as Nykyfor Kalchenko, vice-chairman of the Ukrainian government, informed the Ukrainian Central Committee plenum on 22–23 June 1966, the oblasts that were supposed to benefit most from the government's new attention to agriculture were the southern oblasts of Crimea, Kherson, Mykolaiv, Odesa, and Zaporizhzhia, which needed irrigation investment in order to increase production of grain and vegetables on more than 995,000 hectares; and the western oblasts of Lviv, Rivne, Volyn, and Zhytomyr, but also Kyiv, Chernihiv, and some others that would invest in the drainage of lands in Polissia. However, in practice, as Shelest explained, the all-union melioration programme aimed to expand irrigation in large grain-producing regions: the north Caucasus, the Volga region, and southern Ukraine. More importantly, the state required quick returns. Therefore, 'in order not to end up with the dispersion of funds', the republican government was going to invest primarily in economies and oblasts that would have the highest and fastest return.[102]

Thirdly, the central leadership relied primarily on the ministries to implement the melioration programme, such as the Ukrainian Ministry of Melioration and Water Economy, which was allocated 900 million roubles for this programme; the Ukrainian Ministry of Construction (84.8 million roubles); the Ukrainian Ministry of Rural Construction (143.3 million roubles); the Ukrainian Ministry of Energy and Electrification; the Ukrainian Ministry of Montage and Special Construction Works; the Ukrainian Ministry of Automobile Transport and Highways; the Ukrainian Ministry of Communication; and various organizations that were under the direct jurisdiction of the all-union ministries, such as 'Kremenchuggesstroi' and 'Dneprostroi' of the USSR Ministry of Energy and Electrification.[103]

Finally, according to the estimates of the central planners, even the increased investment in agriculture was considered insufficient to fulfil the production plan targets. The kolkhozy and sovkhozy were put in a position when they had to 'construct or get everything themselves', as Aleksei Krasnopivtsev, the head of the USSR Gosplan agricultural department, put it, and the central leadership relied on the republican governments to find additional funds and resources for agricultural development.[104] 'Additional funds' meant non-centralized investments, which included voluntary help, or patronage, by industrial enterprises to kolkhozy and sovkhozy (for more detail, see the previous chapter). In particular, the central leadership relied on industrial enterprises to continue helping kolkhozy and sovkhozy build small irrigation systems, equip villages with electricity, construct and mechanize cattle farms and greenhouses, and produce agricultural equipment and spare parts for agricultural machinery.[105] In 1972, the Ukrainian leadership would even organize patronage assistance of industry to agriculture at the republican level. On 1 March 1972, it provided metallurgical factories with

**Illustration 11**  Petro Shelest visiting the Donetsk oblast, July 1969/© TsDAHOU
(f. 330 op. 1 spr. 23 ark. 12)

At the end of the 1960s, CPU First Secretary Petro Shelest was at the peak of his political career.
In summer 1969, he visited the Donetsk oblast. Right to left: Volodymyr Dehtiariov, the secretary of
the Donetsk obkom (1964–1976), Petro Shelest (4th).

resources to produce spare parts for agricultural machinery. The Ukrainian leadership could not pay for labour, so the party committees of the enterprises that participated in this programme were supposed to explain (*provesti raz"iasnitel'nuiu rabotu*) 'the importance of supplementary output of spare parts for republican agriculture to the collectives of these enterprises' and 'popularize socialist competition for an early fulfilment of the task'.[106]

With the Ukrainian leadership unable to independently distribute investments between the oblasts, and the state relying on industrial enterprises to assist the kolkhozy and sovkhozy with the fulfilment of agricultural plans, Shelest was forced to moderate his criticism of regional party–industry alliances in 1966.[107] So, consolidated under the sovnarkhoz system, the alliances persisted even after the sovnarkhozy were abolished. The main difference now was that the obkoms found themselves indirectly dependent on the all-union industrial ministries.[108] The continued prioritization of heavy industry sealed the pattern of strong regional party–industry alliances in the highly industrialized eastern oblasts of Ukraine and in Lviv.

At the 22–23 June 1966 Ukrainian Central Committee plenum, speakers discussing the implementation of the land melioration programme illustrated this pattern quite clearly. In the period between 1964 and 1966, the kolkhoz 'Zaria komunizmu' in the Zaporizhzhia oblast built an irrigation system on

2,805 hectares of land with the patronage of the trust 'Zaporozhstroi' and the metallurgical factory 'Zaporozhstal'. The industrial enterprises provided assistance amounting to 770,000 roubles, or 3.4 percent of the oblast's centrally allocated funds. The heavy industry of Luhansk helped local kolkhozy and sovkhozy to build small irrigation systems on 3,778 hectares of land. The Luhansk obkom planned to build systems of small irrigation on 19,600 hectares of lands in the next five years.[109] The Kharkiv oblast did not have enough water, and lacked equipment, materials, and pipes that were produced elsewhere. Nonetheless, the oblispolkom '[found] some material locally, [and brought] industrial enterprises to help the kolkhozy and sovkhozy.... By the end of 1966, 16,000 hectares would be under irrigation',[110] estimated the chairman of the Kharkiv oblispolkom, Dmytro Pisniachevsky.

In the Odesa oblast, construction of irrigation systems progressed very slowly. 'In the seven-year period [1959–1965], only 6,000 hectares were irrigated', whereas in the last two years, the kolkhozy and sovkhozy had built irrigation systems on 9,000 hectares with the patronage of local industrial enterprises. The local industrial enterprises could help more, but they needed pipes, which had to be brought in from other oblasts',[111] explained Mykhailo Synytsia, first secretary of the Odesa obkom.

Fedir Golovchenko, first secretary of the Kyiv obkom, relied on enterprises located in the Kyiv oblast to maintain its drainage systems. In 1964, 7,000 hectares of arable land were restored using 'local opportunities'; almost 8.5 hectares were restored in the period between 1963 and 1966.[112]

The oblasts with low levels of industrialization had to rely on the state to implement the land melioration programme. The Kherson oblast did not have the industrial potential of the Dnipropetrovsk oblast, but it was supposed to benefit from the all-union Kakhovka irrigation system project designed to irrigate 320,000 hectares. Still, industrially poor and with a small population, the Kherson oblast relied on the state to build housing, roads, and cultural centres to attract labour from other regions.[113]

The first secretary of the Zhytomyr obkom, Mykhailo Lazurenko, relied on the state to fulfil agricultural plans. 'In 1963, an irrigation system was constructed on 11,300 hectares with state funds in the Zhytomyr oblast.'[114] The Zhytomyr oblast also depended on other oblasts for lime fertilizer and thus required the assistance of the republican authorities to organize the supplies.

The Chernihiv oblast did not have the industrial potential to support local agriculture, either. 'In the forthcoming five-year period, the oblast planned to restore 65,000 hectares, for which it needed almost 14 million roubles in investment. The oblast needed to expand construction organizations; it needed more machinery and fertilizers. For all this, the oblast relied on the republican ministries and the Gosplan.'[115]

The Sumy oblast was in a similar situation. It was not among the priority oblasts for centralized capital investment. To increase the productivity of the agricultural soil and install irrigation systems, the first secretary of the Sumy obkom, Borys Voltovsky, involved 'specialists of agriculture, workers of research administrations, communists, Komsomol, all toilers of the village'. Voltovsky did not rely much on help from Kyiv, though. Rather, considering that 'the Polissia areas had the potential to create pastures and implement the system of hard standings for cattle, as practised in the Estonian SSR', the obkom 'sent a delegation of collective farmers and chairmen of collective farms to Estonia to study the experience of the Estonian kolkhozy'.[116] Voltovsky wanted to implement the Estonian experience in Sumy.

Western Ukraine's low level of industrialization affected the approach of the obkoms in fulfilling the agricultural plans as well. Yakiv Pohrebniak, first secretary of the Ivano-Frankivsk obkom, relied on the state for financing the drainage works that were required on 30 percent of all agricultural lands and about 27 percent of all arable lands. At the same time, similarly to Voltovsky, Pohrebniak sent an agricultural delegation to Estonia, Latvia, and the Leningrad oblast to study sheep milk and meat production, 'the share of which in the total agricultural output of the Ivano-Frankivsk oblast was increasingly growing'. Still, to increase the production of sheep meat and milk, the obkom relied on the republican government to provide the oblast with cement and metal for fences and minerals for high-altitude pastures. Pohrebniak hoped that the Ukrainian leadership would convince the Ministry of Industry of Construction Materials to reverse its refusal to organize local production of high-quality lime flour in the oblast.[117]

While Ivano-Frankivsk could at least hope to increase its production of sheep milk and meat, the situation in the Rivne oblast was more desperate. For this oblast, the programme of land restoration 'not only was of high priority but was existentially necessary for the further development of the regional economy, for the fulfilment of state plans, to increase the material well-being of people, and to solve the problem of unemployment'. Unfortunately, as Ivan Mozghovy, first secretary of the Rivne obkom, explained, the drainage programme as it was implemented did not result in an increase in output. In the last years, 16,000 hectares of land were drained; however, the kolkhozy and sovkhozy could not cultivate these lands because they lacked the necessary machinery. The oblast had only thirty-eight out of 150 necessary tractors adapted to the Rivne type of soil. The kolkhozy lacked ploughs, harrows, mineral fertilizers, and a variety of materials and machinery. With no industrial enterprises that could offer patronage, the kolkhozy and sovkhozy could only rely on local Komsomol.[118]

The situation in the only industrialized oblast in Western Ukraine, Lviv, was different. Local enterprises were not yet fully involved in the construction of drainage systems, but, nonetheless, patronage links between local industrial enterprises and farmers were developing. With them, relations between the party apparatus and the managers grew closer.[119]

Shelest, in his concluding speech at the June 1966 Ukrainian Central Committee plenum, unwittingly admitted that the western oblasts did not have sufficient industrial capacity to facilitate the fulfilment of agricultural plans. He praised the party organizations and enterprises of the Donetsk and Dnipropetrovsk oblasts, the Ukrainian Ministry of Ferrous Metallurgy (located in Dnipropetrovsk), and the Ukrainian Ministry of the Coal Industry (located in Donetsk) for 'tangible help to the countryside'. He reprimanded the managers of the Kharkiv, Luhansk, Zaporizhzhia, Odesa, and Lviv oblasts for not doing enough and finished his speech with the general idea that 'the party organizations should consider patronage work to the countryside as one of the most important areas of their everyday activity. The work should be organized in such a way that each industrial enterprise and each construction organization provided tangible assistance to kolkhozy and sovkhozy'.[120] Considering chronic lack of investment in agriculture and the republic's direct responsibility for the fulfilment of agricultural plans, Shelest could not but encourage a full mobilization of resources, regardless of whether or not it meant consolidating regional party–industry alliances.

Being dependent on industrial enterprises for the fulfilment of agricultural plans, the obkoms could not 'control and supervise' them at the same time,[121] which Shelest duly acknowledged. In 1969, Shelest encouraged the obkoms to assist ministers and industrial managers in fulfilling production tasks, rather than controlling or supervising them. If the production enterprise was lagging behind, it was the ministry that should address the problems. The obkoms should assist the ministries and the managers in fulfilling the plans.[122]

Still, Shelest's acceptance of the regional party–industry alliances did not stop him from pursuing his goal of imposing party control over industry or consolidating the authority of the republican leadership over the regions. As he failed to break regional party–industry alliances, Shelest focused on empowering the Ukrainian Central Committee.

## Empowering the Ukrainian Apparatus

In the period between September 1966 and March 1969, the Ukrainian Central Committee asked the Central Committee several times to expand the apparatus of the Ukrainian Central Committee.[123] For example, on 16 April 1969, the Ukrainian Central Committee explained to the Central Committee that because of the growth of the mining industry and non-ferrous metallurgy in Ukraine, there should be a separate section of mining and non-ferrous metallurgy within the Ukrainian Central Committee department of heavy industry. Shelest did not ask for much, just to allocate one additional staff member to lead the new section. Generally, the Central Committee was supportive, and Shelest's requests were approved.[124]

Starting in September 1969, Shelest's requests became more substantial. In a long letter on 30 September, Shelest argued for the further expansion of the party apparatus in Ukraine. Shelest wanted to expand the Ukrainian Central Committee department of defence industry and create a separate section that would supervise the fulfilment of the so-called 'mobilization tasks' (*mobilizatsionnye zadaniia*) by production enterprises, regardless of their branch affiliation.[125] Shelest wanted to mirror the division of the Ukrainian Ministry of Construction into two ministries, the Ministry of Construction of Enterprises of Heavy Industry and the Ministry of Industrial Construction, and split the Ukrainian Central Committee department of construction and urban infrastructure into two, as well. Shelest wanted to systematize and centralize the supervision of financing and planning, and he asked to expand the staff of the obkoms.[126]

Most revealing of Shelest's intention to impose the authority of the Ukrainian Central Committee over the regions was his request to increase the number of Ukrainian Central Committee inspectors responsible for work with the obkoms from eight to between twenty-eight and thirty. Twenty-six inspectors 'would be attached to the [twenty-five] oblast party organizations and the Kyiv city organization, and the others [two to four] would carry out the tasks assigned to them by the Ukrainian Central Committee.'[127]

While the decision on Shelest's September request was still pending, on 13 October 1969, the Central Committee issued an instruction to work out measures 'to improve the structure of administration of chemical, oil, and coal industries'. To protect Ukrainian ministries from being abolished, Shelest promised Moscow to place them under tighter supervision by the Ukrainian Central Committee. For that, on 13 December 1969, Shelest suggested splitting the Ukrainian Central Committee department of chemical and oil industries into two sections, one to supervise chemical industry and organic synthesis and the other to supervise oil and petrochemical industries.[128] At the beginning of February 1970, the Central Committee approved Shelest's request to expand the Ukrainian Central Committee, except instead of twenty-eight to thirty inspectors, it agreed only to nineteen.[129]

Neither Shelest's extensive request to expand the Ukrainian Central Committee apparatus nor Moscow's amenability was accidental. At the 15 December 1969 Central Committee plenum, Brezhnev announced that economic growth had slowed and blamed it on the ministries.[130] In his concluding speech, Brezhnev called for an increase in labour, party, and state discipline. As for methods, Brezhnev rejected a Stalin-like atmosphere of fear. He called 'to widely develop criticism and self-criticism, to improve the work of the people's control and organs of the party control,... [and] to increase the accountability of the cadres'. 'We have the potential to successfully fulfil the 1970 plan. [But] we ought to work seriously [for this]. The party organizations, Soviet and economic organs, trade unions, and Komsomol have a great deal of organizational and educational work to do.'[131]

In the meantime, while Brezhnev called for a boost to party control over the economy, the ministries continued to recentralize industrial administration. In May 1970, Ukraine had to agree to abolish the republican coal and oil ministries. At the end of that summer, the central leadership suggested abolishing the Ukrainian Ministry of Geology and placing geology under the administration of the USSR Ministry of Geology. In the spring of 1971, the USSR Ministry of Construction Materials Industry suggested transforming the Ukrainian republican ministry into union-republican. One of the explanations for further recentralization was the Ukrainian ministries' failure to fulfil the plans, to which Shelest, when arguing against the abolition of the Ukrainian Ministry of Chemical Industry, insisted that the success of the chemical industry had been impeded by delays in the implementation of technological innovation and the low quality of new technological processes.

> The technical level of the majority of production enterprises lags considerably behind the achievements of modern science and technology. Scientific, research, and project institutes of the USSR Ministry of Chemical Industry systematically make a large number of serious mistakes and miscalculations in technical documentation, selection of equipment, and designs of chemical enterprises.[132]

Shelest implicitly reminded the central leadership that he had opposed the recentralization of control over the implementation of new technology in production in 1965. Even USSR Minister of Agriculture Vladimir Matskevich would make several attempts to concentrate planning, administration, and distribution of resources for agriculture in his ministry. In all of his attempts, he was rebuffed by the republican governments, as well as by the USSR Gosplan. One of the attempts was made around the time Shelest was removed, and it would fall to Volodymyr Shcherbytsky to categorically oppose Matskevich's idea on 14 June 1972.[133]

In continuation of the December 1969 Central Committee plenum, the Twenty-Fourth Party Congress in March–April 1971 changed the party rules 'in order to give the PPOs [Primary Party Organizations] of ministries the right of control "of the apparatus in carrying out the directives of the party and government and the observance of Soviet laws".'[134] At the 22–23 November 1971 plenum, Brezhnev criticized the ministries for persistent failure to implement technological innovations in production and for low labour productivity, which was twice as high in the United States as in the Soviet Union. So 'considering the increasing role of labour productivity, there [was] a decision to set plan targets again for the growth of labour productivity for the ministries and enterprises'. It was based on this criterion that the work of the leading cadres should be evaluated.[135]

Once Brezhnev started pushing to empower local party organizations, Shelest embarked on what ended up being his final campaign to assert Kyiv's authority in the republic. As in 1965, he started with an attempt to convince the obkoms to prioritize duty to the party over regional economic interests. At the 24–25 June 1971 plenum of the Ukrainian Central Committee, Shelest reverted to criticizing the obkoms for industry's regular failure to meet plan targets: 1,180 enterprises, or 14.3 percent, did not meet the labour productivity target in the period between January and June 1971. Shelest blamed the enterprises' party organizations for being soft on the management of their enterprises, and the obkoms for being soft on the enterprises' party organizations. In reaction to the criticism of consumer goods shortages that sounded at the Twenty-Fourth Party Congress, Shelest insisted that 'the party organizations had to establish day-to-day control over the construction and reconstruction of factories of light, food, meat, and milk indus-tries, and of the local industry and other factories that produce consumer goods'. Of course, the party had to perform its direct function of 'working with the masses'. However, insisted Shelest,

> it was important that while solving any production problem, the party organisa-tions and all our cadres skilfully combined economic and party-political work.... The party cannot take the position of a bystander when enterprises, construction sites, or kolkhozy use reserves inefficiently or violate state or labour discipline, when the labour productivity grows slowly, when the plans are not fulfilled, and there are shameful incidents of whitewashing [ochkovtiratel'stvo], false statistics, or unjustifiable increases in prices.[136]

Then Shelest criticized regional party–industry alliances.

> A considerable shortcoming in the work of some gorkoms and raikoms is their attempt to replace Soviet and economic organs. Some obkoms commit the same sin. Substitution [podmena][137] and guardianship often create with some Soviet and economic workers the feeling of reassurance and a desire to secure the approval of the party organ in order to evade responsibility [for their actions] later.

Shelest criticized the obkoms for petite tutelage and lacking a relationship with grassroots party organizations.

> In a number of obkoms, the branch committees still have a poor connection with the grassroots [party] organisations and insufficiently study their work.... [V]ery often, the party leaders, when they visit enterprises, kolkhozy, or sovkhozy, discuss the issues mainly with the khoziaistvenniki, instead of with the party aktiv, the communists. Sometimes they do not even meet with the secretaries of [the grassroots] party organisations [at these enterprises]. Unfortunately, certain party functionaries of the Ukrainian Central Committee have the same shortcomings. We must increase the role of the grassroots party organisations.[138]

Yet, instead of controlling industrial enterprises, the obkoms continued to defend and cooperate with them. At the 28 September 1971 Ukrainian Central Committee plenum, there was a consensus that the task set by the Twenty-Fourth Party Congress to increase production of consumer goods and food products could not be achieved without the help of the all-union ministries and their enterprises. At the same time, as a stimulus to increase production of consumer goods, Pavlo Kozyr, first secretary of the Odesa obkom, suggested allowing local organs to sell a share of the excess production inside their oblasts above the quantities that the state plan allowed the oblast to sell.[139] They did not discuss who would instruct the enterprises to produce above the plan and determine how the profits would be divided between the industrial enterprises that produced the goods and local trade organizations, which were predominantly under the jurisdiction of the oblispolkoms. That the relationship between the obkoms and industrial enterprises would tighten, however, was certain.

On 23 November 1971, Ivan Lutak, secretary of the Ukrainian Central Committee and member of the Ukrainian Politburo, submitted to the Central Committee a request for additional staff positions for the Ukrainian Central Committee departments of propaganda and agitation, heavy industry, defence industry, machine construction, light industry, and food, as well as for construction and municipal services, the agricultural department, trade, and cadres. In attempt to place the industrial cadres under tight party control, Lutak asked the Central Committee to form personnel departments in seventeen obkoms and to keep close track of the nomenklatura. In the other eight obkoms (Donetsk, Dnipropetrovsk, Odesa, Kharkiv, Kyiv, Zaporizhzhia, Lviv, and Luhansk (Voroshylovhrad)), the personnel departments had been created in 1970. Lutak also argued that the departments of administrative, trade, and financial organs should exist as separate departments in all obkoms.[140]

For the third time since 1965, on 21 December 1971, Shelest asked the Central Committee to allow him to increase party control over the defence industry in Ukraine. 'In 1958, departments of the defence industry were created in the Ukrainian Central Committee and seven obkoms, Donetsk, Dnipropetrovsk, Zaporizhzhia, Kyiv, Lviv, Mykolaiv, and Kharkiv. At the time, the republic had seventy-four enterprises and organizations of the defence industry branches with the labour of 231,000 people.' By 1971, the number of enterprises had tripled, the volumes of production had increased fivefold, and the labour force now constituted 832,000 people. Shelest asked to provide funding for a deputy head of the Ukrainian Central Committee department of defence and to create defence industry departments in the obkoms of Voroshylovhrad, Crimea, Sumy, and Kherson, and sectors for the defence industry in the obkoms of Zakarpattia, Kirovohrad, Odesa, and Khmelnytskyi.[141] Fifteen out of twenty-five Ukrainian obkoms would now have either a department or a sector of the defence industry.

By the end of 1971, despite his intention to expand the party apparatus, Shelest was no longer relying on the reluctant obkoms to impose party discipline on industrial managers. At a meeting with the Ukrainian Central Committee apparatus on 14 January 1972, Shelest indicated that he believed that only the Ukrainian Central Committee and the grassroots organizations could hold the ministries and industrial managers accountable for plan failures.[142]

Shelest started the 14 January meeting with a reminder of the importance of the party apparatus in state administration and a poorly veiled claim that the industrial managers subordinated the party apparatus to their interests.

> As we know from history, the Trotskyists and other opportunists tried to sow discord between the party apparatus and the party [and]...weaken the role of the party apparatus in managing party, state, and economic construction. There were even attempts to use the apparatus to undermine the general party line and the party leadership.[143]

Then Shelest explained what he expected from the apparatus of the Ukrainian Central Committee. 'First of all, it is necessary to strengthen control by the [Ukrainian] Central Committee apparatus over the fulfilment of the party and government's decisions', and to tackle all problems with the party's political approach. 'It is not enough for the functionaries of the [Ukrainian] Central Committee to establish that such and such enterprises or branches are working poorly', specified Shelest. 'What should interest them first is why setbacks happen and how the managers [*rukovodiashchie rabotniki*] of the ministries or administrations, but also the party committees [in these ministries and administrations], analyse and evaluate these setbacks.'[144] This was necessary for the party to establish whom to hold responsible and how to punish them.

The reason why the Ukrainian Central Committee apparatus had to take a stance against the malpractices of the managers was that the Ukrainian Central Committee—not the party in general—was the defender of the people. When ministries rejected requests and suggestions coming from the periphery, explained Shelest, 'people have no choice but to go to the Central Committee, to the [Ukrainian government]'. Of course, it was difficult to control the ministries, acknowledged Shelest. The Ukrainian Central Committee often made appointments without consulting the grassroots organizations. 'The departments [of the Ukrainian Central Committee] should actively react and resolutely insist on eliminating bureaucratic perversions in the work of separate links of the state and economic apparatus.' To achieve these tasks, the Ukrainian Central Committee apparatus had to improve the circulation of information. 'This does not mean that we should invent additional forms of information [*formy informatsii*]', explained Shelest. 'What is important is that not a single event passes by the

[Ukrainian] Central Committee....It is also important to remember that not a single opinion can replace exact information.'[145]

The secretaries and heads of various departments of the Ukrainian Central Committee shared Shelest's enthusiasm but pointed to the difficulties in their work. Thus, Anatolii Ulanov noted that the work of his department in the oblasts was impeded by the existence of numerous commissions from various all-union, but also republican, organizations and administrations. 'Two teams from the [Ukrainian] Central Committee recently worked in the Donetsk oblast; but besides the Central Committee, [our] question was prepared by the Ukrainian government, the Presidium of the Supreme Soviet of Ukraine, [the Ukrainian Republican Soviet of Trade Unions], [and various] ministries and administrations.' The instructor of the Ukrainian Central Committee department of machine construction pointed to the specifics of the branch that he supervised: machine construction enterprises were run by the all-union ministries. The all-union ministry was not sharing information on the work of its enterprises, so his department had

> to look for other sources of communication [with enterprises] and other methods of work in order to stay well informed about the situation at the branch main enterprises and promptly react to shortcomings in their work. For this purpose, [they] involved the obkoms and the party organisations at these enterprises, and often visit[ed] these enterprises [them]selves, because [even] the information that [his department] receive[d] from the Gosplan and the Central Statistical Agency [was] often incomplete.[146]

In contrast, I. A. Palatny, secretary of the Ukrainian Central Committee department of party-organizational work, optimistically insisted that with sufficient effort, the Ukrainian Central Committee could achieve tangible results. His department systematically controlled the fulfilment of the resolution on increasing the output of consumer goods by using production reserves and local resources more efficiently in Kharkiv enterprises. The persistence of the Ukrainian Central Committee department motivated local party organizations to seek production reserves 'even more aggressively'. As a result, 'due to the aggressiveness of local party organizations, the industry of the Kharkiv oblast increased production of consumer goods by 53 million roubles'.[147]

The report of the head of the Ukrainian Central Committee defence industry department, Yakiv Rudenko, must have been music to Shelest's ears. Similar to machine construction, the defence industry in Ukraine was run directly from Moscow. However, apparently in contrast to his counterparts from the machine-construction department, Rudenko's department maintained close contact with the central apparatus. The description of Rudenko's achievements deserves extensive quotation, particularly since two years after Shelest's removal from Ukraine, Rudenko, at the age of sixty-three, would retire.

RUDENKO: The staff-members of our department regularly go to Moscow, and they regularly visit the minister [of the defence industry], regularly visit the [USSR] Gosplan. When our comrades go there, they have an assignment. I must say that when our instructor comes to the minister—and the instructor comes with a note indicating what the minister has to resolve—the minister welcomes him with great pleasure. (Laughter and excitement in the audience)...

SHELEST: And do you know why he [welcomes our instructor] with great pleasure?

RUDENKO: Yes. Because not a single question, not a single minister can solve a problem in Ukraine successfully without the [Ukrainian] Central Committee, without Pyotr Efimovich [Shelest], without our department. (Excitement in the audience)

...Very often—this is from our experience—a vice-minister would come to Kyiv, visit a factory, make promises, leave, and then do nothing. We do not ignore such cases. We always call the minister and say: Have some influence [*vozdeĭstvuĭte*] on this vice-minister! If a senior official from the ministry comes to Kyiv or Kharkiv and does not visit [our] central committee department in Kyiv, we always call the minister and tell him that if your head of the glavk expects to fulfil a state assignment without the party organs and without [our] department, he will fail.

...I do not want to exaggerate, but we have such a relationship [with the minister in Moscow] that when I call and say 'Aleksandr Ivanovich Shchekin, hello, this is Yakov Kuz'mich Rudenko speaking....I am asking to solve this and that matter'...he says: 'Yakov Kuz'mich, I am in Moscow on the fifth floor, whereas you are there. Whatever you decide, that is the decision. Thank you.' So we are solving the problem as [we see] necessary.

SHELEST: This is not just a job, this is a real fairy-tale. (Laughter in the audience)[148]

Shelest could only hope the other ministers in Moscow would follow the example of Aleksandr Ivanovich Shchekin (if Shchekin did indeed behave the way Rudenko described).

On 22 February, the Ukrainian Politburo discussed the planners. After the ritual praise of certain achievements, Shelest criticized them for paying insufficient attention to the combination of branch and territorial planning.[149]

At the 31 March 1972 Ukrainian Central Committee plenum, the Voroshylovhrad and Cherkasy obkom secretaries were personally criticized for the economic failures of their oblasts. The Dnipropetrovsk, Lviv, Odesa, and Kharkiv obkom first secretaries defended their counterparts by insisting that the fault for the non-fulfilment of the production plans lay solely with the ministries. In response,

Shelest insisted that it was now necessary to increase the personal responsibility of all functionaries for the fulfilment of their tasks, for the fulfilment of state plans.[150] The motive of 'personal responsibility' was not new. Brezhnev mentioned it briefly in his closing speech at the 1969 December Central Committee plenum and the Twenty-Fourth Party Congress in March–April 1971.[151] However, framed in the context of increasing the authority of the Ukrainian Central Committee, and of Shelest personally, over industry and the regions, it could legitimately be viewed as something more than lip-service to the official rhetoric on the role of the party in society.

On 6 April, Shelest reported to the Central Committee on the improvement of organizational and party work in Ukraine and the 'increased responsibility of the cadres'. 'Obkoms were starting to inform the Ukrainian Central Committee more regularly about the fulfilment of the decisions of the party congresses, party plenums, and resolutions of the Central Committee, about their experience of organizational and ideological work, about the reaction of the toilers to the most important political events.'[152] If true, the Ukrainian leadership had finally got what it had wanted since 1921: information on the party work in the periphery. As described in Chapter 2, with the gubkoms and later obkoms delivering regular reports directly to the Central Committee, the Ukrainian republican leadership had struggled to obtain up-to-date information on the situation in the periphery.

Shelest continued to assert party control. On 11 April 1972, in continuation of a discussion held at the 28 September 1971 Ukrainian Central Committee plenum on opportunities to increase the supply of consumer goods and food products, the Ukrainian Politburo formally established the failure of the all-union enterprises to participate in fulfilling the task set by the Twenty-Fourth Party Congress. The Ukrainian leadership issued a resolution instructing the oblispolkoms to establish control over the fulfilment of this task by enterprises of all-union jurisdiction and report the results to the Ukrainian Central Committee every six months. Moreover, Shelest wanted to tackle the problem of consumer goods shortages at the republican level and, arguably, independently of the all-union ministries. 'Ministries and administrations of Ukraine were instructed to hold competitions during 1972 for the best innovatory proposal on the production of consumer goods from industrial wastes and local raw materials.' Imposing party control over enterprises with the aim of increasing production and supplies of consumer goods was a legitimate 'involvement' since it was the party that was responsible for meeting the needs of the population.[153]

At the end of April, Shelest tried to impose party control over the holy grail of the Ukrainian economy: ferrous metallurgy. On 28 April, the Ukrainian Politburo studied the results of an audit of the Ukrainian Ministry of Ferrous Metallurgy that had been held by the Ukrainian Central Committee department of heavy industry. The report found that despite positive results, the ministry did not fully use production capacities at its enterprises. The Dnipropetrovsk, Donetsk,

Zaporizhzhia, and Voroshylovhrad obkoms, and some gorkoms and raikoms, in their turn, insufficiently controlled the metallurgical and mining production enterprises. They did not sufficiently demand that managers fulfil plans to implement new technology or increase productivity. The Ukrainian Politburo decided that the Ukrainian Ministry of Ferrous Metallurgy should examine the causes of low productivity growth and that the Ukrainian Central Committee department of ferrous metallurgy should supervise the fulfilment of this resolution.[154]

Whatever plans Shelest might have had with regard to the ministries, they were cut short. At the Ukrainian Politburo meeting on 24 May 1972, Volodymyr Shcherbytsky replaced Petro Shelest as first secretary of the CPU. Shelest was transferred to Moscow as vice-chairman of the Soviet government.

## Conclusion

From Shelest's perspective, Khrushchev's removal was supposed to lead to the consolidation of the republican first party secretaries' power. Instead, it was followed by the restoration of the ministerial system, which in turn resulted in the curtailment of the Ukrainian republican leadership's authority and of the power of the first secretary in any republic. Ministries deprived republican first secretaries of access to financial and material funds. After 1965, Shelest was in no position to assist the obkoms, which remained accountable not only for the fulfilment of agricultural plans and social programmes, but also for the 'industrial' performance of their oblasts. To regain authority, Shelest needed access to industry. In theory, Brezhnev's rhetoric about party control over the economy provided Shelest with a perfect context to insist that the obkoms demand the subordination of industrial managers. Had the obkoms imposed control over managers, as the official rhetoric called for, Shelest would have had access to the Ukrainian industrial enterprises. However, in practice, without alternative sources, the obkoms simply were not in a position to 'break up' with their local managers. With regional party–industry alliances intact, Shelest's main value to the obkoms and their managers was his position in lobbying for resources. The prioritization of heavy industry and the dominance of ferrous metallurgy, in particular, led Shelest to prioritize this branch over other branches in his requests to Moscow. Yet even this service was of marginal value to the regions. By 1972, Shelest, after fruitless efforts to bring industry under party control through the obkoms, concentrated his energy on empowering the Ukrainian Central Committee.

While restoration of the ministerial system weakened the office of the CPU first secretary, it did not weaken regional party–industry alliances or consolidate the CPU. In the process of the organizational reshuffle that accompanied the abolition of the sovnarkhoz system, the incentive system that dictated the relationship between the obkoms and industrial managers and the priority of economic tasks for the obkoms remained intact. As a result, with industry under Moscow's direct control, the obkoms found themselves, or rather remained, indirectly dependent on the various ministries in Moscow. The continuous prioritization of heavy industry and its concentration in eastern Ukraine deepened the lines of fracture between the oblasts and between the obkoms.

*The Institutional Foundations of Ukrainian Democracy: Power Sharing, Regionalism, and Authoritarianism*. Nataliya Kibita, Oxford University Press. © Nataliya Kibita 2024. DOI: 10.1093/9780191925351.003.0006

# 6

# Shcherbytsky's Leadership between Moscow and the Regions

## Introduction

When Volodymyr Shcherbytsky became first secretary of the Communist Party of Ukraine (CPU) in 1972, the Soviet Union was entering a period which Gorbachev later famously described as the era of stagnation. Stagnation was not all-encompassing. Rising consumerism, a third wave of migration, 'new woman' literature, new trends in art and informal culture, and even the survival of political dissent despite the KGB's increased prosecutions demonstrated some evolution of Soviet society and the development of individualism.[1] But while society was moving ahead, the state did enter a phase of stagnation. Kosygin's 1965 reform was curtailed. Economic growth slowed. The annual growth rate of income dropped from 3.7 percent in 1970–1975 to 2.0 percent in 1980–1985.[2] According to Gorbachev's own admission, in January–February 1985, the growth rate had fallen 'to a level below that of 1981 and constituted 1.7 percent, while the plan was for 3.9 percent per year'.[3] Brezhnev's policy of 'trust in cadres' stifled the initiative of the party and state apparatus and normalized the officials' irresponsibility and non-accountability for tasks assigned to them. It bred corruption and caused moral decay within the party and state apparatus.[4] Inertia took hold of the system, by now under the dual power of the party and state apparatus, with ministries in a position to decide important political questions.[5] Problems were duly noted but remained unaddressed. The system rejected change.[6]

The Ukrainian leadership, being part of the system, rejected change as well. Hence it remained institutionally weak. Shcherbytsky had an image of a strong leader, but that image had little to do with the actual authority of the Ukrainian leadership, which remained defined by its ability to provide resources. Such ability was limited and shrank further by the end of 1989 when Shcherbytsky retired. The CPU remained fragmented. The persistent absence of mechanisms to incorporate the needs of the regions into policies specific to Ukraine, the absence of a formal framework to enable formal horizontal relationships between the oblasts, and the continuous dependence of the obkoms on local managers and Moscow-controlled ministries for their own success or failure provided poor conditions for consolidating the CPU into a united regional division of the CPSU.

## A Strong Leader with Weak Powers

### The Image of Strong Leader

Shcherbytsky's image as 'the Politburo's Untouchable', as *Newsweek* called him in its 18 May 1987 edition, was not unfounded. It was based partly on Shcherbytsky's political longevity and his personal links to Brezhnev.[7] Before becoming CPU first secretary, he had served as the chairman of the Ukrainian government for a total of nine years (28 February 1961 to 28 June 1963 and 15 October 1965 to 8 June 1972). He outlived Soviet leaders Brezhnev, Yurii Andropov, and Konstantin Chernenko, and by the end of his tenure was working with the fourth, Mikhail Gorbachev. His image was also based on his political astuteness and superb administrative skills. From the start of his tenure, Shcherbytsky positioned himself not only as a loyal ally of Brezhnev—nothing less was expected of him anyway—but also as a firm and disciplined executive for Brezhnev and, more importantly, for the central industrial ministries. By the beginning of the 1970s, the ministries had centralized resource allocation and planning not only for union-republican but also for republican-level ministries.[8] 'A proponent of "the party of order"',[9] according to his aide Vitalii Vrublevsky, and a 'genius in working not with a person, but with an [administrative] position', as writer Vitalii Korotych described him, Shcherbytsky knew what to ask, what not to ask, and when and how to ask.[10] He would not always receive what he asked for, but his efforts, or his refusal to make any effort, certainly projected power.

'Shcherbytsky knew how to accommodate any leadership, he was able to adjust to anyone', argued Korotych. Well, not quite to anyone: Shcherbytsky did not adjust to Khrushchev, who removed Shcherbytsky from the chairmanship of the Ukrainian government in 1963 and exiled him back to Dnipropetrovsk as the first obkom secretary. He remained there until Brezhnev brought him back to the Ukrainian government in 1965.[11] For Brezhnev, Shcherbytsky was the perfect leader for Ukraine. Rumour had it that Brezhnev even viewed Shcherbytsky as his successor.[12] Whereas his predecessor, Shelest, resisted centralization and challenged Moscow's policies and decisions, Shcherbytsky was willing to play by the rules dictated by Moscow. However, he, too, resisted centralization and challenged Moscow's decisions. In June 1972, Shcherbytsky joined first secretaries from other republics who rejected the initiative of all-union Minister of Agriculture Vladimir Matskevich, to deprive the republican governments of their authority in planning agricultural production and manipulating agricultural resources inside the republic. Shcherbytsky found such a reorganization 'unnecessary'.[13] In 1973, Shcherbytsky spoke against the liquidation of the Ukrainian Ministry of Energy.[14] But contrary to Shelest, Shcherbytsky did not challenge the prerogative of Moscow in policymaking. He did not seek to expand the margins of authority of the Ukrainian centre and did not insist on formalizing the relationship between the republican and central state apparatuses. In a departure from

Shelest's view of Ukraine as one economic complex, Shcherbytsky did not insist on the complex development of the Ukrainian economy, either. He accepted the superiority of branch interests over regional and the central ministerial apparatus's continuous prioritization of heavy and defence industry, despite Brezhnev's efforts to 'create the fullest possible satisfaction of the people's material and cultural needs'.[15]

Playing by the rules also meant not insisting on placing managers under party supervision in the periphery, the futility of which Shcherbytsky must have known all too well. As a former first obkom secretary, he had personal experience of the party organizations' dependence on the ministries and local managers for success in industrial and agricultural growth and the socio-economic development of the territories under their responsibility.[16] As a former chairman of the Ukrainian government, he experienced the limitations of the CPU first secretary's office. Now he had to report to the Central Committee on the republic's accomplishments. Hence, he dropped Shelest's policy of holding the managerial apparatus personally responsible for failures to fulfil party directives.[17]

## The Campaign for Discipline

To steer the Ukrainian apparatus away from Shelest's ideas, and to signal to Moscow that the centre could rely on him, Shcherbytsky launched a campaign to restore discipline at the very start of his tenure. At the 27 July 1972 Ukrainian Central Committee plenum, Shcherbytsky instructed the party apparatus and the production managers to take measures to ensure that industrial growth and productivity increased as planned. 'Taking measures' included two components which central ministries could only welcome: mobilizing locally available labour and materials, and letting khoziaistvenniki do their job. To improve production processes, explained Shcherbytsky, 'it [was] necessary to release specialists from the extrinsic functions and not to distract them from work [ot dela] during their working hours. It [was] necessary to create conditions for specialists to concentrate their entire attention on technological progress and on increasing economic efficiency of production.'[18]

To those who might have been confused by the lack of clearly formulated instructions on what to do and what not to do, Shcherbytsky's close ally, Oleksii Vatchenko, who had been a member of the Ukrainian Politburo since 1966 and was the first secretary of the Dnipropetrovsk obkom, explained that the party should not meddle in economic administration. Alluding to the removal of Shelest, he emphasized that it was precisely the focus of the party organizations on economic problems and the 'frequent replacement of soviet and economic organs' that allowed the party organizations to overlook such fundamental aspects of the party's work as the selection and education of cadres, control over execution of the decisions made by the highest authorities, and the organization of socialist competition to mobilize producers for plan fulfilment.[19]

The calls for fulfilling plan assignments were nothing new and were as a rule ignored by the apparatus. However, Shcherbytsky had good reason to believe that this time, the periphery apparatus would not dismiss lightly his call for discipline, at least not with regard to the mobilization of locally available resources for the fulfilment of production plans. Shcherbytsky took on the post of first secretary at the beginning of the 1972–1974 party cards exchange—a process during which members were supposed to turn in their party cards and then receive new ones, if applicable. The campaign was first announced by Brezhnev at the Twenty-Fourth Party Congress in March–April 1971, but Brezhnev launched the process at the 19 May 1972 Central Committee plenum. Brezhnev assured the party that the exchange of party cards was not a concealed purge, although he still expected that the exchange would not be reduced to an automatic reissuing of party cards.[20] For Shcherbytsky, the exchange of party cards provided an opportunity to bring concealed resources into circulation.

At the 30 November 1973 Ukrainian Central Committee plenum, Vatchenko illustrated how this mechanism worked in practice. In the Dnipropetrovsk oblast, he reported, the exchange of party cards was intentionally delayed for 320 communists on whom the party organizations had various claims, effectively suspending their membership until they fulfilled their obligations. '[As a result], demands [*trebovatel'nost'*] on the managers [on the part of the party organs] to fulfil plans increased.' Shevchenko, chairman of the kolkhoz 'Dnipro', was one of the officials whose career was affected by a party card suspension. 'Comrade Shevchenko had a passive attitude to work', reported Vatchenko.

[He] broke discipline which led to a decrease in milk production per cow. In August [1973] the party organisation issued him a warning and decided to delay the exchange of his party card. This influenced him. He drastically changed his attitude to work, … became more demanding of his subordinates, brought order to the farm and, at present, the production of milk has increased.[21]

In October 1973, Shcherbytsky could report to the Central Committee that

the increase of discipline and mobilisation in the collectives allowed for the successful fulfilment of economic plans. Since the start of the five-year plan in 1971, the republic's industry [had] produced and sold above-plan production worth 3.8 billion roubles. Industrial workers began to mobilise to fulfil the Directives of the Twenty-Fourth Party Congress. They now aimed to increase the volume of industrial output ahead of schedule, by September 1975, and supply above-plan production for more than 5 billion roubles.[22]

In November 1973, Shcherbytsky expanded the Ukrainian Central Committee party commission, indicating his intent to maintain focus on discipline.[23]

**Illustration 12** The Ukrainian leadership with the group of communists awarded
state decorations, 1978/© TsDAEA (2-154580)

Ukrainian Soviet leaders in 1978. Sitting left to right: first secretary of the Zaporizhzhia obkom
Oleksii Titarenko (2nd), first secretary of the Dnipropetrovsk obkom Oleksii Vatchenko, Volodymyr
Shcherbytsky, Chairman of the Ukrainian Government Oleksandr Liashko (6th), first secretary of the
Kharkiv obkom Ivan Sokolov, Central Committee secretary Yakiv Pohrebniak, first secretary of the
Lviv obkom (1987–1990).

It is important to emphasize that, just as Shcherbytsky demanded discipline
from the Ukrainian apparatus with regard to Ukraine's obligations to the Union,
he also expected the all-union agencies to fulfil their obligations to Ukraine. In
his numerous letters to Moscow, Shcherbytsky insisted that the central apparatus
respect central plans and the resolutions and directives passed by the central
leadership.[24] If the Ukrainian leadership was held accountable for the fulfilment
of its obligations, the all-union apparatus should be accountable for its own.[25]

As economic growth continued to slow and the possibilities for mobilizing
locally available resources subsided, Shcherbytsky had to write more letters
demanding that the all-union agencies supply what they owed to the republic. At
the same time, Shcherbytsky became more insistent that Moscow consider Kyiv's
economic proposals.[26]

## Institutional Weakness of the First Secretary

As was the case with Shelest, the decisions of the central apparatus to fulfil or to
dismiss Shcherbytsky's requests had little to do with the fact that it was

Shcherbytsky who asked. Shcherbytsky, 'while being "the master of Ukraine", did not have real influence at the all-union level.'[27] The Ukrainian leadership controlled only limited resources generated in Ukraine and could not use the inputs as leverage to prompt Ukrainian producers to pressure the central apparatus. By the mid-1980s, 95 percent of Ukrainian enterprises had all-union status (as compared to 93 percent in Russia and 90 percent in the Baltic states).[28] Inter-republican deliveries were managed by the central apparatus.

Hence, the Ukrainian leadership's complaints in 1979 about supplementary above-plan tasks given to the Ukrainian coal mines, 'which had been practised for 15 years', were ignored. Investments in Ukrainian coal were allocated when and in the amount that the USSR Ministry of Coal was convinced were economically or politically justified. Ukrainian estimates of the necessary investment sums were dismissed.[29] Shcherbytsky's repeated requests to allocate sufficient fertilizers, fodder for husbandry, and agricultural machinery—a chronic problem all over the country—were not met, either.[30] The republic could manoeuvre agricultural machinery inside the republic, but only so long as the USSR Gosplan did not need it. Given the different schedules of agricultural works all over the Union, the USSR Gosplan commonly moved machinery from one republic to another. In August 1972, for example, it moved 3,200 grain combines that had been manufactured in Ukraine to Kazakhstan. In January 1973, Shcherbytsky had to ask central planners to return these combines to Ukraine.[31]

The Ukrainian leadership remained dependent on Moscow for the socio-economic development of Ukrainian regions as well, even though this development was its direct responsibility. In 1975, Shcherbytsky had to appeal to central planners and central ministries to address the socio-economic backwardness of the Polissia region, the geographic zone that included parts of the oblasts of Rivne, Volyn, Zhytomyr, Kyiv, Khmelnytskyi, Chernihiv, Sumy, Lviv, and Ternopil.[32] Polissia remained marginal to Moscow's economic interests. In January 1989, the periphery apparatus would ask the Ukrainian leadership to launch a programme to develop Ukrainian Polissia that would include the construction of paved roads, schools, and kindergartens in the villages, as well as 'culture and healthcare' facilities.[33]

As elsewhere in the Soviet Union, local soviets relied on industrial enterprises and their ministries for housing and urban infrastructure.[34] 'In the USSR in 1985, of the 72 per cent of housing in the state sector, ministries owned 46 per cent compared with only 26 per cent owned by the local soviets.'[35] In 1976, the Ukrainian Central Committee instructed the obkoms to speed up the relocation of people from barracks, basements, and run-down houses into safe housing; in 1981, the obkoms were instructed to ensure that the ministries shared housing they constructed with local soviets. Such instructions and resolutions were meaningless unless the ministries were willing to cooperate, which to an extent they were. 'Barracks were liquidated in 1984, and in 1985, people living in basements received new housing.'[36] However, the housing problem was not solved.[37] The waiting list for housing in the cities of Ukraine increased from 1.4 million families in 1980 to 2 million families in 1985 and 2.5 million families by 1991.[38] With perestroika in progress, the ministries felt no obligation to fund housing. 'One apartment building a year for 32,000 workers [at a Leningrad factory]!'[39] complained Gorbachev to the central Politburo on 14 July 1989. The Donetsk oblast authorities reported in 1989 that '82 percent of the miners' residences were under the jurisdiction of the Ministry of Coal and that their condition was deplorable.... 20 percent of residences lacked water supply, 26 percent were not connected to a sewage system, 28 percent did not have central heating, 63 percent lacked hot water.'[40] Yet there was little the Ukrainian leadership could do to assist local authorities, in Donbas, Odesa, Chernihiv, or Lviv.[41]

In the 1970s and 1980s, some people in the Ukrainian Central Committee apparatus still believed that the obkom secretaries could 'solve all questions in the Ukrainian Central Committee, [and] the republican government', and that 'they addressed the all-union organs extremely rarely'. They believed that the obkom secretaries visited Brezhnev and other Central Committee secretaries only 'out of respect', 'but business issues were solved in Kyiv'.[42] The reality was the opposite. The obkom secretaries maintained direct communication with the Moscow-based offices of the ministries that administered enterprises in their oblasts.[43] Addressing all-union ministries for resources did not guarantee a positive outcome, nor that the central ministry would refrain from redirecting the request to the Ukrainian Gosplan or a Ukrainian ministry. However, resources remained with the all-union apparatus in Moscow, and addressing the Ukrainian Central Committee or the Ukrainian government often delayed obtaining a reply.[44]

### The Chornobyl revelation
The limits of the Ukrainian leadership's authority became visible for all to see with the Chornobyl (Rus.: Chernobyl) nuclear catastrophe in 1986. Perestroika had yet to reach Ukraine. The system was solid, Shcherbytsky was firmly in his seat, and the Ukrainian leadership played by the rules.

The revelation of their own weakness befell the Ukrainian leadership from the first moments of the catastrophe. The nuclear power plant was situated 130 kilometres from Kyiv. The first responders, the firemen, and the militia were subordinated to Ukrainian Minister of the Interior Ivan Hladush, who was doubly subordinated to the republic and the Union. Yet Chairman of the Ukrainian Government Oleksandr Liashko received the news of the accident from his boss in Moscow, Chairman of the Soviet Government Nikolai Ryzhkov, at 2.40 a.m. on 26 April. Before the scale of the accident was fully understood, Liashko gave instructions to Hladush to prepare transportation to evacuate the local population from the plant area. His personal order, however, was not enough. He needed the approval of both Shcherbytsky and Ryzhkov, both of whom needed convincing. By 2 p.m. on 26 April, 1,200 buses and 240 trucks were ready to move people from the city of Prypyat where the Chornobyl plant was located; but they could not move until the central leadership authorized the evacuation. Once Moscow was convinced that the population had to be removed from the contaminated area, the evacuation could begin.[45]

Liashko's intuition explained his early decision to prepare for mobilization; intuition based on his long experience of managing industry when urgent orders had to be implemented under conditions of uncertainty, shortages, or bottlenecks, which taught him to be as prepared for unforeseen eventualities as possible. This advance preparation must have saved precious hours for the evacuees when the central authorities in Moscow finally gave the green light (although it was less helpful for the bus drivers, who had to wait for the order in the contaminated area outside Prypyat). No such preparations could be undertaken for the inhabitants of Kyiv. The general public remained uninformed of the catastrophe or of the protective measures that people could take on their own. 'Liashko, mindful of the monopoly on information exercised by Moscow, was reluctant to make any public statement on the accident.' To avoid spreading panic, Gorbachev ordered Shcherbytsky to go ahead with the May Day parade. Shcherbytsky obeyed.[46]

Still, in the early days of May, acting on the recommendation of Kyiv scientists, Shcherbytsky was prepared to evacuate children from Kyiv. However, his initiative was not welcomed. Two Moscow guests, academician Leonid Ilin and Director of the State Committee on Hydrology and Meteorology Yurii Izrael, who were present at the Ukrainian Politburo meeting where this suggestion was brought up, did not give their permission. Shcherbytsky and Liashko decided to proceed anyway.

> But when the [Ukrainian] government officials asked all-union authorities for additional trains to transport the children, they got a negative response from Moscow. Boris Shcherbina [deputy chairman of the Soviet government in charge of the energy sector] personally sent an angry telegram asking the Kyiv authorities to stop spreading panic and cancel preparations for the partial evacuation.[47]

When the central and republican leadership finally admitted to the scale of the catastrophe, first to the world and then to their own population, they jointly started mobilizing the workforce and resources necessary for the relief effort in Chornobyl. The refugee crisis and protection of the civilian population from radiation, however, was placed fully and solely on the shoulders of the Ukrainian leadership.[48]

**Illustration 13** Chornobyl nuclear power plant, 1979/© TsDAEA (0-241988)

**Illustration 14** Ukrainian Soviet leaders at the May Day parade, 1 May 1986/© TsDAEA (2-161602)

Five days after the Chornobyl catastrophe, the Soviet leadership ordered the Ukrainian leadership to carry on business as usual and hold the May Day parade. On 1 May 1986, the Ukrainian leadership held the parade. Left to right: Chairman of the Ukrainian Government Oleksandr Liashko, CPU First Secretary Volodymyr Shcherbytsky, Chairman of the Presidium of the Supreme Soviet of the Ukrainian SSR Valentyna Shevchenko, first deputy of the Chairman of the Ukrainian Government Ivan Mozghovy, Central Committee secretary Borys Kachura, first secretary of the Lviv obkom Yakiv Pohrebniak, first secretary of the Kyiv gorkom Yuri Yelchenko, chairman of the Kyiv gorispolkom Valentyn Zghursky.

The way the catastrophe was handled on the Ukrainian side revealed that sub-servience to Moscow was in the DNA of the Ukrainian political elite, concluded Serhii Plokhy; that fear of being reprimanded by the central leadership prevented Liashko and Shcherbytsky from taking an assertive stance and fulfilling their direct duty to protect the population.[49] Yet the catastrophe revealed more than fears of reprimand.

The crisis revealed inconsistency between the rights, responsibilities, and options of the Ukrainian leadership. Responsible for the well-being of the population, and prepared to act, it had no authority, resources, or access to information to act accordingly, which in this case had a particularly devastating cost for the population. Still, unwilling or unable to learn, the centre did not increase the Ukrainian leadership's capacity to protect the local population from the radiation in the contaminated zone in the following years. The central government retained the prerogative to classify areas as contaminated, a classification that made the population from these areas eligible for food subsidies, and to distribute production.[50]

## Perestroika: The Change of Context

Gorbachev's perestroika undermined what little authority the Ukrainian leadership had acquired by the mid-1980s. In his address to the Twenty-Seventh Party Congress on 25 February 1986, Gorbachev announced perestroika by declaring the course towards democratization, decentralization, and glasnost. The context in which the Ukrainian leadership operated, however, transformed most after the enactment of two notorious laws designed to liberalize economic relations. The Law on the State Enterprise came into force on 30 June 1987 and was enacted in January 1988. It granted vast autonomy to enterprises, including the freedom to export. In May 1988, the central Politburo enacted the Law on Cooperatives. Both laws allowed transactions between state enterprises and cooperatives, state enterprises received the right to create cooperatives, and both could accumulate profits and create commercial banks. The laws were designed to weaken ministerial control over producers. Thus, the declared formal role of the ministries changed from directive planning to overall strategic guidance of the economy, which allowed some economists to call these laws 'decentralization'.[51] The extent of decentralization was debatable. Industrial ministries retained tight control over the economy until the autumn of 1991, although by then the control operated through associations they created. Regardless, as economic relations between the ministries and enterprises liberalized, Kyiv's control over the Ukrainian economy was reduced.[52]

In 1987, Shcherbytsky had to oversee the liquidation of Ukrainian union-republican ministries of electric and energy industry, coal, ferrous and non-ferrous metallurgy, and geology. (The Ukrainian leadership argued that these ministries connected Ukrainian enterprises with republican and local organs of the industries involved, and were important for the republic's further economic development, but these arguments were dismissed in Moscow.)

From Moscow's perspective, the administrative value of Ukrainian ministries remained low. The problems related to production were resolved in Moscow anyway, which the Ukrainian leadership could not deny. The Ukrainian leadership lost what little say it had in the development of Ukraine's main industries. Control over heavy industry, still prioritized, was fully centralized.[53]

Thus, Ukraine retained its ministries for food and light industries. However, it still had no influence on Moscow's investment policies for these branches. Equipment for them was produced by all-union ministries. The Ukrainian republican ministries did have jurisdiction over all enterprises that produced for local consumption as well as any enterprises that had solely republican status. For the first time, the Ukrainian government received material and financial funds allocated to the republic in bulk and could freely distribute these resources. However, the caveat was that the Ukrainian government had jurisdiction over a mere 5 percent of enterprises located in Ukraine.[54]

Ukrainian production continued to provide an increasing share of Soviet exports, but the Ukrainian leadership could influence neither the nomenclature of products for export nor the volumes of exports. The Ukrainian Ministry of Food Industry could expect a share of the profits from exporting Ukrainian agricultural produce. However, because the centre fixed low prices for agricultural exports, rather than permitting republics to sell independently at world market prices, Ukraine estimated that it lost 140 billion roubles on the export of its food production.[55]

Additionally, the Ukrainian leadership had to make use of the same resources for agriculture, despite a certain degree of decentralization in the administration of agriculture in 1985. To implement the Central Committee's 15 March 1985 order 'to overcome the backlog in state procurements of meat production', the Ukrainian leadership received more flexibility in manipulating available resources and could now redistribute livestock feed.[56] Through the newly established State Agro-Industrial Committee (Gosagroprom) of Ukraine—the Ukrainian branch of the USSR Gosagroprom, formed in November 1985 and placed under dual subordination of Moscow and Kyiv—the Ukrainian leadership retained dictatorial administrative power over farms. In 1987, the central leadership allocated funds and material resources for agriculture to the Ukrainian government in bulk, which increased its flexibility in manipulating resources inside the republic. However, the volume of resources did not increase. Republican governments received the right to change procurement prices for agricultural produce, but they could not exceed the total amount of funds allocated to the republic by the central leadership.[57] In March 1989, the USSR Gosagroprom was abolished. The majority of its enterprises were transferred to republican gosagroproms. However, agricultural machinery remained under Moscow's control, as did fertilizers, as well as fuel for combines and tractors. A new system of wholesale prices would be introduced only in 1990. Nonetheless, the republic still had plan targets to meet, now called 'state orders', or *goszakazy*, since January 1988, and the *goszakaz* for grain production was now up to 30 percent of estimated gross production, taking into account transportation and storage losses. 'The republic owned the grain produced above the volumes destined for *goszakaz*',[58] yet the potential to increase republican reserves remained limited.

At this low point of the economic relationship between Moscow and Kyiv, Shcherbytsky received good news from Moscow. At the Nineteenth Party Conference (28 June–1 July 1988), Gorbachev announced that the Soviet leadership had decided to proceed with correcting deformations which had accumulated in the nationality policy—the course was declared at the Twenty-Seventh Party Congress in 1986—and called for increasing independence of the Union republics and autonomous entities as a way of strengthening the state.[59] Gorbachev suggested formalizing the relationship between the centre and the republics. Shcherbytsky, following in the footsteps of Rakovsky and Shelest, could not miss this opportunity. On 31 December 1988, he wrote a letter that must have alarmed Gorbachev. If it did not, it should have. The letter showed that the institution of centralized administration of Ukraine for Ukraine had its own dynamic, no matter who was at the head of Ukraine. Yet before presenting this letter, it is necessary to discuss the state of the CPU. It was Gorbachev's public support for the idea of a renewed federation that provided a formal opportunity for Shcherbytsky to stand up to Moscow's agencies and defend the institutional interests of the Ukrainian leadership without being accused of localism or nationalist deviations. But it was pressure from below that shaped Shcherbytsky's vision of the future federation and created the content of his letter.

## Fragmentation in the 'Era of Stagnation'

Throughout Shcherbytsky's tenure, the CPU remained a fragmented organization. On the formal level, the status of the Ukrainian Central Committee remained that of an obkom. The Ukrainian obkom first secretaries remained doubly subordinated to the Central Committee and the Ukrainian Central Committee. 'The authority of the Ukrainian Central Committee as the party centre remained illusory', remembered Vrublevsky. It had no power over party matters, the party budget, or the structure of the periphery party organs. The first secretary of Ukraine still needed the Central Committee's approval to appoint a first obkom secretary.[60] Such approvals were a formality, but it emphasized the institutional weakness of the Ukrainian Central Committee.[61] Besides, Moscow could appoint an obkom secretary without Shcherbytsky's approval.[62] The Ukrainian Central Committee did not control communication between the Ukrainian regions and Moscow, either. The obkom secretaries maintained direct communication with the Central Committee secretaries and wrote directly to the republican and all-union ministers asking for resources for industries or the social needs of workers. The new party cards issued after 1972 no longer mentioned the Communist Party of the Union republic on the cover or the front page, 'because the Party [was] one centralized organization with one programme and one statute' (although the new card still mentioned the party organization of the republic that issued it).[63] 'Kommunisticheskaia Partiia Ukrainy' disappeared from the letterhead of the official stationery of the obkoms, as well. These decorative changes were consistent with Brezhnev's concept of a new historical community, the Soviet people, or sovetskii narod, but, like Brezhnev's concept of sovetskii narod, they were of little practical significance.

As elsewhere in the Soviet Union, in the 1970s and 1980s, Ukrainian obkom first secretaries continued to be held accountable for the economic performance of the territories under their supervision. Plan fulfilment by industrial and agricultural producers in their territories and the socio-economic development of the territories remained the two main tasks of the territorial party organizations and the main criteria for evaluating the work of the obkom first secretaries. An oblast's failure to fulfil the plan did not necessarily mean that the obkom secretary would be immediately removed,[64] but if the leadership decided to remove a party secretary, non-fulfilment of plans could be used as a reason.[65]

Before perestroika, industrial enterprises 'disposed of 70–80 percent of the financial and other resources in a region'.[66] Whether it was for 'environmental control, housing, distribution of goods, transport, infrastructure, labour resources, [or] urban development', or for the fulfilment of production plans by industrial enterprises, kolkhozy, and sovkhozy, the success or failure of the obkom secretaries remained dependent on industrial enterprises and the ministries that controlled resources for production and the social agenda of their enterprises.[67] Local industry, formally subordinated to local soviets and the Ukrainian Ministry of Local Industry, was dependent on centrally distributed material inputs, equipment and financial investments, as well. In Ukraine in the mid-1970s, only 4 percent of local industry output was produced from local inputs. By the end of the 1980s, Ukraine would be producing between 15 and 20 percent of its output solely from Ukrainian inputs.[68]

The enterprises' patronage of the farms remained important for improving the material-technical base of agriculture and for increasing agricultural production until as late as 1989. It was encouraged by the leadership.[69] At the meeting of the party-state aktiv of Ukraine on 26 July 1973, in the presence of Brezhnev, Shcherbytsky instructed enterprises 'to find additional capacities to increase the production of machinery and equipment, mineral fertilizers, materials; increase the supply of these products to the countryside; and increase the efficiency of industries that process agricultural produce'.[70] In the years that followed, central financial allocations to the agricultural sector increased but yielded modest results.[71] In 1985, Gorbachev encouraged the apparatus 'to put pressure on the partners that service[d] agricultural production' and 'to involve *shefy*', or patrons, to increase meat production.[72] In 1986, the Ukrainian leadership called the obkoms to organize *shefy* to mechanize farm labour and build roads, housing, schools, and clubs in rural areas. The size of the oblast industrial sector, although not decisive in meeting agricultural plans or improving infrastructure in rural areas, nonetheless mattered. The larger it was, the more help the farms of that oblast could expect.[73] Consequently, in both Kyiv and Moscow, the obkom first secretaries continued to defend and lobby for the economic interests of industries in their territories.

Throughout the period, regional party–industry alliances remained in place. The territorial party secretaries' dependence on industrial managers reflected their local party leaders' 'connivance and lack of control over the soviet and managerial cadres'. As discussions at the periphery party conferences at the end of 1985 revealed, instead of demanding that managers/communists fulfil their direct duties, periphery party secretaries often 'begged them' to fulfil their duties.[74] Industrial managers, in their turn, did not hesitate to influence the cadre appointments in the party organizations of their enterprises.[75] The Ukrainian Central Committee was powerless to put an end to it.[76]

## Important versus Non-important

While the obkom first secretaries remained focused on the economic situation in their oblasts, the leadership continued to treat the oblasts as either 'important' or 'not so important'.[77] Important were all the industrialized oblasts and large agricultural oblasts, such as Vinnytsia. At the same time, in the Ukrainian Politburo, there was no place for an obkom secretary from an agricultural oblast. First secretaries of the Donetsk, Dnipropetrovsk, and Lviv obkoms and first secretary of the Kyiv gorkom retained regular seats throughout 1972–1989. Ivan Sokolov, the Kharkiv obkom first secretary, served on the Politburo until 1976. Sokolov's political successor in Kharkiv, Ivan Sakhniuk, did not receive a seat on the Ukrainian Politburo,[78] but Sokolov, who was appointed CPU second secretary in 1976, was promoted from candidate-member to full member of the Ukrainian Politburo. In 1989, under the pressure of a changing political environment, whereby Kyiv's importance as the capital of Ukraine was growing, the Kyiv gorkom secretary was joined on the Politburo by the Kyiv obkom first secretary. On 31 March 1990, the Politburo also included Hryhorii Kharchenko, first secretary of the Zaporizhzhia obkom, as a member, and his counterpart from the Crimean obkom, Mykola Bahrov, as a candidate-member.

Important obkoms hosted large delegations from the republican and central apparatus at their local conferences.[79] Obkom secretaries and oblispolkom chairmen from important oblasts often spoke at the Ukrainian party forums. There, they could publicly express the difficulties that their oblasts faced in fulfilling plans, often in the presence of representatives from the all-union state apparatus.[80] Such public declarations, which often included complaints that the central apparatus did not fulfil its obligations to enterprises, served both the regional authorities and the Ukrainian leadership as a certain security in case the plans were not fulfilled. Publicly declaring an oblast's achievements and potential failures at the party forums was so useful to the Ukrainian leadership that it permitted obkom first secretaries of important oblasts to address the audience even when a secretary's leadership style was unsatisfactory.[81]

Consistent with the economic contribution of the region, the obkom secretaries from the western oblasts remained rare speakers at political forums. At the 14–15 September 1972 party functionary meeting that discussed the exchange of party cards and that was still being held in the context of the struggle against Ukrainian nationalism, out of a total of nineteen speakers, three were from western oblasts: the first secretary of the Rivne obkom, Ivan Mozghovy; the head of the organizational department of the Khust raikom (Zakarpattia oblast), G. Svarichevska; and the second secretary of the Lviv obkom, V. Sviatotsky. The head of the organizational department of the Chortkiv raikom (Ternopil oblast), P. Kravchuk, and the head of the organizational department of the Zaliznychnyi raikom (Lviv oblast), R. Korytko, were two of seven speakers who did not get a chance to speak at the plenum but who had submitted written reports. At the 14 September 1973 Ukrainian Central Committee plenum that discussed agriculture and the exchange of party cards, not a single secretary from western obkoms spoke. At the 30 November 1973 meeting of the party and state apparatus, not a single obkom first secretary from the western oblasts spoke, either. That meeting discussed the agricultural performance of the republic in 1973, the production plan, the budget for 1974, and organizational party matters. In his reports to Moscow, Shcherbytsky likewise paid little attention to Western Ukraine.[82]

### Western Ukraine

Western Ukraine remained a distinct region. By the February 1986 party congress, during which Gorbachev introduced the policy of glasnost, the region had not yet achieved the level of sovietization of central or eastern Ukraine.[83] Soviet state and party infrastructure was well in place, the economy was state controlled, the population lived a Soviet life. Yet industrialization, with its proletarianization of the workforce and the integration of the worker into the centralized ministerial system, lagged behind the rest of Ukraine. Compared to the industrialized oblasts of south-eastern and central Ukraine, the population in Western Ukraine depended on themselves for their well-being much more than on the state.

When Shcherbytsky took office, he inherited the acute problem of unemployment in the region. Despite Shelest's efforts, investments allocated to Western Ukraine were insufficient, and people still struggled to find state employment. In Zakarpattia, unemployment manifested in seasonal migration, 'even among communists'. Almost 10,000 residents of the Ivano-Frankivsk oblast 'emigrated abroad'.[84] It remains to be researched how many of these emigrated due to an absence of employment. Still, the proportion of available labour in this region was sufficiently large for the Ukrainian leadership to ask Moscow to increase investment allocations.[85] The increase obtained, however, was small. Of the capital investments allocated to Ukraine, the share allocated to the Chernivtsi, Zakarpattia, Ternopil, Volyn, Rivne, and Ivano-Frankivsk oblasts increased from 9.7 percent in 1976–1980 to 10.4 percent in 1981–1985 and 10.8 in 1986–1990. Including the Lviv oblast, the numbers were 14.1, 15.0, and 15.4 percent, respectively.[86]

The share of these oblasts in the total industrial output of Ukraine increased from 5.7 percent in 1963 to 9.5 percent in 1990 (see Table 1 on p. 154). With Lviv, the numbers were 10.7 and 15.3 percent, respectively. The gap between the most economically developed oblast in eastern Ukraine and the least economically developed oblast in Western Ukraine fell by more than 25 percent in the period between 1970 and 1985. Nonetheless, Chernivtsi, Volyn, Ternopil, Rivne, and Zakarpattia remained the least economically developed oblasts in Ukraine.[87] By the mid-1980s, Lviv was the only western oblast that had developed above the Ukrainian average. Ukrainian economists classified the oblasts of Volyn, Rivne, Ternopil, Zakarpattia, and also Khmelnytskyi as regions that 'fell behind in their development'. The oblasts of Ivano-Frankivsk and Chernivtsi, along with Crimea, Vinnytsia, and Zhytomyr, developed below the average level of economic development in Ukraine.[88] The geographic proximity of the poorly developed oblasts suggested that the entire western region was economically marginalized, with the highly industrialized outlier Lviv highlighting the general backwardness of other six oblasts. Following the trajectory of its recent history, the region remained 'nationalist' until the end of the Soviet Union.[89]

## Perestroika in Action: Fragmentation Revealed

As long as the system remained stable, the fragmentation of the CPU and the institutionally weak Ukrainian Central Committee remained concealed behind formal procedures and reports, party forums where Shcherbytsky and Liashko told the apparatus what to do, instructions and directives sent by the Ukrainian Central Committee and the Ukrainian government to the periphery party and state apparatus, and various formal and informal rituals. Once the system was destabilized, the CPU's fragmentation was unveiled and further solidified.

Along with the above-mentioned economic reforms that upset economic relations, Gorbachev began to work on political reform in early 1988 with the ultimate aim of democratizing Soviet politics and turning the soviets (councils) into permanent governing bodies.[90] At the Nineteenth Party Conference, Gorbachev announced the restoration of the soviet system as the basis of self-government, declared a course towards subordination of party bodies to the elected soviets, and called for democratization of the party through 'full restoration of the Leninist principle of collective discussion and decision making' and free election of members and secretaries of all party committees.[91]

Contested elections for the local soviet and party organs put pressure on elected officials to build up local support among the population and managers. The socio-economic development of the oblasts thus transformed from an administrative to a political task.[92] A secretary's political career relied on his success in meeting the needs of common people in food and consumer goods supplies, housing, urban and rural infrastructure (including roads, schools, and hospitals), water supplies, and ecological management.[93] At the same time, Gorbachev did not release the party apparatus from its responsibility for fulfilling the goszakaz. Hence, elected officials in the periphery had to continue combining responsibility for production plan fulfilment with the suddenly urgent need to address the social agenda in their territories. As a result, despite the political and ideological change that attended perestroika, 'there was remarkably little change in the economic role being played by party officials on the ground'.[94] Most notably, the regional apparatus now had greater incentive to protect local interests rather than republican or all-union interests.

As economic relations continued to liberalize, the obkoms and oblispolkoms increasingly lost their formal access to resources managed by enterprises.[95] The Law on the State Enterprise and the Law on Cooperatives in 1987–1988, and the radical liberalization of foreign trade in 1989, increased the operational autonomy of industrial and agricultural producers and allowed the directors of state enterprises and private cooperatives to increase their control over material supplies and cash flows, as well as to accumulate profits.[96] From 1988, enterprises were instructed to pay a share of their profits into the local budgets. However, the industrial ministries withdrew the lion's share of the enterprises' profits and, at the same time, reduced allocations for social programmes, including housing.[97] Regional authorities 'received much less from Moscow by way of either help or instructions than they did prior to 1988'.[98] By the end of the 1980s, the obkoms were struggling to enforce patronage relationships between industrial enterprises and the farms of their oblasts. With prices for agricultural produce below the cost of production, it was impossible for many farms to pay for extra help, while an increasingly small number of enterprises were willing or able to cover the cost of patronage.[99]

The regional authorities' informal access to resources accumulated at enterprises increased, however, as 'the initially modest fiscal and organizational reforms of 1986–1987' enabled local bureaucrats 'to opportunistically pursue self-interested agendas' and increase private gains.[100]

More opportunities to increase their own gains, combined with increased incentives to satisfy the demands of the population and the formal requirement to fulfil the plans, motivated local authorities to continue assisting producers with their needs, defending the economic interests of industries in their territories, and lobbying for those industries in Kyiv and Moscow. As a result of growing disruptions in the fulfilment of contracts, the obkoms supported the enterprises' practice of substitution to correct their production plans downwards and tolerated the practice of falsifying reports even more than before.[101] In return, producers continued to assist local authorities with their official socio-economic and private agendas. Party–industry alliances grew stronger, as did regionalism and CPU fragmentation.[102]

While regionalism grew stronger, the economic situation in the country continued to deteriorate and the regions could not survive independently. The list of problems that the obkoms needed to address was long. Traditionally, requests for material and financial resources had been sent to the Moscow-based ministries. The obkoms expected the Ukrainian leadership to pressure the central leadership to introduce systemic changes, changes that would ultimately consolidate the authority of the Ukrainian leadership, unify the CPU, and bolster the popularity of communism.

## Shcherbytsky and the Regions

### What the Regions Wanted

Since 1985, and more so after Gorbachev's call to create favourable conditions to increase the self-governing of Soviet society at the Nineteenth Party Conference,[103] Ukraine's regions spoke of the need to regulate and formalize the relationship between local soviets, local producers, and the ministries. A matter of urgent concern was the ability of local authorities to address shortages of consumer goods in their territories. As one gorispolkom chairman explained, local authorities had the right to order consumer goods from local enterprises for their regions, but at the same time, the total plan target for these enterprises 'should not exceed the targets originally approved by the ministries and administration of USSR and Ukrainian SSR. The state was giving with one hand, and then taking away with another.'[104]

A source of frustration was the lack of clarity in dividing the enterprise profits between enterprises, local budgets, and ministries. Not only did different enterprises pay different shares of their profits to the ministries, but also it was not clear how these shares were calculated. At the end of 1988, enterprises could pay as much as 91 percent of their profits to their ministry. In the Cherkasy oblast, the USSR Ministry of Chemical Industry 'broke its promises' and reduced the share of profits left to its enterprises from 30 to 26 percent.[105] The Ministry of Road Construction left 21 percent of the profits generated by the plant 'Stroimash' in Pryluky in the Chernihiv oblast. 'Why not less or at least not more?' asked local authorities. Even more angering were the situations when people were asked to work more for less. 'How do we explain to workers that in the plan for 1989, the production volumes are growing, whereas profits that remain at the disposal of enterprises reduce almost two times[?],[106] asked Mykhailo Hur'ev, director of the Odesa railway. The increase in production targets did not mean that the ministries suddenly diligently supplied inputs to their enterprises or abandoned the practice of changing plan targets. (Extraction of maximum profits from enterprises was characteristic of all ministries, regardless of their all-union or republican status. Ukrainian ministries were just as keen as the all-union ministries to assign state orders without providing the inputs or to ignore requests coming from factories for the necessary equipment. Ukrainian ministries were just as keen to expropriate the profits of enterprises as well, leaving sometimes as little as 9 percent of gained profits to enterprises.[107])

The first secretary of the Nedryhailiv raikom (Sumy oblast) urged the Ukrainian Central Committee's socio-economic department to make corrections in the distribution of above-plan production and profits in a way that would incentivize workers to produce more, and 'more rationally correlate the interests of workers' collectives with the interests of the state'. The Poltava authorities urged the Ukrainian Gosplan to respect The Law on the State Enterprise and stop distributing local construction materials. Some secretaries hoped for some logic and fairness in food distribution. Others urged the Ukrainian leadership to address the root of the problem and finally resolve the long-standing imbalance between the local soviets' responsibilities and access to resources by making them independent of the branch ministries.[108]

In a drastic departure from the past, authorities of some regions no longer agreed to an arbitrary distribution of centrally allocated resources among oblasts. They insisted that the Ukrainian leadership formalize the process. Distribution of resources among the oblasts should be based on a normative method, transparent and fair. The norms of distribution of food and consumer goods should be the same for large cities and small towns, and the planned surplus should be divided between the regions and the union-republican funds. Hryhorii Revenko, first secretary of the Kyiv obkom, had a very specific request to the Ukrainian leadership: that the city and the oblast of Kyiv be treated as one region, like Moscow and the Moscow region, *Podmoskov'e*, and that the food supplied to the Ukrainian capital be organized based on the same principle as for Moscow.[109]

The Kharkiv authorities asked the Ukrainian Central Committee to assist in correcting structural deformations of regional economies. They also suggested that the Ukrainian Central Committee address the consequences caused by the central ministries neglecting the local supplies of consumer goods and the social agenda.[110]

At the end of 1988, the authorities of the Zakarpattia oblast brought the idea of a special economic zone to the attention of the Ukrainian leadership. They hoped to organize trans-border trading and manufacturing with enterprises from Hungary, Romania, and Czechoslovakia.[111] Special economic zones were officially allowed by the central government in December 1988. The idea had been embraced by Anatolii Sobchak, the mayor of Leningrad, by the Estonian leadership, and by the regional leadership in the Far East.[112] The Zakarpattia party aktiv was sure that their region was also ready.

On the political front, with glasnost changing the public environment to one less hospitable for communists, the obkoms required guidance from the Central Committee, not the Ukrainian Central Committee, as to how to prepare for the election campaign. They urged the Ukrainian Central Committee to formally decentralize the administration of the CPU and thus give communists the leeway to struggle against political opposition in their own oblasts. In another significant departure from the past, at the oblast party conferences held in December 1988, a number of regional party organizations from various parts of Ukraine suggested that a share of party fees should remain with the regional party organizations 'for their own needs'. Among the supporters of this idea was Revenko, who had been moved from the Central Committee apparatus to head the Kyiv obkom in 1985. Revenko also argued against the Ukrainian Central Committee's monopoly on information. Regions, he argued, also needed up-to-date information on the political and socio-economic situation in their oblast and the republic. 'At the moment, neither the Academy of Social Sciences [of Ukraine], nor the Kyiv Highest Party School produce meaningful summarizing materials about processes in the party and society.' Indeed, 'the time had come for the obkoms, gorkoms, and raikoms to have mobile groups that would study sociological issues, summarize this information and provide the party organizations with objective information on problems that concerned people [in their regions]'.[113]

Regional authorities understood very well that the Ukrainian leadership did not have the power to draft policies or solve Ukraine's myriad economic and administrative problems. Nonetheless, they expected the Ukrainian leadership to perform its function as the main intermediary agency between the periphery and the central agencies. Instead of focusing on assisting the ministries in extracting resources from the regions, or 'transmitting the message' from Moscow to the regions, or sending down directives and instructions, the regions needed the

Ukrainian leadership to focus on assisting them with the implementation of economic reforms, with meeting the socio-economic needs of the population, and with confronting growing political opposition. Instead of acting on behalf of Moscow, the regions urged the Ukrainian leadership to accept the increasing importance of addressing regional problems before branch interests and to act on behalf of the regions.

Shcherbytsky felt the pressure from the regions. At the end of 1988, the Ukrainian leadership was not prepared to prioritize the interests of the Ukrainian regions over those of the branch ministries, as the regions wanted. However, Gorbachev's project to 'reformat' the Soviet federation provided Shcherbytsky with an opportunity to change the rules of interaction between the centre and the republic, to increase the power of the republican centre, and, thus, to increase the authority of the Ukrainian leadership within the republic.

## Shcherbytsky's Letter

Shcherbytsky's 31 December 1988 letter to the Central Committee, 'On perfection of inter-national relations in the USSR', included the Ukrainian Central Committee's suggestions and was written as a formal response to Gorbachev's call at the Nineteenth Party Conference to correct deformations which had accumulated in the nationality policy, at a time of lively debates on federalism in Moscow and in anticipation of the Central Committee plenum on nationality policy.

In the document, the Ukrainian leadership agreed with Gorbachev that it was for the sake of the Union, first and foremost, that the central leadership should revive the main Leninist principles of the Soviet federation, formalize the relationship between the centre and the republics, and expand republican rights. The specifics of Shcherbytsky's letter, however, suggested that the Ukrainian leadership had more radical changes in mind than Gorbachev expected.

The document began with a general statement that 'the USSR Constitution should clearly divide the functions of the Union of SSR and the Union republics', but then immediately specified that the Constitution should include full lists of issues that 'fall into the sole competence of the Union of SSR and the joint competence of the Union of SSR and the Union republics'. Any issue not mentioned in the two lists should 'fall into the sole competence of the republic to be addressed as it pleases'.[114] The letter advocated the formalization of the relationship between the Union and republican organs and a clear division of their functions in the area of foreign relations. It was the prerogative of the Union to define the main direction of Soviet foreign policy, agreed Shcherbytsky. However, there was a place for the republics 'to participate in forming the main directions of the USSR's foreign policy and foreign trade'.[115]

Consequently, and echoing previous Ukrainian leaders, Shcherbytsky wanted a 'qualitatively new mechanism for the formation of republican and local budgets'. Republican budgets should be predictable, and the republic should have full control of them. More importantly, in a departure from Soviet tradition, the budget should be formed from the bottom up. The republic, not the Union, should collect all taxes paid by the population, organizations, cooperatives, and enterprises, 'regardless of their departmental subordination', argued Shcherbytsky, and it is for the republic to pay a tax to the all-union budget 'for common Union tasks', 'based on a stable normative', not for the Union to allocate funds to the republics based on Moscow's whim.[116]

Like Shelest before him, Shcherbytsky insisted on formalizing the republics' food deliveries to the all-union funds and distributing them fairly. In 1981–1987, the growth in the Ukraine's contribution of meat products to the all-union fund exceeded the growth of the meat product supply in Ukraine. Thus, the republic consumed 49 percent of the meat it produced in 1987, whereas Russia consumed 66 percent of its output of meat products, and Belorussia consumed 64 percent of its meat production. The Union average of locally produced meat consumption was 64 percent.[117]

Under pressure from an increasingly important environmental agenda after the Chornobyl disaster, Shcherbytsky criticized the all-union agencies for turning Ukraine 'into one of the most <u>ecologically</u> tense [*napriazhennyĭ*] regions of the country [underlined in the document]', which was under 'the highest level of anthropogenic and technogenic pressure'.[118]

In reaction to complaints from the obkoms, Shcherbytsky criticized the all-union agencies for focusing on industrial expansion while neglecting the social agenda. As a result, the Ukrainian periphery authorities of large industrial oblasts such as Kharkiv, Odesa, Lviv, Dnipropetrovsk, Kryvyi Rih, and Zhdanov (renamed Mariupol in 1989) had 'to find local resources to keep up with the social infrastructure'. At the same time, while authorities in large industrial centres could at least find local resources, the authorities from regions with a low level of industrialization could not. As a result, 'social infrastructure in many oblasts of Ukraine was at 62–66 percent of the accepted norm'.[119]

The Ukrainian leadership blamed the all-union agencies for structural deformations in Ukraine. With the excessive growth of heavy industry, the republic had to import almost one-third of consumer goods from other republics to satisfy local demand and balance the income and expenditures of the population. Shcherbytsky explained:

> Because of the deformation of the branch structure of the Ukrainian economy allowed by central agencies, the inconsistencies in taxation of manufactured and sold production, and shortcomings in the pricing policy, the republic is ranked only sixth based on per capita production, and seventh based on income

per capita, which clearly does not correspond to the republic's place in the economic complex of the country.

Speaking of personal income, Shcherbytsky emphasized that the average monthly wage in Ukraine ranked eighth in the Union and was inconsistent with Ukraine's contribution to the Union economy. The wages of the kolkhozniks did not correspond to the intensity of their labour and their output. Ukraine ranked twelfth among the republics for kolkhoznik wages.[120]

More generally, again similarly to his predecessors, Shcherbytsky was frustrated with unjustified hyper-centralization and the inconsistency between the rights and responsibilities of the Ukrainian leadership. The republic was responsible for the implementation of industrial programmes that were composed without consultation and 'without considering the real capabilities' of the republic. Hence, he agreed with the Ukrainian Central Committee's conclusion that 'it is impossible to accomplish fundamental success in socio-economic development without considerable expansion of the republican administrations' powers [underlined in the document]'; and such expansion should include Ukraine's access to information. The Ukrainian leadership should have direct access to raw statistical data, and not receive information on Ukraine 'after the centre [had] processed it'.[121]

'In short, transferring the republics and the regions to the principles of khozraschet is an objectively urgent need', Shcherbytsky agreed with Gorbachev. This did not mean replacing the *diktat* of the branch ministries with the *diktat* of the republics, Shcherbytsky reassured the central leadership. 'The work of the republican organs will be directed to the fulfilment of the state order.' Only when the issue concerned nature and ecology should the territorial principle prevail over branch. But a new arrangement meant that the Ukrainian government would be able to produce what it needed at any enterprise regardless of its subordination, supervise 'the direction of capital investments from the all-union budget', and 'independently decide where to allocate capital investments that are financed from the republican and local budgets'. Consequently, Shcherbytsky expected 'mutually beneficial trade' between the republics, based on formal contractual obligations.[122]

In contrast to Shelest and Rakovsky, Shcherbytsky did not include economic relations in 'the national question'. Shcherbytsky did not view Ukraine as a self-sufficient economic complex. He remained a proponent of economic integration of the republics into one all-union complex. But he did view this integration as a process that was still in progress. Hence, the republics should assist the centre with this transition.[123]

In a drastic departure from his past convictions, Shcherbytsky no longer supported the policy of Russification in Ukraine, although this was not because of a newfound love for Ukrainian culture or support for 'the national question' in the traditional narrow interpretation of the Soviet leaders. He simply believed that the party needed to drop the thesis 'about the forthcoming merger of nations, their languages, [and] cultures', and increase the status of the national language, expand its usage, and develop national culture through educational and cultural programmes in order to increase the chances for communists to win elections.[124]

The Ukrainian leadership drafted these suggestions based on Gorbachev's vague guidance points. Broadly, Shcherbytsky's letter reflected the principle of a strong centre, but also strong republics, that Gorbachev and his entourage defended at a time when scholars from the USSR Academy of Sciences deemed it absurd. However, the letter arguably took this principle further than Gorbachev intended and played into the fears of central Politburo conservatives that the *diktat* of the republics might replace the *diktat* of the centre.[125] In addition to its openly anti-ministerial stance, the Ukrainian proposal emphasized the importance of formalizing relations between the republics and the centre, which for conservatives meant an end to the principle of indisputable domination of the central apparatus over the republics.

Theoretical debates aside, nobody in Moscow, neither Gorbachev nor the central party nor the state bureaucracy in Moscow, was ready for the practical implementation of Leninist federalism, not to mention Shcherbytsky's interpretation of it. The draft of the party platform 'On ways to harmonize inter-national relations in the USSR', discussed at the central Politburo meeting on 14 July 1989, remained vague in defining the competences and rights of the republics.[126]

Hence, the Ukrainian leadership's margins of authority remained as limited as before, which meant that in 1989, as in previous years, it had limited opportunity to assist the regions or consolidate the CPU. The pressure from the regions, however, only increased, including from the obkom secretaries, who were loyal and 'ideologically pure' but felt they were no longer protected from the anger of the population.

## Shcherbytsky under Pressure from Below

Heorhii Kriuchkov, after years in the Ukrainian Central Committee as the head of the party work department, was already in the Central Committee apparatus when in October 1988 Shcherbytsky asked him to return to Ukraine and become first secretary of the Odesa obkom. Kriuchkov had no experience of running an oblast. However, the region was economically and strategically very important, and Shcherbytsky believed that a strong (read: 'well-connected') leader would be able to halt the region's economic decline and prevent it from falling into the wrong hands (read: 'national-democratic' or 'democratic').[127] When Kriuchkov arrived in Odesa, he found that the city 'had poor food supplies compared to other Ukrainian oblasts, and that food prices [there] were higher than elsewhere'. 'The oblast ranked twenty-first based on housing supply.' It ranked twenty-second based on the availability of hospital beds. Only 0.4 percent of rural houses had central gas supplies, an abysmal number even compared to the equally abysmal 6.1 percent central gasification throughout rural Ukraine. The population did not have a regular supply of drinking water (more than 200 villages in the Odesa oblast had to rely on the transportation of fresh water from elsewhere), and environmental issues were high on the agenda of the obkom.[128]

After more than six months of efforts to 'mobilize locally available resources' to improve the socio-economic situation in the oblast, Kriuchkov concluded that his connections and authority were not enough. 'The oblast needed considerable help from the republican and all-union organs.' At the 7 August 1989 Ukrainian Central Committee meeting, Kriuchkov asked Shcherbytsky to include regional needs in the republican plan. Only then 'would there be more guarantee that [the obkom] will not allow some undesirable developments in this very sensitive region [neprostoi region]'. On 31 August 1989, Kriuchkov and the chairman of the oblispolkom, Andrii Pechiorov, sent a detailed follow-up letter to the Ukrainian Central Committee and the Ukrainian government repeating the importance of republican help in the political struggle.[129]

Kriuchkov's counterpart from Lviv, Yakiv Pohrebniak, was in a similar situation but in a politically more complex oblast in under-sovietized Western Ukraine. Appointed in 1987, the former Ukrainian Central Committee secretary discovered a region with particularly disproportionate structural development and a particularly politically active population that openly discussed such problems as shortages of food, consumer goods, water supplies, schools, and pre-school establishments, as well as the low quality of health services and a deteriorating ecological situation.[130] At the Lviv obkom plenum on 10–11 December 1988, Pohrebniak was elected the obkom first secretary. By then, he faced growing political opposition in the region from the national-democratic movement. Like Kriuchkov, Pohrebniak believed that the struggle for minds had to be waged in the socio-economic arena. But for help, Pohrebniak addressed Gorbachev directly.

On 6 March 1989, Pohrebniak wrote a letter to Gorbachev in which he, echoing Shcherbytsky's criticism of central ministries, argued against the domination of branch development. The branch approach, explained Pohrebniak, led to the irrational exploitation of natural resources of the Carpathian region and a high ecological and social cost. As a result, air and water resources were polluted, soil was eroded, social infrastructure in rural areas fell behind in its development, and pendulum migration increased as the population sought jobs. 'The number of oncological diseases and respiratory illnesses increased', he wrote. The city of Lviv had food shortages and a difficult situation with drinking water and transportation. The oblast occupied one of the last places in Ukraine in terms of housing, pre-school establishments, and hospitals. Pohrebniak argued that to correct structural disbalances, the Soviet leadership should follow the principle of

**Illustration 15**  Mikhail Gorbachev in Lviv, 22 February 1989/© TsDAEA (0-215087)
Less than a month before the elections to the USSR Supreme Soviet, Gorbachev visited Ukraine.
In the photo, Gorbachev and his wife, Raisa Gorbacheva (in the centre) meet with Lviv residents.
Volodymyr Shcherbytsky, to the left of Gorbachev, accompanied him.

regional administration of the economy and 'pass a resolution on the complex socio-economic development of the Carpathian region'.[131] The letter was most likely written with the permission of Gorbachev himself, who together with Shcherbytsky visited Lviv on 22–24 February. Obkom secretaries writing formal letter requests after the visits of higher functionaries was not an uncommon practice.

While waiting for a reply from Gorbachev, Pohrebniak faced intensifying pressure from the political opposition. The country was preparing for the 26 March 1989 elections to the USSR Supreme Soviet. On 16 February 1989, the national-democratic movement *Narodnyĭ Rukh Ukraïny* (hereafter, 'Rukh'), which was strong in Western Ukraine, published its programme. In the section '*Ekonomika*', it called for 'an equivalent exchange between the republics, for development of direct economic connections, [and]…for independent access to world markets'.[132] One of the Rukh leaders, Viacheslav Chornovil, actively defended the idea of federalization in Ukraine.[133] As the letter to Gorbachev showed, Pohrebniak tried to stay ahead of Rukh on economic matters without calling for federalization, while hinting at the need for wide decentralization.

With no central resolution on the complex socio-economic development of the region in sight, Pohrebniak brought the problem of regional development to the June 1989 Ukrainian Central Committee plenum. There, he tried to convince the Ukrainian leadership that Ukraine needed 'a new model of territorial administration', and regional development could 'be the first stage in forming it'.

In order to provide rational administration [of the economy], it is necessary to accelerate the establishment of new economic relations between the centre, the republic, the oblasts, [and] primary production units [i.e., enterprises] based on regional khozraschet. The republic [i.e., the republican leadership] should show more initiative in this matter. Not so long ago, the suggestion of the [Lviv] oblast to create a regional production-construction association did not find its due support. There are today examples of similar associations and concerns at the Union level, [but] it is not clear why such associations do not exist in the republic.[134]

According to Pohrebniak, by mid-1989 the situation in Lviv had deteriorated to the point that 'it became difficult for [the Lviv authorities] to solve the problems that life put in front of them on their own'. The Lviv obkom needed assistance from Shcherbytsky or Gorbachev. None was forthcoming. In the summer of 1989, nobody in the Ukrainian leadership 'fully realized the complexity of the situation or understood how serious everything that was happening in Lviv and other western oblasts was'.[135] Western Ukraine was traditionally on the periphery of the leadership's attention. Regional development more generally was not its priority either. Besides, in July 1989, the Ukrainian leadership had to deal with a 'sectoral' crisis in the coal industry, one of the main industries of Ukraine. Ukrainian miners in Donbas and the Lviv-Volyn coalfield, in Chervonohrad, went on strike.[136]

## Shcherbytsky's Clash with the Regions

The Ukrainian leadership, and Shcherbytsky personally, were of little help to Kriuchkov, Pohrebniak, or any other obkom secretary.[137] On the one hand, Kyiv was unable to provide meaningful help; resources in quantities sufficient to change the situation in a branch or a region were outside the reach of the Ukrainian leadership. It could not issue its own regulations to affect the centralized distribution of resources, either. On the other hand, Shcherbytsky was not particularly eager to help. He was not convinced that systemically empowering local authorities, as the emphasis on regional development dictated, was the way for the CPSU to stay in power.

Shcherbytsky viewed the rise of the oppositional movement as alarming. It certainly required the party and law-enforcement organs to 'activate the struggle against anti-societal extremist manifestations'.[138] With 70 percent of Rukh party cells located in Western Ukraine, this region was particularly vulnerable,[139] but he did not see the rise of the opposition as threatening as long as it had no access to resources.[140] Without 'financial capabilities and material possibilities', political forces have no real power.[141] So far, the centralized communist state still controlled the economy. Empowering local soviets when the oppositional forces had

a possibility of winning in local elections meant increasing the risk of oppositional forces obtaining 'financial capabilities and material possibilities'.

Shcherbytsky had another reason to resent the idea of empowering the regions.
Empowering the regions meant revising the existing dynamic between the
Ukrainian leadership and the periphery. The Ukrainian leadership was institutionally weak with limited decision-making authority, and the regions maintained
direct communication with Moscow. Nonetheless, the Ukrainian leadership was
the representative of the all-union leadership in Ukraine. With no meaningful
control over resources, it still had administrative authority that neither Moscow
nor the regions could ignore. Empowering the regions by supporting regional as
opposed to sectoral development, by increasing the resources at their disposal, or
by formalizing administrative relationships meant changing the balance of power
between the Ukrainian leadership and the Ukrainian regions in favour of the latter. The Ukrainian leadership would no longer be able to impose a top-down
*diktat*, the only model that Shcherbytsky accepted. In his 31 December 1988 letter
to the Central Committee, Shcherbytsky clearly signalled his readiness to replace
Moscow in administering Ukraine, but not to increase the powers of the
Ukrainian regions.[142]

Therefore, while unable to assist the regions tangibly with their agendas, the
Ukrainian leadership continued urging them to focus on the importance of the
human factor, better cadres selection, and the mobilization of locally available
resources.[143] By July 1989, Shcherbytsky was ready to make concessions on education in Ukrainian and allowing 'cultural-educational societies for small national
groups'. He was prepared to change the Ukrainian Constitution to grant
Ukrainian language the status of a state language in Ukraine, and to support long-
term programmes for the development of Ukrainian national culture and historical research, all in line with glasnost.[144] But he was not prepared to empower the
regions to enable them to fight for their own socio-economic survival. The product of the Soviet authoritarian model of administration, he had the same fear of
empowering the Ukrainian regions as Moscow had of empowering the republics.

Shcherbytsky's reluctance to empower the very same regional secretaries who
defended communist control over the economy in the periphery even manifested
in his anecdotal refusal to share information that the Ukrainian Central
Committee received from Moscow with the obkom first secretaries, which could
not but puzzle the latter. How could they work with their 'eyes shut?'[145]

In line with Shcherbytsky's 31 December 1988 letter to Moscow, at the June
1989 Ukrainian Central Committee plenum and at its 7 August 1989 meeting,
Kriuchkov, Pohrebniak, and other obkom first secretaries tried to convince
Shcherbytsky that the rapidly deteriorating economic situation and rapid liberalization of political life called for empowering regional authorities to enable them
to fight the opposition and maintain party control over the state.[146] The situation
required higher authorities to trust the regional authorities. It required the

decentralization of decision making. Shcherbytsky was neither prepared nor wanted to participate in such a drastic change. On 28 September 1989, based on his request, the Ukrainian Central Committee plenum relieved him of his duties.

## Conclusion

The stability of the Soviet system until the end of Shcherbytsky's leadership and the secrecy that surrounded the workings of the apparatus concealed the Ukrainian leadership's weakness and the CPU's fragmentation. The introduction of contested elections in 1988–1989 increased the bottom-up pressure from the regions on the Ukrainian leadership. Still accountable for meeting plan targets, yet obligated to concentrate on the local agenda and deprived of its former access to resources, the periphery apparatus turned to the Ukrainian leadership for resources, procedures, formalization of the agencies' administrative relationships, and enforcement of existing contracts. Playing by the rules, the principle to which Shcherbytsky adhered in his political career, had made him a master of political survival and allowed him to create an image of a strong Ukrainian leader, but it could no longer provide the Ukrainian leadership with secure authority and power over the regions. Under pressure from the regions, but also in response to Gorbachev's openness to reconsider federal relations, Shcherbytsky asked the central leadership to change the rules and expand the Ukrainian leadership's margins of authority. Moscow was not ready for such a drastic step, not just yet. As a result, by the end of Shcherbytsky's leadership, just like before perestroika, the institutionally weak Ukrainian leadership had no means to accommodate the needs of the regions. Each obkom together with its oblispolkom was left to work out its own strategy to stay in power.[147]

*The Institutional Foundations of Ukrainian Democracy: Power Sharing, Regionalism, and Authoritarianism.* Nataliya Kibita,
Oxford University Press. © Nataliya Kibita 2024. DOI: 10.1093/9780191925351.003.0007

# 7

# The Ukrainian Leadership's
# Experiment with *Diktat*

## Introduction

The years 1990–1991 were arguably the most favourable years for the Ukrainian leadership to consolidate its power. Since the early days of the Bolshevik control of Ukraine, the Soviet leadership had administered the Ukrainian republican centre and the Ukrainian regions directly from Petrograd and then Moscow. The Ukrainian leadership had a small, but secure niche in the party and state administration, and Moscow was a reliable source of power for the Ukrainian leadership. But in 1990, the all-union centre began to crumble.[1] The Central Committee's political authority rapidly decayed. The economic control maintained by the Soviet government and the central planning organs decayed by the day, as well.[2] The Ukrainian Central Committee and the Ukrainian government were still the highest administrative organs in the republic. After the March 1990 elections to the Supreme Soviet of the Ukrainian Soviet Socialist Republic (the Verkhovna Rada), the Presidium of the Verkhovna Rada joined the Ukrainian Central Committee and government to form a new Ukrainian leadership, but neither of the three institutions could rely on the central leadership for power.[3] The Ukrainian regional authorities, which after democratic elections also expanded to include not only the apparatus of territorial party organizations and directors of large state enterprises but also the soviet and ispolkom chairmen and the regional deputies to the Verkhovna Rada (MPs),[4] could not rely on Moscow for power, either. In 1990–1991, they increased the pressure that the obkoms had been putting on the Ukrainian leadership since 1989 to consolidate its grip on Ukraine.

The shared goal of the Ukrainian leadership and the Ukrainian regions to consolidate centralized administration in Ukraine for Ukraine found its expression in the Verkhovna Rada's declaration of sovereignty on 16 July 1990.[5] However, as this chapter shows, there remained a fundamental disagreement between the regions and the Ukrainian leadership as to *how* to consolidate the Ukrainian centre.

For the regions, which were now able to defend their interests in the Verkhovna Rada, sovereignty meant the ability to fulfil their socio-economic, political,

and private agenda in Kyiv instead of Moscow. For them, sovereignty meant consolidating the regions as a precondition for consolidating the republican centre,
overcoming regionalism, and consolidating Ukraine into one polity. Hence, they
wanted the Ukrainian centre to focus on their agenda.

Faced with growing political opposition, the communist majority in the
Verkhovna Rada and the periphery apparatus needed the Ukrainian Central
Committee to consolidate the CPU and lead the political struggle, particularly
against the familiar and formidable foe, Ukrainian nationalism.[6] The national-
democratic movement Rukh dominated in Western Ukraine, but the rapidly
deteriorating economic situation created fears that Rukh and democratic
opposition could spread across Ukraine and remove the communists from
power. Regional communists also needed the Ukrainian Central Committee to
defend them in the soviets. Back in September 1988, Gorbachev had initiated a
political reform that aimed to replace the party with the soviets and turn the
soviets into permanently governing bodies.[7] To defend the communist cause,
and protect their personal careers, the periphery apparatus gradually migrated
to the soviets. Yet, the soviets as institutions remained weak and did not allow
communists to defend their own agenda in the same way they had in the territorial
party organizations. To defend communists in the soviets, the periphery
apparatus needed the Ukrainian Central Committee to expand and formalize
the power of the soviets.

Authorities from all regions, regardless of their ideological convictions, needed
a strong republican centre that would prioritize their economic needs over the
fulfilment of the all-union agenda, regulate their relationships inside and outside
Ukraine, enforce contract discipline to ensure supplies of inputs for enterprises,
and thereby preserve the jobs and supplies of consumer goods to their voters, on
whom they depended for re-election and personal prosperity.

The regions were not alone in wanting the Ukrainian centre to focus on fulfilling their agenda. The 'old guard', which continued to dominate in the Verkhovna
Rada and in the regions, also insisted on changing the relationship between the
regions and the Ukrainian centre.[8] Adding to the morass of an increasingly deregulated economy, Gorbachev's political reform put democratically elected soviets
alongside obkoms bound by centralism, creating administrative chaos. With the
Ukrainian leadership unable to control this morass, the regions insisted on the
decentralization of administration down to the level of oblasts and even raions. In
place of *diktat*, to which they had submitted throughout the entire Soviet period,
the regions expected to cooperate with the Ukrainian centre in elaborating and
implementing policies. The regions also encouraged the Ukrainian leadership to
break with the centre's practice of refusing any responsibility for its policies and
decisions. As a new power centre, Kyiv should share responsibility for the situation in Ukraine with the regions.

To the Ukrainian leadership, on the other hand, Ukraine's sovereignty meant the decentralization of decision- and policymaking from the level of all-union administration to the level of the republican centre, but also the unquestioned submission of the regions to the authority of Kyiv, the unquestioned priority of Ukrainian republican needs as defined by the Ukrainian leadership over regional needs, and the continued infallibility of the leadership. The Ukrainian leadership had gradually come to the realization that Moscow was an unreliable source of power. It also realized that, as a group, the regions were stronger than the republican centre. However, it resented the very idea of building its power from the bottom up and in cooperation with the regions. It chose to attempt to impose its authority through *diktat*.

As this chapter shows, such an approach to consolidating centralized power was inadequate for Ukraine. Both the Ukrainian leadership and the periphery operated in a deregulated environment that motivated and indeed compelled regionalism. As a group, the regions were stronger than the Ukrainian leadership. The Ukrainian leadership had neither the mechanisms nor any leverage to impose its authority over the regions. It was up to the regions to decide whether to accept Kyiv's *diktat* or not. The regions desired and had an objective need for a strong Ukrainian leadership. They supported the idea of Ukrainian sovereignty. On 24 August 1991, the same old-new Verkhovna Rada that was elected by the regions issued an Act of Declaration of Independence of Ukraine.[9] However, the regions had no desire, nor an objective reason, to accept the *diktat* of Kyiv in an independent Ukraine, any more than they desired the *diktat* of Moscow in the reformed Soviet Union.

In 1990–1991, the Ukrainian leadership refused to accept the institutional realities of Ukraine and deviate from Soviet-style *diktat* to find a new modus operandi in its relationship with the periphery. As a result, it remained weak, while the regions grew stronger. Regionalism prevailed over a centralized vertical administration.

## Part I: 1990

### Regions Urging Kyiv to Lead

As the Ukrainian periphery party apparatus entered 1990, the CPU was dominated by a defeatist mood and the sentiment of being abandoned by the party leadership.[10] At the CPU forum in March 1990 there was hardly any obkom secretary who would not openly criticize the Central Committee and the Ukrainian Central Committee for passivity and lack of leadership. Some asked uncomfortable questions, such as 'What role do the Central Committee and the Ukrainian

Central Committee play? Why does the ruling party not use its right of legislative initiative?'[11] All were waiting for 'thought-through political decisions' and 'a concept of perestroika'. Gorbachev's insistence on the party's withdrawal from economic administration at the Nineteenth Party Conference (28 June–1 July 1988) particularly confused the obkom secretaries, as it contradicted the very raison d'être of the obkoms. After all, the leadership was still demanding that they ensure the fulfilment of state orders, and people still came to the obkoms with their problems. If continued, party withdrawal from the economy 'would lead to the creation of parallel structures to whom workers would entrust the defence of their interests',[12] they argued.

The obkom secretaries insisted that if the Central Committee could not organize the Ukrainian obkoms for political struggle, then the Ukrainian Central Committee should.

In February, in preparation for the 4–18 March 1990 elections to the Verkhovna Rada, Ukrainian obkom secretaries had already urged Shcherbytsky's successor, Volodymyr Ivashko, to take an assertive stance vis-à-vis the Central Committee. Three months before Russia declared its sovereignty, and four months before Ukraine did, they insisted that the Ukrainian Central Committee should instruct the communist-dominated Verkhovna Rada and the Ukrainian government to stop rewriting the all-union laws and instead write original laws that, while not contradicting the all-union laws, would reflect republican needs.[13] After the elections, the pressure increased. At the 30 March Ukrainian Central Committee meeting, 'after three meetings with the obkom secretaries in the past 10 months', obkoms insisted that the Ukrainian Politburo should advance beyond 'just talking' and provide 'a quality analysis of the political situation, a political forecast, and a specific programme of action'.[14] And not only should the Ukrainian Central Committee lead, it should lead in a fundamentally new way, drastically different from the way the Central Committee managed the party.

First and foremost, the CPU should be formalized. The time had come to turn the CPU from an ephemeral and 'in some sense illegal organization' into a 'real', legal, united, and disciplined party organization. The CPU should be an autonomous part of the CPSU with its own statute and programme. The CPU programme should not simply list instructions to the periphery apparatus. The programme should be drafted from below, be discussed with the obkoms, and 'express a common and coordinated position of the obkoms', and it should address 'the daily problems of common people'. The Ukrainian Central Committee should abandon the practice by which the party congress rubber stamped the decisions of the central Politburo. The CPU should be democratized. If the obkom secretaries were elected, the CPU first secretary should be elected, too. Finally, instead of sending Ukrainian Central Committee instructors to supervise the obkoms, the Ukrainian Central Committee should offer 'real' help, like funds for local party newspapers, or qualified party workers to assist the obkoms in their relationship with the population.[15]

The obkom secretaries had a strong view on decentralizing the implementation of the yet-to-be-drafted CPU programme. The socio-economic situation in their oblasts remained the cornerstone of the obkoms' institutional existence. The situation varied from one oblast to another, so, they argued, they should be free to implement the programme and the decisions of the Ukrainian Central Committee in the way they considered most suitable to the socio-economic and political situation in their regions, without seeking the Ukrainian Central Committee's permission. Restoring order by traditional top-down *diktat* could not bring results—not because the obkoms rejected or resisted *diktat* per se, but because instructions from the top that were drafted with no input from the obkoms were outdated and did not help the obkoms address local problems or lead a proactive struggle against political opposition. For example, in some regions, obkoms were open to cooperating with various political groups, which the Ukrainian Central Committee was not yet authorizing.[16]

Related to decentralizing the implementation of the future party programme was the request of the obkom secretaries to review the budget of the CPU. Echoing their suggestions from the end of 1988, the periphery party secretaries suggested that they should be told what share of collected membership fees to transfer to the Central Committee and the Ukrainian Central Committee and be allowed to keep what remained and spend these sums without consulting Kyiv.[17] At the March 1990 Ukrainian Central Committee plenum, the Lviv obkom secretary took the discussion about party finances further and suggested that, considering that the party was 'heading towards difficult financial times', it could invest a share of membership fees 'either in profitable businesses, or into expanding the network of party enterprises'.[18]

As a by-product of the democratization of politics, the obkoms no longer agreed to be held solely responsible for the deteriorating state of the country, something they signalled in 1989. The party leadership should be also held accountable, for the instructions it issued. In line with Shcherbytsky's proposal from December 1988 on the division of responsibilities between the union and the republican centres, the obkoms insisted on a formal division of responsibilities between the party committees and the party leadership, as well as a formalized correlation between the rights and responsibilities of the obkoms.[19]

Finally, to gain political victories, the periphery party apparatus urged the Ukrainian leadership to assert its control over the economy and assist the regions with their agendas. In particular, they hoped the Ukrainian leadership would secure an equivalent exchange of goods between the republics and create an economic system that would guarantee the fulfilment of contracts. Establishing a fair and transparent system for distributing state-controlled products inside Ukraine, something the obkoms had been hoping for since the end of 1988, would help their efforts to maintain control over the economic situation in their territories, as well. All in all, the Ukrainian leadership should proceed with economic reforms towards a market economy.[20]

## Kyiv Resisting the Pressure

At the 30 March 1990 meeting with the obkom secretaries in the Ukrainian Central Committee, Ivashko and his guest, Valerii Nakonechny, the head of the Central Committee department for Ukraine and Moldavia (Moldova), rejected any accusation of non-leadership. Ivashko refused to lead the CPU autonomously and confirmed his reliance on the Central Committee as the main source of authority for the Ukrainian Central Committee. He saw nothing wrong with Gorbachev's agenda to remove the party from the economy, something the Central Committee had repeatedly tried but failed to do before perestroika. But he was in favour of leaving 50 percent of the collected membership fees to the primary party organizations and encouraged the party organizations to earn money. Ivashko even suggested that the obkoms should make money on party hotels and cars. To the other demands of the periphery apparatus, he replied philosophically that some would be studied. However, the periphery secretaries should not have any illusions that all their suggestions would be implemented: 'This never happened before and will not happen any time soon, because this does not happen.'[21]

Ivashko supported the idea of Ukraine controlling its own economy. 'Anyway, direct relations between the republics would become dominant in the future [Soviet] federation.'[22] But together with the chairman of the Ukrainian government, Vitalii Masol (July 1987–October 1990), he was inclined to take control over the economy gradually, without undermining inter-republican deliveries or Ukraine's deliveries to the all-union funds, and in coordination with the all-union centre, not the regions.[23] Besides, on 16 April 1990, the new president of the Soviet Union, Mikhail Gorbachev, signed a law on dividing responsibilities between the USSR and the subjects of federation. At the Twenty-Eighth Party Congress, on 2 June 1990, the chairman of the Soviet government, Nikolai Ryzhkov, declared that the central government would take a completely new approach to its relationship with the republics. Ryzhkov stopped short of promising that none of the main socio-economic issues would be solved without coordinating with the republics.[24] Nonetheless, Ukrainian leaders were hopeful that Moscow would be responsive to their power ambitions and share control over the economy with them.

**Illustration 16** CPU First Secretary Volodymyr Ivashko addresses the Verkhovna Rada, 16 May 1990/© TsDAEA (0-220409)

As perestroika stalled, the economic situation deteriorated and democratic movement intensified, the power of the Verkhovna Rada increased. By May 1990, CPU First Secretary Volodymyr Ivashko (addressing the MPs) had no other choice but to accept the new reality. In the photo, Ivashko addresses the Supreme Soviet of the UkSSR, from now on referred to as the Verkhovna Rada.

**Illustration 17** Pickets during the first session of the Supreme Soviet of the UkSSR of the twelfth convocation, also known as first session of the Verkhovna Rada of the first convocation, 15 May 1990/© TsDAEA (0-220392)

Banner bottom left: 'God! Give wisdom and force to the deputies of the UkSSR Verkhovna Rada to stop the genocide of the Ukrainian people!'; banner in the centre 'Khmelnytskyi territorial Rukh demands the approval of the decision by the Khmelnytskyi oblast soviet about the moratorium on the construction of the Khmelnytskyi nuclear power plant. Political hunger strike in Khmelnytskyi continues.' Banners at the top say that the elections held in Bila Tserkva were forged.

**Illustration 18**  Viacheslav Chornovil, June–July 1990/© TsDAEA (0-220464)

Member of the Verkhovna Rada and leader of the national-democratic movement Rukh, Viacheslav Chornovil, greets pickets in front of the Verkhovna Rada during its first session.

Yet in June, the context in which Ivashko operated had already changed. Firstly, on 4 June 1990, he was elected the chairman of the Verkhovna Rada. A new institution, one that according to Gorbachev's political reform was supposed to replace the Ukrainian Central Committee as the central institution, dictated new interests. Secondly, on 12 June, Russia declared sovereignty. Declaration of Russian sovereignty weakened the all-union centre, the power source for the Ukrainian leadership. Facing uncertainty, the Ukrainian leadership now needed the support of the Ukrainian regions to assert its authority both within the republic and vis-à-vis the new Russian authorities. The Ukrainian leadership began by recognizing its own weakness.

At the 23 June 1990 Ukrainian Central Committee plenum, Masol admitted that each Ukrainian oblast 'had its own system' and that the Ukrainian leadership could not forge these systems into one republican system without the good will of the regions.[25] Echoing Masol, at the Twenty-Eighth CPU Congress held on 19–23 June 1990, Ivashko admitted to the weakness of the Ukrainian Central Committee and the fragmentation of the CPU. 'The Ukrainian Central Committee did not manage to organize strong working connections with local party organizations and committees, or to overcome such negative phenomena as the fall of party discipline.' Crucially, the Ukrainian Central Committee could no longer protect the obkom secretaries from being removed. Ivashko recognized that the Ukrainian leadership was politically and administratively passive, did not always critically assess the decisions of the centre, did not anticipate the social effect of these decisions, and did not show the necessary resolve, courage, if you want, in defending the interests of the republic when solving the most urgent problems. Exactly this clearly manifested in the situation with the Chornobyl tragedy when the republican leadership could not resist the *diktat* of the ministries when all rescue efforts were dictated by the centre.[26]

Ivashko finally caught up with the obkoms and agreed to increase the autonomy of the CPU within the CPSU, 'so that [it] could, disregarding the centre, take responsibility for solving the political, socio-economic, and spiritual development of the republic, define the priorities, [and] choose forms for the realization of common party [i.e., CPSU] decisions, as dictated by the declaration of state sovereignty of the Ukrainian SSR'. He admitted that the CPU could take such responsibility only if it could affect policymaking and policy implementation. He now also agreed with the obkoms that Gorbachev's idea of removing the party from economic administration, formalized on 12 March 1990 in the revised version of article 6 of the USSR Constitution, undermined the political struggle of communists in Ukraine. Hence the CPU should deviate from it. In response to Russia's declaration of sovereignty, Ivashko now supported the idea that 'the new Ukrainian Central Committee should organize the elaboration of a new effective investment policy[,] and introduce it to the Verkhovna Rada in the form of a legislative initiative'. Social policies and the agricultural sector, both traditionally under party control, should be its priority.[27]

The Ukrainian leadership arrived to Shcherbytsky's view from late 1988 that the relationship between Moscow and Kyiv needed to be formalized. Although for Shcherbytsky this was a preventive measure, implemented top-down, and 'Moscow' meant the all-union centre, Ivashko and Masol had to act in response to Russian nationalism and Boris Yeltsin's rise in popularity, and to them 'Moscow' meant both the all-union and the Russian centres. So, on 25 June, Masol promised to prioritize establishing direct economic relations with Russian enterprises and a treaty with Russia.[28] Ivashko, in his turn, in private as well as in public, spoke of the need to legally strengthen Ukraine's economic sovereignty, to introduce 'citizenship of the Ukrainian SSR as "an inalienable attribute of statehood and sovereignty"'.[29] Ivashko took Shcherbytsky's thesis about Ukraine's participation in drafting Soviet foreign policy and advanced it to a thesis about 'the right of the republic to "enter into relations with foreign states, to make agreements with them"'. He viewed Ukraine as an actor 'in the general European process'.[30]

However, little from Ivashko's emphatic speech was implemented. On 9 July 1990, Ivashko suddenly resigned from the Verkhovna Rada and moved to Moscow to support Gorbachev and become his deputy. On 16 July, the Verkhovna Rada declared sovereignty. Yet it could not compete with the Ukrainian Central

Committee as the leading institution just yet. The context in which the new CPU First Secretary Stanislav Hurenko operated had changed once again. In July, Gorbachev and Yeltsin made a tactical alliance to jointly seek adequate economic reforms for the Soviet Union. Grigorii Yavlinsky, a young economist born in Lviv, drafted an economic programme which both Gorbachev and Yeltsin were ready to support. The two leaders failed to form one team of reformers; two rival teams of economists were created.[31] Still, from Hurenko's perspective, Moscow was searching for a correct concept of economic reforms and there was the possibility that once it was formulated, the central leadership would regain control over the entire economy and federation.[32] The consolidation of the all-union centre would allow the Ukrainian leadership to continue relying on Moscow as the sole source of power and save it from aligning its interests with the regions and yielding to the demands of the regions to decentralize, democratize, share responsibility, and so on.

The regions did not want to wait. They continued putting pressure on the Ukrainian Central Committee to assert Ukraine's sovereignty. They needed the Ukrainian leadership to defend Ukrainian producers and customers, and secure the necessary supplies now, not in the ephemeral future. 'Already today we see that the central government is powerless to help us in all of the most important issues. Yeltsin gave the order to not supply fuel to Ukraine until 25 July [and it was not supplied]', complained the first secretary of the Zaporizhzhia obkom at the 1 August Ukrainian Central Committee meeting. 'We must get ready for contract relations with other republics, for wood, for gas, for everything else.' The industrial ministries increasingly ignored their social agenda, and Ukrainian regions were 'already losing [control over] construction, social and cultural services'. To address shortages of consumer goods and interruptions of other supplies, the Ukrainian Central Committee should mobilize communists who worked in the Ukrainian government and 'demand results from them',[33] insisted the obkom secretaries.

On the political front, as well, the Ukrainian Central Committee should be more proactive, the obkom secretaries believed. Persistent lack of political leadership undermined the obkoms' efforts to retain authority in their regions. 'Good wishes and the directives that the centre [was] sending [were] not enough' to fight against Rukh. The Ukrainian Central Committee should step up and stop the party from free falling. The Ukrainian Central Committee should work out a political line and a strategy to unite and defend the Communist party and the periphery apparatus. Otherwise, the opposition that was moving from the west would reach Ukrainian eastern oblasts and 'we will be killed like quails one by one'.[34] The chronic handicap of the Soviet system, circulation of information, finally had to be addressed as well. So far, each obkom was informed about the situation in its own and the neighbouring oblasts, but it lacked knowledge of the situation throughout Ukraine. Echoing discussions in August 1989, first secretary of the Kharkiv obkom Anatolii Mialytsia and second secretary of the Kyiv gorkom Heorhii Nechytovsky suggested that the Ukrainian Central Committee should regularly collect, summarize, and distribute to the obkoms information on the latest developments related to Rukh.[35] To improve the financial situation of the obkoms and stop the exodus of the party cadres to the soviets and enterprises, the obkoms urged the Ukrainian Central Committee to allow them to run their own businesses. The decision to cut the party apparatus by 60–70 percent and reduce the wages of the party functionaries, due to the CPU budget deficit of 177 million roubles in 1990, was wrong. Obkoms were already engaged in entrepreneurship, but they should expand their commercial activity. Mialytsia suggested that the obkoms be allowed to organize subsistence farms, 'similar to the one that the Ukrainian Central Committee had', and asked the Ukrainian government to assist the Kharkiv obkom to 'procure a plot of land'. The first secretary of the Ivano-Frankivsk obkom, too, had land plots in mind to be 'purchased' by the obkom.[36]

The Ukrainian Central Committee should also hold law enforcement forces responsible for the developing political crisis and the staggering growth of crime. 'Only 10 percent of laws are enforced today. Ten percent! What do we want to discuss, then?' asked Mialytsia rhetorically. The relationship between the CPU and the KGB and militia needed to be improved, as well, because 'it was not clear who was following whom'. Finally, the time came for Hurenko to overcome his resentment of the Verkhovna Rada and forge the CPU into a parliamentary party. If communists in the Verkhovna Rada were not organized, then Rukh would take over.[37]

The Ukrainian leadership resisted the pressure from the regions as best as it could. The CPU statute, which the obkoms hoped would unite the CPU and arm the periphery apparatus in its political struggle against the opposition, was put on hold. Convinced that the 'time will come for Ukraine to supply to the all-union funds what Ukraine was withdrawing today', Hurenko insisted that the CPU should focus on fulfilling agricultural plans by reverting to the old method of mobilizing the urban population and local enterprises for agricultural works. Masol echoed the Ukrainian Central Committee. He put on hold the establishment of direct economic relations with the Russian leadership that he had promised to the regions on 25 June. In return for Russia's refusal to supply petrol, Masol 'could close all [sea] ports, and Russia would not receive grain. But this [was] a serious political step' that Masol was not prepared to take, either. Anyway, Ukraine had enough diesel for its agricultural machines. In his view, the obkoms should 'just deliver' and 'stop creating a conflict between the urban and rural population'.[38]

## Kyiv's Efforts to Control Resources

At the end of August 1990, the prospects of Moscow expanding the power of the Ukrainian leadership reduced considerably. The Ukrainian leadership received Gorbachev's long-awaited new economic programme, the so-called 500 Days programme.[39] The research institute of the Ukrainian Gosplan and the Verkhovna Rada commission for economic reform, both dominated by the old cadres, found the programme unacceptable for Ukraine. The programme did not separate the economic responsibilities of the centre and the republics, something which the Ukrainian leadership had occasionally insisted on since the early 1920s. Nor did it correlate the republics' rights and responsibilities, particularly on the social agenda. The programme ignored the Declaration about the Sovereignty of Ukraine, as well as the law 'On the Economic Independence [*samostiïnist'*] of the UkSSR' passed by the Verkhovna Rada on 3 August 1990. Economic administration remained strictly centralized. The newly formed all-union structures, such as the Economic Council of the President of the USSR and the Financial Reserve System of the Union, 'receive[d] broad rights to defend the interests of the Union. However, their responsibility for the results of their policies, or for protecting interests of the sovereign republics, were not defined.' The Verkhovna Rada commission found the Union's monopoly on foreign trade 'unacceptable', and the powers attributed to the president dictatorial.[40]

Being squeezed between the incessant pressure from the regions and the obvious unwillingness of the union centre to expand and formalize the division of economic power between the republics and the centre, the Ukrainian government was motivated to take a more active position in asserting control over the Ukrainian economy independently from Moscow.[41] Thus, Masol took the advice the obkom secretaries had given in February and proposed to the Verkhovna Rada 'to cancel article 71 of the Constitution of the Ukrainian SSR that stated the superiority of all-union laws on the territory of Ukraine. Our full-fledged state sovereignty, [and] the constitutional priority of republican laws will provide us with the practical possibility to implement own economic policy', he argued. On 24 October 1990, the Verkhovna Rada amended article 71 to state that republican laws were superior to all-union.[42]

With control over resources remaining the main definition of power, the Ukrainian government mimicked the central government and established Ukrainian *goszakaz* (state orders) for all Ukrainian enterprises and organizations, regardless their status or type of ownership.[43] Similarly to the all-union *goszakaz* that was also in force in the territory of Ukraine, the Ukrainian *goszakaz* was introduced for the purpose of fulfilling the needs of the republic, which included intra-republican distribution of goods produced in Ukraine, fulfilment of inter-republican agreements, and exports. To motivate Ukrainian producers to fulfil its *goszakaz*, the Ukrainian government promised the necessary inputs.[44]

But to promise did not mean having the ability to deliver. By October 1990, hoping for a country-wide economic programme, the Ukrainian leadership had practically no contacts with the leadership of Russia, the main supplier for Ukraine.[45] In March 1989, Gorbachev increased the share of industry managed by the republics, varying between 27 percent in the Russian Federation to 75 percent

**Illustration 19** President of the Russian Federation Boris Yeltsin addresses the Verkhovna Rada of Ukraine, 19 November 1990/© TsDAEA (0-216048); for video footage, see https://www.youtube.com/watch?v=mcYb4-Eshas, accessed on 15 August 2023

On 19 November 1990, Boris Yeltsin addressed the Verkhovna Rada, presenting himself as a democratic leader who understood and respected the national aspirations of the Ukrainian people: 'How do we see the relationship between Ukraine and Russia[?] Our relationship can develop only based on the principle of equality....I categorically reject accusations that Russia today claims some sort of a special role [in the Soviet state]. Russia does not aim to become the centre of some new empire and have special privileges....History shows that a nation that dominates other nations cannot be happy...'

in Moldavia. The official share of industrial production under the Ukrainian government's control rose from 6–7 percent in 1987 to 42–44 percent in 1989. However, the de facto control over resources remained divided between the all-union agencies and the regions. Monetary, fiscal, foreign trade, transport, and communication systems remained under central control. The basic industries, such as fuel-energy, metallurgical, and machine-building complexes, as well as most chemical branches, continued to be administered by the all-union agencies, as well. Consequently, the oblasts of Donetsk, Luhansk, Dnipropetrovsk, Zaporizhzhia, Kharkiv, and to a lesser extent Kyiv, where the basic industries

**Illustration 20**  Pickets from Kherson, Odesa, and Mykolaiv oblasts in front of the building of the Verkhovna Rada, November 1990/© TsDAEA (0-245593)

In the final years of the Soviet Union, pickets regularly gathered in front of the Verkhovna Rada. During Yeltsin's visit to Kyiv, many came to express their support for Ukraine's union with Russia. Banner in Russian, top centre: 'Our future is in the Union of sovereign republics'; banner in Ukrainian, to the right: 'The one who is with Bandera is not with God'; bottom right, in Ukrainian: 'Who asked the people?'

were concentrated, continued to be tightly connected to Moscow. The central apparatus in Moscow controlled the inputs. There was no system in place that would enable Ukrainian ministries to secure supplies from other republics.[46] The regions, on the other hand, controlled actual production forces and output. Whether it was to fulfil inter-republican deliveries, deliveries to all-union funds, or deliveries within Ukraine, the Ukrainian leadership depended on the willingness of the regional authorities and enterprises to share their resources with Kyiv. The enterprises had nothing against signing contracts with the Ukrainian Gossnab, or even with the all-union Gossnab, but only if 'the chairman of the [Ukrainian government] guaranteed that the Gossnab would supply them with the necessary inputs.'[47]

The regions and the Ukrainian leadership had the classic chicken-and-egg problem. The regions would supply to Kyiv, but only if Kyiv provided the inputs that the regions and Moscow controlled.

How to secure the necessary inputs to the regions was *the* fundamental question to which the Ukrainian leadership would be seeking a response for years to come. Without control over supplies from Russia and other republics, but also from the Ukrainian regions, the Ukrainian leadership would remain weak and unable to impose its authority over the Ukrainian regions.

## The Regions' 'Dream' Scenario

The solution that the regions offered to the Ukrainian leadership in October 1990 was unorthodox by Moscow's standards, but relevant to Ukrainian realities. The regions suggested that the Ukrainian leadership accept the fact that the regions as a group were stronger than the Ukrainian leadership, focus on the needs of producers and the regions, and switch from a top-down to a bottom-up approach to stabilization of the Ukrainian economy. In particular, the Ukrainian leadership should decentralize economic administration and formally empower local authorities. It should 'launch mechanisms to fulfil its own decisions'. Unlike the central leadership and apparatus in Moscow, it should take responsibility for its own policies and decisions. The members of the Ukrainian government should be held personally responsible for fulfilling the tasks they were assigned. Given the dramatic situation with agriculture, Masol should be personally responsible for fulfilling the government's resolution to prioritize agricultural development. And if the government insisted on a centralized distribution of resources, the government should assign those responsible for providing the inputs to producers, and not just hold producers solely responsible for failing to fulfil the *goszakaz*. (Only 213 MPs voted for this amendment; it did not pass.)[48]

## The Growth of Regionalism

The decay of the all-union centre would have been less dramatic for the Ukrainian leadership had the central leadership guided Ukraine through the transition and had Kyiv simply needed to take over Moscow's functions. As discussed in the previous chapters, Moscow directly controlled Ukrainian regions. Combined with the deteriorating economic situation against the background of liberalized politics, the decay of the all-union centre boosted regionalism in Ukraine.

### Barter

The entire Soviet economy descending into chaos was the most important factor that not only motivated but also enabled regional authorities, which mostly comprised communists, to increase their efforts to protect local economic interests. Non-deliveries of inputs risked increasing unemployment; unemployment destabilized the political situation in the regions, which was already difficult due to a growing lack of consumer goods.[49] As elsewhere in the Soviet Union, to secure inputs for enterprises, or consumer goods for the population, Ukrainian regions hoarded goods for direct horizontal exchange in the form of inter-regional barter. Hoarding and barter had existed before perestroika, but by 1990, as the regulatory role of the ministries decreased, inter-regional barter began to dominate over inter-branch exchange. The struggle between economic actors 'centered around efforts to capture goods that were in particularly sharp shortage and had the status of virtual currencies. These were such things as food, fuel, paper, tires, construction materials (cement, bricks, etc.), and consumer durables.'[50] The regional authorities, being in close proximity and connected to the enterprises in their territories, found themselves better positioned to prioritize regional inter-ests over all-union or republican interests than they were before 1990.[51]

In 1990, with agricultural produce in high demand and easier for the regions to control, the oblasts of Khmelnytskyi, Ternopil, Volyn, Rivne, and Ivano-Frankivsk did not deliver full amounts of meat to the state fund and instead consumed 39 more tonnes of meat from the state fund than in 1989. The oblasts of Kyiv, Crimea, Odesa, Mykolaiv, and Zaporizhzhia did not supply vegetables to the city of Kyiv, but supplied 11,000 tonnes of vegetables to customers outside Ukraine who paid better prices. By the beginning of August 1990, the regions were fulfilling only 11 percent of the total *goszakaz* for vegetables.[52] 'In absolute majority, the chairmen of the kolkhozy and directors of the sovkhozy and enterprises of the APK [agro-industrial complex] [were] communists', but in 1990, the state did not receive 2.2 million tonnes of grain, while the 'pay with grain' for labour in the kolkhozy increased by 1 million tonnes in 1990 as com-pared to 1989.[53]

### Transfer of Power to the Soviets

In the periphery, the growth of the barter economy was accompanied by an accel-erating transfer of power from territorial party committees to the soviets. The process was initiated by Gorbachev in 1988.[54] In 1989, it stalled. The powers of the soviets remained limited. At the beginning of 1990, the periphery party apparatus realized that the soviets' limited powers impeded their own political survival. Elections provided them with an opportunity to remain in power by switching institutions. Indeed, in the March 1990 elections, fifteen out of twenty-five obkom secretaries and 66 percent of raikom secretaries became chairmen of the oblast and raion soviets.[55] However, in soviets with limited powers, communists would be unable to address local problems. The electoral victory of the com-munists would only allow 'the population again to blame "the nomenklatura" for the economic crisis'. At the Ukrainian Central Committee meeting on 30 March 1990, the obkom secretaries argued that the Verkhovna Rada should pass a law on local self-administration for Ukraine. The Ukrainian leadership should set mechanisms to regulate the interaction between communists and representatives of various public and political organizations in the soviets, and it should clearly separate the economic functions of the republic from the functions of the Union centre whereby the soviets, not the republican apparatus, would take over the socio-economic agenda that had previously been fulfilled by the all-union ministries in the regions but was increasingly neglected by them.[56]

The Ukrainian leadership resented the idea of expanding the soviets' administrative authority and shrugged off the obkoms' suggestions until the October 1990 Central Committee plenum, when the central leadership recognized the superiority of the soviets over the territorial party committees and defined the work of the party in the soviets as 'most important'.[57] The Ukrainian leadership followed the lead. On 7 December 1990, the Verkhovna Rada passed a law on local soviets and self-administration.

The law formalized the administrative framework for regionalism. It granted limited formal powers to the soviets, but it formalized the long-standing tradition of one-man rule in the periphery and granted the soviets the functions previously performed by the territorial party committees. Now the soviets were responsible for providing for their territories' socio-economic development and ensuring that all enterprises, organizations, and administrations under their jurisdiction respected the legislation.[58] The law reflected the 28 August 1990 resolution of the Central Committee Secretariat that reaffirmed the local authorities' double task to fulfil state plans and meet local demand for scarce produce at the same time.[59] Both documents ignored that, with local authorities depending on popular support, and under the conditions of a deregulated economy, scarcity of centrally allocated resources, and growing barter, this double task caused an acute conflict of interests whereby local considerations could not but dominate over all-union or republican ones.

Hence, the soviets found themselves facing the same dependence on producers for meeting the local agenda as the territorial party committees had experienced, but, due to the barter economy, to an even greater degree. In June 1991, unable to assist the regions with resources, the Ukrainian leadership would formalize this dependence through article 126 of the Constitution. The article allowed the soviets to make 'agreements' with enterprises and organizations that did not belong to the communal property—that is, any enterprise—'in the interest of fulfilling the needs of the population and the socio-economic development of the territory'.[60]

As a result, along with taking over territorial party committees, the soviets inherited the inconsistency between their rights and responsibilities, between weak formal powers that limited their ability to fulfil the local agenda, and strong incentives and informal powers which motivated and enabled them to do so. The inconsistency would be well articulated by Mykhailo Voloshchuk, the head of the Zakarpattia oblast soviet and oblispolkom, at a meeting with the Ukrainian government on 22 July 1991 when he asked the Ukrainian leadership to expand the powers of the soviets and at the same time praised the Ukrainian government for 'paying great attention to the oblast soviets' and for acknowledging that 'all power belonged to the oblasts'.[61]

## The CPU Fragmented

While the soviets as institutions were consolidated, the CPU as a politico-administrative organization continued to disintegrate. At the second stage of the

Twenty-Eighth CPU Congress, which was held on 13–14 December 1990, the CPU was legitimized and received its own statute. The dream of the Bolsheviks of Ukraine in the 1920s finally materialized. The CPU could independently implement the CPSU programme documents and pursue its own agenda. However, the statute came too late and was of little practical value to the CPU in the new historical context. The CPU was already haemorrhaging members, and, besides, the statute was not accompanied by the new socio-economic programme that Ivashko had promised in June 1990, behind which the communists could have united. Hence, communists in the periphery and the Verkhovna Rada continued the struggle, but 'did not know what [they were] struggling for'.[62]

In a further blow to the party, Hurenko announced to the congress that the unofficial policy of the Ukrainian Central Committee was that if an obkom secretary had to combine his obkom work with his soviet work, and there was a worthy replacement for the party work, 'then the obkom secretary should choose soviet work. If the replacement could not happen, then it was necessary to combine the two posts.' The party apparatus was well ahead of its leadership. Those elected to the Verkhovna Rada ignored the Twenty-Eighth CPU Congress, 'calling it secondary'.[63]

**Illustration 21**  Stanislav Hurenko at the Twenty-Eighth CPU Congress, 14 December 1990/© TsDAEA (0-214752)

CPU First Secretary Stanislav Hurenko (in the centre) among delegates to the second stage of the Twenty-Eighth CPU Congress during the break between sessions.

Of greater impact on the integrity of the party was the instruction to the Ukrainian party committees to take their finances into their own hands. Starting in 1991, the Central Committee no longer allowed the Ukrainian Central Committee to subsidize obkoms to make up for non-collected membership fees. The party committees had to adjust their apparatus to their financial situation. The Ukrainian Central Committee allowed the party to lead commercial activity, create its own enterprises, and invest.[64] Gorbachev's idea to separate the party from the commercial managers had completely degenerated. Not only was the party apparatus more motivated to seek financial gains in their regions, but their efforts were also encouraged. In effect, the CPU was instructed to fragment itself.

By the beginning of 1991, there was no periphery institution with an incentive to defend all-union or republican interests. With the periphery party apparatus and the soviets controlling barter exchange and aligned in their effort to defend local interests, Ukraine was set on a tide of regionalism. In 1991 this tide would only gain force.

## Part II: 1991

### Ukrainian Leadership: Controlling Politics

In the spring and summer of 1991, the Ukrainian leadership continued asserting its authority in the republic. The Ukrainian Central Committee maintained its control over the Ukrainian government, the Ukrainian government continued to deliver reports to the Ukrainian Central Committee, and the Verkhovna Rada publicly appointed the ministers. But behind closed doors, the Ukrainian Politburo still approved the Ukrainian ministers.[65] Leonid Kravchuk, the chairman of Verkhovna Rada, was a member of the Politburo.

At the April 1991 Ukrainian Central Committee plenum, Hurenko admitted that 'previously, the parliamentary function of the party was underestimated'.[66] By June 1991, after one year of neglecting the growing importance of the Verkhovna Rada and now coming to accept the reality, the Ukrainian Central Committee was prepared to recognize it as the highest legislative organ in Ukraine, where the communist majority could pass the policies drafted in the Ukrainian Central Committee into law. On 17 June 1991, for the first time since they were elected, Hurenko invited communist MPs and announced that the Ukrainian Central Committee would boost its leadership over the communist majority in the parliament.[67] He expressed hope that in future they would vote unanimously on the main issues and warned them that if they allowed themselves to have their own opinion 'that contradicted the party line', such opinion 'will obtain principled political evaluation by all party committees, including the Ukrainian Central Committee'. Hurenko reminded those who accused the

Ukrainian Central Committee of *diktat* or violations of party democracy that 'strict, moreover, iron discipline in the parliament was the prerequisite condition of party life in any parliamentary society'. Hurenko instructed them to create a communist faction and, in a departure from his previous position, to 'increase cooperation with other parliamentary groups'.[68] In spring, Hurenko had already realized that although communists, 'true or fake', constituted 75 percent in the Verkhovna Rada, the overall popularity of communists was rapidly decreasing.[69] People blamed communists for the economic crisis. Cooperation with the parties that did not stand on a firm anti-communist position was thus necessary to show that communists were ready for 'a dialogue with all factions and groups' and 'mutual compromises to protect the general interests of the people', and that they would continue with political liberalization. Such cooperation could also diffuse the republican leadership's responsibility for the growing economic crisis.[70]

Hurenko also reached out to the regions. Echoing Ivashko in June 1990, he admitted at the 15 February 1991 Ukrainian Central Committee plenum, and again in April 1991, that 'the party position of non-involvement in the socio-economic area was wrong and dangerous'. Economic crisis was a key political problem. At the same time, he insisted that the obkoms and the soviets 'take measures' to restore contract discipline and enforce the fulfilment of *goszakaz*.[71]

## Ukrainian Leadership: Not Controlling the Regions

Leading the republican organs was relatively easy, as such leadership did not require organizing economic relations. As the periphery party apparatus reminded the Ukrainian leadership in February 1991, its power claims over the regions could be accepted only after Kyiv controlled the economy and secured supplies to the regions. How could any obkom restore labour discipline 'if enterprises [were] in a critical situation through no fault of their own?' they wondered.[72] The Ukrainian Central Committee and the Ukrainian government focused on inter-republican deliveries, and rightly so. However, intra-republican deliveries were already within the leadership's jurisdiction, and they were not managing it satisfactorily. 'Is it normal when, say, the Kamianets-Podilskyi cement factory, or metallurgical enterprises from the Dnipropetrovsk oblast, with the knowledge of the Ukrainian government, demand a tax on the funded materials, in kind or money [from their customers?]', wondered Yevhen Marmazov, first secretary of the Kirovohrad obkom, in February 1991. Likewise, although the Ukrainian Central Committee declared restoration of the countryside and the development of the agro-industrial complex one of its priorities, they were not supporting this goal with proper distribution of goods. How could obkom secretaries explain to the rural population that even though their oblast supplied the required wheat to the state in 1990, the government did not take responsibility for supplying villages with the simplest consumer goods? The regions also urged the

Ukrainian leadership to react to Moscow delaying the introduction of new whole-sale and retail prices. The shop shelves were empty, but the warehouses were full. The population knew this, which risked social explosion.[73]

In 1991, the central ministries were reluctant to release control over the economy,[74] so the Ukrainian leadership launched several initiatives to increase the resources under its control. On 27 March 1991, a non-budgetary fund was created to stabilize the economy of Ukraine. Echoing Rakovsky's unfulfilled idea, the fund was to be filled by enterprises. (A share of this fund was allocated to the all-union stabilization fund, probably in return for permission to create a Ukrainian fund.) On 16 April 1991, the Verkhovna Rada passed a law, 'On Foreign Economic Activity'. The Ukrainian government was instructed to divide the functions related to foreign trade between the all-union and republican agencies and to create a Ukrainian state organ by 1 July to regulate the foreign economic con-nections of Ukraine.[75] However, the process required the cooperation of the relevant all-union agencies, and the latter were reluctant to cooperate. Hence in July 1991, the central ministries still managed Ukrainian exports, and the USSR Ministry of Foreign Trade retained the profits. In July 1991, the Ukrainian leadership established a moratorium on a number of all-union laws.[76] Finally, in a major breakthrough, on 3 July the Verkhovna Rada voted for the Programme for Economic Stabilization. This programme was a long-awaited document that many hoped would consolidate the Ukrainian economy into a coherent economic complex.

However, while the regions in general welcomed the efforts of the Ukrainian leadership in establishing control over the economy, they did not consider the specific changes to be the most adequate for Ukraine. At a meeting on 17 June 1991, echoing their suggestions from October 1990, the obkoms and Oleksandr Moroz, the leader of communists in the Verkhovna Rada, again argued that the Ukrainian leadership should focus on rebuilding the economy from the bottom up rather than attempting to control it top-down, and should design a market infrastructure that would let the regions increase production. 'Only then should the planning-distribution system that exists today be imposed.'[77] Cooperation and decentralization, or 'de-concentration' of economic administration, as the leaders from the western oblasts of Lviv, Zakarpattia, and Ternopil put it, remained for many the most obvious answer to the economic crisis.[78] Descending policies upon the regions was certainly possible. However, 'decisions have force only when they are implemented,'[79] explained Vasyl Stepenko, first secretary of the Poltava raikom and Poltava oblast deputy to the Verkhovna Rada. In the absence of effective formal mechanisms or leverage, the Ukrainian government will have difficulty implementing its policies unless it considers the interests of the regions, he noted. One solution to align the interests of the regions with the policies that the Ukrainian leadership sought to implement was to 'create a per-manent working organ that would include one representative from each oblast' to solve urgent problems.[80]

Kyiv must have promised cooperation, as the Ukrainian leadership and the regions formed a consensus, and the Verkhovna Rada voted in favour of the programme on 3 July. However, soon after the programme was legalized, it became clear that the Ukrainian leadership was not prepared to cooperate. It aimed for maximum extraction of resources from the regions and the priority of distribution over production. The needs of producers were secondary to its plans for distribution.

The official programme for stabilization reflected the Ukrainian Central Committee's approach to the economic crisis, which was to stop the economy from declining before transitioning to a market economy,[81] which the majority accepted. It also reflected the Ukrainian government's ambition to centralize control over the economy through mandatory *goszakaz* and centralized distribution of state subsidies,[82] which the majority welcomed, because the programme included the government's pledge to provide 'main material-technical and raw material supplies' to support the fulfilment of the *goszakaz*.[83] However, once the programme was legalized, the government revoked its promise to guarantee supplies for the *goszakaz*. As Ukrainian State Minister of Defence Complex and Conversion Viktor Antonov, who was also a member of the Presidium of the Cabinet of Ministers of Ukraine, succinctly explained to the periphery apparatus on 22 July 1991, 'the supplies were never guaranteed before, [and] they will not be guaranteed now'.[84]

In another blow to the regions, the Ukrainian government broke the promise that Prime Minister Vitold Fokin (23 October 1990–1 October 1992) had given to the regions in April not to replace 'the *diktat* of Moscow' with 'the *diktat* of Kyiv'. At the meeting on 22 July, the government announced that economic stabilization would be implemented under the watchful eye of a newly formed extraordinary commission. Under Fokin's chairmanship, the commission would coordinate the work of regional extraordinary commissions and branch commissions.[85]

The suggestion by some regional authorities, such as Volodymyr Shevchenko, the head of the Sumy oblast soviet and the chairman of the oblispolkom, and Anatolii Butenko, first deputy of the Odesa oblispolkom, that instead of creating a new vertical executive the government should decentralize administration, grant extraordinary power to the local apparatus, and rely on the oblispolkoms to implement the programme, was duly heard and ignored.[86]

The reluctance of the Ukrainian leadership to cooperate and entrust the regional authorities with the implementation the programme reflected its firm adherence to the traditional Russian and Soviet top-down *diktat*. In the Ukrainian context, *diktat* was, to put it mildly, unwise because in 1991, like in 1990, the resolve of the Ukrainian leadership to centralize control over the economy did not mean it had the capacity to do so.[87] Moscow retained its share of control over the economy, while the institutional dynamic towards regionalism that was boosted in 1990 accelerated further in 1991.

## Consolidation of Regionalism in 1991

The motivation, opportunities, and objective need for the regions to defend local interests had increased in 1991. The growing economic crisis, chaos in economic administration, and growth of the barter economy remained of pivotal importance. The Ukrainian leadership was unable to secure inputs for production or consumer goods. In search of supplies, Ukrainian state enterprises often turned to local party committees, the soviets, the oblispolkoms, and their MPs. The cohort of elected officials, already dependent on the managers, was willing to oblige, in return for help from enterprises with the fulfilment of their own agenda, such as financial help to the unemployed, or supplies of food and goods to local stores, not to mention personal gains that this discussion omits. 'From the perspective of an enterprise director, influence over his actions had more to do with who could supply needed resources and less with fealty to governmental elites in [Kyiv].'[88] Mutually beneficial cooperation was widespread.

For example, to provide local construction enterprises with supplies and thus accelerate housing construction in the Rivne oblast, one of the poorest oblasts in Western Ukraine, deputies of the Rivne oblast soviet helped these enterprises 'to partially solve the problem of lumbar supplies', and to secure contracts for deliveries of pipes from Azerbaijan and cable from Estonia. In 1991, the Rivne oblispolkom expected the oblast's industrial enterprises to 'further cooperate' with the kolkhozy and sovkhozy to build food-processing factories. So, the Rivne soviet and oblispolkom negotiated with the union and union-republican ministries to set quotas for locally produced construction materials, 'which allowed them to double resources for the organizations of the agro-industrial complex'. In return for their services, the Rivne authorities relied on all 'rich enterprises, kolkhozy, organizations, and associations' to finance the healthcare system and several programmes related to the aftermath of the Chornobyl catastrophe, to increase salaries for workers in education, for culture, and for other programmes. As a result of close cooperation between the oblispolkom and local enterprises and businesses, the Rivne oblast fully covered its 19 million rouble budget deficit in 1990. Financial contributions to the local budget and funds were expected to continue in 1991.[89]

In May 1991, the Zaporizhzhia obkom mobilized the directors of industrial enterprises to overcome the economic crisis. First deputy chairman of the Zaporizhzhia oblispolkom and MP Oleksandr Bilousenko created a council of directors that later grew into a council of industrialists and entrepreneurs. Bilousenko was actively involved in the development of the infrastructure of the Zaporizhzhia oblast. MPs from all regions 'acted as petitioners, bringing the petitions [*chelobitnye*] to the ministries, administrations, and the Cabinet of Ministers'. After all, the MPs were not released from their original posts and had their jobs, which paid them salaries, in their regions.[90]

No less important for the consolidation of regionalism was the permission to the soviets and ispolkoms to lead economic activity.[91] Like the obkoms, the soviets were encouraged to create enterprises to serve their own agendas. In the chaos and fiscal crisis of 1991, they had little choice but to get actively involved in the economic life of their regions. The dynamic that merged the interests of the elected officials and industrial managers was the same all over Ukraine, regardless of the level of industrialization in the region.

By spring 1991, the foundations of the system that merged the interests of elected politicians and economic managers, the very same system that in the 1990s would turn oligarchic, were institutionalized and fully in effect. Kyiv had limited or no control over the regions and was painfully aware of its impotence. The CPU as a coherent organization that tied the regions to the Ukrainian centre was fragmented. The freedoms given to the soviets, not to be confused with their formal powers, were unchecked. Communists prevailed in the majority of the soviets, yet by April 1991 the total number of unlawful decisions passed by the oblast soviets and the soviet of Kyiv city was already 230. The Verkhovna Rada could not cancel them 'in bulk', and, even if it could, it had no mechanisms to enforce the cancelations. At the meeting with the obkom secretaries in April 1991, Kravchuk admitted the de facto paralysis of the Kyiv-regions vertical.[92]

## Pleading for Goodwill

With the Ukrainian leadership unable to guarantee supplies, and the regions motivated to prioritize local interests, the volume of resources that the Ukrainian leadership could control was determined by the regions. Hence, the regions determined the strength of the Ukrainian leadership's power.

The stabilization fund that the Ukrainian government established on 27 March 1991 received little support from the regions. When it was set up, the government expected the fund to have 13.8 billion roubles in 1991. By the end of July, the fund had accumulated only 0.9 billion roubles and the government had to adjust its expectations to 4.7 billion roubles by the end of the year.[93] Enterprises, cooperatives, and organizations violated existing export regulations and kept the profits. The regions freely replaced export–import operations with barter arrangements, and thus avoided paying taxes.[94]

The *goszakaz* that the Ukrainian government viewed as 'a contract between the state and the regions' was ignored by some communist-dominated ispolkoms and violated by others.[95] At the beginning of 1991, the Odesa oblast received *goszakaz* and agreed to supply 1,275,000 tonnes of grain to the state in 1991. 'Then in March–April [1991], the Odesa soviet decided that the contract would now be 800,000 tonnes.' 'The majority of the oblispolkoms established for themselves the *goszakaz* they considered necessary.'[96] Even then, at the end of July 1991, the oblasts of Zaporizhzhia, Mykolaiv, Odesa, and Kherson, among others, informed

Kyiv that they would be delivering between 25 and 50 percent of the *goszakaz* for grain. The oblispolkoms of these oblasts intended to manage the grain that the Ukrainian government considered a state resource and vetoed deliveries of their grain outside their oblasts. Such behaviour of the regions 'terrified' Mykola Kompanets, the head of the Ukrainian State Committee for Bread (cereal) Products. However, the regions had little choice but to 'terrify' the government. Agricultural machinery, spare parts, and other inputs necessary for agricultural production remained scarce. The government failed even to begin the pro-gramme of reorienting Ukrainian industrial producers from non-Ukrainian to Ukrainian inputs, as some regions insisted it could and should do.[97] Despite Fokin's June 1991 promises to increase the procurement prices for grain, in September, the state was still paying 1990 prices.

As a result, in 1991, the ability of the Ukrainian leadership to perform its tradi-tional function of regulating food supplies to the cities had shrunk considerably.[98] By 5 September, the government had secured 4.2 million tonnes less grain than it had by the same time in 1990, or 9.6 million tonnes of grain out of the 17 million that was 'absolutely necessary' for the Ukrainian government to avoid social unrest and not become 'a former government'. 'The grain was leaving the repub-lic by various means.'[99] The government faced the fact that it had lost the monop-oly on grain distribution in 1991.

At a meeting on 22 July 1991, Fokin echoed Kravchuk and admitted that the vertical executive was weak. Lack of mechanisms to enforce republican policies and decisions on the producers and local soviets undermined what little author-ity the Ukrainian leadership had. The government introduced fines and sanctions for violation of the leadership's instructions. However, they had little effect. Thus, the soviets shut down enterprises whenever they considered it necessary.[100]

Fokin and his cabinet members pleaded with the regions for support. Minister of Finances Oleksandr Kovalenko pleaded with the chairmen of the oblispolkoms 'to provide all possible help to the financial organs to find additional resources to reduce the [budget] deficit and finance the government's programmes'.[101] Minister of Agrarian Policy and Food Oleksandr Tkachenko admitted that 'today all power [was] with the heads of the oblasts' and asked them to mobilize urban dwellers for the harvest campaign. Fokin appealed to the wheat-producing regions to fulfil the *goszakaz* to avoid 'a famine, similar to the one Ukraine had in 1932–1933'. Fourteen oblasts of Ukraine depended on wheat subsidies from the Ukrainian government.[102]

And still, while acknowledging its own powerlessness and asking the periphery apparatus to share its conviction that only the Ukrainian government could regu-late the circulation of commodities in the republic and ensure that the republic did not starve, the Ukrainian leadership could not understand that the regions would only accept its *diktat* in return for supplies, and only after the leadership had organized production and satisfied their own demand for consumer goods and inputs. Instead of pleading with the regions for their good will to submit themselves to the *diktat* of Kyiv, Kyiv should secure supplies, explained the regions. It should secure supplies not by demanding centralized control over resources and then manually distributing them, but by creating a system that would guarantee deliveries. Centralized allocation did not guarantee supplies. And Fokin himself admitted at a meeting with the regional authorities in June 1991 that a lot of the resources that the government allocated to the country-side did not reach it because 'some sort of association' to distribute state supplies was beyond the reach of the government.[103] If the government could not ensure that the centrally allocated goods reached state enterprises, kolkhozy, and sovkhozy, why then did it take upon itself centralized distribution of pipes, metal, plastic, and wood? Why did it ban agricultural producers from procuring the necessary supplies themselves? Before the moratorium, the oblasts could create local exchanges to enable local producers to procure small and large goods, such as thread for flour bags, lumbar, and pipes in return for the agricultural produce from local kolkhozy and sovkhozy. The moratorium made such exchange impossible.[104]

Fokin did not seem ignorant of the fundamental problems that were undermining the power of the Ukrainian leadership. Yet he did little or nothing to organize production. A system for enforcing contracts within Ukraine, upon which the obkoms had insisted since early 1990, remained a wish. Even at the very basic level, despite the amendments made to the Ukrainian Constitution and the leadership's newly established priorities, Ukraine still did not have its own mechanisms for communicating the laws and policies passed by the Ukrainian leadership.[105]

### No Change in Sight

After the Verkhovna Rada declared the independence of Ukraine on 24 August 1991, the government continued to seek control over the regions by doing more of the same: demanding obedience and at the same time begging the regions for their unconditional acceptance of Kyiv's control over resources.

At a meeting of the Cabinet of Ministers on 9 September, the government issued reprimands to some chairmen of the oblispolkoms and threatened legal investigations of others for non-deliveries of food to the government. Fokin urged the chairmen of the oblispolkoms to use 'unpopular methods and expropriations' to collect the necessary amounts of products. 'We will not mention this in the resolution [of this meeting], but each present here should draw the appropriate conclusions.'[106] Verkhovna Rada Chairman Kravchuk, also present at the meeting on 9 September, pleaded with them 'to explain to the kolkhozy that tragedy was about to happen [if the government did not receive the grain], a social explosion might happen.'[107] Not to mention that 'without the grain [the Cabinet of Ministers] was worth nothing.'[108]

The regional authorities explained that they could not expropriate grain, nor were they willing to confront those on whom they depended for their political careers and personal well-being. The countryside needed a correct pricing policy, fair trade, and industrial supplies such as fuel, wood, machinery, spare parts for the machinery, etc. No producer would act against his own interests. Why would a kolkhoz supply its grain to the state, if 'for all grain that it delivered to the state, it would be able to purchase 0.8 of a tractor?'[109] asked Ivan Hopei, chairman of the Poltava oblispolkom. I. Sichuk from the Odesa oblispolkom explained that when the state could not provide the countryside with the inputs that it promised, the kolkhozy had to procure the supplies on their own, in exchange for their grain.[110] The chairmen of the Odesa, Dnipropetrovsk, Khmelnytskyi, and Poltava oblispolkoms said the same. Only economic measures, transparent distribution of material supplies, and equal terms for receiving material supplies that the Ukrainian government insisted on distributing centrally would make the kolkhozy willing to supply the state.[111] Administrative measures such as the closure of oblast borders did not work and could not work because 'the causes and conditions [that motivated the suppliers to violate the state moratorium on the sale of grain] were not eliminated', explained Roman Vasylyshyn, the chairman of the Rivne oblispolkom.[112]

Regions were in a strong bargaining position and were hardly scared of Kyiv's administrative measures. With regional authorities elected, not only could the regions withhold grain from the government, but they also possessed the hard currency that was urgently needed to buy the necessary grain abroad. Liberalization of the economy had allowed Ukrainian enterprises and organizations to accumulate 465 million convertible roubles by September 1991. The Ukrainian government had 2.3 million convertible roubles. In September, Fokin had no other choice but to instruct the chairmen of the oblispolkoms of Donetsk, Dnipropetrovsk, Zaporizhzhia, Kyiv, Lviv, Luhansk, and Kharkiv and the city of Kyiv to collect 230–240 million convertible roubles from industrial enterprises to purchase grain and protein supplements for fodder.[113]

The message the regions conveyed could not have been clearer: they will prioritize their own economic needs until the government convinces them to prioritize the state as a customer.

For a brief moment, Fokin seemed prepared to reduce the government's claims for full control over the economy and focus on the needs of the regions. On 24 September, at a meeting with the oblispolkoms, the gorispolkoms of Kyiv and Sevastopol, and the government of the Crimean Autonomous Soviet Socialist Republic, Fokin proposed that the regions submit lists of all-union enterprises over which they would like to assume ownership. Fokin promised that *goszakaz* would be voluntary and would be imposed only for a limited nomenclature of goods. 'Just name us the number [you are willing to supply for the *goszakaz*] and it will be accepted without any discussion.' The government intended to keep agriculture under tighter state control than industry. Still, it promised not to claim more than 55–60 percent of agricultural output.[114]

Fokin's views, however, were corrected by the Ministry of Economy a few weeks later. In its draft of the Concept and Forecast for Economic and Social Development of Ukraine for 1992, the ministry repeated Fokin's promise to secure the inputs for the *goszakaz*. However, the ministry stated that the bottom-up principle would not be implemented for forming *goszakaz*. At the same time, it promised that directive assignments to producers would concern only an 'inconsiderable number of indices'. The ministry did not anticipate any changes in the branch structure of the republican economy and thus the specialization of the regions. The draft did not reflect any independent economic policy in Ukraine, nor did it anticipate an acceleration in the formation of market structures. The draft did not include a section on regional development, either.[115]

On 29 October, the State Economic Council of the Cabinet of Ministers of Ukraine, chaired by its vice chairman, Oleksandr Yemelianov, qualified the Concept and Forecast for 1992 as 'old by style and thinking'. But the revised version from 5 November 1991 remained just as 'old'. The Ministry of Economy promised to combine administrative and economic levers to regulate the economy. Economic levers would include taxes and interest rates fixed by the National Bank. Administrative levers would include licences and quotas for certain types of products and services, as well as a customs regime. The ministry qualified *goszakaz* as a market mechanism. The idea of a voluntary *goszakaz* was abandoned, aside from the plan that 'in the next year or two, the state will move away from the distribution of the *goszakaz* and will instead provide preferential conditions to those producers who win in the competition for *goszakaz*'. To reflect the criticism that the government neglected regional development, the new draft included a section, 'Main directions in regional policy and distribution of production forces'. However, by tradition, regional development was to be orchestrated in Kyiv, not determined by the regions.[116] Thus Fokin's brief urge to rebuild the Ukrainian economy in cooperation with the regions was not going to materialize.

## Conclusion

Had the Soviet leadership managed Ukraine through the Ukrainian government and the Ukrainian Central Committee, the disintegration of the Soviet system would have meant simply cutting ties between Kyiv and Moscow. In reality, perestroika cut the ties between Moscow, Kyiv, and the Ukrainian regions. The Ukrainian leadership thus faced the task of establishing its control over the regions.

The Ukrainian leadership did not lack the ambition to assert itself as the highest authority in the republic. However, the decay of the central leadership in Moscow that had been its source of power further undermined the traditionally weak Ukrainian leadership. In the last two years of the Soviet Union, the Ukrainian Central Committee failed to unite the CPU under its leadership; the Ukrainian government failed to replace the all-union government for Ukrainian regions.

The environment for consolidating regionalism, on the other hand, was favourable. The regional authorities' incentives to prioritize local over republican needs increased. Their access to regional material and financial resources increased as well. The conflicting agenda of the regional authorities, to fulfil the economic agenda of the state and, at the same time, to ensure socio-economic development of their territories, remained in place.

Objectively in need of a strong administrative centre, the regions suggested that the Ukrainian government should depart from the Soviet top-down *diktat* and build the Ukrainian economy from below. Deprived of any meaningful leverage against the regions, the Ukrainian leadership should motivate the regions to cooperate and support the Ukrainian leadership. In other words, the regions urged the Ukrainian leadership 'to transform a political system rooted in fear and inertia into one based on consent'.[117]

Consolidating Ukrainian sovereignty from the bottom up did not appeal to the Ukrainian leadership. Whether from the euphoria of the 1 December 1991 Ukrainian referendum in which 92.3 percent of voters, regardless of their ethnicity, supported independence for Ukraine, or from the victory of Leonid Kravchuk, who was 'one of their own', as the first president of Ukraine, or from the relatively peaceful dissolution of the Soviet Union, or its 'genetic predisposal for *diktat*', the Ukrainian government chose in 1992 to continue with the 'good old' Soviet model of manual centralized administrative control over the economy. This was the same model that allowed the Ukrainian leadership to project an image of being the republican centre, but not to consolidate its power. Why Kravchuk and Fokin decided that it would suddenly work remains unclear. But as the next years showed, *diktat* remained inadequate for consolidating the government's control over the economy or Ukrainian statehood. Kyiv's centralized administrative control over the economy left the 'old guard' who remained in power in the regions no choice but to continue protecting regional interests. The years 1992–1994 in Ukrainian history were a time of social, political, and economic change, but also of strong inertia of institutional fundamentals.[118] The change has been extensively analysed elsewhere. How the institutional inertia prevailed over the forces for change after the collapse of the Soviet state is discussed in the next chapter.

*The Institutional Foundations of Ukrainian Democracy: Power Sharing, Regionalism, and Authoritarianism*. Nataliya Kibita, Oxford University Press. © Nataliya Kibita 2024. DOI: 10.1093/9780191925351.003.0008

# 8

# 'The More We Centralize, the Less Order There Is in the State'

## Introduction

On 1 December 1991, Leonid Kravchuk, former Ukrainian Central Committee secretary for ideology and later chairman of the Verkhovna Rada, won the first Ukrainian presidential elections against his main rival, Viacheslav Chornovil, former dissident from Western Ukraine and leader of Rukh. Kravchuk would preside over Ukraine for two-and-a-half years of turbulent economic crisis.

With the acknowledgement of the break-up of the Soviet Union in the Belavezha Accords signed by Russia, Ukraine, and Belorussia on 8 December 1991, the Ukrainian leadership took the entire economy of Ukraine under its jurisdiction.[1] The new dual executive branch, the President and the Cabinet of Ministers, faced the task of establishing de facto control over the Ukrainian economy and the regions. The task was monumental, but, as discussed in the previous chapter, not new. New was the urgency. The Ukrainian leadership could no longer hide behind Moscow. With the popular mandate and the support of the elites, it *had* to establish control over the Ukrainian state. And yet, as this chapter shows, to accomplish this task, the newly formed executive branch chose the old Soviet *diktat*, ignoring the fact that it had been tested in 1990–1991 and had proved inadequate for Ukraine. From the early days of independence, the Ukrainian leadership neglected economic reforms.[2] It focused on actively testing the limits of extracting resources from the regions through regulation and administrative control over the economy.[3] At the same time, ironically, and continuing the Soviet bureaucratic tradition, it ignored such technicalities as the rule of law,[4] control and constraint of the bureaucratic apparatus, and formalizing the relationship between the capital and the regions.

The Soviet model of heavily regulated centralized administration was an unfortunate choice; the government could not save the economy from its freefall. Despite having a peacetime economy, Ukraine saw more than 10,300 percent hyperinflation in 1992 and 1993. Administrative *diktat* through a dysfunctional administrative apparatus provided a favourable environment for severe corruption and rent seeking. By 1994, almost half the economy was in the shadow.[5]

The Soviet model did not allow the Ukrainian leadership to overcome regionalism and assert its power over the regions, either. The industrial structure was preserved; there was no active regional policy.[6] Throughout Kravchuk's presidency, the executive branch continued to prioritize heavy industry.[7] Traditionally administered from Moscow, large enterprises of heavy industry saw less administrative intervention from the Ukrainian government and more direct and indirect state subsidies than agricultural producers, which were traditionally under the tighter administration of Kyiv.[8] The Ukrainian government maintained nearly full control over agriculture through *goszakaz* and the centralized distribution of inputs and output.[9] In the words of Vasyl Romaniuk, an MP from the Khmelnytskyi oblast, some branches worked in market conditions, while others had fixed low sale prices.[10] As a result, while the share of industry in gross domestic product declined from 44.6 percent in 1992 to 35 percent in 1994, the share of agriculture declined from 20.6 percent in 1992 to 14.3 percent in 1994.[11] Economic disparities between the oblasts remained intact.[12] The continuous prioritization of heavy industry meant the political elites from the wealthier industrialized oblasts of Dnipropetrovsk, Donetsk, Zaporizhzhia, Luhansk, and Kharkiv continued to dominate over political elites from poorer oblasts of Western Ukraine. The industrialized oblasts remained relatively less dependent on Kyiv than the agricultural oblasts.[13]

The executive branch's decision to embrace institutional inertia was based on an erroneous understanding of the Soviet institutional system in general and Ukrainian regionalism more specifically.[14] The president and prime minister believed that with the disappearance of Moscow from the 'Moscow–Kyiv–regions' administrative triangle, Kyiv was free to dictate its decisions and policies to the regions, and the regions would accept the authority of the Ukrainian executive branch over the regions, prioritize government needs over regional, and place their resources at Kyiv's disposal. The assumption was not completely incorrect in that the Ukrainian regions needed a strong Ukrainian policy- and decision-making central administration.[15] As discussed in the previous chapters, some had insisted on it since 1988. By the end of 1991, even the regions with least nationalist sentiments, the eastern and southern oblasts, had realized that Moscow was unable to run the economy efficiently and urged Kyiv to take over Moscow's administrative functions. After all, by then, state structures already existed in Ukraine, such as the parliament, ministries, and branches of financial institutions, even though they were not formed into a fully coherent system.[16]

But, as this chapter shows, the executive branch was wrong to assume that the regions would accept Kyiv's *diktat* unconditionally. Indeed, as Janusz Bugajski observed,

> just as the 'nationalised' Ukrainian nomenklatura preferred to be leaders of an independent state rather than provincial bosses of a centralised federation, so also regional elites sought to maximise their autonomy, especially in economic

matters, through the devolution of powers to local governments rather than to become mere administrators of a new political center.[17]

To rephrase what Peter Boettke formulated as a paradox in perestroika, Ukrainian regions wanted to obtain strong central control through the devolution of economic decision making.[18]

Throughout 1992–1994, the regions continued explaining to the government that the command-administrative *diktat* was not the way to consolidate centralized control over the economy in Ukraine, build a strong economy, or consolidate Ukrainian statehood. *Diktat* might have worked if Kyiv had institutional, financial, and/or material levers at its disposal or resources to distribute, but Kyiv had neither. Although politically independent from Moscow, the Ukrainian leadership still depended for its distribution plans on the willingness of both non-Ukrainian and Ukrainian producers to share their output. Without Ukrainian currency and still in the rouble zone, it remained dependent on the Russian government for fiscal and monetary policies. Ukraine needed to increase production but, the regions insisted, under the circumstances, *diktat* would not bring about an increase in production. To increase production, the state needed market reforms. The state needed a system that would secure supplies of inputs, consistent fiscal and monetary policies, and transparent mechanisms for implementing central policies and laws. As they had been saying since 1988, the Ukrainian economy had to be built from the bottom up, by prioritizing the needs of the regions and producers.

In the context of uncontrolled economic liberalization and full-fledged economic crisis, legal nihilism, corruption, and the inherited Soviet tradition of evading responsibility by policy- and decision-makers, but also the new legal opportunities for public officeholders and directors of state enterprises to seek personal enrichment, regionalism was unavoidable. The permanent threat of early elections pushed local authorities to seek ever closer cooperation with local businesses and the 'open for business' state apparatus in Kyiv to provide food and consumer goods. Devolution of power was the only solution the Ukrainian regions believed was available to the Ukrainian leadership to overcome regionalism and consolidate its power. And because the regions controlled resources and, as an uncoordinated group, were stronger than the Ukrainian leadership, it was up to the Ukrainian leadership to convince the regions to accept its authority, rather than for the regions to unconditionally accept Kyiv's *diktat*.

As this chapter shows, at this critical historical juncture, institutional inertia prevailed over institutional change. Despite the hyperinflation, economic chaos, and the paralysis of power, the Ukrainian executive continued to believe in the potential of *diktat*. It resented any cooperation with the regions right up until regionalism threatened the functioning of the Ukrainian state, a logical result of *diktat* in Ukraine.[19]

## Part I: Old Problem—Old Solution

When the Soviet Union dissolved, Ukraine finally had its policymaking centre free to respond to the needs of the regions. Central planning mechanisms disintegrated. Market regulatory mechanisms were not yet established. Both the economy and the state in general were in chaos. Unemployment, empty shelves, and inflation caused social discontent, which in turn generated fears of new elections in which the victory of politicians occupying their offices in the periphery and in the Verkhovna Rada was not at all secured.[20]

Hence, if the government needed to accumulate reserves of resources through *goszakaz* to regulate relations among producers, their suppliers, and customers, or to provide affordable consumer goods and food products to the population, the regions were happy to support it. After all, around 70 percent of exchange in Ukraine in the first half of 1992 constituted barter.[21] (In Russia, the main economic partner of Ukraine, the share of barter in economic transactions in some industries reached as high as 58 percent by the end of the first quarter of 1992.[22])

The task was not easy. On 31 January 1992, Ivan Pliushch, the chairman of Verkhovna Rada, explained why.

> I just spoke to Vitold Fokin....There was a long (more than four-hour) meeting between him and...Yeltsin who immediately, in [Fokin's] presence, gave instructions to several ministers [regarding oil supplies to Ukraine]. However, yesterday our representatives returned from Tyumen and other oil-producing Russian regions where they were told: 'We have not heard about your talks [i.e., between Fokin and Yeltsin] and don't want to hear. If you want oil, don't go to Moscow, go to Tyumen. We will negotiate what Ukraine can offer in return for oil.' Then they gave a price...in roubles and in USD. 'And if you do not have dollars, then give us butter and meat, [or] something else', and so on. As you can see, what happened is what we expected would happen: those who produce oil control the sale of oil; those who produce coal control the sale of coal, those who produce lumbar control the sale of lumbar.[23]

The independent Ukrainian leadership was in a two-year-old vicious circle: to provide resources to Ukrainian producers it needed resources held by Ukrainian producers. To solve the old problem, it used old approaches: administrative control over the economy[24] and priority of distribution over production.[25]

Thus, once hoped to be a mechanism of state support of producers, *goszakaz* remained an instrument for extracting resources from producers. At the same time, while industrial producers could often negotiate their sales to the state and even evade signing state *goszakaz*,[26] agricultural producers and the regional authorities generally could not. The original law on local soviets guaranteed the regions the right to decide the volumes they wished to supply to the state.[27]

However, on 30 December 1991, the Cabinet of Ministers de facto revoked this right when it forced agricultural producers to choose between supplying to the state at fixed prices or shutting down their production.[28] The old Soviet budgetary system whereby revenues and expenditures of the local budgets were defined by Kyiv and the central government collected all main taxes was preserved as well.[29] The government positioned itself as the sole protector of the population from economic crisis. It refused to denationalize industry and agriculture, and continued to centrally distribute food and consumer goods to the cities.[30]

## Regions: An Old Problem Needs a New Solution

As before independence, the regions recognized the difficulties faced by the government as it was establishing itself as an economic actor in post-Soviet realities. But as before, they resented the replacement of the old Moscow-centralized system that prioritized central interests over regional ones with a new Kyiv-centralized system that did the same thing. It was inadequate before and it was even more inadequate now. The regions viewed the process of state building as something to be done in cooperation and in coordination with the new central leadership. They indicated this unambiguously on 5 July 1991 when the Verkhovna Rada, at that time the representative organ of the territories rather than parties,[31] voted for the parliamentary-presidential system. The provisions of the law 'On the President of the Ukrainian SSR' passed that day granted limited powers to the president.

> The Verkhovna Rada maintained important levers of influence over the president, including...the parliamentary right to veto executive decrees, the simple majority vote to override a presidential veto (which in essence means no presidential veto), the right to reject the appointment of key ministers, and the right to dismiss the government.

Importantly, 'the president had no right to dissolve the parliament or call new elections.'[32]

The 'old guard' that dominated in the Verkhovna Rada might have been predisposed to 'authoritarianism, and command-administrative methods, and clan connections.'[33] Yet the interests of the majority remained in their regions. In defence of their traditional interests, the 'old guard' in the Verkhovna Rada sought maximum inclusion of the regions in policymaking and maximum devolution of decision making to the periphery. The 'old guard' wanted the government to change its approach to administering the state.

Besides, they believed this was also the position of the newly elected president, Leonid Kravchuk, widely viewed by the ex-communists who dominated the

Verkhovna Rada as first among equals.[34] In an interview on Ukrainian television on 17 June 1991 in his capacity as the chairman of the Verkhovna Rada, Kravchuk argued that 'to change everything in the economy, it is necessary to change the economy itself, relations in the economy[,] so that there is real responsibility of the collectives for their rights and [so that there was real] delegation of power'. He believed that

> the most real delegation of power [was] from the top to the bottom. The lower [the administration,] the more the power it should have. Then we will build something. The collectives should have full power, the raions [and] the oblasts[.] As for the highest echelons of power, they must create the legislative and other conditions so that the administration at the bottom and the collectives work. Then it is real business. If all power is in the centre, as it was before, and raions, oblasts, cities, collectives have no power, believe me, nothing will come out of that...[35]

At the time, Kravchuk was speaking on behalf of the institution that represented the regions, and the interview was given during the Novo-Ogaryovo process of the devolution of power from the central government to the republics. It was important for Kravchuk to ensure that the principle of devolution prevailed over centralization in the restructured Union, and, at the same time, that the oblasts and the Crimean Autonomous Soviet Socialist Republic (formed on 12 February 1991), received decision-making powers. But Kravchuk also argued that not only did the responsibilities of the centre and the republics have to be clearly separated, but also it was the republics who should delegate powers to the Union. Kravchuk echoed the ideas of Rakovsky from 1922 that the margins of power of the union organs should be defined by the republics.[36] Little did the regions know that once in the office of the President of Ukraine, Kravchuk would change his views of the principles of power distribution.

After the presidential elections, the regions resumed their efforts to convince the government to consult the regions before adopting policies and, generally, to focus on helping the regions.[37] Producers needed coherent policies, certainty, and clear rules to optimize production. The liberalization of prices that Ukraine was forced to implement in response to the price liberalization in Russia was not a reform, as the Ukrainian government claimed, but an 'administrative act' that impeded economic growth. Ukraine had no Ukrainian currency, no new taxation or land policy, no privatization, no liberalization of foreign trade, no reform of state administration in sight, and no 'decisive struggle with speculation'. Combined with confiscatory taxes introduced in December 1991, the main economic and political cost from the liberalization of prices was put on enterprises and local authorities. Enterprises and kolkhozy had to find resources to increase their employees' salaries.[38] Local authorities had to provide food and consumer goods to voters who were angered by the unfair distribution of goods and the failure of law enforcement organs to fight speculation.[39]

Regardless of their ideological convictions, proponents of both market reforms and central administrative control needed the government to enforce contract discipline. The government could not, understandably, enforce the fulfilment of contracts by non-Ukrainian partners, but what prevented it from enforcing contract discipline within Ukraine? The government was urged to organize systemic enforcement of bans, particularly on the export of vital inputs for agriculture.[40]

Budgetary relations needed to be revised as well. The existing budgetary system did not reward the economic initiative of local organs. The distribution of income from centrally collected taxes varied from region to region, and 'it was not clear if a region would have more if it worked better'.[41] Oblasts had to beg Kyiv for funds, some more than others. As Robert Kravchuk observed, the highly industrialized oblasts of eastern Ukraine 'were relatively fiscally independent of the central government in 1992, [but] by 1995 [they] approached or even exceeded the average for regional budgetary dependence upon Kyiv'.[42] Days before the official dissolution of the Soviet Union, echoing Kravchuk's June 1991 interview and the debates on the party budget, some soviets suggested that all taxes should be paid to the local budget and then the localities should transfer money to the top.[43] At the very least, the Ministry of Finance should stop changing the budgets of local soviets 'after the local soviets approved them', insisted Bilousenko from the Zaporizhzhia oblast. 'We hope that such methods, characteristic of the former centre, will not be used by the government of Ukraine. If an extraordinary situation requires such changes, then they should be discussed with the participation of the oblasts beforehand.'[44]

Centralized distribution of food to the cities was unviable. By January, three months after the Fokin government confirmed state control over agriculture and food supplies, the food situation in the cities had deteriorated. Local authorities tried to tackle the problem themselves. 'Before, we received [butter] from thirteen oblasts of Ukraine. Today, only three oblasts [deliver butter to the Donetsk oblast], Sumy, Cherkasy, and Chernihiv. The deliveries of meat have reduced by 64 percent [since 1990]—this is a catastrophe', explained the head of the Donetsk oblast soviet and ispolkom Yurii Smirnov in January 1992. Appealing to the government for help did not bring results. So, to force the oblast-suppliers to respect their obligations, in December 1991, the Donetsk authorities stopped delivering mineral fertilizers, salt, and metal to the oblasts that owed them food produce. 'We will have to do the same in January', warned Smirnov. 'But is this the method? Is this what we aimed for when we declared independence?' The Donetsk authorities tried to resolve the problem of food supplies by suggesting that the government leave to the oblast 2 percent of the agricultural output that the oblast supplied through *goszakaz*. Kyiv refused. Consequently, they passed their own resolution on the issue.[45] Zaporizhzhia authorities, too, had to organize food supplies themselves and 'seek compromises with the kolkhozy, sovkhozy, and the population' to make sure people had enough food, shared Volodymyr Demianov, the head of the Zaporizhzhia oblast soviet and ispolkom. The authorities of the Dnipropetrovsk oblast were in a similar situation. 'The Kirovohrad oblast owed 1,700 tonnes of meat to the city and oblast of Dnipropetrovsk but supplied only 3 tonnes. Who in the government or the Verkhovna Rada was accountable for this?'[46] they wondered.

In January 1992, many regions viewed the formal decentralization of food supplies to the cities as the most obvious solution to the Ukrainian government's inability to regulate the increasingly chaotic and wild market. Anyway, regional authorities already relied on the directors of enterprises, kolkhozy, and sovkhozy, as well as personal networks, for food supplies.[47] In the meantime, the government could 'urgently gather all heads of the oblasts and find common mechanisms' to resolve problems with food supplies, proposed Smirnov in early January 1992.[48]

While the regions argued in favour of devolution, the situation in Ukraine was rapidly evolving closer to anarchy than democratic transformation. The country urgently needed a solid vertical executive, and executive discipline. All eyes turned towards the head of the new executive branch, the president. As discussed below, although a democratic institution, the presidency had been designed based on the Soviet blueprint of the CPU first secretary; hence, from the start it was in an unfavourable position to overcome the regionalism that rapidly evolved in the following two years.

## Soviet Origins of the Presidency in Ukraine

Although the presidency was created by the Verkhovna Rada,[49] the institution of the presidency and the president's governors in Ukraine was originally suggested by the Ukrainian communists. In 1990, several obkom secretaries suggested replacing the 'CPU first secretary–obkom first secretary' vertical structure with a 'president–governors' vertical structure.[50] In September 1990, the Ukrainian International Institute of Management submitted to the Verkhovna Rada its second draft of the Concept of the System of State Administration in Ukraine, the first draft of which had been submitted in June. The institute commission introduced the president as the head of the state and the executive branch, subordinated to the Verkhovna Rada.[51]

Apart from the adjustment for democratic development, whereby the president was elected by the population of Ukraine and could not be a member of any party, the institution of the presidency was designed based on the basic principle of the CPU first secretary: it would be responsible and accountable for the situation in the republic, but would not have control over the economy. Similar to the first secretary, the president was 'alone responsible for fulfilling the material and spiritual needs of the people of Ukraine'. The first secretary of the CPU reported to the Central Committee for the situation in Ukraine; the president reported to the Verkhovna Rada. The Verkhovna Rada was supposed to replace the old central Soviet leadership as the superior institution for the new Ukrainian executive. Just as the CPU first secretary of Ukraine did not appoint the chairman of the Ukrainian Soviet government, so too the president did not appoint the prime minister. The president could suggest a candidate for prime minister to the Verkhovna Rada, but it was up to the Verkhovna Rada to confirm or reject the candidate. In other words, the person who would administer the economy had to be approved by the regions. Indeed, in this concept, the MPs were to be elected 'by the people, not the parties'. In the envisioned two-tier parliament, the lower People's House was 'a gathering of representatives of the regions [oblasts]'.[52]

To formalize the actual situation in Ukraine, the 1990 draft included a provision stating that 'the oblast level of economic administration should become the main centre for solving issues related to the organization of production'. The proposed design was a thinly veiled effort by the regional authorities, communist in their majority, to use the presidency to secure their power. At the end of 1990 and in early 1991, public opinion was against a communist-sponsored presidency, and this draft, to the best knowledge of this author, was not put to a vote.[53]

But the communists did not drop the idea. On 21 February 1991, communist MPs wrote to Hurenko that since Gorbachev had created the presidency 'to increase the efficiency of executive power', Ukraine too should 'create republican presidential structures of administration that would pull Ukraine out of the difficult political and economic situation'. Hurenko did not act. On 17 June 1991, five days after the election of Boris Yeltsin as President of the Russian Federation, at a meeting in the Ukrainian Central Committee, the regions put the institution of the presidency back on the agenda.[54] This time, the idea materialized into a law that the Verkhovna Rada passed on 5 July 1991, 'On the President of the Ukrainian SSR'. The institution of the presidency was presented as a necessary attribute of Ukrainian statehood.[55]

The functions initially assigned to the president in autumn 1990 'migrated' into constitutional amendments: representation of Ukraine abroad, responsibility for the socio-economic situation in the republic, and reporting to the Verkhovna Rada. 'The president was granted sweeping powers to nullify central decisions, but the law was less precise about the president's prerogatives vis-à-vis republican institutions.'[56] Control over the economy remained with those who controlled resources, and that was neither the first secretary then nor the president now.

The Verkhovna Rada adapted the Soviet dual executive to new political realities. The 'Ukrainian Central Committee–Ukrainian Soviet government' duo was replaced with the 'Presidency–Cabinet of Ministers'. Like the first secretary in the Soviet system, the president was the head of the executive branch.[57] Just as the

Ukrainian Soviet government was accountable to both the Ukrainian Central Committee and the central leadership in Moscow, the Cabinet of Ministers was accountable to two power centres, the president and the Verkhovna Rada. The government administered the economy. However, the programmes on economic, social, and national-cultural development, the state budget, the programmes for supplies of food to the population, and other aspects of socio-economic development had to be approved by the Verkhovna Rada before the government could implement them.[58]

## Building the Vertical Executive

At the beginning of January 1992, there was a consensus on the need to enforce the vertical executive, but there was no consensus as to how. Some supported decentralizing the state administration and consolidating the soviets. Proponents of decentralization argued that the soviets should enforce the government's resolutions and the president's instructions. Others insisted on installing a presidential vertical structure. The MPs urged the president to protect producers and the consumers' market and to take over the government, 'like comrade Yeltsin did'. Kravchuk himself was sceptical about empowering the soviets. As he told the Verkhovna Rada on 28 January 1992, 'numerous facts show that at this crucial point, local soviets are detached from people, have lost connection with workers' collectives. Even worse, many officials do not take responsibility, are too cautious, and sometimes even slow down the reforms.'[59]

By the end of January 1992, there was consensus on 'how'. By then, following the liberalization of prices in Russia, prices in Ukraine had risen by 285 percent. The degree of administrative chaos increased as well, not all due to the inflation. The bureaucracy's lack of responsibility for its policy and decision making, inherited from Soviet political culture, remained unaddressed. Lack of accountability and irresponsibility were endemic. The government could not enforce its own decisions. It did not bother to establish regular communication with the oblispolkoms, either, thus 'leaving them in an extreme situation on their own, without giving them any help'.[60] As economic and administrative chaos increased, so did political uncertainty.[61] Hence, the majority in the Verkhovna Rada agreed to support the idea of a vertical presidential structure and to expand presidential powers. The belief was that, once empowered, the president would enforce the laws and directives of the government, protect the population from impoverishment and promote market reforms. Empowered, the president would be able to stabilize prices and improve the lives of the people.[62]

Disagreement remained as to whether the vertical executive should be built top-down or bottom-up. In the first case, the president would appoint his representatives in the regions and hold them to account for implementing the laws.

In the second case, the president would work with the existing oblispolkoms, whose chairmen were elected. (Curiously, the latter provision was included in the Ukrainian Central Committee draft of the Constitution from June 1991. Article 117 stated that the chairman of the soviet, who was also the head of the ispolkom, was also the representative of the president.[63]) Proponents of the latter approach were against governors with personal loyalty to the president and independence from local elites, even though in the recent past the majority had belonged to the same party.[64]

Kravchuk was prepared to become the head of the government, but after the Verkhovna Rada expanded the president's constitutional rights. Kravchuk observed sarcastically, yet correctly:

> Paragraph 9 of article 114 states that 'if the president violated the Constitution and the laws of Ukraine, based on the decision of the Supreme Court...' (it is good that it does not yet exist) '...he can be removed from his post by the Verkhovna Rada of Ukraine'. This we did not forget to put down, but what the president can do, we forgot [to put down]....Should I issue decrees that contradict the Constitution, the Verkhovna Rada would correctly ask [me] why was [I] violating Constitutional Laws? So, make changes to the Constitution, then everything will fall into place.[65]

Kravchuk did not mention that it was under his leadership that the Verkhovna Rada amended the Constitution. As the chairman of the legislative organ, he was not interested in a strong executive. Now he had the interests of the executive branch to protect. Kravchuk was nonetheless correct to insist that the rights of the president should be correlated with his responsibilities and 'allow him to implement the existing laws, make radical decisions in the interest of the people, [and] be a true guarantor of the rights and freedoms of the citizens'. The president already had the right of legislative initiative. Now he was asking for a temporary constitutional right to issue normative acts on certain issues not regulated by legislation, which he received.[66]

Kravchuk viewed the chaos in the relationship between the capital and the territories and between various levels of power in the localities as one of the subjective factors that had contributed to the economic crisis. From the start, Kravchuk rejected the idea of cooperating with the soviets and the ispolkoms. For the former Ukrainian Central Committee secretary for ideology, the sector where the Ukrainian Central Committee did have power, the Ukrainian Central Committee–obkom vertical was an effective structural connection between the oblasts and Kyiv. Kravchuk was prepared to restore it under the guise of the vertical between the president and the president's representatives to the oblasts. Kravchuk agreed for the soviets to propose the candidates and promised that the function of the president's representatives would be to control the socio-economic situation in their territories, not to directly administer the oblasts like the obkom secretaries did. But still, the oblispolkoms had to transfer executive power to the president's representatives.[67]

The majority in the Verkhovna Rada supported Kravchuk. In the absence of the rule of law and the destruction of the party apparatus vertical, the loyalty of the president's representatives to the president was viewed as a guarantee that they would enforce the vertical executive regardless of whether the government set new mechanisms for the implementation of laws, decrees, and instructions. Given that at the end of January 1992 the president expressed his full trust and support of Prime Minister Fokin, whom the Verkhovna Rada was prepared to remove for inefficiency, nobody expected a power struggle between the two executive branches over the subordination of the president's representatives. It was assumed that since the president was the head of the executive branch, his representatives would implement the government's orders.

On 5 March 1992, the Verkhovna Rada passed the law 'On the Representative of the President of Ukraine'.[68] To ensure that the new cohort of oblast heads focused on *implementing* the laws and instructions, article 3 prohibited them from combining their new posts with the mandate of MP. The law placed the

**Illustration 22**  Delegation from Sevastopol city council at the meeting with President of Ukraine Leonid Kravchuk, 11 March 1992/© TsDAEA (0-215908)

On 11 March 1992, a group of delegates from Sevastopol city council met with Leonid Kravchuk. On that day, President Kravchuk signed a decree that subordinated the state executive power of the city of Sevastopol directly to the central executive organs of Ukraine.

ispolkoms of the oblasts and raions under the direct jurisdiction of the president's representatives and transferred to them certain functions performed by the soviets.[69] Indeed, for all appearances, the law 'On the Representative of the President of Ukraine' 'effectively formalize[d] Kravchuk's dominance of local government'.[70] However, throughout 1992–1993, the president's representatives demonstrated that in the institutional system of Ukraine, the factor of personal loyalty to the president was perfectly compatible with the factor of regionalism.[71]

## Part II: The Unbeatable Force of Regionalism

### The President's Representatives as 'Guards' of Regionalism

By September 1992, it had become clear that instead of enforcing the executive vertical by implementing the laws, central policies, and instructions, the president's representatives, still personally loyal to the president, had chosen to protect their own interests which were often aligned with regional agendas. If a policy did not suit their interests, it was not implemented. The government programme of small-scale privatization, for example, completely failed as it remained up to the regions whether to implement it or not. In the absence of general mechanisms for privatization common to the entire country, only four oblasts, Lviv, Khmelnytskyi, Rivne, and Kharkiv, held small privatizations in 1992. The majority of the oblasts did not have a programme of privatization and did not even form administrative bodies to organize it. The fund of state property formally in charge of privatization had no influence on regional administrations.[72] In a reflection of the regions' resentment towards implementing privatization, the latter was repeatedly halted by the government in 1992.[73]

In some territories, the chairmen of the soviets and the president's representatives cooperated. In others, local soviets and their ispolkoms were in conflict with the president's representatives. In such conflicts, the latter generally came out as the winners.[74] As Oleksandr Borzykh from the Luhansk oblast argued at the end of September 1992, the president's representative became 'not only the president's but, judging by how his rights expanded, God's representative on earth, as they say'. Importantly, as viceroys, they not only suppressed local elected organs, but released themselves from the duty to implement the laws and instructions of the government and the president, which was their raison d'être in the first place. Instead of commercializing the retail trade, explained Borzykh,

> which was your decree, Leonid Makarovych [Kravchuk], the representative of the president in the Luhansk oblast created a trade-coordinating centre where the oblast administration is the main founding member. This centre has the

right to make contracts, fix prices, and so on. Is this the function of the oblast administration or those structures that should implement the very decree about commercialisation?![75]

Taras Nahulko from the Khmelnytskyi oblast insisted that many of the president's representatives contributed to lawlessness.[76] Volodymyr Shcherbyna from the Kharkiv oblast illustrated Nahulko's argument with a story of the inhabitants in the Boyarsky raion of the Kyiv oblast who felt they had no choice but to appeal to the United Nations with the complaint that their soviet had refused them land for housing and private plots. 'The law [was] violated, but the president's representative support[ed] this violation',[77] observed Shcherbyna.

As Chornovil explained, 'the institution of the representatives of the president [was] controlled by no one, not even the president. Now we have neither soviet power, nor any other functional form of people's representation, and the economy is practically unmanageable, neither by the central organs, nor by the territorial authorities.' Ironically, Chornovil was among the strongest opponents of soviet power. In January 1992, he insisted that 'the system of soviets destroyed the single vertical executive'.[78]

None of the criticism of the president's representatives that sounded in September–October 1992 had any effect. Kravchuk continued cultivating the loyalty of his representatives in the regions and remained reluctant to hold them accountable for violations of laws and instructions. Loyalty remained the only criterion to which the president held his representatives accountable. As a result, by May 1993, instead of controlling the implementation of laws, the president's representatives had turned into local lords who violated the laws and made their own policies.[79]

A popular explanation of the autonomy of the president's representatives at the time was their subordination to the president even after the president's 27 October 1992 decree placed them under dual subordination to the president and the Cabinet of Ministers.[80] On 18 May 1993, when reporting to the Verkhovna Rada on work done by the government in the past six months, Prime Minister Leonid Kuchma, who succeeded Fokin on 13 October 1992, insisted that a strong vertical executive could be established only if local state administrations were subordinated to the government.[81]

Administrative reorganization was a traditional Soviet approach to administrative problems. Yet, the underlying reason that motivated the president's representatives to consolidate regionalism instead of the vertical executive was the same as it had been for the obkom secretaries, or the soviets after them. Their institutional and personal interests were best served by pursuing regionalism rather than the centre's policies.

By law, the president's representatives were assigned the functions previously performed by the obkom secretaries and later the chairmen of the soviets and oblispolkoms: responsibility for, firstly, the implementation of the centre's orders, which included the laws of Ukraine, decrees of the president, resolutions of the Verkhovna Rada and the Cabinet of Ministers, and other acts of legislative and executive power, and secondly, 'economic and social development on the territory under his[/her] jurisdiction'.[82] The second task was not defined in quantitative or qualitative terms and broadly meant social peace and stability. It was the second task that was more important for the president's representatives, as it was for the soviets, although each had a slightly different reason. The chairmen of the soviets needed peace and stability in their territories to secure their re-election to soviets and/or the Verkhovna Rada. The president's representatives needed peace and stability in the oblasts under their jurisdiction to secure the re-election of the president who appointed them. The economic weakness of the Cabinet of Ministers made the president dependent on the regions for his political survival. Hence, he put no pressure on his representatives to implement the government's instructions and decrees. As long as they maintained order in their territories and remained loyal, they were immune from being punished for violations of the laws and decrees.

This tacit contract between the president and his representatives was formalized in article 12 of the law: 'The representative of the president can be brought to criminal or administrative responsibility by the court, with mandatory notification of the president of Ukraine about *the circumstances that were the reasons* for the violation [italics added].' Similar to their institutional predecessors, the president's representatives, too, had to inform their direct superior about the state of affairs in their territory and 'report to him about their activity'. A president's representative could be removed from his post only by the president (articles 4 and 5). Mimicking the relationship between the CPU first secretary and obkom first secretaries, there was no formal mechanism that would have allowed, or forced, the president to hold his representatives responsible for their activity.

Aligned with institutional interests were the personal interests of the president's representatives. The paralysis of the legal system, corruption, loopholes in legislation, and reluctance of the government and the Verkhovna Rada to prohibit state and elected officials from commercial activity opened vast opportunities to the president's representatives for collusion with local producers and various businesses, including banking institutions, for personal enrichment.[83] The permanent threat of social upheaval only further motivated the president's representatives to secure personal gains and establish a safe transition into business before their political patron lost power. The president's representatives had a personal interest to protect the interests of producers or banks which could give them material and financial help to alleviate the burden of the economic crisis on the population or increase their own personal wealth. To ensure that businesses responded to the calls of the president's representatives, paragraph 3 of article 6 of the law granted them the right of control over enterprises, regardless of their jurisdiction or the form of the property.

Since both institutional and personal incentives motivated the president's representatives to prioritize regional interests over central policies, since there was no punishment for failure to implement the centre's orders, and since the government could not satisfy the needs of the regions and had 'regional economic affairs on the back burner', as Ivan Salii, the president's representative to the city of Kyiv, put it, the president's representatives, like the soviets and the obkom secretaries before them, had little choice but to address regional problems independently from the government in 1992–1993.[84]

## Part III: In Search of a Consensus

### 'Fifth Power, the Power of Mafia'

By the beginning of autumn 1992, the Ukrainian government had proved completely incapable of taking control over the economy. The political configuration, discussed in detail elsewhere, made governance unstable and confused.[85] The Ukrainian state still did not have functional mechanisms for the implementation of legislative acts, decrees, resolutions, or instructions issued by either the Verkhovna Rada or the government.[86] According to Chornovil, the chairman of the Lviv oblast soviet, about 70–80 percent of Ukrainian laws were not implemented. 'Some of them were halted [by the Verkhovna Rada], others did not have mechanisms for implementation, yet others were violated by the instructions or decrees of the government.'[87] The mechanisms regulating *goszakaz* were still pending.[88] The very definition of what constituted *goszakaz* remained unclear; and the general idea of *goszakaz* as a contract between the state and the producer, particularly agricultural producers, was discredited. The regions agreed that without a government with resources, there was no state. The government needed resources for kindergartens, schools, hospitals, Chornobyl victims, the army and security forces, and other recipients of subsidies. But while focusing on extraction and distribution, the government had not done anything 'so that there was something to distribute'.[89]

Selectively implemented bans, high taxes, licences, tariffs, and manually distributed state subsidies based on murky criteria, combined with the government's inability to secure the supplies of industrial inputs it had promised, signalled to the regions that the government had no interest in supporting production and preferred to perform its old Soviet function of extracting and distributing. Who needed such a government? 'State licences established barriers for producers. I have sugar, but I cannot exchange it for petrol', explained Oleksii Cherniavsky from the Sumy oblast at the Verkhovna Rada session on 15 October 1992. 'Excuse me, but I would not need you if you hadn't established such a regime. I fulfilled *goszakaz*. Why can't [I] freely exchange what [I] produced in excess to the *goszakaz* [for what I need]?'[90]

Yet even while focused on distribution, the government failed to secure sales of state resources at fixed prices, which allowed many to conclude that the government had allied with the mafia structures that got their hands on the supplies delivered through *goszakaz*. In October 1992, some regions insisted that the government name those personally responsible for ensuring that the products the government received from the regions through *goszakaz* would not end up with the mafia structures. Others, like Zhytomyr, Kharkiv, and Poltava, no longer supported the idea of the government distributing agricultural production.[91] In 1992, the regions supplied 10.6 million tonnes of grain to the state, 1 million tonnes more than in 1991, but still only 62 percent of 'the 17 million tonnes that were absolutely necessary for Ukraine to survive', as Fokin put it in 1991.[92]

If the government was unable to organize the production or distribution of food, why should it decide on the regions' expenditures? Why should the regions procure food only in the amounts allocated to them by the Ukrainian government? The regions accepted that the government insisted on budget constraints and refused to pay off the debts of the soviets, but the regions could not understand why the government could not establish mechanisms to allow the regions to trade directly with each other and why the regions were not allowed to use extra-budgetary funds to meet their own needs.[93]

Echoing the debates from 1990, the regions urged the government to formally empower the soviets, giving them formal rights, obligations, and financial/material resources so that they could be fully responsible for the situation in their territories.[94] Similarly, if the Ukrainian government was unable to organize the implementation of legislative acts, it should 'allow local soviets...to implement [them]', suggested Chornovil. For example, if the government failed to set a mechanism for implementing the law on privatizing the housing fund, 'the Lviv, Donetsk, Kharkiv, and other oblasts should work out their own mechanisms within the margins of the law and begin work'.[95]

By the autumn of 1992, economic crisis and popular demand to punish those responsible for it submerged the executive and legislative branches in the blame game. Since responsibility for policy- and decision making was still not formalized in the new state, it was a murky issue to determine whose fault it was, and to what degree, that the population of Ukraine was living in a worse condition than the population in the neighbouring post-Soviet countries.

**Illustration 23**  Prime Minister Vitold Fokin addressing the government of Ukraine
on the occasion of his removal, 2 October 1992/© TsDAEA (0-215992)

By September 1992, the economic crisis had reached a new height. President Kravchuk could no
longer protect Prime Minister Fokin. In the photo, Kravchuk is next to Fokin (standing) who is saying
his goodbyes to the government.

Prime Minister Leonid Kuchma ignored the calls 'to investigate the former
government' and did not promise 'to hold those responsible for the current situation to account'.[96] The president, too, was reluctant to hold Prime Minister Fokin,
widely held to be the culprit for the economic disaster, to account—possibly
because this would have given the Verkhovna Rada an opportunity to examine
the president's own contribution to the crisis. On 28 January 1992, during heated
debates in the Verkhovna Rada on Prime Minister Fokin's ability to run the economy, Kravchuk publicly supported Fokin and refused to remove him.[97] At the
time, Kravchuk admitted that it was the government which resisted the reforms
and that it was with the Cabinet's permission that the state committees 'did not let
enterprises breathe'. Kravchuk assured the MPs that Fokin personally was a supporter of market reforms.

I already had a conversation with Vitold Pavlovych [Fokin] about this. Indeed,
many of the [state] committees changed their title, turned into associations, various corporations, yet still receive money from the government. So we [i.e.,
Kravchuk and Fokin] will put things in order. They will not stop us advancing to
the market. We guarantee you this.[98]

In that, Kravchuk and Fokin failed. A market economy remained a distant dream, as did 'order'. Instead, corruption reached such dimensions that Kuchma broke political correctness in his 27 October 1992 speech in the Verkhovna Rada and publicly recognized that a 'fifth power, the power of mafia' existed in the country. For the first time, the highest government official publicly recognized that there was corruption at all levels of state administration and that it was necessary 'to immediately activate the work of law-enforcing organs'. Kuchma promised that with extraordinary legislative powers, he would bring order to economic life.[99]

## New Government: New Promises, Old Habits

A candidate from the group of 'red directors', or directors of state enterprises, Kuchma was viewed as someone who understood that the government should concentrate on assisting producers, and that to produce, the government needed not only to draft the correct policies, but also to ensure that the policies were implemented.[100] Indeed, the main task for the new government was 'to make sure that the laws and resolutions were fulfilled', said Volodymyr Dorofeev from the Luhansk oblast. 'We will never have the rule of law if the government does not respect the laws passed by the Verkhovna Rada and does not fulfil its own resolutions.'[101]

Kuchma indicated that he understood what was expected of him. He promised, in addition to fighting corruption, to reduce the list of export goods and products regulated through quotas and licences, and to establish customs control that would allow the enforcement of a ban on exports of the goods urgently needed in Ukraine. He reassured regional authorities that he understood the power of the regions. He emphasized the importance of developing regional economies and urged 'each region to concentrate its resources on developing the production of goods that would be competitive on the world market'. The economy of Ukraine would recover if the regional economies did. Kuchma received applause for saying that he 'intentionally did not include the Ministry of Trade in the list [of ministries]. Such an organ should not exist in the Cabinet of Ministers. These functions should be passed to the local administrations, to the Ministry of Economy as the last resort.' Only then could the privatization of the retail trade be implemented.[102]

To speed up the implementation of market reforms, the Verkhovna Rada granted extraordinary legislative powers to Kuchma's Cabinet of Ministers. On 18 November, and then on 19 December 1992, the Verkhovna Rada temporarily, until 12 May 1993, delegated the right of legislative regulation of economic relations to the government. At the same time, the president lost the right to regulate the economy by decree.[103]

## The Power of Inertia

Very soon it became clear that Kuchma was not immune to the powers of institution. Having moved from the Verkhovna Rada where he was an MP into the office of the Prime Minister, Kuchma prioritized 'bringing order' through centralized administrative state control over the economy rather than responding to the needs of the regions.

Following Fokin's path, Kuchma concentrated on establishing control over physical resources. With its 22 January 1993 decree, 'About state contract and state order for 1993' legalized, the government announced in the Verkhovna Rada on 15 October the provision that the Cabinet was no longer responsible for providing inputs in return for output. Producers supplying to the state had to procure the inputs themselves. The voluntary principle, already violated by Fokin in January 1992, was also officially abandoned.[104] The state now officially dictated who would produce what.

Kuchma recognized the urgency to restore the vertical executive and executive discipline, and that it was not enough for the government to send down its decrees, resolutions, and instructions to the periphery. The fulfilment of these instructions had to be enforced and controlled. However, as Vice Prime Minister Viktor Pynzenyk revealed in the new economic programme to the Verkhovna Rada on 2 February 1993, instead of empowering the soviets, inducing the regions to comply, and reinforcing the 'government–ispolkom' vertical structure, the government decided to force the regions into compliance and empower vertical branch relationships. Mimicking the Soviet ministerial system, in which the ministries administered their enterprises through glavks, Kuchma intended for the Ukrainian ministries to administer enterprises through periphery branch departments and administrations of local ispolkoms.[105] Kuchma also intended to restore the nomenklatura system for the directors of state enterprises, although he planned to update it by introducing a contract system and granting 10 percent ownership shares to directors who would turn their state enterprises into corporations.[106] In 'good old' Soviet tradition, the programme did not include 'general mechanisms to ensure that those responsible for the non-fulfilment of laws would be brought to account'. The ministers were free to violate the laws and legislative norms and to put administrative pressure on producers.[107]

The new economic programme did not reflect Kuchma's rhetoric about regional development, not to mention the regions' expectations. The regions viewed regional policy as decentralization, 'as the right of local organs to act independently, depending on local conditions and possibilities, in correlation with state interests'. However, 'so far, the decrees of the government aimed at centralization,'[108] explained Mykhailo Hryshko, the head of the Verkhovna Rada commission on soviets and development of local administration from the Chernihiv oblast, in February 1993.

The programme did not address the regions' urgent issues. In January 1992 Fokin identified the commercialization of retail trade as the most urgent problem, 'to be solved in two to three weeks maximum', but in February 1993, the commercialization of retail trade was still pending. Property needed to be divided between communal and state ownership.[109] Some regional leaders were categorically against the government's idea of combining state and communal property under the management of the ministries, central administrations, and local administrations, which, according to Kuchma's plan, were subordinated directly to the central administration. Since regional authorities relied on state enterprises for local socio-economic agendas, 'this will lead to *diktat* of the centre and deprive local organs of the possibility to independently solve specific regional issues and take expedient measures for providing for raions and towns', insisted Yukhym Zviahilsky, the chairman of the Donetsk city soviet.[110]

The contested issue of budgetary relations between the centre and the regions was not resolved, either. The soviets did not draft their budgets, nor did they have formal authority to solve social issues.[111] The regions did not agree that republican programmes should be financed by local budgets and returned to the idea of forming the state budget from the bottom up. Why couldn't the government make it clear what share of collected taxes went to the state budget and what share remained to the local soviet, wondered Hryshko while echoing the old discussion on the principle of forming the party budget. The state budget should 'reflect the specificity of the regions as well as the needs of the state. Hence, local authorities should have the legal right to introduce local taxes', argued Zviahilsky.[112]

The regions were also against the government's proposal to include non-budgetary funds in the general state budget. This initiative 'contradicted article 13 of the law on local soviets and local self-administration.[113] More importantly, it deprived the soviets of the incentive to fill these funds because local soviets were removed from managing non-budgetary funds in the government's proposal',[114] clarified Hryshko. The regions should have financial resources to be able to fulfil their responsibilities.

The producers, in their turn, waited for a coherent pricing policy, a monetary reform, and introduction of a permanent Ukrainian currency.[115] Some suggested that the government should replace administrative control with a taxation system to regulate state orders, exports, and the budget. 'Give enterprises maximum freedom and help them without producing additional institutions of [central] power',[116] urged Mykola Riabchenko, the director of the Kryvyi Rih cement-mining plant. That would include, for example, regulation of the banking sector. The National Bank shared assets with commercial banks, which charged businesses high interest rates that enterprises were not always able to afford. Furthermore, 'while before, banking operations took hours or one day, now [they] take] weeks or months'. Untimely payments froze the capital and brought down businesses. The absurdity of the banking system reached the point where, instead of earning interest on their foreign currency bank deposits, enterprises had to pay the bank for keeping their money there. 'This is why the money settles abroad', concluded Dorofeev from Luhansk.[117]

**Illustration 24**  Ukrainian entrepreneurs at a meeting with President Kravchuk,
24 March 1993/© TsDAEA (0-217289)

**Illustration 25**  President Kravchuk at a meeting with Ukrainian entrepreneurs,
24 March 1993/© TsDAEA (0-217288)

**Illustration 26**  Representatives of the Ukrainian National Assembly of Entrepreneurs
at a meeting with President Kravchuk, 30 March 1993/© TsDAEA (0-217287)

As the economic situation deteriorated and dissatisfaction with the President's representatives to the
oblasts increased, President Kravchuk tried to forge support of businessmen and directors of
industrial enterprises.

When discussing Kuchma's programme, the regions repeated what they had been telling the Ukrainian leadership for several years now, that unless the Ukrainian government incentivized the regions, which remained stronger than the Ukrainian centre, it would be constrained in its ability to implement any of its programmes. A strong incentive could be devolution of decision making. 'You should understand, if we abandon [the idea of] decentralization and you lose the support of local organs, your reforms will not progress fast', explained Hryshko.[118] The regions would continue prioritizing local interests until the government aligned its policies with them. And so far, the government's efforts to establish a centralized top-down system of administrative control had only consolidated regionalism.

On 18 May 1993, the emergency powers that Prime Minister Kuchma had obtained from the Verkhovna Rada in November 1992 expired. The expectations of the regions and the 'red directors' that Prime Minister Kuchma would liberalize the economy and pursue cooperation with the regions instead of *diktat*, as he had promised in his inaugural speech in October 1992, did not materialize.

The approach to economic management did not change. Instead of reforms and cooperation, producers saw a command-administrative system of economic administration.[119] Formal liberalization was minimal. The share of planned figures during 1993 was reduced compared to 1992, but 'still indicated a coverage of about 60 percent of goods'.[120] 'Quotas and other quantitative and tax measures continued to restrict more than 70 percent of all exports'.[121] Government policies did not support producers. Like before, most decrees issued by the Kuchma government were directed towards extracting from enterprises before giving them either inputs or functional regulations in return. Certainty and clear rules remained lacking as well.[122] The government had no scruples or rules against 'passing a decree on 1 April, then publishing it on 15 April, but declaring it active since 1 January of the same year', a practice deemed by many as pure 'banditry'.[123]

Kuchma restored state control over 94 percent of the economy. But distribution remained privatized and corrupt. 'Stealing became the main way of making money', not manufacturing.[124] The regions agreed with Kuchma that the decline in economic growth had slowed down. But national income in the first quarter of 1993 was still 11 percent lower compared to the first quarter of 1992. 'The living standards of citizens fell three times since [Kuchma's] government received extraordinary powers.... Up to 80 percent of the population lived below poverty level'.[125] (Economic output declined by 38 percent from 1990 to 1993.[126])

After six months of command-directive management, there was the same vacuum of power and deficit of responsibility within the apparatus as before Kuchma took office. Instead of implementing the laws issued by the Verkhovna Rada, the government amended them with decrees. Yet the government decrees were not enforced, either. Crucially, the government did not possess accurate information about the economy. The local soviets did.[127]

Echoing his predecessor, Kuchma could not but admit that 'executive power did not extend beyond the doors of the government's building'.[128] Ironically, the very ministries that the Ukrainian government protected were autonomous from the government. The apparatus in the periphery and in the capital were free to choose which instructions to implement. The audit of the periphery apparatus held in spring 1993 revealed that 'in some local administrations, particularly in raions, the [envelopes with] decrees from the government were not opened'.[129] The connections between Kyiv and the regions remained weak. The president failed to replace the old party vertical structure with a new executive one, and Kuchma was not sure who was the highest authority in the regions to 'be held responsible for failed agricultural work'.[130] Since the government did not have periphery administrations subordinate to it, control over resources remained in the regions.

Yet, Kuchma believed that the main destabilizing factor in the Ukrainian economy was a 'deficit of energy resources and unbalanced economic relations with the states of the former Soviet Union'.[131] Hence, like his predecessors, he insisted that the centre should be consolidated before the regions. 'Ukraine is not Bankova or Hrushevskoho.[132] Ukraine is first of all the regions with their unlimited economic and political potential', admitted Kuchma. 'Today, the main task of regional policy is to balance the interests of the regions with the interests of the state and to transfer maximum power from Kyiv to the regions.' However, he argued, 'before empowering the regions, we should create a normal vertical administration between Kyiv and the regions'.[133]

A 'normal vertical administration' and consolidation of the centre was more than welcomed by the regions, as they had indicated to the government on numerous occasions, but not until the government assisted them in alleviating the social cost of the economic crisis that affected their political careers, as they had also indicated to the government on numerous occasions. When Kuchma asked for an extension of the Cabinet's legislative powers, the Verkhovna Rada gave a firm 'no'. When Kravchuk asked for extra-constitutional rights for the president, the legislature voted to give the president power to sign decrees on economic reform that were not regulated by the laws. His decrees would be in effect until the Verkhovna Rada passed the relevant laws. Apart from the necessary liberation of producers from excessive quotas, tariffs, licences, and taxes, and demonopolization of foreign trade, the MPs urged the executive branch to focus on increasing the responsibility of the government for the quality of its policies and their implementation, on cooperation with the regions when making policies, and on fighting corruption.[134]

## No Consensus on Decentralization

By the end of spring 1993, dissatisfaction at the government's inability to restore order and stop the economic crisis had reached such a scale that even in the highly industrialized oblasts, including Lviv, public opinion was 'most strongly in favour of delegating decision powers to regional authorities'.[135] Donbas demanded autonomy. The trade union of workers in metallurgy that was concentrated in the Dnipropetrovsk and Zaporizhzhia oblasts was prepared to put forward political demands for autonomy of Prydniprovsk if the government failed to meet its demands.[136] Northern and eastern oblasts of Ukraine actively sought cross-border cooperation with the border regions of Russia, observed Nemiria. But there was no strong secessionist political force in Ukraine. Regional authorities still saw 'more prospects for themselves within the boundaries of independent Ukraine than in a situation of "furious competition for scarce resources" with their stronger counterparts in Russia'.[137] Still, although there was no strong secessionist political force, there were concerns that the idea of secession might gain force. To prevent this from happening, some MPs, like Andrii Bondarchuk from the Volyn oblast, argued that the government and the Verkhovna Rada should consider giving more autonomy to all regions.[138]

In June, in the middle of the Donbas miners' strike and amidst growing calls from the regions to hold a referendum on confidence in the president and new elections to the Verkhovna Rada, Kuchma invited regional authorities from all oblasts to sit at the negotiation table and together seek solutions to the economic crisis. After the legislature rejected his request to extend the extra-constitutional rights of the government, Kuchma signalled his readiness to make concessions to the regions. On 20 May, the Cabinet of Ministers issued a decree 'About local taxes and levies' that increased the financial independence of local budgets. Then, on 23 June, Kuchma presented a new programme that proposed to liberalize taxation policy, to move on with the corporatization of medium-sized and large state enterprises and the privatization of small and medium-sized enterprises, to auction 1,432 unfinished industrial sites, and, significantly, to allow local authorities to use communal property as collateral to obtain bank loans.[139]

Yet like earlier government programmes, this one was not implemented. The system of centralized administration of the economy remained in place. The Ukrainian government was steadily heading towards what Daniel Kaufmann described as 'its own "threshold" point beyond which increasing administrative controls result in a loss of effective administrative control over the overall economy', or what Dmytro Dorchynets from Zakarpattia described at the time as 'a paradoxical situation where the more we centralize, the less order there is in the state'.[140]

By the autumn of 1993, the economic crisis and social tensions had reached a level that made early elections unavoidable. Kuchma had to resign. Once again, this time in his final speech as prime minister on 21 September 1993, Kuchma could not but recognize that there was no strong centralized power in Ukraine and that the power lay with the regions. He accepted that the idea of extra-judicial powers was discredited. But he was unprepared to admit his own mistake of neglecting the interests of the regions or failing to hold the state apparatus to account for its decisions.

For Kuchma, formerly part of the nomenklatura himself, the anarchy in economic administration was a result of the chaotic dismantling of the administrative mechanism and the inability of the executive branch to establish *diktat* over the regions. After eleven months as prime minister, during which he made almost thirty trips to the regions, Kuchma concluded:

> [It was] long absence of ironclad instructions from Kyiv [that] allowed regional administrative teams to consolidate themselves and even spread their wings. They [ran] their economies based on their possibilities and understanding, sometimes well, sometimes poorly. But one should admit that today, a considerable share of practical work and responsibility [was] in the regions, at the level of oblasts and large industrial cities.[141]

Kuchma then indicated that he understood the fundamental motives for regionalism in Ukraine: weak central administration and the objective need for regional authorities and producers to fulfil local socio-economic agendas. He no longer rejected decentralization as a way to consolidate central power.

> Regional teams, I think, long since recognised that there was a power vacuum in Kyiv, and do not hurry to ask someone sick with AIDS for health advice. The power in the periphery, of democratic or of post-communist origin,…stopped jangling with terminology like 'socialism' and 'capitalism' and concerned itself first and foremost with daily bread for people, with free economic zones, with technological innovation of production, with development of strong commercial structures. Such seemingly ideology-less daily work of regional administrators will bring, I think, Ukraine out of political and economic crisis.…[M]aybe it is time to consider delegating as much power as possible to the regions, for the sake of political stability? I am sure, numerous directors will not head the strikes because it won't be Verkhovna Rada, but local organs of administration who would be the object of attention of the strikers.[142]

Why he ignored the calls of MPs from the regions to do exactly that while he was still in office, Kuchma preferred not to discuss.

The MPs did not miss the chance to remind Kuchma that it was because he promised to promote market reforms and cooperate with the regions that he was appointed in the first place. So, why then did his 'government go back to the command methods of administration'? The president, who engaged in this discussion with MPs instead of Kuchma, must have understood this question as rhetorical, so he replied philosophically: 'There were objective and subjective reasons, and there were faults in the legislation. All this [was] there.' He was, though, very clear that in the blame game with the legislature as to who was responsible for the economic and political crisis, he, as the head of the executive branch, was not going to hold his prime ministers to account for any failures. 'I belong to those who suggest examining the activity of the government, and the president, and the Verkhovna Rada. But I do not belong to those who think that it is necessary to...bring those guilty to criminal, or other responsibility.'[143] President Kravchuk did not support the idea of investigating the Fokin government in the autumn of 1992, and he was not going to investigate the Kuchma government in the autumn of 1993, either.

At the same time, Kravchuk could not neglect the fact that Kyiv did not control the regions and Kravchuk himself needed their support in the forthcoming elections. Hence, he had little choice but to follow the example of Kuchma and flirt with the regions.

Vitalii Chernenko from the Donetsk oblast asked the president:

Kuchma said that the regions are gradually beginning to solve economic problems independently. It is simpler that way than to solve them through the centre. Don't you think that it would be wiser to give the regions the opportunity to solve their problems more actively and [allow them to] choose their own partners in economic, communal, and social areas? Maybe this is a real solution?

Kravchuk agreed.

The idea of providing vast powers to the regions was actively discussed a year ago when we began discussing the draft of the Constitution....I strongly support this. Moreover, there are my decrees and instructions that the Donetsk and Prydniprovsk regions should receive such powers. The problem remains, with the help of what mechanism should we realise this idea[?][144]

While the search for proper mechanisms continued, President Kravchuk remained faithful to the command-administrative system. The next de facto prime minister, but de jure acting first deputy prime minister, Yukhym Zviahilsky, turned out to be just the right man. He went further than Fokin or Kuchma. Supported by Kravchuk, Zviahilsky (22 September 1993–4 June 1994) introduced more regulations and tried to rebuild the command economy.[145] Zviahilsky was yet another victim of the power of institutions. As mentioned above, he had been among the strong and vocal proponents of empowering the soviets when he was the chairman of the Donetsk city soviet. With the change of institution came a change of interests.

**Illustration 27** Acting First Deputy Prime Minister, Yukhym Zviahilsky (left) and President Kravchuk in the Verkhovna Rada, September 1993/© TsDAEA (0-249487)

In a desperate effort to stop the economic crisis, on 22 September 1993, President Kravchuk appointed his third prime minister, Yukhym Zviahilsky. After his predecessors' desperate and futile efforts to stabilize the economy, Zviahilsky returned to 'good old' administrative control. His methods and policies drove the Ukrainian economy to near collapse. In the photo: Zviahilsky (left) and Kravchuk in the government box in the Verkhovna Rada.

**Illustration 28** People's deputies to the Verkhovna Rada from the Dnipropetrovsk oblast during the ninth session of the Verkhovna Rada of the first convocation, February 1994/© TsDAEA (0-221429)

The Dnipropetrovsk regional elites retained a dominant position in independent Ukraine. In reflection of the importance of their region, the MPs from the Dnipropetrovsk oblast occupied the front rows. Six months later, Leonid Kuchma (right end of the second row) became the second president of Ukraine.

Reflecting the priority of heavy industry over light industry or agriculture, Kravchuk's support for providing vast powers to the regions did not expand beyond highly industrialized Donetsk and Prydniprovsk. On 29 November 1993, he enacted a decree that provided the oblasts of Dnipropetrovsk, Donetsk, Luhansk, and Zaporizhzhia with greater economic autonomy for a two-year period.[146] On 21 February 1994, with presidential elections approaching, Kravchuk continued to flirt with the four industrial regions and issued another decree that extended their property and entrepreneurial legislative powers. He did not show similar generosity to other oblasts. Still, in March 1994, he 'ordered the wholesale transfer of the ownership of all state assets in housing and communal services, personal services, trade, public restaurants, urban roads, education, culture, fitness and sports, healthcare, and other social welfare functions to the oblast capital city governments by 1 July 1994'. According to presidential adviser Vasyl Rudenko, this decree was a 'serious step towards decentralization and power sharing between ministries and oblast administrations'.[147]

**Illustration 29** Second President of Ukraine Leonid Kuchma (left) and his predecessor Leonid Kravchuk, 19 July 1994/© TsDAEA (0-230038)

In the midst of economic and political crisis, Ukraine succeeded in holding democratic elections. On 19 July 1994, President Kravchuk peacefully transferred power to President Kuchma.

**Illustration 30**  President Kuchma at a meeting with the chairmen of city soviets, December 1994/© TsDAEA (0-236843)

Leonid Kuchma began his presidency by seeking consensus with the regions. In December 1994, he held a meeting with the chairmen of city soviets. First Vice Prime Minister Viktor Pynzenyk (left) had the task of implementing economic reforms.

As had often been the case in Ukrainian history since 1917, faced with uncertainty, the leader pulled out the decentralization card to gain the support of the regions. For the president, this time it was no help. Kravchuk's competitor Leonid Kuchma defeated him in the second round of presidential elections on 10 July 1994. Kuchma, too, ran on a platform of greater regional autonomy, but also of greater representation of regional interests in national politics, closer economic ties with Russia, and a looser official language policy. All three issues appealed to the regions, although to different degrees.[148]

## Conclusion

Efforts by the Ukrainian executive branch to adapt Soviet *diktat* to the Ukrainian context of the early 1990s brought it to the verge of political death. The Ukrainian government did not control the economy. It did not have command authority over the regions. By the beginning of 1994, the Ukrainian executive was still relying on the good will of the regions to fulfil its orders. The regions, on the other hand, progressed from pleading with the Ukrainian leadership to establish strong centralized power that would protect their interests to demanding devolution of decision making.

'The desire for greater autonomy in Ukraine's regions often coincide[d] with the greatest need for help from Kyiv.'[149] Yet the help the regions needed from the Ukrainian government and president was not just decrees or instructions handed down to them, but a functional state, secure supplies, and mechanisms for the implementation of decrees and instructions. They needed a system that would help them to fulfil their agendas.

By mid-1993, 'the inability of the state to function…contributed to the upsurge of separatism in the periphery.'[150] By 1994, the Ukrainian economy had reached a point deemed by the Central Intelligence Agency as threatening the survival of the Ukrainian state.[151] Regionalism triumphed. The triumph of regional clans would soon follow with a devastating effect on the Ukrainian state and society.[152]

In 1992–1994, the Ukrainian government understood that the regions controlled the resources and that there could be no political authority without economic power. It understood that it depended on the regions to a greater extent than they depended on the government.[153] But the government failed to understand that in the absence of repressive methods, in order to assert its authority, its demands had to be compatible with the interests of the regions. In the 'good old' tradition of prioritizing heavy industry, the Ukrainian government was sensitive to the interests of the highly industrialized regions, but it was not guided by the general principle of considering regional interests in policymaking. The government failed to appreciate that while the incentives that motivated the regions to prioritize their own interests during Soviet times remained intact after 1991, the opportunities for the regions to defend their own interests had increased. It was not by *diktat* that the Ukrainian government could interest the regions in implementing its policies, but by adequate assistance, cooperation, and inclusion in policymaking. President Kuchma, having brought the state close to collapse under his jurisdiction, would try to strike a balance between the need to consolidate centralized administration in Ukraine and the need to meet the interests of the regions. This, however, is another story that lies beyond the scope of this monograph.

*The Institutional Foundations of Ukrainian Democracy: Power Sharing, Regionalism, and Authoritarianism.* Nataliya Kibita, Oxford University Press. © Nataliya Kibita 2024. DOI: 10.1093/9780191925351.003.0009

# Conclusion

This book started with the observation that viewing late perestroika and the fall of the Soviet Union as the starting point in Ukraine's state building leaves students of independent Ukraine with a number of unposed questions that, if left unasked, would continue preventing scholars from forming an accurate understanding of the key institutional configuration that, along with a number of other factors that came into play after 1991, have been protecting Ukraine from becoming authoritarian. The key configuration of 'weak centre, strong regions' placed Ukraine in a 'league of its own' among post-Soviet states. How did Ukraine find itself in this unique position? Seeking answers to this question in the fall of the Soviet centralized party-state and Ukraine's post-Soviet development does not provide a good sense of the distinct political system in Ukraine. Such an approach does not answer specific questions related to the presidency of Leonid Kravchuk, either. More importantly, treating 1991 as a clean start leaves students of Ukraine with the understanding that including the Ukrainian nation in the autocratic Russian empire interrupted its historical evolution as a liberal and democratic polity, and it was only thanks to Ukraine's historic heritage that the Russian authoritarian interlude did not cause Ukraine to completely abandon democracy and liberalism after the fall of the Soviet Union.

This monograph has shown that the concept of 1991 as a break point for Ukraine is not as solid as conventional thinking suggests. But the insignificance of the fall of the Soviet centralized party-state system for Ukraine's institutional set-up becomes clear only if one deviates from the Moscow-centric interpretation of the Soviet-era history of Ukraine, which focuses on a relationship between Kyiv and Moscow in which Moscow dictates and Kyiv implements, and instead analyses the power of the Ukrainian leadership from what can tentatively be called a republic-centred perspective. As this book has shown, the inclusion of the Ukrainian regions into analyses of the margins of power of the Ukrainian centre reveals that Ukraine had its own specific institutional dynamic, and that this dynamic influenced the post-Soviet transformation to a far greater extent than the collapse of the unitary party-state system.

Of course, the political dynamic in Soviet Ukraine was shaped by the policies and decisions devised in Moscow. However, it was also susceptible to the developments on the ground. From the beginning, it was the decision of the Ukrainian nationalists to create the first all-Ukrainian administrative and political central institution, the Ukrainian Central Rada, and unite all Ukrainian lands into a single polity that proved truly historic. By creating the Central Rada, they initiated a new institutional and political dynamic in Ukraine and in Russia. Ukraine as one polity proved too much of a temptation for the Bolsheviks of Ukraine. They ideologically resented 'bourgeois nationalism' which, as they claimed, motivated Ukrainians to create the Central Rada in the first place, but their resentment of Ukrainian nationalism did not prevent them from realizing and grasping power opportunities that Ukraine as one polity opened to them. Lenin had no choice but to accept the political realities that dictated the survival of Ukraine as a territorial polity created by Ukrainians.

During the genesis of the Soviet party-state system, had Stalin accepted the pleas of Rakovsky and Manuilsky and made the Ukrainian leadership a real power with sufficient authority, resources, and decision- and policymaking powers, the Ukrainian leadership would have been much less vulnerable to pressures from the regions. But he did not. Stalin's reluctance to delegate powers to the Ukrainian leadership and formalize the relationship between the Union centre and the republics exposed the Ukrainian leadership to pressure from below. Deprived of its own tools of repression against regional elites, deprived of control over resources and independent access to information, the Ukrainian republican leadership was forced to cooperate, particularly with the most economically important regions, which maintained a direct relationship with and were directly subordinated to the all-union agencies. The leadership did not cooperate in order to impose its policies, as it did not have any policies of its own. Instead, it had to cooperate to justify its own economic administrative usefulness to the eastern and southern oblasts, as well as to Moscow. As discussed in Chapters 2 and 3, such a justification was particularly pertinent under Stalin's dictatorship. To some degree, as discussed in Chapters 4, 6, and 7, in the context of Khrushchev's and Gorbachev's reforms, the Ukrainian leadership realized that cooperation with the regions allowed it to take an assertive stance as 'the protector of the regions' and justify its demands to Moscow to expand its powers. Besides, as Ukrainian leaders argued in the 1950s and 1960s, and then again during perestroika, expansion of the powers of the Ukrainian leadership was as much in the interest of Moscow, as Moscow was incapable of efficiently running a Soviet economy that stretched over eleven time zones. However, it was only by positioning itself as a 'valuable partner' for the industrialized eastern and southern oblasts that the Ukrainian leadership could make such demands in the first place, as these regions had no objective need for Kyiv's assistance to solve their immediate problems while they maintained a direct relationship with the central party-state apparatus.

The prioritization of heavy industry and, in particular, the uneven distribution of heavy industry that facilitated Moscow's direct and tight control over the most important regions of Ukraine only further reinforced the 'cooperative stance' of the Ukrainian Soviet leadership towards the regions. Throughout its entire existence as a Soviet republican administrative centre, Kyiv had to learn to balance not only between Moscow and the regions as a group, but also between the industrialized and non-industrialized regions. As Chapter 5 illustrated, Petro Shelest, faced with the recentralization of the economy after Khrushchev's removal from power, tried to convince Moscow not to completely curtail the economic rights of the republics by highlighting the Ukrainian leadership's usefulness in balancing regional interests. His successor, Volodymyr Shcherbytsky, as shown in Chapter 6, was not prepared to demand the expansion of republican powers for the purpose of balancing the economic development of the regions, but when Gorbachev's reforms deregulated the economic and political system, he too faced an objective need to perform this balancing act. By 1991, this balancing act, or rather, to be more precise, the need to perform the balancing act inside Ukraine, became part of the political agenda of the Ukrainian central elites that was reflected in political culture. The consensus seeking in late-perestroika Kyiv that has been detected by scholars thus has solid institutional foundations. And yet, as Chapter 7 showed, consensus seeking as an instrument for consolidating the Ukrainian centre was dismissed by the final Ukrainian Soviet leadership. The unique window of opportunity to consolidate the Ukrainian administrative centre based on the support of the regions, as opposed to the 'blessing' from Moscow, was not even examined. Building Ukrainian statehood, which was the priority of the Ukrainian Soviet leadership in 1990–1991, whether it realized it or not, from the bottom up required formal concessions to the regions and cooperation with the regions in policymaking. Kyiv was neither willing nor ready to make any concessions to the Ukrainian regions. Building the Ukrainian statehood bottom-up meant a drastic departure from Soviet state-building practice, which the late Soviet and early post-Soviet Ukrainian leadership was unable to conceive.

As the institutional set-up that determined the relationship between Kyiv and the regions shows, throughout the entire Soviet period, while the Ukrainian leadership wanted Moscow to consolidate its power over the Ukrainian regions and thus enable it to impose its *diktat* over them, Moscow preferred to keep Kyiv institutionally weak. Throughout the entire Soviet period, through its policies and institutions, Moscow did not allow Kyiv's interests to prevail over regional interests. Stalin's successors Khrushchev, Brezhnev, and Gorbachev diligently followed the principle laid out by Stalin and also prevented the Ukrainian leadership from becoming the de facto highest authority in the republic, an authority that would be in a position to 'collude' with the regions against Moscow. (This concern was not without good reason, as Khrushchev learned during the Sovnarkhoz reform.) By following this principle, however, Moscow inadvertently consolidated Ukrainian Soviet statehood from the bottom up, which, of course, was the last thing Moscow wanted to do in any republic. The reasons why the most active Soviet reformers, Khrushchev and Gorbachev, chose to follow Stalin's principles remains beyond the scope of this book. Such an investigation, however, could provide us with a clearer understanding of the constraints that the Soviet leaders faced. (The case of Khrushchev is particularly puzzling. He had first-hand experience of struggling against the super-centralized bureaucracy as the first secretary of Ukraine in 1939–1949. Yet, as highlighted in Chapter 4, he refused to empower Kyiv in the 1950s to enable it to become the de facto main authority for the regions. Gorbachev's reluctance to follow Shcherbytsky's advice at the end of 1988 also deserves further investigation. Whether Shcherbytsky was the only republican leader who urged Moscow to return to the Leninist federalist principles in 1988 is another research question that might interest students of Soviet history.)

Finally, in 1992–1994, when Ukraine became politically independent but remained economically dependent on Russia, the Ukrainian leadership concentrated on accumulating dictatorial powers over the regions. The leadership's old desire to become the single point of communication between the Ukrainian regions and the all-union party-state agencies suggests that in 1992–1994, while in a semi-dependent relationship with Moscow, Kyiv must have felt that it had finally achieved the decentralization it had always dreamt of. What the new executive branch failed to realize, after it shrugged off Moscow's excessive 'supervision', was, firstly, that Ukraine did not have the institutional foundations for authoritarianism, and secondly, that the dominance of the barter economy did not allow it to develop. Deviation from consensus in the direction of authoritarianism in 1992–1994 was practically impossible. Kyiv's refusal to embrace consensus-seeking politics did not mean that the regions would accept Kyiv's *diktat*. Indeed, in the system that they inherited from Soviet Ukraine, regional authorities *could not* accept it. The new executive branch refused to accept reality. Hence by 1994, the attempt to impose *diktat* had brought the Ukrainian state to the brink of destruction.

Neither the choice between *diktat* and cooperation, nor the outcome of this choice, was new. The Ukrainian Soviet leadership always preferred *diktat*, or an authoritarian stance, over consensus, unless, as illustrated in Chapters 2 and 4, there was a threat to its authority, as was the case in 1923 and in 1963–1964. It was at times when Moscow threatened to curtail Kyiv's powers that the Ukrainian leadership reached out to the regions, seeking to cooperate with them and to position itself as a defender of their interests. In 1994, when the survival of the Ukrainian state was threatened, but only after futile efforts to impose its *diktat*, the new Ukrainian executive branch was also ready to make concessions to the regions and cooperate with them.

The bulk of this book contributes to the discussion of the effect of institutions on the behaviour of leaders in the Soviet case.[1] At the same time, for the first time in historiography, the book scrutinizes institutional continuity in a post-Soviet state and demonstrates that Soviet and post-Soviet Ukrainian leaders were susceptible to similar incentives and constraints. The book suggests that ideology had little effect on the power ambitions of Ukrainian Soviet or post-Soviet leaders. It is this author's understanding that even after 1994, institutional constraints and incentives had more effect on Ukrainian central and regional leaders than their ideology. But this remains for future research to substantiate.

It is this author's contention, which remains to be confirmed by future comparative study, that when the Soviet Union collapsed, Ukraine was in a unique position compared to other republics. The uniqueness of Ukraine was not determined by the broken Moscow-centric party-state. Uniqueness was in the balance between the Ukrainian centre and the Ukrainian regions. Regionalism was founded on a fragmented Communist Party of Ukraine and the fact that the obkoms were economic administrators. Russia had obkoms, but it did not have its own central committee. Only four republics, Belorussia, Uzbekistan, Kazakhstan, and Ukraine, had central committees and obkoms.[2] Of these four, Ukraine was the closest economically to Russia, by size and diversification. As David Dyker observed, Ukraine represented a microcosm of the Soviet economy.[3] The behaviour of the regions in Russia and Ukraine was similar in 1990–1993, yet the institutional weight of the regions as a group within their respective new states vis-à-vis their capitals was different. In Ukraine, not only were resources at the disposal of the regions, but there was no single leading region in the industrialized east within the uncoordinated group of regions. While economically weak and industrially inferior, Western Ukraine provided the ideology for the Ukrainian republican leadership to recreate itself and survive the fall of its original source of administrative power, the all-union centre in Moscow.

The configuration 'weak centre, strong regions' that was founded by Ukrainians in 1917 and institutionalized during the Soviet period provided independent Ukraine with a solid basic framework to resist authoritarianism after 1991. Ironically, it was the central leadership of the Soviet Union that, by denying the Ukrainian leadership powers consistent with its functions and by consolidating the Ukrainian regions, left Ukraine with a structural legacy that allowed for the survival of the well-observed tradition of pluralism and political accommodation characteristic of Ukrainian land for centuries.[4] Therefore, from a broad historical perspective, the Soviet period appears to have been not an interruption, but a deviation from Ukraine's centuries-long historic path to democracy and liberalism through space and time. As the post-Soviet transition progressed, a variety of factors, including increasing mass participation in politics and growing civil society, superposed this configuration. Interlinked, they all contributed to Ukraine's slow, sometimes interrupted, but certain path away from authoritarianism and dictatorship towards democracy. In 2013–2014 and then again in 2022, the differences between Russia and Ukraine were laid bare for everyone to see.

It is not for nothing that Ukraine gained the reputation of a republic of regional clans; strong regions were a historical legacy of the centralized Russian and Soviet state imposing control in Ukraine. However, since 1990, instead of capitalizing on the strength of its regions and using regionalism to build a strong, democratic, centralized state, Ukraine allowed the regions to compete for control over the state. Instead of building the Ukrainian state from the bottom up, those groups who held power insisted on building the state top-down. Whereas President Kuchma tried to balance the interests of the regions, President Viktor Yanukovych took this 'top-down' approach to its extreme and tried to impose the dominance of the Donetsk clan over the entirety of Ukraine. Euromaidan in 2013 and the Revolution of Dignity in 2014 were as much a reaction to his pro-Russian choice as they were a reaction to his efforts to build an authoritarian regime founded on one regional clan. Yanukovych's approach to state building was unnatural to Ukraine, and Ukrainians naturally revolted. This political shock, followed by the invasion of Donbas and Crimea by Russia in 2014, unequivocally prompted Ukraine to boost decentralization. The new Ukrainian leadership had finally accepted the long-standing historic configuration of the balance of power between the centre and the regions and proceeded with its formalization. The optimal distribution of power between the centre and the regions is, arguably, yet to be found. It remains to be seen what long-term effect the war that Russia escalated against Ukraine on 24 February 2022 will have on the relationship between the Ukrainian state and its regions. But at the very least, a reversal of the decentralization reforms seems highly unlikely, certainly from the standpoint of December 2022 when this conclusion is being written.

'Much of what has been described as the "change" of a regime into something else', observed Hale, 'actually reflects predictable dynamism within a single regime type.'[5] With a traditional analysis of Ukraine's political development, this might be taken to mean that authoritarianism was a predictable dynamism for Ukraine. The evidence in this book shows, in contrast, that in Ukraine, behind the façade of Soviet authoritarianism, a system incompatible with it was conceived and matured. Despite being fully integrated in the Soviet centralized party-state, Soviet Ukraine was a subject in its own right, even at the 'best times' of totalitarianism and authoritarianism. 'Ukraine is not Russia', said Leonid Kuchma, the second president of Ukraine.[6] Indeed it is not. It never was. And the differences spread beyond culture, language, or historical heritage, as abundant scholarly and popular literature shows. They include the institutional configuration that is at the foundation of the Ukrainian state. This keystone configuration not only allows but forces Ukraine to engage in a hard struggle against Russia's efforts to impose direct control on Ukrainian politics, but also allows Ukraine to lead a 'soft' struggle against Moscow's *diktat* of historical knowledge and memory.[7]

No state is secure from falling into dictatorship, and Ukraine today has yet to build a fully functional democracy with the rule of law, inclusive institutions, a strong economy, a prosperous state and society, and happy citizens. Ukraine has yet to solidify its democratic path. Yet, it has never before seen and perceived this path as clearly as today, at this tragic and critical moment of its history when it is fighting a war against Russia and paying a colossal price for its right to make its own choices.

*The Institutional Foundations of Ukrainian Democracy: Power Sharing, Regionalism, and Authoritarianism.* Nataliya Kibita, Oxford University Press. © Nataliya Kibita 2024. DOI: 10.1093/9780191925351.003.0010

# Notes

## Introduction

1. Way (2015: 8–12); Stoner-Weiss (2006); Fairbanks, Jr (1996: 341–374).
2. Snyder (2005: 5, 6).
3. Casanova (2005).
4. Levitsky and Way (2010: 26–28).
5. Way (2005); Minakov (2019: 233–239); Harasymiw (2002: 35–79); Markov (1993: 35).
6. Diamond (2002: 22, 30); Hale (2015: 4–6); Sedelius (2015).
7. Whitmore (2019: 1478); Hale (2015: 5–6).
8. On national communists, see Haran (2013: 68–69); Kuzio (2000: 181–186).
9. On Russian events, see, for example, Zimmerman (2014: 196–219); Reuter (2017: 74–79); Tucker (1995: 13–27).
10. D'Anieri et al. (1999: 192–195); Way (2015: 53–55); Roeder (1994: 79–80). It would take another five years for Ukraine to adopt its first post-Soviet Constitution. And still, the Constitution of 1996, just like the constitutional agreement from 1995 that preceded it, was the product of compromises between various factions in the Verkhovna Rada and the president. Wolczuk (2001); Whitmore (2005: 8).
11. Smith (2013: 3–4); Prizel (1997: 331, 337); Roeder (1988: 254–257).
12. Wilson (2015: 156–157).
13. Way (2021); Kubicek (2000: 42).
14. Åslund (2013: 32); Prizel (1997: 344).
15. Karmazina (2007: 123).
16. Roeder (1994: 79–80); Karmazina (2007: 128–135, 141–143); Way (2015: 1, 5–6).
17. Brooker (2008); Hale (2015: 130–131); Kubicek (2000: 42–43, 47).
18. Way (2015: 50).
19. Way (2015: 1, 26).
20. McFaul (2010: 192–193); Way (2005: 140–144); Way (2015: 8–15, 39–42, 44, 47–48, 53, 55–56); Hale (2015: 130–132).
21. Herrera (2005: 98–101); Stoner-Weiss (1997: 56–89); Stoner-Weiss (2006); Roeder (2007: 188–199).
22. Moses (2019: 218–220); Hahn (2003: 344–347).
23. Minakov (2012); Minakov (2019: 228–229); Sasse (2010: 102).
24. Quote from Myshlovska et al. (2019: 4). For more, see also Moses (1992); Adamovych (2009: 258–270, 357–429, 533–582, 637–661, 721–817).
25. Sasse (2010); Barrington and Herron (2004); Katchanovski (2006). On regional identity, see, for example, Birch (2000a); Fournier (2002).
26. Kuzio (1997: 8–10, 22–24); Wilson and Bilous (1993: 693); Arel (1990–1991); Potichnyj (1992a).
27. D'Anieri (2011: 31); Whitmore (2004: 32–35); Way (2015: 53).
28. See, for example, Birch (2000b: 1030–1036); Hesli (1995); D'Anieri (2007a); Wolchik and Zviglyanich (2000).
29. Whitmore (2004: 34–35).
30. Minakov (2019: 221).
31. Minakov (2019: 222–224, 227–228).
32. On the ideological splits of the elites, see Åslund (2015: 60–61); Wilson (2015: 174–193); Kuzio (2000: 167–173, 185–188).
33. Minakov (2019: 221, 230–231).
34. Turovsky (1999); Kravchuk (1999); Kuzio (1997: 42–43).
35. D'Anieri et al. (1999: 161–162; see also, fn. 61 on p. 303).
36. Sasse (2010); Minakov (2019: 232–233); Way (2015: 19–22, 45–47, 50–57).
37. Whitmore (2004: 24–36).
38. The historiographic view of Ukraine as one region is based on the view of the Soviet Union as an empire that appoints its governor for each periphery.

39. Accessed on 26 September 2022 at http://www.encyclopediaofukraine.com/display.asp?linkpath=pages%5CK%5CR%5CKravchukLeonid.htm.
40. Kubicek (1999a: 29–30).
41. Wolczuk (1997: 154).
42. Beissinger (2002: 37); Wilson (2015: 161–169, 174–178); Karmazina (2007: 110–115).
43. Kubicek (1999a: 33–34).
44. Wolczuk (1997: 155); Markov (1993: 32–35); Wilson (1999); Motyl (1995: 116–119); Whitmore (2004: 32–33).
45. On the Cossack and Habsburg legacy, see Schmid (2020: 23, 32–40); Hrytsak (2004: 245–247); Plokhy (2015: 58, 100–101, 158–159); Plokhy (2012: 26–27, 32–41, 79–87, 149–152); Kavanagh (1991: 487).
46. Hale (2015: 7).
47. Snyder (2005: 1). See, for example, Beissinger and Kotkin (2014); Kuzio (1998a); Hartwell (2016); Pop-Eleches and Tucker (2017); Minakov et al. (2021); Krylova (2014); Minakov (2019).
48. Minakov (2018); Hale (2015: 4–7, 110–122); Kuzio (2015); Libman and Obydenkova (2021); Leitner and Meissner (2018).
49. Beissinger and Kotkin (2014: 5).
50. Hall (2016); Pierson (2004).
51. Unless specified in the text, 'region' in this study means the administrative units in Ukraine named after anchoring cities: gubernia(s) (1917–1922(23)), okruha(s) (1922(23)–1930(32)), oblast(s), and raion(s) (1932–present), and the autonomous republic of Crimea after February 1991. By 1963, after a number of reorganizations, there were twenty-five oblasts in Ukraine. For more details on the administrative division of Ukraine and the definition of regions (see Map 2), see Myshlovska (2020: 21–27).
52. Nemiria (2000: 185, 188). In the context of Ukraine, regionalism can also be interpreted as regional divisions, or regional diversity based on cultural traditions, ethnic development, language, historical legacy of belonging to different states, level and composition of economic development, urbanization, or demographics. For a detailed overview, see Myshlovska (2020); Schmid and Myshlovska (2019); Kubicek (2002).
53. On the full structure of regional groups, see Minakov (2019: 225–226).
54. Harris (2018); Kushnir (2018); Beissinger and Kotkin (2014).
55. On the Soviet federation, see Slezkine (1994); Martin (2001); Smith (2013); Hirsch (2014). On the centralized system, see Gill and Pitty (1997); Whitefield (1993); Ōgushi (2008).
56. Thelen and Steino (1992: 2).
57. Based on Fioretos et al. (2016: 5); Conran and Thelen (2016).
58. For more on Ukraine as a pluralistic but unstable democracy, see Minakov and Rojansky (2021); Kudelia and Kasianov (2021).
59. North (1990: 4–5); Fioretos et al. (2016: 7–8); Capoccia (2016a: 89–90).
60. North (1990: 6, 89–91, 100–101, 112); Acemoglu and Robinson (2012); Pierson (2004: 11–16, 153–157).
61. Gorlizki and Khlevniuk (2020: 8–9). See also Steinmo (2008: 136); Conran and Thelen (2016: 53–57); North (1990: 112).
62. Gorlizki and Khlevniuk (2020: 5); Gill and Pitty (1997: 45–71).
63. Gorbachev believed Shcherbytsky led Ukraine firmly. Gorbachev (1995: 125–126). This view is also shared by, for example, Kuzio (2000: 43, 48–51); Shapoval and Yakubets (2016); Bilinsky (1983).
64. As quoted in Kuzio (2000: 51).
65. Also known as premier-presidential system. According to Wilson (1999: 260), semi-presidentialism was the optimal political system to adopt in Ukraine because it 'provided an attractive form of political compromise in Ukraine's ethnically, linguistically, and regionally divided society'. For more, see Meleshevich (2007: 144–147).
66. Tucker (1995: 11).
67. Kuzio (2000: 51).
68. Hough (1969: 256–271); Fortescue (1988a: 16–18); Ōgushi (2008: 30–73); Rutland (1993).
69. Kirkow (1998: 30–31); Gorlizki and Khlevniuk (2020: 2–3); Rutland (1993: 49–72).
70. Gorlizki and Khlevniuk (2020); Easter (2000); Khlevniuk (2004: 7–10).
71. Anderson and Boettke (1993: 102). In the literature, this view is examined through the prism of the 'party versus ministries' relationship (Gorlizki 2002; Gregory 2004); or through the prism of 'region versus branch ministry' confrontation (Fortescue 1988a; Harris 1999; Whitefield 1993).
72. Nemiria (2000: 193).
73. Gorlizki and Khlevniuk (2020: 13).
74. Gordon (2000: 122).

75. Stoner-Weiss (2006: 14).
76. Capoccia (2016b: 1098, 1100); Mahoney and Thelen (2010).
77. For the theoretical framework, see Hall (2016).
78. Hough (1969); Armstrong (1959).
79. As argued in Chapter 8, the barter economy was one of the defining factors that influenced early post-Soviet Ukrainian politics.
80. Snyder (2005: 6–7).

## Chapter 1

1. The regions across the Russian Empire saw the February Revolution as an opportunity to reshape centre–periphery relations. Dickins (2019: 227).
2. *Ukraïns'ka Tsentral'na Rada* (1996: 38–39, 44–45, 50–51).
3. Plokhy (2015: 159). See also Rudnytsky (1987: 128–134).
4. Plokhy (2015: 162–167).
5. Konyk (2013: 307–308).
6. *Ukraïns'ka Tsentral'na Rada* (1996: 67).
7. *Ukraïns'ka Tsentral'na Rada* (1996: 74–76, 84); Hrushevsky (1989: 122).
8. *Ukraïns'ka Tsentral'na Rada* (1996: 86–87, 92–93, 99). On 19 May, Kerensky visited the Central Rada and gave an ambiguous comment on the question of Ukraine's autonomy: 'It is necessary to organize a new Russia in the way that would exclude possibilities for deeply sad misapprehensions which might disturb our revolutionary upsurge....I don't know what you mean when you are talking about the autonomy of Ukraine. I can categorically declare that the Provisional Government has the willingness to do everything possible,...and permissible, including everything regarding the autonomy of Ukraine.' *Ukraïns'ka Tsentral'na Rada* (1996: 90–92).
9. Stojko (1977: 4–32).
10. Gol'denveizer (1922: 180–181).
11. For more on the Ukrainian Bolsheviks, see Riga (2012: 123–154).
12. Mace (1983: 21); *VII (Aprel'skaia)* (1958: 212–216, 224–226, 281–283).
13. *VII (Aprel'skaia)* (1958: 217).
14. On Lenin's support for Ukraine's autonomy in 1917, Szporluk (2006: 611–626).
15. TsDAHOU f. 51 op. 1 spr. 9 ark. 5–7.
16. TsDAHOU f. 51 op. 1 spr. 10 ark. 12–14, 94–96.
17. In April, the oblast committee of RSDRP(b) of the south-western region sent invitations to Bolsheviks in seven gubernias: Kyiv, Chernihiv, Podillia, Volyn, Poltava, Kherson, and Katerynoslav. Representatives of only the first four came to the founding meeting. Bosh (1925: 20–21).
18. *Bol'shevistskie organizatsii Ukrainy* (1990: 405, 409–410); also, Borys (1980: 142–145); Sullivant (1962: 30–34).
19. *Bol'shevistskie organizatsii Ukrainy* (1990: 414, 417–418); Soldatenko (2017: 174); *Ukraïns'ka Tsentral'na Rada* (1996: 458).
20. Borys (1980: 143).
21. Soldatenko (2017: 175–176). For an alternative view of Lenin's support for the Ukrainian Bolshevik Party, see, for example, Sullivant (1962: 32).
22. Soldatenko (2017: 176).
23. Velychenko (2015: 45–46).
24. Velychenko (2015: 71).
25. Szporluk (2006: 617).
26. *Ukraïns'ka Tsentral'na Rada* (1996: 456).
27. *Ukraïns'ka Tsentral'na Rada* (1996: 457, 458).
28. Vasiliev (2014: 55); Yefimenko (2008: 48).
29. The text of the ultimatum can be found in Chamberlin (1987: 486–488). The original text of the ultimatum and the answer of the General Secretariat can be found in Bosh (1925: 81–82). For further discussion of the ultimatum, see Pipes (1997: 118–120); Reshetar Jr (1952: 95–96).
30. For earlier efforts of Ukraine's Bolsheviks to adjust to the Ukrainian context, see Borys (1980: 141–143).
31. *Ukraïns'ka Tsentral'na Rada* (1996: 460–475); Khrystiuk (1921: 14–15, 66–67).
32. As Velychenko (2015: 24) established, 'by December 1917, the Bolsheviks did not yet dominate Ukraine's approximately three hundred soviets. In 1917 they controlled the soviets only in the large cities—they were 88 per cent of members in Luhansk, 60 per cent in Kyiv, 48 per cent in Kharkiv, 47 per cent in Katerynoslav, 40 per cent in Odesa.'

33. TsDAHOU f. 1 op. 1 spr. 1 ark. 15; for an alternative interpretation, see Soldatenko (2017: 178–179).
34. TsDAHOU f. 1 op. 1 spr. 1 ark. 13–15; Mace (1983: 24–25).
35. TsDAHOU f. 1 op. 1 spr. 1 ark. 11zv, 12.
36. TsDAHOU f. 1 op. 1 spr. 1 ark. 15zv.
37. TsDAHOU f. 1 op. 1 spr. 1 ark. 16zv.
38. Pipes (1997: 120–122); Borys (1980: 182–184).
39. Kravchenko (2020: 186–187); Friedgut (1994b: 5–42).
40. Yefimenko (2008: 53–57); Khrystiuk (1921: 69); Borys (1980: 182–184, 188–189).
41. The full text of the telegram is in Bosh (1925: 89–90).
42. Cited in *Bol'shevistskoe rukovodstvo* (1996: 30).
43. Vasiliev (2014: 57).
44. Borys (1980: 143–144).
45. Lenin (1970a: 408, n. 26); Ordzhonikidze (1967: 198); Mace (1983: 26–27).
46. *Bol'shevistskie organizatsii Ukrainy* (1990: 522); TsDAVOU f. 1 op. 1 spr. 2 ark. 4.
47. Velychenko (2015: 57).
48. Vasiliev (2014: 57–58); Borys (1980: 191); Ordzhonikidze (1967: 203–205, 207); Lenin (1970a: 22–23, 29, 30, 33, 35, 49–51).
49. *Grazhdanskaia voĭna na Ukraine* (1967: 44–45, 46–48).
50. *Bol'shevistskie organizatsii Ukrainy* (1962: 61–63).
51. Erde (1927: 232–236). See also Borys (1980: 191–193).
52. *Grazhdanskaia voĭna na Ukraine* (1967: 101–102, 762).
53. For more on the workings of the delegation and the financial aspect of the relationship between the Sovnarkom and the People's Secretariat, see Yefimenko (2008: 81–88).
54. TsDAVOU f. 1 op. 1 spr. 7в ark. 57, 64; also Yefimenko (2008: 82–84).
55. Erde (1927: 256); Vasiliev (2014: 61–62).
56. The name of the RSDRP(b) after the Seventh Congress (6–8 March 1918).
57. Erde (1927: 264); Ravich-Cherkasskii (1923: 62).
58. Velychenko (2015: 56, 63).
59. Cited in Yefimenko (2008: 78).
60. Swain (2020: 336–339).
61. Vasiliev (2014: 63).
62. *Bol'shevistskie organizatsii Ukrainy* (1990: 666–667). For more on the competition between the left dominated by the Kyiv Bolsheviks and the right led by the Bolsheviks from Kharkiv and Katerynoslav, see Pipes (1997: 126–136).
63. Vasiliev (2014: 63–64); Pipes (1997: 134–135).
64. Velychenko (2015: 71); Rakovsky (1925: 6).
65. Cited in Wandycz (1969: 66–67).
66. Cited in Wandycz (1969: 66–67).
67. *Dokumenty vneshneĭ politiki* (1959: 566–567); Velychenko (2015: 74, 97); Mace (1983: 31).
68. Adams (1958: 296).
69. Borys (1980: 209).
70. Vasiliev (2014: 68); Mace (1983: 32).
71. *Revoliutsiia na Ukraine* (1930: 409); Adams (1958: 297); Vasiliev (2014: 69); Sullivant (1962: 47).
72. Pipes (1997: 139–140) explains this delay by Lenin's unwillingness to rush a military action in Ukraine, thus linking the Ukrainian Provisional Soviet Government to the invasion.
73. Pipes (1997: 139–140); Adams (1958: 298–305); Borys (1980: 209–212).
74. Zatonsky, as quoted in Adams (1958: 300).
75. Zatonsky (1925: 142–144).
76. Zatonsky (1925: 143).
77. Zatonsky (1925: 147–149); Adams (1958: 305).
78. Adams (1958: 205); Zatonsky (1925: 149).
79. Adams (1958: 305–306).
80. *Leninskiĭ sbornik* (1942: 54).
81. Wandycz (1969: 67).
82. Cited in Kulchytsky (2013: 197).
83. Yefimenko (2008: 109).
84. Graziosi (1992: 136, 137).
85. Kulchytsky (2013: 328).
86. Graziosi (1992: 140, 149–150, 154, 157, 158–159); Soldatenko (2017: 160–162).

87. Soldatenko (2017: 277–279); Martin (2001: 2–3).
88. Kulchytsky (1996: 76–77).
89. Yefimenko (2008: 111–112).
90. Borys (1980: 215–216).
91. For more, see Yefimenko (2008: 142–145).
92. Yefimenko (2012: 70–71, 72).
93. TsDAHOU f. 1 op. 1 spr. 15 ark. 113.
94. TsDAHOU f. 1 op. 1 spr. 15 ark. 119–120, 121–122.
95. TsDAHOU f. 1 op. 1 spr. 15 ark. 138.
96. *V. I. Lenin* (2000: 273).
97. Kulchytsky (1996: 132); Velychenko (2015: 68).
98. Cited in Yefimenko (2008: 145).
99. TsDAHOU f. 1 op. 1 spr. 15 ark. 189, 192zv–193.
100. TsDAHOU f. 1 op. 1 spr. 15 ark. 189–190.
101. Yefimenko (2008: 145).
102. Conte (1989: 149, 150–151).
103. Velychenko (2015: 102).
104. Lenin (1969: 34–35).
105. *V. I. Lenin* (2000: 269–270).
106. Velychenko (2015: 52, 67–68).
107. Swain (2008: 69–88).
108. Yefimenko (2008: 155–156).
109. Lenin (1969: 400–401, 481).
110. RGASPI f. 17 op. 3 d. 11 ll. 5–6.
111. TsDAHOU f. 1 op. 20 spr. 129 ark. 15–16.
112. RGASPI f. 17 op. 3 d. 11 ll. 2–3.
113. Lenin (1970b: 14–15).
114. On 3 March, the Supreme Sovnarkhoz introduced the practice of channelling finances for the Ukrainian commissariats along branch lines through the All-Russian commissariats, as opposed to through the Ukrainian Sovnarkom. Yefimenko (2008: 144).
115. RGASPI f. 17 op. 3 d. 11 l. 3.
116. RGASPI f. 17 op. 3 d. 11 ll. 3, 7, 8.
117. Yefimenko (2012: 73).
118. TsDAHOU f. 1 op. 20 spr. 129 ark. 33.
119. TsDAHOU f. 1 op. 20 spr. 129 ark. 32.
120. Borotbists, Borbists, and Bolsheviks cooperated in Ukraine against Denikin. The anti-peasant Bolshevik policies strained the relationship between the Bolsheviks and the Ukrainian left. In August 1919, the Borotbists formed a Ukrainian Communist Party (Borotbists). On Borotbists and Borbists, see Mace (1983: 53–62); Borys (1980: 263–278).
121. TsDAHOU f. 1 op. 20 spr. 129 ark. 33.
122. RGASPI f. 17 op. 3 d. 20 l. 1; Yefimenko (2012: 77).
123. *Revoliutsiia na Ukraine* (1930: 414); Pipes (1997: 144); Yefimenko (2012: 81 82).
124. On federalists, Pipes (1997: 145–147); Borys (1980: 154–155); Mace (1983: 49–53); their Memorandum from 5 November 1919 in Velychenko (2015: 183–186).
125. TsDAHOU f. 1 op. 20 spr. 23 ark. 18.
126. *The Unknown Lenin* (1996: 76–77).
127. *Vos'maia konferentsiia RKP(b)* (1934: 185); Velychenko (2015: 52).
128. *Vos'maia konferentsiia RKP(b)* (1934: 185–187); *The Unknown Lenin* (1996: 76–77).
129. Vasiliev (2014: 80).
130. *Vos'maia konferentsiia RKP(b)* (1934: 95–96).
131. *Vos'maia konferentsiia RKP(b)* (1934: 95–97).
132. *Vos'maia konferentsiia RKP(b)* (1934: 101–104).
133. *Vos'maia konferentsiia RKP(b)* (1934: 106–107).
134. *Vos'maia konferentsiia RKP(b)* (1934: 110).
135. *V. I. Lenin* (2000: 314).
136. Velychenko (2015: 52).
137. *Nestor Makhno* (2006: 112–113).
138. RGASPI f. 17 op. 3 d. 55 l. 3.
139. Yefimenko (2012: 232–235); Velychenko (2015: 186–189).
140. Croll (2008: 26); *The Unknown Lenin* (1996: 178–180).

141. Croll (2008: 28, 101, 102–103).
142. Borzecki (2019: 657).
143. Yefimenko (2012: 223); Velychenko (2015: 48).
144. RGASPI f. 17 op. 3 d. 62 l. 1; Yefimenko (2012: 235).
145. RGASPI f. 17 op. 3 d. 62 l. 1.
146. Conte (1989: 108, 149, 150–152). The Constitution of the UkSSR that was adopted by the All-Ukrainian Congress of Soviets on 10 March 1919 allowed Ukraine to have relationships with foreign countries. Borzecki (2019: 658).
147. TsDAHOU f. 1 op. 1 spr. 57 ark. 7, 12.
148. TsDAHOU f. 1 op. 1 spr. 57 ark. 13; Yefimenko (2012: 229).
149. Borzecki (2019: 656).
150. *Dokumenty i materialy* (1965: 301–304); Borzecki (2019: 658).
151. *Dokumenty i materialy* (1965: 302, 304).
152. For the Soviet leadership's evaluation of the outcome of the Soviet–Polish War in September 1920, see Croll (2008: 57–60, 131–132, 190–191).
153. *Protokoly Prezidiuma* (2000: 89).
154. From 1919 (formally 1923) until 1934, Kharkiv was the capital of Soviet Ukraine.
155. TsDAHOU f. 1 op. 1 spr. 42 ark. 116; Yefimenko (2012: 140–141).
156. Yefimenko (2012: 290).
157. Yefimenko (2012: 292).
158. Cited in Yefimenko (2012: 292). This was not the first time the Ukrainian Sovnarkom had suggested that Ukraine could print money. At the beginning of May 1919, Rakovsky asked Moscow to allow the Ukrainian Sovnarkom to continue monetary emission, which started in Odesa and Kyiv in January 1919. Moscow refused. Yefimenko (2008: 151–154).
159. Yefimenko (2012: 226, 241, 286–287).
160. TsDAHOU f. 1 op. 1 spr. 28 ark. 53–54.
161. TsDAHOU f. 1 op. 1 spr. 28 ark. 52, 53–54; *Chetverta konferentsiia KP(b)U* (2003: 69–72).
162. TsDAHOU f. 1 op. 1 spr. 42 ark. 173–175, 210.
163. TsDAHOU f. 1 op. 1 spr. 42 ark. 206–207.
164. TsDAHOU f. 1 op. 1 spr. 42 ark. 237.
165. TsDAHOU f. 1 op. 1 spr. 42 ark. 43, 51, 52.
166. TsDAHOU f. 1 op. 1 spr. 42 ark. 50.
167. TsDAHOU f. 1 op. 1 spr. 42 ark. 116.
168. TsDAHOU f. 1 op. 1 spr. 42 ark. 115. On the views of national communists on the nationality policy, see Velychenko (2015: 142–143).
169. Malle (1985: 274, 275).
170. Malle (1985: 275); Velychenko (2015: 63, 67, 68, 92–97).
171. Borzecki (2019: 662–663).
172. Graziosi (1996: 14).

## Chapter 2

1. Kulchytsky (1996: 75–83); Yefimenko (2012: 251–314).
2. For a detailed discussion of Ukrainian politics in the 1920s which are not covered in this chapter, see, for example, Frolov (2003); Frolov (2004); Sullivant (1962: 80–84). For an overview of primary sources on the relations between Ukraine and Russia, see Yefimenko (2015: 307–337).
3. Sullivant (1962: 80).
4. Cited in Kulchytsky (1996: 76).
5. For more, see 'Ukraïnizatsiia' (2003: 33–39); Chernev (2014); Borisënok (2006); Sullivant (1962: 84–148).
6. *Vos'maia konferentsiia RKP(b)* (1934: 185–187); *V. I. Lenin* (2000: 306).
7. TsDAHOU f. 1 op. 6, spr. 13 ark. 6zv–8.
8. *Desyatyi s"ezd RKP(b)* (1963: 204, 205).
9. TsDAHOU f. 1 op. 1 spr. 85 ark. 2, 9.
10. TsDAHOU f. 1 op. 6 spr. 13 ark. 100.
11. TsDAHOU f. 1 op. 6 spr. 13 ark. 100, 109.
12. Yefimenko (2010: 119–159). For broader discussion, see Blank (1994: 65–105); Doroshko (2012: 183–204).
13. For more, see Malle (1985: 396–456); on war communism in Ukraine, see Kulchytsky (1996: 21–158).
14. Gimpelson (2000: 24).

15. Mau (2013: 283–284).
16. Mau (2013: 292–303).
17. On Ukraine's foreign trade in the 1920s, see Conte (1989: 150–173).
18. Gimpelson (2000: 29–32); O'Connor (1992: 173–192).
19. TsDAHOU f. 1 op. 6 spr. 13 ark. 35, 36.
20. TsDAHOU f. 1 op. 1 spr. 80 ark. 3. Narkomfin pursued fiscal centralization throughout 1921. Until the beginning of 1921, the local accounts of the whole of Ukraine were unknown or unavailable to the RSFSR Sovnarkom. Royt (2018: 14, 16, 18). The first post-civil war balance sheet for the state budget of the RSFSR was composed only in April 1921. However, it remains to be researched whether Ukraine was included on this sheet.
21. *Dekrety Sovetskoĭ vlasti* (1999: 169–172).
22. *Dekrety Sovetskoĭ vlasti* (2006: 204–207).
23. Yefimenko (2010: 126).
24. TsDAHOU f. 1 op. 7 spr. 10 ark. 140zv.
25. Cited in Yefimenko (2010: 125).
26. Yefimenko (2010: 125–126).
27. TsDAHOU f. 1 op. 1 spr. 59 ark. 22, 23.
28. TsDAHOU f. 1 op. 7 spr. 13 ark. 3–4zv. Tensions ran high between the Ukrainian Central Committee and the gubkoms regarding the cadre appointments. The Ukrainian Central Committee tried to establish a monopoly. The gubkoms resisted its involvement in their territorial organizations. TsDAHOU f. 1 op. 1 spr. 59 ark. 37; op. 6 spr. 13 ark. 31, 34, 35, 42, 96, 104; op. 7 spr. 10 ark. 3zv, 10, 19, 100zv–101, 103, 148–148zv, 149zv, 150, 153, 154, 160, 173, 173zv.
29. TsDAHOU f. 1 op. 7 spr. 10 ark. 154, 163.
30. TsDAHOU f. 1 op. 1 spr. 59 ark. 27.
31. Pavlova (1993: 64); Gimpelson (2000: 50, 51); Frolov (2004: 213–333).
32. TsDAHOU f. 1 op. 1 spr. 59 ark. 26.
33. TsDAHOU f. 1 op. 1 spr. 59 ark. 8.
34. TsDAHOU f. 1 op. 1 spr. 59 ark. 8, 9.
35. According to the All-Russian TsIK resolution from 30 June 1921, the rights of local economic councils were considerably expanded as well. As periphery organs of the STO, they controlled two-thirds of all nationalized enterprises. *Istoriia Ukrainskoĭ SSR* (1984: 38).
36. TsDAHOU f. 1 op. 1 spr. 59 ark. 52.
37. TsDAHOU f. 1 op. 1 spr. 59 ark. 51; spr. 80 ark. 3, 11, paragraph 6.
38. TsDAHOU f. 1 op. 1 spr. 59 ark. 29, 37, 38, 51–52, 55, 59, 60, 61, 64, 65, 70, 72.
39. TsDAHOU f. 1 op. 1 spr. 59 ark. 51.
40. TsDAHOU f. 1 op. 1 spr. 59 ark. 54.
41. TsDAHOU f. 1 op. 1 spr. 59 ark. 50, 56, 57, 72, 73, 82, 83. On the 1921–1923 famine, see Rudnytskyi et al. (2020).
42. TsDAHOU f. 1 op. 1 spr. 59 ark. 70.
43. TsDAHOU f. 1 op. 1 spr. 59 ark. 58.
44. TsDAHOU f. 1 op. 1 spr. 59 ark. 40, 93.
45. TsDAHOU f. 1 op. 1 spr. 59 ark. 58.
46. The complexities of politics in Donbas in 1921 are explained in great detail by Graziosi (1995: 95–138).
47. Yefimenko (2010: 124).
48. TsDAHOU f. 1 op. 6 spr. 29 ark. 1a–1д; 32zv.
49. Yefimenko (2010: 127).
50. TsDAHOU f. 1 op. 20 spr. 1247 ark. 8.
51. TsDAHOU f. 1 op. 20 spr. 1247 ark. 8zv; Yefimenko (2010: 126–127).
52. TsDAHOU f. 1 op. 20 spr. 1247 ark. 46zv.
53. TsDAHOU f. 1 op. 6 spr. 29 ark. 5в.
54. TsDAHOU f. 1 op. 6 spr. 29 ark. 5б; op. 1 spr. 87 ark. 32.
55. TsDAHOU f. 1 op. 20 spr. 1247 ark. 9zv.
56. TsDAHOU f. 1 op. 20 spr. 1247 ark. 16zv; Chattopadhyay (1986: 47, 123).
57. TsDAHOU f. 1 op. 1 spr. 87 ark. 14, 32, 34, 35; op. 6 spr. 29 ark. 17, 22zv; spr. 31 ark. 136. On foreign trade of Ukrainian cooperatives in the 1920s, see Onipko (2013).
58. TsDAHOU f. 1 op. 6 spr. 29 ark. 22zv.
59. TsDAHOU f. 1 op. 1 spr. 87 ark. 28, 30.
60. TsDAHOU f. 1 op. 6 spr. 29 ark. 30zv, 32, 32zv, 50, 50zv, 51, 59, 61, 76, 78–79, 93zv; Yefimenko (2010: 145–148).

61. TsDAHOU f. 1 op. 6 spr. 29 ark. 5г.
62. TsDAHOU f. 1 op. 1 spr. 87 ark. 16, 30. For more on food rations for the party workers, see Pavlova (1993: 68–69).
63. TsDAHOU f. 1 op. 1 spr. 87 ark. 27; op. 20 spr. 982 ark. 9, 23, 31.
64. TsDAHOU f. 1 op. 20 spr. 982 ark. 24–27zv.
65. TsDAHOU f. 1 op. 1 spr. 87 ark. 8a.
66. TsDAHOU f. 1 op. 1 spr. 87 ark. 3–4, 5zv, 6zv, 7.
67. TsDAHOU f. 1 op. 1 spr. 87 ark. 5zv, 6.
68. TsDAHOU f. 1 op. 1 spr. 87 ark. 6zv.
69. TsDAHOU f. 1 op. 6 spr. 29 ark. 49.
70. Yefimenko (2010: 153–154).
71. *Politburo TsK RKP(b)-VKP(b)* (2000: 175); *TsK RKP(b)-VKP(b) i natsional'nyĭ vopros* (2005: 67–69).
72. *TsK RKP(b)-VKP(b) i natsional'nyĭ vopros* (2005: 68). To protect financing for the Ukrainian offices of the All-Russian commissariats, the Ukrainian Sovnarkom instructed Ukraine's representatives in the Federal Russian–Ukrainian Commission, Frunze, Manuilsky, and Skrypnyk, to secure a provision according to which the RSFSR Narkomfin would automatically transfer 15 percent of the funding that it allocated to the All-Russian commissariats directly to the Ukrainian Sovnarkom. The request would be refused. According to the regulations published in August 1922 about the relationship between the Representative of the RSFSR Narkomfin at the Ukrainian Sovnarkom and the Ukrainian Narkomfin, the budget of Ukraine included only the income/expenses of the republican commissariats. The budget of the Ukrainian offices of the All-Russian commissariats was not included in Ukraine's budget. TsDAHOU f. 1 op. 20 spr. 1247 ark. 61–61zv; Yakubovskaia (1959: 140–141).
73. TsDAHOU f. 1 op. 20 spr. 982 ark. 111zv.
74. TsDAHOU f. 1 op. 6 spr. 36 ark. 129–129zv.
75. TsDAHOU f. 1 op. 20 spr. 982 ark. 121, 133, 137, 139–139zv, 141, 142, 149, 152, 165, 167; spr. 986 ark. 32, 33, 58–58zv, 83; spr. 998 ark. 21, 23; op. 6 spr. 29 ark. 95, 100zv; RGASPI f. 572 op. 1 d. 3 ll. 1, 36; see also, Harris (2005: 68–74).
76. TsDAHOU f. 1 op. 20 spr. 998 ark. 23.
77. In July, the Ukrainian Central Committee forbade the gubkoms from randomly taxing local economic or soviet organs. Instead, it decided to tax all commissariats in Kharkiv. TsDAHOU f. 1 op. 20 spr. 983 ark. 181–181zv; Lyakh (2018: 150–151). The situation in Ukraine was not considerably different from elsewhere in the Soviet Federation. 'To cover the deficit, party committees took loans' and 'resorted to irrevocable seizure of financial means from local budgets'. Dolgikh (2015: 43–46). For more, see also Lyakh (2018: 151–154).
78. Letter from D. Z. Manuilsky to I. V. Stalin (1989: 193-195); TsDAHOU f.1 op. 6 spr. 38 ark. 123–124; op. 1 spr. 112 ark. 113.
79. Stalin did not label this policy as the party-state reform. There were no clearly set deadlines, either, with some measures introduced as early as 1919 and some implemented after 1923. However, the coherence, intensity, and persistence of the measures pursued by Stalin to impose the superiority of the party in state administration allowed Pavlova to qualify these measures as a reform. One of the main elements of the reform was the monopoly of the Central Committee Orgburo and the Secretariat on all important state and party posts at the All-Russian, regional, republican, and gubernia levels through the nomenklatura system.
    Officially, the nomenklatura system would be legitimized in April 1923 with the resolution of the Twelfth Party Congress. On 12 June 1923, the Orgburo established a procedure for selection and appointment of functionaries of the party-state apparatus. Detailing of the nomenklatura system would be continued by Molotov and Kaganovich in 1923–1925. Pavlova (1993: 66–96); Schapiro (1970: 245–255); Gill (1990: 23–50, 121–134, 160–165); Harris (2005: 63–82); Anfert'ev (2017: 58–78). On the power, or lack thereof, of the Central Committee Secretariat over the appointments, see Monty (2012: 169–191).
80. *Vserossiĭskaia konferentsiia* (1922: 1–4, 41).
81. Manuilsky seemed not to be particularly interested in placing the trade unions under party control. Manuilsky considered that the trade unions in Ukraine were in a similarly difficult situation to the party, particularly the trade unions in the metallurgical industry that went through massive worker redundancies in 1921–1922. RGASPI f. 49 op. 1 d. 7 ll. 84–88.
82. RGASPI f. 49 op. 1 d. 9 l. 34; *Vserossiĭskaia konferentsiia R.K.P.(b). Biulleten'* No. 3, 27.
83. Curiously, the Central Committee did not have a copy of the 1919 Constitution of Ukraine. In September 1922, Stalin requested a copy from the Ukrainian Central Committee. TsDAHOU f. 1 op. 20 spr. 983 ark. 95.

84. TsDAHOU f. 1 op. 20 spr. 1063 ark. 20.
85. RGASPI f. 17 op. 3 d. 306 l. 1.
86. RGASPI f. 17 op. 3 d. 306 l. 1; TsDAHOU f. 1 op. 20 spr. 1247 ark. 107zv.
87. Letter from I. V. Stalin to V. I. Lenin, 22 September 1922 (1989: 198–200); *Taĭny natsional'noĭ politiki* (1992: 4–11, 57–58, 107–110); Blank (1994: 176–80); Chattopadhyay (1986: 120–129); Borys (1980: 313–341).
88. RGASPI f. 49 op. 1 d. 9 ll. 34, 67ob; Kulchytsky (1996: 235).
89. TsDAHOU f. 1 op. 20 spr. 983 ark. 36, 37, 79.
90. TsDAHOU f. 1 op. 20 spr. 986 ark. 70, 70zv.
91. TsDAHOU f. 1 op. 20 spr. 982 ark. 167; spr. 983 ark. 130.
92. TsDAHOU f. 1 op. 20 spr. 983 ark. 69; spr. 986 ark. 83.
93. TsDAHOU f. 1 op. 20 spr. 998 ark. 79; op. 1 spr. 92 ark. 5.
94. TsDAHOU f. 1 op. 1 spr. 92 ark. 43.
95. TsDAHOU f. 1 op. 20 spr. 998 ark. 58.
96. TsDAHOU f. 1 op. 20 spr. 983 ark. 77, 181; spr. 998 ark. 94; Lyakh (2018: 154).
97. TsDAHOU f. 1 op. 20 spr. 983 ark. 36, 79.
98. TsDAHOU f. 1 op. 20 spr. 983 ark. 117.
99. TsDAHOU f. 1 op. 20 spr. 982 ark. 167.
100. TsDAHOU f. 1 op. 20 spr. 998 ark. 58.
101. TsDAHOU f. 1 op. 6 spr. 30 ark. 76zv, 79.
102. On 8 October, Frunze informed Lebid that the October Central Committee plenum placed military affairs, roads, postal, and telegraph services, as well as foreign affairs and foreign trade, under the centralized administration of the relevant all-union commissariats. The plenipotentiaries of these commissariats would exist in each republic. Land affairs, justice, internal affairs, social security, education, and health services would be exclusively under the management of the republican governments. Commissariats for food, finances, and labour, and the sovnarkhozy would exist in the republics 'with the obligation to implement the directives of the centre'. TsDAHOU f. 1 op. 6 spr. 38 ark. 133.
103. TsDAHOU f. 1 op. 1 spr. 92 ark. 1–2, 46, 73.
104. TsDAHOU f. 1 op. 1 spr. 92 ark. 45. At the Twelfth RKP(b) Conference, Molotov explained the difference between 'the oblast party committees, to which belongs, for example, the Central Committee [of the Ukrainian] Communist Party' and the oblast buros. The former reported to the oblast party conferences, whereas the latter 'were fully subordinated directly to the Central Committee of the Party' (RKP(b)). *Vserossiĭskaia konferentsiia* (1922: 27).
105. TsDAHOU f. 1 op. 6 spr. 39 ark. 42.
106. Pavlova (2001: 54).
107. TsDAHOU f. 1 op. 20 spr. 998 ark. 85.
108. TsDAHOU f. 1 op. 20 spr. 998 ark. 95.
109. Lack of trust in the republican leadership was not limited to Ukraine. At the Twelfth Party Congress in April 1923, Filipp Makharadze from the Georgian organization accused the Central Committee of not trusting local comrades who had worked for a long time in the revolutionary movement to implement central directives, and asked Stalin to clarify whether the Central Committees of the republics 'had the right of initiative and the right to discuss certain Central Committee resolutions if local conditions required revision or temporary suspension of these resolutions'. *Dvenadtsatyĭ s"ezd RKP(b)* (1968: 173–174). For more, see Smith (2005: 59–60).
110. TsDAHOU f. 1 op. 6 spr. 30 ark. 98; op. 20 spr. 986 ark. 93, 93zv, 101, 179; op. 7 spr. 24 ark. 46; spr. 1063 ark. 1, 29, 31, 86–108.
111. TsDAHOU f. 1 op. 6 spr. 30 ark. 85zv; op. 20 spr. 983 ark. 158, 237; spr. 998 ark. 94.
112. TsDAHOU f. 1 op. 20 spr. 983 ark. 181; op. 6 spr. 38 ark. 142.
113. TsDAHOU f. 1 op. 20 spr. 983 ark. 179, 248.
114. TsDAHOU f. 1 op. 20 spr. 983 ark. 181–181zv.
115. TsDAHOU f. 1 op. 20 spr. 983 ark. 237.
116. TsDAHOU f. 1 op. 6 spr. 30 ark. 97.
117. TsDAHOU f. 1 op. 20 spr. 998 ark. 101.
118. Pavlova (2001: 59).
119. Pavlova (2001: 53).
120. TsDAHOU f. 1 op. 20 spr. 1637 ark. 32–33.
121. TsDAHOU f. 1 op. 1 spr. 100 ark. 117–118.
122. TsDAHOU f. 1 op. 1 spr. 100 ark. 19–21.
123. TsDAHOU f. 1 op. 1 spr. 100 ark. 10–11, 94–95, 128, 129.

124. TsDAHOU f. 1 op. 1 spr. 100 ark. 129; spr. 101 ark. 103.
125. TsDAHOU f. 1 op. 1 spr. 100 ark. 10–11, 134.
126. TsDAHOU f. 1 op. 1 spr. 100 ark. 139.
127. TsDAHOU f. 1 op. 1 spr. 100 ark. 138, 139.
128. TsDAHOU f. 1 op. 1 spr. 100 ark. 118, 136.
129. TsDAHOU f. 1 op. 1 spr. 100 ark. 47.
130. TsDAHOU f. 1 op. 1 spr. 101 ark. 101, 191–192, 197, 202.
131. That Ukrainization was viewed as serving specifically the Ukrainian government was indirectly indicated by Stalin. On the one hand, at the Tenth Party Congress, he insisted that 'the Ukrainian nationality exists and it [was] the communist duty to develop it'. *Protokoly X s"ezda RKP(b)* (1933: 216). However, he did not show as much zeal in forcing the Ukrainian gubkoms to perform this 'duty', as he showed in forcing them to report directly and regularly to the Central Committee. Only in the spring of 1923, after he established centralized control over the Ukrainian gubkoms and was half-way to defeating Rakovsky's autonomy project, and even more so, in 1925, when the Ukrainian republican centre lost any meaningful authority and Stalin needed to increase the authority of the Ukrainian Central Committee, did he make an explicit and clear effort to enforce Ukrainization on the Ukrainian periphery apparatus, not least by appointing Kaganovich. For more on Ukrainization, see Liber (1991: 15–23); Perri (2014: 131–154); 'Ukraïnizatsiia' (2003); Palko (2020: 163–171).
132. TsDAHOU f. 1 op. 1 spr. 100 ark. 85.
133. *Dvenadtsatyĭ s"ezd RKP(b)* (1968: 672); Pavlova (2001: 60).
134. Pavlova (1993: 71–73).
135. *Dvenadtsatyĭ s"ezd RKP(b)* (1968: 55–69).
136. The issue of the budgetary rights of the Ukrainian government was brought up by Frunze at the meeting of the congress section on the nationality question, 25 April 1923. Stalin accepted Frunze's suggestion. *XII s"ezd RKP(b)* (1991: 171–172).
137. *XII s"ezd RKP(b)* (1991: 168); *Dvenadtsatyĭ s"ezd RKP(b)* (1968: 482).
138. *Dvenadtsatyĭ s"ezd RKP(b)* (1968: 65).
139. TsDAHOU f. 1 op. 1 spr. 112 ark. 11, 109zv; op. 20 spr. 1698 ark. 5–8.
140. Gill (1990: 246).
141. Confederalism in its meaning of 'independence' was an accusation thrown at Rakovsky and Skrypnyk by Stalin. According to Frolov, Stalin's accusation of confederalism had political, 'not real meaning. In other words, these accusations were groundless.' Frolov (2004: 210).
142. TsDAHOU f. 1 op. 1 spr. 112 ark. 2zv–3.
143. TsDAHOU f. 1 op. 1 spr. 112 ark. 2zv–3.
144. Frolov (2004: 199).
145. Frolov (2004: 209).
146. Yugostal', State South metallurgical trust of the Supreme Sovnarkhoz, existed from autumn 1921 until beginning of 1930. Yugomashtrest, State South machine-construction trust of the Ukrainian Sovnarkhoz, was formed in 1922. On trusts in Ukraine, see Hrynchuts'kyi (1997).
147. TsDAHOU f. 1 op. 20 spr. 1648 ark. 122; Frolov (2004: 204–205).
148. TsDAHOU f. 1 op. 20 spr. 1639 ark. 102.
149. TsDAHOU f. 1 op. 20 spr. 1648 ark. 168, 174, 206; spr. 1637 ark. 39; Frolov (2004: 205); Cheberiako (2012a: 350–362).
150. In December 1924, the central Politburo, based on the STO decision, decided to form a special fund for the Commissariat of Railways to regulate its financial relationship with metallurgical industry and enable timely payment of salaries. At the same time, the Central Committee delegated the power to enforce timely payments of salaries to the Supreme Sovnarkhoz, not the republican governments or republican sovnarkhozy. TsDAHOU f. 1 op. 20 spr. 1828 ark. 136; spr. 1920 ark. 119; spr. 1925 ark. 140zv, 143, 143zv; RGASPI f. 17 op. 3 d. 480 ll. 3, 10.
151. TsDAHOU f. 1 op. 1 spr. 118 ark. 149, 152.
152. Despite the pleas from both the Ukrainian Central Committee and the Donbas local authorities, on 9 April 1925, Moscow raised prices for workers in Donbas by 1 kopeck. Bread prices in Moscow, Leningrad, and some other workers' centres had been kept the same. Curiously, on 7 April, at the Ukrainian Central Committee plenum, the newly appointed General Secretary of Ukraine, Lazar Kaganovich, expressed certainty that 'the Central Committee will take measures to preserve prices of bread in workers' regions of Ukraine no matter what, because it is clear that the increase of bread prices would lead to the increase of other prices and the reduction of [the real] salary'. On 10 April 1925, the Ukrainian Politburo chaired by Kaganovich had already

'considered and implemented' Moscow's instruction about the increase of bread prices in Donbas. TsDAHOU f. 1 op. 1 spr. 158 ark. 123–124; op. 6 spr. 60 ark. 13zv, 27zv, 59; RGASPI f. 17 op. 3 spr. 496 ark. 3.

153. TsDAHOU f. 1 op. 1 spr. 118 ark. 312, 374–376.
154. TsDAHOU f. 1 op. 1 spr. 153 ark. 243; op. 6 spr. 60 ark. 5; f. 237 op. 1 spr. 4 ark. 101.
155. TsDAHOU f. 1 op. 6 spr. 60 ark. 21; op. 1 spr. 158 ark. 11, 102.
156. TsDAHOU f. 1 op. 1 spr. 153 ark. 6, 26.
157. TsDAHOU f. 1 op. 1 spr. 153 ark. 263; spr. 158 ark. 109.
158. TsDAHOU f. 1 op. 1 spr. 153 ark. 263–264.
159. TsDAHOU f. 1 op. 1 spr. 153 ark. 260, 263.
160. TsDAHOU f. 1 op. 1 spr. 118 ark. 282, 229.
161. TsDAHOU f. 1 op. 1 spr. 158 ark. 93, 136.
162. V. Khramov, writing at the time, qualified these gubernias as 'weak', with their budgets of between 2 and 4 million roubles in 1923–1924. 'Strong' gubernias were Kyiv, Odesa, and Kharkiv with 20–24 million roubles; 'middle' gubernias were Poltava, Donetsk, and Katerynoslav with budgets of between 10 and 13 million roubles. Cheberiako (2012b: 148).
163. Alternative currencies circulated in other cities, such as Donetsk, as well. TsDAVOU f. 1 op. 2 spr. 2187 ark. 6–8zv; TsDAHOU f. 1 op. 20 spr. 1812 ark. 16, 46.
164. For more, see Oliinyk (2015: 104–131, 175–247).
165. TsDAHOU f. 1 op. 1 spr. 153 ark. 173; RGASPI f. 17 op. 163 d. 467 l. 25.
166. TsDAHOU f. 1 op. 1 spr. 153 ark. 263–264.
167. TsDAHOU f. 1 op. 1 spr. 153 ark. 264.
168. TsDAHOU f. 1 op. 6 spr. 60 ark. 42; Frolov (2002: 70–79); Doroshko (2003: 92–103); Rees (2012: 61–62).
169. That the decision was not Stalin's and that *trotskyism* might not have been the primary cause for his removal is suggested by the decision of the central Politburo meeting on 14 April 1925. In Stalin's presence and with his approval, while 'not objecting' to removing Kviring from Ukraine, the central Politburo 'pointed out to the Ukrainian Central Committee that before removing Kviring, it should have consulted the Central Committee'. Then, the central Politburo immediately accepted the suggestion of Dzerzhinsky to appoint Kviring the second vice-chairman of the Supreme Sovnarkhoz. RGASPI f. 17 op. 3 d. 497 l. 6; op. 163 d. 484 l. 47.
170. On the NEP in Ukraine, see Kulchytsky (1996: 161–367); Pyrih (2001); Somchynsky (1988: 52–69).
171. TsDAHOU f. 1 op. 1 spr. 158 ark. 114, 145, 152. For more, see Pauly (2018).
172. For more, see Brovkin (2005: 57–80); Anfert'ev (2017: 93–119); Hudson (2012: 34–57).
173. TsDAHOU f. 1 op. 1 spr. 118 ark. 93, 238; spr. 158 ark. 120; op. 20 spr. 1920 ark. 5, 6; spr. 1925 ark. 1; spr. 1971 ark. 23.
174. TsDAHOU f. 1 op. 1 spr. 153 ark. 160, 183.
175. At the end of 1924, the party and state apparatus in Ukraine regularly used administrative measures against private traders. Stalin described the practice as equivalent to banning and destroying private trade, issuing a circular on 19 December 1924 that confirmed the directive of the Thirteenth Party Congress on domestic trade. RGASPI f. 558 op. 11 d. 32 l. 138.
176. TsDAHOU f. 1 op. 1 spr. 158 ark. 26, 40, 131, 132, 133.
177. Apart from the Unified State Political Administration (OGPU), which regularly informed Stalin on the situation in the country, Stalin could hear about the party's difficulties in the countryside from Kviring himself, whom Stalin saw twice before replacing him with Kaganovich, and/or from the chairman of the Ukrainian TsIK, Petrovsky, who visited Stalin on the same days as Kviring, 23 February and 16 March; and/or Chubar on 16 March. *Na priëme u Stalina* (2010: 749, 751); Hudson (2012).
178. RGASPI f. 17 op. 163 d. 484 ll. 27, 28–31.
179. RGASPI f. 17 op. 3 d. 425 l. 6.
180. RGASPI f. 17 op. 3 d. 426 l. 5.
181. TsDAHOU f. 1 op. 1 spr. 118 ark. 223.
182. TsDAHOU f. 1 op. 1 spr. 153 ark. 13, 14; spr. 158 ark. 20, 23,103, 129–130; op. 6 spr. 60 ark. 58; op. 20 spr. 1971 ark. 23.
183. TsDAHOU f. 1 op. 1 spr. 158 ark. 128.
184. TsDAHOU f. 1 op. 1 spr. 118 ark. 94, 100–105.
185. At the Eighth CP(b)U Conference in May 1924, the gubkom secretaries refused to pass the December 1923 Central Committee regulation that required the gubkoms to hold elections every six months and rejected the Ukrainian Central Committee resolution prepared on

Molotov's instruction. The removals, not sanctioned by either the Ukrainian Central Committee or the Central Committee, and the appointments of the gubkom secretaries were viewed as a sign of a 'healthy organization' that practised democracy. TsDAHOU f. 1 op. 1 spr. 118 ark. 380–381; spr. 153 ark. 14.

186. TsDAHOU f. 1 op. 6 spr. 60 ark. 42.

187. TsDAHOU f. 1 op. 1 spr. 158 ark. 24–25, 28, 33, 85–86. In absence of capital, goods, or consistent instructions, the gubkoms did not feel compelled to report to the Ukrainian Central Committee 'on what the gubkoms and the [gubernia] cooperation boards [*kooperatsoveshchaniia*] did to implement the [January 1925] resolutions on cooperation'. TsDAHOU f. 1 op. 1 spr. 158 ark. 102.

188. TsDAHOU f. 1 op. 1 spr. 158 ark. 12, 127. In accordance with the all-union policy, the resolution of the Ukrainian Politburo from 13 October 1925 instructed the State Bank to finance fully any agent that was procuring agricultural raw materials for industry, including non-centralized cooperatives, private trade, and private industry. TsDAHOU f. 1 op. 6 spr. 59 ark. 39; spr. 76 ark. 1zv.

189. Gill (1990: 113–198).

190. Anfert'ev (2016: 119).

191. RGASPI f. 17 op. 3 d. 416 ll. 1–2; d. 476 l. 2.

192. TsDAHOU f. 1 op. 1 spr. 118 ark. 288.

193. Gill (1990: 123).

194. In January 1924, the Ukrainian Central Committee reprimanded the secretary of the Katerynoslav gubkom, V. Ivanov, for 'practically failing to explain the extent to which the gubkom influenced the development of industry'. TsDAHOU f. 1 op. 20 spr. 1920 ark. 33.

195. RGASPI f. 558 op. 1 d. 2411 ll. 1–3.

196. RGASPI f. 17 op. 163 d. 459 ll. 25ob, 26.

197. RGASPI f. 17 op. 163 d. 459 l. 26.

198. TsDAHOU f. 1 op. 1 spr. 118 ark. 142.

199. The central leadership relied on local party apparatus to collect taxes, procure grain, implement the currency reform, and so on. The implementation of central policies was framed as a campaign, not least because of their ad hoc character and the lack of funds for their implementation. The central leadership relied on the enthusiasm of local party members to implement these campaigns. TsDAHOU f. 1 op. 1 spr. 118 ark. 122; RGASPI f. 558 op. 1 d. 2484 ll. 1–18; f. 17 op. 3 d. 422 l. 6.

200. TsDAHOU f. 1 op. 20 spr. 1925 ark. 4, 5, 69.

201. This circular followed a discussion of Piatakov's complaint that the Omsk gubkom had issued a resolution ordering the salt syndicate, Solesindikat, in Omsk to contribute 300 roubles to a peasant organization. The central Politburo found this resolution unlawful and ordered the Omsk gubkom to return the money. RGASPI f. 17 op. 163 d. 459 ll. 25–25ob.

202. RGASPI f. 17 op. 3 d. 720 l. 1; d. 768 l. 11.

203. TsDAHOU f. 1 op. 1 spr. 153 ark. 65; op. 20 spr. 1971 ark. 17.

204. TsDAHOU f. 1 op. 1 spr. 158 ark. 37, 69.

205. In the industrialized areas, the party committees tried not to completely ignore their controlling function, although they often assigned the role of controller to the trade unions and instructed them 'to be careful to avoid a tendency of permanent bickering between the trade unions and the managers'. TsDAHOU f. 1 op. 20 spr. 1925 ark. 126–126zv. For more, see Chase (1986: 149–185).

206. TsDAHOU f. 1 op. 20 spr. 1925 ark. 13, 73–74.

207. TsDAHOU f. 1 op. 20 spr. 1925 ark. 76, 78, 80.

208. TsDAHOU f. 1 op. 20 spr. 1925 ark. 73–74.

209. RGASPI f. 17 op. 3 d. 460 l. 2.

210. TsDAHOU f. 1 op. 20 spr. 1925 ark. 74–75.

211. Werth (1977: 341–355).

212. TsDAHOU f. 1 op. 6 spr. 60 ark. 21zv.

213. TsDAHOU f. 1 op. 20 spr. 1828 ark. 216.

214. TsDAHOU f. 1 op. 1 spr. 153 ark. 25, 42, 55.

215. TsDAHOU f. 1 op. 6 spr. 76 ark. 259. According to Belova and Lazarev (2012: 39–67), state subsidies to the party faded by the mid-1960s, when the party was able to generate nearly 90 percent of its revenue. By 1991, the party had created a reserve fund of some 2 billion roubles.

216. Prylutskyi (2004: 101, 110). According to Kulchytsky (2015: 28), heavy industry in Ukraine received 86.7 percent of all investments allocated to the republic during the NEP.

217. TsDAHOU f. 1 op. 1 spr. 158 ark. 137; op. 20 spr. 1812 ark. 50zv, 53–55; spr. 1943 ark. 32zv, 43.

218. TsDAHOU f. 1 op. 20 spr. 1662 ark. 8–9.

219. TsDAHOU f. 1 op. 20 spr. 1812 ark. 56; spr. 1920 ark. 7; spr. 1925 ark. 69, 131, 133–133zv.

220. Before the 1917 revolution, Podillia accounted for 10 percent of all Ukrainian industry. Podillia did not have large industrial enterprises. By December 1925, when the central leadership announced its course towards industrialization, the industry of the Podillia gubernia had been restored to about 50 percent of its pre-First World War level. Much of the investment allocated to the region during industrialization was directed towards restoring the pre-war industrial base. Oliinyk (2015: 175, 196–197, 207–208).
221. Osokina (1999: 147–148).
222. RGASPI f. 17 op. 3 d. 487 l. 3.
223. TsDAHOU f. 237 op. 1 spr. 4 ark. 259.
224. TsDAHOU f. 237 op. 1 spr. 4 ark. 259.
225. TsDAHOU f. 1 op. 6 spr. 59 ark. 27zv. In 1932, the territorial administrative units were again enlarged. Ukraine was divided into six oblasts, Kharkiv, Kyiv, Odesa, Dnipropetrovsk, Vinnytsia, and Donetsk. For more on regionalization in Ukraine, see Kulchytsky (2015: 9–11).

## Chapter 3

1. Rees (2001: 52).
2. Swain (2016: 36–37).
3. Gregory and Harrison (2005: 721–761).
4. In the earlier period, observes Thomas Rigby (1981: 7), personalized networks were often formed from 'trusted and readily available revolutionaries eager to give loyal service to the precarious regime'.
5. Rigby (1981: 7–9).
6. Lewin (2003: 219–251).
7. On the institutional weaknesses of the Soviet Communist Party, see Getty (1985); Gill (1990); Khlevniuk (1996).
8. Rees (2004a: 19–58); Rees (2004b: 200–239); Wheatcroft (2004: 79–107).
9. See, for example, Lynne et al. (2005).
10. Davies et al. (1994: 6–8).
11. Boterbloem (1999: 259–260); Gregory and Harrison (2005: 748).
12. Tikhonov and Gregory (2001: 175).
13. Rees (2001: 35–60); Carr and Davies (1969–[1978]: 353–355).
14. Westlund (1998: 214). For more on the regional policy, see Dunmore (1980a: 26–94); Pallot and Shaw (1981).
15. Tikhonov and Gregory (2001: 191).
16. Lenin (1970b: 287).
17. Davies et al. (1994: 136–137).
18. Kaplan (1983: 3); *TsK VKP(b) i regional'nye komitety* (2004: 6); Armstrong (1959: 61).
19. Mokhov (2003: 12).
20. Kaplan (1983: 3); Hough (1969: 2–3); Rigby (1964: 546).
21. Harris (2018: 3–4); Lewin (2003: 228–238).
22. Harris (2018: 2–3).
23. Dunmore (1984: 10–41); Rees and Watson (1997: 9–31). On the party's 'depolitisation' and 'economization', see Lewin (2003: 228–238, 250 251); Hough (1969: 102, 107).
24. Khrushchev (2006: 14).
25. Kirkow (1998: 30–31); Armstrong (1959: 68).
26. Siroshtan et al. (1967: 40–41).
27. On lobbying, see Boterbloem (1999); Stotland (2015: 353–354, 357–362); Armstrong (1959: 68); Khlevniuk (2004: 7–10). For documentary evidence, see *TsK VKP(b) i regional'nye komitety* (2004: 319–384).
28. On informal politics and personalized political groups in the Soviet system, see Rigby (1981); Miller (1989: 54–69); Gill (1990); Willerton (1992); Hughes (1996: 551–568); Harris (1999: 146–190 in particular); Easter (2000); Getty (2013); Khlevniuk (2004: 1–17).
29. On the persistence of personalized politics in Russia, see Getty (2013: 9–11).
30. TsDAHOU f. 1 op 1 spr. 158 ark. 212, 213; Rees (2012: 64).
31. Rees (2012: 61–63).
32. TsDAHOU f. 1 op. 20 spr. 2031 ark. 1–2.
33. TsDAHOU f. 1 op. 20 spr. 2031 ark. 2.
34. TsDAHOU f. 1 op. 20 spr. 2031 ark. 2–3. According to Robert Davies (1958: 309), 'from 1926 onwards, 99 percent of the income tax, industrial tax, and agricultural tax collected on the territory of each republic was transferred to its own revenue'.
35. TsDAHOU f. 1 op 20 spr. 2031 ark. 3.

36. TsDAHOU f. 1 op 20 spr. 2031 ark. 3.
37. TsDAHOU f. 1 op 20 spr. 2031 ark. 4.
38. TsDAHOU f. 1 op. 6 spr. 59 ark. 26–27; Rees (2012: 65).
39. Cheberiako (2011: 49).
40. TsDAHOU f. 1 op. 1 spr. 174 ark. 129–131, 183.
41. TsDAHOU f. 1 op. 1 spr. 174 ark. 133–134.
42. TsDAHOU f. 1 op. 1 spr. 174 ark. 141–142, 152–153, 154–155, 156, 167.
43. TsDAHOU f. 1 op. 1 spr. 174 ark. 182–186.
44. TsDAHOU f. 1 op. 1 spr. 174 ark. 147–148, 176–177.
45. TsDAHOU f. 1 op. 1 spr. 174 ark. 114, 119–124, 187–197, 201–202.
46. TsDAHOU f. 1 op. 20 spr. 1639 ark. 100–118.
47. TsDAHOU f. 1 op. 20 spr. 1639 ark. 114, 117, 118.
48. Sokyrska (2019: 154–155).
49. Davies (1958: 81, 84).
50. Sokyrska (2019: 155).
51. At the June 1926 plenum of the Ukrainian Central Committee, the Ukrainian leadership expressed the intent to extend Ukrainization beyond culture and education, to include the army, urban proletariat, and territorial administrative structure. The programmes it developed intended 'to increase the regional attachments of these important groups and to diminish their identification with the Union as a whole'. Sullivant (1962: 113–114).
52. Cheberiako (2012c: 91); on centralization, see Carr and Davies (1969–[1978]: 360–369).
53. Carr and Davies (1969–[1978]: 353–355).
54. Carr and Davies (1969–[1978]: 368).
55. For more, see Vasil'ev (2014: 167–172); Rees (2012: 72–75).
56. Rees (2012: 73); Rassweiler (1988: 35).
57. Vasil'ev (2014: 173–176).
58. Davies (1958: 300).
59. Cheberiako (2011: 50); Cheberiako (2012c: 96).
60. For purges at the end of the 1930s in Ukraine, see Doroshko (2012: 329, 336, 339, 354).
61. Of the three leaders, it is on Khrushchev's leadership style that the literature is not unanimous. According to such scholars as Lozytsky (2005: 82–83), Khrushchev was an authoritarian leader. Geoffrey Swain (2016) has a less categorical view. As he argued in a conversation with this author, 'Khrushchev was at the less arbitrary end of an arbitrary system'; 'Khrushchev's style was authoritarian when applying a policy, but he was prepared for a discussion before a policy was adopted'. Kaganovich and Melnikov were less prone to consultations. Rees (2012: 79); Lozytsky (2005: 87, 93–94).
62. Cheberiako (2012c: 93–94); Cheberiako (2011: 50).
63. Davies (1958: 299).
64. On republican funds, see Davies (1958: 310–311).
65. RGASPI f. 17 op. 3 d. 883 l. 10.
66. RGASPI f. 17 op. 3 d. 882 l. 9.
67. Liber (2016: 136).
68. RGASPI f. 17 op. 3 d. 877 l. 5.
69. On restoration of the Ukrainian economy after the war, see Smolii (2011: 366–405).
70. Lanovyk (2006: 431).
71. Tomilina (2009a: 123–124).
72. TsDAHOU f. 1 op. 24 spr. 718 ark. 101–103, 104–110.
73. For more, see Satskyi (2017: 181–182).
74. RGASPI f. 17 op. 3 d. 937 l. 44; Vasil'ev (2004: 175).
75. Taubman (2003: 125).
76. Cited in Lozytsky (2005: 89).
77. Gregory and Harrison (2005: 735).
78. Liber (2016: 136).
79. For a detailed discussion on the oversight of Ukrainian agriculture on the part of the central leadership, see Vasil'ev (2014: 252–285).
80. Doroshko (2012: 330–331); Gill (1990: 211).
81. Vasil'ev (2014: 256–257); RGASPI f. 17 op. 3 d. 912 ll. 8, 44; d. 929 l. 27.
82. Khrushchev (2006: 5).
83. For more, see Swain (2016: 47–49); Taubman (2003: 199–203).
84. The Holodomor of 1932–1933 is one of the most researched episodes of Ukraine's history. To name a few studies, see Kulchytsky (2018); Rudnytskyi et al. (2020); Graziosi, Haida and Hryn (2013).

85. RGASPI f. 17 op. 3 d. 912 l. 25; TsDAHOU f. 1 op. 24 spr. 718 ark. 98–99, 285–286.
86. RGASPI f. 17 op. 3 d. 946 l. 25; d. 948 l. 16.
87. TsDAHOU f. 1 op. 24 spr. 716 ark. 78; spr. 718 ark. 193; spr. 721 ark. 204–205.
88. For documentary evidence, see *Ukrainskie natsionalisticheskie organizatsii* (2012: 600–603, 613–624, 731–735, 846–849).
89. *Politicheskoe rukovodstvo Ukrainy* (2006: 68–69).
90. *Politicheskoe rukovodstvo Ukrainy* (2006: 136–137). On 30 March 1953, the Ukrainian leadership would ask Khrushchev to abolish this commission in order to increase the responsibility of the ministries for economic and cultural construction in Western Ukraine. TsDAHOU f. 1 op. 24 spr. 3473 ark. 141.
91. TsDAHOU f. 1 op. 24 spr. 718 ark. 6–12, 13–31, 32–35.
92. RGASPI f. 17 op. 3 d. 733 l. 5–6; TsDAHOU f. 1 op. 24 spr. 716 ark. 57–59, 128–129, 162, 168, 178, 185–186; spr. 721 ark. 9–10, 31.
93. RGASPI f. 17 op. 3 d. 928 ll. 15, 16.
94. For a discussion of the powers of the Ukrainian Politburo in the 1930s, see Vasil'ev (2004: 168–199).
95. Mobilization of local resources was particularly relevant after the war. Tomilina (2009a: 180–181, 200–202, 245–251).
96. *Politicheskoe rukovodstvo Ukrainy* (2006: 150–151).
97. *The Stalin-Kaganovich Correspondence* (2003: 152). For more on the resistance of the Ukrainian leadership, the Ukrainian periphery apparatus, and Ukrainian peasantry to the grain procurement targets in summer 1932, see Vasil'ev (2014: 227–257, 266–285).
98. On Khrushchev's leadership in Ukraine, see Swain (2016: 47–51).
99. RGASPI f. 17 op. 3 d. 787 l. 3; TsDAHOU f. 1 op. 24 spr. 721 ark. 240–244.
100. TsDAHOU f. 1 op. 1 spr. 293 ark. 194, 195, 197–199, 202–203.
101. TsDAHOU f. 1 op. 1 spr. 293 ark. 210.
102. Khlevniuk (2004: 11–12).
103. RGASPI f. 572 op. 2 d. 23 ll. 101–125ob.
104. RGASPI f. 17 op. 3 d. 925 l. 19; d. 929 l. 8–9; d. 930 l. 26; d. 943 l. 17; Khlevniuk (2004: 9).
105. RGASPI f. 17 op. 3 d. 738 ll. 3, 12–14; d. 799 l. 18; d. 842 ll. 5, 19–26; d. 932 l. 28.
106. Westlund (1998: 237).
107. Kulchytsky (2015: 28–29).
108. Liber (2016: 135).
109. Amar (2015: 185, 186, 188).
110. Kubijovyc (1969: 780).
111. Liber (2016: 267).
112. Rodgers (1974: 229).
113. Kubijovyc (1969: 777).
114. In 1933, the Kharkiv enterprises organized 327 stationary and 208 mobile shops for repairing agricultural machinery. In the Volyn oblast, 96 enterprises, organizations, and administrations provided *shefstvo* to kolkhozy and sovkhozy. Siroshtan et al. (1967: 40); Tron'ko et al. (1970: 77). In the Kalinin province in Russia, which had few vital industries, *shefstvo* was rather limited. Boterbloem (1999: 19, 173–178, 211).
115. Filtzer (2010: 27, 57).
116. Khlevniuk (2004: 9).
117. Krasnopiorova (2013: 206–212).
118. As Kees Boterbloem (1999: 260) established, Moscow allocated 'extremely limited' resources to the Kalinin party organization, 'for few vital industries were located in the province'. See also *Regional'naia politika N.S. Khrushcheva* (2009: 131–135).
119. *Politicheskoe rukovodstvo Ukrainy* (2006: 51–53); Kulchytsky (1988: 16).
120. Belova and Lazarev (2012: 12, 17, 18, 33).
121. Lewin (2003: 229).
122. Westlund (1998: 233).
123. Lozytsky (2005: 246, 279, 298–304); Vasil'ev (2004: 169); Shteinle (2012: 155–158).
124. The privilege given to the Vinnytsia obkom might have been due to the personal connections of its secretary, Volodymyr Cherniavsky, with Kaganovich and the chairman of the all-union commission for food industry and trade, Anastas Mikoian, and/or the fact that, although agricultural, the Vinnytsia oblast produced between 30 and 40 percent of Soviet sugar. Vasil'ev (2002: 175, 181).
125. Lozytsky (2005: 89).
126. Lozytsky (2005: 63–64, 55–56, 93–94); Armstrong (1959: 149).
127. *TsK VKP(b) i regional'nye komitety* (2004: 10).

## Chapter 4

1. On de-Stalinization before Khrushchev's secret speech at the Twentieth Party Congress in 1956, see Swain (2016: 60–83); Chernyshova (2021: 387–409); Loader (2016: 1759–1792); Zubkova (2000: 67–84); Gorlizki (1996: 1307, 1279–1318).
2. On territorial versus branch dimensions in Soviet planning, see Shaw (1985: 401–412).
3. Fursenko et al. (2004: 990).
4. Kibita (2013: 37).
5. Hough (1969); Gregory (1990: 123–145). See also Gorlizki and Khlevniuk (2020: 131–141); Harris (2018: 45–68, 96–99, 125–126, 141–160, 172–173, 176–183).
6. On the administration of defence enterprises, see Simonov (1996: 285–294).
7. Kirkow (1998: 32).
8. Kibita (2013: 55–56).
9. RGAE f. 4372 op. 57 d. 167 l. 49; d. 203 l. 63.
10. Mieczkowski (1967: 214). Documents 72, 73, 75, 77 in *Regional'naia politika N.S. Khrushcheva* (2009: 402–403, 404–410, 415–417, 424–427).
11. Document 72 in *Regional'naia politika N.S. Khrushcheva* (2009: 375).
12. TsDAVOU f. 582 op. 3 spr. 5011 ark. 142.
13. Kirkow (1998: 33). Some scholars argued that Khrushchev decentralized economic administration to gain the support of the regional party secretaries in his political struggle in Moscow. 'After that contest ended in 1957, Khrushchev attempted to reign in regional authority.' Herrera (2005: 109 and n. 25).
14. On the political implications of economic decentralization, such as the flourishing of national communism, see Motyl (1990: 87–99); also Gorlizki and Khlevniuk (2020: 171–193).
15. On the outreach of de-Stalinization under Khrushchev, see Bohn (2014).
16. TsDAVOU f. 2 op. 8 spr. 10234 ark. 12, 15.
17. Tomilina (2009b: 232–237).
18. Carr and Davies (1969–[1978]: 353).
19. Kibita (2013: 13–15).
20. Kibita (2013: 16–18).
21. Kibita (2014: 162–163).
22. TsDAHOU f. 1 op. 24 spr. 3755 ark. 93.
23. TsDAVOU f. 2 op. 9 spr. 329 ark. 97–99.
24. TsDAVOU f. 2 op. 9 spr. 329 ark. 108–111.
25. Kibita (2013: 18–19); Simon (1991: 233–236).
26. TsDAHOU f. 1 op. 24 spr. 3753 ark. 114–115; spr. 3755 ark. 59. In January 1956, the central leadership abolished the plenipotentiaries of the Ministry of Procurements in the oblasts and raions. Collection of state procurements was transferred to the machine-tractor stations. The Ukrainian Ministry of Finance procured agricultural produce from individuals. TsDAHOU f. 1 op. 24 spr. 4248 ark. 140–142.
27. Kibita (2013: 18–22).
28. TsDAHOU f. 1 op. 3 spr. 573 ark. 40–50; Kibita (2013: 27–28).
29. Kibita (2013: 26–27).
30. TsDAHOU f. 1 op. 24 spr. 4310 ark. 38.
31. TsDAHOU f. 1 op. 24 spr. 4248 ark. 130–133.
32. Kibita (2013: 23–29).
33. Kibita (2013: 32–34).
34. Kibita (2013: 55, 67–68).
35. The sovnarkhozy did not always welcome direct orders from Moscow, either, particularly when the ad hoc delivery orders were not supported with production plan targets, when production capacities were not available, or when the order was issued directly to enterprises. In November 1959, the chairman of the Kharkiv sovnarkhoz, Mykola Sobol, described the existing management of the supply system as 'a "great evil" for enterprises-suppliers, as well as for the consumers'. Dyadyk, the chairman of the Stalino sovnarkhoz, complained about the USSR Gosplan performing managerial functions. RGAE f. 4372 op. 57 d. 138 l. 143. Kibita (2013: 67, 85).
36. TsDAVOU f. 582 op. 3 spr. 5011 ark. 142.
37. Harris (2018: 151–152).
38. Kibita (2013: 68–70).
39. TsDAVOU f. 4820 op. 1 spr. 1896 ark. 14.
40. Kibita (2013: 72–73).

41. Kibita (2013: *passim*).
42. Kibita (2013: 73–78).
43. On misappropriation of state funds by local authorities for personal housing, see Kulick (2017: 154–157).
44. TsDAHOU f. 1 op. 24 spr. 4778 ark. 83.
45. TsDAHOU f. 1 op. 24 spr. 4687 ark. 13.
46. TsDAVOU f. 337 op. 2 spr. 874 ark. 113.
47. Kibita (2013: 47).
48. Ironically, while protesting regional localism, the Ukrainian leadership demonstrated the same tendency to defend local interests in its 1958 plan draft. The draft addressed the imbalance in the development of Ukrainian economy by increasing the shares of the light, food, and machine-construction industries in Ukraine's economy. This was not what central planners envisaged for Ukraine. RGAE f. 4372 op. 57 spr. 167 ark. 118–121; Kibita (2013: 55–62, 132).
49. TsDAHOU f. 1 op. 24 spr. 4023 ark. 225–226.
50. TsDAHOU f. 1 op. 24 spr. 4687 ark. 44; spr. 4778 ark. 76–77, 82.
51. TsDAHOU f. 1 op. 24 spr. 4778 ark. 85 for quote.
52. TsDAHOU f. 1 op. 24 spr. 4778 ark. 89–90. For details, see Kibita (2013: 63–67, 77–83, 84, 86).
53. Kibita (2013: 91–93).
54. TsDAVOU f. 2 op. 13 spr. 33 ark. 235.
55. TsDAVOU f. 2 op. 13 spr. 410 ark. 187–240; spr. 7.
56. TsDAVOU f. 2 op. 13 spr. 1 ark. 11.
57. Kibita (2013: 76).
58. A common violation was that of the deadline. Instead of reviewing the plan forty-five days before the end of the quarter, the sovnarkhozy, ministries, and various administrations could review the targets after the end of the quarter. TsDAVOU f. 2 op. 13 spr. 1 ark. 11–13.
59. TsDAVOU f. 2 op. 13 spr. 1 ark. 74.
60. TsDAHOU f. 1 op. 53 spr. 4109 ark. 66. After 1963, Ukrsovnarkhoz actively helped the sovnarkhozy to obtain resources that they were allocated but did not receive. TsDAVOU f. 2 op. 13 spr. 33 ark. 149.
61. TsDAHOU f. 1 op. 31 spr. 2340 ark. 2–3.
62. TsDAVOU f. 2 op. 13 spr. 1 ark. 73–74, 98, 184–197, 269.
63. TsDAHOU f. 1 op. 31 spr. 762 ark. 3–4; spr. 1880 ark. 146.
64. Kibita (2013: 56–58).
65. Mieczkowski (1965: 481–482).
66. For more on Ukrsovnarkhoz, see Kibita (2013: 79–87, 99–105, 118–119).
67. For more, see Swain (2016: 135–139, 165–166); Fursenko et al. (2004: 597–616).
68. Kibita (2013: 109); Fursenko et al. (2004: 649).
69. Kibita (2013: 108–109); Fursenko et al. (2004: 611).
70. Kibita (2013: 110–112).
71. Kibita (2008: 433, 434).
72. TsDAVOU f. 4820 op. 1 spr. 1848 ark. 116–117.
73. Kibita (2013: 119–120).
74. TsDAHOU f. 1 op. 6 spr. 3527 ark. 242, 243, 245.
75. Kibita (2013: 119–123).
76. TsDAVOU f. 4820 op. 1 spr. 1676 ark. 247.
77. In 1960, when the Ukrainian leadership accumulated 242 million roubles due to new prices and wanted to invest this amount in the construction sites that were not included in the central plan, it had to ask the USSR Gosplan and the USSR Ministry of Finance for permission. The permission was not given. Such an investment in construction, explained central planners, would increase investment into Ukrainian economy, 'which [was] not necessary at the moment'. GARF f. 5446 op. 94 d. 1148 l. 31.
78. TsDAVOU f. 4820 op. 1 spr. 1762 ark. 296.
79. TsDAVOU f. 2 op. 9 spr. 4304 ark. 1.
80. TsDAVOU f. 2 op. 10 spr. 407 ark. 453. In 1966, the reserve fund was 1.5 percent of Ukraine's budget. For 1967, the USSR Gosplan planned a 1 percent reserve fund for Ukraine. Ukraine still needed authorization to spent it. TsDAVOU f. 2 op. 13 spr. 1123 ark. 248.
81. TsDAVOU f. 2 op. 10 spr. 407 ark. 449, 453.
82. TsDAVOU f. 4820 op. 1 spr. 1762 ark. 24–25.
83. 'Institutionally stronger' here means that the dependence of the sovnarkhozy on the Ukrainian leadership for the fulfilment of plans was lower than the dependence of the Ukrainian leadership on the regions for the fulfilment of its power agenda.
84. TsDAVOU f. 2 op. 9 spr. 7201 ark. 84.

85. Hough and Fainsod (1979: 223–224).
86. TsDAHOU f. 1 op. 24 spr. 5646 ark. 199.
87. TsDAVOU f. 2 op. 13 spr. 7 ark. 13.
88. Kibita (2013: 120).
89. TsDAHOU f. 1 op. 31 spr. 2312 ark. 2–3, 10–21, 114–124; op. 6 spr. 3658 ark. 11–18.
90. Kibita (2013: 121–123); Allen (2003: 206); TsDAVOU f. 4820 op. 1 spr. 1848 ark. 116–117.
91. Shelest (2011: 332).
92. TsDAVOU f. 2 op. 13 spr. 410 ark. 140–153.
93. TsDAVOU f. 2 op. 13 spr. 33 ark. 140–143, 151–152.
94. TsDAVOU f. 2 op. 13 spr. 33 ark. 118–123.
95. Hough cited in Ōgushi (2008: 27).
96. Markevich and Zhuravskaya (2011: 1551, 1555).
97. Ōgushi (2008: 25) traces the rise of periphery khoziaistvenniki to the Brezhnev period.
98. Gorlizki and Khlevniuk (2020: 138–140). On agriculture during the Khrushchev years, see Nove (1992: 372–377); Zelenin (2011: 44–70). On financing of social programmes including housing, see Ivanova (2011: 36–103).
99. Gorlizki and Khlevniuk (2020: 134–135, 141).
100. The view that the reform allowed the obkoms to influence the managers is based on the fact that an economic region was generally confined to an oblast/krai and that the party made the cadres appointments in the sovnarkhozy. Consequently, when the regions were amalgamated, the influence of the party on the managers decreased. Hough (1969: 108); Ballis (1961: 162); Markevich and Zhuravskaya (2011: 1552); Clark (2013: 283).
101. Ballis (1961: 163).
102. In 1959, the number of Ukrainian oblasts was reduced to twenty-five. The Drohobych oblast was merged with the Lviv oblast.
103. TsDAHOU f. 1 op. 24 spr. 4570 ark. 51, 59, 78; Kibita (2013: 46–48).
104. In 1963, the share of capital investments that the Soviet state allocated to Ukraine in the non-production sector, which included construction of housing, hospitals, and urban infrastructure, was 29 percent, as compared to 34 percent in the entire Soviet Union, 35.8 percent in Russia, 36.5 percent in Belorussia, and 32.2 percent in Kazakhstan. The share of state capital investments allocated to the non-productive sector reduced from 25.3 percent of total investment allocations in 1956–1960 to 20.6 percent in 1961–1965. For 1966–1970, central planners suggested reducing that number to 15 percent. In the period between 1958 and 1963, the per capita volume of capital allocations to state and cooperative enterprises and organizations (excluding kolkhozy) in the non-productive sector had increased in Ukraine by a mere 5 roubles per capita, as compared to 15 roubles in Russia or the Soviet Union average of 13.5 roubles. The Ukrainian leadership estimated that housing construction was insufficient, 'based on minimum norms based on growth of urban population related to the development of industry'. TsDAVOU f. 2 op. 13 spr. 7 ark. 6, 26, 73. On the obkoms' reliance on managers throughout the 1950s, see TsDAHOU f. 1 op. 6 spr. 2493 ark. 11; op. 24 spr. 3755 ark. 59; spr. 6043 ark. 377–378; TsDAVOU f. 2 op. 13 spr. 408 ark. 54; DAZO f. 102 op. 4 spr. 13 ark. 71; see also Sobol (1995: 167); Zhuk (2010: 22–23).
105. TsDAHOU f. 1 op. 24 spr. 4570 ark. 58.
106. TsDAHOU f. 1 op. 6 spr. 2701 ark. 146.
107. TsDAHOU f. 1 op. 24 spr. 4570 ark. 16, 17.
108. TsDAHOU f. 1 op. 24 spr. 4570 ark. 66.
109. TsDAHOU f. 1 op. 24 spr. 4778 ark. 89, 92.
110. Harris (2018: 99–106).
111. Harris (2018: 102–103, 158–159).
112. TsDAHOU f. 1 op. 24 spr. 4727 ark. 59, 146, 207.
113. Kibita (2013: 121).
114. TsDAHOU f. 1 op. 24 spr. 6040 ark. 12–13, 22–23.
115. TsDAHOU f. 1 op. 24 spr. 6040 ark. 17–18.
116. TsDAHOU f. 1 op. 24 spr. 6040 ark. 27. Anatolii Yeriomenko, the chairman of the Lviv sovnarkhoz; Ivan Prybylsky, the chairman of the Chornomorsky sovnarkhoz; Hryhorii Lubenets, the Minister of Construction of Ukraine.
117. TsDAHOU f. 1 op. 24 spr. 6040 ark. 120, 126.
118. TsDAHOU f. 1 op. 24 spr. 6040 ark. 99, 100–101.
119. TsDAHOU f. 1 op. 24 spr. 6040 ark. 117–118.
120. TsDAHOU f. 1 op. 24 spr. 6040 ark. 65, 67, 69.

121. Kulick (2017: 132–144).
122. TsDAHOU f. 1 op. 24 spr. 6040 ark. 84.
123. TsDAHOU f. 1 op. 53 spr. 4107 ark. 60; spr. 4108 ark 14; TsDAVOU f. 2 op. 13 spr. 33 ark. 221.
124. TsDAHOU f. 1 op. 24 spr. 6040 ark. 102.
125. After the November 1962 plenum, the Kyiv sovnarkhoz discussed its forthcoming enlargement mainly with the Kyiv obkom. The opinion of the obkoms of Chernihiv, Zhytomyr, and Cherkasy that together with Kyiv would form the new Kyiv economic region, if it were to exist, was not included in the proposal that the Kyiv obkom and the Kyiv sovnarkhoz submitted to the Ukrainian Central Committee on 29 December 1962, nor were these obkoms mentioned. TsDAHOU f. 1 op. 31 spr. 2105 ark. 149–153.
126. The Podillia sovnarkhoz was formed in 1962–1963. In 1963, it accounted for 5.6 percent of Ukraine's total industrial output and 8.5 percent of Ukraine's total agricultural and industrial production. It administered industries in the oblasts of Chernivtsi, Ternopil, Khmelnytskyi, and Vinnytsia. The Podillia sovnarkhoz was located in Vinnytsia. From 1957 until 1962, Vinnytsia had hosted the Vinnytsia sovnarkhoz. TsDAHOU f. 1 op. 6 spr. 3911 ark. 46, 47.
127. TsDAHOU f. 1 op. 1 spr. 1927 ark. 127.
128. TsDAVOU f. 2 op. 13 spr. 2 ark. 69–70.
129. TsDAHOU f. 1 op. 1 spr. 1927 ark. 197.
130. TsDAVOU f. 2 op. 13 spr. 2 ark. 61–62, 71–72, 73–74, 75–76, 77–78, 81–82.
131. TsDAHOU f. 1 op. 24 spr. 5885 ark. 72; op. 6 spr. 3911 ark. 72.
132. Kulick (2017: 28). The average annual rate of investments in food industry increased from 104.7 percent in 1952–1956 to 119.2 percent in 1959–1964. The respective numbers for light industry were 118.4 percent and 131.5 percent. At the same time, the share of light industry in Ukraine's total gross output reduced from 2.45 percent in 1958 to 1.75 percent in 1965; the share of the food industry reduced from 28.6 percent in 1958 to 24.6 percent in 1965. TsDAVOU f. 582 op. 3 spr. 5011 ark. 143; f. 4820 op. 1 spr. 1896 ark. 34–35; Kyrylenko (2012: 163).
133. TsDAVOU f. 582 op. 3 spr. 5011 ark. 143; f. 4820 op. 1 spr. 1896 ark. 34–35; TsDAHOU f. 1 op. 24 spr. 4518 ark. 24.
134. In 1958, the authorities of the Cherkasy oblast complained that the Kyiv sovnarkhoz that administered the Cherkasy's industry prioritized the industry of the Kyiv oblast. TsDAHOU f. 1 op. 24 spr. 4778 ark. 146. For more, see Kibita (2013: 96–98).
135. TsDAHOU f. 1 op. 31 spr. 2105 ark. 201.
136. On the transfer of local industry to sovnarkhozy, see Kibita (2013: 116–118).
137. TsDAHOU f. 1 op. 31 spr. 2105 ark. 112, 126, 146–147.
138. RGAE f. 4372 op. 64 d. 941 ll. 222, 259.
139. TsDAVOU f. 2 op. 13 spr. 7 ark. 13; Lozytsky (2005: 305).
140. Armstrong (1959: 145).
141. Kazanets and Khudosovtsev focused on the needs of heavy industry, although they occasionally spoke of 'the republican needs' as well. TsDAVOU f. 2 op. 13 spr. 408 ark. 53–315 (passim).
142. For more on Dnipropetrovsk regional politics, see Kulick (2017: 46–47, 166–185); Moses (1976: 63–89).
143. Western obkoms received particular attention in their 1953 address in the context of Beria's nationality policy and in their 1956 address in the context of the events in Hungary.
144. Lozytsky (2005: 170, 306); Vasil'ev (2009: 321).
145. TsDAHOU f. 1 op. 31 spr. 2105 ark. 197.
146. TsDAHOU f. 1 op. 31 spr. 2105 ark. 186. For more on the stratification of salaries in the party and soviet apparatus in 1957, see Kulick (2017: 65–74).
147. TsDAHOU f. 1 op. 6 spr. 3911 ark. 10–15, 16–26.
148. Khlevniuk (2007: 10).
149. Westlund (1998: 223).
150. TsDAVOU f. 2 op. 13 spr. 1 ark. 73–74, 98, 184–197, 269.
151. TsDAHOU f. 1 op. 24 spr. 5648 ark. 130–142; Belova and Lazarev (2012: 39).

## Chapter 5

1. On the events of October 1964, see, for example, Swain (2016: 186–191); Tompson (1991: 1101–1121).
2. On bifurcation, see Chotiner (1982: 154–188); Khlevniuk (2012: 164–179).
3. Whitefield (1993: 121).
4. Motyl and Krawchenko (1997: 245).
5. Kibita (2013: 124–125, 128).

6. In his report, dated 23 June 1964, the head of the Ukrainian delegation to the first UN Conference on Trade and Development, Minister of Commerce of Ukraine Sakhnovsky suggested that Ukraine should open an office in Geneva, start training cadres for foreign trade, and create its own chamber of commerce that would not only organize exhibits of Ukrainian production, but also study world trade. In July 1964, Ukrainian planners wrote to Shelest in support of Sakhnovsky's proposals. In August 1964, the Ukrainian Ministry of Foreign Affairs expressed its support. At the end of summer, Shelest instructed Olha Ivashchenko, who was the Ukrainian Central Committee secretary and the head of the Economic Commission of the Soviet of Nationalities of the USSR Supreme Soviet, to study Sakhnovsky's suggestions and draft relevant proposals for Moscow. On 25 September 1964, Ivashchenko informed Shelest that Ukraine's request to create a Ukrainian Chamber of Commerce had already been submitted to the central government. The Ukrainian leadership expected a positive response from Moscow, as it had already completed the formalities for constructing a building for the Chamber of Commerce in Kyiv. TsDAHOU f. 1 op. 24 spr. 6028 ark. 14–15, 17–35, 36–38, 39–42.
7. Kibita (2013: 125–126).
8. Pyzhikov (2002: 175).
9. Since 1955, Ukraine had been asking to retain surplus production. In 1956, the Ukrainian government hoped that it could sell the above-plan production directly on the foreign market. Kibita (2013: 27, 53–54).
10. TsDAHOU f. 1 op. 24 spr. 5990 ark. 166–169.
11. In 1965, the above-plan production was managed according to the regulations adopted in December 1959. 'The largest share of the above-plan production that the republics could keep was 60 percent of ferroalloy.' The republics could not keep any material or equipment produced above the plan that would have allowed them to increase the output of consumer goods. Still, the 1959 regulations were considered a big victory for the republican governments. In the summer of 1959, central planners tried but failed to secure control of 100 percent of the above-plan production. Kibita (2013: 76–78).
12. At the 19 June 1965 meeting of the Ukrainian party and state apparatus, Shelest denied the rumours about the forthcoming reversal of excessive centralization: '[Increasing centralization of industrial administration] is a dangerous thing, we think.... [T]hese times had passed. Is it at all possible to run any economic branch from Chukotka to the Black Sea from Moscow[?] This is impossible to do, impossible.' TsDAHOU f. 1 op. 24 spr. 6040 ark. 127, 129.
13. Shelest (2011: 332).
14. Shelest (2011: 963).
15. TsDAHOU f. 1 op. 24 spr. 5991 ark. 18–19, 25.
16. TsDAHOU f. 1 op. 24 spr. 5991 ark. 38–39.
17. Interestingly, Shelest did not mention the letter from Ukrainian Vice-Minister of Commerce A. Romanov from 29 July 1965. Romanov gave Shelest a report on his conversations with the Canadian delegation that visited Kyiv on 25–26 July. Canadians indicated, wrote Romanov, that the reason they came to the Soviet Union was to activate Canada's trade with it. Canadians had high hopes for the forthcoming World Fair in 1967—that is, the 1967 International and Universal Exposition or Expo 67. 'In the Soviet pavilion, we would like to see not only the exhibit items that show the progress of your country, but also businesspeople who are empowered to sign trade agreements', they said. Romanov suggested that the Ukrainian Gosplan and Ukrsovnarkhoz prepare suggestions (agreed with the USSR Ministry of Trade) for concluding trade agreements between Ukrainian and Canadian organizations for exports of goods that were manufactured in Ukraine. TsDAHOU f. 1 op. 24 spr. 6028 ark. 3–4.
18. TsDAHOU f. 1 op. 24 spr. 5991 ark. 81–82.
19. The first to suggest decentralizing Soviet foreign trade was Christian Rakovsky. In 1921–1922, he argued that Ukraine's autonomy in foreign trade would increase the Soviet state's income and benefit Soviet foreign propaganda. In 1923 and 1925, Chubar and Kaganovich argued that Ukrainian cooperatives should have autonomy in foreign trade. Conte (1989: 150–174); TsDAHOU f. 1 op. 20 spr. 1637 ark. 32–33; TsDAHOU f. 1 op. 6 spr. 59 ark. 10zv; op. 20 spr. 2031 ark. 1–4.
20. Kibita (2013: 26–27).
21. TsDAHOU f. 1 op. 24 spr. 4310 ark. 199–200.
22. TsDAHOU f. 1 op. 24 spr. 5991 ark. 21.
23. On 12 February 1963, at the Ukrainian Presidium meeting, Pidhorny, to counteract the recentralization efforts of the all-union bureaucracy, passed a resolution 'On the improvement and coordination of scientific research in economics in the Ukrainian RSR'. Pidhorny criticized Ukrainian planners for the low level of economic research in the republic. 'The level of economic research in the republic does not correspond to the scale and tempos of economic development of the

Ukrainian RSR.' 'The main reason for considerable shortcomings in the organization and development of economic science and particularly of branch economies is the fact that there is no republican state organ that would coordinate the work of the branch economic organizations and perform common methodical leadership.' With this resolution, the Ukrainian leadership instructed the Ukrainian government State Committee to centralize control over economic research done in the republic. TsDAHOU f. 1 op. 6 spr. 3516 ark. 39–43; Kibita (2013: 110–112).

24. TsDAHOU f. 1 op. 6 spr. 3854 ark. 14, 37, 40, 44, 45–46.
25. On unemployment in Soviet Ukraine after the Second World War, see Khomyn and Kravchuk (2013: 274–276). On unemployment in the Soviet Union, see Ivanova (2011); Malle (1990: 36–38, 78–79, 200); Granick (1987: 83–84).
26. TsDAHOU f. 1 op. 24 spr. 5283 ark. 383–388. The full document and its translation in English are annexed in Kibita (2008: 540–551).
27. TsDAHOU f. 1 op. 6 spr. 3516 ark. 39, 40, 41, 42.
28. TsDAHOU f. 1 op. 6 spr. 3911 ark. 82.
29. TsDAHOU f. 1 op. 6 spr. 3911 ark. 36, 83.
30. On the territorial limits on employment, particularly in the 1980s, see Malle (1990: 206–212). Granick (1987: 84), however, shows that in small urban areas of the Kyrgyz Republic, hirings sometimes occurred beyond the plan limits. He suggests that this happened due to pressure from local party authorities.
31. TsDAHOU f. 1 op. 24 spr. 5885 ark. 71–73.
32. TsDAHOU f. 1 op. 6 spr. 3911 ark. 44–51, 52–58, 59–72.
33. By 12 January 1965, the Ukrainian committee of party-state control and the Ukrainian government, with the participation of other Ukrainian republican agencies, drafted a plan of action to study employment systematically in the republic. On 23 January 1965, the Ukrainian Gosplan submitted its report on unemployment to Shelest. TsDAHOU f. 1 op. 6 spr. 3911 ark. 73, 78–90.
34. The south-western region included the following oblasts: Vinnytsia, Volyn, Zhytomyr, Zakarpattia, Ivano-Frankivsk, Kyiv, Lviv, Rivne, Ternopil, Khmelnytskyi, Cherkasy, Chernihiv, Chernivtsi, and the city of Kyiv.
35. The western oblasts were those of Volyn, Zakarpattia, Ivano-Frankivsk, Lviv, Rivne, Ternopil, and Chernivtsi.
36. TsDAHOU f. 1 op. 6 spr. 3911 ark. 80, 86, 88.
37. According to Malle (1990: 61), the main reason for creating the buros was 'connected with the imminent fall in the rate of growth of the working-age population'. For more, see Arnot (1988: 131–155).
38. TsDAHOU f. 1 op. 6 spr. 3911 ark. 86, 89.
39. TsDAHOU f. 1 op. 6 spr. 3911 ark. 93, 98, 99, 100.
40. TsDAHOU f. 1 op. 24 spr. 5990 ark. 273–274, 276–299.
41. TsDAHOU f. 1 op. 6 spr. 3911 ark. 35, 36; spr. 3854 ark. 24–26; op. 1 spr. 1927 ark. 198, 199.
42. TsDAHOU f. 1 op. 6 spr. 3854 ark. 24–26.
43. The transfer of industry from the sovnarkhozy to the ministries continued until the spring of 1966. TsDAVOU f. 4820 op. 1 spr. 1894 ark. 14.
44. TsDAHOU f. 1 op. 6 spr. 3854 ark. 10–11.
45. TsDAHOU f. 1 op. 6 spr. 3823 ark. 168; spr. 3858 ark. 11; spr. 3911 ark. 38–39. The restoration of the system of local industry was within the purview of the Kosygin reform.
46. Shelest (2011: 332–333).
47. Kriuchkov (2004: 50–51).
48. Shelest (2011: 333–336).
49. Kriuchkov (2004: 47).
50. TsDAHOU f. 1 op. 25 spr. 345 ark. 40.
51. Tillet (1975: 752–768); Palko (2014: 36–40).
52. Harrison (2002: 55, also 54–67). On the Kosygin reform, see Tompson (2003: 64–69); Whitefield (1993: 29–33); Feygin (2017: 155–242); Kähönen (2014: 23–40).
53. RGANI f. 2 op. 1 d. 789 l. 15; Nove (1977: 40–45).
54. TsDAHOU f. 1 op. 1 spr. 1927 ark. 16–18.
55. RGANI f. 2 op. 1 d. 789 ll. 21–22, 53–54, 62.
56. While the sovnarkhozy, or territorial economic administrations, were abolished, the economic regions were not.
57. RGANI f. 2 op. 1 d. 789 l. 53.
58. On the rights of the Ukrainian government as defined by the Ukrainian Constitution, see Koropeckyj (1977: 43–56).

59. At the same time, Kosygin encouraged the ministries to use foreign technology more actively. 'We often spend years to develop new machinery or equipment. However, it would have been much faster and cheaper to buy the relevant licences abroad.' RGANI f. 2 op. 1 d. 789, ll. 5, 8, 16, 17, 20, 54. Only in 1971, at the Twenty-Fourth Party Congress, would Brezhnev declare 'the rapid development of scientific technical revolution' a priority for the Soviet economy. Until then, as Kaufman (1994: 376) observed, 'for Kosygin and Brezhnev, the bureaucratic advantage was the transfer of technology from the West'. *XXIV s"ezd* (1971: 90–94).
60. RGANI f. 2 op. 1 d. 789 ll. 18–19.
61. RGANI f. 2 op. 1 d. 790 ll. 21–22.
62. RGANI f. 2 op. 1 d. 790 l. 15.
63. RGANI f. 2 op. 1 d. 790 l. 7.
64. RGANI f. 2 op. 1 d. 790 ll. 17–18.
65. RGANI f. 2 op. 1 d. 797 ll. 83, 87–88.
66. RGANI f. 2 op. 1 d. 792 l. 8.
67. RGANI f. 2 op. 1 d. 797 l. 93.
68. Whitefield (1993: 120).
69. Kramer (2018: 289, 304 n. 32).
70. Resolution of the Soviet leadership no. 728 from 30 September 1965 reduced the economic authority of the republican governments to ensuring correct territorial planning and drafting plan projects for all enterprises, including those for local industry. The text of the law can be found at http://www.libussr.ru/doc_ussr/usr_6302.htm (accessed on 9 March 2019).
71. TsDAHOU f 1 op. 1 spr. 1927 ark. 128, 151, 184, 193.
72. TsDAHOU f. 1 op. 1 spr. 1927 ark. 205–206.
73. TsDAHOU f. 1 op. 24 spr. 6127 ark. 39.
74. TsDAHOU f. 1 op. 24 spr. 6127 ark. 83–96.
75. TsDAHOU f. 1 op. 24 spr. 6128 ark. 20, 36–37.
76. TsDAHOU f. 1 op. 24 spr. 6128 ark. 17.
77. RGANI f. 2 op. 3 d. 171 l. 171; TsDAHOU f. 1 op. 25 spr. 168 ark. 158. It is worth mentioning another complaint that Shelest addressed to central planners. He insisted that the central planners had allocated funds to Ukraine for consumption, housing construction, health services, etc., based on an inaccurate estimate of Ukraine's population, systematically lowering it. The discrepancy between the estimates of the USSR Gosplan and the actual size of the Ukrainian population was 119,000 people in 1966, 235,000 in 1967, 339,000 in 1968, and 421,000 in 1969. 'The USSR Gosplan defined Ukraine's population size by the end of 1975 at 48,504,000 people, or 979,000 people fewer than estimates of the republic.' TsDAHOU f. 1 op. 25 spr. 168 ark. 159–160.
78. Other areas included communications (29.23 million), trade and public catering (40.44 million), science (12.92 million), education and culture (101.5 million), healthcare, physical education, and social security (47.1 million), and housing construction (501.1 million). These areas were not included in total industrial output. TsDAVOU f. 2 op. 13 spr. 1123 ark. 272–273.
79. In the total output generated in Ukraine—that is, including industry subordinated directly to the all-union ministries—the share of the gross output produced by the republican industry in 1966 was 9.7 percent. In 1966, the share of the gross output manufactured by enterprises of the all-union jurisdiction was 29 percent; 61.3 percent of the industrial output was produced by enterprises of union-republican status. TsDAVOU f. 2 op. 13 spr. 1123 ark. 267.
80. At the June 1966 Ukrainian Central Committee plenum, the Presidium was renamed 'Politburo'.
81. By the September 1965 Central Committee plenum, the Ukrainian Ministry of Local Industry already existed. TsDAHOU f. 1 op. 6 spr. 3858 ark. 11.
82. TsDAHOU f. 1 op. 24 spr. 6174 ark. 57–58.
83. TsDAHOU f. 1 op. 1 spr. 1927 ark. 151.
84. TsDAHOU f. 1 op. 24 spr. 6174 ark. 57–58.
85. TsDAVOU f. 2 op. 13 spr. 1123 ark. 267; TsDAHOU f. 1 op. 25 spr. 500 ark. 79; op. 31 spr. 2105 ark. 158.
86. In the 1950s, the Ukrainian leadership insisted on clearly dividing rights and responsibilities between economic agencies. Kibita (2013: 23, 85, 99, 104, 112, 119, 167 (n. 12)); Koropeckyj (1977: 46). As discussed in Chapter 8, lack of clarity in rights and responsibilities persisted in post-Soviet Ukraine.
87. By the beginning of the 1970s, the legal status of twenty-eight Ukrainian union-republican ministries varied from one ministry to another: 'Nineteen had individual charters issued to them by the Ukrainian Council of Ministers, while the rest operated without any legal document'. Koropeckyj (1977: 45).
88. TsDAHOU f. 1 op. 24 spr. 6270 ark. 1–2; op. 25 spr. 1 ark. 51, 52.

89. TsDAHOU f. 1 op. 25 spr. 2 ark. 120–121.
90. On 20 January 1969 Shelest argued that the decision not to transfer the production of the DT-20 tractor to Ternopil was based on inflated estimates and again insisted on the social benefits of moving this production to Ternopil. TsDAHOU f. 1 op. 25 spr. 168 ark. 6–7.
91. TsDAHOU f. 1 op. 24 spr. 6270 ark. 19; spr. 6271 ark. 227–231; spr. 6272 ark. 30–33, 150–151; op. 25 spr. 1 ark. 67, 207; spr. 2 ark. 136–137; spr. 500 ark. 24–25; spr. 641 ark. 83. The longest and most detailed section of Ukraine's comments on the five-year plan for 1971–1975 from 14–15 May 1970 was a four-page request for more investment in metallurgy, as opposed to a half-page request for investment in machine construction, which was of all-union status, and a two-page request for agriculture. TsDAHOU f. 1 op. 25 spr. 345 ark. 192–195, 200–202.
92. TsDAHOU f. 1 op. 25 spr. 641 ark. 83. Shelest's instructions with regard to other industries often carried little weight. For example, in 1969, after several years of trying to obtain permission to build a steam-boiler room at a cannery in the Poltava oblast, the director of this cannery asked Shelest for help in making sure that the steam-boiler room was included in the construction plan for 1970. Shelest, in turn, asked the Ukrainian Ministry of Food Industry to resolve the issue. The minister replied that his ministry had requested the Ukrainian Ministry of Rural Construction to construct the boiler room. However, the all-union Ministry of Rural Construction, which drafted the plans for the Ukrainian ministry, overruled the decisions of all agencies and administrations involved in this construction, although it promised to include it in the plan for 1971. TsDAVOU f. 4743 op. 1 spr. 908 ark. 65–68.
93. See, for example, correspondence of the Zaporizhzhia obkom in 1965–1972. DAZO f. 102 op. 4 spr. 13 ark. 12; spr. 246 ark. 20, 23–24, 25, 28, 45, 46, 47, 48, 55–60; spr. 372; spr. 970; spr. 1308 ark. 12; spr. 1317 ark. 17.
94. Naidis (1966: 17–26).
95. TsDAVOU f. 2 op. 13 spr. 1123 ark. 286. Furthermore, union-republican ministries allocated investments to their branch enterprises that remained under the jurisdiction of the oblispolkoms. TsDAVOU f. 4743 op. 1 spr. 193 ark. 79, 100, 101.
96. TsDAHOU f. 1 op. 1 spr. 1927 ark. 211.
97. TsDAHOU f. 1 op. 1 spr. 1927 ark. 20–27, 211. The idea that the party organs should 'control' and 'lead' the managers without replacing them was widely shared by the party functionaries. Hough (1969: 116–120).
98. TsDAHOU f. 1 op. 1 spr. 1927 ark. 205, 207, 208, 210, 211.
99. RGANI f. 2 op. 1 d. 780 l. 41. The resolution of the Central Committee from 1 April 1965 allocated 41 billion roubles to the construction of agricultural production facilities for 1966–1970. RGANI f. 2 op. 1 d. 771 l. 121. According to Alec Nove (1970: 388), 'total state and kolkhoz agricultural investments of 71 billion roubles were planned for the 1966–1970 quinquennium, as against 34.2 billion in 1961–65'. In 1969, Shelest claimed that state capital investments in agriculture in 1966–1970 were about 37 billion roubles, or 12 percent of the total capital investments in the Soviet economy in 1966–1970. TsDAHOU f. 1 op. 25 spr. 168 ark. 154. In addition to increasing investment in agriculture, in 1965, the Soviet leadership introduced a subsidy system to cover the increases in procurement prices paid to farmers. Within years, subsidies increased, reaching 37 billion roubles in 1980. Wegren (1992: 8). On agriculture in Ukraine in the 1970s, see, for example, Ozornoy (1983: 79–88).
100. TsDAHOU f. 1 op. 25 spr. 168 ark. 154.
101. TsDAHOU f. 1 op. 1 spr. 2011 ark. 6–7, 8, 28–29, 240, 244, 245, 246, 250, 254.
102. TsDAHOU f. 1 op. 1 spr. 2011 ark. 28, 240, 244, 245, 246, 250, 254.
103. TsDAHOU f. 1 op. 1 spr. 2011 ark. 29–30.
104. Krasnopivtsev (2013: 79); RGANI f. 2 op. 1 d. 771 l. 121.
105. TsDAHOU f. 1 op. 1 spr. 2011 ark. 35–36; DAZO f. 102 op. 4 spr. 237 ark. 26–27; spr. 240 ark. 70; spr. 1306 ark. 155–156.
106. DAZO f. 102 op. 4 spr. 1306 ark. 43–44.
107. From the early 1970s, the practice of patronage would be formally encouraged as 'agro-industrial integration'. Ozornoy (1983: 84). On agro-industrial complexes and inter-farm cooperation, see Stebelsky (1975: 119–121). This also meant that more farms would be directly subordinated to the ministries. At the meeting of the Ukrainian Ministry of Food Industry on 11 March 1969, the director of the Kherson cannery combine (*ob"edinenie*) stated that the two sovkhozy that were included in this combine produced as many vegetables as fifty non-specialized enterprises in their region and 'had productivity higher than in the kolkhozy or sovkhozy of the Ministry of Agriculture or the Ministry of Melioration'. He asked to transfer another three or four sovkhozy to the combine. TsDAVOU f. 4743 op. 1 spr. 852 ark. 57–58.
108. TsDAVOU f. 4743 op. 1 spr. 193 ark. 63, 108.

109. TsDAHOU f. 1 op. 1 spr. 2011 ark. 36, 179, 181.
110. TsDAHOU f. 1 op. 1 spr. 2011 ark. 225, 227, 228, 229, 230.
111. TsDAHOU f. 1 op. 1 spr. 2011 ark. 101–102.
112. TsDAHOU f. 1 op. 1 spr. 2011 ark. 77–78, 80.
113. TsDAHOU f. 1 op. 1 spr. 2011 ark. 58, 61–62.
114. TsDAHOU f. 1 op. 1 spr. 2011 ark. 38.
115. TsDAHOU f. 1 op. 1 spr. 2011 ark. 136, 137, 138, 139, 140.
116. TsDAHOU f. 1 op. 1 spr. 2011 ark. 169, 171, 172, 173, 174, 175.
117. TsDAHOU f. 1 op. 1 spr. 2011 ark. 231, 232, 235, 236, 237.
118. TsDAHOU f. 1 op. 1 spr. 2011 ark. 113–114, 117, 119.
119. TsDAHOU f. 1 op. 1 spr. 2011 ark. 213, 214, 215, 217.
120. TsDAHOU f. 1 op. 1 spr. 2011 ark. 240, 244, 245, 246, 250, 254, 257.
121. On the accountability of the party organs for the economic performance of their regions and the collusion of their interests with the interests of industrial managers and state administrators, see Andreev (1989: 144–173); Hough (1969: 5–6); Whitefield (1993: 123–131).
122. TsDAHOU f. 1 op. 1 spr. 2093 ark. 18–19.
123. TsDAHOU f. 1 op. 24 spr. 6128 ark. 117; spr. 195 ark. 1, 6.
124. TsDAHOU f. 1 op. 25 spr. 195 ark. 9.
125. TsDAHOU f. 1 op. 25 spr. 195 ark. 15. This would be at least Shelest's second request to expand the Ukrainian Central Committee department of defence industry. The first request was made in 1967 when he asked to expand the department from nine staff members, as approved in 1963, to fifteen because they could not cope with the volume of work: the output of production for defence had increased twofold compared to 1963. TsDAHOU f. 1 op. 24 spr. 6271 ark. 180–181.
126. TsDAHOU f. 1 op. 25 spr. 195 ark. 15, 16–21.
127. TsDAHOU f. 1 op. 25 spr. 195 ark. 14.
128. TsDAHOU f. 1 op. 25 spr. 195 ark. 29; spr. 345 ark. 184.
129. Interestingly, in 1962, Khrushchev approved the bifurcation of nineteen, instead of twenty-five, Ukrainian obkoms; the obkoms of the western oblasts remained united. One of the reasons for this decision was the low level of industrialization among the western oblasts, aside from Lviv. In 1970, Moscow must have added the city of Kyiv to the group of six oblasts that were without a separate inspector. Assigning a Ukrainian Central Committee inspector to the Kyiv gorkom would mean de facto recognition of Kyiv as a city with special status. Although Kyiv was the capital of the Ukrainian SSR, the Kyiv city party organization was part of the Kyiv oblast party organization. (In 1957–1962, Shelest was first secretary of the Kyiv obkom.) Only in 1975 would the Kyiv gorkom be carved out of the Kyiv obkom and be directly subordinated to the Ukrainian Central Committee. TsDAHOU f. 1 op. 25 spr. 195 ark. 12–13; spr. 2038 ark. 113; Kibita (2008: 416–420).
130. RGANI f. 2 op. 3 spr. 171 ark. 167, 185–192.
131. RGANI f. 2 op. 3 d. 171 ll. 194–196.
132. TsDAHOU f. 1 op. 25 spr. 345 ark. 182–185; spr. 346 ark. 171; spr. 499 ark. 160.
133. Krasnopivtsev (2013: 94); TsDAHOU f. 1 op. 25 spr. 642 ark. 5.
134. Fortescue (1988b: 33).
135. RGANI f. 2 op. 3 d. 248 ll. 5, 7, 8–10. In line with Brezhnev's criticism, in December 1971, the USSR Gosplan instructed the ministries to rework their proposals on new management techniques and structural changes. Feygin (2017: 241).
136. TsDAHOU f. 1 op. 1 spr. 2253 ark. 12, 21, 22. *XXIV s"ezd* (1971: 73, 79); Chernyshova (2013: 17–42).
137. As Whitefield (1993: 130–131) explains, '*podmena*, or the involvement of the party in the affairs of state, arose from the symbiosis of personnel, structures, and interests.'
138. TsDAHOU f. 1 op. 1 spr. 2253 ark. 48. On 17 August 1971, Shelest asked Moscow for funds to organize party education for the grassroots party organizations. TsDAHOU f. 1 op. 25 spr. 500 ark. 39.
139. TsDAHOU f. 1 op. 25 spr. 500 ark. 78. In 1969, the Lviv oblispolkom suggested that large heavy industry enterprises should provide patronage to enterprises of the food industry in order to improve the technological base of the food industry and 'boost its progress'. TsDAVOU f. 4743 op. 1 spr. 852 ark. 85–86.
140. TsDAHOU f. 1 op. 25 spr. 505 ark. 127–130.
141. TsDAHOU f. 1 op. 25 spr. 500 ark. 156, 158.
142. Yet, while the obkoms colluded with the industrial management, the grassroots organizations were often passive and/or powerless. TsDAHOU f. 1 op. 54 spr. 1885 ark. 29.

143. TsDAHOU f. 1 op. 25 spr. 818 ark. 1–2.
144. TsDAHOU f. 1 op. 25 spr. 818 ark. 8–9.
145. TsDAHOU f. 1 op. 25 spr. 818 ark. 11, 13–14, 17, 18.
146. TsDAHOU f. 1 op. 25 spr. 818 ark. 46, 57–58.
147. TsDAHOU f. 1 op. 25 spr. 818 ark. 96, 97.
148. TsDAHOU f. 1 op. 25 spr. 818 ark. 85–87.
149. TsDAHOU f. 1 op. 10 spr. 1072 ark. 15–21.
150. TsDAHOU f. 1 op. 10 spr. 1108 ark. 123–127; op. 25 spr. 641 ark. 91.
151. RGANI f. 2 op. 3 d. 171 l. 196; f. 582 op. 1 d. 1 l. 107.
152. TsDAHOU f. 1 op. 25 spr. 641 ark. 98.
153. TsDAHOU f. 1 op. 10 spr. 1098 ark. 60–62.
154. TsDAHOU f. 1 op. 10 spr. 1108 ark. 13–18, 24–29.

## Chapter 6

1. See, for example, Yurchak (2006); Chernyshova (2013); Klumbytė and Sharafutdinova (2013); Fainberg and Kalinovsky (2016).
2. Allen (2003: 189–211).
3. TsDAHOU f. 1 op. 25 spr. 2824 ark. 83.
4. Gill (2018: 213–252); Hanson (2003: 128–154).
5. Whitefield (1993: 105, 135).
6. A good illustration of the rigidity of the system was the environmental agenda that Brezhnev tried but failed to implement. Josephson et al. (2013: 197–213).
7. Willerton (1987: 175–204).
8. Barabash et al. (2011: 265).
9. Vrublevsky (1993: 44).
10. Cited in Shapoval (2003: 122).
11. For more on the political career of Shcherbytsky, see Shapoval (2003: 118–129, 122 for quote).
12. Schattenberg (2022: 353). According to Zubok (2021: 14), Brezhnev viewed Andropov as his successor.
13. TsDAHOU f. 1 op. 25 spr. 642 ark. 5; Krasnopivtsev (2013: 94).
14. TsDAHOU f. 1 op. 25 spr. 833 ark. 68–69.
15. For a discussion of the power of the ministries over the party in 1965–1985, see Whitefield (1993: 123–137); Fortescue (1988a: 11–23).
16. Whitefield (1993: 119–131); Fortescue (1988a: 19–20).
17. At the 14 September 1973 Ukrainian Central Committee plenum, during the discussion of the plenum resolution, someone suggested making the phrase 'to produce more fodder and organize production of machines for this purpose' more specific and indicating who exactly should produce these machines. Shcherbytsky said: 'Let's leave it as it is.' TsDAHOU f. 1 op. 2 spr. 76 ark. 151.
18. TsDAHOU f. 1 op. 2 spr. 23 ark. 15–16.
19. TsDAHOU f. 1 op. 2 spr. 23 ark. 23. On the debate on the party's role in Soviet industry in Brezhnev's period, see Dunmore (1980b).
20. For more, see Rigby (1976: 320–321).
21. TsDAHOU f. 1 op. 2 spr. 93 ark. 186.
22. TsDAHOU f. 1 op. 25 spr. 834 ark. 193.
23. TsDAHOU f. 1 op. 2 spr. 93 ark. 235. In July 1972, Shcherbytsky appointed a new chairman of the Ukrainian Central Committee party commission, Leontii Naidek. TsDAHOU f. 1 op. 25 spr. 642 ark. 49.
24. TsDAHOU f. 1 op. 25 spr. 834 ark. 1–2; 92–93, 96–97; spr. 1024 ark. 7–8; Tolochko et al. (2018: 524–525, 572–574, 592–593).
25. TsDAHOU f. 1 op. 25 spr. 642 ark. 76–78; spr. 833 ark. 138–139.
26. *Politicheskoe rukovodstvo Ukrainy* (2006: 398–99).
27. Portnov and Portnova (2014: 78).
28. Lanovyk (2006: 437, 438).
29. TsDAHOU f. 1 op. 25 spr. 1873. On the role of the Ukrainian Ministry of Coal in administration of the industry, see Marples (1991: 175–206).
30. To meet the plan targets for agricultural production in 1981, Ukraine needed 1 million more tons of fertilizers than planned by the USSR Gosplan, at least 25,000 combines instead of the 12,000 planned, and at least 62 percent of fodder instead of the 56 percent planned. TsDAHOU f. 1 op. 25 spr. 2038 ark. 54–55.
31. TsDAHOU f. 1 op. 25 spr. 833 ark. 60.

32. *Politicheskoe rukovodstvo Ukrainy* (2006: 399).
33. TsDAHOU f. 1 op. 25 spr. 3307 ark. 146.
34. DARO f. 400 op. 121 spr. 84 ark. 119.
35. Whitefield (1993: 146); TsDAHOU f. 1 op. 25 spr. 3273 ark. 18.
36. DARO f. 400 op. 121 spr. 84 ark. 118, 119–120. Kriuchkov (2004: 44–45).
37. Lanovyk (2006: 451).
38. Danylenko (2018: 38).
39. Cherniaev et al. (2008: 511).
40. Cited in Marples (1991: 208).
41. For a variety of problematic issues for which the periphery authorities sought assistance from republican and all-union administrations, see, for example, TsDAHOU f. 1 op. 25 spr. 3306, 3307; op. 32 spr. 2437.
42. Kriuchkov (2004: 94–95).
43. Gregory (1992: 137) argues that 'local party officials [could] address [central bureaucratic institutions] only indirectly through the relevant instructor of the Central Committee'.
44. DAZO f. 102 op. 4 spr. 1712–1716; DARO f. 400 op. 106 spr. 73; op. 108 spr. 78; op. 132 spr. 87, 88. First secretary of the Zakarpattia obkom in 1962–1980, Yurii Ilnytsky, observed that for the expansion of industry in the Zakarpattia oblast, 'Moscow helped more than Kyiv because it had more money'. Ilnytsky (2007: 171).
45. Plokhy (2019: 122–142).
46. Plokhy (2019: 182–183, 184–188, 196).
47. Plokhy (2019: 212–214).
48. Plokhy (2019: 194–195, 207, 210, 219–229).
49. Plokhy (2019: 196).
50. In May 1987, Liashko would be requesting the inclusion of additional inhabited localities of the Kyiv and Zhytomyr oblasts in the list of localities eligible for financial assistance. RGANI f. 89 op. 56 reel 1.1008 file 5, in the Register of the Archives (2012).
51. For more, see Zubok (2021: 27–33); Sakwa (1991: 277–282).
52. Hanson (2003: 194–217); Whitefield (1993: 186–187).
53. TsDAHOU f. 1 op. 32 spr. 3273 ark. 156, 158; Masol (1993: 30).
54. Danylenko (2018: 24).
55. Marchenko (2013: 149).
56. TsDAHOU f. 1 op. 25 spr. 2824 ark. 114.
57. Dyker (1992b: 114–120); Danylenko (2018: 25–26).
58. RGANI f. 89 op. 22 d. 19 ll. 5, 8; Dyker (1992b: 122–123).
59. *Documents and Materials* (1988: 146–151).
60. Vrublevsky (1993: 79). Pohrebniak (1999: 183) argued that 'it would be a mistake to overestimate the power of the republican leaders'.
61. Ironically, Shcherbytsky became notorious precisely for his power over nomenklatura appointments in the party apparatus. In his memoirs (1999: 246), Pohrebniak mentioned an anecdotal case when Valentyn Malanchuk, vice-minister of higher and middle special education of Ukraine and later the Ukrainian Central Committee secretary, had to go to Moscow under an invented name in secret from Shcherbytsky.
62. Barabash et al. (2011: 265).
63. TsDAHOU f. 1 op. 2 spr. 13 ark. 19.
64. Gregory (1992: 124–125).
65. For example, 'Considerable shortcomings in administering economy' were mentioned when Kochubei was removed from the post of first secretary of the Kherson obkom in September 1972. When appointing the first secretary of the Rivne obkom, Mozghovy, in his place, Shcherbytsky referred to 'considerable achievements of the Rivne oblast in economic development'. TsDAHOU f. 1 op. 25 spr. 642 ark. 102, 103. During perestroika, non-fulfilment of plans was interpreted by the leadership as the result of the resistance of the obkom first secretary to new administrative methods and democratization of leadership. TsDAHOU f. 1 op. 25 spr. 3273 ark. 42–48, 54–57, 60–61, 63–78; Harasymiw (1989: 33).
66. Ellman and Kontorovich (1998: 97).
67. Whitefield (1993: 138–167, 128–129); Kirkow (1998: 35–38); Gregory (1992: 121–140).
68. In 1973, local industry enterprises in the agricultural oblasts of Vinnytsia and Rivne used less than 2 percent of raw material inputs of local origin. The industrialized oblast of Lviv produced less than 2 percent of industrial output from local resources. Lviv ranked last in the list of the Ukrainian oblasts based on the volume of output from local resources. TsDAHOU f. 1 op. 25 spr. 3273 ark. 71; spr. 834 ark. 78; Danylenko (2018: 32); Vrublevsky (1993: 140).

69. TsDAHOU f. 1 op. 2 spr. 93 ark. 61; Rutland (1993: 214).
70. TsDAHOU f. 1 op. 25 spr. 834 ark. 139.
71. As Gorbachev acknowledged at the central Politburo in July 1988, the technical base of agriculture grew by 40–50 percent from 1970 to 1985. However, production increased by only 10 percent. For more, see Miller (2016a: 113–114).
72. TsDAHOU f. 1 op. 25 spr. 2824 ark. 112.
73. Thus, construction of housing in rural areas per capita was half as much in the Voroshylovhrad oblast as in the Kharkiv or Dnipropetrovsk oblast. Still, enterprises in Voroshylovhrad could afford to cover the expenses of the kolkhozy and sovkhozy where their workers and employees fulfilled patronage obligations. For example, the production association 'Voroshilovgradteplovoz' paid for 300,000 person-days that its workers worked in the sovkhoz that it patronized during 1985, which mounted to almost 4 million roubles. TsDAHOU f. 1 op. 25 spr. 3083 ark. 17, 18.
74. TsDAHOU f. 1 op. 25 spr. 2824 ark. 54, 56; spr. 2038 ark. 123–124.
75. Khotin (1992: 74–85, 81–83); TsDAHOU f. 1 op. 2 spr. 93 ark. 159–160; op. 25 spr. 3306 ark. 91.
76. TsDAHOU f. 1 op. 25 spr. 3083 ark. 19.
77. On the classification of the obkoms in the RSFSR, see Frank (1974: 217–230); McAuley (1974: 473–501).
78. Lozytsky (2005: 307–311). The loss of the seat in the Ukrainian Politburo held by the Kharkiv obkom first secretary after 1976 might be related to the fact that Chairman of the Presidium of the USSR Supreme Soviet Nikolai Podgorny (Ukr.: Mykola Pidhorny), who patronized Kharkiv regional elites, was removed from his post.
79. TsDAHOU f. 1 op. 25 spr. 2835 ark. 38–40.
80. Biddulph (1983: 28–52); Breslauer (1986: 650–672).
81. TsDAHOU f. 1 op. 2 spr. 93 ark. 212.
82. TsDAHOU f. 1 op. 1 spr. 2076 ark. 217–226, 260; spr. 2253; op. 2 spr. 3; spr. 76; spr. 93 ark. 92–241; op. 25 spr. 642 ark. 141–147; spr. 677 ark. 242; spr. 834 ark. 72.
83. Magocsi (2007: 269, 290).
84. TsDAHOU f. 1 op. 25 spr. 673 ark. 67; spr. 677 ark. 101.
85. The Soviet Union as a whole was running out of labour reserves. During 1971–1975, the average annual rate of increase in total non-agricultural employment was 2.5 percent, and that of industrial employment was 1.3 percent. Grossman (1976: 18). According to the Ukrainian Academy of Sciences, at the end of the 1970s, 'there were large possibilities for attracting additional working people in the small and mid-sized towns, particularly in the South-Western economic region'. Bem et al. (1979: 13).
86. Popovkin et al. (1994: 39).
87. TsDAHOU f. 1 op. 6 spr. 3911 ark. 47; Popovkin et al. (1994: 31–32, 41).
88. Popovkin et al. (1994: 58).
89. Farmer (1980: 176); Risch (2011); Chura (2012).
90. For more on the demolition of the Soviet system, see Zubok (2021: 35–38, 40–42); Kotkin (1997: 104–120).
91. *Documents and Materials* (1988: 130–135, 137–139).
92. Wilson (1997: 106, 107); D'Anieri (1999: 88–91). On the growth of populism during the elections of directors of enterprises and the effect this had on economy, see Ellman and Kontorovich (1998: 143–149, 156–157, 187–190).
93. Rutland (1993: 206).
94. Rutland (1993: 208); see also Ellman and Kontorovich (1998: 190–210).
95. According to Gregory (1992: 135–136), in 1990, there was a 'change in the attitudes of enterprise directors toward local party organizations. They show that the party committee no longer plays the role of placing pressure on enterprises that are threatened with plan failure'.
96. Åslund (2009: 24–25); Herrera (2005: 131, 139–141); Kravchuk (2002: 41–42).
97. TsDAHOU f. 1 op. 25 spr. 2824 ark. 64–65, 76; spr. 3307 ark. 108.
98. Rutland (1993: 208–209). A researcher at the Gossnab Research Institute, Lev Freinkman, had an opposite view of the economic powers of the local authorities, arguing that in the mid-1980s, 'regional authorities received significant new [managerial] freedoms'. Ellman and Kontorovich (1998: 188).
99. TsDAHOU f. 1 op. 25 spr. 3307 ark. 3; Nadtoka (1990).
100. Solnick (1998: 7).
101. DARO f. 400 op. 141 spr. 18 ark. 7, 80–81; TsDAHOU f. 1 op. 25 spr. 3083 ark. 137; spr. 3272 ark. 68, 76, 89; spr. 3273 ark. 20.
102. As Herrera (2005: 140) noted, 'appropriation of resources by the nomenklatura did not entirely favour the regions'. 'Through amendments to the Law on [the] State Enterpris[e] in

1989, ministries were transformed into holding companies in the form of interbranch state associations (MGO), concerns, and state associations.... In this process, the property under the control of ministries became the property of the ministry leadership...' However, Ukrainian ministries were not in the same position as the all-union ministries. They were administratively weaker and unable to provide for Ukrainian enterprises as the Moscow-based MGOs could.

103. *Documents and Materials* (1988: 130).
104. TsDAHOU f. 1 op. 25 spr. 2824 ark. 77, 115; spr. 3307 ark. 163, 172; op. 32 spr. 2437 ark. 2.
105. TsDAHOU f. 1 op. 25 spr. 3306 ark. 99, 126; spr. 3307 ark. 71, 130, 132.
106. TsDAHOU f. 1 op. 25 spr. 3307 ark. 21, 156.
107. TsDAHOU f. 1 op. 25 spr. 3306 ark. 99, 126; spr. 3307 ark. 15, 67, 70, 71, 72, 73, 74, 108, 130, 131, 133, 159; op. 32 spr. 2437 ark. 12, 13.
108. TsDAHOU f. 1 op. 25 spr. 2824 ark. 172; spr. 3307 ark. 67, 127, 147; op. 32 spr. 2437 ark. 16. On the pressure of the ministries on the local soviets in the 1970s, see Little (1980: 233–246).
109. TsDAHOU f. 1 op. 25 spr. 3307 ark. 127, 13; op. 32 spr. 2437 ark. 24.
110. TsDAHOU f. 1 op. 32 spr. 2437 ark. 23.
111. TsDAHOU f. 1 op. 25 spr. 3306 ark. 47.
112. Miller (2016b: 107–117).
113. The list of regional party organizations included those of Kyiv city and the oblasts of Kyiv, Vinnytsia, Lviv, Kharkiv, Khmelnytskyi, Cherkasy, Chernihiv, and Chernivtsi. TsDAHOU f. 1 op. 25 spr. 3306 ark. 7, 76, 91, 92, 93, 130, 136; spr. 3307 ark. 90, 114, 124, 151, 171.
114. TsDAHOU f. 1 op. 1 spr. 3321 ark. 23.
115. TsDAHOU f. 1 op. 1 spr. 3321 ark. 38–40.
116. TsDAHOU f. 1 op. 1 spr. 3321 ark. 24, 33.
117. TsDAHOU f. 1 op. 1 spr. 3321 ark. 28.
118. TsDAHOU f. 1 op. 1 spr. 3321 ark. 25–26.
119. TsDAHOU f. 1 op. 1 spr. 3321 ark. 26, 28.
120. TsDAHOU f. 1 op. 1 spr. 3321 ark. 26, 27, 28.
121. TsDAHOU f. 1 op. 1 spr. 3321 ark. 27, 28–29.
122. TsDAHOU f. 1 op. 1 spr. 3321 ark. 29, 30–32, 33.
123. TsDAHOU f. 1 op. 1 spr. 3321 ark. 34–35.
124. TsDAHOU f. 1 op. 1 spr. 3321 ark. 35–38.
125. Zubok (2021: 58–59).
126. Cherniaev et al. (2008: 512, 513).
127. On Rukh in Odesa, see Kozachenko (2011: 89–95).
128. Kriuchkov (2004: 187, 190, 192, 194).
129. Kriuchkov (2004: 192–193, 252 for quote).
130. Pohrebniak (1999: 319–321). For more, see Chura (2016: 251–260). More broadly on democratic developments in Ukrainian society during perestroika, see Danylenko (2018: 81–129).
131. DALO f. II-3 op. 62 spr. 547 ark. 7–14.
132. Haran (1993: 29).
133. Sasse (2001: 80).
134. Pohrebniak (1999: 358–359).
135. Pohrebniak (1999: 356).
136. Marples (1991: 206–211).
137. In the spring–summer of 1989, Anatolii Vinnyk, first secretary of the Donetsk obkom, had to navigate between the growing discontent of miners over living conditions and wages (which culminated in a strike in July) and the oblast's failure to meet plan targets for coal production. Marples (1991: 207–208).
138. *Politicheskoe rukovodstvo Ukrainy* (2006: 460–461 n. 1).
139. *Politicheskoe rukovodstvo Ukrainy* (2006: 455).
140. *Politicheskoe rukovodstvo Ukrainy* (2006: 450–453; 455–461); Pohrebniak (1999: 356).
141. Cited in Kriuchkov (2004: 255).
142. Shcherbytsky supported the Ukrainian oblasts' demand that the relations between enterprises and local soviets should be formalized. However, while he agreed that the all-union budget should be formed bottom-up, he reserved the right for Kyiv to dictate to the regions which types of income would form the local budget. TsDAHOU f. 1 op. 1 spr. 3321 ark. 30, 33.

143. On the principal party cadre appointments in 1982–1988, see Harasymiw (1989: 28–39); TsDAHOU f. 1 op. 25 spr. 3273 ark. 137.
144. It was on 28 October 1989, one month after Shcherbytsky's removal, that the Supreme Soviet of the Ukrainian SSR (the Verkhovna Rada) adopted a law that elevated Ukrainian to the status of state language in the Ukrainian republic. *Politicheskoe rukovodstvo Ukrainy* (2006: 452).
145. From the extract of the records of the meeting in the Ukrainian Central Committee on 7 August 1989 published in Kriuchkov (2004: 256–257).
146. Among other secretaries who argued in favour of decentralization was Vinnyk, first secretary of the Donetsk obkom, http://www.ukrregion.j.u-tokyo.ac.jp/data/176.html, accessed on 15 August 2023.
147. Pohrebniak (1999: 341).

## Chapter 7

1. To name a few titles on the last years of the Soviet Union particularly relevant to this discussion, see Boettke (1993); Gill (1994); Kotz and Weir (1997: 63–130); Solnick (1998); Beissinger (2002); Kotkin (2009); Seliktar (2015: 172–202); Zubok (2021: 140–142).
2. Ōgushi (2008: 30–111); Dyker (1992b: 171–191).
3. Bugajski (2000: 167).
4. Whitmore (2004: 50, 56–57).
5. Until 1990, the Supreme Soviet of the Ukrainian SSR was a Soviet-type parliament that had no legislative power. After parliamentary elections in 1990, the Verkhovna Rada assumed its formal responsibility of writing the laws; 373 out of 450 MPs were communists at the time of their election. After the August 1991 coup in Moscow and the ban on the Communist Party, communist MPs declared themselves independent. Wise and Pigenko (1999: 30).
6. On the ideological split within the CPU between conservatives and national communists, see Sochor (1996: 147–163); Wilson (1997: 100–110); Kuzio (2000: 166–173).
7. Zubok (2021: 33–36, 41–42).
8. More generally on the March 1990 election to the Verkhovna Rada, see Arel (1990–1991: 108–154); Szporluk (1992: 176–214, 215–231); Kuzio (2000: 128–157).
9. On Ukraine's path to independence, see Nahaylo (1999: 109–399). For an overview, see D'Anieri et al. (1999: 22–33); Wilson (2015: 161–171). On the last years of perestroika in Ukraine, see Kuzio (2000: 103–213); Wolczuk (2001: 59–101); Kasianov (2008: 13–39); Plokhy (2014); Danylenko (2018: 194–242).
10. TsDAHOU f. 1 op. 2 spr. 1121 ark. 4, 26, 37, 79, 85–87.
11. TsDAHOU f. 1 op. 2 spr. 1122 ark. 29–32, 38–39, 48, 50–52, 60–61, 83–84, 125.
12. TsDAHOU f. 1 op. 2 spr. 1119 ark. 50; spr. 1122 ark. 37; Ōgushi (2008: 33–37).
13. TsDAHOU f. 1 op. 2 spr. 1121 ark. 82, 85, 90.
14. TsDAHOU f. 1 op. 2 spr. 1122 ark. 61, 119–120.
15. TsDAHOU f. 1 op. 2 spr. 1119 ark. 100, 105–106, 114; spr. 1120 ark. 45, 46, 60; spr. 1122 ark. 65–66, 87, 117.
16. TsDAHOU f. 1 op. 2 spr. 1119 ark. 21, 49, 114, 115; spr. 1121 ark. 82; spr. 1122 ark. 31–32.
17. TsDAHOU f. 1 op. 2 spr. 1119 ark. 113, 151; spr. 1120 ark. 76.
18. TsDAHOU f. 1 op. 2 spr. 1122 ark. 128.
19. TsDAHOU f. 1 op. 2 spr. 1122 ark. 55–56.
20. TsDAHOU f. 1 op. 2 spr. 1122 ark. 40; spr. 1107 ark. 12; spr. 1126 ark. 33, 34–35.
21. TsDAHOU f. 1 op. 2 spr. 1122 ark. 18–22, 182.
22. TsDAHOU f. 1 op. 2 spr. 1121 ark. 49–50; spr. 1126 ark. 9–12, 17.
23. Cited in Masol (1993: 58); Wilson (1997: 101–103).
24. RGASPI f. 646 op. 1 d. 2 l. 24.
25. TsDAHOU f. 1 op. 2 spr. 1107 ark. 27.
26. TsDAHOU f. 1 op. 2 spr. 1021 ark. 67–68.
27. TsDAHOU f. 1 op. 2 spr. 1021 ark. 82, 104, 108–112.
28. Ukrainian Soviet Socialist Republic (until 24 August 1991). Ukraine. Verkhovna Rada, *Biuleten'* 11 (10 October 1990), [hereafter, *Biuleten'*], 90–91.
29. Wilson (1997: 101).
30. Wilson (1997: 101).
31. Zubok (2021: 132–134).

32. The Central Committee resolution from 28 August created this impression by stating that there were reserves in the periphery and the problem was that the 'Councils of Ministers of the Union republics' and the producers 'had reduced dynamism, often ignored general interests of the state'. The Central Committee secretaries were instructed to talk with first secretaries of the republican central committees, kraikoms, and obkoms about 'specific measures on the part of the party organizations to stabilize the socio-political situation in each region', and 'to pay particular attention to increasing the discipline in procurements and supplies of agricultural produce, [and] to the fulfilment of the planned production volumes of all consumer goods'. 'Ob usilenii politicheskoĭ napriazhennosti' (1990: 13–19).
33. TsDAHOU f. 1 op. 2 spr. 1127 ark. 50, 62.
34. TsDAHOU f. 1 op. 2 spr. 1127 ark. 49, 51, 55–56, 59. For more on the 'Popular Movement in Support of Perestroika', or Rukh, and political opposition more generally, see Wilson (2015: 156–161).
35. TsDAHOU f. 1 op. 2 spr. 1127 ark. 11, 45–46, 62.
36. TsDAHOU f. 1 op. 2 spr. 1127 ark. 18, 52, 63, 68.
37. TsDAHOU f. 1 op. 2 spr. 1127 ark. 17, 54, 56, 60, 61, 62.
38. TsDAHOU f. 1 op. 2 spr. 1127 ark. 6, 23–27, 75–76.
39. For more on the '500 Days', see Zubok (2021: 131–140).
40. TsDAVOU f. 1 op. 22 spr. 1762 ark. 61–69, 88.
41. By the beginning of October, the Ukrainian government had signed bilateral agreements declaring the intention to cooperate with twelve Union republics and had begun direct negotiations with foreign suppliers of inputs for light and food industries. *Biuleten'* 11 (10 October 1990: 26).
42. VVR (45/1990: 606).
43. Contrary to traditional plan targets, *goszakaz* was not meant to take up the full production capacity of the enterprise.
44. VVR (44/1990: 596).
45. *Biuleten'* 11 (10 October 1990: 90–91).
46. Kravchuk (2002: 42); Dienes (1992: 138); Lukinov (1992: 31); Dolishnii (1992: fig. 14–3, 306–307).
47. TsDAHOU f. 1 op. 2 spr. 1126 ark. 32, 35; spr. 1107 ark. 24, 25; *Biuleten'* 14 (15 October 1990: 39).
48. *Biuleten'* 11 (10 October 1990: 65–66, 80); 14 (15 October 1990: 54–55).
49. *Biuleten'* 11 (10 October 1990: 86).
50. Woodruff (1999: 56–68). For more on the barter economy, see Ledeneva (2006: 115–141); Seabright (2000).
51. Woodruff (1999: 68–78); Herrera (2005: 98–142). On the growth of regionalism, see Moses (1992: 479–509).
52. TsDAHOU f. 1 op. 2 spr. 1127 ark. 25–27.
53. TsDAHOU f. 1 op. 2 spr. 1130 ark. 15.
54. For more on the political reform, see Zubok (2021: 33–36, 41–42).
55. TsDAHOU f. 1 op. 2 spr. 1130 ark. 15, 17; spr. 1142 ark. 254.
56. TsDAHOU f. 1 op. 2 spr. 1119 ark. 113; spr. 1120 ark. 76; spr. 1122 ark. 30, 83, 86, 102, 118; Kravchuk (1999: 170–171).
57. RGANI f. 89 op. 8 d. 26 ll. 2–3, 4.
58. This provision would be introduced in article 116 of the draft of the Constitution of Ukraine from 12 June 1991 that was commissioned by the Ukrainian Central Committee and voted by the Verkhovna Rada into the Constitution on 19 June 1991 as article 125. TsDAHOU f. 1 op. 32 spr. 2902 ark. 55–57; VVR (35/1991: 467).
59. 'Ob usilenii politicheskoĭ napriazhennosti' (1990: 13).
60. VVR (35/1991: 467).
61. TsDAVOU f. 2 op. 15 spr. 2186 ark. 255. On difficulties faced by local authorities, see Friedgut (1994a: 169–183).
62. In June 1991, after MPs put pressure on Hurenko to provide them with a clear party programme of economic reforms and reforms of state administration that would be understandable to the entire population, Hurenko promised to draft a CPU programme that would reflect the party vision of further social and political development of Ukraine. TsDAHOU f. 1 op. 2 spr. 1143 ark. 228; spr. 1146 ark. 64, 88, 121.
63. TsDAHOU f. 1 op. 2 spr. 1069 ark. 8–9, 105.
64. TsDAHOU f. 1 op. 2 spr. 1142 ark. 49; op. 32 spr. 2956.
65. In April–May 1991 the Ukrainian government drafted, and the Ukrainian Central Committee approved, a new structure for the state administration of Ukraine that did not include industrial branch state ministries. Supervision over the branches was transferred to branch state committees. The chairmen of state branch committees were appointed by the Cabinet of Ministers of

Ukraine, not the Verkhovna Rada. TsDAVOU f. 2 op. 15 spr. 2186 ark. 11, 257; TsDAHOU f. 1 op. 2 spr. 1146 ark. 161.
66. TsDAHOU f. 1 op. 2 spr. 1142 ark. 34.
67. TsDAHOU f. 1 op. 2 spr. 1146 ark. 11, 16, 117, 122–125; spr. 1142 ark. 27.
68. TsDAHOU f. 1 op. 2 spr. 1146 ark. 19, 20, 31.
69. In 1990, some members of the CPU joined a democratic group called 'Narodna Rada' (People's Council). Some joined the group (later Party) of Democratic Revival of Ukraine. 'Formally members of the CPSU, they appeared in the opposition to the party.' There was a similar situation in the local soviets. Only in nine oblasts—Luhansk, Mykolaiv, Odesa, Poltava, Kherson, Khmelnytskyi, Cherkasy, Chernivtsi, and Chernihiv—'none of the communists-deputies left the party.' TsDAHOU f. 1 op. 2 spr. 1146 ark. 31, 98. See also Wilson and Bilous (1993: 693–703).
70. TsDAHOU f. 1 op. 2 spr. 1142 ark. 33; spr. 1146 ark. 22–23.
71. TsDAHOU f. 1 op. 2 spr. 1130 ark. 14, 15, 17; spr. 1142 ark. 13, 29, 45–46, 254.
72. TsDAHOU f. 1 op. 2 spr. 1130 ark. 36.
73. TsDAHOU f. 1 op. 2 spr. 1130 ark. 26, 37, 38, 49; spr. 1146 ark. 93.
74. Whitefield (1993: 246).
75. VVR (29/1991: 377, 378).
76. TsDAVOU f. 2 op. 15 spr. 2186 ark. 190, 205, 221, 218; VVR (17/1991: 205).
77. TsDAHOU f. 1 op. 2 spr. 1146 ark. 64.
78. TsDAHOU f. 1 op. 2 spr. 1146 ark. 94; TsDAVOU f. 2 op. 15 spr. 2186 ark. 214, 228, 234, 255.
79. TsDAHOU f. 1 op. 2 spr. 1146 ark. 82.
80. TsDAHOU f. 1 op. 2 spr. 1146 ark. 88.
81. TsDAVOU f. 2 op. 15 spr. 2186 ark. 194.
82. See articles 7, 44, 45 of the Programme, VVR (36/1991: 473).
83. As before, the realization of *goszakaz* for agricultural production was placed on local authorities, now the soviets. As before, local authorities had to organize the urban population for agricultural work (articles 54 and 59). VVR (36/1991: 473).
84. TsDAVOU f. 2 op. 15 spr. 2186 ark. 244.
85. TsDAVOU f. 2 op. 15 spr. 2186 ark. 24, 191, 256.
86. TsDAVOU f. 2 op. 15 spr. 2186 ark. 195, 238, 256.
87. On 30 August 1991, after the coup against Gorbachev in Moscow and after the Verkhovna Rada declared independence, Kravchuk signed a decree on the transfer of all-union enterprises and organizations under the administration of the Ukrainian Cabinet of Ministers. All former all-union enterprises and organizations were instructed to 'unconditionally fulfil *goszakaz* and contract obligations for 1991.' VVR (44/1991: 581). On 11 September 1991, the Cabinet of Ministers formed a special commission to implement the decree. The text of the instruction accessed on 30 October 2021 at https://zakon.rada.gov.ua/laws/show/237-91-%D1%80#Text.
88. Wise and Brown (1999: 32).
89. DARO f. 204 op. 4 spr. 2208 ark. 71, 72, 85, 89, 222, 224, 233. Not all oblasts could find the funds locally to cover their budgetary needs. The Ternopil oblast soviet, for example, relied on the republic to cover its budget deficit. For 248 million roubles of revenue in 1990, the oblast budget had 318 million roubles of expenses. The oblispolkom could not find 7.5 million of roubles for education, 12 million roubles for health care, and 3 million roubles for social programmes. TsDAVOU f. 2 op. 15 spr. 2186 ark. 228.
90. TsDAHOU f. 1 op. 2 spr. 1146 ark. 74; Barabash et al. (2011: 164, 171, 173–174).
91. Article 24, paragraph 3 of the December 1990 law. VVR (2/1991: 5).
92. TsDAHOU f. 1 op. 2 spr. 1142 ark. 101–102, 208. On 16 February 1991 in Lviv, the Lviv, Ternopil, and Ivano-Frankivsk soviets held a joint session, the so-called Galicia Assembly. In the presence of their guests, representatives from the Rivne, Volyn, Chernivtsi, Zhytomyr, Odesa, and Zakarpattia oblasts, and three deputies from the RSFSR, the deputies discussed the political situation in the region, the forthcoming all-union referendum and a general concept for economic cooperation in the region. At their second session on 5 September 1991 in Ternopil, they discussed an economic policy in the region that would reflect national and regional priorities and interests. TsDAHOU f. 1 op. 32 spr. 2975 ark. 63; Kobuta (2011: 21–32); Adamovych (2009: 744–749); Davymuka (2015–2016: 89–90).
93. TsDAVOU f. 2 op. 15 spr. 2186 ark. 204.
94. In 1990 and the first quarter of 1991, the customs of the Donetsk oblast processed more than 11,000 customs declarations for goods banned for export. TsDAHOU f. 1 op. 32 spr. 2975 ark. 50–51; spr. 2976 ark. 32–33, 34–35.
95. By mid-February 1991, the oblasts of Volyn, Sumy, Poltava, Ternopil, and Khmelnytskyi were poorly delivering agricultural produce to the state. Rivne had not even started delivering to the state. 'Out of 66 percent of quarter deliveries to the union-republican fund, in January–February

[1991], the Mykolaiv oblast delivered 50.4 percent of meat products, Crimea delivered 38.5 percent, Odesa delivered 36.2 percent, Lviv delivered 17.2 percent of the plan. Only four oblasts delivered 100 percent of dairy products, only five oblasts fulfilled the plan target for eggs.' TsDAHOU f. 1 op. 32 spr. 2975 ark. 77, 103, 124.

96. TsDAVOU f. 2 op. 15 spr. 2187 ark. 91.
97. TsDAVOU f. 2 op. 15 spr. 2186 ark. 222, 233.
98. TsDAHOU f. 1 op. 32 spr. 2975 ark. 103, 107, 124.
99. TsDAVOU f. 2 op. 15 spr. 2186 ark. 224–225.
100. TsDAVOU f. 2 op. 15 spr. 2186 ark. 193, 232; TsDAHOU f. 1 op. 2 spr. 1143 ark. 191; *Biuleten'* 11 (10 October 1990: 44).
101. TsDAVOU f. 2 op. 15 spr. 2186 ark. 205.
102. TsDAVOU f. 2 op. 15 spr. 2186 ark. 232, 250, 254.
103. TsDAHOU f. 1 op. 2 spr. 1146 ark. 111.
104. TsDAHOU f. 1 op. 2 spr. 1146 ark. 94; TsDAVOU f. 2 op. 15 spr. 2186 ark. 229.
105. TsDAVOU f. 2 op. 15 spr. 2186 ark. 213, 228.
106. TsDAVOU f. 2 op. 15 spr. 2186 ark. 224; spr. 2187 ark. 9–10, 77–78, 98.
107. TsDAVOU f. 2 op. 15 spr. 2187 ark. 90.
108. TsDAVOU f. 2 op. 15 spr. 2186 ark. 224.
109. TsDAVOU f. 2 op. 15 spr. 2187 ark. 95.
110. TsDAVOU f. 2 op. 15 spr. 2187 ark. 86, 87, 89.
111. TsDAVOU f. 2 op. 15 spr. 2187 ark. 78, 83, 84, 86, 87, 89, 92, 95.
112. TsDAVOU f. 2 op. 15 spr. 2187 ark. 97.
113. US$70 million was expected from the Kyiv oblast and the city of Kyiv; $60 million from Odesa, $30 million from Donetsk, $20 million from Dnipropetrovsk, $16 million from Kharkiv, $14 million from Lviv, $10 million from the Crimean autonomous republic, $7 million from Luhansk, and $3 million from Zaporizhzhia. TsDAVOU f. 2 op. 15 spr. 2187 ark. 12–14, 99.
114. TsDAVOU f. 2 op. 15 spr. 2187 ark. 91, 99, 400; spr. 2193 ark. 126.
115. TsDAVOU f. 2 op. 15 spr. 2187 ark. 148zv, 179zv; spr. 2185 ark. 36.
116. TsDAVOU f. 2 op. 15 spr. 2187 ark. 389–391; spr. 2188 ark. 14, 51zv–52zv, 60–61zv.
117. Lieven (1990: 90).
118. On the transformation of Ukrainian state and society in the first half of the 1990s, see Nahaylo (1999: 400–550); Wilson (2015: 172–193); Kasianov (2008: 40–66). On institutional change and inertia, see Motyl (1997: 433–447); Nordberg (1998: 41–55); Kuzio (1998b; 1998c); D'Anieri et al. (1999: 90–140); D'Anieri (2007b: 74–83).

## Chapter 8

1. With the activization of the Verkhovna Rada, the chairman of the Verkhovna Rada, the president, and the prime minister formed a triumvirate. Wilson (1999: 263).
2. Åslund (2009: 44); Von Hirschhausen (1998: 452); Wittkowsky (1998: 35); Kravchuk (2002: 10, 13–34); Havrylyshyn (2000: 54–60).
3. Kaufmann (1994: 51–69); Ménil (2000: 28–58).
4. Way (2015: 7).
5. D'Anieri et al. (1999: 172–173); Banaian (1999: 31–40); Zon (2000: 30–43); Kravchuk (2001: 40–54); Åslund (2009: 47, 54–56); Havrylyshyn (2017: 61–84); Kasianov (2009: 160–165).
6. Von Hirschhausen (1998: 452–453); Nemiria (2000: 183–197).
7. By the beginning of 1993, light industry had fallen to the level of the 1970s and 1980s. Zon (2000: 74, 77); *Biuleten'* 1 (2 February 1993: 103–106).
8. Zon (2000: 74, 78, 141); Kravchuk (2002: 39).
9. Zon (2000: 91).
10. *Biuleten'* 2 (28 January 1992: 41).
11. Von Hirschhausen (1998: 453); Zon (2000: 87).
12. Kravchuk (1999: 160–162); Nemiria (2000: 186–188).
13. Kravchuk (1999: 187, 192, 195).
14. For alternative reasons for delayed reforms, see Havrylyshyn (2017: 69–84).
15. Wolczuk (2001: 140).
16. Havrylyshyn (2017: 72); Bugajski (2000: 167).
17. Bugajski (2000: 167); Sasse (2001: 82, 83).
18. 'The paradox in perestroika', observed Boettke (1993: 38), 'was that [Gorbachev] needed strong central control to accomplish a great decentralization of economic decision-making.' See also Bugajski (2000: 168).

19. On regionalist sentiments in specific regions, see Solchanyk (1994: 47–68); Bugajski (2000: 168–181); Nemiria (2000: 183–197).
20. Whitmore (2004: 31–32). Fear of social unrest was a leitmotif at the sessions of the Verkhovna Rada. *Biuleten'* 52 (17 December 1991: 34); 56 (19 December 1991: 51); 59 (4 January 1992: 37, 60, 84); 60 (4 January 1992: 34); 1 (28 January 1992: 66). The functionaries of the state apparatus, too, lived with permanent sense of uncertainty, remembered Ursula Woolley (Griffiths) in conversation with this author on 17 December 2021. In 1992, in her capacity in the British Embassy in Ukraine, she observed that the state apparatus was reluctant to implement the instructions handed down to them, on the basis that the person who had given the instruction might already have lost their authority, or be soon to lose it, or their job, anyway—and it was very hard to be certain what was the case in any given situation.
21. Cacace (1993: 136). The share of barter transactions varied by sector but remained high in the first half of the 1990s. According to Marin et al. (2000: 207), in 1997, it constituted 51 percent in total industrial sales. Kravchuk (2002: 253) estimated this share to be lower, still, 'exceeding 40 percent in total in 1997'.
22. Ledeneva (2006: 119).
23. *Biuleten'* 7 (31 January 1992: 4–5).
24. *Biuleten'* 55 (19 December 1991: 17–18); 57 (20 December 1991: 77).
25. *Biuleten'* 59 (4 January 1992: 87–89); 60 (4 January 1992: 23); 8 (30 September 1992: 77).
26. See, for example, *Biuleten'* 58 (20 December 1991: 50, 52–54); 21 (27 October 1992: 11–12).
27. *Biuleten'* 2 (28 January 1992: 40–41).
28. Resolution from 30 December 1991 no. 395 accessed on 20 January 2022 at https://zakon.rada.gov.ua/laws/show/395-91-%D0%BF/ed19911230#Text; *Biuleten'* 2 (28 January 1992: 41).
29. Law from 8 October 1991 accessed on 20 October 2021 at https://zakon.rada.gov.ua/laws/show/512-12/ed19911008#Text. For more details on the Ukrainian budgetary system in 1992–1994, see Martinez-Vazquez et al. (1995: 281–319). On expenditures assigned to local soviets, see Kravchuk (1999: 170–192).
30. *Biuleten'* 59 (4 January 1992: 69).
31. *Biuleten'* 2 (2 February 1993: 65); 43 (20 May 1993: 63). Wilson and Bilous (1993: 693–694); Kasianov (2008: 56–57); Whitmore (2004: 34–35, 50–57); Arel (1990–1991: 108–154); Clem (1995). Throughout the entire post-Soviet period, the Verkhovna Rada remained 'extremely susceptible to external stimuli' from 'regional patronal networks that shaped parties' and deputies' interests'. Whitmore (2019: 1484). For the nascent multi-party system in Ukraine in 1991–1994, see also Kuzio (1994: 109–127); Potichnyj (1992b: 13–36).
32. D'Anieri (1999: 94).
33. Kubicek (2000: 42).
34. Wise and Pigenko (1999: 32).
35. TsDAHOU f. 1 op. 2 spr. 1145 ark. 12.
36. TsDAHOU f. 1 op. 2 spr. 1145 ark. 12–13. For the Novo-Ogaryovo process, see Zubok (2021: 206–210).
37. *Biuleten'* 59 (4 January 1992: 68–69, 94). For a detailed discussion of the power of the local authorities, see Boukhalov and Ivannikov (1995: 126–136).
38. *Biuleten'* 59 (4 January 1992: 91–93); 60 (4 January 1992: 59–60); 8 (30 September 1992: 77). On taxes, see Åslund (2009: 54); D'Anieri et al. (1999: 172–173).
39. *Biuleten'* 52 (17 December 1991: 53–55).
40. *Biuleten'* 52 (17 December 1991: 60–61).
41. *Biuleten'* 53 (18 December 1991: 59); 55 (19 December 1991: 19); Martinez-Vazquez et al. (1995: 298–299, 313).
42. Kravchuk (1999: 187).
43. In an interview in 1995, President Kuchma's former regional policy adviser, Volodymyr Hryniov, said that he would 'overturn the taxation pyramid to place its foundation not in the center but in the regions'. Cited in Kravchuk (1999: 176).
44. *Biuleten'* 55 (19 December 1991: 21).
45. *Biuleten'* 59 (4 January 1992: 67–68).
46. *Biuleten'* 59 (4 January 1992: 83, 97).
47. *Biuleten'* 57 (20 December 1991: 50); 59 (4 January 1992: 69, 83); 1 (28 January 1992: 96); 2 (28 January 1992: 24).
48. *Biuleten'* 59 (4 January 1992: 68).
49. Wise and Brown (1999: 28); Wilson (1999: 3); D'Anieri (2007b: 80); Whitmore (2004: 30–31).
50. TsDAHOU f. 1 op. 2 spr. 1127 ark. 52.

51. TsDAVOU f. 1 op. 22 spr. 1761 ark. 2–13.
52. TsDAVOU f. 1 op. 22 spr. 1761 ark. 4–6.
53. TsDAVOU f. 1 op. 22 spr. 1761 ark. 3–4; TsDAHOU f. 1 op. 2 spr. 1146 ark. 84.
54. TsDAHOU f. 1 op. 32 spr. 2899 ark. 84, 88; op. 2 spr. 1146.
55. Wilson (1999: 261–266); Whitmore (2004: 30); Wolczuk (2001: 75–76).
56. Whitmore (2004: 30).
57. Roeder (1994: 75); article 114–1, Amendments to the Constitution from 14 February 1992, VVR (20/1992: 271).
58. TsDAHOU f. 1 op. 32 spr. 2902 ark. 41, 50–55; article 117, Amendment to the Constitution from 19 June 1991, VVR (35/1991: 467); from 17 September 1991, VVR (46/1991: 619); Markov (1993: 33). For a detailed discussion, see Wise and Pigenko (1999: 32–39); Markov (1993: 31–35).
59. *Biuleten'* 59 (4 January 1992: 94); 60 (4 January 1992: 54); 1 (28 January 1992: 63). See also Karmazina (2007: 123–125).
60. *Biuleten'* 59 (4 January 1992: 62–63).
61. Åslund (2009: 44).
62. *Biuleten'* 60 (28 Jan 1992: 83–84, 87); 2 (28 January 1992: 56).
63. TsDAHOU f. 1 op. 32 spr. 2902 ark. 55–57.
64. *Biuleten'* 2 (28 January 1992: 21, 48, 49–50).
65. *Biuleten'* 60 (4 January 1992: 88).
66. *Biuleten'* 1 (28 January 1992: 82, 83–86); Roeder (1994: 76); Markov (1993: 33).
67. *Biuleten'* 1 (28 January 1992: 81, 86–87).
68. VVR (23/1992: 335).
69. TsDAHOU f. 1 op. 32 spr. 2902 ark. 55–57.
70. Kravchuk (1999: 164).
71. D'Anieri et al. (1999: 126–127) argued that the president's representatives 'were widely viewed as an obstacle to the fulfilment of some regions' economic aspirations'.
72. *Biuleten'* 39 (18 May 1993: 20); 40 (18 May 1993: 8, 15–16, 22–23, 28–30); Wittkowsky (1998: 108, 124–127).
73. Puglisi (2003: 105).
74. *Biuleten'* 48 (2 June 1993: 37); 9 (30 September 1992: 42); 20 (22 October 1992: 55–59).
75. *Biuleten'* 9 (30 September 1992: 10–11).
76. *Biuleten'* 3 (3 February 1993: 32).
77. *Biuleten'* 2 (2 February 1993: 54–55).
78. *Biuleten'* 9 (30 September 1992: 14); 59 (4 January 1992: 62–63).
79. *Biuleten'* 43 (20 May 1993: 83); 44 (20 May 1993: 37–38, 40–41).
80. *Biuleten'* 9 (30 September 1992: 42); 2 (2 February 1993: 60); 42 (19 May 1993: 62–63); 43 (20 May 1993: 80, 83); 48 (2 June 1993: 36, 62); Markov (1993: 35); Kravchuk (2001: 52–53).
81. *Biuleten'* 39 (18 May 1993: 43–44).
82. *Biuleten'* 43 (20 May 1993: 83).
83. See, for example, Leitner and Meissner (2018: 183–194).
84. Salii vividly described his time in the office of president's representative to the city of Kyiv. Remarkable in his memoirs was, however, not even the description of his efforts to meet the needs of the city, or the omission of his personal gains from his official post, but a complete omission of his efforts to implement any of the president's decrees or instructions, not to mention the government's programmes. Salii (2008: 329–345).
85. Whitmore (2004: 31–34); Wolczuk (2001: 110–116).
86. *Biuleten'* 9 (30 September 1992: 26); 10 (1 October 1992: 53–54); 21 (27 October 1992: 10–12).
87. *Biuleten'* 1 (15 September 1992: 41).
88. *Biuleten'* 18 (15 October 1992: 13).
89. *Goszakaz* was originally planned as a temporary mechanism. The law on state order did not exist until 22 December 1995. Until then, the government had to regularly return to the Verkhovna Rada for an approval of the volumes and the nomenclature of items it wished to purchase at state prices. The delivery volumes approved by the Verkhovna Rada, however, were not iron-clad and could be amended by individual ministries. *Biuleten'* 10 (1 October 1992: 58–60, 64–65); 17 (15 October 1992: 112, 114, 116); 18 (15 October 1992: 8–13).
90. *Biuleten'* 17 (15 Oct 1992: 113).
91. *Biuleten'* 9 (30 September 1992: 34, 41); 17 (15 October 1992: 97–99, 104–107, 115). One raion in the Khmelnytskyi oblast, having delivered 22,000 tonnes of grain in 1991, received a *goszakaz* to deliver 40,000 tonnes in 1992. The quantity was absurd. 'Never once in our history have we supplied such an amount of grain, not even at the harshest times of [the Soviet] administration', complained deputy Romaniuk at the Verkhovna Rada meeting on 28 January 1992. *Biuleten'* 2 (28 January 1992: 40).

92. *Biuleten'* 17 (15 October 1992: 109). In 1993, the state succeeded in procuring 14 million tonnes of grain through *goszakaz*, after it provided an unlimited line of credit to agriculture and promised to provide grain producers with equivalent exchange for industrial goods. Kaufmann (1994: 62, 69).
93. *Biuleten'* 17 (15 October 1992: 105–107).
94. *Biuleten'* 9 (30 Sept 1992: 43).
95. *Biuleten'* 1 (15 Sept 1992: 41).
96. *Biuleten'* 21 (27 October 1992: 68–69).
97. Markov (1993: 34).
98. *Biuleten'* 1 (28 January 1992: 91).
99. *Biuleten'* 21 (27 October 1992: 14, 58–62).
100. As Kubicek (1999b: 71) pointed out, 'several observers [at the time] accused the Ukrainian government of being held hostage to the directors, and Kuchma in particular was singled out for serving the directors' interests and abandoning reform during his tenure as prime minister from 1992 to 1993'.
101. *Biuleten'* 21 (27 October 1992: 54).
102. *Biuleten'* 21 (27 October 1992: 17–19, 29); 1 (2 February 1993: 64).
103. Markov (1993: 33).
104. *Biuleten'* 17 (15 October 1992: 114); VVR (13/1993: 119). Two resolutions accessed on 15 December 2021: of the Cabinet of Ministers from 10 February 1993, at https://zakon.rada.gov.ua/laws/show/100-93-%D0%BF/ed19930210#Text; of the Cabinet of Ministers from 10 February 1993 at https://zakon.rada.gov.ua/laws/show/101-93-%D0%BF/ed19930210#Text.
105. *Biuleten'* 1 (2 February 1993: 66–67, 78). For more on the programme, see D'Anieri et al. (1999: 133–134).
106. On 3 February 1993, the Verkhovna Rada vetoed the decree from 21 January 1993. As P. I. Osadchuk from the Ivano-Frankivsk oblast explained, the directors of state enterprise-monopolies were already treating these enterprises as private and blackmailed the government by putting forward certain conditions. *Biuleten'* 1 (2 February 1993: 70, 71); 2 (2 February 1993: 15); VVR (14/1993: 128).
107. *Biuleten'* 2 (2 February 1993: 17); 3 (3 February 1993: 32, 72, 75–76).
108. *Biuleten'* 2 (2 February 1993: 24–25, 34–35); Kravchuk (1999: 162–164).
109. *Biuleten'* 59 (4 January 1992: 35); 2 (2 February 1993: 25, 64).
110. *Biuleten'* 2 (2 February 1993: 34).
111. *Biuleten'* 2 (2 February 1993: 64); Kravchuk (1999: 170).
112. *Biuleten'* 2 (2 February 1993: 24, 35–36).
113. Article 13 defined non-budgetary funds as one of the sources of local budgets. Non-budgetary funds included various fines, rent payments, and so on. Importantly, this article formalized the old practice whereby party secretaries relied on enterprises to contribute to the socio-economic agenda in their territories. Now the law stipulated that enterprises (associations), organizations, and administrations had to pay a proportional share of their funds for social development to those localities where their employees lived. This article granted local organs of self-administration the right to spend these funds as they saw fit and protected non-budgetary funds from expropriation by the government. Amendment to the law 'On Local Soviets of People's Deputies and Local and Regional Self-Administration', VVR (2/1991: 5).
114. *Biuleten'* 2 (2 February 1993: 24).
115. A permanent new currency, the *hryvnia*, was introduced in September 1996.
116. *Biuleten'* 21 (27 October 1992: 56–57).
117. *Biuleten'* 21 (27 October 1992: 55); 2 (2 February 1993: 35, 48).
118. *Biuleten'* 2 (2 February 1993: 24).
119. *Biuleten'* 39 (18 May 1993: 42–43).
120. Kaufmann (1994: 58).
121. Ménil (2000: 36).
122. *Biuleten'* 42 (19 May 1993: 32–35); Kravchuk (2002: 25).
123. *Biuleten'* 40 (18 May 1993: 51).
124. *Biuleten'* 40 (18 May 1993: 52, 91).
125. *Biuleten'* 40 (18 May 1993: 31, 50–51).
126. Way (2015: 55).
127. *Biuleten'* 56 (19 December 1991: 12–13); 39 (18 May 1993: 19); 42 (19 May 1993: 62–63); 43 (20 May 1993: 74–75, 94); 44 (20 May 1993: 48–49); 45 (21 May 1993: 54); 48 (2 June 1993: 72). See also D'Anieri et al. (1999: 105–110).
128. *Biuleten'* 47 (1 June 1993: 60).
129. *Biuleten'* 39 (18 May 1993: 51); D'Anieri et al. (1999: 109).

130. *Biuleten'* 39 (18 May 1993: 41–42); 42 (19 May 1993: 61–62).
131. *Biuleten'* 1 (2 February 1993: 102). Inter-republic trade and energy usage were two problems particularly acute for Ukraine. Ménil (2000: 33–34).
132. The names of the streets where the president's administration and the Verkhovna Rada are located.
133. *Biuleten'* 39 (18 May 1993: 43–44).
134. *Biuleten'* 40 (18 May 1993: 45–48); 42 (19 May 1993: 44–46); 45 (21 May 1993: 63); 48 (2 June 1993: 72); Markov (1993: 33); Whitmore (2004: 33).
135. Hesli (1995: 105). For more on the political crisis, see Wolczuk (2001: 116–119).
136. For more, see Wilson (1993: 8–13); Oosterbaan (1997: 214–216); Sasse (2001: 84–85); *Biuleten'* 52 (15 June 1993: 44–46).
137. Nemiria (2000: 191–193).
138. *Biuleten'* 51 (14 June 1993: 24). From 1992 to 1995, 'Odesa, Kharkiv, Kherson, Donetsk, Zakarpattia, Sevastopol, and the Crimean Republic' proposed to create free economic zones. Kravchuk (1999: 156, 164); Hesli (1995: 91–121).
139. *Biuleten'* 51 (14 June 1993: 41); 62 (23 June 1993: 45–52); Kravchuk (1999: 171–176).
140. Kaufmann (1994: 63); *Biuleten'* 42 (19 May 1993: 26).
141. *Biuleten'* 1 (21 September 1993: 64–66, 68–69).
142. *Biuleten'* 1 (21 September 1993: 70–71).
143. *Biuleten'* 1 (21 September 1993: 79–81).
144. *Biuleten'* 1 (21 September 1993: 102–103).
145. Åslund (2009: 47); Kaufmann (1994: 58).
146. Kravchuk (1999: 164, 198 n. 27).
147. Cited in Kravchuk (1999: 165). By then, the Verkhovna Rada had established a new structure of local government and eliminated the institute of president's representatives, effective 26 June 1994. Kravchuk (2001: 53).
148. Kravchuk (1999: 165); Sasse (2010: 102–103). For a detailed discussion on Ukraine's 'Europe' versus 'Russia' vectors of economic cooperation, see, for example, Abdelal (2005: 49–54, 64–65, 112–121).
149. Birch and Zinko (1996: 25).
150. Hesli (1995: 96).
151. Åslund (2009: 56); Zon (2000: 19); Whitmore (2004: 31–32). According to a poll conducted in May–June 1994, 47 percent of respondents in eight eastern oblasts and in the autonomous republic of Crimea would have voted against the independence of Ukraine. Solchanyk (1995: 48).
152. For a detailed discussion of clientelism and regional clans in the 1990s, see Minakov (2018: 135–150).
153. Hesli (1995: 96).

## Conclusion

1. Gorlizki and Khlevniuk (2020).
2. Frank (1974: 220).
3. Dyker (1992a: 151). See also Havrylyshyn (2017: 25–30); Ioffe (2004: 85–89); Bishimbaev (2010: 144); Lubin (1989).
4. Kavanagh (1991: 487).
5. Hale (2015: 8).
6. Kuchma (2003).
7. I am grateful to Ursula Woolley (Griffiths) for sharing a draft of her PhD dissertation (2023).

# Bibliography

## Archives

References for Ukrainian archives refer to f., *fond*; op., *opis'*, or inventory; spr., *sprava*, or file; ark., *arkush* (plural *arkushi*), page number. For Russian archives, the references refer to f., *fond*; op., *opis'*, or inventory; d., *delo*, or file; and l., page number.

### Ukrainian Archives

*Central State Archive for Audiovisual and Electronic Materials (TsDAEA)*

*Central State Archive of Public Organisations of Ukraine (TsDAHOU)*

Fond 1. Central Committee of the Communist Party of Ukraine (CC CPU). 1918–1991
    Opys 1, 2, 3, 6, 7, 10, 20, 24, 25, 31, 32, 53, 54.
Fond 237. Collection of documents about G. I. Petrovsky
    Opys 1.

*Central State Archive of Supreme Bodies of Power and Government of Ukraine (TsDAVOU)*

Fond 1. The Verkhovna Rada of Ukraine. 1917–2017
    Opys 1, 2, 22.
Fond 2. Cabinet of Ministers of Ukraine
    Opys 8, 9, 10, 13, 15.
Fond 582. State statistics committee of Ukraine (Derzhkomstat). 1920–2003
    Opys 3.
Fond 4820. Ukrainska Rada Narodnoho Hospodarstva (Ukrradnarhosp, or Ukrsovnarkhoz). 1960–1966
    Opys 1.
Fond 4743. Ministry of the food industry of URSR and its main administrations
    Opys 1.
Fond 337. Ministry of economy of Ukraine. 1921–2005
    Opys 2.

*State Archive of Zaporizhzhia Oblast (DAZO)*

Fond 102. Zaporizhzhia obkom of the Communist Party of Ukraine
    Opys 4.

*State Archive of Rivne Oblast (DARO)*

Fond 204. Rivne oblast Rada (Soviet) of people's deputies
    Opys 4.
Fond 400. Rivne obkom of the Communist Party of Ukraine
    Opys 106, 108, 121, 132, 141.

*State Archive of Lviv Oblast (DALO)*

Fond П-3. Lviv obkom of the Communist Party of Ukraine
    Opys 62.

### Russian Archives

*Russian State Archive of the Russian Federation (GARF)*

Fond 5446. USSR Council of Ministers
    Opys' 94.

*Russian State Archive of Social and Political History (RGASPI)*

Fond 17. Central Committee
  Opis' 3, 163.
Fond 49. Records of the Twelfth Conference of the RKP(b). 1922
  Opis' 1.
Fond 572. Records of the Central Auditing Commission of the RKP(b)-KPSS
  Opis' 1, 2.
Fond 558. Stalin archive, accessed through Stalin Digital Archive, https://www.stalindigitalarchive.com/frontend/
  Opis' 1, 11.
Fond 646. Records of the Twenty Eighth Congress of the KPSS. 1990
  Opis' 1.

*Russian State Archive of Contemporary History (RGANI)*

Fond 2. Stenographic Reports and Materials of Central Committee Plenums
  Opis' 1, 3.
Fond. 89. Communist Party of the Soviet Union on Trial records. 1919–1992
  Opis' 8, 22.
Fond 582. Twenty-fourth Congress of the CPSU. 1971
  Opis' 1.

*Russian State Archive of the Economy (RGAE)*

Fond 4372. USSR Gosplan
  Opis' 57, 64.

## Databases

Political Elite of Ukrainian regions, http://www.ukrregion.j.u-tokyo.ac.jp/surnames.html
Ukraine. Verkhovna Rada, Shorthand record reports of the Plena meetings of the Verkhovna Rada, [*Biuleten'*], https://www.rada.gov.ua/meeting/stenogr/
Ukraine. Legislative acts, *Vidomosti Verkhovnoi Rady URSR* [VVR], https://zakon.rada.gov.ua/laws/main

# References

## Published Documents

*Bol'shevistskie organizatsii Ukrainy: organizatsionno-partiïnaia deiatel'nost', fevral' 1917–iiul' 1918: sbornik dokumentov i materialov.* 1990. Compiled by P. L. Vagratiuk et al. Kyiv: Izdatel'stvo politicheskoï literatury Ukrainy.
*Bol'shevistskie organizatsii Ukrainy v period ustanovleniia i ukrepleniia sovetskoï vlasti: noiabr' 1917–aprel' 1918 gg.: sbornik dokumentov i materialov.* 1962. Compiled by P. V. Zamkovoi et al. Kyiv: Gosudarstvennoe Izdatel'stvo politicheskoï literatury UkSSR.
*Bol'shevistskoe rukovodstvo. Perepiska. 1912–1927.* 1996. Compiled by A. V. Kvashonkin et al. Moscow: ROSSPEN.
*Chetverta konferentsiia Komunistychnoï Partiï (bil'shovykiv) Ukraïny 17–23 bereznia 1920 r. Stenograma.* 2003. Compiled by V. S. Lozytsky et al. Kyiv: Alternatyvy.
*Dekrety Sovetskoï vlasti. T. XV. Mai 1921g.* 1999. Compiled by Yu. A. Akhapkin et al. Moscow: Editorial URSS.
*Dekrety Sovetskoï vlasti. T. XVII. Iiul' 1921g.* 2006. Compiled by Yu. A. Akhapkin et al. Moscow: ROSSPEN.
*Desyatyĭ s"ezd RKP(b), mart 1921. Stenograficheskiĭ otchet.* 1963. Compiled by T. G. Breneizen et al. Moscow: Gospolitizdat.
*Documents and Materials: 19th All-Union Conference of the CPSU: Reports and Speeches by Mikhail Gorbachev, General Secretary of the CPSU Centre Committee: Resolutions.* 1988. Washington, DC: Embassy of the Union of Soviet Socialist Republics.

*Dokumenty i materialy po istorii Sovetsko-Pol'skikh otnosheniĭ tom III, aprel' 1920 g.–mart 1921 g.* 1965. Compiled by S. Vronsky et al. Moscow: Nauka.

*Dokumenty vneshneĭ politiki SSSR, tom 1.* 1959. Compiled by I. N. Zemskov et al. Moscow: Gospolitizdat.

*Dvenadtsatyĭ s"ezd RKP(b) 17–25 aprelia 1923 goda. Stenograficheskiĭ otchet.* 1968. Compiled by S. I. Elkina et al. Moscow: Izdatel'stvo politicheskoĭ literatury.

Fursenko, A. A. et al., eds. 2004. *Prezidium TsK KPSS. 1954–1964. Chernovye protokol'nye zapisi zasedaniĭ. Stenogrammy. Postanovleniia. T.1, Chernovye protokol'nye zapisi zasedaniĭ. Stenogrammy. 2-e izd.* Moscow: ROSSPEN.

*Grazhdanskaia voĭna na Ukraine 1918–1920. Sbornik dokumentov i materiialov v 3-kh tomakh i 4-kh knigakh, tom 1, kniga 1.* 1967. Compiled by Ivan K. Rybalko. Kyiv: Naukova dumka.

Lenin V. I. 1969. *Polnoe sobranie sochineniĭ, izd. 5-e, tom 38.* Moscow: Izdatel'stvo Politicheskoĭ Literatury.

Lenin V. I. 1970a. *Polnoe sobranie sochineniĭ, tom 50.* Moscow: Izdatel'stvo Politicheskoĭ Literatury.

Lenin V. I. 1970b. *Polnoe sobranie sochineniĭ, tom 51.* Moscow: Izdatel'stvo Politicheskoĭ Literatury.

*Leninskiĭ sbornik. XXXIV.* 1942. Compiled by I. A. Gladkov. Moscow: OGIZ.

Letter from D. Z. Manuilsky to I. V. Stalin, 4 September 1922. 1989. *Izvestiia TsK KPSS* 9: 193–195.

Letter from I. V. Stalin to I. I. Lenin, 22 September 1922. 1989. *Izvestiia TsK KPSS* 9: 198–200.

*Na priëme u Stalina: tetradi (zhurnaly) zapiseĭ lits, priniatykh I.V. Stalinym: 1924–1953 gg.* 2010. Compiled by A. Chernobayev. Moscow: Novyĭ Khronograf.

*Nestor Makhno. Krest'ianskoe dvizhenie na Ukraine. 1918–1921: Dokumenty i materialy.* 2006. Compiled by V. Danilov. Moscow: ROSSPEN.

'Ob usilenii politicheskoĭ napriazhennosti v sviazi s ukhudsheniem obespechenia naseleniia prodovol'stvennymi i drugimi tovarami.' 1990. *Izvestiia TsK KPSS* 10: 13–19.

*Politburo TsK RKP(b)-VKP(b). Povestki dnia zasedaniĭ. 1919–1952. Tom 1. 1919–1929.* 2000. Compiled by G. M. Adibekov et al. Moscow: ROSSPEN.

*Politicheskoe rukovodstvo Ukrainy: 1938–1989.* 2006. Compiled by V. Yu. Vasil'ev [Vasiliev] et at. Moscow: ROSSPEN.

*Protokoly Prezidiuma Vysshego Soveta Narodnogo Khoziaĭstva. 1920 god. Sbornik dokumentov.* 2000. Compiled by A. K. Sokolov. Moscow: ROSSPEN.

*Protokoly X s"ezda RKP(b).* 1933. Compiled by N. Lukina-Bukharina. Moscow: Partiĭnoe izdatel'stvo.

*Regional'naia politika N.S. Khrushcheva. TsK KPSS i mestnye partiĭnye komitety 1953–1964 gg.* 2009. Compiled by O. V. Khlevniuk et al. Moscow: ROSSPEN.

*Register of the Archives of the Soviet Communist Party and Soviet State Microfilm Collection: Russian State Archive of Contemporary History.* 2012. Finding aid prepared by Lora Soroka. Stanford University, Hoover Institution Archives.

*Revoliutsiia na Ukraine po memuaram belykh.* 1930. Compiled by S. A. Alekseev. Moscow: Gosudarstvennoe izdatel'stvo.

*Taĭny natsional'noĭ politiki TsK RKP. 'Chetviortoe soveshchanie TsK RKP s otvetstvennymi rabotnikami natsional'nykh respublik I oblasteĭ v g. Moskve 9–12 iiunia 1923 g.' Stenograficheskiĭ otchet.* 1992. Compiled by B. F. Sultanbekov. Moscow: INSAN.

*The Stalin-Kaganovich Correspondence, 1931–36.* 2003. Compiled and edited by R. W. Davies et al. New Haven, CT; London: Yale University Press.

*The Unknown Lenin: From the Secret Archive.* 1996. Compiled by Richard Pipes. New Haven, CT; London: Yale University Press.

Tomilina, N. G., ed. 2009a. *Nikita Sergeevich Khrushchev: dva tsveta vremeni, dokumenty iz lichnogo fonda N.S. Khrushcheva: v 2-kh tomakh, tom 1.* Moscow: Mezhdunarodnyi fond 'Demokratiia.'

Tomilina, N. G., ed. 2009b. *Nikita Sergeevich Khrushchev: dva tsveta vremeni, dokumenty iz lichnogo fonda N.S. Khrushcheva: v 2-kh tomakh, tom 2.* Moscow: Mezhdunarodnyi fond 'Demokratiia.'

*TsK RKP(b)-VKP(b) i natsional'nyĭ vopros. Kniga 1. 1918–1933.* 2005. Compiled by L. S. Gatagova et al. Moscow: ROSSPEN.

*TsK VKP(b) i regional'nye partiĭnye komitety, 1945–1953.* 2004. Compiled by V. V. Denisov et al. Moscow: ROSSPEN.

*Ukrainskie natsionalisticheskie organizatsii v gody vtoroĭ mirovoĭ voĭny: Dokumenty, tom 2.* 2012. Compiled by T. V. Tsarevskaia-Diakina et al. Moscow: ROSSPEN.

*Ukraïns'ka Tsentral'na Rada, dokumenty i materiialy u dvokh tomakh, vol. 1.* 1996. Compiled by Petro P. Tolochko et al. Kyiv: Naukova Dumka.

*V. I. Lenin. Neizvestnye dokumenty, 1891–1922.* 2000. Compiled by Yu. N. Amiantov et al. Moscow: ROSSPEN.

*VII (Aprel'skaia) Vserossiĭskaia konferentsiia RSDRP(b). Protokoly.* 1958. Compiled by M. A. Zotov et al. Moscow: Gosudarstvennoe izdatel'stvo politicheskoĭ literatury.

*Vos'maia konferentsiia RKP(b), dekabr' 1919.* 1934. Compiled by N. N. Popov. Moscow: Partiĭnoe izdatel'stvo.

*Vserossiĭskaia konferentsiia R.K.P. (bol'shevikov). Biulleten' No. 3. 8 August 1922.* Moscow.

*XII s"ezd RKP(b). Stenogramma zasedaniia sektsii s"ezda po natsional'nomu voprosu 25 aprelia 1923 goda.* 1991. *Izvestiia TsK KPSS* 5: 155–176.

*XXIV s"ezd Kommunisticheskoĭ Partii Sovetskogo Soiuza,* Biulleten' 1. 1971. Moscow: Pravda.

**Memoirs**

Barabash, Oleksandr et al., eds. 2011. *Zdobuttia nezalezhnosti Ukraïny 1991. Istoriia proholoshennia, dokumenty, svidchennia u dvokh tomakh. Tom 2.* Zhytomyr: Ruta.

Bosh, Evgeniia. 1925. *God bor'by: bor'ba za vlast' na Ukraine s aprelia 1917 g. do nemetskoĭ okkupatsii.* Moscow: Gosudarstvennoe izdatelstvo.

Cherniaev, A. et al. 2008. *V Politburo TsK KPSS…Po zapisiam Anatoliia Cherniaeva, Vadima Medvedeva, Georgiia Shakhnazarova (1985–1991), izd. 2-e.* Moscow: Gorbachev-Fond.

Gol'denveizer, Aleksei Aleksandrovich. 1922. 'Iz Kievskikh vospominaniĭ.' In G. B. Gessen, ed. *Arkhiv Russkoĭ Revoliutsii, tom VI,* 161–303. Berlin: Slowo-Verlag.

Gorbachev, Mikhail. 1995. *Memoirs.* New York: Doubleday.

Hrushevsky, Mykhailo. 1989. 'Spomyny.' *Kyiv* 9: 108–149.

Ilnytsky, Yu. V. 2007. *Spomyny: iz prozhytoho i perezhytoho.* Uzhhorod: Mystetska liniia.

Khrushchev, Sergei, ed. 2006. *Memoirs of Nikita Khrushchev: Reformer, 1945–1964.* University Park, PA: Pennsylvania State University Press.

Krasnopivtsev, Aleksei. 2013. *Zhazhda spravedlivosti. Politicheskie memuary. Tom 1.* Moscow: Algoritm.

Kriuchkov, Georgii. 2004. *Trudnye uroki: razdum'ia byvshego partiĭnogo rabotnika.* Kyiv: Oriany.

Masol, Vitalii. 1993. *Upushchennyĭ shans: nebespristrastnye razmyshleniia eks-prem'era Ukrainy o tom, chto proizoshlo v byvshem Sovetskom Soiuze.* Kyiv: Molod'.

Ordzhonikidze, Zinaida. 1967. *Put' Bol'shevika. Stranitsy iz zhizni G.K. Ordzhonikidze.* Moscow: Izdatelstvo politicheskoi literatury.

Pohrebniak, Yakiv. 1999. *Ne predam zabveniiu: zapiski professional'nogo partiĭnogo rabotnika.* Kyiv: Letopis'-XX.

Rakovsky, Kh. 1925. 'Il'ich i Ukraina.' *Letopis' revoliutsii* 2 (11): 5–10.

Salii, Ivan. 2008. *Oblychchia stolytsi v doliakh ïï kerivnykiv.* Kyiv: Dovira.

Shelest, Petro. 2011. 'Spravzhniĭ sud istoriï shche poperedu': spohady, shchodennyky, dokumenty, materialy.* Yuri Shapoval, ed. Kyiv: Adef-Ukraina.

Sobol, N. A. 1995. *Vospominaniia direktora zavoda.* Kharkov: Prapor.

Vrublevsky, V. K. 1993. *Vladimir Shcherbitskiĭ: pravda i vymysly: zapiski pomoshnika: vospominaniia, dokumenty, slukhi, legendy, fakty.* Kyiv: Dovira.

Zatonsky, Vladimir. 1925. 'K voprosu ob organizatsii vremennogo raboche-krest'ianskogo pravitel'stva Ukrainy.' *Letopis' revoliutsii* 1 (10): 139–49.

**PhD and Master's Dissertations**

Clem, James Ivan. 1995. *The Life of the Parties: Party Activism in L'viv and Donetsk, Ukraine.* PhD dissertation. University of Michigan.

Croll, Kirsteen Davina. 2008. *Soviet-Polish Relations, 1919–1921.* PhD dissertation. University of Glasgow.

Feygin, Yakov. 2017. *Reforming the Cold War State: Economic Thought, Internationalization, and the Politics of Soviet Reform, 1955–1985*. PhD dissertation. University of Pennsylvania.

Kibita, Nataliya. 2008. *The Sovnarkhoz Reform in Ukraine: Evolution of the Economic Administrative System (1957–1965)*. PhD dissertation. University of Geneva.

Kulick, Orysia Maria. 2017. *When Ukraine Ruled Russia: Regionalism and Nomenklatura Politics after Stalin*. PhD dissertation. Stanford University.

Nadtoka, G. M. 1990. *Shefskaia pomoshch goroda selu (1971–1980 gg.) na materialakh partiĭnykh organizatsiĭ Ukrainy*. Kandidatskaia dissertattsiia. Kyiv.

Royt, Alex. 2018. *Businesslike Communists: Soviet Finance and the Crisis of International Capital, 1921–1924*. MSc dissertation. London School of Economics and Political Science.

Woolley (Griffiths), Ursula. (2023). *'Where's your Mannerheim Line?': On the 'History Front' in Ukraine. Interventions in Civic Discourses of Public History (2012–2021). Tackling Russia's Revanchist 'Dominion of Meaning'*. PhD dissertation. University College London.

### Books, Articles, Book Chapters

Abdelal, Rawi. 2005. *National Purpose in the World Economy: Post-Soviet States in Comparative Perspective*. Ithaca, NY: Cornell University Press.

Acemoglu, Daron and Robinson, James A. 2012. *Why Nations Fail: The Origins of Power, Prosperity, and Poverty*. London: Profile Books.

Adamovych, Serhii. 2009. *Sobornist' ta rehional'nyĭ rozvytok u suspil'no-politychnomu zhytti nezalezhnoï Ukraïny*. Ivano-Frankivsk: Misto NV.

Adams, Arthur E. 1958. 'Bolshevik Administration in the Ukraine—1918.' *Review of Politics* 20 (3): 289–306.

Allen, Robert C. 2003. *Farm to Factory: A Reinterpretation of the Soviet Industrial Revolution*. Princeton, NJ: Princeton University Press.

Amar, Tarik Cyril. 2015. *The Paradox of Ukrainian Lviv: A Borderland City between Stalinists, Nazis, and Nationalists*. Ithaca, NY; London: Cornell University Press.

Anderson, Gary M. and Boettke, Peter J. 1993. '*Perestroika* and Public Choice: The Economics of Autocratic Succession in a Rent-Seeking Society.' *Public Choice* 75 (2): 101–118.

Andreev, Sergei. 1989. 'Struktura vlasti i zadachi obshchestva.' *Neva* 1: 144–173.

Anfert'ev, I. A. 2016. 'Praviashchaia RKP(b): otkaz ot politiki voennogo kommunizma i rost vlastnykh polnomochiĭ partiĭnogo apparata v upravlenii stranoĭ v 1920-e gody.' In O. S. Porshneva et al., eds. *1917 god v Rossii: sotsialisticheskaia ideia, revoliutsionnaia mifologiia i praktika*, 115–128. Ekaterinburg: Izdatelstvo Ural'skogo Universiteta.

Anfert'ev, I. A. 2017. *Politicheskaia biografiia praviashcheĭ RKP(b)-VKP(b) v 1920–1930-e gody. Kriticheskiĭ analiz*. Moscow: Infra-M.

Arel, Dominique. 1990–1991. 'The Parliamentary Blocs in the Ukrainian Supreme Soviet: Who and What do They Represent?' *Journal of Soviet Nationalitics* 1 (4): 108–154.

Armstrong, John A. 1959. *The Soviet Bureaucratic Elite: A Case Study of the Ukrainian Apparatus*. New York: Praeger.

Arnot, Bob. 1988. *Controlling Soviet Labour: Experimental Change from Brezhnev to Gorbachev*. Armonk, NY: M. E. Sharpe.

Åslund, Anders. 2009. *How Ukraine Became a Market Economy and Democracy*. Washington, DC: Peterson Institute for International Economics.

Åslund, Anders. 2013. *How Capitalism was Built: The Transformation of Central and Eastern Europe, Russia, the Caucasus, and Central Asia*, 2nd edn. Cambridge: Cambridge University Press.

Åslund, Anders. 2015. *Ukraine: What Went Wrong and How to Fix It*. Washington, DC: Peterson Institute for International Economics.

Ballis, William B. 1961. 'Political Implications of Recent Soviet Economic Reorganisations.' *The Review of Politics* 23 (2): 153–171.

Banaian, King. 1999. *The Ukrainian Economy since Independence*. Cheltenham, UK; Northampton, MA: Edward Elgar.

Barrington, Lowell W. and Herron, Erik S. 2004. 'One Ukraine or Many? Regionalism in Ukraine and Its Political Consequences.' *Nationalities Papers* 32 (1): 53–86.

Beissinger, Mark R. 2002. *Nationalist Mobilization and the Collapse of the Soviet State.* Cambridge: Cambridge University Press.

Beissinger, Mark R. and Kotkin, Stephen, eds. 2014. *Historical Legacies of Communism in Russia and Eastern Europe.* New York: Cambridge University Press.

Belova, Evgeniia and Lazarev, Valery. 2012. *Funding Loyalty: The Economics of the Communist Party.* New Haven, CT; London: Yale University Press.

Bem, I. S. et al., eds. 1979. *Ekonomicheskiĭ potentsial regionov (problemy razvitia i ispol'zovaniia).* Kyiv: SOPS USSR.

Biddulph, Howard L. 1983. 'Local Interest Articulation at CPSU Congresses.' *World Politics* 36 (1): 28–52.

Bilinsky, Yaroslav. 1983. 'Shcherbytskyi, Ukraine, and Kremlin Politics.' *Problems of Communism* 32 (4): 1–20.

Birch, Sarah. 2000a. *Elections and Democratization in Ukraine.* London: Palgrave Macmillan.

Birch, Sarah. 2000b. 'Interpreting the Regional Effect in Ukrainian Politics.' *Europe-Asia Studies* 52 (6): 1017–1041.

Birch, Sarah and Zinko, Ihor. 1996. 'Ukraine: The Dilemma of Regionalism.' *Transition* 2 (22): 22–25.

Bishimbaev, Kuandyk. 2010. 'Osobennosti politiki industrial'nogo rosta v Kazakhstane.' *KazKKA Khabarshysy* 4 (65): 143–148.

Blank, Stephen. 1994. *The Sorcerer as Apprentice: Stalin as Commissar of Nationalities, 1917–1924.* Westport, CT; London: Greenwood Press.

Boettke, Peter J. 1993. *Why Perestroika Failed: The Politics and Economics of Socialist Transformation.* London; New York: Routledge.

Bohn, Thomas M., Einax, Rayk and Abeßer, Michel, eds. 2014. *De-Stalinisation Reconsidered: Persistence and Change in the Soviet Union.* Frankfurt am Main: Campus.

Borisënok, Elena. 2006. *Fenomen sovetskoĭ Ukrainizatsii. 1920–1930-e gody.* Moscow: Evropa.

Borys, Jurij. 1980. *The Sovietization of Ukraine, 1917–1923: The Communist Doctrine and Practice of National Self-Determination.* Edmonton, AB: Canadian Institute of Ukrainian Studies.

Borzecki, Jerzy. 2019. 'Foreign Policy as a Factor in the Establishment of the Soviet Union: The Cases of Ukraine and Belarus.' *Diplomacy and Statecraft* 30 (4): 652–680.

Boterbloem, Kees. 1999. *Life and Death under Stalin: Kalinin Province, 1945–1953.* Montreal, QC: McGill-Queen's University Press.

Boukhalov, Oleksandr and Ivannikov, Sergei. 1995. 'Ukrainian Local Politics after Independence.' *Annals AAPSS* 540: 126–136.

Breslauer, George. 1986. 'Provincial Party Leaders' Demand Articulation and the Nature of Centre-Periphery Relations in the USSR.' *Slavic Review* 45 (4): 650–672.

Brooker, David C. 2008. 'Kravchuk and Yeltsin at Reelection.' *Demokratizatsiya* 16 (3): 294–304.

Brovkin, Vladimir. 2005. *Russia after Lenin: Politics, Culture and Society, 1921–1929.* London; New York: Routledge.

Bugajski, Janusz. 2000. 'Ethnic Relations and Regional Problems in Independent Ukraine.' In Sharon L. Wolchik and Volodymyr Zviglyanich, eds. *Ukraine: The Search for a National Identity,* 165–181. Lanham, MD; London: Rowman & Littlefield.

Cacace, Paolo. 1993. 'Ukraine: Countertrade and Commodity Exchanges.' *Most* 3 (2): 135–143.

Capoccia, Giovanni. 2016a. 'Critical Junctures.' In Orfeo Fioretos, Tulia G. Falleti, and Adam Sheingate, eds. *The Oxford Handbook of Historical Institutionalism,* 89–106. Oxford: Oxford University Press.

Capoccia, Giovanni. 2016b. 'When Do Institutions "Bite"? Historical Institutionalism and the Politics of Institutional Change', *Comparative Political Studies* 49 (8): 1095–1127.

Carr, E. H. (Edward Hallett) and Davies, R. W. (Robert William). *Foundations of a Planned Economy, 1926–1929,* volume 1. London: Macmillan, 1969–[1978].

Casanova, José. 2005. 'Ethno-linguistic and Religious Pluralism and Democratic Construction in Ukraine.' In Barnett Rubin and Jack Snyder, eds. *Post-Soviet Political Order: Conflict and State Building,* 2nd edn, 75–96. London: Taylor & Francis.

Chamberlin, William Henry. 1987. *The Russian Revolution, volume I, 1917–1918.* Princeton, NJ: Princeton University Press.

Chase, William. 1986. 'The Dialectics of Production Meetings, 1923–29.' *Russian History* 13 (2/3): 149–185.

Chattopadhyay, Kunal. 1986. 'Christian Rakovsky and the 1923 Ukrainian Opposition in the RCP(b).' *Proceedings of the Indian History Congress* 47: 123.

Cheberiako, Oksana. 2011. 'Diial'nist' biudzhetnoï komissiï pry VuTsVK (1922–1929r.).' *Visnyk Kyïvs'koho Universytetu* 108: 44–51.

Cheberiako, Oksana. 2012a. 'Stanovlennia i rozvytok biudgetnoï systemy SRSR u 1923–1929 rr.' *Visnyk Kam'ianets-Podil's'koho Universytetu* 5: 350–362.

Cheberiako, Oksana. 2012b. 'Biudgety USRR 1920-kh rr: struktura, funktsiï, evoliutssia.' *Visnyk Kharkivs'koho Universytetu* 45: 145–156.

Cheberiako, Oksana. 2012c. 'Dzherela finansuvannia derzhavnoï promyslovosti v USRR druhoï polovyny 1920-kh rr.: priorytety biudzhetnoï polityky.' *Visnyk Cherkas'kogo Universytetu* 9 (222): 88–98.

Chernev, Borislav. 2014. 'Ukrainization and Its Contradictions in the Context of the Brest-Litovsk System.' In Eric Lohr et al., eds. *The Empire and Nationalism at War*, 163–188. Bloomington, IN: Slavica.

Chernyshova, Natalya. 2013. *Soviet Consumer Culture in the Brezhnev Era*. New York: Routledge.

Chernyshova, Natalya. 2021. 'De-Stalinisation and Insubordination in the Soviet Borderlands: Beria's Attempted National Reform in Soviet Belarus.' *Europe-Asia Studies* 73 (2): 387–409.

Chotiner, Barbara Ann. 1982. 'Institutional Innovation under Khrushchev: The Case of the 1962 Reorganisation of the Communist Party.' *The Soviet and Post-Soviet Review* 9 (1): 154–188.

Chura, Oleksandra. 2016. 'L'viv naperedodni perebudovy: sotsial'no-ekonomichnyï i poli-tychnyï dyskurs.' *Proceedings of History Faculty of Lviv University* 17: 251–260.

Chura, Vasyl'. 2012. *Ostanniï komunistychnyï eksperyment. Perebudova narodnohospodars'koho kompleksu zakhidnykh oblasteï URSR na zlami 80kh-90kh rokiv XX stolittia. Monografiia.* Lviv: Liga-Pres.

Clark, William A. 2013. 'Khrushchev's "Second" First Secretaries: Career Trajectories after the Unification of Oblast Party Organisations.' *Kritika: Explorations in Russian and Eurasian History* 14 (2): 279–312.

Conran, James and Thelen, Kathleen. 2016. 'Institutional Change.' In Orfeo Fioretos, Tulia G. Falleti, and Adam Sheingate, eds. *The Oxford Handbook of Historical Institutionalism*, 51–70. Oxford: Oxford University Press.

Conte, Francis. 1989. *Christian Rakovski (1873–1941): A Political Biography*. New York: East European Monographs.

D'Anieri, Paul J. 1999. 'The Impact of Domestic Divisions on Ukrainian Foreign Policy: Ukraine as a "Weak State".' In Taras Kuzio, Robert S. Kravchuk, and Paul D'Anieri, eds. *State and Institution Building in Ukraine*, 83–105. Basingstoke: Macmillan.

D'Anieri, Paul J. 2007a. 'Ethnic Tensions and State Strategies: Understanding the Survival of the Ukrainian State.' *Journal of Communist Studies and Transition Politics* 23 (1): 4–29.

D'Anieri, Paul J. 2007b. *Understanding Ukrainian Politics: Power, Politics, and Institutional Design*. Armonk, NY: M. E. Sharpe.

D'Anieri, Paul J. 2011. 'Structural Constraints in Ukrainian Politics.' *East European Politics and Societies* 25 (1): 28–46.

D'Anieri, Paul, Kravchuk, Robert, and Kuzio, Taras. 1999. *Politics and Society in Ukraine*. Boulder, CO: Westview Press.

Danylenko, Viktor. 2018. *Ukraïna v 1985–1991 rr.: ostannia glava Radians'koï istoriï.* Kyiv: Instytut Istoriï NAN Ukraïny.

Davies, R. W. (Robert William). 1958. *The Development of the Soviet Budgetary System*. Cambridge: Cambridge University Press.

Davies, R. W. (Robert William), Harrison, Mark, and Wheatcroft, Stephen G. 1994. *The Economic Transformation of the Soviet Union 1913–1945.* Cambridge; New York: Cambridge University Press.

Davymuka, Stepan. 2015–2016. 'Ekonomichni osnovy Galyts'koï asambleï.' *Novitnia Doba* 3–4: 89–103.

Diamond, Larry J. 2002. 'Thinking About Hybrid Regimes.' *Journal of Democracy* 13 (2): 21–35.

Dickins, Alistair. 2019. 'Local Studies of Revolutionary Russia: Towards a Third Wave.' *European Review of History: Revue européenne d'histoire* 27 (1/2): 222–235.

Dienes, Leslie. 1992. 'Energy, Minerals, and Economic Policy.' In Ivan S. Koropeckyj, ed. *The Ukrainian Economy: Achievements, Problems, Challenges*, 123–147. Cambridge, MA: Harvard Ukrainian Research Institute.

Dolgikh, Fiodor. 2015. 'Finansirovanie deiatel'nosti RKP(b)-VKP(b) v pervoĭ polovine 1920-kh gg.' *Probely v Rossyĭskom Zakonodatel'stve* 4: 43–46.

Dolishnii, Miriian. 1992. 'Regional Aspects of Ukraine's Economic Development.' In Ivan S. Koropeckyj, ed. *The Ukrainian Economy: Achievements, Problems, Challenges*, 290–311. Cambridge, MA: Harvard Ukrainian Research Institute.

Doroshko, Mykola. 2003. 'Borot'ba za vladu rad u Bol'shovyts'kiĭ partii v 1923–1925 rokakh ta ïï vplyv na rozstanovku syl u partiĭno-derzhavniĭ verkhivtsi USRR.' *Problemy istoriï Ukraïny: fakty, sudzhennia, poshuky* 10: 92–103.

Doroshko, Mykola. 2012. *Nomenklatura: kerivna verkhivka Radianskoï Ukraïny (1917–1938 rr.).* Kyiv: Nika-Tsentr.

Dunmore, Timothy. 1980a. *The Stalinist Command Economy: The Soviet State Apparatus and Economic Policy, 1945–1953.* London: Macmillan.

Dunmore, Timothy. 1980b. 'Local Party Organs in Industrial Administration: The Case of the Ob''edinenie Reform.' *Soviet Studies* 32 (2): 195–217.

Dunmore, Timothy. 1984. *Soviet Politics, 1945–1953.* London: Macmillan.

Dyker, David A. 1992a. 'Capital Formation, Capital Stock, and Capital Productivity.' In Ivan S. Koropeckyj, ed. *The Ukrainian Economy: Achievements, Problems, Challenges*, 148–170. Cambridge, MA: Harvard Ukrainian Research Institute.

Dyker, David A. 1992b. *Restructuring the Soviet Economy.* London; New York: Routledge.

Easter, Gerald M. 2000. *Reconstructing the State: Personal Networks and Elite Identity in Soviet Russia.* Cambridge; New York: Cambridge University Press.

Ellman, Michael and Kontorovich, Vladimir, eds. 1998. *The Destruction of the Soviet Economic System: An Insiders' History.* Armonk, NY: M. E. Sharpe.

Erde, David. 1927. *Revoliutsiia na Ukraine: ot Kerenshchiny do nemetskoĭ okkupatsii.* Kharkiv: Proletarii.

Fainberg, Dina and Kalinovsky, Artemy, eds. 2016. *Reconsidering Stagnation in the Brezhnev Era: Ideology and Exchange.* Lanham, MD: Lexington Books.

Fairbanks, Charles H., Jr. 1996. 'Clientelism and the Roots of Post-Soviet Disorder.' In Ronald Grigor Suny, ed. *Transcaucasia, Nationalism, and Social Change: Essays in the History of Armenia, Azerbaijan, and Georgia*, revised edn, 341–374. Ann Arbor, MI: University of Michigan Press.

Farmer, Kenneth C. 1980. *Ukrainian Nationalism in the Post-Stalin Era: Myth, Symbols, and Ideology in Soviet Nationalities Policy.* Dordrecht: Springer Netherlands.

Filtzer, Donald. 2010. *The Hazards of Urban Life in Late Stalinist Russia: Health, Hygiene, and Living Standards, 1943–1953.* Cambridge: Cambridge University Press.

Fioretos, Orfeo, Faletti, Tulia G., and Sheingate, Adam. 2016. 'Historical Institutionalism in Political Science.' In Orfeo Fioretos, Tulia G. Falleti, and Adam Sheingate, eds. *The Oxford Handbook of Historical Institutionalism*, 3–28. Oxford: Oxford University Press.

Fortescue, Stephen. 1988a. 'The Regional Party Apparatus in the "Sectional Society".' *Studies in Comparative Communism* 21 (1): 11–23.

Fortescue, Stephen. 1988b. 'The Primary Party Organizations of Branch Ministries.' In Peter J. Potichnyj, ed. *The Soviet Union: Party and Society*, 26–47. Cambridge; New York: Cambridge University Press.

Fournier, Anna. 2002. 'Mapping Identities: Russian Resistance to Linguistic Ukrainisation in Central and Eastern Ukraine.' *Europe-Asia Studies* 54 (3): 415–433.

Frank, Peter. 1974. 'Constructing a Classified Ranking of CPSU Provincial Committees.' *British Journal of Political Science* 4 (2): 217–230.

Friedgut, Theodore H. 1994a. 'Perestroika in the Provinces: The Politics of Transition in Donetsk.' In Theodore H. Friedgut and Jeffrey W. Hahn, eds. *Local Power and Post-Soviet Politics*, 162–183. Armonk, NY: M. E. Sharpe.

Friedgut, Theodore H. 1994b. *Iuzovka and Revolution, Volume II: Politics and Revolution in Russia's Donbass, 1869–1924*. Princeton, NJ: Princeton University Press.

Frolov, Mykola. 2002. 'Rozlam bil'shovyts'koï elity: osoblyvosti borot'by proty prykhyl'nykiv L. Trots'kogo v Ukraïni 20-kh rokiv XX st.' *Zaporizhzhia Historical Review* 1 (15): 70–79.

Frolov, Mykola. 2003. *Kompartiïno-Radians'ka elita v USRR (1917–1922 rr.): stanovlennia i funktsionuvannia*. Zaporizhzhia: Premier.

Frolov, Mykola. 2004. *Kompartiïno-Radians'ka elita v Ukraïni: osoblyvosti isnuvannia ta funktsionuvannia v 1923–1928 rrï*. Zaporizhzhia: Premier.

Getty, J. Arch. 1985. *Origins of the Great Purges: The Soviet Communist Party Reconsidered, 1933–1938*. Cambridge; New York: Cambridge University Press.

Getty, J. Arch. 2013. *Practicing Stalinism: Bolsheviks, Boyars, and the Persistence of Tradition*. New Haven, CT: Yale University Press.

Gill, Graeme J. 1990. *The Origins of the Stalinist Political System*. Cambridge: Cambridge University Press.

Gill, Graeme J. 1994. *The Collapse of a Single-Party System: The Disintegration of the Communist Party of the Soviet Union*. Cambridge; New York: Cambridge University Press.

Gill, Graeme J. 2018. *Collective Leadership in Soviet Politics*. Cham, Switzerland: Palgrave Macmillan.

Gill, Graeme and Pitty, Roderic. 1997. *Power in the Party: The Organization of Power and Central-Republican Relations in the CPSU*. Basingstoke: Macmillan; New York: St Martin's Press.

Gimpelson, Efim. 2000. *NEP i sovetskaia politicheskaia sistema: 20-e gody*. Moscow: Institut Rossiĭskoĭ istorii RAN.

Gordon, Claire. 2000. 'Institutions, Economic Interests and the Stalling of Economic Reform.' In Neil Robinson, ed. *Institutions and Political Change in Russia*, 106–129. Basingstoke: Macmillan.

Gorlizki, Yoram. 1996. 'Anti-ministerialism and the USSR Ministry of Justice, 1953–56: A Study in Organisational Decline.' *Europe-Asia Studies* 48 (8): 1279–1318.

Gorlizki, Yoram. 2002. 'Ordinary Stalinism: The Council of Ministers and the Soviet Neopatrimonial State, 1946–1953.' *The Journal of Modern History* 74: 699–736.

Gorlizki, Yoram and Khlevniuk, Oleg. 2020. *Substate Dictatorship: Networks, Loyalty, and Institutional Change in the Soviet Union*. New Haven, CT: Yale University Press.

Granick, David. 1987. *Job Rights in the Soviet Union: Their Consequences*. Cambridge; New York: Cambridge University Press.

Graziosi, Andrea. 1992. 'G. L. Piatakov (1890–1937): A Mirror of Soviet History.' *Harvard Ukrainian Studies* 16 (1/2): 102–166.

Graziosi, Andrea. 1995. 'At the Roots of Soviet Industrial Relations and Practices: Piatakov's Donbass in 1921.' *Cahiers du Monde russe* XXXVI (1–2): 95–138.

Graziosi, Andrea. 1996. *The Great Soviet Peasant War: Bolsheviks and Peasants, 1917–1933*. Cambridge, MA: distributed by Harvard University Press for the Ukrainian Research Institute.

Graziosi, Andrea, Haida, Lubomyr A., and Hryn, Halyna, eds. 2013. *After the Holodomor: The Enduring Impact of the Great Famine on Ukraine*. Cambridge, MA: distributed by Harvard University Press for the Ukrainian Research Institute.

Gregory, Paul R. 1990. *Restructuring the Soviet Economic Bureaucracy*. Cambridge; New York: Cambridge University Press.

Gregory, Paul R. 1992. 'The Communist Party and the Economic Bureaucracy in the USSR.' In James R. Millar, ed. *Cracks in the Monolith: Party Power in the Brezhnev Era*, 121–140. Armonk, NY: M. E. Sharpe.

Gregory, Paul R. 2004. *The Political Economy of Stalinism: Evidence from the Soviet Secret Archives*. Cambridge; New York: Cambridge University Press.

Gregory, Paul and Harrison, Mark. 2005. 'Allocation under Dictatorship: Research in Stalin's Archives.' *Journal of Economic Literature* 43 (3): 721–761.

Grossman, Gregory. 1976. 'An Economy at Middle Age.' *Problems of Communism* 25 (2): 18–33.

Hahn, Gordon M. 2003. 'The Past, Present, and Future of the Russian Federal State.' *Demokratizatsiya* 11 (3): 343–362.

Hale, Henry E. 2015. *Patronal Politics: Eurasian Regime Dynamics in Comparative Perspective.* New York: Cambridge University Press.

Hall, Peter A. 2016. 'Politics as a Process Structured in Space and Time.' In Orfeo Fioretos, Tulia G. Falleti, and Adam Sheingate, eds. *The Oxford Handbook of Historical Institutionalism*, 31–50. Oxford: Oxford University Press.

Hanson, Philip. 2003. *The Rise and Fall of the Soviet Economy: An Economic History of the USSR from 1945.* London; New York: Longman.

Haran, Oleksii V. 1993. *Ubyty drakona: z istoriï Rukhu ta novykh partiï Ukraïny.* Kyiv: Lybid'.

Haran, Oleksii V. 2013. 'Ukraine.' *Russian Social Science Review* 54 (3): 68–89.

Harasymiw, Bohdan. 1989. 'Political Patronage and Perestroika: Changes in Communist Party Leadership in Ukraine under Gorbachev and Shcherbytsky.' In Romana M. Bahry, ed. *Echoes of Glasnost in Soviet Ukraine*, 28–39. North York, ON: Captus.

Harasymiw, Bohdan. 2002. *Post-Communist Ukraine.* Edmonton, AB: Canadian Institute of Ukrainian Studies Press.

Harris, James R. 1999. *The Great Urals: Regionalism and the Evolution of the Soviet System.* Ithaca, NY: Cornell University Press.

Harris, James R. 2005. 'Stalin as General Secretary: The Appointments Process and the Nature of Stalin's Power.' In Sarah Davies and James Harris, eds. *Stalin: A New History*, 63–82. Cambridge: Cambridge University Press.

Harris, Jonathan. 2018. *Party Leadership under Stalin and Khrushchev: Party Officials and the Soviet State, 1948–1964.* Lanham, MD: Lexington Books.

Harrison, Mark. 2002. 'Economic Growth and Slowdown.' In Edwin Bacon and Mark Sandle, eds. *Brezhnev Reconsidered*, 38–67. Basingstoke; New York: Palgrave Macmillan.

Hartwell, Christopher A. 2016. *Two Roads Diverge: The Transition Experience of Poland and Ukraine.* New York: Cambridge University Press.

Havrylyshyn, Oleh. 2000. 'The Political Economy of Delayed Reform in Ukraine.' In Sharon L. Wolchik and Volodymyr Zviglyanich, eds. *Ukraine: The Search for a National Identity*, 49–68. Lanham, MD; London: Rowman & Littlefield.

Havrylyshyn, Oleh. 2017. *The Political Economy of Independent Ukraine: Slow Starts, False Starts, and a Last Chance?* London: Palgrave Macmillan.

Herrera, Yoshiko M. 2005. *Imagined Economies: The Sources of Russian Regionalism.* Cambridge; New York: Cambridge University Press.

Hesli, Vicki L. 1995. 'Public Support for the Devolution of Power in Ukraine: Regional Patterns.' *Europe-Asia Studies* 47 (1): 91–121.

Hirsch, Francine. 2014. *Empire of Nations: Ethnographic Knowledge and the Making of the Soviet Union.* Ithaca, NY: Cornell University Press.

Hough, Jerry F. 1969. *The Soviet Prefects: The Local Party Organs in Industrial Decision-Making.* Cambridge, MA: Harvard University Press.

Hough, Jerry F. and Fainsod, Merle. 1979. *How the Soviet Union Is Governed.* Cambridge, MA: Harvard University Press.

Hrynchuts'kyi, Valerii. 1997. *Promyslovi tresty Ukraïny v dvadtsiati roky.* Kyiv: Nova dumka.

Hrytsak, Yaroslav. 2004. 'On Sails and Gales, and Ships Sailing in Various Directions: Post-Soviet Ukraine.' *Ab Imperio* 1: 229–254.

Hudson, Hugh D. 2012. 'The Kulakization of the Peasantry: The OGPU and the End of Faith in Peasant Reconciliation, 1924–1927.' *Jahrbücher für Geschichte Osteuropas* 60 (1): 34–57.

Hughes, James. 1996. 'Patrimonialism and the Stalinist System: The Case of S. I. Syrtsov.' *Europe-Asia Studies* 48 (4): 551–568.

Ioffe, Grigory. 2004. 'Understanding Belarus: Economy and Political Landscape.' *Europe-Asia Studies* 56 (1): 85–118.

*Istoriia Ukrainskoï SSR v desiati tomakh, tom sed'moï.* 1984. Edited by V. A. Godlevskaya. Kyiv: Naukova Dumka.

Ivanova, Galina M. 2011. *Na poroge 'gosudarstva vseobshchego blagosostoianiia. Sotsial'naia politika v SSSR (seredina 1950-kh–nachalo 1970-kh godov).'* Moscow: RAN, Institut Rossiïskoï Istorii.

Josephson, Paul et al., eds. 2013. *An Environmental History of Russia.* Cambridge; New York: Cambridge University Press.

Kähönen, Aappo. 2014. 'Optimal Planning Optimal Economy Optimal Life? The Kosygin Reforms, 1965–72.' In Katalin Miklóssy and Melanie Ilic, eds. *Competition in Socialist Society,* 23–40. Abingdon; New York: Routledge.

Kaplan, Cynthia S. 1983. 'The Communist Party of the Soviet Union and Local Policy Implementation.' *The Journal of Politics* 45 (1): 2–27.

Karmazina, Maria. 2007. *Prezydentstvo: Ukraïns'kyi variant.* Kyiv: NAN Ukraïny, Instytut politychnykh i etnonatsional'nykh doslidzhen' im. I.F. Kurasa.

Kasianov, Georgiy. 2008. *Ukraina 1991–2007: ocherki noveïcheï istorii.* Kyiv: Nash Chas.

Kasianov, Georgiy. 2009. 'Systema vladnykh vidnosyn u suchasniï Ukraïni: grupy interesu, klany ta oliharkhiia.' *Ukrainskyi istorychnyi zhurnal* 1: 160–180.

Katchanovski, Ivan. 2006. 'Regional Political Divisions in Ukraine in 1991–2006.' *Nationalities Papers* 34 (5): 507–532.

Kaufman, Stuart J. 1994. 'Organizational Politics and Change in Soviet Military Policy.' *World Politics* 46 (3): 355–382.

Kaufmann, Daniel. 1994. 'Diminishing Returns to Administrative Controls and the Emergence of the Unofficial Economy: A Framework of Analysis and Applications to Ukraine.' *Economic Policy* 9 (19): 51–69.

Kavanagh, Dennis. 1991. 'Why Political Science Needs History.' *Political Studies* 39 (3): 479–495.

Khlevniuk, O. 1996. *Politburo. Mekhanizmy politicheskoï vlasti v 30-e gody.* Moscow: ROSSPEN.

Khlevniuk, O. 2004. 'Tsentr-regional'nye otnosheniia v 1930-e gody. Lobbirovanie i klientelizm v stalinskoï sisteme upravleniia.' *Vestnik Moskovskogo universiteta* 3: 1–17.

Khlevniuk, O. 2007. 'Regional'naya vlast' v SSSR v 1953-kontse 1950-kh godov. Ustoïchivost' i konflikty.' *Otechestvennaya istoriya* 3: 31–49.

Khlevniuk, O. 2012. 'Rokovaya reforma N. S. Khrushcheva: razdelenie partiïnogo apparata i ego posledstviya, 1962–1964 gody.' *Rossiiskaya istoriya* 4: 164–179.

Khomyn, Oksana Io. and Kravchuk, S. Z. 2013. 'Bezrobittia v Ukraïni pislia Druhoï svitovoï viïny do nezalezhnosti.' *Visnyk Kam'ianets'-Podil's'koho natsional'noho universytetu* 8: 274–276.

Khotin, Leonid. 1992. 'Manager and Primary Party Organization Secretary: The Distribution of Responsibility within the Soviet Enterprise.' In James R. Millar, ed. *Cracks in the Monolith: Party Power in the Brezhnev Era,* 63–88. Armonk, NY: M. E. Sharpe.

Khrystiuk, Pavlo. 1921. *Zamitky i materiialy do istoriï Ukraïns'koï revoliutsiï. 1917–1920 rr., tom 2.* New York: Vydavnytstvo Chartoryïs'kykh.

Kibita, Nataliya. 2013. *Soviet Economic Management under Khrushchev: The Sovnarkhoz Reform.* London; New York: Routledge.

Kibita, Nataliya. 2014. 'De-Stalinising Economic Administration: Ukrainian Alternative Sision (1953–1965).' In Thomas M. Bohn et al., eds. *De-Stalinisation Reconsidered: Persistence and Change in the Soviet Union,* 161–173. Frankfurt am Main: Campus.

Kirkow, Peter. 1998. *Russia's Provinces: Authoritarian Transformation Versus Local Autonomy?* Basingstoke: Macmillan; New York: St Martin's Press.

Klumbytė, Neringa and Sharafutdinova, Gulnaz, eds. 2013. *Soviet Society in the Era of Late Socialism, 1964–1985.* Lanham, MD: Lexington Books.

Kobuta, Stepan. 2011. ''Galyts'ka asambleia'' 1991 roku: politychnyï proekt chy sproba rehional'noho spivrobitnytstva?' *Visnyk Prykarpats'koho universytetu* 19: 21–32.

Konyk, Oleksandr O. 2013. *Deputaty Derzhavnoï Dumy Rosiïs'koï imperiï vid huberniï Naddniprians'koï Ukraïny (1906–1917 rr.).* Dnipropetrovsk: Herda.

Koropeckyj, Ivan S. 1977. 'Economic Prerogatives.' In Ivan S. Koropeckyj, ed. *The Ukraine within the USSR: An Economic Balance Sheet,* 13–64. New York: Praeger.

Kotkin, Stephen. 1997. 'In Search of the Nomenklatura: Yesterday's USSR, Today's Russia.' *East European Constitutional Review* 6 (4): 104–120.

Kotkin, Stephen. 2009. *Uncivil Society: 1989 and the Implosion of the Communist Establishment*. With a contribution by Gross, Jan T. New York: Modern Library.

Kotz, David M. with Weir, Fred. 1997. *Revolution from Above: The Demise of the Soviet System*. London; New York: Routledge.

Kozachenko, O. M. 2011. 'Diial'nist Odes'koï kraiovoï orhanizatsiï NRU ta ïï vidnosyny z mistsevymy orhanamy vlady i partiïnym kerivnytstvom v kintsi 1989-kh–na pochatku 1990-kh rokiv.' In *Inteligentsiia i Vlada* 21: 89–95. Odesa: Astroprynt.

Kramer, Mark. 2018. 'Foreign Policymaking and Party-State Relations in the Soviet Union During the Brezhnev Era.' In Rüdiger Bergien and Jens Gieseke, eds. *Communist Parties Revisited: Sociocultural Approaches to Party Rule in the Soviet Bloc, 1956–1991*, 281–312. New York: Berghahn.

Krasnopiorova, L. O. 2013. 'Ob'emy ta napriamky zhytlovoho budivnytstva na Donbasi v period pisliavoennoï vidbudovy ta "khrushchovs'koï vidlyhy".' *Istorychni i politologichni doslidzhennia* 4 (54): 206–213.

Kravchenko, Volodymyr. 2020. 'Borderland City: Kharkiv.' Translated from Ukrainian by Marta Olynyk. *East/West: Journal of Ukrainian Studies* 7 (1): 169–196.

Kravchuk, Robert S. 1999. 'The Quest for Balance: Regional Self-Government and Subnational Fiscal Policy in Ukraine.' In Taras Kuzio, Robert S. Kravchuk, and Paul D'Anieri, eds. *State and Institution Building in Ukraine*, 155–211. Basingstoke: Macmillan.

Kravchuk, Robert S. 2001. 'Administrative Reform and Centre-Local Relations.' *Journal of Ukrainian Studies* 26 (1–2): 37–75.

Kravchuk, Robert S. 2002. *Ukrainian Political Economy: The First Ten Years*. New York: Palgrave Macmillan.

Krylova, Anna. 2014. 'Soviet Modernity: Stephen Kotkin and the Bolshevik Predicament.' *Contemporary European History* 23 (2): 167–192.

Kubicek, Paul. 1999a. 'What Happened to the Nationalists in Ukraine?' *Nationalism and Ethnic Politics* 5 (1): 29–45.

Kubicek, Paul. 1999b. 'Ukrainian Interest Groups, Corporatism, and Economic Reform.' In Taras Kuzio, Robert S. Kravchuk, and Paul D'Anieri, eds. *State and Institution Building in Ukraine*, 57–81. Basingstoke: Macmillan.

Kubicek, Paul. 2000. *Unbroken Ties: The State, Interest Associations, and Corporatism in Post-Soviet Ukraine*. Ann Arbor, MI: University of Michigan Press.

Kubicek, Paul. 2002. 'Regionalism in Post-Soviet Ukraine.' In Daniel R. Kempton and Terry D. Clark, eds. *Unity or Separation: Center-Periphery Relations in the Former Soviet Union*, 227–249. Westport, CT; London: Praeger.

Kubijovyc, Volodymyr. 1969. *Concise Encyclopaedia Ukraine*. Toronto, ON: University of Toronto Press.

Kuchma, Leonid. 2003. *Ukraina—ne Rossia*. Moscow: Vremia.

Kudelia, Serhiy and Kasianov, Georgiy. 2021. 'Ukraine's Political Development after Independence.' In Mykhailo Minakov, Georgiy Kasianov, and Matthew Rojansky, eds. *From 'the Ukraine' to Ukraine: A Contemporary History, 1991–2021*, 9–52. Stuttgart: Ibidem-Verlag.

Kulchytsky, Stanislav. 1988. 'Kartografichna interpretatsiia protsesiv sotsialistychnoï industrializatsiï v Ukraïns'kiï RSR.' *Istoryko-geografichni doslidzhennia v Ukraïni: zbirka naukovykh prats'*, 12–18. Kyiv: Instytut Istoriï NAN Ukraïny.

Kulchytsky, Stanislav. 1996. *Komunizm v Ukraïni: pershe desiatyrichchia (1919–1928)*. Kyiv: Osnovy.

Kulchytsky, Stanislav. 2013. *Chervonyĭ vyklyk. Istoriia komunizmu v Ukraïni vid ioho narodzhennia do zahybeli. Knyha 1*. Kyiv: Tempora.

Kulchytsky, Stanislav. 2015. *Radians'ka industrializatsiia na Donbasi: 1926–1938*. Kyiv: Instytut Istoriï NAN Ukraïny.

Kulchytsky, Stanislav. 2018. *The Famine of 1932–1933 in Ukraine: An Anatomy of the Holodomor*, translated by Ali Kinsella. Edmonton, AB: Canadian Institute of Ukrainian Studies Press, University of Alberta.

Kushnir, Ostap. 2018. *Ukraine and Russian Neo-imperialism: The Divergent Break*. Lanham, MD: Lexington Books.

Kuzio, Taras. 1994. 'The Multi-party System in Ukraine on the Eve of Elections: Identity Problems, Conflicts and Solutions.' *Government and Opposition* 29 (1): 109–127.

Kuzio, Taras. 1997. *Ukraine under Kuchma: Political Reform, Economic Transformation and Security Policy in Independent Ukraine*. Basingstoke: Macmillan; New York: St Martin's Press.

Kuzio, Taras. 1998a. 'Ukraine: Coming to Terms with the Soviet Legacy.' *Journal of Communist Studies and Transition Politics* 14 (4): 1–27.

Kuzio, Taras. 1998b. 'Ukraine: A Four-Pronged Transition.' In Taras Kuzio, ed. *Contemporary Ukraine: Dynamics of Post-Soviet Transformation*, 165–180. Armonk, NY: M. E. Sharpe.

Kuzio, Taras. 1998c. *Ukraine: State and Nation Building*. London; New York: Routledge.

Kuzio, Taras. 2000. *Ukraine: Perestroika to Independence*, 2nd edn. New York: St Martin's Press.

Kuzio, Taras. 2015. *Ukraine: Democratization, Corruption, and the New Russian Imperialism*. Santa Barbara, CA: Praeger Security International.

Kyrylenko, A. O. 2012. 'Promyslovist' pivdnia Ukraïny v period 'Khrushchovs'koï vidlyhy.' *Naukovyi visnyk Mykolaivs'koho natsional'noho universytetu* 3 (33): 161–165.

Lanovyk, Bohdan D. ed. 2006. *Ekonomichna istoriia Ukraïny i svitu*. Kyiv: Vikar.

Ledeneva, Alena. 2006. *How Russia Really Works: The Informal Practices that Shaped Post-Soviet Politics and Business*. Ithaca, NY: Cornell University Press.

Leitner, Johannes and Meissner, Hannes. 2018. 'Corruption in Ukraine: Soviet Legacy, Failed Reforms and Political Risks.' In Berney Warf, ed. *Handbook on the Geographies of Corruption*, 183–194. Cheltenham, UK: Edward Elgar.

Levitsky, Steven and Way, Lucan A. 2010. *Competitive Authoritarianism: Hybrid Regimes after the Cold War*. Cambridge: Cambridge University Press.

Lewin, Moshe. 2003. 'Rebuilding the Soviet Nomenklatura, 1945–1948.' *Cahiers du Monde russe* 44 (2/3): 219–251.

Liber, George. 1991. 'Korenizatsiia: Restructuring Soviet Nationality Policy in the 1920s.' *Ethnic and Racial Studies* 14 (1): 15–23.

Liber, George. 2016. *Total Wars and the Making of Modern Ukraine, 1914–1954*. Toronto, ON: University of Toronto Press.

Libman, Alexander and Obydenkova, Anastassia V. 2021. *Historical Legacies of the Communism: Modern Politics, Society, and Economic Development*. Cambridge; New York: Cambridge University Press.

Lieven, Dominic. 1990. 'Crisis in the Soviet Union: The Historical Perspective.' *The World Today* 46 (5): 90–93.

Little, Richard D. 1980. 'Regional Legislatures in the Soviet Political System.' *Legislative Studies Quarterly* 5 (2): 233–246.

Loader, Michael. 2016. 'Beria and Khrushchev: The Power Struggle over Nationality Policy and the Case of Latvia.' *Europe-Asia Studies* 68 (10): 1759–1792.

Lozytsky, Volodymyr. 2005. *Politburo TsK Kompartiï Ukraïny: istoriia, osoby, stosunky (1918–1991)*. Kyiv: Geneza.

Lubin, Nancy. 1989. 'Uzbekistan: The Challenges Ahead.' *Middle East Journal* 43 (4): 619–634.

Lukinov, Ivan. 1992. 'Radical Reconstruction of the Ukrainian Economy.' In Ivan S. Koropeckyj, ed. *The Ukrainian Economy: Achievements, Problems, Challenges*, 21–43. Cambridge, MA: Harvard Ukrainian Research Institute.

Lyakh, Serhii. 2018. 'Nevidomyï NEP, abo iak zaporiz'ki komunisty led've nepmanamy ne staly.' *Scholarly Works of the Faculty of History, Zaporizhzhia National University* 50: 149–154.

Lynne, Viola et al., eds. 2005. *The War Against the Peasantry, 1927–1930: The Tragedy of the Soviet Countryside*. New Haven, CT: Yale University Press.

Mace, James E. 1983. *Communism and the Dilemmas of National Liberation: National Communism in Soviet Ukraine, 1918–1933*. Cambridge, MA: distributed by Harvard University Press for the Harvard Ukrainian Research Institute.

Magocsi, Paul. 2007. *Ukraine: An Illustrated History*. Seattle, WA: University of Washington Press.

Mahoney, James and Thelen, Kathleen. 2010. 'A Theory of Gradual Institutional Change.' In James Mahoney and Kathleen Ann Thelen, eds. *Explaining Institutional Change: Ambiguity, Agency, and Power*, 1–37. Cambridge; New York: Cambridge University Press.

Malle, Silvana. 1985. *The Economic Organization of War Communism, 1918–1921*. Cambridge; New York: Cambridge University Press.

Malle, Silvana. 1990. *Employment Planning in the Soviet Union: Continuity and Change*. London: Palgrave Macmillan.

Marchenko, S. D. 2013. 'Superechlyvi protsesy rozvytku agrarnogo vyrobnytstva ta prodovol'chi trudnoshchi u 1980-ti roky.' *Visnyk agrarnoï istoriï* 6–7: 142–152.

Marin, Dalia, Kaufmann, Daniel, and Gorochowskij, Bogdan. 2000. 'Barter in Transition Economies: Competing Explanations Confront Ukrainian Data.' In Paul Seabright, ed. *The Vanishing Rouble: Barter Networks and Non-monetary Transactions in Post-Soviet Societies*, 207–235. Cambridge; New York: Cambridge University Press.

Markevich, Andrei and Zhuravskaya, Ekaterina. 2011. 'M-form Hierarchy with Poorly-Diversified Divisions: A Case of Khrushchev's Reform in Soviet Russia.' *Journal of Public Economics* 95: 1550–1560.

Markov, Ihor. 1993. 'The Role of the President in the Ukrainian Political System.' *RFE/RL Research Report* 2 (48): 31–35.

Marples, David R. 1991. *Ukraine under Perestroika: Ecology, Economics and the Workers' Revolt*. New York: St Martin's Press.

Martin, Terry. 2001. *The Affirmative Action Empire: Nations and Nationalism in the Soviet Union, 1923–1939*. Ithaca, NY: Cornell University Press.

Martinez-Vazquez, Jorge, McClure Jr, Charles E., and Wallace, Sally. 1995. 'Subnational Fiscal Decentralization in Ukraine.' In Richard M. Bird, Robert D. Ebel, and Christine I. Wallich, eds. *Decentralization of the Socialist State: Intergovernmental Finance in Transition Economies*, 281–319. Washington, DC: The World Bank.

Mau, Vladimir. 2013. *Reformy i dogmy. Gosudarstvo i ekonomika v epokhu reform i revoliutsiï (1861–1929), 3-e izdanie*. Moscow: Delo.

McAuley, Mary. 1974. 'Hunting the Hierarchy: RSFSR Obkom Secretaries and the Central Committee.' *Soviet Studies* 26: 473–501.

McFaul, Michael. 2010. 'Importing Revolution: Internal and External Factors in Ukraine's 2004 Democratic Breakthrough.' In Valerie Bunce, Michael McFaul, and Kathryn Stoner-Weiss, eds. *Democracy and Authoritarianism in the Postcommunist World*, 189–225. Cambridge; New York: Cambridge University Press.

Meleshevich, Andrey A. 2007. *Party Systems in Post-Soviet Countries: A Comparative Study of Political Institutionalization in the Baltic States, Russia, and Ukraine*. New York: Palgrave.

Ménil, Georges de. 2000. 'From Hyperinflation to Stagnation.' *Russian and East European Finance and Trade* 36 (1): 28–58.

Mieczkowski, Zbigniew. 1965. 'The 1962–1963 Reforms in Soviet Economic Regionalization.' *Slavic Review* 24 (3): 479–496.

Mieczkowski, Zbigniew. 1967. 'The Economic Administrative Regions in the U.S.S.R.' *Tijdschrift voor economische en sociale geografie* 58 (4): 209–219.

Miller, Chris. 2016a. 'Gorbachev's Agriculture Agenda: Decollectivization and the Politics of Perestroika.' *Kritika* 17 (1): 95–118.

Miller, Chris. 2016b. *The Struggle to Save the Soviet Economy: Mikhail Gorbachev and the Collapse of the USSR*. Chapel Hill, NC: University of North Carolina Press.

Miller, John H. 1989. 'Putting Clients in Place: The Role of Patronage in Cooption into the Soviet Leadership.' In Archie Brown, ed. *Political Leadership in the Soviet Union*, 54–95. London: Palgrave Macmillan.

Minakov, Mykhailo (Mikhail). 2012. 'Postsovets'ka nesuchasnist' respubliky rehioniv.' *Krytyka* XVI (9–10): 2–4.

Minakov, Mykhailo. 2018. *Development and Dystopia: Studies in Post-Soviet Ukraine and Eastern Europe*. Stuttgart: Ibidem.

Minakov, Mykhailo. 2019. 'Republic of Clans: The Evolution of the Ukrainian Political System.' In Bálint Magyar, ed. *Stubborn Structures: Reconceptualizing Post-Communist Regimes*, 217–245. Budapest; New York: Central European University Press.

Minakov, Mykhailo and Rojansky, Matthew. 2021. 'Democracy in Ukraine.' In Mykhailo Minakov, Georgiy Kasianov, and Matthew Rojansky, eds. *From 'the Ukraine' to Ukraine: A Contemporary History, 1991–2021*, 321–357. Stuttgart: Ibidem.

Minakov, Mykhailo, Kasianov, Georgiy, and Rojansky, Matthew, eds. 2021. *From 'the Ukraine' to Ukraine: A Contemporary History, 1991–2021*. Stuttgart: Ibidem.

Mokhov, Viktor P. 2003. *Regional'naia politicheskaia elita Rossii (1945–1991 gg.)*. Perm: Permskoe knizhnoe izdatel'stvo.

Monty, Christopher S. 2012. 'The Central Committee Secretariat, the Nomenklatura, and the Politics of Personnel Management in the Soviet Order, 1921–1927.' *The Soviet and Post-Soviet Review* 39: 166–191.

Moses, Joel C. 1976. 'Regional Cohorts and Political Mobility in the USSR: The Case of Dnepropetrovsk.' *The Soviet and Post-Soviet Review* 3 (1): 63–89.

Moses, Joel C. 1992. 'Soviet Provincial Politics in an Era of Transition and Revolution, 1989–91.' *Soviet Studies* 44 (3): 479–509.

Moses, Joel C. 2019. 'Russian Center-Periphery Relations from Khrushchev to Putin, 1957–2018.' *Demokratizatsiya: The Journal of Post-Soviet Democratization* 27 (2): 215–236.

Motyl, Alexander J. 1990. *Sovietology, Rationality, Nationality: Coming to Grips with Nationalism in the USSR*. New York: Columbia University Press.

Motyl, Alexander J. 1995. 'The Conceptual President: Leonid Kravchuk and the Politics of Surrealism.' In Timothy J. Colton and Robert C. Tucker, eds. *Patterns in Post-Soviet Leadership*, 103–121. Boulder, CO: Westview Press.

Motyl, Alexander J. 1997. 'Structural Constraints and Starting Points: The Logic of Systemic Change in Ukraine and Russia.' *Comparative Politics* 29 (4): 433–447.

Motyl, Alexander and Krawchenko, Bohdan. 1997. 'Ukraine: From Empire to Statehood.' In Ian Bremmer and Ray Taras, eds. *New States, New Politics: Building the Post-Soviet Nations*, 235–275. Cambridge; New York: Cambridge University Press.

Myshlovska, Oksana. 2020. 'Regionalism in Ukraine: Historic Evolution, Regional Claim-Making, and Centre-Periphery Conflict Resolution.' In Hanna Shelest and Maryna Rabinovych, eds. *Decentralisation, Regional Diversity, and Conflict: The Case of Ukraine*, 17–47. Cham, Switzerland: Palgrave Macmillan.

Myshlovska, Oksana, Schmid, Ulrich, and Hofmann, Tatjana. 2019. 'Introduction.' In Ulrich Schmid and Oksana Myshlovska, eds. *Regionalism without Regions: Reconceptualizing Ukraine's Heterogeneity*, 3–23. Budapest; New York: Central European University Press.

Nahaylo, Bohdan. 1999. *The Ukrainian Resurgence*. Toronto, ON: University of Toronto Press.

Naidis, Isaak G. 1966. *Partiĭnoe rukovodstvo khoziaĭstvom na novom etape*. Moscow: Moskovskiĭ rabochiĭ.

Nemiria, Grigory. 2000. 'Regionalism: An Underestimated Dimension of State-Building.' In Sharon L. Wolchik and Volodymyr Zviglyanich, eds. *Ukraine: The Search for a National Identity*, 183–197. Lanham, MD; London: Rowman & Littlefield.

Nordberg, Marc. 1998. 'State and Institution Building in Ukraine.' In Taras Kuzio, ed. *Contemporary Ukraine: Dynamics of Post-Soviet Transformation*, 41–55. Armonk, NY: M. E. Sharpe.

North, Douglass C. 1990. *Institutions, Institutional Change and Economic Performance*. Cambridge; New York: Cambridge University Press.

Nove, Alec. 1970. 'Soviet Agriculture under Brezhnev.' *Slavic Review* 29 (3): 379–410.

Nove, Alec. 1977. *The Soviet Economic System*. London: George Allen & Unwin.

Nove, Alec. 1992. *An Economic History of the USSR: 1917–1991*, 3rd edn. London: Penguin.

O'Connor, Timothy Edward. 1992. *The Engineer of Revolution: L. B. Krasin and the Bolsheviks, 1870–1926*. Boulder, CO: Westview Press.

Ōgushi, Atsushi. 2008. *The Demise of the Soviet Communist Party*. London; New York: Routledge.

Oliinyk, Mykola. 2015. *Transformatsiïni protsesy na Podilli v dobu nepu (1921–1928 rr.)*. Khmelnytsky: Polihrafist-2.

Onipko, Tetiana. 2013. *Spozhyvcha kooperatsiia Ukraïny v konteksti mizhnarodnoho kooperatyvnoho rukhu: 20-ti rr. XX st.* Poltava: PUET.

Oosterbaan, Gwynne. 1997. 'Clan Based Politics in Ukraine and the Implications for Democratization.' In John S. Micgiel, ed. *Perspectives on Political and Economic Transitions after Communism*, 213–233. New York: Institute on East Central Europe, Columbia University.

Osokina, Elena. 1999. *Za facadom 'Stalinskogo izobiliia': raspredelenie i rynok v snabzhenii naseleniia v gody industrializatsii, 1927–1941.* Moscow: ROSSPEN.

Ozornoy, Gennady. 1983. 'The Ukrainian Economy in the 1970s.' In Bohdan Krawchenko, ed. *Ukraine after Shelest*, 73–100. Edmonton, AB: Canadian Institute of Ukrainian Studies, University of Alberta.

Palko, Olena. 2014. 'Ukrainian National Communism: Challenging History.' *Debatte: Journal of Contemporary Central and Eastern Europe* 22 (1): 27–48.

Palko, Olena. 2020. 'Debating the Early Soviet Nationalities Policy: The Case of Soviet Ukraine.' In Lara Douds et al., eds. *The Fate of the Bolshevik Revolution: Illiberal Liberation, 1917–41*, 163–171. London: Bloomsbury.

Pallot, Judith and Shaw, Denis J. B. 1981. *Planning in the Soviet Union.* London: Croom Helm.

Pauly, Matthew. 2018. *Breaking the Tongue: Language, Education, and Power in Soviet Ukraine, 1923–1934.* Toronto, ON: University of Toronto Press.

Pavlova, Irina. 1993. *Stalinism: stanovlenie mekhanizma vlasti.* Novosibirsk: Sibirskii Khronograf.

Pavlova, Irina. 2001. *Mekhanizm stalinskoï vlasti: stanovlenie i funktsionirovanie.* Novosibirsk: SO RAN.

Perri, Giuseppe. 2014. 'Korenizacija: An Ambiguous and Temporary Strategy of Legitimization of Soviet Power in Ukraine (1923–1933) and Its Legacy.' *History of Communism in Europe* 5: 131–154.

Pierson, Paul. 2004. *Politics in Time: History, Institutions, and Social Analysis.* Princeton, NJ: Princeton University Press.

Pipes, Richard. 1997. *The Formation of the Soviet Union: Communism and Nationalism 1917–1923.* Cambridge, MA; London: Harvard University Press.

Plokhy, Serhii. 2012. *The Cossack Myth: History and Nationhood in the Age of Empires.* Cambridge; New York: Cambridge University Press.

Plokhy, Serhii. 2014. *The Last Empire: The Final Days of the Soviet Union.* New York: Basic Books.

Plokhy, Serhii. 2015. *The Gates of Europe: A History of Ukraine.* London: Allen Lane.

Plokhy, Serhii. 2019. *Chernobyl: History of a Tragedy.* London: Penguin.

Pop-Eleches, Grigore and Tucker, Joshua. 2017. *Communism's Shadow: Historical Legacies and Contemporary Political Attitudes.* Princeton, NJ: Princeton University Press.

Popovkin, V. A., Kalytenko, A. P., and Rozynka, V. O. 1994. *Rivni sotsial'no-ekonomichnoho rozvytku rehioniv Ukraïny, vyp. 24.* Kyiv: Natsional'nyĭ instytut stratehichnykh doslidzhen'.

Portnov, Andrei and Portnova, Tatiana. 2014. 'Stolitsa zatsoia? Brezhnevskiĭ mif Dnepropetrovska.' *Politika kul'tury* 5 (97): 71–87.

Potichnyj, Peter J. 1992a. 'Elections in the Ukraine, 1990.' In Zvi Gitelman, ed. *The Politics of Nationality and the Erosion of the USSR*, 176–213. Basingstoke: Macmillan; New York: St Martin's Press.

Potichnyj, Peter J. 1992b. *The Multi-party System in Ukraine.* Köln: BOIS.

Prizel, Ilya. 1997. 'Ukraine between Proto-democracy and "Soft" Authoritarianism.' In K. Dawisha and B. Parrott, eds. *Democratic Changes and Authoritarian Reactions in Russia, Ukraine, Belarus, and Moldova*, 330–370. West Nyack, NY: Cambridge University Press.

Prylutskyi, Viktor. 2004. 'Modernizatsiia promyslovosti radians'koï Ukraïny u mizhvoennyĭ period (1921–1938 rr.).' *Problemy istoriï Ukraïny: fakty, sudzhennia, poshuky* 11: 94–128.

Puglisi, Rosaria. 2003. 'The Rise of the Ukrainian Oligarchs.' *Democratization* 10 (3): 99–123.

Pyrih, Oleksandra. 2001. *NEP: bil'shovyts'ka polityka improvizatsiï*. Kyiv: Kyïvs'kyï natsional'nyï torgovo-ekonomichnyï universytet.

Pyzhikov, Aleksandr V. 2002. *Khrushchevskaya 'Ottepel'*. Moscow: Olma-Press.

Rassweiler, Anne D. 1988. *The Generation of Power: The History of Dneprostroi*. New York; Oxford: Oxford University Press.

Ravich-Cherkasskii, Moisei Efimovich. 1923. *Istoriia kommunisticheskoĭ partii (b-ov) Ukrainy*. Kyiv: Gosudarstvennoe izdatel'stvo Ukrainy.

Rees, E. Arfon. 2001. 'Leaders and Their Institutions.' In Paul R. Gregory, ed. *Behind the Façade of Stalin's Command Economy: Evidence from the Soviet State and Party Archives*, 35–60. Stanford, CA: Hoover Institution Press, Stanford University.

Rees, E. Arfon. 2004a. 'Stalin as Leader 1924–1937: From Oligarch to Dictator.' In E. A. Rees, ed. *The Nature of Stalin's Dictatorship: The Politburo, 1924–1953*, 19–58. London: Palgrave Macmillan.

Rees, E. Arfon. 2004b. 'Stalin as Leader, 1937–1953: From Dictator to Despot.' In E. A. Rees, ed. *The Nature of Stalin's Dictatorship: The Politburo, 1924–1953*, 200–239. London: Palgrave Macmillan.

Rees, E. Arfon. 2012. *Iron Lazar: A Political Biography of Lazar Kaganovich*. London: Anthem Press.

Rees, E. Arfon and Watson, Derek H. 1997. 'Politburo and Sovnarkom.' In E. A. Rees, ed. *Decision-Making in the Stalinist Command Economy, 1932–37*, 9–31. Basingstoke: Macmillan; New York: St Martin's Press.

Reshetar Jr, John S. 1952. *The Ukrainian Revolution, 1917–1920: A Study in Nationalism*. Princeton, NJ: Princeton University Press.

Reuter, Ora John. 2017. *The Origins of Dominant Parties: Building Authoritarian Institutions in Post-Soviet Russia*. Cambridge; New York: Cambridge University Press.

Riga, Lilian. 2012. *The Bolsheviks and the Russian Empire*. Cambridge: Cambridge University Press.

Rigby, T. H. (Thomas Henry). 1964. 'Traditional, Market, and Organizational Societies and the USSR.' *World Politics* 16 (4): 539–557.

Rigby, T. H. 1976. 'Soviet Communist Party Membership under Brezhnev.' *Soviet Studies* 28 (3): 317–337.

Rigby, T. H. 1981. 'Early Provincial Cliques and the Rise of Stalin.' *Soviet Studies* 33 (1): 3–28.

Risch, William Jay. 2011. *The Ukrainian West: Culture and the Fate of Empire in Soviet Lviv*. Cambridge, MA: Harvard University Press.

Rodgers, Allan. 1974. 'The Locational Dynamics of Soviet Industry.' *Annals of the Association of American Geographers* 64 (2): 226–240.

Roeder, Philip G. 1988. *Soviet Political Dynamics: Development of the First Leninist Polity*. New York: Harper & Row.

Roeder, Philip G. 1994. 'Varieties of Post-Soviet Authoritarian Regimes.' *Post-Soviet Affairs* 10 (1): 61–101.

Roeder, Philip G. 2007. *Where Nation-States Come From: Institutional Change in the Age of Nationalism*. Princeton, NJ: Princeton University Press.

Rudnytsky, Ivan L. 1987. *Essays in Modern Ukrainian History*. Edited by Rudnytsky, Peter L. Edmonton, AB: Canadian Institute of Ukrainian Studies.

Rudnytskyi, Omelian, Kulchytskyi, Stanislav, Gladun, Oleksandr, and Kulyk, Natalia. 2020. 'The 1921–1923 Famine and the Holodomor of 1932–1933 in Ukraine: Common and Distinctive Features.' *Nationalities Papers* 48 (3): 549–568.

Rutland, Peter. 1993. *The Politics of Economic Stagnation in the Soviet Union: The Role of Local Party Organs in Economic Management*. Cambridge; New York: Cambridge University Press.

Sakwa, Richard. 1991. *Gorbachev and His Reforms, 1985–1990*. Englewood Cliffs, NJ: Prentice Hall.

Sasse, Gwendolyn. 2001. 'The "New" Ukraine: A State of Regions.' *Regional and Federal Studies* 11 (3): 69–100.

Sasse, Gwendolyn. 2010. 'The Role of Regionalism.' *Journal of Democracy* 21 (3): 99–106.

Satskyi, Pavlo V. 2017. 'Ratsionalizatsiia resursnoho zabespechennia budivnytstva Kakhovs'koï HES i Pivdenno-Ukraïns'koho i Pivnichno-Kryms'koho kanaliv ta hospodars'ke osvoennia pivdennykh raioniv Ukraïny i Krymu (1950–1953 rr.).' *ZNU* 47: 178–182.

Schapiro, Leonard. 1970. *The Communist Party of the Soviet Union*, 2nd edn. New York: Random House.

Schattenberg, Susanne. 2022. *Brezhnev: The Making of a Statesman*. London; New York: I. B. Tauris, Bloomsbury.

Schmid, Ulrich. 2020. *Ukraine: Contested Nationhood in a European Context*. Translated by Roy Sellars. London; New York: Routledge.

Schmid, Ulrich and Myshlovska, Oksana, eds. 2019. *Regionalism without Regions: Reconceptualizing Ukraine's Heterogeneity*. Budapest; New York: Central European University Press.

Seabright, Paul, ed. 2000. *The Vanishing Rouble: Barter Networks and Non-monetary Transactions in Post-Soviet Societies*. Cambridge; New York: Cambridge University Press.

Sedelius, Thomas. 2015. 'Party Presidentialization in Ukraine.' In Gianluca Passarelli, ed. *The Presidentialization of Political Parties: Organizations, Institutions and Leaders*, 124–141. Basingstoke: Palgrave Macmillan.

Seliktar, Ofira. 2015. *Politics, Paradigms, and Intelligence Failures: Why So Few Predicted the Collapse of the Soviet Union*. London; New York: Routledge.

Shapoval, Yuri I. 2003. 'V.V.Shcherbytskyï: osoba polityka sered obstavyn chasu.' *Ukrainskyï istorychnyï zhurnal* 1: 118–129.

Shapoval, Yuri and Yakubets, Olexandr. 2016. 'Ostannia barykada: Volodymyr Shcherbytskyï pid chas "perebudovy".' *Ukraïna XX stolittia: kul'tura, ideologiia, polityka: zbornyk statei* 21: 12–27.

Shaw, Denis J. B. 1985. 'Spatial Dimensions in Soviet Central Planning.' *Transactions of the Institute of British Geographers* 10 (4): 401–412.

Shteinle, Oleksii. 2012. 'Buro TsK Kompartiï Ukraïny v 1952–1953 rr.: personal'nyï sklad.' *ZNU*, 33: 155–158.

Simon, Gerhard. 1991. *Nationalism and Policy toward the Nationalities in the Soviet Union: From Totalitarian Dictatorship to Post-Stalinist Society*. Translated by Karen Forster and Oswald Forster. Boulder, CO: Westview Press.

Simonov, Nikolai S. 1996. *Voenno-promyshlennyï kompleks SSSR v 20-50-e gody: tempy ekonomicheskogo rosta, struktura, organizatsiia proizvodstva i upravlenie*. Moscow: ROSSPEN.

Siroshtan, Mykola A. et al., eds. 1967. *Istoriia mist i sil Ukraïns'koi RSR. Kharkivs'ka oblast'*. Kyiv: Golovna redaktsiia Ukraïns'koï Radians'koï entsyklopediï AN URSR.

Slezkine, Yuri. 1994. 'The USSR as a Communal Apartment, or How a Socialist State Promoted Ethnic Particularism.' *Slavic Review* 53 (2): 414–452.

Smith, Jeremy. 2005. 'Stalin as Commissar for Nationality Affairs, 1918–1922.' In Sarah Davies and James Harris, eds. *Stalin: A New History*, 45–62. Cambridge: Cambridge University Press.

Smith, Jeremy. 2013. *Red Nations: The Nationalities Experience in and after the USSR*. Cambridge; New York: Cambridge University Press.

Smolii, Valerii A. et al., eds. 2011. *Ekonomichna istoriia Ukraïny: istoryko-ekonomichne doslidzhennia, t.2* Kyiv: Nika-Tsentr.

Snyder, Jack. 2005. 'Introduction: Reconstructing Politics amidst the Wreckage of Empire.' In Barnett Rubin and Jack Snyder, eds. *Post-Soviet Political Order: Conflict and State Building*, 2nd edn, 1–12. London: Taylor & Francis.

Sochor, Zenovia A. 1996. 'From Liberalization to Post-Communism: The Role of the Communist Party in Ukraine.' *Journal of Ukrainian Studies* 21 (1): 147–163.

Sokyrska, Vladylena V. 2019. 'Ukraïnska SRR v systemi 'zahal'nofederatyvnoho biudzhetu' RSFSR/SRSR 1920-kh rr.' *Gileia: naukovyï visnyk* 141 (2/1): 151–156.

Solchanyk, Roman. 1994. 'The Politics of State Building: Centre-Periphery Relations in Post-Soviet Ukraine.' *Europe-Asia Studies* 46 (1): 47–68.

Solchanyk, Roman. 1995. 'Ukraine: The Politics of Reform.' *Problems of Post-Communism* 42 (6): 46–51.

Soldatenko, Valerii. 2017. *Georgiĭ Piatakov: Opponent Lenina, Sopernik Stalina*. Moscow: ROSSPEN.

Solnick, Steven. 1998. *Stealing the State: Control and Collapse in Soviet Institutions*. Cambridge, MA: Harvard University Press.

Somchynsky, Bohdan. 1988. 'National Communism and the Politics of Industrialization in Ukraine, 1923–1928.' *Journal of Ukrainian Studies* 13 (2): 52–69.

Stebelsky, Ihor. 1975. 'Ukrainian Agriculture: The Problems of Specialization and Intensification in Perspective.' In Peter J. Potichnyj, ed. *Ukraine in the Seventies. Papers and Proceedings of the McMaster Conference on Contemporary Ukraine, October 1974*, 103–126. Oakville, ON: Mosaic Press.

Steinmo, Sven. 2008. 'Historical Institutionalism.' In Donatella Della Porta and Michael Keating, eds. *Approaches and Methodologies in the Social Sciences: A Pluralist Perspective*, 118–138. Cambridge; New York: Cambridge University Press.

Stojko, Wolodymyr. 1977. 'Ukrainian National Aspirations and the Russian Provisional Government.' In Taras Hunczak, ed. *The Ukraine, 1917–1921: A Study in Revolution*, 4–32. Cambridge, MA.: Harvard Ukrainian Research Institute.

Stoner-Weiss, Kathryn. 1997. *Local Heroes: The Political Economy of Russian Regional Governance*. Princeton, NJ; Chichester: Princeton University Press.

Stoner-Weiss, Kathryn. 2006. *Resisting the State: Reform and Retrenchment in Post-Soviet Russia*. Cambridge; New York: Cambridge University Press.

Stotland, Daniel. 2015. 'The War Within: Factional Strife and Politics of Control in the Soviet Party State (1944–1948).' *Russian History* 42 (3): 343–369.

Sullivant, Robert S. 1962. *Soviet Politics and the Ukraine, 1917–1957*. New York; London: Columbia University Press.

Swain, Geoffrey. 2008. *Russia's Civil War*. Stroud: The History Press.

Swain, Geoffrey. 2016. *Khrushchev*. London; New York, NY: Palgrave Macmillan.

Swain, Geoffrey. 2020. 'A Soviet Government?' In Daniel Orlovsky, ed. *A Companion to the Russian Revolution*, 331–339. Hoboken, NJ: Willey-Blackwell.

Szporluk, Roman. 1992. 'The Strange Politics of Lviv: An Essay in Search of an Explanation.' In Zvi Gitelman, ed. *The Politics of Nationality and the Erosion of the USSR*, 215–231. Basingstoke: Macmillan; New York: St Martin's Press.

Szporluk, Roman. 2006. 'Lenin, "Great Russia," and Ukraine.' *Harvard Ukrainian Studies* 28 (1/4): 611–626.

Taubman, William. 2003. *Khrushchev: The Man and His Era*. New York: Norton.

Thelen, Kathleen and Steino, Sven. 1992. 'Historical Institutionalism in Comparative Politics.' In Sven Steinmo, Kathleen Thelen, and Frank Longstreth, eds. *Structuring Politics: Historical Institutionalism in Comparative Analysis*, 1–32. Cambridge; New York: Cambridge University Press.

Tikhonov, Aleksei and Gregory, Paul R. 2001. 'Stalin's Last Plan.' In Paul R. Gregory, ed. *Behind the Façade of Stalin's Command Economy: Evidence from the Soviet State and Party Archives*, 159–192. Stanford, CA: Hoover Institution Press, Stanford University.

Tillet, Lowell. 1975. 'Ukrainian Nationalism and the Fall of Shelest.' *Slavic Review* 34 (4): 752–768.

Tolochko, Petro et al. 2018. *Shcherbytskyĭ Volodymyr Vasyl'yovych. Politychnyĭ portret na foni epokhy*. Kyiv: Adef-Ukraina.

Tompson, William J. 1991. 'The Fall of Nikita Khrushchev.' *Soviet Studies* 43 (6): 1101–1121.

Tompson, William J. 2003. *The Soviet Union under Brezhnev*. Harlow: Routledge.

Tron'ko, Petro T. et al., eds. 1970. *Istoriia mist i sil Ukraïns'koi RSR. Volyns'ka oblast'*. Kyiv: Golovna redaktsiia Ukraïns'koï Radians'koï entsyklopediï AN URSR.

Tucker, Robert C. 1995. 'Post-Soviet Leadership and Change.' In Timothy J. Colton and Robert C. Tucker, eds. *Patterns in Post-Soviet Leadership*, 5–28. Boulder, CO: Westview Press.

Turovsky, Rostislav. 1999. 'Sravnitel'nyĭ analiz tendentsiĭ regional'nogo razvitiia Rossii i Ukrainy.' *Polis* 6: 1–13.

'Ukraïnizatsiia' 1920-1930-kh rokiv: peredumovy, zdobytky, uroky. 2003. Edited by V. A. Smolii. Kyiv: Instytut Istoriï NAN Ukraïny.

Vasil'ev [Vasiliev], Valerii. 2002. 'Vinnitsa oblast'.' In E. A. Rees, ed. Centre-Local Relations in the Stalinist State, 1928–1941, 167–190. London: Palgrave Macmillan.

Vasil'ev, Valerii. 2004. 'The Ukrainian Politburo, 1934–1937.' In E. A. Rees, ed. The Nature of Stalin's Dictatorship: The Politburo, 1924–1953, 168–199. London: Palgrave Macmillan.

Vasil'ev, Valerii. 2009. 'Pershi sekretari obkomiv Kompartiï Ukraïny v radians'kiï upravlins'kiï systemi (ser. 50-kh–pochatok 60-kh rr. XX st.).' In Valerii Smolii, ed. Ukraïna XX st.: kul'tura, ideologiia, polityka. Zbirnyk stateĭ, 15 (1): 318–331. Kyiv: Institut Istoriï Ukraïny NAN Ukraïny.

Vasil'ev, Valerii. 2014. Politychne kerivnytstvo URSR i SRSR: dynamika vidnosyn tsentr-subtsentr vlady (1917–1938). Kyiv: Instytut Istoriï NAN Ukraïny.

Velychenko, Stephen. 2015. Painting Imperialism and Nationalism Red: The Ukrainian Marxist Critique of Russian Communist Rule in Ukraine, 1918–1925. Toronto, ON; Buffalo, NY; London: University of Toronto Press.

Von Hirschhausen, Christian. 1998. 'Industrial Restructuring in Ukraine Seven Years after Independence: From Socialism to a Planning Economy?' Communist Economies and Economic Transformation 10 (4): 451–465.

Wandycz, Piotr S. 1969. Soviet-Polish Relations, 1917–1921. Cambridge, MA: Harvard University Press.

Way, Lucan Ahmad. 2005. 'Kuchma's Failed Authoritarianism.' Journal of Democracy 16 (2): 131–145.

Way, Lucan Ahmad. 2015. Pluralism by Default: Weak Autocrats and the Rise of Competitive Politics. Baltimore, MD: Johns Hopkins University Press.

Way, Lucan Ahmad. 2021. '"The Party of Power": Authoritarian Diaspora and Pluralism by Default in Ukraine.' Democratization 28 (3): 484–501.

Wegren, Stephen K. 1992. 'Dilemmas of Agrarian Reform in the Soviet Union.' Soviet Studies 44 (1): 3–36.

Werth, Nicolas. 1977. 'Structure Sociale du Parti Communiste de Biélorussie sous la NEP (D'après l'Enquête du Bureau Biélorusse Temporaire).' Cahiers du Monde russe et soviétique 18 (4): 341–355.

Westlund, Hans. 1998. 'The Limits of Spatial Planning: Regional Experiences of the Soviet Epoch.' Papers in Regional Science: The Journal of the RSAI 77 (3): 213–240.

Wheatcroft, Stephen G. 2004. 'From Team-Stalin to Degenerate Tyranny.' In E. A. Rees, ed. The Nature of Stalin's Dictatorship: The Politburo, 1924–1953, 79–107. London: Palgrave Macmillan.

Whitefield, Stephen. 1993. Industrial Power and the Soviet State. Oxford: Clarendon Press; New York: Oxford University Press.

Whitmore, Sarah. 2004. State-Building in Ukraine: The Ukrainian Parliament, 1990–2003. London: Routledge; New York: Curzon.

Whitmore, Sarah. 2005. 'State and Institution Building under Kuchma.' Problems of Post-Communism 52 (5): 3–11.

Whitmore, Sarah. 2019. 'Disrupted Democracy in Ukraine? Protest, Performance and Contention in the Verkhovna Rada.' Europe-Asia Studies 71 (9): 1474–1507.

Willerton Jr, John P. 1987. 'Patronage Networks and Coalition Building in the Brezhnev Era.' Soviet Studies 39 (2): 175–204.

Willerton Jr, John P. 1992. Patronage and Politics in the USSR. Cambridge; New York: Cambridge University Press.

Wilson, Andrew. 1993. 'The Growing Challenge to Kiev from the Donbas.' RFE/RL Research Report 2 (33): 8–13.

Wilson, Andrew. 1997. Ukrainian Nationalism in the 1990s: A Minority Faith. Cambridge: Cambridge University Press.

Wilson, Andrew. 1999. 'Ukraine.' In Robert Elgie, ed. Semi-Presidentialism in Europe, 260–280. Oxford; New York: Oxford University Press.

Wilson, Andrew. 2015. The Ukrainians: Unexpected Nation, 4th edn. New Haven, CT; London: Yale University Press.

Wilson, Andrew and Bilous, Artur. 1993. 'Political Parties in Ukraine.' *Europe-Asia Studies* 45 (4): 693–703.

Wise, Charles R. and Brown, Trevor L. 1999. 'The Separation of Powers in Ukraine.' *Communist and Post-Communist Studies* 32: 23–44.

Wise, Charles R. and Pigenko, Volodymyr. 1999. 'The Separation of Powers Puzzle in Ukraine: Sorting Out Responsibilities and Relationships between President, Parliament, and the Prime Minister.' In Taras Kuzio, Robert S. Kravchuk, and Paul D'Anieri, eds. *State and Institution Building in Ukraine*, 25–55. Basingstoke: Macmillan.

Wittkowsky, Andreas. 1998. *Piatiletka bez plana: Ukraina: 1991–1996: formirovanie natshion-al'nogo gosudarstva, ekonomika, elity*. Kyiv: Sfera.

Wolchik, Sharon L. and Zviglyanich, Volodymyr, eds. 2000. *Ukraine: The Search for a National Identity*. Lanham, MD; London: Rowman & Littlefield.

Wolczuk, Kataryna. 1997. 'Presidentialism in Ukraine: A Mid-term Review of the Second Presidency.' *Democratization* 4 (3): 152–171.

Wolczuk, Kataryna. 2001. *The Moulding of Ukraine: The Constitutional Politics of State Formation*. Budapest: Central European University Press.

Woodruff, David. 1999. *Money Unmade: Barter and the Fate of Russian Capitalism*. Ithaca, NY; London: Cornell University Press.

Yakubovskaia, Sofia. 1959. *Stroitelstvo Soyuznogo Sovetskogo Sotsialisticheskogo gosudarstva 1922–1925*. Moscow: Izdatel'stvo Akademii Nauk SSSR.

Yefimenko [Efimenko], Hennadii. 2008. *Vzaemovidnosyny Kremlia ta Radians'koï Ukraïny: ekonomichnyĭ aspect (1917–1919 rr.)*. Kyiv: Instytut Istoriï NAN Ukraïny.

Yefimenko, Hennadii. 2010. 'Za lashtunkamy komisiï zi z'iasuvannia vzaemovidnosyn mizh RSFRR ta USRR (sichen'-traven' 1922 r.).' *Problemy istoriï Ukraïny: fakty, sudzhennia, poshuky* 19 (1): 119–159.

Yefimenko, Hennadii. 2012. *Status USRR ta ïï vzaemovidnosyny z RSFRR: dovhyĭ 1920 rik*. Kyiv: Instytut Istoriï NAN Ukraïny.

Yefimenko, Hennadii. 2015. 'Dokumenty i materialy z istoriï vidnosyn mizh USRR ta RSFRR u 1917–1923 rr.: dzhereloznavchyĭ analiz.' In *Problemy istoriï Ukraïny: fakty, sudzhennia, poshuky*, 23: 307–337. Kyiv: Instytut Istoriï NAN Ukraïny.

Yurchak, Alexei. 2006. *Everything Was Forever, Until It Was No More: The Last Soviet Generation*. Princeton, NJ: Princeton University Press.

Zelenin, Il'ia E. 2011. 'N.S. Khrushchev's Agrarian Policy and Agriculture in the USSR.' *Russian Studies in History* 50 (3): 44–70.

Zhuk, Sergei. 2010. *Rock and Roll in the Rocket City: The West, Identity, and Ideology in Soviet Dniepropetrovsk, 1960–1985*. Washington, DC: Woodrow Wilson Center Press.

Zimmerman, William. 2014. *Ruling Russia: Authoritarianism from the Revolution to Putin*. Princeton, NJ: Princeton University Press.

Zon, Hans van. 2000. *The Political Economy of Independent Ukraine*. London: Palgrave Macmillan.

Zubkova, Elena. 2000. 'The Rivalry with Malenkov.' In William Taubman et al., eds. *Nikita Khrushchev*, 67–84. New Haven, CT: Yale University Press.

Zubok, Vladislav M. 2021. *Collapse: The Fall of the Soviet Union*. New Haven, CT; London: Yale University Press.

# Index

Since the index has been created to work across multiple formats, indexed terms for which a page range is given (e.g., 52–53, 66–70, etc.) may occasionally appear only on some, but not all of the pages within the range.

# List of Symbols

| | |
|---|---|
| ĭ | quite a few |
| ï | quite a few |
| Å | in Åslund |
| É | a few |
| ê | in raison d'être |
| ė | in Klumbytė |
| Ō | in Ōgushi |
| Π | in bibliography (Fond Π-3...) and ch. 6, ft 128 |
| ö | in bibliography, Köln |